To the Student

This modern text is designed to prepare you for your future professional career. While theories, ideas, techniques, and data are dynamic, the information contained in this volume will provide you a quick and useful reference as well as a guide for future learning for many years to come. Your familiarity with the contents of this book will make it an important volume in your professional library.

A Study Guide for this textbook is available through your college bookstore. It has been written to enhance your understanding of the process of managing. Ask the bookstore manager to order a copy for you if it is not in stock.

MANAGEMENT
Principles and Functions

MANAGEMENT
Principles and Functions

John M. Ivancevich
University of Houston

James H. Donnelly, Jr.
University of Kentucky

James L. Gibson
University of Kentucky

1989   Fourth Edition

Homewood, IL 60430
Boston, MA 02116

Cover photo: © *Roberto Brosan*

Executive editor: *Gary L. Nelson*
Project editor: *Rita McMullen*
Production manager: *Bette Ittersagen*
Designer: *Michael Worrell*
Artist: *Art Force*
Compositor: *J. M. Post Graphics, Corp.*
Typeface: *10/12 Times Roman*
Printer: *R. R. Donnelley & Sons Company*

Library of Congress Cataloging-in-Publication Data

Ivancevich, John M.
  Management: principles and functions.
  Rev. ed. of: Managing for performance. 3rd ed.
1986.
  Includes bibliographies and indexes.
  1. Management. I. Donnelly, James H. II. Gibson,
James L. III. Ivancevich, John M. Managing for
performance. IV. Title.
HD31.I89 1989   658   88–7469
ISBN 0-256-06671-X

Printed in the United States of America
  2 3 4 5 6 7 8 9 0 DO 6 5 4 3 2 1 0 9

PREFACE

The major goal in writing *Management: Principles and Functions* is to provide students and instructors a comprehensive, systematic, and relevant introduction to the field of management. An important means for achieving our goal is the presentation of the material according to the four managerial functions of *planning, organizing, leading,* and *controlling*. This presentation enables us to emphasize *the attainment of effective organizational performance through management*. Effective managerial performance in the context of this book means that managers do those things and make decisions required to plan, organize, lead, and control effectively. This edition of *Management: Principles and Functions* reflects our commitment to offer students of management a comprehensive perspective on the work of managers.

The previous three editions of this text were titled *Managing for Performance*. There were students and instructors interested in the book who could not determine its theme or orientation from the title. Thus, to reduce any potential confusion we decided to retitle the book. The new title reflects exactly the theme and content of the book. The principles of management serve as guides for managers who engage in carrying out specific functions to solve problems and make decisions.

AUTHORS' GUIDELINES FOR THIS EDITION

This thoroughly revised edition covers the major managerial topics that contemporary students need and expect of an introductory course in management. The content surveys the common body of knowledge comprising the field of management as outlined by the American Assembly of Collegiate Schools of Business and also reflects our experience and contacts with such professional organizations as the Academy of Management and the American Management Association. As students' needs change and as the subject matter expands, authors of textbooks must make difficult choices: What new topics should be included? What topics should be deleted? What topics should be expanded or contracted? The responses to these questions indicated the need for new materials and the elimination of some material. Thus, while not tampering with the basic outline and thrust of the book, this edition does reflect a major revision. As authors, we have dedicated our careers to preparing textbooks and conducting research that has meaning and is readable. We strongly believe that meaning and readability can be achieved without sacrificing scholarship. Each chapter was crafted with the student in mind and with the intent of providing a realistic, relevant, and challenging view of management.

A MAJOR REVISION

Contemporary management theory and practice are changing rapidly, and these changes must be presented to students if they are to obtain an accurate understanding of management. Consequently, we have added one new chapter, added new material to every other chapter, and reformatted the order of presentation of various chapters.

The new chapter is Chapter 21: Management and Entrepreneurship. Chapter 21 covers entrepreneurship and how specific management skills must be applied to be successful in creating and managing a new business.

The previous additions and extensions to this edition are too voluminous to include in the Preface. We took reviewers' suggestions, student recommendations, colleague statements and ideas, and our own thoughts, experience, and beliefs and crafted this fourth edition to fit current thinking, themes, and trends about management. A sample of some of the additions and extensions are:

- The introduction of international examples of the use of principles and functions of management throughout the book.
- New examples of systems theory and applications.
- More coverage of the external environment and how it influences management decision making.
- A close look at needed managerial skills for the 1990s.
- Computer-assisted decision making, covered in terms of how it will impact management practice.
- Strategic planning discussed from a real-world perspective.
- Downsizing and restructuring examined in actual organizations.
- More emphasis on nonverbal communications.
- The introduction of McClelland's achievement motivation theory.
- Employee stock ownership plans examined in terms of use, effectiveness, and limitations.
- The concept of quality and its relationship to effectiveness examined in detail.
- New applications of linear programming.
- Just-in-time inventory management defined and evaluated.
- Political risk analysis, terrorism in the corporate world, and host government influence covered in detail.
- Company approaches to social responsibility and the current state of business ethics.

FRAMEWORK FOR PRESENTING THE MATERIAL

A beginning student can be overwhelmed by the numerous concepts and theories comprising the field of management. The systematic approach taken in *Management: Principles and Functions* overcomes this problem. The material is presented in six parts, each consisting of two to four chapters. Each of the five major parts begins with a substantial discussion explaining the rationale for the inclusion of the material there rather than elsewhere. As instructors of management courses know so well, the order in which material is presented, while not entirely arbitrary, lends itself to a variety of patterns. No doubt there are many appropriate ways to present the material in the beginning course. We claim no hold on the truth of this matter, but we do believe that it makes sense to tell the reader why the material comes in the sequence it does. The part openers serve that purpose.

    Part I of the book consists of two chapters which together introduce the subject matter and the themes that will carry forward throughout the remainder of the book. Chapter 1 establishes the importance of management in the lives of the readers. An important feature of this chapter is the presentation of the plan for the book. Chapter 2 describes aspects of the relevant environments which are the sources of challenges to which managers must respond.

    Part II contains four chapters that focus on the managerial function of planning. Separate chapters are devoted to the elements of planning, managerial decision making, decision support systems, and strategic planning. This part is integrated through the concept of decision making as it applies to planning.

    Part III consists of three chapters devoted to analyzing the managerial function of organizing. The three chapters present the elements of organizing, job design, and organization design. This part treats job and organization design as separate but interrelated issues managers must confront.

    Part IV presents the managerial function of leading. The part has four chapters which analyze the elements of leading, interpersonal and organizational communications, motivation, and work groups. The theme of the discussion is that managerial leadership is an inherently people-oriented process which requires considerable interpersonal and communication skills as well as technical ability.

    Part V contains four chapters that present the function of controlling. The chapters present the elements of controlling, production and financial control, human resources control, and organizational change and development. This part emphasizes the importance of developing an integrated control system which enables managers to monitor the performance of all resources devoted to the achievement of organizational performance.

    Part VI presents four important and pervasive challenges: managing the multinational corporation, responding to expectations of society for socially responsible corporate and managerial behavior, developing conditions for the fulfillment of useful and satisfying careers in management, and meeting the unique challenges of creating and managing a new organization. These four topics are presented as settings and opportunities for applying the principles and functions developed in the preceding chapters.

LEARNING ELEMENTS AVAILABLE IN THIS TEXTBOOK

We have either revised, extended, or replaced the learning elements from previous editions. We have also provided several new features to encourage learning. The presentation of material in each chapter encourages the reader to take an active role. The key features that involve the reader are as follows:

Learning objectives.   Clearly stated and attainable learning objectives are spelled out at the start of each chapter. These objectives permit the reader to monitor progress while reading the material.

Management incident and solution.   This edition introduces the idea of using reports of real incidents that managers have faced and resolved as openers and closers of each chapter. The student reads the incident, reads the chapter material, and then reads the actual management solution. This sequence encourages critical consideration of the chapter material in light of the applicability of that material.

Management applications.   Each chapter contains two to four appropriately placed descriptions of real-world issues and problems managers have confronted. These are dynamic examples of how management is conducted within organizations.

Figures and tables.   Important points are illustrated with well-designed visuals. These visuals reinforce the importance of key ideas by presenting them in a different perspective.

Management summaries.   Summaries of key points of each chapter appear at the end of each chapter. These summaries are patterned after the Executive Summary concept so widely used in organizations.

Review and discussion questions.   All chapters conclude with pertinent questions that serve as reinforcers of the material. Readers can monitor their own progress by answering these questions.

Cases.   A total of 39 cases appear in this edition. Placed at the end of the 20 major chapters, they feature issues that large and small organizations have faced as reported in periodical literature. The reader will immediately recognize the organizational settings of these cases.

Learning exercises.   Experiential learning exercises appear at the end of 13 of the book's 21 chapters. These exercises allow the reader to apply management concepts and theories through both individual and group efforts. Class participation in using the exercises adds to the realism of the content being covered in each chapter.

Comprehensive cases.   At the end of each of the four major parts of the book is a comprehensive case. These four cases enable the reader to apply the full range of material presented in that part of the book.

Comprehensive Cases.   At the end of each of the four major parts of the book is a comprehensive case. These four cases enable the reader to apply the full range of material presented in that part of the book.

Glossary.   Learning the language of management is important in the management course. Thus, important terms that make up the language of management appear in a glossary at the end of the book. There the terms are defined consistently with their use in the text discussions.

Indexes.   Comprehensive author, company, and subject indexes will assist the reader in locating information in the text.

Supplemental Study Guide.   In addition to the student-oriented learning approaches that appear in the text, a Study Guide is available. The guide reinforces and extends the text material. It includes a summary and outline of each chapter as well as definitions of key terms. The guide contains objective questions and essay questions for each text chapter to help the reader check comprehension of the material. It extends each chapter by providing additional references and timely articles from *The Wall Street Journal*.

INSTRUCTIONAL AIDS AVAILABLE WITH THIS TEXTBOOK

Instructors who use this textbook benefit from the availability of supplemental material prepared especially for this edition.

Instructor's Manual.   This aid has been significantly enhanced over each previous edition. For this edition the Instructor's Manual can be described as thorough, relevant, and scholarly. In addition to the chapter synopses, the manual includes lecture, exercise, and project ideas for all chapters and lecture outline notes. Other features include suggested answers to end-of-chapter questions and cases, 10 additional chapter questions and answers, suggested transparency masters and films, term paper topics, and a student handout exercise.

Lecture Resource Manual.   This instructional aid provides background material for supplemental and innovative lecture topics. These topics are keyed to the chapter material and can be used in combination with the material in the Instructor's Manual.

Transparencies.   Two- and four-color transparencies of important text figures are available to instructors. Also available are transparency masters of text figures and tables that are included in the Instructor's Manual.

Videotapes.   An exciting and personal approach to viewing management in action is the use of videotapes. These are available for use to stimulate classroom discussion, present management incidents and solutions, and review management topics.

Test Bank.   This testing resource contains two test forms for each chapter. Each form contains multiple choice, true/false, and matching questions, plus essay questions. The Test Bank is available on discs for IBM and Apple personal computers.

Automated Test Service.   A complete high-quality teletest service is available.

These instructional aids will enable the instructor to present a relevant learning experience for the benefit of students in the class.

CONTRIBUTORS TO THIS EDITION

This and each of the editions reflect many suggestions provided by the reviewers. The authors acknowledge the contributions of Marcia Kassner, The University of North Dakota; Lowell Lamberton, Central Oregon Community College; Garry Veak, Southern Alberta Institute of Technology; Eileen Kaplan, Montclair State College; Thomas M. Calero, Illinois Institute of Technology; John Drexler, Oregon State University; Philip C. Grant, Husson College; Peter L. Irwin, Richland College; W. R. Nelson, Old Dominion University; John Rogers, Onondaga Community College; and Stanley Stough, University of Dayton.

The authors also wish to acknowledge the specific contributions of other reviewers of previous editions and ideas. Development of a useful textbook is a cumulative process that combines the efforts of all who contribute to it. In this context, we pay thanks to Eric S. Emory, Sacred Heart University; Charles A. Gallagher, University of Central Florida: John H. Howe, Santa Ana College, Edward B. Lee, Allegheny County Community College; Boyce Campus; Vincent T. Luchsinger, Texas Tech University; Ronald Lundstrom, Kearney State College; Nicholas J. Mauro, Kinsborough Community College; Arlyn J. Melcher, Kent State University; Jan Muczyk, Cleveland State University; Warren J. Sprick, Kellogg Community College; and James Thomas, University of Houston.

We also acknowledge Anne Highfill and Judy Haywood for their special efforts to coordinate, word process, edit, review, and schedule details associated with this book. The role played by these competent assistants is appreciated by each author. We know how vital they are to our success. Thank you to two special individuals who are competent, professional, and pleasant.

A final thank you to the students too numerous to list who have commented about the book, helped us shape a student-friendly book, and have expressed ideas that made our revision work enjoyable and worthwhile. It is to students that we dedicate this new edition.

John M. Ivancevich
James H. Donnelly, Jr.
James L. Gibson

CONTENTS

Part V
The Controlling Function   444

Part VI
Managing for Performance: Trends and Perspectives 596

PART I

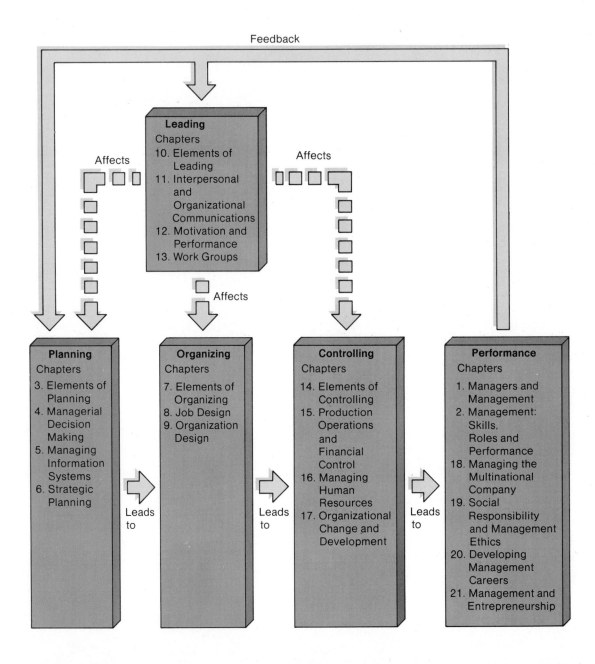

Feedback

Leading
Chapters
10. Elements of Leading
11. Interpersonal and Organizational Communications
12. Motivation and Performance
13. Work Groups

Affects

Affects

Affects

Planning
Chapters
3. Elements of Planning
4. Managerial Decision Making
5. Managing Information Systems
6. Strategic Planning

Leads to

Organizing
Chapters
7. Elements of Organizing
8. Job Design
9. Organization Design

Leads to

Controlling
Chapters
14. Elements of Controlling
15. Production Operations and Financial Control
16. Managing Human Resources
17. Organizational Change and Development

Leads to

Performance
Chapters
1. Managers and Management
2. Management: Skills, Roles and Performance
18. Managing the Multinational Company
19. Social Responsibility and Management Ethics
20. Developing Management Careers
21. Management and Entrepreneurship

MANAGERS AND PERFORMANCE

INTRODUCTION TO PART I

The chapters that comprise Part I of this text introduce the reader to the study of management. The purpose of this part is to convey to the reader the importance of management as a force for achieving the good things of life. Managers are found in any and all organizations that societies create to produce goods and services; to deliver health care, social support, and education; and to provide settings for worship, public service, and government. Managers perform the difficult task of seeing to it that these organizations do in fact accomplish the purposes that societies expect of them.

The process that managers undertake to achieve organizational performance is the underlying theme of the entire text. In Chapter 1 we introduce this process and suggest that it can be understood and studied by dealing with four separate functions that make up the total process. These four functions are *planning, organizing, leading,* and *controlling.* Managers' jobs consist of activities that can be classified according to these four functions; with this classification we are better able to study and,

consequently, practice management. The discussion in Chapter 1 demonstrates that the management process has been the subject of considerable theory development and research. Many students and practitioners of management have contributed to the growing body of literature of the field. This literature provides a rich source of information for those who wish to learn more about the problems, practice, and promise of management.

What does it take to be an effective manager? This question has been at the heart of the study of management throughout the history of the field. Chapter 2 presents information from important studies which have sought answers to this important question. The findings from these studies indicate that managers play particular roles in organizations and that playing these roles requires certain skills. Through the application of managerial skills, the managerial process can be the source of high levels of organizational, managerial, and individual performance. *Managing for performance* is what this text is all about, and Part I begins the discussion.

ONE

Managers and Management

LEARNING OBJECTIVES

After completing Chapter 1, you should be able to:

Define: what is meant by the term *management*.

State: the four basic management functions and provide an activity that is performed in each function.

Describe: the different meanings of management.

Explain: the contributions and limitations of the classical, behavioral, and management science approaches to management.

Discuss: the systems theory and contingency approaches to management and their importance in practicing management today.

J ohn Risen captains a large transport ship and exchanges food products for furniture and silk goods in foreign ports. On his way to these ports of call, John usually encounters storms, lulls, and crew members who sometimes seem to be slowing down the business instead of helping. Unless John has a plan, uses his experience, and practices sound navigational procedures, his ship may waste valuable time, flounder, or even become lost before it reaches safe harbor.

The above metaphor includes a number of crucial assumptions. First, the voyage is considered a success if John's ship reaches the port of destination and not some other. Second, the faster and straighter the ship sails, the better. Third, getting to the specific ports of call requires skill, patience, and experience. Fourth, there is no single, best way for John to get to the ports. He must develop his own management plan.

This book deals with the functions that managers must perform to be successful. A manager of an organization, like the ship captain above, must integrate the efforts of people to be successful. The primary objective in this textbook is to help managers and students of management perform more effectively. By studying this book, you will gain an increased understanding of the attributes of organizations and leaders that help them achieve their mission. The book's thesis is that to be successful, a manager must use an integrated approach. In other words, the successful captains of ships and captains of industry do not rely on a single management skill or principle to achieve their goals. They use a combination of existing tools and principles.

Peter Drucker, a management consultant and philosopher, postulates three major tasks of management: (1) to decide the purpose and mission of the organization, (2) to make work productive, and (3) to manage social impacts and responsibilities. About the second task, Drucker has stated: "The second task of management is to make work productive and the worker achieving."[1] In essence, Drucker has claimed, and we agree, that the one true resource of any organization is the *human resource*. Managers must work effectively with their subordinates to achieve maximum performance.

---

[1] Peter F. Drucker, *Management: Tasks, Responsibilities, Practices* (New York: Harper & Row, 1973), p. 41.

MANAGEMENT INFLUENCES EVERYONE

In our society, important work is done by individuals with such titles as restaurant manager, production manager, marketing manager, chairperson, dean, superintendent, ship captain, mayor, and governor. These individuals may work in different types of organizations with different purposes, but they all have one thing in common: They practice management. Furthermore, our society depends on the goods and services provided by the organizations these individuals manage.

Each of us is influenced by the actions of managers every day because we come into contact with organizations every day. Our experiences may be as students in a college, patients in a hospital, customers of a business, or citizens of a state. Whether we are *satisfied* with our experiences, however, depends greatly on the individuals who manage the organization. *All* organizations are guided and directed by the decisions of one or more individuals who are designated *managers*.

MANAGEMENT HAS DIFFERENT MEANINGS

The term *management* can have different meanings, and it is important that you understand these different definitions. They will be the focus of the remainder of this chapter. First, however, they will be introduced and briefly examined, so you can put them into perspective.

Management as a process.   Have you ever said, "That is a well-managed company" or "That organization has been mismanaged"? If you have, what did you mean by such statements? They seem to imply that: (1) management is some type of work or set of activities; and (2) sometimes the activities are performed quite well, and sometimes not so well.

You may not be able to define management exactly, but you are saying that it is a *process* involving certain functions and activities that managers must perform. Managers also use principles in managing which are generally accepted tenets that guide their thinking and actions. This is what managers do. They engage in the process of management. This book, *Management: Principles and Functions* focuses on this management process, the functions managers perform, and the principles they apply in managing organizations.

Management as a discipline.   If you say that you are a student of management or majoring in management, you are referring to the discipline of management. Classifying management as a discipline implies that it is an accumulated body of knowledge that can be learned. Thus, management is a subject with principles, concepts, and theories. A major purpose of studying the discipline of management is to learn and understand the principles, concepts, and theories of management and how to apply them in the process of managing.

Management as people.   Whether you say, "That company has an entirely new management team" or "She* is the best manager I've ever worked for," you are

---

*As yet, there is no convenient, generally accepted pronoun that means either *he* or *she*. Therefore, we will use, on a random basis, either the masculine or feminine pronoun to refer to both genders.

referring to the people who guide, direct, and, thus, manage organizations. The work *management* used in this manner refers to the people, *managers,* who engage in the process of management. Managers are the people primarily responsible for seeing that work gets done in an organization.

The perspective of management as people has another meaning. It refers to, and emphasizes, the importance of the employees who managers work with and manage in accomplishing an organization's objectives. People are an organization's lifeblood; successful organizations—indeed the well-being of society—require a strong, mutually satisfying partnership of managers and the people they manage.

Management as a career.   "Mr. Johnson has held several managerial positions since joining the bank upon his graduation from college." "After receiving her degree in business, Ms. Teruya entered the company's management training program." Such statements imply that management is a career. People who devote their working lives to the process of management progress through a sequence of new activities and, often, new challenges. More than ever before, today's business environment is fast-changing and competitive, posing challenges, opportunities, and rewards for individuals pursuing management as a career. Chapter 20 of this book is devoted entirely to the career of management.

A DEFINITION OF MANAGEMENT

The different meanings of the term *management* can be related as follows: *People* who wish to have a *career* as a manager must study the *discipline* of management as a means toward practicing the *process* of management. Thus, a book about managing for performance must emphasize the process. In this textbook, we define management as follows:

> Management is the process undertaken by one or more persons to
> coordinate the activities of other persons to achieve results not attainable
> by any one person acting alone.

THE PROCESS OF MANAGEMENT

The process of management consists of certain basic *management functions*. The entire process and the individual management functions are presented in Figure 1–1.

Figure 1–1 indicates that the management process is an integrated whole. However, something as complex as the management process is more easily understood when it is described as a series of separate activities or functions making up the entire process. The model of management used throughout this book identifies the management functions as *planning, organizing,* and *controlling,* linked together by *leading.* Planning determines *what* results the organization will achieve; organizing specifies *how* it will achieve the results; and controlling determines *whether* the results are achieved. Throughout planning, organizing, and controlling, managers exercise leadership.

Figure 1–1   The managerial process.

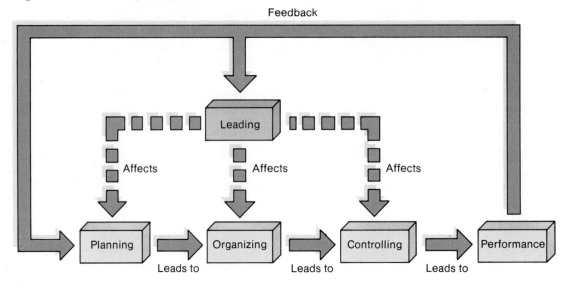

Planning

The planning function is the capstone activity of management. Planning activities determine an organization's objectives and establish the appropriate strategies for achieving those objectives. The organizing, leading, and controlling functions all derive from planning in that these functions carry out the planning decisions.

Planning is done by all managers at every level of the organization. Through their plans, managers outline what the organization must do to be successful. While plans may differ in focus, they are all concerned with achieving organizational goals in the short and long term. Taken as a whole, an organization's plans are the primary tools for preparing for and dealing with changes in the organization's environment.

Organizing

After managers develop objectives and plans to achieve the objectives, they must design and develop an organization that will be able to accomplish the objectives. Thus, the purpose of the organizing function is to create a structure of task and authority relationships that serves this purpose.

The organizing function takes the tasks identified during planning and assigns them to individuals and groups within the organization so that objectives set by planning can be achieved. Organizing, then, can be thought of as turning plans into action. The organizing function also provides an organizational structure that enables the organization to function effectively as a cohesive whole.

Leading

Once objectives have been developed and the organizational structure has been designed and staffed, the next step is to begin to move the organization toward the objectives. The leading function serves this purpose. Sometimes called *directing* or *motivating,* leading involves influencing the members of the organization to perform in ways that accomplish the organization's objectives.

The leading function focuses directly on the people in the organization, since its major purpose is to channel human behavior toward accomplishing organizational goals. Effective leadership is a highly prized ability in organizations and is a skill that some managers have difficulty in developing. The ability requires both task-oriented capabilities and the ability to communicate, understand, and motivate people.

Controlling

Finally, a manager must make sure that the actual performance of the organization conforms with the performance that was planned for the organization. This is the controlling function of management, and it requires three elements: (1) established *standards* of performance, (2) *information* that indicates deviations between actual performance and the established standards, and (3) *action* to correct performance that does not meet the standards. Simply speaking, the purpose of management control is to make sure the organization stays on the path that was planned for it.

At this point, you should note that the management process does not involve four separate or unrelated activities but a group of closely related functions. Also, the four functions do not necessarily occur in the sequence we have presented. In fact, the only time they might do so is when a new organization is being formed. In reality, various combinations of the four activities usually occur simultaneously.

LEARNING HOW TO MANAGE

Reading a book is not the only way to learn about management. It is unlikely that a book alone can make you a manager. This text, however, can provide you with the *knowledge, attitudes, and skills to apply to your experience once you become a manager.* You would probably learn these attitudes and skills on the job, but the process would certainly take longer and not be as well organized. The important thing to remember is that no one is born with management knowledge. So, while this book may not make you an effective manager by itself, it will help you accomplish this goal. At this point, then, it seems appropriate to discuss the major sources of the management knowledge on which this book is based.

MANAGEMENT KNOWLEDGE—THE EVOLVING DISCIPLINE OF MANAGEMENT

Knowledge about management comes from the field of management itself as well as many other fields. Most of the early writers were practicing executives who described their own experiences from which they developed broad principles. They wanted to share with others the practices that seemed to work for them. A great deal of management knowledge comes from the autobiographies and memoirs of people who practiced management.

On the other hand, many individuals whose interest in management was or is strictly scientific have contributed knowledge to the field. Many psychologists, sociologists, and anthropologists consider management to be a very important social phenomenon and managers to be an important social resource. Their interest, then, is strictly scientific; they want to understand and to explain the process of management. Numerous other professions such as mathematics, accounting, economics, law, political science, engineering, and philosophy also have contributed to the discipline of management.

With so many individuals with different purposes, and so many diverse fields of study contributing to our knowledge of management, we face a problem: How can we approach the study of the discipline of management in some coherent way? We must organize the knowledge so that it is meaningful to the student of management.

Contemporary management knowledge is the product of three basic approaches: the *classical approach,* the *behavioral approach,* and the *management science approach.* We believe that the ideas of each approach contribute positively to the total body of knowledge of the discipline of management. Through these three approaches, you can see an evolution of what *is* known and what *should be* known about management. Let us examine each one.

The Classical Approach

Serious attention to management began in the early years of this century. One of the critical problems facing managers at that time was how to increase the efficiency and productivity of the work force. The effort to resolve these issues marked the beginning of the study of modern management. It was eventually labeled *the classical approach,* as is usually the case with the beginning efforts of every field of study.

We believe that the classical approach to management can be better understood by examining it from two perspectives. These two perspectives are based on the problems each examined. One perspective concentrated on the problems of lower-level managers dealing with the everyday problems of the work force. This perspective is known as *scientific management.* The other perspective concentrated on the problems of top-level managers dealing with the everyday problems of managing the entire organization. This perspective is known as *classical organization theory.* For the student of management, the contributions of the classical approach are critical. These insights, in fact, constitute the core of the discipline of management and the process of management and comprise a major part of this book. Let us briefly examine each.

Scientific management. At the turn of the 20th century, business was expanding and creating new products and new markets, but labor was in short supply. Two solutions were available: (1) substitute capital for labor or (2) use labor more efficiently. Scientific management concentrated on the second solution.

Probably the greatest contributor to scientific management was Frederick W. Taylor. Taylor joined the American Society of Mechanical Engineers in 1886 and used this organization to develop and test the ideas he formulated while working in various steel firms. It was in one of these firms, Midvale Steel Company, that he observed men producing far less than their capacities. Taylor believed this waste was due to ignorance of what constituted a fair day's work. At that time, there were no studies to determine expected daily output per worker (work standards) and the relationship between work standards and the wage system. Taylor's personal dislike for waste caused him to rebel at what he interpreted as inefficient labor and management practices based solely on hunch, common sense, and ignorance.

Taylor tried to find a way to combine the interests of both management and labor to avoid the necessity for sweatshop management. He believed that the key to harmony was seeking to discover the one best way to do a job, determine the optimum work pace, train people to do the job properly, and reward successful performance by using an incentive pay system. Taylor believed that cooperation would replace conflict if workers and managers knew what was expected and the positive benefits of achieving mutual expectations.[2]

To the modern student of management, Taylor's ideas may not appear to be pioneering. Given the times in which he developed them, however, his ideas were, and continue to be, lasting contributions to the way work is done at the shop floor level. He urged managers to take a more systematic approach in performing their job of coordination. His experiments with stopwatch studies and work methods stimulated many others at that time to undertake similar types of studies.[3]

An interesting fact about scientific management is that if it were evaluated in terms of its impact on management practice at the time of its development, it would receive a low grade. While some firms adopted scientific management, the methods of Taylor and his followers were largely ignored. One cause of the seeming failure is the fact that Taylor and other supporters of scientific management failed to understand fully the psychological and sociological aspects of work. For example, scientific management made the implicit assumption that people are motivated to work primarily by money. In the late 19th century, this was undoubtedly a valid assumption. To assume this today, however, is far too simplistic.

Classical organization theory.   As noted above, another body of ideas developed at the same time as scientific management. These ideas focused on the problems faced by top managers of large organizations. Since this branch of the classical approach focused on the management of organizations while scientific management focused on the management of work, it was labeled *classical organization theory*. Its two major purposes were to (1) develop basic principles that could guide the design, creation, and maintenance of large organizations and (2) identify the basic functions of managing organizations.

----

[2]Lyndall Urwick, *The Golden Book of Management* (London: Newman Neame, Ltd., 1956), pp. 72–79.

[3]Frederick W. Taylor, *Principles of Scientific Management* (New York: Harper & Row, 1911), pp. 36–37. Also see Claude S. George, Jr., *The History of Management Thought* (Englewood Cliffs, N.J.: Prentice–Hall, 1968); and Edwin A. Locke, "The Ideas of Frederick W. Taylor: An Evaluation," *Academy of Management Review,* January 1982, pp. 14–24.

Engineers were the prime contributors to scientific management; practicing executives were the major contributors to classical organization theory. As with scientific management, there were many contributors to classical organization theory. Henri Fayol should be singled out for discussion, however, because his ideas reflect classical organization theory.[4]

For 50 years, Henri Fayol practiced management and reflected on just what it was that he did as managing director of a French coal company. He began writing articles about his experiences around 1916 and published a book in 1925, translated into English in 1929.[5]

Fayol wanted to develop principles of management that would be flexible and adaptable to a wide variety of circumstances. Deciding which principle to use was, in Fayol's judgment, the art of managing. He believed that a great number of principles might exist and described the ones that he most frequently applied in his own experience. In addition to *principles*, Fayol also presented what he believed were *functions* of managers. We shall discuss them in that order.

Principles of management.   Fayol proposed 14 principles to guide the thinking of managers in resolving problems. He never suggested total obedience to the principles but suggested that a manager's "experience and sense of proportion" should guide the degree of application of any principle in a particular situation. They are presented in capsule form in Figure 1–2. As with scientific management, the reader should keep in mind the time in which Fayol developed his principles and his intent. His work probably was the first major effort devoted to problems of managing large-scale business organizations. At that time in our history, they were relatively new phenomena.

Functions of management.   Fayol was perhaps the first individual to discuss management as a process with specific functions that all managers must perform. He proposed four management functions:

1. *Planning*.   Fayol believed that managers should make the best possible forecast of events that could affect the organization and draw up an operating plan to guide future decisions.

2. *Organizing*.   Fayol believed that managers must determine the appropriate combination of machines, material, and humans necessary to accomplish the task.

3. *Commanding*.   In Fayol's scheme, commanding involved directing the activities of subordinates. He believed that managers should set a good example and have direct, two-way communication with subordinates. Finally, managers must continually evaluate both the organizational

---

[4]Other very important contributors to classical organization theory include James D. Mooney and Alan C. Reiley, who wrote *Onward Industry* (New York: Harper & Row, 1931), and Lyndall F. Urwick, who wrote *The Elements of Administration* (New York: Harper & Row, 1943).

[5]Henri Fayol, *General and Industrial Management,* trans. J. A. Conbrough (Geneva: International Management Institute, 1929). Another more widely available translation is by Constance Storrs (London: Pitman Publishing, 1949).

Figure 1–2   Fayol's 14 principles of management.

```
 1. Division of labor
 2. Authority
 3. Discipline
 4. Unity of command
 5. Unity of direction
 6. Subordination of individual interest to the common good
 7. Remuneration of personnel
 8. Centralization
 9. Hierarchy of authority
10. Order
11. Equity
12. Stability of staff
13. Initiative
14. Espirit de corps
```

structure and their subordinates, and they should not hesitate to change the structure if they consider it faulty, or to fire subordinates who are incompetent.

4. *Controlling*.   Controlling ensures that actual activities are consistent with planned activities. Fayol did not expand the idea except to state that everything should be "subject to control."

The reader can see that Fayol's description of the management process is very similar to the one presented in Figure 1–1 as the focus of this book. Fayol's *commanding* function is our *leading* function.

Contributions and Limitations of the Classical Approach

Contributions.   The greatest contribution of the classical approach was that it identified management as an important element of organized society. Management has, if anything, increased in importance today. The fact that management skills must be applied in schools, government, and hospitals, as well as business firms, will be stressed throughout this book. Advocates of the classical approach believed that management, like law, medicine, and other occupations, should be practiced according to principles that managers can learn.

The identification of management functions such as planning, organizing, and controlling provided the basis for training new managers. The manner in which the management functions are presented often differs, depending upon who is presenting them. But any listing of management functions acknowledges that managers are concerned with *what* the organization is doing, *how* it is to be done, and *whether* it was done.

The contributions of the classical approach, however, go beyond the important work of identifying the field of management and its process and functions. Many management techniques used today are direct outgrowths of the classical approach. For example, time and motion analysis, work simplification, incentive wage systems, production scheduling, personnel testing, and budgeting are all techniques derived from the classical approach.

Limitations.   One major criticism of the classical approach is that the majority of its insights are too simplistic for today's complex organizations. Critics argue that scientific management and classical organization theory are more appropriate for the past, when the environments of most organizations were very stable and predictable. The changing environment, changing workers expectations, and changing expectations of society today will be discussed in the next chapter.

The Behavioral Approach

The behavioral approach to management developed partly because practicing managers found that following the ideas of the classical approach did not achieve total efficiency and workplace harmony. Managers still encountered problems because subordinates did not always behave as they were supposed to. Thus, an increased interest in helping managers become more effective grew.

The behavioral approach to management has two branches. The first branch, the *human relations approach,* became very popular in the 1940s and 1950s. The second branch, the *behavioral science approach,* became popular in the 1950s and still receives a great deal of attention today.

The human relations approach.   The term *human relations* refers to the manner in which managers interact with subordinates. To develop good human relations, followers of this approach believed, managers must know why their subordinates behave as they do and what psychological and social factors influence them.

Students of human relations brought to the attention of management the important role played by individuals in determining the success or failure of an organization. They tried to show how the process and functions of management are affected by differences in individual behavior and the influence of groups in the workplace. Thus, while scientific management concentrated on the *physical* environment of the job, human relations concentrated on the *social* environment.

Human relations experts believe that management should recognize the need of employees for recognition and social acceptance. They suggest that since groups provide members with feelings of acceptance and dignity, management should look upon the work group as a positive force which could be utilized productively. Therefore, managers should be trained in people skills as well as in technical skills.

The behavioral science approach.   Other individuals who were university trained in social sciences such as psychology, sociology, and anthropology began to study people at work. They had advanced training in applying the scientific approach to the study of human behavior. These individuals have become known as *behavioral scientists* and their approach is considered to be distinct from the human relations approach.

The individuals in the behavioral science branch of the behavioral approach believe that man is much more complex than the "economic man" description of the classical approach and the "social man" description of the human relations approach. The emphasis of the behavioral science approach concentrates more on the nature of work itself, and the degree to which it can fulfill the human need to use skills and abilities. Behavioral scientists believe that an individual is motivated to work for many reasons in addition to making money and forming social relationships.

Contributions and Limitations of the Behavioral Approach

Contributions.   For the student of management, the behavioral approach has contributed a wealth of important ideas and research results on the people-managing aspect of the discipline of management. The basic rationale is that since management must get work done through others, management is really applied behavioral science, because a manager must motivate, lead, and understand interpersonal relations.

Limitations.   The basic assumption that managers must know how to deal with people appears valid. But management is more than applied behavioral science. For the behavioral approach to be useful to managers, it must make them better practitioners of the process of management. It must help them in problem situations. In many cases, this objective has not been achieved because of the tendency of some behavioral scientists to use technical terms when trying to communicate their research findings to practicing managers. Also, in some situations, one behavioral scientist (a psychologist) may have a different suggestion than another (a sociologist) for the same management problem. Human behavior is complex and is studied from a variety of viewpoints. This complicates the problem for a manager trying to use insights from the behavioral sciences.

The Management Science Approach

The management science approach is in one sense a modern version of early emphasis on the "management of work" by those interested in scientific management. Its key feature is *the use of mathematics and statistics to aid in resolving production and operations problems*. Thus, the approach focuses on solving technical rather than human behavior problems. The computer has been of tremendous value to this approach because it has enabled analyses of problems that would otherwise be too complex.

The management science approach has only existed formally for approximately 45 years. It began during the early part of World War II when England was confronted with some complex military problems that had never been faced before, such as antisubmarine warfare strategy. To try to solve these kinds of problems, the English formed teams of scientists, mathematicians, and physicists. The units were named *operations research* teams, and they proved to be extremely valuable. When the war was over, American business firms began to use the approach.

Today the operations research approach has been formalized and renamed the management science approach. Basically, it involves mixed teams of specialists from whatever fields the problem being attacked calls for. The team members analyze the problem and often develop a mathematical representation of it. Thus, they can change certain factors in the equations to see what would happen if such a change was actually made in the real world. The results of their work often become useful to management in making a final decision. One of their important purposes is to provide management with *quantitative bases* for decisions.

Contributions and Limitations of the Management Science Approach

Contributions.   Today, the most important contributions of management science are in the areas of production management and operations management. *Production management* focuses on manufacturing technology and the flow of material in a manufacturing plant. Here, management science has contributed techniques that help solve production scheduling problems, budgeting problems, and maintenance of optimal inventory levels.

Operations management is very similar to production management except that it focuses on a wide class of problems and includes organizations such as hospitals, banks, government, and the military, which have operations problems but do not manufacture tangible products. For these types of organizations, management science has contributed techniques to solve such problems as budgeting, planning for work force development programs, and aircraft scheduling.

Limitations.   We noted in our discussion of the behavioral approach that management is more than applied behavioral science. At this point, we should stress that management science is not a substitute for management. The techniques of the management science approach are especially useful as aids to the manager performing the management process. However, while it is used in many problem areas, management science does not deal with the people aspect of an organization.

ATTEMPTS TO INTEGRATE THE THREE APPROACHES TO MANAGEMENT

Recently, there have been some attempts to aid managers in integrating the three approaches to management. One of these attempts, the *systems approach,* stresses that organizations must be viewed as total systems with each part linked to every other part. The other, the *contingency approach,* stresses that the correctness of a managerial practice is contingent on how it fits the particular situation to which it is applied; in other words, it "depends on the situation." Let us briefly examine each approach.

The Systems Approach

The systems approach to management is essentially a way of thinking about organizations and management problems. The approach views an organization as a group of interrelated parts with a unified purpose: surviving and ideally thriving in an environment.

From the systems perspective, management involves managing and solving problems in each part of the organization but doing so with the understanding that actions taken in one part of the organization affect other parts of the organization. For example, implementing a solution to a problem in the production department of a company will likely affect other aspects of the company such as marketing, finance, and personnel. Each part is tightly linked to other organizational parts; no single part of an organization exists and operates in isolation from the others. Thus, in solving problems, managers must view the organization as a dynamic whole and try to anticipate the unintended as well as the intended impacts of their decisions.

The systems approach views the elements of an organization as interconnected. The approach also views the organization as linked to its environment. Organizational effectiveness, even survival, depends on the organization's interaction with its environment. To further your understanding of these ideas, let's consider Apple Computer, Inc., as an example. As a computer manufacturer, Apple Computer is an *open system* that actively interacts with its environment. (For now, consider the environment as comprised of such factors as customers, competitors, financial institutions, suppliers, and the government. The environment will be discussed in more detail in Chapter 2.) The basic elements of Apple Computer as an open system are shown in Figure 1–3.

Active interaction means that Apple both obtains resources from and provides resources to its environment. For example, in order to function, Apple must obtain *inputs* from the environment. The company needs motivated and skilled employees with the ability to design and manufacture innovative, high-quality personal and business computers. Apple obtains this resource from the environment—specifically from the graduating classes of universities nationwide, from competitors, and from other organizations.

Financial resources (money) are needed to build manufacturing facilities, to fund Apple's R&D efforts, and to meet any number of other expenses. Apple obtains the funds from the environment—from banks, other lending institutions, and from people who buy shares of Apple's stock. Raw materials (e.g., computer parts) are obtained from outside suppliers in the environment. Information about the latest computer product technology and about the latest products developed by Apple's competitors is also needed. This information substantially influences the design and manufacture of Apple's computers. Information is obtained from the environment; that is, from research journals, computer conferences, and other external contacts.

These inputs are employed, used, coordinated, and managed in a *transformation* process that produces *output*—in this case, personal and business computers. However,

Figure 1–3 The four parts of an open system organization (e.g., Apple Computer, Inc.).

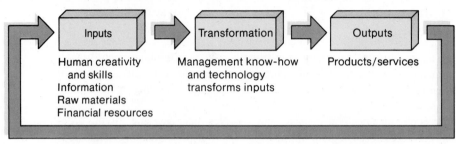

Inputs

Human creativity
and skills
Information
Raw materials
Financial resources

Transformation

Management know-how
and technology
transforms inputs

Outputs

Products/services

Environmental feedback serves as a response to products/services

the company's task is not complete. Apple provides this resource (output) to the environment by delivering its computers to retail outlets for sale to customers. Does the company survive? Only if the customer reacts to Apple's computers and decides to purchase the product. The customer's decision to buy or look elsewhere (for an IBM, AT&T or Compaq computer) provides Apple with *feedback*.

If the feedback is positive (the customers buy Apples), the environment provides a critical input to Apple—cash which the company uses to obtain other inputs from the environment such as top-quality employees, materials, and knowledge. Negative feedback (no sales) provides Apple with a serious problem. Regardless, Apple Computer must closely monitor feedback and act upon it (e.g., changing a failing product's design or features based on customer responses). As an open system in a dynamic environment, Apple cannot afford to ignore the environment. Neglecting developments in the environment (e.g., technological innovations, competitor's moves) will, over time, doom the company.

However, not all organizations are open systems. Some, like a Catholic monastery, are *closed systems*. The organization pays little attention to the environment. A monastery, for example, obtains some resources from the Catholic Church. However, beyond this relationship, the monastery has little need to closely monitor its environment. Its members remain in the monastery for their adult life, with no active interaction with the outside world. Developments in the outside world have little impact on the organization.

Importantly, today most organizations must operate as open systems to survive, and utilize a systems perspective to management. Managers must think broadly about a problem and not concentrate only on the desired results because these results will impact other problems and parts of the organization and even in the environment beyond the organization. The age-old confrontation between the production objective of low manufacturing costs (achieved by making one product in one color and style) and the marketing objective of a broad product line (requiring high production costs) is a good example. Both objectives cannot be achieved at the same time. In this situation, a compromise is necessary for the overall system to achieve its objective.

And in seeking a compromise, the organization must always be mindfully aware of the environment (e.g., will customers accept fewer models?). The objectives of the individual parts must be compromised for the objective of the entire firm.

Using the systems approach in the above example, you can see that individual managers must adopt a broad perspective. With a systems perspective, managers can more easily achieve coordination between the objectives of the various parts of the organization and the objectives of the organization as a whole.[6]

The Contingency Approach

The systems approach to management advocates that managers recognize that organizations are systems comprised of interdependent parts and that a change in one part affects other parts. This insight is important. Beyond this, however, it is useful for managers to see how the parts fit together. The contingency approach can help you better understand their interdependence.

Our discussion of the contingency approach is presented within the context of a continuum of views on management effectiveness which is shown in Figure 1–4. Much of the theory in the management discipline has differed on a major question: whether there exists a "one best way" to apply principles and to conduct the functions of management to achieve organizational effectiveness. For example, managers are interested in determining if there is one superior way to lead and motivate individuals, to structure an organization, or to institute change in an organization.

In the early years of the development of management theory, some theorists advocated the "universalistic" view of management effectiveness. They argued that there indeed exists a one best way to perform different management functions. In their view, the task of management theorists is to identify these superior management prescriptions by developing and then testing theory via research.

However, other management theorists, who can be referred to as *situationalists,* disagreed. In the view of situationalists, no one best approach to management exists because each situation that a manager faces is too different. No one principle or prescription is supremely applicable across totally unique situations. In fact, very few principles and concepts are useful across situations. Because each managerial situation is unique, a manager must approach each situation with few if any guidelines to follow. Management effectiveness first requires that a manager evaluate each situation from scratch before deciding which action to take.

The contingency approach attempts to bridge the extreme points on this continuum of views. Like the situationalists, contingency theorists do not subscribe to any one best approach to management. In their view, the situations that managers face do differ and thus prohibit any one best prescription. However, the contingency theorists stop short of asserting that all managerial situations are totally unique. Rather, they argue that situations are often similar to the extent that some principles of management can

---

[6]See Fremont E. Kast and James E. Rosenzweig, "General Systems Theory: Applications in Organizations and Management," *Academy of Management Journal,* December 1972, pp. 447–65; and Daniel Katz and Robert L. Kahn, *The Social Psychology of Organizations* (New York: John Wiley & Sons, 1966).

Figure 1–4 A continuum of views on approaches to management effectiveness.

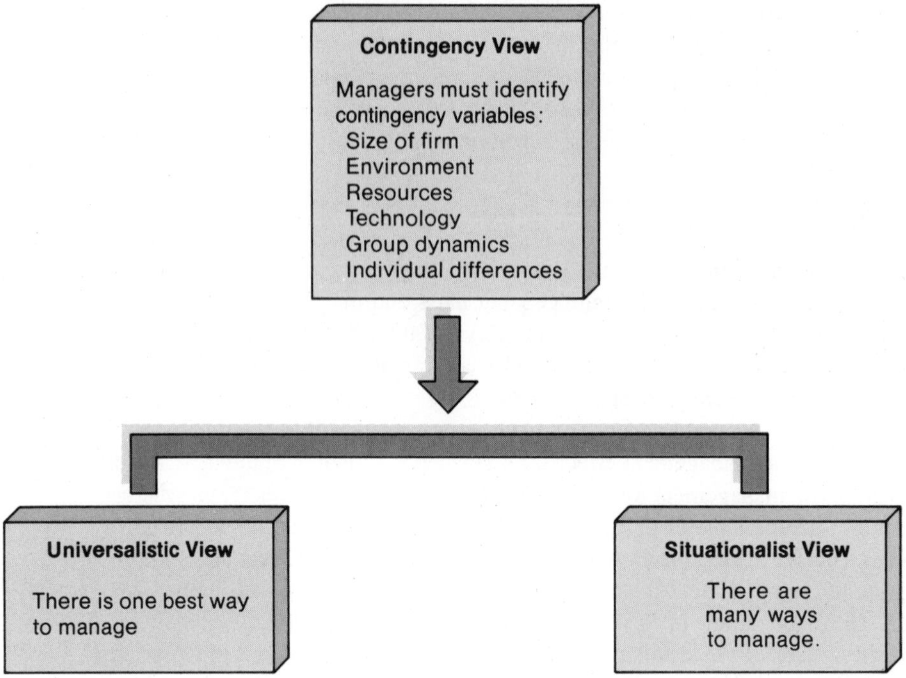

Contingency View

Managers must identify
contingency variables:
Size of firm
Environment
Resources
Technology
Group dynamics
Individual differences

Universalistic View

There is one best way
to manage

Situationalist View

There are
many ways
to manage.

be effectively applied. However, the appropriate principles must be identified. This is done by first identifying the relevant *contingency variables* in the situation and then evaluating those factors.[7]

For example, consider a manager's frequent and often perplexing task of determining an effective leadership approach in a particular situation. According to research, subordinate characteristics (individual differences in Figure 1–4) is a relevant contingency variable. The characteristics of the subordinate's task is another contingency factor to consider. Certain principles of leadership apply when the task is well structured; others apply when the task is unstructured (where there are many alternative ways to perform the job).

International Business Machines Corp. (IBM) is one example of a company where management has applied the contingency approach in implementing major organizational change. In recent years, the computer giant has experienced an earnings slump in the intensely competitive computer industry. This problem is due to many factors,

---

[7]See Fred Luthans, "The Contingency Theory of Management: A Path out of the Jungle," *Business Horizons,* June 1973, pp. 63–72; and Harold Koontz, "The Management Theory Jungle Revisited," *Academy of Management Review,* April 1980, pp. 175–88.

notably a bureaucratic organizational structure that has hindered the company's ability to quickly develop and market new products. In many observers' view, IBM was also losing touch with its customers' computer needs and problems.

In his effort to turn around IBM, CEO John Akers did not apply any one best approach. Nor did he start from scratch, analyzing the situation without any guidelines to follow. Instead, Akers identified key contingency variables in the situation and applied principles based on his evaluation of the contingency factors. For example, the environment is a primary contingency variable in IBM's situation. The computer industry is a dynamic environment where change is fast-paced (in product characteristics, competitors' strategies, and product prices). A primary management principle concerning the environment is that an organization's structure must be flexible in a dynamic environment, enabling a firm to quickly adapt and respond to changes in the environment. Akers applied this principle. He decentralized the company, delegating decision-making authority to managers in the lower levels of the organization. With this change, decisions are more quickly made by individuals who are closer to the company's product markets and customers. Akers also trimmed the "fat" from the company's structure by eliminating redundant jobs (without any employee layoffs).

IBM has identified and evaluated other important contingency variables before implementing organizational changes. For example, individual differences and group dynamics have influenced actions taken to promote an entrepreneurial spirit among managers and employees.[8] IBM is one of many organizations that have used a contingency approach to management. Managers in all organizations need to know and consider contingency variables in managing their organizations.

In essence, the contingency approach to management involves identifying the important contingency variables in different situations, evaluating the variables and then applying appropriate management knowledge and principles in selecting an effective approach to the situation. Principles and guidelines do exist in the management discipline; the task is knowing when and how to use them. Contingency variables are vital in this regard. One major purpose of this book is to develop your understanding of these variables and the knowledge and principles that are relevant to them.

Both the systems approach and the contingency approach have developed valuable insights for students of management. At this point, however, they are in rather early stages of development. Thus, it is too soon to know if either or both approaches will achieve the objective of integrating the three approaches of management thought which comprise the discipline of management.

PLAN FOR THIS BOOK

It is hoped, at this point, that you can see that writing a management book for future managers is not an easy task. Management is a discipline in continual evolution. Three well-established approaches—classical, behavioral, and management science—have made contributions to our ability to manage different aspects of organizations, namely work and organizations, people, and production and operations.

---

[8]Geoff Lewis, "Big Changes at Big Blue," *Business Week*, February 15, 1988, pp. 92–98.

Figure 1–5 Plan for the book.

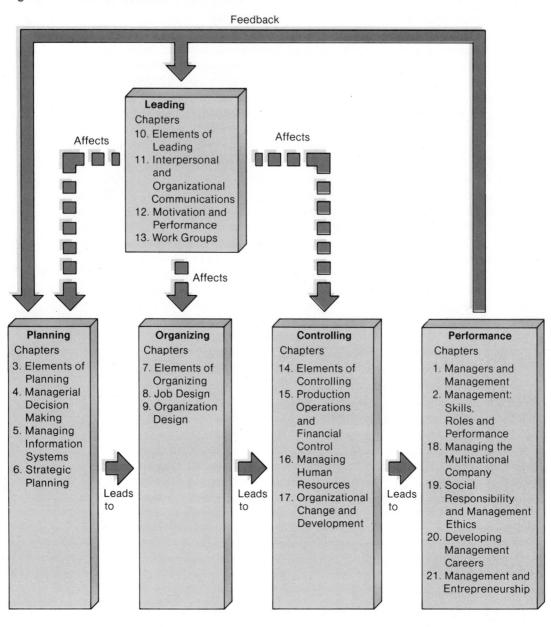

Thus, it would be virtually impossible to write a management book without including contributions from all approaches. In addition, wherever possible, the book should try to encourage "systems thinking" and a "contingency perspective." The plan for our book is outlined in Figure 1–5, which is an expansion of Figure 1–1.

Figure 1–5 indicates that the *process* of management is the focus of the book. Indeed it should be. This contribution of the classical approach produced the core *functions* of management and has endured throughout the evolution of the discipline of management. Figure 1–5 indicates that the bulk of the material in the book is organized around the management functions of planning, organizing, leading, and controlling. Throughout our discussions of the management process and each of the management functions, the contributions of the classical approach will be evident. Indeed, those contributions have produced much of the knowledge that is specific to the discipline of management as opposed to being drawn from other disciplines.

Figure 1–5 indicates that the contributions of the behavioral approach should in no way be viewed separately from the classical approach. Examining the topics covered indicates that the behavioral approach has made contributions to the human aspects of the *organizing, leading,* and *controlling* functions. In subsequent chapters on career development, motivation, leadership, communications, organizational change, and performance evaluation, we will draw upon the contributions of the behavioral approach.

The contributions of the management science approach are seen in various facets of the *planning* and *controlling* functions. In subsequent chapters on planning, decision making, managerial control and information, and production/operations and financial control, we will draw upon the contributions of the management science approach.

In summary, the management process is the focus of our book. We have selected only that knowledge which we believe will help improve the performance of a management function. Thus, while management draws upon relevant aspects of other disciplines, it also has certain identifiable characteristics, such as the process and functions of management, that are its own.

You should know that merely learning the many techniques and concepts that other disciplines have contributed to the discipline of management will not necessarily produce an effective manager. To be effective you must know which technique is appropriate for which situation. This view is clearly stated by Peter Drucker:

> Managers practice management. They do not practice economics. They
> do not practice quantification. They do not practice behavioral science.
> These are tools for the manager. . . . As a specific discipline,
> management has its own basic problems . . . specific approaches . . .
> distinct concerns. . . . A man who only knows the skills and techniques,
> without understanding the fundamentals of management, is not a
> manager; he is, at best, only a technician.[9]

When you finish this book, you will be equipped with the knowledge, attitudes, and skills that will enable you to evaluate which management practice fits which situation.

---

[9]Drucker, *Management,* p. 17.

MANAGEMENT SUMMARY

- ☐ A successful manager does not rely on a single managerial skill, but rather a combination of skills.
- ☐ Management can be thought of as multi-dimensional in nature. It can be defined as a process, a discipline, people, and a career.
- ☐ Four key functions make up the process of management: planning, organizing, leading, and controlling.
- ☐ The discipline of management is continually evolving and is addressed through three primary approaches to the subject. They are the classical approach, the behavioral approach, and the management science approach.
- ☐ The classical approach focuses on ways to increase the efficiency and productivity of workers; the behavioral approach focuses on the human dynamics of the workplace. The management science approach addresses the use of math and statistics in solving production and operations problems.
- ☐ More recently, attempts have been made to integrate the three approaches to the study of management. These integrative approaches are known as the systems approach and the contingency approach.
- ☐ The systems approach stresses the interrelatedness of all aspects of organizations and the links between the organization and its environment. The contingency approach emphasizes the need to evaluate contingency variables in selecting approaches to managerial situations.

REVIEW AND DISCUSSION QUESTIONS

1. What does Drucker mean when he states that "A man who only knows the skills and techniques, without understanding the fundamentals of management, is not a manager; he is, at best, only a technician"?

2. Clearly distinguish between the process of management and the functions of management. How are they related?

3. Why is there no one best way to manage?

4. List the organizations that influence your life. In what ways do they influence you?

5. Someone has said that managers are a very important social resource in the United States. Why do you think this person made this statement? Do you agree or disagree? State your reasons.

6. Apply the systems theory concepts to an organization with which you are familiar. What are the inputs and outputs? How are the outputs transformed? What are the challenges in managing an organization from the systems theory perspective?

7. Can you think of any reasons why three approaches to management thought comprise the discipline of management?

8. Have you ever been a manager? Can you think of a situation in which you played a managerial role? Outline your planning, organizing, leading, and controlling functions.

9. As the chapter's figure of the management process indicates, planning leads to organizing which leads to controlling which leads to performance, and leading activities affect the three managerial functions. Is it possible that the controlling function can affect the organizing and planning functions? Or that the organizing function can affect the leading function? Explain.

10. Although Taylor received little credit at the time he introduced his thinking about scientific management, his contributions to management certainly have withstood the test of time. Why have Taylor's views of management had a lasting impact?

TWO

Management: Skills, Roles, and Performance

LEARNING OBJECTIVES

After completing Chapter 2, you should be able to:

Define: the different roles that managers assume and provide an example of each role.

State: the crucial management skills that must be applied if an organization is to be successful.

Describe: the types of external environments that influence the management process in an organization.

Explain: what is meant by performance (organizational, managerial, and individual).

Discuss: the three levels of management and the relative importance of different skills at each level.

THE TOBACCO INDUSTRY: THE HEAT IS ON

Few industries in the United States are as profitable as the $35 billion tobacco industry. A U.S. cigarette maker generally earns 30 percent pretax profit on every pack of cigarettes sold. However today, social, political, and legal forces in the industry's external environment are threatening to diminish the industry's sales and profits.

Ever since medical evidence emerged that linked smoking to several serious illnesses, pressure has been mounting to make America a "smokeless society"—an objective that the U.S. Surgeon General hopes to achieve by the year 2000. Concerned about the health hazards of inhaling others' smoke, antismokers have lobbied government to ban smoking in public places. So far, 42 states and over 1,000 communities have responded, passing laws that restrict smoking in these areas. More than 30 percent of America's corporations limit smoking on the job (an estimated 80 percent will have restrictions by 1990).

Some companies, such as Atlanta's Turner Broadcasting System, will not hire smokers. In this environment, many smokers are experiencing social pressure to stop smoking.

Congress and state governments are threatening to boost the excise taxes on cigarettes that would reduce sales and profits. In the courts, over 125 suits against cigarette makers are pending, with most filed by the relatives of now-deceased smokers, seeking damages. Tobacco companies are spending $100 million each year fighting these suits.

Because of these pressures, cigarette consumption has dropped almost 10 percent in the last six years and continues to decline. Cigarette manufacturers are facing the question of how to remain profitable when a society increasingly does not want its product.

(The Management Solution to this Management Incident can be found at the end of this chapter.)

Performance in an organization does not just happen. Dedicated and skillful managers carrying out specific roles make it happen. Managers influence performance by defining objectives, recognizing and minimizing obstacles to the achievement of these objectives, and effectively planning, organizing, leading, and controlling all available resources to attain high levels of performance. This chapter focuses on management skills and roles that must be aggressively applied to everyday organizational situations. The skillful manager is able to manage and monitor performance in such a way that objectives are achieved because he or she is action oriented and doesn't simply sit back and let things happen.

If one closely examines most organizational problems, sooner or later the people element will come into play. This is certainly the case with achieving performance. As we stated in Chapter 1, to perform means "to do, to accomplish." The term *productivity* has been used to indicate specifically what is being accomplished. Productivity is defined in a general sense as the relationship between real inputs and real outputs, or the *measure* of how well resources (human, technological, financial) are combined and utilized to produce a result desired by management. Productivity is a component of performance, not a synonym for it.[1] As the highest order of resources, human beings are responsible for utilizing all other resources. People design and operate the technology and work flow; they purchase and use raw materials; they produce the product or service; they sell the product or service. People make a company effective or ineffective, and they must be skillfully managed if an organization is to function and survive.

In most organizations, managers are simultaneously subordinates and superiors. They are subordinate to a "boss" or a board of directors or shareholders and are therefore accountable to others, while at the same time depending on their own subordinates to perform the job. Even Lee Iacocca, the chief executive officer of Chrysler Corp., and John Sculley, president of Apple Computer, Inc., must depend on the work efforts of their subordinates to accomplish goals. Iacocca doesn't produce and sell cars, he manages the system. He sits at the top of a management hierarchy and attempts to effectively apply various skills and perform specific roles.

A successful manager possesses certain qualities in applying his or her skills and carrying out various managerial roles. One study conducted by Harbridge House, a Boston consulting firm, identified the qualities of a successful manager.[2] The profile seems to fit managers regardless of age, sex, industry, size of the organization, or the corporate culture. The study identified the following qualities:

1. *Provides clear direction.* An effective manager needs to establish explicit goals and standards for people. He must communicate group goals, not just individual goals. The manager must involve people in setting these goals and not simply dictate them himself. She must be clear and thorough in delegating responsibility.

2. *Encourages open communication.* The manager must be candid in dealing with people. He must be honest and direct. "People want straight information from

---

[1]D. Scott Sink, Thomas C. Tuttle, and Sandra J. DeVries, "Productivity Measurement and Evaluation: What Is Available?" *National Productivity Review,* Summer 1984, p. 265.

[2]"A Checklist of Qualities That Make a Good Boss," *Nation's Business,* November 1984, p. 100.

their bosses," the study says, "and managers must establish a climate of openness and trust."

3. *Coaches and supports people.* This means being helpful to others, working constructively to correct performance problems, and going to bat with superiors for subordinates. This last practice "was consistently rated as one of the most important aspects of effective leadership," says Robert Stringer, senior vice president of Harbridge.

4. *Provides objective recognition.* The manager must recognize employees for good performances more often than she criticizes them for problems. Rewards must be related to the quality of job performance, not to seniority or personal relationships. "Most managers don't realize how much criticism they give," the study says. "They do it to be helpful, but positive recognition is what really motivates people."

5. *Establishes ongoing controls.* This means following up on important issues and actions and giving subordinates feedback.

6. *Selects the right people to staff the organization.*

7. *Understands the financial implications of decisions.* This quality is considered important even for functional managers, such as those in personnel/human resources and research and development, who do not have responsibility for the bottom line.

8. *Encourages innovation and new ideas.* Employees rate this quality important in even the most traditional or conservative organizations.

9. *Gives subordinates clear-cut decisions when they are needed.* "Employees want a say in things," the report says, "but they don't want endless debate. There's a time to get on with things, and the best managers know when that time comes."

10. *Consistently demonstrates a high level of integrity.* The study shows that most employees want to work for a manager they can respect.

If any one quality stood out in the study, it was the importance of open and honest communication. Above all other things, a manager must be honest when dealing with employees.

THE MANAGEMENT SYSTEM

As any organization increases in size and complexity, its management must adapt by becoming more specialized. This section addresses some results of specialization of the management process.

Types of Managers

The history of most ongoing firms reveals an evolution through which the management has grown from one manager with many subordinates to a team of many managers with many subordinates. The development of different types of managers has occurred as a result of this evolution. For example, Figure 2–1 illustrates a one-manager–many-subordinate firm. In this situation, the manager performs all of the management functions. Let us assume that the firm is successful, and the manager decides to add some new products and sell to some new markets. As the manager becomes overworked

Figure 2–1 One manager and many subordinates.

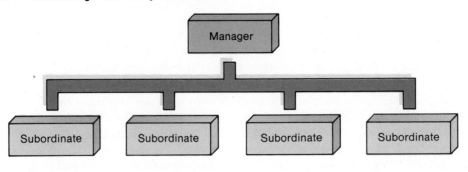

Figure 2–2 Vertical specialization of the management process.

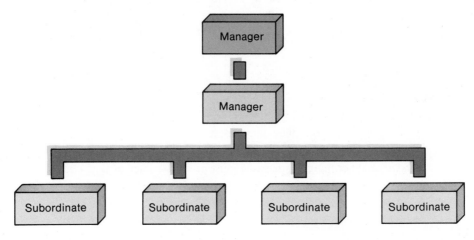

because of the increased complexity of the job, he may decide to specialize *vertically* by assigning the task of supervising subordinates to another person (Figure 2–2) or *horizontally* by assigning certain tasks, such as production or marketing, to another person (Figure 2–3). Whichever method is chosen, the management process is now shared, specialized, and thus more complex.

As the management system develops an even higher degree of specialization (Figure 2–4), relationships among the managers and nonmanagers become even more complex. In Figure 2–4, it is clear that the managers in production, marketing, accounting, and research not only manage their own subordinates, but are managed by *their* superiors as well. Figure 2–4 illustrates three types of managers.

Figure 2–3 Horizontal specialization of the management process.

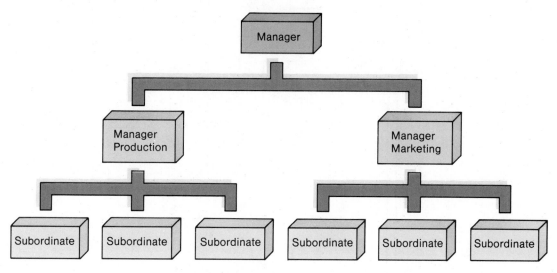

First-line management.   These managers coordinate the work of others who are not themselves managers. Those at the level of *first-line management* are often called *supervisors, office managers,* or *foremen.* These are typically the entry-level line positions of recent college graduates. The subordinates of a first-line manager may be blue-collar workers, salespersons, accounting clerks, or scientists, depending on the particular tasks that the subunit performs: for example, production, marketing, accounting, or research. Whatever the case, first-line managers are responsible for the basic work of the organization according to plans provided by their superiors. First-line managers are in daily or near daily contact with their subordinates, and they are ordinarily assigned the job because of their ability to work with people. They must work with their own subordinates and with other first-line supervisors whose tasks are related to their own.

Middle management.   The middle manager is known in many organizations as the departmental manager, plant manager, or director of operations. Unlike first-line managers, those in *middle management* plan, organize, lead, and control the activity of other managers; yet, like first-line managers, they are subject to the managerial efforts of a superior. The middle manager coordinates the activity (for example, marketing) of a subunit.

Top management.   A small cadre of managers, which usually includes a chief executive officer, president, or vice president, constitutes the *top management.* Top management is responsible for the performance of the entire organization through the

Figure 2–4 Vertical and horizontal specialization of the management process.

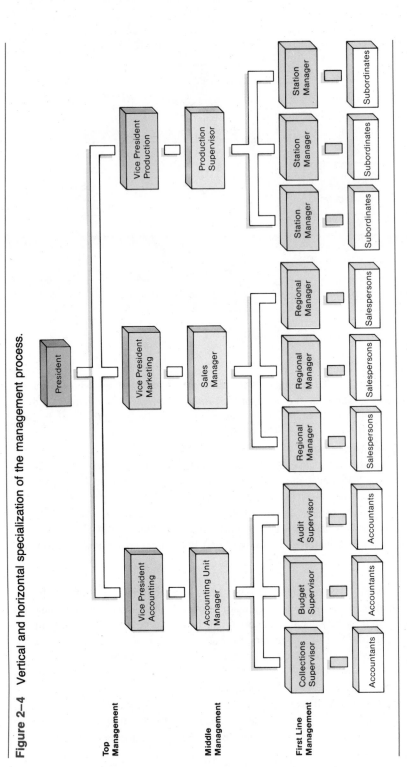

Figure 2–5   Management level and the management functions.

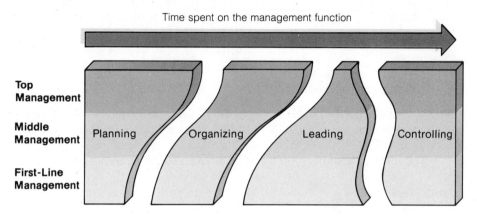

Time spent on the management function

Top Management				
Middle Management	Planning	Organizing	Leading	Controlling
First-Line Management				

middle managers. Unlike other managers, the top manager is accountable to none other than the owners of the resources used by the organization.[3] Of course, the top-level manager is dependent on the work of all of her subordinates to accomplish the organization's goals and mission.

The designation *top, middle, first-line,* classifies managers on the basis of their vertical rank in the organization. The completion of a task usually requires the completion of several interrelated activities. As these activities are identified, and as the responsibility for completing each task is assigned, that manager becomes a functional manager.

Functional management.   As the management process becomes horizontally specialized, a functional manager is responsible for a particular activity. In Figure 2–4 the management process has been divided into three functions: production, marketing, and accounting.

Thus, one manager may be a first-line manager in production, while another may be a middle manager in marketing. The function refers to what *activities* the manager actually oversees as a result of horizontal specialization of the management process. The level of the manager refers to the *right to act and use resources* within specified limits as a result of vertical specialization of the management process.

Management level and management functions.   In the last chapter, we noted that the management functions of planning, organizing, leading, and controlling are performed by all managers. However, the amount of time and effort devoted to each function depends on the manager's level in the organization. Figure 2–5 attempts to

---

[3]There are signs across America's corporate landscape of the beginnings of a challenge to top management's power in managing organizations. Constituents such as corporate investors, employees, and unions are challenging how top management is running the company. For a discussion of this issue, see Bruce Nussbaum and Judith H. Dobrzynski, "The Battle for Corporate Control," *Business Week,* May 18, 1987, pp. 102–9.

illustrate this relationship. For example, first-line managers usually spend less time planning than do top managers. However, they spend much more time and effort leading and controlling. At high levels in the organization, far more time is spent planning and less time is spent leading. The amount of time and effort devoted to organizing and controlling are usually fairly equal at all levels of management.

Managerial Skills

Regardless of the level of management, managers must possess and seek to further develop many critical skills.[4] A *skill* is an ability or proficiency in performing a particular task. Management skills are learned and developed. Various skills classifications have been suggested as being important in performing managerial roles.

Technical skills.   Technical skill is the ability to use *specific* knowledge, techniques, and resources in performing work. Accounting supervisors, engineering directors, or nursing supervisors must have the technical skills to perform their management jobs. Technical skills are especially important at the first-line management level, since daily work-related problems must be solved.

Merck & Co., Inc., is one example of the importance of technical skills. Considered by many management experts to be one of the best managed companies in America, Merck & Co. manufactures drugs for medical use. The company's key resource is a top-notch team of scientists. Their technical skills have developed a consistent stream of major, productive pharmaceuticals. Merck attracts top talent by paying well and maintaining first-rate lab facilities and a campuslike working environment. Many of its managers possess the same skills; the company's CEO, Roy Vagelos, has a doctorate in medicine.[5]

Analytical skills.   This skill involves using scientific approaches or techniques to solve management problems. In essence, it is the ability to identify key factors, and understand how they interrelate, and the roles they play in a situation. The analytical skill is actually an ability to diagnose and evaluate. It is needed to understand the problem and to develop a plan of action. Without analytical proficiency, there is little hope for long-term success.

Decision-making skills.   All managers must make decisions or choose from among alternatives, and the quality of these decisions determines their degree of effectiveness. A manager's decision-making skill in selecting a course of action is greatly influenced by his or her analytical skill. Poor analytical proficiency will inevitably result in inefficient, spotty, or inadequate decision making.

John F. Welch, chairman and CEO of General Electric, has been credited with having exceptional analytical and decision-making abilities. In the first seven years of

---

[4]See Robert L. Katz, "Skills of an Effective Administrator," *Harvard Business Review,* September–October 1974, pp. 90–102.

[5]See Gordon Bock, "Merck's Medicine Man," *Time,* February 22, 1988, pp. 44–45; and Stephen W. Quickel, "The Drugs Culture," *Business Month,* December 1987, p. 35.

his tenure as CEO, Welch made several major decisions that produced massive changes at GE. Welch eliminated 100,000 jobs, and sold billions of dollars worth of GE businesses, taking the company out of the housewares and television industries. He moved GE into high-tech manufacturing and other higher risk, though more profitable industries. Welch acquired RCA Corporation, reduced the number of layers in GE's structure, and set high objectives for GE's businesses (number one or two standing in their respective markets). Some observers believe that Welch's decisions have transformed GE into an able, fleet-footed competitor. Others believe his cost cutting and standards are excessive and have pushed many talented employees out GE's door.[6]

Computer skills.   Managers who are computer skilled have a conceptual understanding of computers and, in particular, know how to use the computer and software to perform many aspects of their jobs. Computer ability is a valuable managerial skill; in one survey study of 100 personnel directors from America's largest corporations, 7 of every 10 directors believe that computer skills are important, very important, or essential for advancement in management.[7]

Computer abilities are important because using computers substantially increases a manager's productivity. Computers can perform in minutes tasks in financial analysis, human resource planning, and other areas that otherwise take hours, even days to complete. The computer is an especially helpful tool for decision making. The computer instantly places at a manager's fingertips a vast array of information in a flexible and usable form. Software enables managers to manipulate the data and perform "what if" scenarios, looking at the projected impact of different decision alternatives. Northwest Industries, a banking and financial services conglomerate, is one of a growing number of companies that have developed a decision support system to help their executives make financial and planning decisions. Computer skills are essential to make full use of the considerable advantages that computers provide management. The use of decision support systems for planning decisions will be discussed in detail in Chapter 5.[8]

Human relations skills.   Since managers must accomplish much of their work through other people, their ability to work with, communicate with, and understand others is most important. The human relations skill is essential at every organizational level of management; it is a reflection of a manager's leadership abilities.

James F. Lincoln, founding CEO of Lincoln Electric Co., was an individual endowed with considerable human relations skills. Based near Cleveland, Ohio, Lincoln Electric is the world's leading manufacturer of arc welding equipment. With 3,000 employees, the company has 40 percent of the world's market. The company's ex-

---

[6]See Russell Mitchell, "Jack Welch: How Good a Manager?" *Business Week,* December 14, 1987, pp. 92ff; and Peter Petre, "What Welch Has Wrought at GE," *Fortune,* July 7, 1986, pp. 43–47.

[7]"Trying to Climb the Corporate Ladder? Without Basic Computer Skills, You Risk Falling Off, Survey Reports," *PR Newswire,* January 20, 1988.

[8]Nat Sakowski and Leslie Baker, "Will Middle Management Survive the PC?" *PC Magazine,* April 17, 1984, pp. 262–67; and "How Computers Remake the Manager's Job," *Business Week,* April 25, 1983, pp. 68ff.

ceptional success has been attributed to James Lincoln's attitudes toward employees and his relationship with them. Lincoln believed that employees have a basic desire to work productively as members of a company that contributes to society. He believed that pay must be directly linked to performance to reward employees for good performance, and a relationship of complete honesty and understanding must be maintained between employees and managers. Lincoln incorporated these beliefs into the company's unique compensation system and management practices. His human relations-oriented philosophy is still alive today at Lincoln Electric, some 20 years after his death.[9]

Jimmy Treybig, CEO of Tandem Computers, is also credited with having a unique, human relations-oriented leadership style. However, as the following Management Application notes, his leadership style has recently changed.

MANAGEMENT APPLICATION

A CHANGE IN LEADERSHIP STYLE

In the early 1980s, CEO Jimmy Treybig managed Tandem Computers with a unique leadership style. At the company's main location in Silicon Valley, California, Treybig motivated employees by giving inspired speeches about Tandem's future in tents erected on the company parking lots. He stressed hard work and commitment but also flexibility, trust, and communication. No time clocks were installed; few regular meetings with subordinate managers were held. The company's goals were communicated to all employees. Beer busts were held every Friday afternoon on the company grounds to encourage employees to discuss new ideas. Yoga classes, a swimming pool, and jogging trails were built at Tandem.

In sum, Treybig strived to create a demanding but comfortable work environment. The Tandem environment came to symbolize the new corporate culture of Silicon Valley's upstart computer companies. Profits were high; employee turnover was low. Treybig's "cheerleading" leadership style appeared to work.

However, when the computer industry slumped, so did Tandem's profits. Other problems surfaced; Tandem was suffering from poor cost control and many managers weren't meeting their objectives. Treybig made the decision to change his laid-back leadership style. He implemented a cost-cutting program, reassigned many employees, imposed restrictions on corporate-paid travel, and required salaried workers to put in some overtime without pay.

Treybig ended consensus management and established authoritative management. Although he dislikes meetings, weekly staff meetings and quarterly reviews are now the norm. Managers are strictly held to their goals, and receive occasionally harsh critiques from the CEO on their performance.

Treybig's style hasn't totally changed. The Friday beer busts continue, and employ-

---

[9]Harvey Shore, "Mr. Lincoln and His System," *Business Quarterly*, Summer 1986, pp. 10–13; David Whiteside, "Why This 'Obsolete' Company Is a 'Great Place to Work,'" *International Management*, April 1986, pp. 46–50; and William Serrin, "The Way That Works at Lincoln: Its Labor Approach Paid Off in the Welding Industry. Can More Follow?" *The New York Times*, January 15, 1984, p. F4.

ees can still scribble their names on his calendar for a meeting with the CEO. Open communication is still stressed; most of Tandem's 6,200 employees have electronic mail terminals at their desks to communicate with each other. But the emphasis has changed, from inspiration to accountability. So far, his changed style seems to fit the bill. Tandem recently reached the $1 billion mark in yearly sales.

Source: Adapted from Brian O'Reilly, "How Jimmy Treybig Turned Tough," *Fortune,* May 25, 1987, pp. 102–4.

Communication skills.   Effective communication—the written and oral transmission of common understanding—is vital for effective managerial performance. The skill is critical to success in every field, but it is crucial to managers who must achieve results through the efforts of others. Communication skills involve the ability to communicate in ways that other people understand, and to seek and use feedback from employees to ensure that one is understood.

Lewis Lehr, chairman and CEO of 3M, emphasizes open communication among managers and employees. Lehr spends six months of every year away from 3M headquarters in St. Paul, Minnesota, visiting 3M employees at the company's numerous plant locations. There, he participates in question-and-answer sessions with employees. Lehr requires that executives who run 3M operations frequently visit with media, government, and education officials in their regions to talk about 3M. Lehr believes that frequent communication is the only way to build employee trust and cooperation which is essential to 3M's success.[10]

Conceptual skills.   These skills consist of the ability to see the big picture, the complexities of the overall organization, and how the various parts fit together. Recall that in our discussions of the systems approach as a way of thinking about organizations, we stressed the importance of knowing how each part of the organization interrelates and contributes to the overall objectives of the organization.

Many CEOs combine analytical and conceptual skills in developing long-range plans for their companies. Both enable a CEO to look forward and project how prospective actions may affect a company 5, 10, or even 20 years in the future. At Matsushita, a Japanese electronics corporation, Chairman Konosuke Matsushita has used considerable conceptual and analytical skills in developing a 250-year plan for his company.[11]

While the above skills are all-important, the relative importance of each will vary according to the level of the manager in the organization. Figure 2–6 illustrates the skills required at each level. For example, note that technical and human relations skills are more important at lower levels of management. These managers have greater contact with the work being done and the people doing the work. Communication and computer skills are equally important at all levels of management. Analytical skills

---

[10]Del Marth, "Keeping All the Lines Open," *Nation's Business,* October 1984, pp. 85–86.

[11]Walter Kiechel III, "How Executives Think," *Fortune,* February 4, 1985, pp. 127–128.

Figure 2–6   Managerial skills and management level.

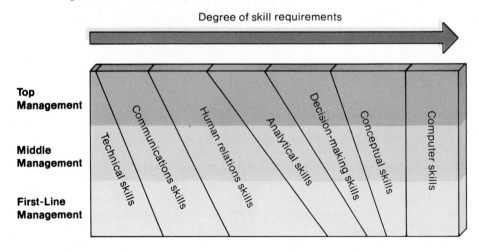

are slightly more important at higher levels of management where the environment is less stable and problems are less predictable. Finally, decision-making and conceptual skills are extremely critical to the performance of top managers. Top management's primary responsibility is to make the key decisions that are executed or implemented at lower levels. This requires that top management see the big picture in order to identify opportunities in the environment and develop strategic plans to capitalize on these opportunities. The many skills required of an effective manager is one of the reasons so many individuals find the field so challenging.

Managerial Roles

We now know that different managers perform at different levels and require different skills. At this point, we want to examine what managers actually do and how they spend their time. One of the most frequently cited studies of *managerial roles* was conducted by Henry Mintzberg. He observed and interviewed five chief executives from different industries for a two-week period. He determined that managers serve in 10 different but closely related roles.[12] These are illustrated in Figure 2–7. The figure indicates that the 10 roles can be separated into three categories: interpersonal roles, informational roles, and decisional roles.[13] Table 2–1 briefly describes each role and lists the specific activities each comprises.

---

[12]Henry Mintzberg, *The Nature of Managerial Work* (Englewood Cliffs, N.J.: Prentice-Hall, 1980).

[13]Henry Mintzberg, "The Manager's Job: Folklore and Fact," *Harvard Business Review,* July–August 1975, pp. 49–61; Jay W. Lorsch, James P. Baughman, James Reece, and Henry Mintzberg, *Understanding Management* (New York: Harper & Row, 1978), p. 220; and Neil Snyder and William F. Glueck, "How Managers Plan—The Analysis of Managers' Activities," *Long-Range Planning,* February 1980, pp. 70–76.

Figure 2–7 Managerial roles.

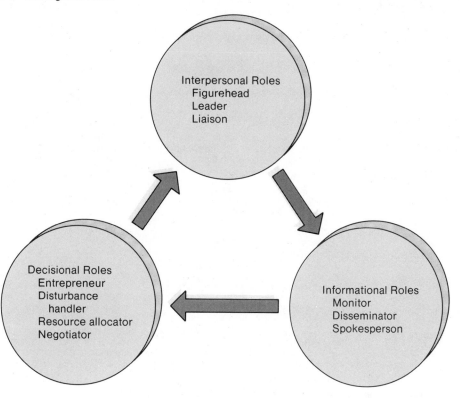

Interpersonal roles.   The three roles of figurehead, leader, and liaison grow out of the manager's formal authority and focus on interpersonal relationships. By assuming these roles, the manager is also able to perform informational roles which, in turn, lead directly to the performance of decisional roles.

All managerial jobs require some duties that are symbolic or ceremonial in nature. Some examples of the *figurehead role* include a college dean who hands out diplomas at graduation, a shop supervisor who attends the wedding of a subordinate's daughter, and the mayor of New York who gives the key to the city to an astronaut.

The manager's *leadership role* involves directing and coordinating the activities of subordinates. This may involve staffing (hiring, training, promoting, dismissing) and motivating subordinates. The leadership role also involves controlling, making sure that things are going according to plan.

The *liaison role* involves managers in interpersonal relationships outside of their area of command. This role may involve contacts both inside and outside the organization. Within the organization, managers must interact with numerous other managers and other individuals. They must maintain good relations with the managers who send work to the unit as well as those who receive work from the unit. For example, a

Table 2–1 Mintzberg's 10 management roles: description and activities.

Roles	Description	Identifiable Activities
A. Interpersonal		
1. Figurehead	Symbolic head; obliged to perform a number of routine duties of a legal or social nature	Ceremony, status, requests, solicitations
2. Leader	Responsible for the motivation and activation of subordinates; responsible for staffing, training, and associated duties	Virtually all managerial activities involving subordinates
3. Liaison	Maintains self-developed network of outside contacts and informers who provide favors and information	Acknowledgments of mail, external board work, other activities involving outsiders
B. Informational		
1. Monitor	Seeks and receives wide variety of special information (much of it current) to develop a thorough understanding of the organization and environment; emerges as nerve center of internal and external information of the organization	Handling all mail and contacts, which are primarily informational, such as periodical news and observational tours
2. Disseminator	Transmits information received from outsiders or from subordinates to members of the organization; some information factual, some involving interpretation and integration	Forwarding mail into the organization for informational purposes, verbal contacts involving information flow to subordinates including review sessions and spontaneous communication
3. Spokesperson	Transmits information to outsiders on the organization's plans, policies, actions and results; serves as expert on the organization's industry	Board meetings, handling mail and contacts involving transmission of information to outsiders
C. Decisional		
1. Entrepreneur	Searches the organization and its environment for opportunities and initiates "improvement projects" to bring about change; supervises design of certain projects as well	Strategy and review sessions involving initiation or design of improvement projects
2. Disturbance Handler	Responsible for corrective action when the organization faces important, unexpected disturbances	Strategy and review involving disturbances and crises
3. Resource Allocator	Responsible for the allocation of organizational resources of all kinds—in effect the making or approving of all significant organizational decisions	Scheduling, requests for authorization, any activity involving budgeting and the programming of subordinates' work
4. Negotiator	Responsible for representing the organization at major negotiations	Negotiation

Adapted from: H. Mintzberg, *The Nature of Managerial Work* (Englewood Cliffs, N.J.: Prentice-Hall, 1980), pp. 91–92.

college dean must interact with individuals all over the campus, a supervisory nurse in an operating room must interact with supervisors of various other groups of nurses, and a production supervisor must interact with engineering supervisors and sales managers. Managers also often have interactions with important people outside of the organization. It is easy to see that the liaison role can often consume a significant amount of a manager's time.

Informational roles.   The *informational role* establishes the manager as the central point for receiving and sending nonroutine information. As a result of the three interpersonal roles discussed above, the manager builds a network of interpersonal contacts. The contacts aid him in gathering and receiving information as a monitor and transmitting that information as the disseminator and spokesperson.

The *monitor role* involves examining the environment in order to gather information, changes, opportunities, and problems that may affect the unit. The formal and informal contacts developed in the liaison role are often useful here. The information gathered may be competitive moves that could influence the entire organization or the knowledge of whom to call if the usual supplier of an important part cannot fill an order.

The *disseminator role* involves providing important or privileged information to subordinates. The president of a firm may learn during a lunch conversation that a large customer of the firm is on the verge of bankruptcy. Upon returning to the office, the president contacts the vice president of marketing, who in turn instructs the sales force not to sell anything on credit to the troubled company.

In the *spokesperson role,* the manager represents the unit to other people. This representation may be internal when a manager makes the case for salary increases to top management. It may also be external when an executive represents the organization's view on a particular issue of public interest to a local civic organization.

Decisional roles.   Developing interpersonal relationships and gathering information are important, but they are not ends in themselves. They serve as the basic inputs to the process of decision making. Some people believe *decisional roles*—entrepreneur, disturbance handler, resource allocator, and negotiator—are a manager's most important roles.

The purpose of the *entrepreneur role* is to change the unit for the better. The effective first-line supervisor is continually looking for new ideas or new methods to improve the unit's performance. The effective college dean is continually planning changes that will advance the quality of education. The effective marketing manager continually seeks new product ideas.

In the *disturbance handler role,* managers make decisions or take corrective action in response to pressure that is beyond their control. Usually the decisions must be made quickly, which means that this role takes priority over other roles. The immediate goal is to bring about stability. When an emergency room supervisor responds quickly to a local disaster, a plant supervisor reacts to a strike, or a first-line manager responds to a breakdown in a key piece of equipment, they are dealing with disturbances in their environments. They must respond quickly and must return the environment to stability.

The *resource allocator role* places a manager in the position of deciding who will get what resources. These resources include money, people, time, and equipment. Invariably there are not enough resources to go around, and the manager must allocate the scarce goods in many directions. Resource allocation, therefore, is one of the most critical of the manager's decisional roles. A first-line supervisor must decide whether an overtime schedule should be established or whether part-time workers should be hired. A college dean must decide which courses to offer next semester, based on available faculty. The president of the United States must decide whether to allocate more to defense and less to social programs.

In the *negotiator role,* a manager must bargain with other units and individuals to obtain advantages for her unit. The negotiations may concern work, performance, objectives, resources, or anything else influencing the unit. A sales manager may negotiate with the production department over a special order for a large customer. A first-line supervisor may negotiate for new typewriters, while a top-level manager may negotiate with a labor union representative.

Mintzberg suggests that recognizing these 10 roles serves three important functions. First, they help explain the job of managing while emphasizing that all the roles are interrelated. Neglecting one or more of the roles hinders the total progress of the manager. Second, a team of employees cannot function effectively if any of the roles is neglected. Teamwork in an organizational setting requires that each role be performed consistently. Finally, the magnitude of the 10 roles points out the importance of managing time effectively, an essential responsibility of managers if they are to successfully perform each of the 10 roles.

Managerial level and roles.   As you might expect, the level in the organization will influence which managerial roles are emphasized, although at every level, each role must be performed to some degree. Obviously, top managers spend much more time in the figurehead role than do first-line supervisors. The liaison role of top and middle managers will involve individuals and groups outside the organization, while at the first-line level, the liaison will be outside the unit but inside the organization. Top managers must monitor the environment for changes that can influence the entire organization. Middle managers monitor the environment for changes likely to influence the particular function (for example, marketing) that they manage, and the first-line supervisor is concerned about what will influence his unit.

THE EXTERNAL ENVIRONMENT

Thus far in this chapter, we have examined three important factors—types of managers, managerial skills, and managerial roles—which influence managerial behavior and performance. We know the value of each of these factors will differ from situation to situation and manager to manager. Another factor influencing a manager's ability to perform is the external environment, a set of outside forces that are difficult to control. These factors may have a profound impact on how well a manager performs.

Recall from our discussion of the open-systems concept in the previous chapter that an organization interacts with the external environment and receives feedback. The open-systems view encourages managers to examine the world and events outside the organization. Much of what occurs inside the organization in terms of performance is affected by the external environment. The organization's goals, structure, staffing program, reward and discipline system, and performance evaluation programs reflect external environmental factors.

The tobacco industry (discussed in this chapter's Management Incident) is one example of the external environment's impact on an industry's organizations. The airline industry is another insightful illustration of the environment's considerable influence. Until recent years, the airline industry's operations were regulated by the U.S. government, a quite powerful external constituency. Government regulations determined the fares an airline charged for flights, the airline's flight routes, and even the size of its fleet of planes.

Once these controls were lifted by deregulation, another external force—competition—became a critical factor. An airline's existence depended on closely monitoring the moves of its competitors and responding quickly and effectively. Obeying this new rule of survival, the industry quickly plunged into a fare-cutting war with each airline matching or beating another's fare reductions. Matching competitor moves in flight discount promotions (such as red-eye flights and frequent-flyer programs) was also essential to attract customers.

When lower fares forced airlines to cut costs to stay competitive, discontent among two other external forces—national union organizations and customers—substantially affected airline companies. The airlines conducted tough negotiations with unions to secure wage cuts and endured labor strikes in several instances. With lower-quality service resulting from severe internal cost cutting, customers complained loudly about service problems (lost baggage, canceled flights) and about increased risks of flying. As a result, the federal government is considering passing laws to protect the consumer's interests, laws that will affect airline operations. In sum, several external forces have critically affected the operations and performance of companies in the airline industry.[14]

Like the airlines, organizations must continually scan and evaluate the forces in the external environment. Beyond the forces discussed, factors such as the economy, culture, technology, and the availability of information and money must be monitored. To ensure survival, organizations must respond to environmental developments with speed and effectiveness.

It is not possible for us to discuss each of the important environmental influences in detail in these few pages. However, it is necessary to outline the broad impacts of environmental influences on the job of managing. Our discussion of environmental effects will focus on the different types of environments in which organizations compete. An organization's environment may be classified as *turbulent, hostile, diverse,* or *technically complex.*[15]

A Turbulent Environment

An organization in a turbulent environment faces rapid changes on a regular basis. These changes may come from technological innovations, changes in government regulations, or economic or competitive shifts. Because of a lack of environmental stability, this is an extremely difficult environment in which to manage.

The soft drink industry is an example of a turbulent environment. There, Coca-Cola Co. and PepsiCo are engaged in the so-called cola wars, an intense battle for

---

[14]See Tom Brown, "Up in the Air but Losing Ground," *Industry Week,* September 7, 1987, p. 13; and Jo Ellen Davis, "Showdown Time at Eastern," *Business Week,* February 8, 1988, pp. 20–21.

[15]Pradip N. Khandwalla, *The Design of Organizations* (New York: Harcourt Brace Jovanovich, 1977), pp. 326–40.

market leadership. Both giants have introduced new products at a dizzying rate, continuously implemented new pricing policies, launched advertising blitzes, and made major acquisitions of other companies. Coca-Cola is buying many of its independent bottlers to build up its distributing system; PepsiCo has purchased the Seven-Up Co. in a megamerger. These speedy and often major changes have affected the sales and strategies of Dr Pepper, Diet Rite, and other soft drink competitors.[16]

A Hostile Environment

When an organization faces intense competition for customers, resources, or both, it is operating in a hostile environment. The U.S. automobile industry faces such an environment. General Motors, Ford Motor Company, and Chrysler are engaged in fierce competition with each other and with tough Japanese and Korean automakers. Intense competition has affected literally every aspect of management, from pricing and car warranty policies, to plant location and operations, and union contracts.[17]

As the following Management Application discusses, the market for overnight air mail delivery is another intensely competitive environment. There, Federal Express and United Parcel Service are competing for the market's leadership.

MANAGEMENT APPLICATION

THE BATTLE FOR LEADERSHIP IN OVERNIGHT DELIVERY

Few markets are as intensively competitive as overnight mail delivery service. The market's growth rate has declined and competitors are fiercely fighting for a larger share of customers and profits. Leading the battle are Federal Express, the Memphis-based company that pioneered overnight delivery, and United Parcel Service, a powerful contender that is challenging Federal Express's leadership.

The two companies are quite different. With 58 percent of the overnight market, Federal Express uses high technology to ensure that all packages picked up as late as 6 P.M. are delivered nationwide by 10:30 the next morning. Its bright white, orange, and purple-colored pickup/delivery vans are each equipped with a computer terminal that is linked to the company's mainframe computers. Such equipment enables headquarters to continually update the van's pickup schedule. While on the road, the courier simply checks his terminal screen for any changes. At each pickup, every package is bar-coded and the code is entered into the main computer network. As a result, the company can locate in an instant any package at every step of its journey from initial pickup to final delivery.

[16]See Thomas Moore, "He Put the Kick Back into Coke," *Fortune,* October 26, 1987, pp. 45ff; Betsy Morris, "Coca-Cola's Corporate Strategy Is Divide and Conquer," *The Wall Street Journal,* October 8, 1987, p. 6; and Amy Dunkin, "Pepsi's Marketing Magic: Why Nobody Does It Better," *Business Week,* February 10, 1986, pp. 52ff.

[17]For an overview of the U.S. and international auto industry, see James B. Treece, "Will the Auto Glut Choke Detroit?" *Business Week,* March 7, 1988, pp. 54ff.

Every night, all pickups are flown to the company's central hub in Memphis where 3,000 employees frantically sort the some 880,000 letters and packages for transport on Federal Express planes to their final destinations. High technology speeds the sorting process. Federal Express maintains an easygoing, velvet-gloved management style; employees are nonunion and well paid. The company emphasizes clever, entertaining television commercials to attract business.

With 15 percent of the market, United Parcel Services (UPS) does not use high technology; most jobs are performed manually. However, the company uses scientific management principles of time-motion study to obtain exceptional productivity from its employees. Tough productivity standards are based on a study of all regular stops on delivery routes. An industrial engineer travels the route with the courier in UPS's dark brown van, studies the courier's movements with a stopwatch, and devises ways to make delivery more efficient. All jobs at UPS's sorting centers are studied the same way.

The UPS work force is unionized and highly committed to the company. Management is conservative, and traditionally has shunned national advertising. But no longer. Three times the size of Federal Express, UPS is putting its considerable resources to the task of snaring the market's top spot from Federal Express. Its television commercials are frequent, its fleet of planes are larger, and its overnight delivery prices are lower. UPS is also investing funds to implement the kind of technology that has given Federal Express some competitive advantages (because of technology, Federal Express comes when you call; UPS must maintain strict pickup schedules).

Federal Express's response: it is working on new ways to lower prices and stay profitable and it is emphasizing the larger package (and more profitable) segment of the overnight market (a segment that historically has been UPS's domain). Who will win? Federal Express is the leader, but UPS is considered the best-managed company in the transportation business. The race is too close to call.

Source: Adapted from Larry Reibstein, "Federal Express Faces Challenges to Its Grip on Overnight Delivery," *The Wall Street Journal*, January 8, 1988, pp. 1, 8; and Kenneth Labich, "Big Changes at Big Brown," *Fortune*, January 18, 1988, pp. 56ff.

A Diverse Environment

An international organization such as McDonald's Corporation is a good example of a firm facing a diversity of languages, consumers, governments, cultures, and food tastes. This diverse environment influences not only what the organization does and how it does it, but when it makes certain moves, as well.

For example, because of cultural taste differences, McDonald's alters its Big Mac and menu in different countries. In Tokyo, slight changes are made in the amount of onions and salt added to a Big Mac and to the amount of catsup put on a regular hamburger. In Brazil, McDonald's sells a soft drink made from guarana, a berry produced in the Amazon. In Malaysia, Singapore, and Thailand, a McDonald's milk shake contains durian, an unpleasant-smelling Southeast Asian fruit that is believed by customers to be an aphrodisiac.[18]

---

[18]Kathleen Deveny, "McWorld?" *Business Week*, October 13, 1986, pp. 78–82, 86.

Domestic companies that produce numerous products which are sold to different markets also face a diverse environment. For example, Philip Morris produces cigarettes, Miller Beer, a wide variety of food products, paper products, and develops real estate properties. Tenneco, Inc., produces food products, automobile parts, aircraft carriers, natural gas, and chemicals. Each product requires different technology and raw materials, and each is sold to a different market.

A Technically Complex Environment

The electronics, computer, and telecommunications industries operate in technically complex environments. They demand sophisticated information and the recruitment of highly technical personnel to survive. New developments can occur quickly, and present products can fast become obsolete as technological breakthroughs occur.

This frenetic pace of technological change is evident in the computer industry. IBM, Apple, Compaq Computer, and other computer makers must not only develop new products quickly and continually; they must meet if not beat their competitors' developments. IBM is currently experiencing the problems of fast technological change. Because personal computers have quickly become more powerful in functions and memory capacity, the market for large, mainframe computers is declining. Mainframes provide 60 percent of IBM's profits.[19]

MANAGERIAL RESPONSES TO A CHANGING EXTERNAL ENVIRONMENT

Since an organization must operate in a world that includes changing environmental forces, managers must respond to them. There are no sure methods of coping with environmental forces, but there are some that can be used with varying degrees of success. An organization can attempt to change the external environmental forces in a way that is suitable to its needs and goals.[20] Or, through its management team it can develop suitable internal responses for coping with the changes. We will describe a few of the internal responses used to maintain and sustain performance.

Fire Fighting

The fire-fighting response to environmental forces, though not recommended or particularly effective, is surprisingly popular. Following this approach means sitting back and letting things happen—and *then* dealing with the result.[21] The problem with this type of response is that the external force—a problem or a competitor—may have

---

[19]Paul B. Carroll and Hank Gilman, "Mainframe Slowdown and Stiff Competition Put Pressure on IBM," *The Wall Street Journal,* November 23, 1987, pp. 1,10. Also see Brian O'Reilly, "Apple Finally Invades the Office," *Fortune,* November 9, 1987, pp. 52ff; and John W. Wilson, "Suddenly the Heavyweights Smell Money in Computer Networks," *Business Week,* April 27, 1987, pp. 110ff.

[20]Richard L. Daft, *Organization Theory and Design* (St. Paul, Minn.: West Publishing, 1983), p. 55.

[21]Grover Starling, *The Changing Environment of Business* (Boston: Kent, 1984), pp. 300–301.

become so big by the time the company reacts that any response is an uphill battle. Because they came late into the small car market (subcompact cars), U.S. automakers allowed foreign market penetration by Toyota and others to become so significant that even today American makers must struggle to survive.

Such observations about fire fighting in the technological environment are also valid when other external environmental forces are considered. For example, the benefits of early reaction to government dissatisfaction with a particular management practice shouldn't be underestimated. If a firm, or even an industry, acts promptly, it can set its own standards and possibly preclude government action. At worst, the firm or industry can have some say in shaping the law and policies that the government imposes. The alternative, ignoring government concern (safety features on cars or in coal mines), can result in laws that are written by legislators with little concern for the problems created for managers.

As the following Management Application notes, a small but growing number of companies are no longer maintaining a fire-fighting attitude toward management crises. Rather, they are developing well-laid plans for handling company disasters should they occur.

MANAGEMENT APPLICATION

PREPARING FOR DISASTER

Deaths from cyanide-laced Tylenol capsules. Union Carbide's industrial accident that killed thousands in Bhopal, India. The near-disaster at the Three Mile Island nuclear plant. These crises have struck organizations and incurred considerable human and financial costs. However, despite their widespread publicity, most companies are poorly prepared to handle management disasters. According to one study, only 38 percent of the major U.S. industrial companies have crisis management teams. In midsize companies, only 32 percent have prepared crisis communications plans, according to another study.

However, a small but growing number of companies are developing just-in-case strategies for handling crises. They are establishing crisis management teams (usually comprised of the CEO, the chief operating and financial officers, public relations officials, and sometimes lawyers). Companies are identifying potential disasters and developing action plans for handling them.

Some organizations such as H. J. Heinz Co., stage mock crises. "We try to say, 'What would we do if the president of the company were kidnapped, if a plant burned down, if somebody alleged tampering with a product,'" said a Heinz official. The company then develops responses and executes them in a simulated emergency. The simulation reduces response time should the crisis actually occur and builds management confidence about handling the crisis.

Mock disasters are also regularly staged at the Niagara Mohawk Power Corp., a utility and nuclear power plant operator. Company officials are given "confrontational training" sessions where reporters aggressively question them about a company crisis during a mock press conference. The company has found that the training has improved spokesperson's skills in handling difficult questions under public pressure. Many companies appoint one crisis spokesperson for the company. Often, the CEO assumes this role.

Some companies with crisis management planning also develop a crisis management manual that describes a step-by-step procedure for handling certain crises. However, some companies such as SmithKline/Beckman Corporation, shun this approach. After the company recalled its Contac capsules after rat poison was found in several capsules, some executives suggested that a detailed manual be developed. However, the company opted for a one-page memo that identifies possible crises and the employees who should be contacted. The reason: too much detail slows the reaction process and muddles thinking.

Source: Adapted from Nancy Jeffrey, "Preparing for the Worst: Firms Set Up Plans to Help Deal with Corporate Crises," *The Wall Street Journal,* December 7, 1987, p. 23; and "Hill and Knowlton Survey Reveals Lack of Preparation of Mid-sized Growth Companies for Corporate Crisis," *PR Newswire,* May 28, 1987.

Organizational Structure

As the complexity in the external environment increases, so does the complexity in organizational structure. Each force in the external environment requires an internal organizational response. For example, customers in the environment are the main responsibility of the marketing department within the organization. Likewise, the technological changes and advancements in the environment are the responsibility of a research and development unit within the firm.

James D. Thompson viewed the organization as a technical core surrounded by *buffers.*[22] The technical core performs the primary activity of an organization. In a university it is the faculty, while at the Ford Motor Co. it is the production workers. The buffers are departments that absorb the uncertainty created by the external environment. Marketing, research and development, and other functional departments are the buffers that a firm needs to make the technical core as efficient as possible. Threats, changes, and other uncertainties that influence the technical core can be buffered by creating additional departments in the organization. Thus, the more complex its environment, the greater the number of departments an organization will need.

The Boundary Spanning Job

A boundary spanning job is one that links two or more systems in different organizations such as a firm and its external environment.[23] An example of a boundary spanning job is that of the Frito-Lay salesperson. He or she is a link between the company and the supermarket customer and can carry information and ideas back and forth between the firm and the environment.

---

[22]James D. Thompson, *Organizations in Action* (New York: McGraw-Hill, 1967), pp. 20–21.

[23]J. Stacy Adams, "The Structure and Dynamics of Behavior in Organization Boundary Roles," in *Handbook of Industrial and Organizational Psychology,* ed. M. Dunnette (New York: John Wiley & Sons, 1976), pp. 1175–99.

The boundary spanner serves two major purposes: She can detect and process information about changes in the external environment and represent the organization to the public. These functions are extremely important because they can provide data, suggestions, and ideas to decision makers who can use the information to devise and implement plans for coping.

Strategic Planning

This subject will be covered in detail in Chapter 6. However, it must be introduced here since it is a crucial managerial response to external environmental forces. In simple terms, *strategic planning* is a management process that involves the determination of the basic long-term objectives of the organization and the adoption of specific action plans for attaining these objectives. The five interrelated elements of strategic planning are: (1) analyzing the environment in terms of mission, threats, changes, and opportunities; (2) establishing objectives; (3) performing a situational analysis focusing on the external environmental forces that play the most significant role in the firm's success; (4) selecting the approach(es) (strategies) that will be used to accomplish the objectives; and (5) implementing and monitoring the actions necessary to accomplish the goals of the strategic plan.

Several studies support the notion that a strategic response to external environmental forces is both needed and beneficial. One group of researchers studied 90 companies that had made concerted efforts to respond strategically to environmental forces.[24] They found that firms using strategic planning outperformed those that did not in earnings growth, sales growth, and earnings per share. In another study, researchers examined strategic planning in 57 corporations.[25] The researchers measured the effects of strategic planning decisions on investment returns. They found that the more systematic the strategic planning, the higher the company's return.

Today's managers will have to consider these and other responses. The fire-fighting response is easy to initiate, but the results are not usually good. Organizational modifications are inevitable and should be given a high priority when developing plans for adjusting to changes. Effective use and support of boundary spanners is crucial for maintaining or achieving high levels of performance. Managers must recognize crucial changes in the external environment and possess the necessary skills to bring about appropriate action.

MEASURING PERFORMANCE: A NECESSITY

One important way to determine how successful managers are is to use a system of performance measurement. Performance measures form the basis on which strengths and weaknesses can be analyzed and against which programs for improvement can be

---

[24]H. Igor Ansoff et al., *Acquisition Behavior of U.S. Manufacturing Firms, 1946–1965* (Nashville, Tenn.: Vanderbilt University Press, 1971).

[25]Sidney Schoeffler et al., "Impact of Strategic Planning on Profit Performance," *Harvard Business Review,* April 1974, pp. 137–45.

made. All members of an organization need some kind of benchmark to provide an indication of how well they are doing, but there is little agreement on how performance should be measured. However, we believe that there are primary measures of performance needed at the organizational, managerial, and individual levels.

Organizational Performance

We regularly judge the performances of various enterprises. For example, most of us would agree that Penn Central Railroad, W. T. Grant, A&P, and Montgomery Ward & Co. did not perform well in the 1970s. American Motors, Financial Corporation of America, Texas Air, and Johns Manville have not performed effectively in the 1980s.[26] As the following Management Application notes, the performances of Merck & Co., PepsiCo, Ford Motor Co., Walt Disney, and Compaq Computer Corp. have been exceptional.

MANAGEMENT APPLICATION

THE WINNERS' CIRCLE

What are the five best-managed companies in America? Each year, *Business Month* magazine convenes a panel of 20 business experts to answer the question by evaluating companies on the basis of managerial excellence and financial performance. Here are the panel's selections, presented in alphabetical order:

Compaq Computer Corp.   This young, Houston-based manufacturer of personal computers made the list because of its exceptional performance while battling toe to toe with the industry giant, IBM. Compaq's primary weapon: the DeskPro 386, a personal computer that runs programs three times faster than any competitor. IBM labored nine months to produce a comparable product. By then, Compaq had debuted a suitcase version of DeskPro; Compaq's portables chased IBM out of the portable market. The company also leads the way in making IBM-compatible machines that offer high quality and many features. In sales to businesses through retailers, Compaq has 25 percent of the PC market second only to IBM's 40 percent. The company is only eight years old.

Ford Motor Co.   The once mediocre maker of American cars now is the most profitable U.S. car manufacturer. While the market declined 8 percent, Ford boosted its market share to 23 percent largely due to big gains in product quality and design. Chairman Donald Petersen successfully implemented a companywide quality improvement program and invested in new technology that boosted plant productivity. Ford plans to continue its success by focusing on sales overseas.

---

[26]American Motors, FCA, Texas Air, and Johns Manville are among the 10 least-admired corporations in America, according to Fortune's 1987 survey. The 10 most-admired are: Merck & Co., Rubbermaid, Dow Jones, Procter & Gamble, Liz Claiborne, 3M, Philip Morris, J. P. Morgan & Co., R. J. Reynolds/Nabisco, and Wal-Mart Stores. See Ellen Schultz, "America's Most Admired Corporations," *Fortune*, January 18, 1988, pp. 32ff.

Merck & Co. This pharmaceutical maker made the grade by investing dollars in basic research that resulted in nine new, important drugs and several other substantially improved ones. Its biggest development: Mevacor, a cholesterol-reducing drug that is expected to become the most profitable drug ever made ($1 billion in annual sales). The company is flexible and attracts top technical talent that produces top-quality prescription drugs. More major breakthroughs are expected from Merck.

PepsiCo. The judges picked PepsiCo because of signs that the company is ending its runner-up status to Coca-Cola. PepsiCo has increased market share by becoming more aggressive in marketing. It also gained on Coke overseas by purchasing The Seven-Up Co. Big gains have also been achieved in its restaurant group (Kentucky Fried Chicken, Pizza Hut) and its snack food group. PepsiCo's formula for success emphasizes managerial autonomy and fierce competitiveness. Its goal: to become the world's largest provider of fast food.

Walt Disney. In recent years, Walt Disney Productions made movies that few came to see. However, with a new CEO, the company launched a dramatic three-year turnaround by improving management, implementing tight cost controls, and pursuing growth. Walt Disney shifted its movie focus to adults and scored some big hits. Successes have also come in network and cable TV with several series and The Disney Channel. Its theme parks are booming; more Disney parks will soon be built in the United States, Europe, and Asia.

In sum, most of the companies in the winners' circle are noted for their aggressiveness and focus on product quality.

Source: Adapted from Arlene Hershman, "A Keen Sense of Boom," *Business Month,* December 1987, pp. 22–23, and profiles on the five companies by Fred V. Guterl, Thomas J. Murray, Lynn Adkins, Stephen W. Quickel, and Aimee L. Stern, pp. 25, 29, 31, 35, 37 respectively.

An obvious criterion of corporate performance is *survival*. Both W.T. Grant and Penn Central are no longer in business. Beyond survival, however, it is not that easy to identify criteria for successful corporate performance.

The primary measure of an organization's success—and its primary responsibility—is the performance of its mission. The key to carrying out this responsibility is making a profit. To make a profit, a firm must create more value than it consumes. Profit means adding, creating, and increasing. Profit is a crucial *organizational performance* measure, but it doesn't provide a total picture of a firm or department's success.

In this book, we shall use four broad criteria of organizational performance. We present them as the overall objectives an organization must achieve to ensure the ultimate objective of survival. These criteria are *profitability, competitiveness, efficiency,* and *flexibility*. Business firms usually develop specific measures of these criteria. Some popular measures are:

- □ *Profitability*—return on equity, return on assets.
- □ *Competitiveness*—percentage growth in sales, market share.
- □ *Efficiency*—labor cost per unit of output, total cost per unit of output.
- □ *Flexibility*—employee satisfaction and turnover, investment in employee development, expenditures on research and development for new products.

Since these criteria for successful organizational performance will be discussed in much detail in the next chapter, it is only necessary at this point that the reader see that they are used throughout this book. We can evaluate organizational performance as good or bad to the degree that measures such as return on investment, market share, and employee turnover improve relative to past performance and/or relative to performance by similar organizations.[27]

We have to this point examined profit-oriented organizations. The not-for-profit organization is today becoming the most common kind of institution in the United States.[28] Conservatively, about 35 percent of all employed people work for not-for-profit organizations—federal, state, and local governments; schools; hospitals; and hundreds of other organizations that qualify under the tax codes for nonprofit status.

The difference between Cook County Hospital and Sears, Roebuck & Co. in Chicago is that the hospital exists for reasons other than to make money. Sears, Roebuck must generate more income from the goods and services it sells than it spends for labor, material, and the use of capital. If Cook County Hospital fails to produce an operating surplus, which it has for years, it must use reserve capital, if available, or raise more capital.

Inherent in the interpretation of organizational performance in the not-for-profit institution is a mandate for efficiency and accountability.[29] Such organizations are accountable for the development of a *clear* mission, the operation of cost-effective programs that accomplish relevant goals, and the proper allocation of funds. There are other useful measures of performance for such organizations, but these are widely applied. As they indicate, managing the organizational performance in a not-for-profit institution is a formidable challenge with no easy answers or formulas for success.

Some criteria of organizational performance in profit-oriented firms are objectively measurable, but we must nevertheless use them with caution. In both types of organizations, there are some important questions to be asked about methods of measurement.

1. How stable is the measure? A measure used one time may not be as valid another time. For example, growth in market share may be important in a rapidly expanding market but not in a stable or shrinking market.

2. How precise is the measure? Not only are many measures difficult to compute, but often there is more than one way to arrive at them. For example, employee satisfaction and investment in employee development can be measured in a variety of ways. How can the clarity of an organization's mission be determined with any degree of precision?

3. How important is time? It is important to evaluate the measures in the short and long run. For example, a measure of profitability or

---

[27]*Forbes, Fortune,* and *Business Week* magazines evaluate corporate performance in this way. For example, in its January issue, *Forbes* measures managerial performance by combining various financial and marketing indexes and rating every major company both within its own industry and in comparison with industry as a whole. *Business Week* develops similar ratings every quarter, and *Fortune* rates the "Fortune 1000" firms.

[28]Philip Kotler, *Marketing in Nonprofit Organizations* (Englewood Cliffs, N.J.: Prentice-Hall, 1982).

[29]Alan Andreasen, "Nonprofits: Check Your Attention to Customers," *Harvard Business Review,* May–June 1982, pp. 105–10.

competitiveness may appear excellent in the short run but may be jeopardizing employee satisfaction or the condition of the plant and its equipment in the long run.

An important step toward measuring organizational performance is the development of stable, precise, and time-sensitive measures. The remainder of the book will show that these are worthwhile measurement criteria—but they can't always be achieved.

Managerial Performance: Line Units

Ideally, managers should strive for consistent results in all four areas of organizational performance: profitability, competitiveness, efficiency, and flexibility. The purpose of managerial performance is to achieve organizational performance. Thus, while performance is influenced by other factors such as technology and the external environment, generally speaking, the more effective managerial performance is, the closer the organization comes to achieving its objectives.

One way to examine managerial performance is to classify jobs into line versus staff functions. A *line manager* manages activities that are central to the organization's core function—the creation and sale of output. A *staff manager* manages activities that support the core or line functions of the organization. Many staff managers are specialists who provide advice to line managers.

We will look at two *line units,* manufacturing and marketing, and two *staff units,* research and development and finance, to illustrate how managerial performance can be measured.

The manufacturing or production function. The primary goal of manufacturing in Procter & Gamble, Digital Equipment Corporation, and General Electric Co. is to produce the company's products on time, within cost, and at acceptable levels of quality. The production unit is a major line unit with managers operating at the top, middle, and first-line managerial levels. General measures of performance include production costs, material costs, and labor costs. Managers are considered good performers if they maintain favorable efficiency ratios (such as cost of goods produced as a percentage of sales), percentage of scrappage, machinery downtime, and number of rejects.[30]

The marketing function. Absolute size and growth of the business are often used as an index of marketing management. Another important measure is market share, which involves estimating the firm's share of total industry sales for products or product lines. Market share is computed by dividing company sales by industry sales. Another common marketing management measure is sales penetration, company sales divided by sales potential.

A marketing manager must measure market responses in the present and estimate them in the future.[31] This year, for example, how will auto buyers respond to model

---

[30]Michael Nash, *Managing Organizational Performance* (San Francisco: Jossey-Bass, 1983), p. 201.

[31]Ibid., pp. 200–201.

changes, price increases, rebates, and promotional campaigns? Will customers continue to select gas-efficient models or will the shift to larger cars continue? Measurement of market responses is used to assess marketing programs.

Sales managers' success is measured by examining the aggregate performance of their subordinates in terms of number of calls made, orders received, and average order size per salesperson. A sales manager whose sales team is not generating sufficient volume or calls is considered to be performing inadequately. However, sales and cost figures do not tell the entire story about a sales manager's performance. These performance dimensions can be affected by competitors' actions, such as price cutting and promotional tactics.

Managerial Performance: Staff Units

Measuring the performance of line managers is difficult, but it is much easier than measuring the performance of staff managers. Since staff units are advisory and consume money, they are considered to be cost centers. Thus, while the units bring money into the organization, staff units consume it. This doesn't mean that the staff manager's performance is unimportant or immeasurable. It is essential in order to improve overall organizational performance to monitor a staff unit's performance.

Research and development. The purpose of a research and development (R&D) unit is to conduct basic and applied research to develop the organization's future products and to improve its existing products.[32] Product improvement and creation are not easy to assess accurately. Specific measures of R&D performance are difficult to find. However, ratios such as the R&D budget as a percentage of sales, sales revenue of products developed in the last three to five years as a percentage of sales, and reduction of cost of goods through product improvement can be used as indexes. The number of patents, amount of research grant money, and number of professional papers prepared by the unit can be calculated. Also, the time and costs required to develop new products or product improvements can be traced over a period of one, two, or three years to examine R&D performance.

Finance. The role of the finance unit is to keep concise records, issue timely and accurate reports, and forecast financial climate in the future.[33] Also, the unit is responsible for raising and managing cash and capital, managing the firm's financial structure, and contributing to organizational profits by making sound financial decisions about taxes and depreciation. In some cases, goals are set to improve the accuracy, timeliness, and clarity of the firm's financial system. Other measures of financial management performance include the hours of labor and cost in dollars required to produce financial reports, the average time required to produce data, and the number of errors in reports. Another measure is the satisfaction with the financial reporting system expressed by line managers.

The identification of relevant management performance dimensions for line and

---

[32]Ibid., pp. 202–3.

[33]Ibid., pp. 204–5.

staff managers follows the description of job responsibilities and duties. The performance dimensions of line unit managers are more conducive to objective measurement than are those of staff unit managers.[34] The few management performance dimensions presented are intended simply to provide a sample, not an exhaustive or recommended list, of how performance is assessed in line and staff units. A manager's performance in a line or staff unit, profit or not-for-profit institution, is largely dependent on the efforts, behavior, and outputs of his or her groups of subordinates.

INDIVIDUAL PERFORMANCE

In Chapter 16, a thorough presentation and discussion is devoted to individual performance measures and techniques. Although managers have always informally evaluated the individual performance of subordinates, systematic appraisal techniques first appeared in the early part of the 20th century.[35] Today individual performance measures are used to make managerial decisions related to salary changes, promotions, and employee development.

Five trends have emerged in individual performance measurement in recent years: (1) involvement of the individual as part of the measurement process; (2) use of individual performance measurements for strategic planning and assessment of managerial effectiveness as well as controlling performance; (3) increase in measurement of individual goal performance; (4) increase in complexity of individual performance techniques; and (5) expansion of litigation involving issues of individual performance. Measuring individual performance correctly is more important than ever because now organizations can be assessed for damages if they make errors in the process.[36] It would be reassuring if using a particular set of individual performance dimensions or techniques would clearly indemnify the employer; unfortunately, as we will see in Chapter 16, although some measures and techniques are better than others, none is ideal or suited to every individual and job.

The fundamental problem in measuring and analyzing the performance of individuals is psychological in nature. People are threatened by measurement of their performance. They know that individual performance assessment can have negative effects on rewards such as salary increases, promotion, and better work assignments. Also a poor assessment can injure self-esteem and discourage an individual in future performances. Although everyone wants some feedback, it is important to hear good news in addition to criticism.[37]

Despite these problems, it is important to develop valid criteria for individual performance measurement. As we stated in the discussion of organizational perform-

---

[34]In increasingly competitive environments, many corporations are reducing the number of staff managers and assigning staff functions to line units or hiring outside consultants to perform specialized staff activities. This trend is particularly evident at the corporate headquarters level of large companies. See Thomas Moore, "Goodbye, Corporate Staff," *Fortune,* December 21, 1987, pp. 65ff.

[35]Richard I. Henderson, *Performance Appraisal* (Reston, Va.: Reston Publishing, 1984), p. 127.

[36]W. F. Cascio and H. J. Bernardin, "Implications of Performance Appraisal Litigation for Personnel Decisions," *Personnel Psychology,* Summer 1981, pp. 211–26.

[37]John M. Ivancevich and William F. Glueck, *Foundations of Personnel/Human Resource Management,* 4th ed. (Plano, Tex.: Business Publications, Inc., 1989).

ance, stability, precision, and timeliness are mandatory features of an individual performance dimension. It is difficult to suggest individual performance dimensions that can be applied to different kinds of work—computer programmer, production line worker, nurse, waitress, laboratory technician, teacher, police officer. However, a starting point in identifying individual performance for most jobs is to think in terms of *quantity, quality,* and *creativity.*[38]

For a production line worker, individual performance can be measured by counting the number of units produced or processed per day, per week, and so on. Similarly, a salesperson's performance can be assessed by the number of sales over a given period of time. These *quantity*-based measures do not apply neatly to all jobs, nor are they complete measures of individual performance. Variability in individual quantity output can be caused by factors beyond the individual's control. One production line worker may produce more because she works with a better machine. A saleswoman may have more sales volume because her territory is bigger or better.

A second problem with the quantity measure is that it doesn't tell the whole story about individual performance.[39] The production line worker who produces more units per day may also be producing more defective units. Quality may be a goal at least as important as quantity. For example, the salesman may spend a lot of time helping customers or potential buyers, and this must be weighed against sales volume. In the long run, new customers may increase sales volume significantly. Attracting new customers is a measure of *creativity* that should be given more recognition and weight in individual performance measurements.

Another type of individual performance measure is usually found in the personnel/human resource data in an organization. Unexcused *absences* and *lateness* are two critical individual performance measures. In most jobs, employees who are unexcused for absence and are late are considered poorer performers than others. In some organizations continued abuse of these two performance indicators can result in being fired. However, the measurement and interpretation of absenteeism and lateness is a thorny area. What should be done with an employee with excessive unexcused absences and lateness who is still judged to be a better performer in terms of quantity, quality, and creativity? Before making a final judgment, managers need to examine the reasons for absence or lateness. (For example, is the problem due to a personality clash with co-workers? a snowstorm? an ill child?)

These five individual performance dimensions are summarized with some examples for each in Figure 2–8. Again, we are not offering these dimensions as the best or only individual performance indicators. They do, however, represent an example of some of the problems associated with measuring individual performance.

A manager's realization of an organization's potential is dependent, in large part, on his or her application of skills in performing the various necessary roles. Managers need technical, analytical, decision-making, human relations, communication, and conceptual skills at each level in the hierarchy. Each of these and other relevant skills

---

[38]Carl R. Anderson, *Management: Skills, Functions, and Organization Performance* (Dubuque, Iowa: Wm. C. Brown, 1984), p. 88.

[39]Paul M. Muchinsky, *Psychology Applied to Work* (Homewood, Ill.: Dorsey Press, 1983), p. 249.

Figure 2–8 Individual performance dimensions.

Dimension	Measurement examples
Quantity	Production line work: Number of units produced. Salesperson: Number of units sold. Nurse: Number of patients cared for. Accountant: Number of reports audited.
Quality	Production line work: Number of defective units produced. Salesperson: Average of sales to customer calls. Nurse: Patient feedback on quality of care. Accountant: Errors found in audited reports.
Creativity	Production line work: Suggestions made for work improvements. Salesperson: Number of new accounts. Nurse: New practices suggested and implemented. Accountant: Modifications made in auditing system that are accepted by management.
Absenteeism	Production line work: Frequency of unexcused absences. Salesperson: Number of days missed because of unexcused absence. Nurse: Frequency of unexcused absences relative to other nurses. Accountant: Timing of unexcused absences during tax season.
Lateness	Production line work: Frequency of lateness. Salesperson: Type of reason cited for lateness. Nurse: Pattern of lateness (Monday-Friday). Accountant: Total time late per month.

are learned and developed as a manager plans, organizes, controls, and leads the work of subordinates.

Figure 2–9 summarizes how the management process, the internal environment, and the external environment are interrelated at the organizational, managerial, and individual levels. Performance assessment provides the basis for gauging how successful the organization, manager, or individual is in conducting the work of the system. In most cases, less than ideal performance measures are used as indicators. This doesn't mean that simplistic or incomplete measures are totally acceptable. It only means that research into understanding, analyzing, and improving performance within organizations must continue.

As the model in Figure 2–9 indicates, both the external and internal environments exert pressure that directly impacts the managerial process. The failure to utilize a systematic set of planning, organizing, controlling, and leading actions would lead to chaos and little focus on the responsibility of the organization to achieve high performance. The application of the management process results in performance. Figure

Figure 2–9 The interrelationships of management process, internal environment, and external environment.

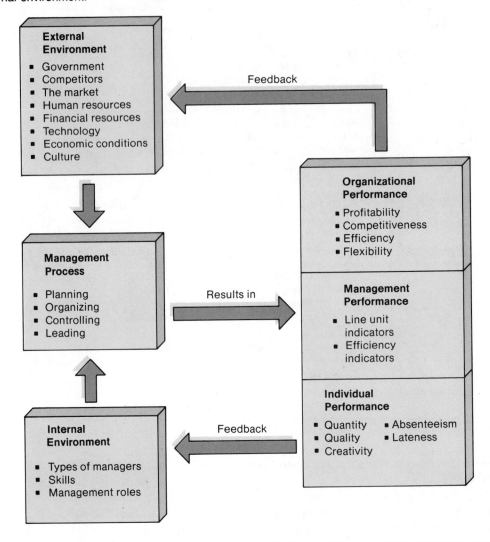

2–9 doesn't provide a complete picture of the process-performance linkage since specific details of each of the processes are not represented. For example, an organizational structure with the necessary buffer units must be established to achieve performance. These are both organizing activities that are not presented. It is not possible to include every process activity in a concise modeling of the interrelationships.

As we will clearly show and report in the following pages, a manager's job is to influence what happens. Acceptable performance at any level will not happen unless the manager is proficient in applying skills. Managers who are willing to put forth the effort, time, and patience, and who possess the needed skills, will achieve and sustain the kind of performance needed to survive.

MANAGEMENT SOLUTION

THE TOBACCO INDUSTRY'S STRATEGY FOR SURVIVAL

R. J. Reynolds/Nabisco and Philip Morris, the industry's two giants, have launched a four-part strategy for survival which other tobacco companies are generally following. The two giants together own over 70 percent of the U.S. cigarette market.

Diversify via acquisition.   Both companies are lessening their financial dependence on the tobacco industry by purchasing companies in other, unrelated industries. In 1985, both companies made major acquisitions. R. J. Reynolds spent $4.9 billion of its cigarette profits to buy Nabisco Brands (the makers of Oreo cookies, Del Monte foods, Planters nuts, and other products). Philip Morris spent $5.6 billion to acquire General Foods, a company of almost equal size. GF makes Oscar Mayer meats, Kool-Aid, and other food products. The trend toward acquiring different companies will continue because most cigarette makers still have much cash from cigarettes to spend.

Cut costs and boost production efficiency. Many companies are spending money to automate their factories. For example, R. J. Reynolds has spent $2 billion in plant modernization. Its totally automated cigarette plant in Tobaccoville, Virginia, cuts, dries, and blends tobacco by machine. The plant makes 110 billion cigarettes each year, about twice the output of an older facility that has three times as many

employees. This strategy is designed to reap a larger profit from every pack of cigarettes sold.

Focus on international markets.   Many companies are targeting countries where pressures to stop smoking are insubstantial and where import barriers have been dropped. Japan recently abolished its 23 percent import tariff on cigarettes. U.S. manufacturers now have 10 percent of the Japanese market which is the second largest free market for cigarettes (after the United States). An even more lucrative market is China where smokers consume 400 billion cigarettes each year. However, import tariffs are high.

Develop tobacco-related products.   R. J. Reynolds's "smokeless" cigarette is a step in this direction. The cigarette emits no smoke after the first few puffs. Many observers believe that this invention, if accepted by smokers, will eventually save the tobacco industry. Other companies are developing a chewing gum that contains finely ground tobacco and nicotine and is flavored (e.g., cinnamon, peppermint).

Some industry observers believe that while sales will dwindle, the tobacco industry will remain relatively strong because cigarettes are addictive. Smokers need to smoke. However, others point to the strength of the growing antismoking movement which could make America smokeless. Rumors abound that companies such as R. J. Reynolds may abandon tobacco. Re-

Continued

(*Concluded*)

gardless, the current plight of the tobacco industry is a convincing illustration of the impact that uncontrollable factors in the external environment can have on an industry and its businesses.

Source: Adapted from Scott Ticer, "Where There's Smoke, There's Trouble," *Business Week*, January 18,

1988, pp. 88–89, and "Big Tobacco's Fortunes Are Withering in the Heat," *Business Week*, July 27, 1987, pp. 47ff; Daniel P. Wiener, "Puffing Up a Second Wind," *U.S. News & World Report*, September 28, 1987, pp. 80ff; and Joan O'C. Hamilton and Emily T. Smith, "'No Smoking' Sweeps America," *Business Week*, July 27, 1987, pp. 40–43, 46.

MANAGEMENT SUMMARY

☐ Certain managerial skills and roles are essential for performance and to enable a manager to respond to the external environment which influences organizations.

☐ Management's response to the increasing complexity of an organization as it develops can be discussed in terms of horizontal and vertical specialization.

☐ Three types of managers are found in most complex organizations. They are first-line management, middle management, and top management.

☐ Seven skills are central to successful management. They can be classified as technical, analytical, decision making, computer, human relations, communication, and conceptual. The relative importance of most of these skills differs across the three levels of management.

☐ In his classic study, Henry Mintzberg identified 10 specific roles of management and grouped them into three categories: interpersonal, informational, and decisional.

☐ Organizations exist and compete in one of four types of external environment: turbulent, hostile, diverse, and technologically complex. To ensure survival, organizations must continually monitor forces in the environment and effectively respond to important environmental changes.

☐ There are four specific managerial responses to a changing external environment. These are discussed as fire fighting, organizational structure, boundary spanning, and strategic planning.

REVIEW AND DISCUSSION QUESTIONS

1. Why would it be important for a manager, in discussing performance at any level, to make sure he or she also discusses whether the short or long run is an important issue?

2. A professional football team like the Miami Dolphins has to be concerned with organizational, managerial (coach), and

   individual performance. Explain these performance variables in terms of the team.

3. A common misconception is that organizations only wish to have managers with technical skills. Why is this viewpoint dangerous and incorrect?

4. If quantity, quality, creativity, absenteeism, and lateness are good individual performance measures, why don't all organizations use them?

5. Some management observers assert that Mintzberg's typology of 10 managerial roles is incomplete. What other roles do managers assume?

6. Of the four types of environment (turbulent, hostile, diverse, and technologically complex), in which environment in your opinion is it most difficult for an organization to succeed?

7. Some management experts assert that computer skills aren't relevant at the top-management level because executives don't use computers. Why might this be the case? Explain.

8. Is there any management situation in which the 10 roles identified by Mintzberg are not important?

9. Some individuals claim that organizations can respond to environmental changes by in turn changing the environment. How can an organization change its environment? Provide examples of such activity.

10. What types of measures would you use to measure the performance of Federal Express? Burger King?

CASES

2–1 TURNAROUND AT TOP GUN

The Tactical Air Command (TAC) is a large unit of the U.S. Air Force charged with protecting U.S. interests in the skies throughout the world. TAC employs over 115,000 individuals in more than 150 worldwide installations. With 3,800 aircraft, its fleet of planes is easily twice as large as all U.S. airlines combined.

In the late 1970s, TAC was in trouble. Half of its planes were not battle ready; well over 200 planes were "hangar queens"—unusable for at least three weeks because needed spare parts were not available or maintenance checkups could not be carried out. More important, poor maintenance of the planes had boosted the rate of accidents and deaths. Many pilots weren't receiving the air time needed to stay sharp. Morale was low. TAC's best pilots and maintenance/technician personnel were leaving the U.S. Air force in considerable numbers.

In 1978, TAC received a new commander, General W. L. (Bill) Creech. A 30-year Air Force veteran, Creech's task was to turn around the now embarrassingly mediocre command.

Creech began by tackling the problem in plane maintenance. The procedures for maintaining or repairing planes at that time were bureaucratic and slow. Because of centralized management, it often took several days to obtain a part and to make a simple repair. Quality was also a problem because often the less-experienced maintenance workers repaired the planes. As a result, more than 80 percent of the planes needing repair were not fixed in an average eight-hour shift.

Delays meant that planes sat idle. In 1969 on average, a plane flew 23 "sorties" (practice and training flights) each year; in 1978, the number was down to 11. With planes waiting in line in hangars, pilots missed their training flights. And when planes were flown, they often weren't repaired or maintained.

To address this problem, Creech restructured TAC. The new operating unit became the squadron (24 planes) instead of the much larger wing unit. Instead of keeping the centralized maintenance group that worked on all planes in an installation, Creech established squadron maintenance crews staffed by technicians from the various maintenance specialities. Each crew worked on its own squadron's planes. The crews, including their office-bound sergeant, also moved directly to the flight lines.

Creech's strategy had an impressive impact on morale. Maintenance crews began sporting their squadron's patches on their fatigues and caps. Crew members, especially the crew chief, developed an identity with their squadron's planes; many of the chiefs were young, in their early 20s. Once given relatively little managerial responsibility, they were now in charge of $27 million jets. Crew discipline tightened up as the chiefs held their technicians strictly accountable.

The squadron's pilots took notice of the crew's commitment, and a camaraderie developed between pilot and crew. To further promote this commitment, Creech allowed each squadron to paint its colors on its planes—a previously prohibited practice. Competition between squadrons emerged on pilot performance and maintenance quality. Creech established a yearly awards banquet for each wing unit where trophies were awarded to the year's top maintenance and supply specialists.

Creech's next step was to improve the planning and scheduling of sorties. This task had traditionally been done by officers at wing headquarters. Creech changed that. Each TAC squadron was given a sortie objective; the squadron set its own schedules as long as the goal was met. To boost crew motivation, Creech established a bonus: if a squadron achieved its monthly objective early, everyone in the squadron received an extra three-day weekend. The squadrons responded. Each year, a squadron earns about 10 extra three-day weekends.

Creech made other changes. He simplified the spare parts system which was very cumbersome (ordering and receiving a part required 243 entries on 13 different forms and 16 hours of administrative work). Creech computerized the spare parts system and purchased minicomputers for the squadron crews. With the computerized system, crews could order parts at their computer terminal in a instant; the part suppliers at the supply station could almost as quickly fill the order. A walk to the supply store normally obtained a part in minutes.

Believing that a high-quality operation should also look high quality, Creech ordered a thorough housecleaning of every TAC facility. All the facilities received a new coat of paint, and many living and working quarters were renovated.

Creech encountered much resistance in implementing his turnaround strategy in part because he decentralized TAC. He moved decision-making authority to the lower levels of the organization. Resistance understandably came from many officers at the higher levels who felt their authority had been diminished.

However, eventually the results of the general's efforts won converts. TAC doubled the number of sorties flown each day. Now on any day, 85 percent of TAC's planes are mission ready. Only a few hangar queens are grounded. Accident rates have been substantially reduced; few accidents occur because of maintenance problems. And fewer of the best pilots and crew members are leaving TAC.

Perhaps the most impressive aspect of TAC's turnaround—these achievements were accomplished with no additional funding, personnel, or planes. The Pentagon is now implementing General Creech's ideas in several other military installations.

Questions

1. In your opinion, what managerial skills (technical, conceptual, analytical, and so on) did Bill Creech utilize the most in accomplishing the turnaround at TAC?

2. What managerial roles were most important in performing the turnaround task?

3. In your opinion, what types of measures are likely used to measure the performance of TAC?

Source: Adapted from Jay Finegan, "Four-Star Management," *Inc*, January 1987, pp. 42ff.

2–2 HELL CAMP

At the foot of Mount Fuji in Japan is the Kanrisha Yosei Gakko, a training school for Japanese executives. In the last eight years, almost 100,000 Japanese managers have attended the 13-day training program. The school's purpose is to teach managers assertiveness and discipline, and to improve their management skills and ability to perform well under considerable stress. The camp is designed to toughen Japanese managers for international competition and the demands of success (which requires "100 liters of sweat, 100 liters of tears").

Most of the camp's recruits are managers on their way up the corporate ladder at such companies as Honda, Toyota, and Hitachi. But moving up requires getting through Hell Camp which isn't easy. The camp begins with an initiation ceremony. There, the recruits recite the school pledge which amounts to admitting serious weaknesses and making a strong commitment to correct them. Each recruit receives the 16 "ribbons of shame" that are pinned to his white uniform shirt. Each ribbon represents a shortcoming (e.g., in writing, speaking, working with others). A ribbon is removed only after passing a rigorous test in the subject each ribbon represents; all ribbons must be removed before a recruit can graduate.

Recruits spend the next 12 days working to remove their ribbons of shame. Each 16-hour day begins at 5 A.M. when the managers rise for a cold shower. To teach discipline, a recruit has a strict time requirement to complete the shower (along with time schedules for washing individual body parts). After breakfast, the recruits proceed to the exercise field for a strenuous round of calisthenics, led by shouting instructors who time the exercisers with stopwatches.

The recruits spend the rest of the day working to remove their ribbons. They memorize and shout long, sometimes nonsensical passages; they write speeches and deliver them before their classmates. They take walking training daily—timed walks across the grounds in single file.

Much time is spent in small work groups where the recruits learn and shout the principles that the school teaches (such as no shilly-shallying, always be punctual, promise yourself to achieve the best results in the shortest time). There is much shouting by instructors and recruits because as a school official explains, "Shouting makes every person know his own force or weakness." To teach humility and discipline, the managers-to-be spend time on such tasks as cutting the lawn with scissors. The instructors are most demanding: they constantly test recruits and harshly correct their shortcomings. There is no room for laggards at Hell Camp.

On the eighth day comes a major test. Dressed in their pinstripes, each recruit goes to the railway station in nearby Fujinomiya. He stands in the middle of the station and sings, loudly and forcefully, the "Salaryman's Song" ("The things I make with the sweat of my brow, I must sell with the sweat of my brow . . ."). The manager sings before onlookers and his instructor, who grades his performance. This exercise induces humility; it also teaches self-confidence. The recruits have practiced the song repeatedly; it is very serious business.

The camp's ultimate test is a 25-mile night hike over mountain trails. If no problems are encountered, the hike takes about eight hours to complete. However, each recruit is given a map as a guide—one that is not accurate. At daybreak, many hikers are still finding their way. All are exhausted; some are in tears.

The camp concludes on the 13th day with the graduation ceremony. Dressed in their pinstripes, those with no ribbons remaining on their chest receive a diploma. Less than 30 percent of the recruits are so honored. The remaining 70 percent must attend the ceremony dressed in their camp uniform and ribbons. They continue at the camp until all ribbons are removed (usually about two additional days).

Hell Camp is a very popular training ground for Japanese managers; it claims an 80 percent success rate. These managers come away from the camp more confident, assertive, better speakers, and more skilled in working with people. By the camp's end, an estimated 12 percent of the managers are hospitalized for mental or cardiac disorders.

In 1988, the school opened a training site in Malibu, California. The school advertised for executive recruits in *The Wall Street Journal* and other major publications. However, after several weeks, no executives signed up. After cancelling several starting dates, the school launched its first 13-day session with 10 recruits. They included several self-employed salespeople, advertising staff members, a massage therapist, and a father-and-son team. These recruits attended at no charge; the camp's regular fee is about $3,000 per recruit.

Yosei Gakko made some changes in its curriculum for American recruits. The 12 ribbons of shame are called the *ribbons of challenge*. Recruits rose at 6 A.M. instead of 5 A.M. Some of the more demeaning tasks were dropped (lawn trimming with scissors). But the tasks were still difficult, and the 10 recruits sang the "Salaryman's Song" one by one outside Vons Supermarket in a shopping mall in nearby Thousand Oaks, before onlookers and their instructor. At the camp's end, several had removed their ribbons and graduated. Said one graduate, "When you turn [a] ribbon in, you feel like you have just climbed Mount Fuji."

Yosei Gakko is hopeful the camp will succeed in the United States as it has in Japan.

Questions

1. In your opinion, will Hell Camp succeed in the United States? Why or why not?

2. Regarding the chapter's discussion of managerial skills, what skills is the camp teaching its manager-recruits?

3. What changes would you make in the school's curriculum to make the training experience more useful to American managers?

Source: Adapted from Edward M. Reingold, "Welcome to 'Hell Camp'" *Time*, March 7, 1988, p. 55; Richard Phalon, "Hell Camp, Malibu-Style," *Forbes*, December 28, 1987, pp. 110, 112; and Peter Waldman, "Japanese-Style Camp for Managers Is Lost in Translation in U.S.," *The Wall Street Journal*, March 1, 1988, pp. 1, 18.

PART II

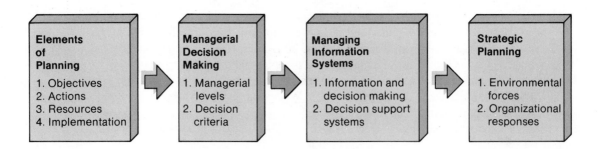

Elements of Planning

1. Objectives
2. Actions
3. Resources
4. Implementation

Managerial Decision Making

1. Managerial levels
2. Decision criteria

Managing Information Systems

1. Information and decision making
2. Decision support systems

Strategic Planning

1. Environmental forces
2. Organizational responses

THE PLANNING FUNCTION

INTRODUCTION TO PART II

Part II, the Planning Function, contains four chapters.

3 **Elements of Planning**
4 **Managerial Decision Making**
5 **Managing Information Systems**
6 **Strategic Planning**

The choice of material in these four chapters is based on the following rationale:

The planning function involves managers in activities which lead them to identify objectives and to determine strategies for achieving those objectives. Planning has become increasingly important as organizations and their environments have become more complex.

Chapter 3 describes the *four elements that are present in any form of planning.*

Chapter 4 discusses planning in the context of decision making. The material in this chapter presents several perspectives on decision making, including the relationship between managerial levels and types of decisions made at each level, and the relationship between degree of uncertainty and de-

cision criteria. Planning requires *choices* of objectives and decisions. Decision making is, therefore, an inherent feature of planning.

Chapter 5 focuses on *information systems*. As organizations grow in size and complexity, managers depend more heavily on various internal and external sources of information for planning and decision making. The material in this chapter emphasizes the need to develop management information systems for the purpose of managerial decision support.

Chapter 6 presents an important planning approach in today's rapidly changing environment—*strategic planning*. Strategic analysis focuses on the organization's environment and the appropriate responses (strategies) to changes, constraints, and opportunities in that environment.

The figure "The Planning Function," on the facing page, presents the four aspects of the planning function. Although these aspects are presented sequentially, it is important to understand that they actually interact.

THREE

Elements of Planning

LEARNING OBJECTIVES

After completing Chapter 3, you should be able to:

Define: each element in the planning process.

State: the factors that contribute to the need for planning.

Describe: the relationship between objectives and strategies.

Explain: why forecasting is a key element of the planning process.

Discuss: the primary purposes served by policies.

TURNING AROUND A FAILING COMPANY

During the last 10 years, rapidly changing financial markets, tough foreign competition, and exciting new technologies have created a dynamic era of change for most American firms. For many, this era has been one of opportunity, hard work, and success. For others, however, it has been an extremely painful era. Many American managers were trained in less volatile times and were used to managing in relatively stable and predictable environments. In an environment of relatively stable technology and stable markets, a manager could assume that the future would look like the present because the present looked like the past. Consequently, in the new environment, some managements have stumbled, and their companies need help.

What happens to a major company when it finds itself in a rapidly deteriorating situation? One increasingly used strategy is for the board of directors to call in a "turnaround specialist." These are individuals who specialize in saving companies that have stumbled. They have been referred to as *a Lone Ranger breed of manager,* and *the Green Berets of corporate management.* Before agreeing to join a firm, these individuals demand, as a condition of employment, total freedom to act and to act quickly.

Some well-known masters of the corporate turnaround are:

1. Terry E. Goldress. An engineer who previously worked for General Motors and General Electric. Currently president of a firm that specializes in turnarounds and claims a 90 percent success rate at 35 midsize companies.
2. Victor N. Palmieri. Manages his own firm of 20 turnaround specialists and concentrates on large companies.
3. Ian B. Sharlit. Cofounder of a firm which has helped rescue 500 small and private companies. Claims a 95 percent success rate.

These and similar rescuers are in great demand in these turbulent times and often achieve near miracles. However, an important question for the student of management at this point should be, "Why could the old management not do earlier what the turnaround specialist did later on?"

(The Management Solution can be found at the end of this chapter.)

Planning is the keystone management function. The functions of organizing, leading, and controlling all carry out the decisions of planning. The increased emphasis on planning can be seen readily in the great number of executive conferences, workshops, and writings on the subject during the past five years.

Although some environments are less predictable than others, *all* organizations operate in uncertain environments. For an organization to succeed, management somehow must cope with, and adapt to, change and uncertainty.[1] Planning is the *only* tool management has to help it adapt to change. If an organization does no planning, its position and fate five years hence will mostly be the result of any momentum built up previously and of luck (hopefully, good). On its own, the organization would follow some kind of course during the next five years. If management wishes to have any control over that course, however, it *must* plan. Otherwise, it will have to rely on defensive reactions rather than on planned actions. Management will be forced to respond to current pressures rather than the organization's long-run needs.

In one way or another, every manager plans. However, the approach to planning, the manner of arriving at plans, and the completeness of plans can differ greatly from organization to organization. Formal planning (as distinguished from the informal planning that we do in thinking through proposed actions prior to their execution) is an activity that distinguishes managers from nonmanagers. Formal planning also distinguishes effective managers from ineffective ones.

If you want to manage effectively the performance of individuals and organizations, you must understand the concept of, and the necessity for, planning. Planning is that part of the management process which attempts to define the organization's future.[2] More formally, *planning includes all the activities that lead to the definition of objectives and to the determination of appropriate courses of action to achieve those objectives.*

To justify the time and resources expended in planning, distinct benefits must accrue to the planner.[3] The major benefits include the following:

1. Planning forces managers to think ahead.
2. It leads to the development of performance standards which enable more effective management control.
3. Having to formulate plans forces management to articulate clear objectives.
4. Planning enables an organization to be better prepared for sudden developments.

---

[1]David A. Fischer, "Strategies toward Political Pressure: A Typology of Firm Responses," *Academy of Management Review,* January 1983, pp. 71–78.

[2]See Dalton E. McFarland, *The Managerial Imperative: The Age of Macromanagement* (Cambridge, Mass.: Ballinger Publishing, 1986).

[3]See A. A. Thompson, Jr. and A. J. Strickland III, *Strategic Management: Concepts and Cases,* 4th ed. (Plano, Tex.: Business Publications, 1987), chaps. 1 and 2 for a related discussion.

UNDERSTANDING THE NEED FOR PLANNING

You cannot develop a sound plan at any level of an organization without first understanding and appreciating the *necessity* for planning. If a manager does not believe in the value of planning (and some managers do not), it is unlikely that he or she will develop a useful plan.

To better appreciate the need for planning, consider the following four important factors.

1. The Increasing Time Spans between Present Decisions and Future Results

The time span separating the beginning of a project and its completion is increasing in most organizations. Managers today must look further into the future than ever before. For example, it took 10 years to develop the supersonic jet and 10 years for General Foods to develop Maxim, a concentrated instant coffee. Meanwhile, Campbell Soup Company spent 20 years in developing a line of dry soup mixes, and Hills Brothers worked 22 years to develop its instant coffee.

Obviously, planning becomes very critical in situations where the results of decisions will occur long after the decisions actually are made. So managers must attempt to consider what *could* happen that might affect the desired outcome. Effective planning can require large commitments of time and money, but management must seek every way possible to minimize uncertainty and its consequences. Planning is the only tool managers have to help them cope with change.

2. Increasing Organization Complexity

As organizations become larger and more complex, the manager's job also becomes bigger and more complicated by the interdependence among the organization's various parts. It is virtually impossible to find an organization (or even a division of a large organization) in which the decisions of the various functions, such as research and development, production, finance, and marketing, can be made independently of one another. The more products an organization offers and the more markets it competes in, the greater the volume of its decisions. One midwestern bank, for instance, offers more than 175 services just for its consumers (not its business customers). Planning, in these circumstances, becomes even more important for survival.

Planning enables each unit in the organization to define the job that needs to be done and the way to go about doing it. With such a blueprint of *objectives,* there is less likelihood of changing direction, costly improvising, or making mistakes.

3. Increased External Change

A major role of managers has always been that of change initiator. A manager must be an innovator and doer, someone in constant search of new markets, businesses, and expanded missions. Rapid rates of change in the external environment will force managers at all levels to focus on larger issues rather than solely on solving internal problems. The faster the pace of change becomes, the greater the necessity for organized responses at all levels in the organization.[4] And organized responses spring from well-thought-out plans.

4. Planning and Other Management Functions

The need for planning also is illustrated by the relationship between planning and the other management functions. We already know that planning is the beginning of the management process. Before a manager can organize, lead, or control, he or she must have a plan. Otherwise, these activities have no purpose or direction.[5] Clearly defined objectives and well-developed strategies set the other management functions into motion.

The effect of planning on the other management functions can be understood by considering its influence on the function of control. Once a plan has been translated from intentions into actions, its relationship to the control function becomes obvious. As time passes, managers can compare actual results with the planned results. The comparisons can lead to corrective action, and this, as we shall see later in the book, is the essence of controlling. The following Management Application describes a company which has only recently recognized the need for formal planning.

MANAGEMENT APPLICATION

COORS RECOGNIZES THE NEED FOR PLANNING

In the mid-1980s, Peter Coors and his brother Jeffrey took over the stagnating family brewery. "My father and uncle had to concentrate on getting beer out the door," says Jeff. "We're in an era where volume, success, and the bottom line do not come automatically."

That may be a profound understatement. Few other major brewers have been hurt as badly by their own blunders or by such giant competitors as Anheuser-Busch, Inc., and Miller Brewing Co. Coors' share of the key California market, for example, has fallen from 44 percent in 1976 to just over 14 percent in the mid-1980s.

Observers say the brothers are likely to move into such new businesses as biotechnology and packaging as well as to introduce some new products at the brewery. But the biggest change they see is that for the first time *formal planning* is taking place at Coors. Planning is one management function previous generations didn't bother with.

By introducing formal planning into the company, Pete and Jeff Coors have recognized the critical importance of this management function. At Coors and elsewhere,

---

[4]William R. Boulton, *Business Policy: The Art of Strategic Management* (New York: Macmillan, 1984), pp. 204–5.

[5]See Arthur C. Beck and Ellis D. Hillmar, *Positive Management Practices: Bringing out the Best in Organizations and People* (San Francisco: Jossey-Bass, 1986).

planning involves setting objectives, determining ways to achieve those objectives, evaluating resource constraints, and implementing the plan.

Source: Adapted from "Can Pete and Jeff Coors Brew up a Comeback?" *Business Week*, December 16, 1985, pp. 86–88.

THE ELEMENTS OF PLANNING

The planning function requires managers to make decisions about four fundamental elements of plans. They are:

1. Objectives.
2. Actions.
3. Resources.
4. Implementation.

Objectives are integral to plans because they specify future conditions that the planner deems satisfactory. For example, the statement "The firm's objective is to achieve a 12 percent rate of return on invested capital by the end of 1990" refers to a future, satisfactory condition.

Actions are the specified, preferred means to achieve the objectives. The preferred course of action to lead to a 12 percent return might be to engage in a product development effort so that five new products are introduced in 1990.

Resources are constraints on the courses of action. For example: "The total cost to be incurred in the development of five new products must not exceed $10 million." A plan should specify the kinds and amounts of resources required, as well as the potential sources and allocations of those resources. Specifying resource constraints also involves *budgeting*—identifying the sources and levels of resources that can be committed to planned courses of action.

Finally, a plan must include ways and means to implement the intended actions. *Implementation* involves the assignment and direction of personnel to carry out the plan.

Establishing objectives and prescribing actions also require *forecasting* the future. A manager cannot plan without explicit consideration of future events and contingencies that could affect what will be possible to accomplish.

Although the four elements of the planning function are discussed separately, they are in fact intertwined. As will be seen, objectives must be set according to what is possible, given the forecasts of the future *and* the budgets of resources. Moreover, availability of resources can be affected by the very actions that management plans. In the previous example, if a 12 percent return is not achieved, $10 million may not be available, because stockholders, bondholders, or other sources of capital will not invest the funds. Then, other action may not be feasible.

In some organizations, planning is the combined effort of managers and staff personnel. In other organizations, planning is done by the top-management group. In still others, it is done by one individual. Planning activities can range from complex, formal procedures to simple and informal ones. Although the *form* of planning activities

Figure 3–1 The planning function.

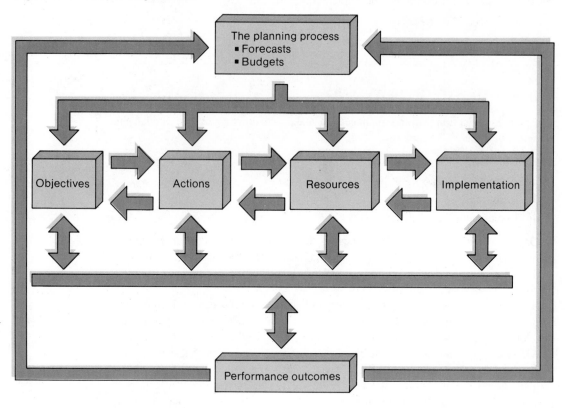

varies from organization to organization, the *substance* is the same. Plans and planning inherently involve objectives, actions, resources and implementation directed toward improving an organization's performance in the future. Figure 3–1 outlines the planning function.

ESTABLISHING OBJECTIVES

The planning function begins with the determination of future objectives, which must satisfy expectations of the organization's environment. Whether the organization is a business, a university, or a government agency, the environment supplies the resources that sustain it. In exchange for these resources, the organization must supply the environment with goods and services at an acceptable price and quality. Because of the increasing interdependence between organizations and their environments, corporate management has turned more and more to formal planning techniques. Moreover, it is clear that organizations that use formal approaches to planning are more profitable than those that do not.[6] Management initiates planning to determine the *priority* and *timing* of objectives. In addition, management also must resolve *conflict* between objectives and provide *measurement* of objectives so results can be evaluated.[7]

Priority of Objectives

The phrase *priority of objectives* implies that at a given time, accomplishing one objective is more important than accomplishing any of the others. For example, the objective of maintaining a minimum cash balance may be more important than achieving minimum profitability to a firm struggling to meet payrolls and due dates on accounts. Priority of objectives also reflects the relative importance of certain objectives, regardless of time. For example, survival of the organization is necessary for the realization of all other objectives.

Managers must establish priorities if they want to allocate resources rationally. Alternative objectives must be evaluated and ranked. Managers of nonbusiness organizations are particularly concerned with the ranking of seemingly interdependent objectives. For example, a university president must determine the relative importance of teaching, research, and community service. Determining objectives and priorities is inherently a judgmental decision—and is inherently difficult.

Time Frame of Objectives

The role time plays in planning is demonstrated in a practice common to many organizations. They develop different plans for different periods of time. For instance, the long-run objective of a business firm could be stated in terms of a desired rate of return on capital, with intermediate and short-run plans stated in terms of objectives that must be accomplished to realize the ultimate goal. Management is then in a position to know the effectiveness of each year's activities in terms of achieving not only short-run but also long-run objectives.

We have not tried to state specific time periods for plans. A bank might consider a long-term loan as one for more than five years and a short-term loan as one for less than one year. Some individuals apply the same logic to planning. In practice, definitions of long-run and short-run plans vary widely. A long-run plan in the aircraft or automobile business could extend to more than five years, while in the volatile world of women's fashion, a long-run plan might extend to only one or two years. In the children's toy business, a production or marketing plan might cover only one selling season. In other words, the organization's product, technology, and market will dictate what long-term and short-term plans are. Here you can see the contingent nature of managerial planning. The major point to remember, however, is that regardless of time spans, all organizations need planning.

---

[6]See Milton Moskowitz, "Lessons from the Best Companies to Work For," *California Management Review,* Winter 1985, pp. 42–47.

[7]Max D. Richards, *Setting Strategic Goals and Objectives,* 2d ed. (St. Paul, Minn.: West Publishing, 1985).

In recent years, the increasing pace of environmental change has prompted many organizations to implement strategic planning. *Strategic planning* focuses on all the activities that lead to the definition of long-term objectives and strategies to achieve those objectives. This is in contrast to *functional* or *operational planning,* which is done in the individual units within the organization and focuses on more immediate objectives and problems. Strategic planning is important and is the focus of Chapter 6 of this textbook.

Conflicts among Objectives

At any time, stockholders (owners), employees (including unions), customers, suppliers, creditors, and governmental agencies are all concerned with the operation of a firm. The process of setting objectives for an organization must not overlook these interest groups. Managers must instead include and integrate all the groups' interests into corporate plans. The form and weight to be given to any particular interest group, however, is a question that precisely illustrates the nature of management's dilemma. Yet management's responsibility is to make these kinds of judgments. Some of the most common planning trade-offs faced by managers in business organizations are:

1. Short-term profits versus long-term growth.
2. Profit margin versus competitive position.
3. Direct sales effort versus development effort.
4. Greater penetration of present markets versus developing new markets.
5. Achieving long-term growth through related businesses versus unrelated businesses.
6. Profit objectives versus nonprofit objectives (that is, social responsibilities).
7. Growth versus stability.
8. Low-risk environment versus high-risk environment.

Management must consider the expectations of diverse groups because the firm's ultimate success depends on them. For example, present and potential customers hold ultimate power over the firm. If they are not happy with the price and quality of the firm's product, they will withdraw their support (stop buying), and the firm will fail through lack of funds. Suppliers, too, hold power over firms. They can disrupt the flow of materials to express disagreement with the firm's activities. Government agencies, meanwhile, have the power to enforce the firm's compliance with regulations. Managers must recognize the existence of all these interest groups and their power to affect the objectives of the firm. The organization will exist only as long as it satisfies the larger society.[8]

---

[8]D. Quinn Mills, "Planning with People in Mind," *Harvard Business Review,* July–August 1985, pp. 97–105.

Studies of objectives that business managers set for their organizations attest to the difficulty of balancing the concerns of interest groups. These studies also suggest that the more successful firms consistently emphasize profit-seeking activities that maximize the stockholder's wealth. This is not to say that successful firms seek only profit-oriented objectives, but merely that such objectives are dominant. Evidently, such firms are managed by persons who value pragmatic, dynamic, and achievement-oriented behavior. These individuals, at the same time, recognize that businesses have an increasing responsibility to do what is best for society.[9] The interrelationship of the managers' values, society's needs, and organizational objectives has been aptly summarized:

> What to make, what to charge, *and* how to market the wares *are*
> *questions that embrace moral as well as economic questions. The answers*
> *are conditioned by the personal value system of the decision maker and*
> *the institutional values which affect the relationships of the individual to*
> *the community.*[10]

The following Management Application describes an organization in which management has sought to achieve a balance among objectives.

MANAGEMENT APPLICATION

AN AIRLINE WITH ITS OWN OBJECTIVES

In the plans of most airlines, expansion of market share is usually an important objective. It is accomplished by expanding their routes and flying to popular, heavily populated cities. Midway Airlines, the first new airline to take to the skies after deregulation nearly 10 years ago, has become the 14th largest U.S. airline as of 1987. Midway has succeeded by bucking conventional wisdom. It offers lower-fare, high-frequency service out of a formerly deserted airport in Chicago, 24 miles from O'Hare International Airport, the city's main airport. In addition, its major objectives are not rapid market share growth through route expansion. The airline has growth objectives but these are "measured growth" objectives because Midway Airlines does not wish to grow too rapidly and become a victim of heavy debt caused by rapid expansion which ruined other airlines such as People Express. One observer commented that Midway Airlines ". . . has missed some opportunities by moving slowly, but it hasn't made a lot of mistakes because of rushing."

Source: Adapted from "Heeding a Gospel of Measured Growth," *Business Week,* September 21, 1987, p. 62.

---

[9]See M. L. Gimpl and S. R. Daken, "Management and Magic," *California Management Review,* Fall 1984, pp. 125–36; R. T. Pascale, "The Paradox of Corporate Culture: Reconciling Ourselves to Socialization," *California Management Review,* Winter 1985, pp. 26–41; Frederick D. Sturdivant, *Business and Society: A Managerial Approach,* 3d ed. (Homewood, Ill.: Richard D. Irwin, 1985), for relevant discussions of these and related management problems.

[10]Clarence C. Walton, *Ethos and the Executive* (Englewood Cliffs, N.J.: Prentice–Hall, 1969), p. 192.

Measurement of Objectives

One important reason for having objectives is to help translate the organization's broad social purposes into measurable terms. *Objectives* serve as guides for action and as starting points for more specific and detailed objectives at lower levels in the organization. Well-managed business organizations have at least four categories of objectives: *profitability, competitiveness, efficiency,* and *flexibility.*[11]

1. *Profitability.* In business organizations, profitability is unquestionably the most important objective. Profitability provides the financial resources for future expansion or innovation. The profitability objective usually is expressed in terms of return on investment—net profit divided by the capital invested in the organization or some similar measure. Every profit-seeking organization should establish a profitability objective. Besides competing for customers, business firms also must compete for resources (particularly capital). An organization's earnings provide the return on investment, and it is for the sake of this return on investment that a shareholder is willing to supply capital. To compete successfully for this capital, an organization usually must earn a return equivalent to the risk of doing business.

2. *Competitiveness.* This objective focuses on the prospects for long-term profitability. It measures the competitive strength of the organization.[12] What is the difference between competitive strength and profitability as stated above? Consider this analogy. Assume that your present normal blood pressure indicates that you are healthy (profitable) today. Assume further that your objective is to remain healthy six months from now. To ensure you will accomplish this profitability objective, you must establish objectives in other areas today (exercise, weight control, proper diet, and so on). Measuring how well you are doing in these other areas will provide you with some idea of your "competitive strength." Each area will be an indicator of how profitable you are likely to be in the long run.

Well-managed organizations establish objectives that concentrate on specific rates of increase in sales and market share. If the economy is expanding at a certain rate, then sales growth objectives should be considerably greater than this percentage.

Clearly, measuring performance in competitive strength is different from measuring performance in profitability. It is entirely possible for an organization to have been profitable in the past but, based on performance in the competitiveness measures, to have poor prospects for long-run profitability.

3. *Efficiency.* An organization must maintain certain types of short-run efficiencies to bring about the prospect of long-run profitability. Measures of efficiency reflect how well the organization's resources are employed. Thus, while it is also a measure of profitability, a ratio such as return on assets (net profit divided by total assets), when compared to that of similar organizations, gives management some indication of how efficient the organization is internally in managing the assets of the organization.

---

[11]See P. P. Pekar, "Setting Goals in the Non-Profit Environment," *Managerial Planning,* March–April 1982, pp. 43–46 for a discussion of objective setting in nonprofit organizations.

[12]Jay B. Barney, "Types of Competition and the Theory of Strategy: Toward an Integrative Framework," *Academy of Management Review,* October 1986, pp. 791–800.

Efficiency directly influences performance and involves both the human and non-human resources of the organization. Well-managed organizations, regardless of size, establish objectives with respect to the quality of management, the succession of management, the depth of critical personnel, and employee turnover. Nonhuman resources such as the age and condition of the plant and equipment also are important indications of efficiency; objectives should be established in these areas, as well.

4. *Flexibility*. We noted earlier that managers plan not to predict the future but to uncover important factors in the present that will ensure that there is a future for the organization.[13] One way managers can guard against unforeseen problems is to maintain certain types of flexibilities. For example, a manufacturer of consumer products operating in a volatile market has a flexibility objective that states the maximum percentage of sales which can be derived from a single product. If this percentage is reached, the firm attempts to introduce a new product. Thus, if customers suddenly change their minds about any one of the organization's products and stop purchasing it, the impact on profitability is minimized. Another organization allows only a certain percentage of sales to be derived from government contracts. This practice ensures that the organization maintains its flexibility and does not become dependent on government contracts.

Other objectives.   Objectives for profitability, competitiveness, efficiency, and flexibility are capable of being measured. However, objectives for such important management concerns as social responsibility and employee attitudes are not so easily identifiable or measurable in concrete terms. This, as we shall see later in the book, is an important problem because without measurement, any subsequent evaluation will be inconclusive if not impossible. For example, vaguely stated objectives such as "to have happy and satisfied employees," or "to become more socially responsible," will be virtually impossible to evaluate whether or not they are accomplished.[14] Table 3–1 presents some selected measures of profitability, competitiveness, efficiency, and flexibility.

One Organization's Use of Objectives in Planning

Establishing specific and measurable objectives is a critical element in the entire planning process. Our discussion of objective setting is summarized in Table 3–2. It is based on one organization's actual experience in establishing objectives. This particular organization established seven objectives and management ranked them in the order of priority as shown in the table. Notice that this organization also developed

---

[13]J. K. Shim and P. McGlade, "Current Trends in the Use of Corporate Planning Models," *Journal of Systems Management,* September 1984, pp. 24–31.

[14]The great management writer Peter Drucker has observed that "the real difficulty lies indeed not in determining what objectives we need, but in deciding how to set them." See the many great works by this writer including *The Practice of Management* (New York: Harper & Row, 1954); *Management: Tasks, Responsibilities, Practices* (New York: Harper & Row, 1974); *Managing in Turbulent Times* (New York: Harper & Row, 1980); and *Innovation and Entrepreneurship* (New York: Harper & Row, 1985).

Table 3–1 Suggested areas of organizational performance and some representative measures.

Profitability	Competitiveness	Internal Efficiency	Flexibility
Return on stockholders' equity Return on assets Earnings per share Ratio of profits to sales	*Growth:* Annual rate of increase in: □ Earnings per share □ Market share □ Sales *Stability:* extent of fluctuations in: □ Sales □ Earnings □ Capacity utilization	□ Return on assets □ Return on sales □ Inventory turnover □ Turnover of working capital □ Personnel turnover □ Depth of management □ Age of plant and machinery	*External:* for example; □ Some maximum percentage of sales and/or profits that can be derived from a single customer market segment or product. *Internal:* Various liquidity and solvency measures. *Liquidity* □ Current ratio □ Acid test ratio □ Inventory to net working capital *Solvency* □ Debt to equity ratio □ Debt to assets ratio □ Long-term debt to equity ratio

objectives in such areas as social responsibility and employee attitudes and development.[15]

An important use of objectives is that they can be converted into specific targets and actions. Note that management also stated each objective in Table 3–2 in more specific secondary objectives which can become objectives for specific departments in the organization.[16] For example, the secondary objective associated with Objective 1 can serve as a financial management objective. Those associated with Objective 2 can become marketing department objectives. And those associated with Objective 3 can become the objectives of the personnel department.

DEVELOPING COURSES OF ACTION

Action is the catalyst that can determine success or failure in meeting objectives. Planned courses of action are called *strategies* and *tactics*. The difference between the two usually involves the scope and magnitude of the action. Strategies typically have long-run, organizationwide implications, while tactics usually have short-run, departmentalwide implications. In either case, a planned action is directed toward changing a present condition; that is, achieving an objective. For example, if an objective is to increase productivity from five units of output per labor-hour to six units per labor-hour, a course of action must be identified and implemented. In some instances,

---

[15]See Thomas I. Chacko, "An Examination of the Affective Consequences of Assigned and Self-Set Goals," *Human Relations,* September 1982, pp. 771–76 for an interesting and related discussion.

[16]L. R. Bittel and J. E. Ramsey, "The Limited Traditional World of Supervisors," *Harvard Business Review,* July–August 1982, pp. 26–37.

Table 3–2 One organization's use of objectives.

Objective	Possible Secondary Objectives	Possible Indicators
1. Achieve a 15 percent return on investment.	a. Earn maximum return on idle funds.	a. Interest income.
2. Maintain a share of the market of 40 percent.	a. Retain 75 percent of old customers. b. Obtain 25 percent of first-time customers.	a. Percent replacement purchases. b. Percent initial purchases.
3. Develop middle managers for executive positions.	a. Develop a merit review system by year-end. b. Select 10 managers to attend industry-sponsored executive school.	a. Report submitted on November 1. b. Number selected by January 1.
4. Help to ensure that clean air is maintained in all geographical areas in which the firm has plant locations.	a. Reduce air pollution by 15 percent.	a. By April 1, pollutants to be 125 pounds/hour measured at stack by electrostatic.
5. Provide working conditions that constantly exceed industrywide safety levels.	a. Automate loading process in Plant B. b. Reduce in-plant injuries by 10 percent by year-end.	a. Installation to be 50 percent complete by January 1. b. Ratio of labor-days lost to total labor-days.
6. Manufacture all products as efficiently as possible.	a. Increase productivity by 5 percent through installation of new punching machine.	a. Installed by August 1. b. Ratio of output to total labor-hours.
7. Maintain and improve employee satisfaction to levels consistent with our own and similar industries.	a. Improve employee satisfaction levels in all functional areas by 15 percent by year-end.	a. Ratio of quits to total employees. b. Attitude survey questionnaires administered to all employees.

managers simply do not know what action to take. When President Kennedy stated as a national objective the placing of an American on the moon by 1970, *no one* knew exactly what was necessary to accomplish that objective. However, the objective had been clearly stated and it set in motion the necessary planning activities that resulted in courses of action that ultimately made the objective a reality.

Other instances can present numerous alternative courses of action. In such cases, managers must select the alternative that is least costly, but most effective. For example, productivity increases can be achieved through a variety of means, including improved technology, employee training, management training, reward systems, and better working conditions. Often, top managers who are planning for the total organization must choose from several viable courses of action. As the plan that is chosen becomes more localized to a single unit in the organization, the number of strategies tends to become smaller, yet more familiar. Table 3–3 illustrates this objective-strategy link for individual departments in a business organization.

Table 3–3 Objectives and some possible strategies.

	Departmental Objective	Possible Strategies
Production	To produce the most maintenance-free product on the market.	1. Install new stamping machine by January 1. 2. Re-evaluate quality control program.
Personnel	To evaluate the managerial potential and the training needs of middle managers by year-end.	1. Conduct a merit review of all middle managers. 2. Evaluate available university executive programs for continuing executive development.
Marketing	To increase the purchase rate by existing buyers of Brand X 10 percent by year-end.	1. Increase the unit of purchase (e.g., larger sizes, 8- and 12-packs). 2. Make product more widely and conveniently available.
Finance	To reduce overdue accounts receivable to five months or less by year-end.	1. Hire part-time college students to analyze all accounts receivable and identify those which are overdue by more than five months.

The following Management Application illustrates the importance of knowing what you want to do and how you expect to do it.

MANAGEMENT APPLICATION

A CLEARLY STATED OBJECTIVE AND A CAREFULLY DEVISED STRATEGY

In 1986, Microsoft was very close to overtaking Lotus® as the leader in personal computer software sales. But Lotus President J. P. Manzi was devising a strategy with top IBM software executives. The two companies each had something which could help the other. Lotus needed to recharge the sales of its Lotus 1-2-3® spreadsheet, the source of 80 percent of the company's profits and IBM needed to sell more of the applications programs that make its computers more useful for buyers.

The result of the meeting: By 1988 Lotus will produce a spreadsheet called 1-2-3/M for IBM minicomputers and mainframes. During the next 10 years, Lotus and IBM will jointly develop and market products for a full range of computers. This strategy is designed to help Lotus achieve an important objective. According to J. P. Manzi, "We don't intend to be the No. 1 company in personal computer software, we intend to be No. 1 in software, period."

Source: Adapted from Anne R. Field and Alex Beam, "Lotus' Dream-Come-True: A Sweet Deal with IBM," *Business Week*, May 25, 1987, p. 116.

The important point is that courses of action and objectives are causally related; that is, the objective is caused to occur by the courses of action. The intellectual effort required in planning involves not only knowing *what* alternatives will accomplish an objective but also *which* one is most efficient. In some instances, managers can test the effects of a course of action by forecasting. Forecasting is *the process of using past and current information to predict future events*.

A typical objective in business planning is to maintain or increase sales volume. Sales volume is a primary source of liquid resources such as cash, accounts receivable, and notes receivable, which managers can use to finance the firm's activities. Courses of action that affect sales include price changes, marketing and sales activities, and new-product development. Factors beyond the control of management also affect sales. Such external factors include the price of competing and substitute products, competitors' marketing/sales activities, and general economic conditions (expansion, recession, inflation). Although managers cannot control many of the factors that determine sales volume, forecasting remains a valuable managerial tool.[17]

Forecasting Sales Volume

Four methods currently are used to forecast future events. Here, they are presented in the context of forecasting sales volume, although the methods generally are applicable to forecasting other events.

1. *Hunches*. Estimates of future sales can be based upon past sales data, comments by salespersons and customers, and instinctive reaction to the "general state of affairs." This approach is relatively cheap and usually effective in firms whose market is stable or at least changing at a predictable rate.

2. *Market survey*. Estimates of future sales can be based upon the opinions customers express to the organization's salespeople. More sophisticated statistical sampling techniques yield more refined information. The forecaster can specify both the range of projected sales and the degree of confidence in the estimates.

3. *Time-series analysis*. Estimates of future sales can be based upon the relationship between sales and time. The movement of sales over time is affected by at least three types of factors: seasonal, cyclical, and trend. That means a firm's sales can vary in response to seasonal factors, in response to cycles common to business activity generally, and to trends of long duration.

The management of a brewery knows that peak sales occur during the summer months. But it also is aware of the cyclical nature of beer consumption, as beer drinkers shift to liquor when their incomes increase and shift back when their incomes decline. For long-term planning, the manager also must know something about the trend in beer consumption. Consumer preferences change with time and with the introduction of new products.

---

[17]S. Makridakis, S. Wheelwright, and V. McGee, *Forecasting Methods and Applications* (New York: John Wiley & Sons, 1982).

4. *Econometric models.* These allow systematic evaluation of the impact of a number of variables on sales. Estimates of future sales can be based upon the relationship between past sales and a number of independent variables. These techniques are the most sophisticated of the methods, yet they offer no hope for the elimination of *all* uncertainty; management judgment is still needed. The econometric approach begins with the identification of those variables that affect the sales of the firm's product. Among the obvious variables are price, competing products, and complementary products. Variables such as the age of existing stocks of the goods, availability of credit, and consumer tastes are less obvious. Measurements of these variables are obtained for previous years and matched with sales of the product for the same years.

No perfect method exists for forecasting future sales. Hunches, market surveys, time-series analysis, and econometric models provide estimates that may or may not be reasonable. They can be no better than the information that goes into them. As technological breakthroughs in information processing occur, we can expect sales forecasts to become more accurate and consequently be better guides for planning. At present, however, forecasting requires a great deal of managerial judgment.

RESOURCES

The sales forecast presumes that a firm has a product to sell, so managers must first utilize resources to acquire or produce that product. And just as managers use forecasts to approximate income from sales, they must also forecast the future availability of major resources including people, energy, raw materials, and money.[18] Techniques for forecasting resources are the same as those employed to forecast sales: hunches, market surveys, time-series analysis, and econometric models. The only difference is that the analyst is seeking to know the quantities and prices of goods that can be purchased rather than those to be sold.

The sales forecast, whether for 1 or 10 years, predicts the firm's level of activity. At the same time, the prediction is conditioned by the availability of resources, by economic and social events beyond the control of management, and by the objectives established. Given an adequate supply of resources, the manager's next task is *the allocation of resources necessary to implement the plan.* The major management technique used in this phase of the planning function is the *budget.*

Developing Budgets

The next facet of managerial planning is the development of budgets for each important element of the organization. Budgets are widely used in business and government. A considerable body of literature deals with *budgeting* techniques. You should understand the close relationship between budgeting as a planning technique and budgeting as a control technique.[19]

---

[18]A. A. Thompson, Jr., "Strategies for Increasing Cost Businesses," *Academy of Management Proceedings,* August 1982, pp. 17–21.

[19]Neil C. Churchill, "Budgeting Choice: Planning vs. Control," *Harvard Business Review,* July–August 1984, pp. 150–64.

Figure 3–2   The financial budgeting process.

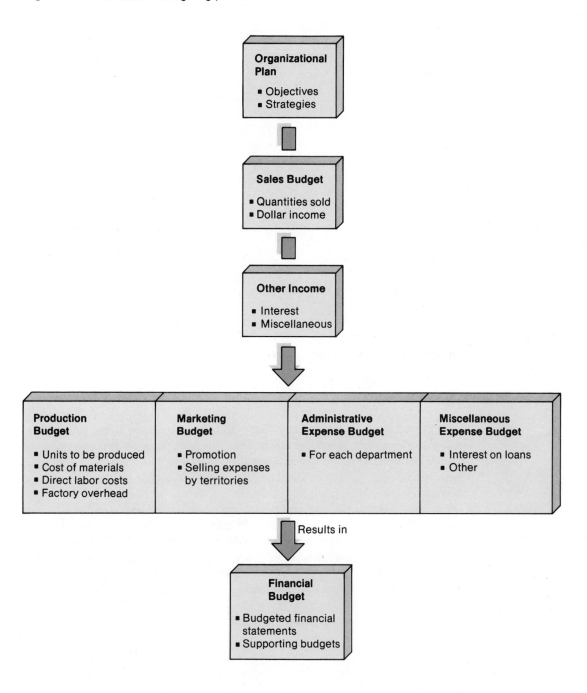

Figure 3–3 The relationship between profit and output.

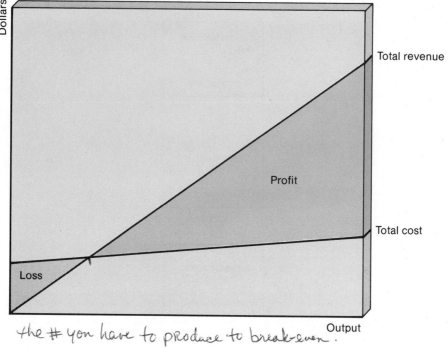

the # you have to produce to break-even.

In this section, we are concerned only with the preparation of budgets prior to operations. From this perspective, budgeting is a part of planning. However, with the passage of time and as the organization engages in its activities, the actual results must be compared with the budgeted (planned) results. Thus, budgets are also a part of management control.[20]

Financial budgeting is the process of implementing the firm's profitability and efficiency objectives and integrating the activities of the firm's various subunits. Budgeting, thus, is an important method for coordinating the efforts of the organization.

The complexity of the financial budgeting process is simplified in Figure 3–2. The sales forecast's key position is evident from the high placement of the sales budget; all other budgets are directly or indirectly related to it. For example, the production budget must specify the materials, labor, and other manufacturing expenses required to support the projected sales level. Similarly, the marketing budget details the costs

[20]Robert N. Anthony, John Dearden, and Norman Bedford, *Management Control Systems,* 5th ed. (Homewood, Ill.: Richard D. Irwin, 1984), pp. 12–13.

Table 3-4   A hypothetical variable budget.

Output (units)		1,000		1,200		1,400		1,600
Sales @ $5		$5,000		$6,000		$7,000		$8,000
Variable costs @ $3	$3,000		$3,600		$4,200		$4,800	
Fixed costs	1,000		1,000		1,000		1,000	
Total costs		4,000		4,600		5,200		5,800
Planned profit		$1,000		$1,400		$1,800		$2,200

associated with the level of sales activity that is projected for each product in each sales region. Administrative expenses also must be related to the predicted sales volume. Finally, the projected sales and expenses are combined in the financial budget, which consists of pro forma financial statements.

The usefulness of financial budgets, however, depends mainly on the degree to which they are adaptable to changes in conditions. The forecast data are based on certain assumptions regarding the future. If these assumptions prove wrong, the budgets are inadequate. Two principal means exist to provide budgetary flexibility—variable budgeting and moving budgeting.

1. *Variable budgeting* provides for the possibility that actual output deviates from planned output. It recognizes that certain costs are related to output (variable costs), while others are unrelated to output (fixed costs). Thus, if actual output is 20 percent less than planned output, actual profit will not necessarily be 20 percent less than planned profit. Rather, the actual profit will vary, depending on the relationship between costs and output. Figure 3-3 demonstrates a hypothetical situation.

The relationships shown in Figure 3-3 take the form of the familiar break-even model. The figure illustrates that profit varies with output variations, but not proportionally. Table 3-4 shows a variable budget that allows for output variations and demonstrates the behavior of costs and profits as output varies.

Variable budgeting requires adjustments in all supporting budgets for completeness. The production, marketing, and administrative expense budgets must likewise allow for the impact of output variation.

2. *Moving budgeting* is the preparation of a budget for a fixed period, perhaps one year, with updating at fixed intervals, such as each month. For example, the budget is prepared in December for the next 12 months, January through December. At the end of January, the budget is revised and projected for the next 12 months, February through January, and so on. In this manner, the most recent information is included in the budgeting process. Assumptions are constantly revised as management learns from experience.

Moving budgets have the advantage of systematic re-examination, but they are costly to maintain. Budgets are important instruments for implementing the objectives of the firm. However, the efforts given to budgets must be kept in perspective because they compete with other demands on managerial time.

IMPLEMENTATION OF PLANS

All the planning in the world will not help an organization realize objectives if plans cannot be implemented. (Implementation of plans involves resources and actions as shown in Figure 3–1.) In some instances, the manager can take all the necessary steps to apply resources in planned actions to achieve objectives. In most instances, the manager must implement plans through *other people,* motivating them to accept and carry out the plan. *Authority, persuasion,* and *policy* are the manager's means of implementing plans.

Authority

Authority is a legitimate form of power, in the sense that it accompanies the position not the person. That is, the nature of authority in organizations is the right to make decisions and to expect compliance to the implications of these decisions. Thus, a manager can reasonably expect subordinates to carry out a plan so long as it does not require illegal, immoral, or unethical behavior. Authority is often sufficient to implement relatively simple plans that involve no significant change in the status quo. But a complex and comprehensive plan can seldom be implemented through authority alone. Persuasion is another important managerial tool.

Persuasion

Persuasion is a process of selling a plan to those who must implement it, communicating relevant information so individuals understand all implications. In this sense, it requires convincing others to base acceptance of the plan upon its merits rather than upon the authority of the managers.

Persuasion does present a hazard. What happens if the plan is not implemented after all persuasive efforts have been exhausted? If the plan is crucial and must be implemented, management must resort to authority. Consequently a manager who has failed once at the use of persuasion must limit use of the technique in the future. Individuals who were the objects of unsuccessful attempts at persuasion and who had thought they had the choice of accepting or rejecting a plan would be skeptical of future persuasive efforts.[21]

Policy

When plans are intended to be rather permanent fixtures in an organization, management develops policies to implement them. Policies usually are written statements that

---

[21]See Toyohiro Kono, "Japanese Management Philosophy: Can It Be Exported?" *Long Range Planning,* Fall 1982, pp. 90–102.

reflect the basic objectives of the plan and provide guidelines for selecting actions to achieve the objectives. Once plans have been accepted by those who must carry them out, policies become important management tools for implementing them. Effective policies have these characteristics:

1. *Flexibility.* A policy must strike a reasonable balance between stability and flexibility. Conditions change, and policies must change accordingly. On the other hand, some degree of stability must prevail if order and a sense of continuity are to be maintained in the organization. A balance of flexibility and stability must exist; only the judgment of management can determine the appropriate balance

2. *Comprehensiveness.* A policy must be comprehensive enough to cover any contingency if plans are to be followed. The degree depends upon the scope of action controlled by the policy itself. If the policy is directed toward very narrow ranges of activity—for example, hiring policies—it need not be as comprehensive as a policy concerned with public relations.

3. *Coordination.* A policy must provide for coordination of the various subunits whose actions are interrelated. Without coordinative direction provided by policies, each subunit is tempted to pursue its own objectives. The ultimate test of any subunit's activity should be its relationship to the policy statement.

4. *Ethical.* A policy must conform to the canons of ethical behavior that prevail in society. The increasingly complex and interdependent nature of contemporary society has resulted in a great number of problems involving ethical dimensions that are only vaguely understood. The manager is ultimately responsible for the resolution of issues which involve ethical principles.

5. *Clarity.* A policy must be written clearly and logically. It must specify the intended aim of the action it governs, define the appropriate methods and action, and delineate the limits of freedom of action permitted to those whose actions are to be guided by it.

The ultimate test of the effectiveness of a policy is whether the objective is attained. If the policy does not lead to the objective, the policy should be revised. Thus, policies must be subjected to re-examination continually. Below are examples of policies an organization might adopt that are consistent with the above criteria:

1. A grocery chain gives store managers authority to buy fresh produce locally rather than purchasing it from a company warehouse whenever they can get a better buy.

2. An oil company decides to lease properties and buildings for its service station operations as a way of minimizing long-term capital requirements.

3. A firm requires each.product division to file weekly sales and profit reports with headquarters as a means of monitoring and evaluating progress toward corporate goals.

4. A hospital requires all patients to make a $100 cash deposit upon admittance, as part of its plan for maintaining financial solvency.

The following Management Application clearly illustrates the effective use of policies in planning.

MANAGEMENT APPLICATION

DEVELOPING POLICIES AND STICKING WITH THEM

In the early 1950s the Sbarros family operated a gourmet Italian deli in Naples, Italy. In 1956 they moved to Brooklyn, New York, with the same objective. Mrs. Sbarro's sandwiches, pasta, and cheesecakes became so popular that the delis evolved into restaurants and the family knew they were on the verge of a great opportunity.

However, they faced an old management problem: How to expand but still keep standards high in order to maintain quality? In the 1970s they decided on a policy not to franchise but to confine their growth to expanding in the New York area. Another policy was that all food served was made fresh daily at the original deli.

In the early 1980s the family continued to look for ways to expand while still maintaining high quality. In keeping with their original plan the family settled on a formula that gave the company ownership of most of its restaurants and awarded productive managers up to 15 percent of a restaurant's net profit. They still closely control service and all ingredients used in their dishes.

Source: Adapted from "Sbarro's Juicy Slice of the Fast-Food Market," *Business Week*, September 7, 1987, pp. 72–73.

ASKING THE RIGHT QUESTIONS

We have seen that planning, a fundamental activity of managers, can cover any time span from the short run to the long run. We also have surveyed some of the more important forecasting and budgeting techniques. These do not encompass the entire range of problems and issues associated with planning.[22] Our discussion has, however, underscored the fact that planning is the essence of management; all other managerial functions stem from planning.

How does a manager begin the planning process? Many professionals agree that much of the task consists of asking the appropriate questions. Table 3–5 suggests the basic ones. Other, more specific questions might well be posed. Yet the fundamental questions are appropriate regardless of the type and size of the organization.

---

[22]See Peter Mills, *Managing Service Industries* (Cambridge, Mass.: Ballinger Publishing, 1986), for discussions of the problems of managing organizations whose product is a human performance and not a tangible product.

Table 3–5 Key planning questions.

Planning Element	Key Managerial Decisions
Objectives	1. What objectives will be sought?
	2. What is the relative importance of each objective?
	3. What are the relationships among the objectives?
	4. When should each objective be achieved?
	5. How can each objective be measured?
	6. What person or organizational unit should be accountable for achieving the objective?
Actions	1. What are the important actions that bear on the successful achievement of objectives?
	2. What information exists regarding each action?
	3. What is the appropriate technique for forecasting the future state of each important action?
	4. What person or organizational unit should be accountable for the action?
Resources	1. What resources should be included in the plan?
	2. What are the interrelationships among the various resources?
	3. What budgeting technique should be used?
	4. Which person or organizational unit should be accountable for the preparation of the budget?
Implementation	1. Can the plan be implemented through authority or persuasion?
	2. What policy statements are necessary to implement the overall plan?
	3. To what extent are the policy statements comprehensive, flexible, coordinative, ethical, and clearly written?
	4. Who or what organizational units would be affected by the policy statements?

MANAGEMENT SOLUTION

TURNAROUND SPECIALISTS HAVE THEIR OWN PLAN

There is no doubt that turnaround specialists or "fixers" are in great demand as companies of all size face turbulent times, international competition, and rapidly changing technology. The success records of these individuals are also quite impressive. One question a student of management should be asking, however, is "Why couldn't the old management do earlier what the turnaround specialist did later on?"

One company success factor of turnaround specialists is that they approach the challenge with their own plan, a new "vision" of what the company could be. Experience suggests that they approach their new jobs without the sentimental

Continued

attachments to "old ways of doing things," to people, or to operations. They often eliminate favorite projects of the past and discard ailing parts of the business. Whenever possible they omit excess executive perks as well as the executives themselves. They establish new objectives to guide the company toward the vision they see. In other words, they are willing to take the actions that are necessary, no matter how

painful or unpopular they may be with employees. Sometimes the new plan does not work, but at least they give companies a possibility of survival—something the earlier management could not do.

Source: Adapted from "The Green Berets of Corporate Management," *Business Week,* September 21, 1987, pp. 110–14.

MANAGEMENT SUMMARY

- The planning function includes those managerial activities that result in predetermined courses of action. Planning necessarily focuses on the future, and management's responsibility is to prepare the organization for the future.

- Planning requires managers to make decisions about objectives, actions, resources, and implementation. These four factors are essential to effective planning.

- Through planning, management coordinates efforts, prepares for change, develops performance standards, and manages development.

- Objectives are statements of future conditions that, if realized, are deemed satisfactory or optimal by the planner. All sets of objectives have three characteristics: Priority, timing, and measurement. How management responds to priority, timing, and measurement issues in setting objectives reflects individual values and economic considerations.

- To be useful in planning, objectives should be stated in measurable terms and should relate to significant organizational performance determinants. In particular,

objectives should be set for profitability, competitiveness, efficiency, and flexibility.

- Courses of action to achieve objectives must be specified. Terms such as strategies and tactics refer to planned courses of action. An important activity in specifying courses of action is that of forecasting future demand for the organization's output and future availability of resources.

- Resource requirements of a plan must be forecast and specified by budgets. Management can select the type of budget that best suits the planning needs of the organization.

- The fourth part of planning is implementation, a phase that takes account of the fact that plans usually are carried out by other people.

- The three approaches to implementation are authority, persuasion, and policy. Approaches can be used individually or in combination.

- Implementation by policy has the advantage of continuously reinforcing the plan for those who must implement it. Effective policies are those that produce the planned course of action.

REVIEW AND DISCUSSION QUESTIONS

1. What is the relationship between the organization's broad purposes and the objectives that are part of its various plans?

2. Why should an objective be specific and measurable?

3. Give an example of a "bad" statement of objective. Point out why the statement is bad, and then reword it to eliminate its defects.

4. Most of us are not good planners. To realize this, we need only to look at what we hoped to accomplish yesterday and what we actually did accomplish. Why do you suppose most of us are ineffective planners?

5. Should the manager responsible for the work be involved in planning the work? Explain.

6. What are some of your instructor's policies in your management class? Why do you think the policies have been established?

7. Consult your school's catalog. Select any school policy statement and evaluate it, using the criteria for a good policy statement discussed in this chapter.

8. What skills do you believe an individual should have to be an effective planner? How do you believe those skills can be acquired?

9. What is the basis for saying that planning is the essential management function? Discuss.

10. A manager was overheard saying, "Plan? I never have time to plan. I live from day to day just trying to survive." Comment.

CASES

3–1   IDENTIFYING PROBLEMS FOR PLANNING

The top management of a large consumer products company was preparing for its annual planning session. Typically at these sessions, management identified the company's significant problems, set priorities, and provided guidelines and policies for the preparation of detailed plans.

The seven functional departments of the company were production, personnel, sales, staff development and training, finance, legal counsel, and engineering. Each of these functions consisted of subunits and operated on annual plans that developed from the planning session. Managers of each of the functional departments had been instructed, in advance of the sessions, to define the single significant problem facing the company from the perspective of that function. Top managers would devise a set of company problems from those enumerated by the functional managers. Problems were ranked in order of priority. The problems presented for discussion are summarized in the following paragraphs.

Excessive downtime of machine-paced operations was the major concern of the production manager; downtime had increased by 20 percent over the previous year. The problem was blamed on the need for more intensive preventive maintenance to stay within quality-control tolerances imposed by new, more restrictive state consumer protection laws.

The manager of the personnel department perceived things differently, seeing the major company problem as the excessive number of grievances that went to the departmental level for arbitration. The personnel manager indicated that the settlement of grievances at that level was usually inappropriate and reflected the inability of first-line managers to deal with problems.

The sales manager said that the major problem was the spiraling cost of product distribution. The company's distribution system was based upon regional warehouses linked to production facilities by a fleet of trucks. The rising cost of fuel was driving up the delivered cost of products and disrupting delivery schedules—all of which indicated the necessity for increasing the delivered price to customers who already were disgruntled by previous price increases.

The manager of staff development and training cited the inability of first-line supervisors to deal effectively with their subordinates as the firm's major problem. The problem grew out of the company's affirmative response to equal opportunity laws that required employment of persons formerly considered marginal. For the most part, these new employees required intensive skill training and close supervision. Moreover, they tended to be sensitive to criticism. The problem resulted in significant expense to train supervisors to manage with greater sensitivity.

To the finance department, the company's primary goal must be to reduce reliance on short-term debt to meet current obligations. The financial manager observed that the company's cash flow was seriously unbalanced, the major cause being the company's liberal credit terms and, subsequently, unpredictable collections from customers.

The chief legal officer said the company must either meet the recently legislated air quality standards or be brought under injunction. The company's principal source of power was coal. The air quality standards required the removal of air pollutants through the use of filter mechanisms, but at heavy expense to the company.

The engineering department's manager considered the company's most significant problem to be the high turnover of engineers who left for better-paying jobs with other companies. He stated that salaries must be upgraded or the company would face a continued drain of engineering talent.

Questions

1. In what order of priority would you place these problems?
2. Is there any basis for interrelating the problems, or is each a separate, unrelated problem? Explain.
3. Once problems are identified, what information is needed for subsequent planning decisions?

3–2 PLANNING AT IBM

In the mid-1980s, International Business Machines Corp. made headline news by announcing that it would invest $350 million in its Lexington, Kentucky, plant. The Lexington plant manufactures typewriters, keyboards, and printers and employs 6,200 people. IBM is the largest private employer in the city, and city officials welcomed the firm's commitment to the plant's future.

John Opel, then president and chief executive officer of IBM, said the $350 million investment would be used to purchase and install automated equipment that will increase the plant's productivity by 30 percent and make the Lexington plant "the most advanced typewriter manufacturing facility anywhere."

IBM's investment in automated manufacturing methods is but one aspect of the company's plan for the 1980s. According to published reports, IBM's plan is based on four primary objectives: (1) achieve low-cost production through investment in automated manufacturing facilities; (2) achieve low-cost distribution by selling small computers and office products through independent distributors, mail orders, catalogs, and company-owned retail stores; (3) position the organization and its products to attack the marketplace, segment by segment; and (4) pursue growth and profit opportunities in every area of the computer business from mainframe computers to home computers. These four objectives reflect IBM's transformation to a high-volume, mass-market business from a one-at-a-time, custom-built, custom-marketed operation.

IBM's plan for the 1980s and its steps to implement the plan result from a sophisticated planning system that enables IBM to react to changes in technology and the marketplace. IBM *expects* change and attempts to stay abreast of it by requiring both line managers and staff specialists to "scan the environment." When they detect a change in technology, competitors' actions, government policy, or economic activity, they alert the management, and a plan of action is initiated. IBM's planning system has two separate, yet interrelated types of plans: program plans and period plans.

Program planning involves efforts to develop a new product, improve an existing product, or improve the performance of a unit within the organization. A program plan usually has a single objective to be accomplished in a brief time span—for example, the decision to upgrade the productivity of the Lexington typewriter plant. When program planning is directed toward product development and improvement, planners first determine customer requirements for information and information processing, then translate those needs into products. If the product is one that IBM has never attempted to produce, planners will rely upon the marketing staff for specifications of the customer's needs.

IBM relies on information obtained from its own econometric model to forecast demand for its products as well as to forecast the U.S. economy. Other sources of forecast data are (1) analysis of growth and replacement patterns for existing and new products, (2) extrapolations of historical information, (3) interviews and questionnaire data obtained from customers, and (4) analysis of backlog for existing products. These forecasts are combined for projections of future product demand, and projections are translated into product targets and plans of action.

Period planning involves the total organization and each unit within the organization. Each unit may have several program plans in various stages of implementation, but only one period plan is in effect at any one moment. The period plan has two components: (1) a long-range corporate plan and (2) short-range unit plans.

The long-range corporate plan covers a five-year period. It results from considerable interaction between line, field, and corporate staff under the direction of the Corporate Management Committee (CMC). The plan specifies corporate and operating-unit profit targets, which then are implemented by specifying corporate and unit strategies that reflect best estimates of economic conditions, competitors' moves, and product development. The corporate plan is the master plan, the basis for action taken throughout the corporation during the five-year period. Four basic objectives—low-cost production, low-cost distribution, product positioning, and wide-spectrum competitive effort—are included in IBM's corporate plan.

The short-range unit plans cover two years and are based upon the corporate plan. Each unit prepares a plan that focuses on budget and implementation issues. The unit's responsibility is to achieve its assigned target by taking appropriate action within the parameters of its operation. (The Office Products Division, for instance, must pursue action that reduces production costs. Investing in automated equipment is appropriate action to take to achieve the corporate objective.) Each unit submits its plan to the CMC, where it is reviewed for compatibility with the corporate plan. When approved, the unit proceeds with implementation.

Questions

1. Evaluate IBM's approach to planning in terms of the four fundamental parts of plans.

2. In what ways does IBM attempt to react to environmental changes in its planning system?

3. Some critics say that IBM moved too slowly into the personal-computer market. If that criticism is valid, can the fault be IBM's planning system? Explain.

FOUR

Managerial Decision Making

After completing Chapter 4, you should be able to:

Define: the major types of managerial decisions.

State: why managers at different levels in the organization concentrate on certain types of decisions.

Describe: the process of decision making and the various phases of the process.

Explain: the importance of the various influences on the decision-making process.

Discuss: group decision making and compare it to individual decision making.

WHAT DO YOU DO WHEN YOUR MAJOR COMPETITOR HITS AND YOU MISS?

Burger King Corporation is a most successful giant in the fast-food burger business. However, even though Americans spend over $13 billion per year on fast-food burgers, the market during the last few years has been rather stagnant, with little growth. In addition, Burger King's sales were flat during the early part of 1987.

For these reasons and others as well, Burger King began to look carefully at its advertising. The company spends $200 million per year on advertising. It has used the same advertising agency for 11 years and was concerned that the agency has been unable to create an advertising campaign in the last few years that would boost the chain's market share. Meanwhile, the No.

1 fast-food burger chain, McDonald's Corporation, has been able to launch several "hit" advertising campaigns.

Most observers agree, however, that it was the widely disliked and unsuccessful "Herb" campaign in 1986 that finally brought Burger King's problem to a head. One expert commented that Burger King's ads have "ranged from horrible to mediocre," while another called the *Herb* campaign a "terrible, terrible campaign." It was clear that Burger King needed to do something.

(The Management Solution to this Management Incident can be found at end of this chapter.)

The focus of this chapter is the decision-making aspects of planning. Planning, in many respects, *is decision making*. Planning involves deciding which objectives to set, which forecasting method to use, which strategies to apply to each objective, how much and what types of resources should be budgeted, and which policies are appropriate. A manager is continually making decisions throughout each stage of planning, and the quality of plans is determined in large part by the decision-making skills of managers.

WHY STUDY DECISION MAKING?

Managers at all levels make decisions. These decisions may ultimately influence the survival of the organization or the starting salary of a new college trainee. All decisions, however, will have some influence—large or small—on performance.[1] Thus, it is important for managers to develop decision-making skills. Like it or not, managers are evaluated and rewarded on the basis of the importance, number, and results of their decisions. The quality of the decisions that managers reach is the yardstick of their effectiveness and of their value to the organization.[2]

TYPES OF DECISIONS

Although managers in large business organizations, government offices, hospitals, and schools may be separated by background, lifestyle, and distance, they all sooner or later must share the common experience of making decisions. They all will face situations involving several alternatives and an evaluation of the outcome. In this section, we will discuss various types of decisions.

Programmed Decisions

Programmed decisions are the decisions managers make in response to repetitive and routine problems. If a particular situation occurs often, managers will develop a routine procedure for handling it.

Nonprogrammed Decisions

When a problem has not arisen in exactly the same manner before, or is complex or extremely important, it may require a *nonprogrammed decision*. Decisions are termed *nonprogrammed* when they are made for novel and unstructured problems. Making such decisions is clearly a creative process.

The two classifications—programmed and nonprogrammed—are broad, yet it is important to clearly differentiate between them.[3]

---

[1]Victor H. Vroom, "Reflections on Leadership and Decision Making," *Journal of General Management*, Spring 1984, pp. 18–36.

[2]Sara Kiesler and Lee Sproull, "Managerial Response to Changing Environments," *Administrative Science Quarterly*, December 1982, pp. 548–70.

[3]Herbert Simon, *The New Science of Management Decision* (New York: Harper & Row, 1960), pp. 5–6. Also see Herbert Simon, *Reason in Human Affairs* (Stanford, Calif.: Stanford University Press, 1983).

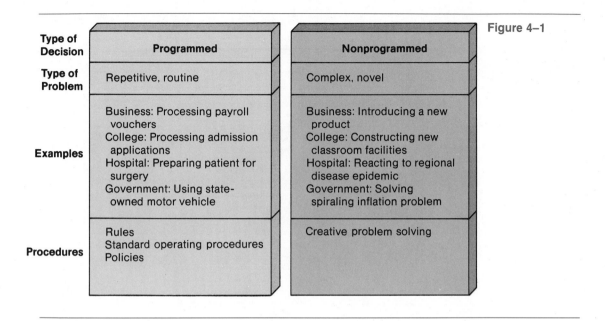

Figure 4–1

Type of Decision	Programmed	Nonprogrammed
Type of Problem	Repetitive, routine	Complex, novel
Examples	Business: Processing payroll vouchers College: Processing admission applications Hospital: Preparing patient for surgery Government: Using state-owned motor vehicle	Business: Introducing a new product College: Constructing new classroom facilities Hospital: Reacting to regional disease epidemic Government: Solving spiraling inflation problem
Procedures	Rules Standard operating procedures Policies	Creative problem solving

The managements of most organizations face great numbers of programmed decisions in their daily operations. Such decisions should be made without expending unnecessary time and effort. Reaching nonprogrammed decisions, however, is more complicated and requires the expenditure of billions of dollars worth of resources every year in our nation. Government organizations make nonprogrammed decisions that influence the lives of every citizen. Business organizations make nonprogrammed decisions to manufacture new products. Hospitals and schools make nonprogrammed decisions that influence patients and students years later. Unfortunately, very little is known about this type of decision making.

Figure 4–1 presents examples of programmed and nonprogrammed decisions in different types of organizations. It shows that programmed and nonprogrammed decisions require different kinds of procedures and apply to very different types of problems.

In most organizations, programmed decisions are handled through policies. In some organizations and industries, management scientists have developed mathematical models that help ease these types of decisions.[4] Nonprogrammed decisions, however, are usually handled by general problem-solving processes, judgment, intuition, and creativity.[5]

---

[4]Paul Shrivastava and Ian I. Mitroff, "Enhancing Operations Research Utilization: The Role of Decision Makers' Assumptions," *Academy of Management Review,* January 1984, pp. 18–26. These authors note that managers have not adopted many of the decision-making methods developed by academics because these methods rarely work in the unstructured situations that managers face.

[5]See Lyle Sussman and Richard Herden, "Dialectical Problem Solving," *Business Horizons,* January–February 1982, pp. 66–71; and W. H. Agor, "Tomorrow's Intuitive Leaders," *Futurist,* August 1983, pp. 49–53.

Figure 4–2

Types of problems, types of decisions, and management level in the organization.

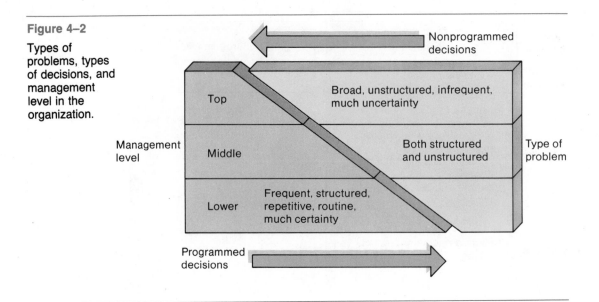

Types of Decisions and Level of Management

Problems that arise infrequently and have a great deal of uncertainty surrounding them are often of a strategic nature and should be the concern of top management. Problems that arise frequently and have fairly certain outcomes should be the concern of lower levels of management.

Middle managers in most organizations concentrate mostly on programmed decisions. As Figure 4–2 indicates, the nature of the problem, how frequently it arises, and the degree of certainty surrounding it should dictate at what level of management the decision should be made.

THE PROCESS OF DECISION MAKING

There are numerous approaches to decision making. Which approach is best will depend on the nature of the problem, the time available, the costs of individual strategies, and the mental skills of the decision maker.[6]

Decisions should be thought of as *means* rather than ends. They are mechanisms by which a manager seeks to achieve some desired state. They are the manager's (and hence the organization's) responses to problems. Every decision is the outcome of a dynamic process influenced by a multitude of forces. Thus, decision making is the process of thought and deliberation that results in a decision; the process influences how good the decision is likely to be.

Decision making is not a fixed procedure, but it is a sequential process.[7] In most

---

[6]Paul C. Nutt, "Types of Organizational Decision Processes," *Administrative Science Quarterly,* September 1984, pp. 414–50.

[7]James C. Hopper and Kenneth J. Euske, "Facilitating the Identification and Evaluation of Decision Objectives," *Cost and Management,* July–August 1985, pp. 36–40.

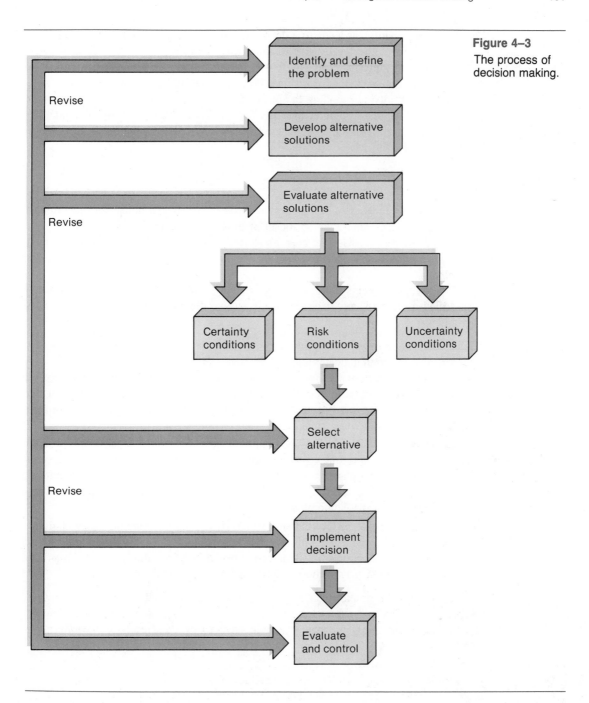

Figure 4–3
The process of decision making.

decision situations, managers go through a number of stages that help them think through the problem and develop alternative strategies. The stages need not be rigidly applied; their value lies in their ability to force the decision maker to structure the problem in a meaningful way. Figure 4–3 enables us to examine each stage in the normal progression that leads to a decision. You may find it helpful to develop your own list of stages for the decision-making process.

The process represented in Figure 4–3 is more applicable to nonprogrammed decisions than to programmed decisions. Problems that occur infrequently with a great deal of uncertainty surrounding the outcome require the manager to utilize the entire process.[8] In contrast, problems that occur frequently are often handled by policies or rules, so it not necessary to develop and evaluate alternatives each time these problems arise.[9]

An Example of the Process

Suppose the vice president of a local bank has established a specific error rate (number of errors per 1,000 transactions) for all of the bank's tellers. At the end of the year, the error rate has consistently been above the desired rate. The vice president must then *identify* and *define the problem* and make some kind of decision to solve the problem.

Identifying problems is not as easy as it may seem. If the problem is incorrectly identified or defined, any decisions made will be directed toward solving the wrong problem.[10] There are several criteria managers use to locate problems:

1. *Deviation from past performance.* A sudden change in some established pattern of performance often indicates that a problem has developed. When employee turnover increases, sales decline, student enrollments decline, selling expenses increase, or more defective units are produced, a problem usually exists. Thus, if the error rate among tellers had always been below the standard until this year, this departure from the historical pattern could signal a problem.

2. *Deviation from the plan.* When results do not meet planned objectives, a problem is likely. For example, a new product fails to meet its market share objective, profit levels are lower than planned, or the production department is exceeding its budget. In our example above, the teller error rate exceeded the performance objective. These occurrences signal that some plan is off course.

3. *Outside criticism.* Outsiders may identify problems: Customers may be dissatisfied with a new product or with their delivery schedules; a labor union may present grievances; investment firms may not recommend the organization as a good investment opportunity; alumni may withdraw their support from an athletic program.

In the above example, once the banker has clearly defined the problem, it will be necessary to *develop* a number of *alternative solutions*—potential strategies or solutions to the problem. Next the banker would have to *evaluate* each of the *alternative*

[8]Jane M. Booker and Maurice C. Bryson, "Decision Analysis in Project Management: An Overview," *IEEE Transactions on Engineering Management*, February 1985, pp. 3–9.

[9]J. W. Boudreau, "Decision Theory Contributions to HRM Research and Practices," *Industrial Relations*, Spring 1984, pp. 198–217.

[10]David A. Cowan, "Developing a Process Model of Problem Recognition," *Academy of Management Review*, October 1986, pp. 763–77.

solutions. Evaluation involves measuring and comparing the potential payoffs and possible consequences of each alternative solution. For example, suppose the banker decides that two possible solutions are (1) to invest in the latest electronic technology for recording teller transactions or (2) to invest in an intensive teller training program. He would carefully consider the potential payoffs and consequences of each solution and *select one alternative*.

Once selected, the decision must be implemented. A decision is only an abstraction if it is not implemented. It is possible that a "good" decision can be damaged by poor implementation. Thus, implementation may be just as important as the actual activity of selecting an alternative.[11]

Finally, the solution must be *evaluated* and *controlled*. The bank vice president would have to continue periodic measurement of the teller error rate, compare the results with the established standard, and if problems still exist, face new decisions.

Terms Used in Decision Making

The term *state of nature* is used to describe an *event beyond a manager's control that could actually happen*. For example, a manufacturer of children's toys knows that the accuracy of sales forecasts will depend in large measure upon the state of the overall economy—an event that is beyond the firm's control. The executive of a tobacco company must make decisions on how much and what type of each of the firm's cigarettes to produce, given the government campaign against certain tobacco products. In each of these examples, the decision maker must make a decision while facing an uncontrollable state of nature.

The term *strategies* is used to describe the alternative solutions available to the decision maker. As noted, decision making involves selecting one of several alternative solutions (*strategies*), which in combination with a future *state of nature* yields some desired result. The desired result may be to maximize profit, revenue, or market share or to minimize some objective such as costs, absenteeism, defective output, or teller error rates.[12]

Now that you are familiar with the process of decision making, we shall devote the next section of the chapter to a detailed analysis of a decision problem.

DECISION MAKING IN ACTION

To illustrate the use of decision making in managerial planning we will develop an example of a book publisher. If a publisher knows exactly how many books will be demanded, then the number of books to produce is obvious. However, this is frequently not the case. Often a book will commemorate a special event such as the Olympics or the nation's bicentennial celebration. Since the book is unique, the publisher may have only sketchy information about its potential sales.

---

[11]Paul C. Nutt, "Tactics of Implementation," *Academy of Management Journal*, June 1986, pp. 232–61.

[12]D. V. Lindley, *Making Decisions* (New York: John Wiley & Sons, 1987).

Table 4–1 Conditional-value payoff table for production decision.

Strategies: Books Printed	States of Nature: Number of Books Demanded			
	.20 5,000	10,000. 40	15,000 .30	.10 20,000
5,000	$ 3,750	$3,750	$ 3,750	$ 3,750
10,000	− 1,250	7,500	7,500	7,500
15,000	− 6,250	2,500	11,250	11,250
20,000	− 11,250	− 2,500	6,250	15,000

Let us assume that the publisher has established the price of the book at $1.75 and that the incremental cost of each book is $1.00. Thus, each book that is sold will contribute $0.75 to overhead and profit. Assume also that there is no secondary market for the book. If it is not sold by the end of the Olympics or bicentennial celebration period, there will be no market for it. With that in mind, we can understand that if the publisher prints one book and one book is demanded, then the contribution is $0.75; if two books are printed and two are demanded, the contribution is $1.50. But if two books are printed and three are demanded, the contribution remains $1.50, and the publisher has no more books to sell. By the same reasoning, if the publisher prints three books and two are demanded, the contribution is $0.50: The revenue is $3.50 (2 × $1.75), the incremental cost is $3.00 (3 × $1.00), and $3.50 − $3.00 = $0.50. The contribution for any combination of production and demand can be calculated in this manner.

Say that the publisher decides it is only necessary to investigate four levels of possible demand, in 5,000-unit intervals (i.e., rather than dealing with the infinite range of production and demand combinations, we will illustrate only four): 5,000, 10,000, 15,000, and 20,000 books. With this information, we can determine the contribution for each of the four levels of sales and each of the four production levels. In the terminology of decision theory, each level of sales is called a *state of nature,* and each production level is a strategy. The contribution associated with each state of nature and strategy is a conditional value because it is conditioned on the demand for books. The conditional values, or payoffs, for each of the four possible combinations of production and demand are presented in Table 4–1.

In the present example, the payoffs associated with each possible strategy and state of nature are based on the previously presented price ($1.75) and cost ($1.00). Thus the payoff associated with producing 5,000 books and selling 5,000 books (Revenue − Cost = Payoff) is:

Revenue (5,000 × $1.75)	$8,750
Cost (5,000 × $1.00)	$5,000
Payoff	$3,750

If, however, the publisher prints 15,000 books and only 10,000 are demanded, the payoff is:

Revenue (10,000 × $1.75)	$17,500
Cost (15,000 × $1.00)	$15,000
Payoff	$ 2,500

Each payoff in Table 4–1 is calculated in the above manner. The fact that some of the values are negative simply reflects the cost of overproducing.

The payoff table is useful, but it does not make the decision; it simply organizes the important information on which to base the decision. But how can the publisher make such a decision? Let's examine three different conditions the publisher might face: certainty, risk, and uncertainty.

Decision Making: Certainty Conditions

If a manager knew exactly which state of nature would occur (e.g., knowing that on April 15 income taxes are due), the decision could be made with certainty. A certainty situation means that a perfectly accurate decision will be made time after time. Of course, decision making under certainty is rare.

For illustrative purposes, however, assume that the publisher knows with certainty that 10,000 books will be demanded. The maximum payoff associated with this state of nature is to produce 10,000 units: The payoff of $7,500 associated with the joint occurrence of 10,000 books produced and demanded is greater than any other payoff associated with that state of nature.

The publisher in this situation is fortunate to have perfect information about future states of nature. In most situations, of course, the publisher will not know with certainty which state of nature will occur. When facing a decision where the state of nature is uncertain, a manager is forced to use probabilities.

Decision Making: Risk Conditions

Probabilities fall into two categories. *Objective* probability is based on historical evidence. For example, the probability of obtaining either heads or tails on the toss of a fair coin is 0.50 (50 percent); the coin is equally likely to come up a head or a tail. In many cases, historical evidence is not available, so a manager must rely on a personal estimate, or *subjective* probability, of the situation outcome.

Even a manager who is able to estimate the likelihood that the various states of nature will occur faces risk conditions. A risk situation requires the use of probability estimates. The ability to estimate may be due to experience, incomplete but reliable information, or intelligence.

Decision making under risk conditions also necessitates the use of expected values. (Recall that the payoffs listed in Table 4–1 are conditional values because they will occur only if a specific state of nature occurs and a specific strategy is chosen.) The

Table 4–2 Expected-value table for production decision.

Strategies: Books Printed	States of Nature: Number of Books Demanded									
	5,000 (.20)*		10,000 (.40)*		15,000 (.30)*		20,000 (.10)*		Expected Value	
5,000	$ 750	+	$1,500	+	$1,125	+	$ 375	=	$3,750	
10,000	− 250	+	3,000	+	2,250	+	750	=	5,750	
15,000	− 1,250	+	1,000	+	3,375	+	1,125	=	4,250	
20,000	− 2,250	+	− 1,000	+	1,875	+	1,500	=	125	

*Estimated probability.

expected value of an alternative is the long-run average return; in other words, you would obtain the same results, on average, if you made the same decision in the same situation over and over again. In decision making, the average return or *expected value,* is found by taking the value of an outcome if it should occur (the conditional value) and multiplying that value by the probability that the outcome will occur. This is a standard and acceptable procedure. Remember that:

$$\text{Expected value} = \text{Conditional value} \times \text{Probability}$$

If the book publisher is able to estimate subjectively the probabilities associated with each of the four levels of demand (states of nature), these estimates can be used to construct a table of expected values. Suppose, for example, that the publisher estimates the following probabilities.[13]

Demand	Probabilities
5,000 books	.20
10,000	.40
15,000	.30
20,000	.10

Table 4–2 presents the expected values for each of the four strategies. For example, the expected value for the strategy of printing 10,000 books (refer to row 2 in Table 4–2) is computed as follows:

$$(.2 \times -\$1,250) + (.4 \times \$7,500) + (.3 \times \$7,500) + (.1 \times \$7,500) = \$5,750$$

The proper decision for the book publisher is to print 10,000 books. The expected value of that strategy exceeds the expected value of any alternative strategy. When given the probabilities of different states of nature, decision theory can aid managers

---

[13]The calculations of such probabilities involve mathematical computations beyond the scope of this book. Interested readers may wish to consult a basic text on statistics or economics.

in making decisions that maximize the value of some outcome. Decision theory has many applications, including decisions that require the minimization of costs.

The following Management Application illustrates the actual use of a payoff matrix by Hallmark Cards, Inc.

MANAGEMENT APPLICATION

HALLMARK USES PAYOFF MATRIX

Hallmark Cards, Inc., and the local newsstand have at least one management problem in common: No one wants to buy leftover inventory. On December 26, there is likely to be little demand for either Christmas cards or December 25 newspapers. Managers at Hallmark Cards and newsstands must somehow produce and order just enough product to satisfy demand without running either short or over. To run short means lost sales; to run over means excessive inventory costs.

Hallmark's production managers face many such decisions each year. The company produces numerous special theme cards and promotional materials that have never before been made. Consequently they have little basis for deciding how many to produce. Prior to 1982, production managers decided how many first-time and specialty cards to produce by applying the "similar experience" approach, a method by which one looks for the most similar past experience and projects that experience to the new one. Thus, the production run for a specialty card featuring a Walt Disney character could be determined by consulting the sales experience of a previously issued Disney character card. These past experiences enabled production managers to obtain "best estimates" as the basis for their production decisions.

Beginning in 1982, Hallmark began to apply somewhat more sophisticated decision-making techniques to their production problems. The new techniques enable production managers to use their judgment to make probabilistic estimates (e.g., the chance that something will happen) of the effects of different production runs. For each level of production, an associated revenue and cost can be combined to obtain a "payoff." When the managers apply probabilistic estimates to each level of production, they can calculate expected payoffs. Such estimates of expected sales and costs enable the managers to take into account all their collective, pertinent information about an uncertain future event—expected sales—to make a production decision.

Source: Adapted from F. Hutton Barron, "Payoff Matrices Pay Off at Hallmark," *Interfaces*, July–August 1985, pp. 20–25.

What if the decision maker has absolutely no basis for estimating probabilities of future states of nature? As we have seen, probabilities are necessary if one is to calculate expected values. But in many instances, decision makers confront problems that do not lend themselves to the application of expected-value methods. The next section presents some ways that decision theory can assist decision makers with such problems.

Decision Making: Conditions of Uncertainty

When no historical data exist concerning the probabilities for the occurrence of the states of nature, the manager faces conditions of uncertainty. A number of different decision criteria have been proposed as possible bases for decisions under uncertainty, including:

1. Maximax criterion (optimistic): maximizing the maximum possible payoff.
2. Maximin criterion (pessimistic): maximizing the minimum possible payoff.
3. Minimax criterion (regret): minimizing the maximum possible regret to the decision maker.
4. Insufficient-reason criterion: assuming equally likely probabilities for the occurrence of each possible state of nature.

As with conditions of certainty and risk, the first step in making decisions under conditions of uncertainty is to construct a conditional-value payoff table. The next step is to select and apply one of the above decision criteria. Using the conditional-value payoffs in Table 4–1, we will illustrate the four criteria for decision making under conditions of uncertainty.

Maximax criterion.   Some decision makers think optimistically about the occurrence of events influencing a decision. A manager with this attitude will examine the conditional-value table and select the strategy allowing the most favorable payoff. But this criterion is dangerous to employ because it ignores possible losses and the chances of making or not making a profit.

Using a maximax criterion, the publisher would assume that no matter what strategy is selected, the best possible state of nature will occur. Therefore, the publisher should print 20,000 books because that strategy is associated with the maximum payoff of $15,000 (see Table 4–1).

Maximin criterion.   Some managers act on the belief that only the worst possible outcome can occur. This pessimism results in the selection of the strategy that maximizes the least favorable payoff. Using this criterion, the publisher would locate the worst possible outcome associated with each alternative. Table 4–1 indicates the worst possible payoffs associated with each strategy and state of nature to be as follows:

Strategy	Worst Outcome
Print 5,000 books	$ 3,750
Print 10,000 books	− 1,250
Print 15,000 books	− 6,250
Print 20,000 books	− 11,250

Table 4-3 Regret table for production decision.

| Strategies: Books Printed | States of Nature: Number of Books Demanded | | | |
	5,000	10,000	15,000	20,000
5,000	0	$ 3,750	$7,500	$11,250
10,000	$ 5,000	0	3,750	7,500
15,000	10,000	5,000	0	3,750
20,000	15,000	10,000	5,000	0

The publisher will minimize the worst possible outcome by selecting the strategy of printing 5,000 books. Of the four worst possible outcomes, that one is the maximum of the minimums—the best of the worst.

Minimax criterion.   If a manager selects a strategy and if a state of nature occurs that does not result in the most favorable payoff, regret occurs. The manager is regretful that the strategy selected did not lead to the best payoff.

A manager who does not know and does not want to guess which state of nature will occur selects a regret strategy. Managerial regret is the payoff for each strategy under every state of nature, subtracted from the most favorable payoff that is possible with the occurrence of the particular event. For example, if the publisher prints 5,000 books and the demand is for 10,000, the publisher will experience regret of $3,750 (the difference between the realized payoff for that strategy and the potential payoff associated with printing 10,000 books). The regret for any particular strategy is the difference between the best possible outcome and the actual outcome.

Applying the minimax criterion requires the development of regret tables. These tables indicate the amount of regret associated with each strategy and state of nature. Table 4-3 presents the amounts of regret associated with the book publisher's production decisions.

Next, the regret values for each strategy are identified:

Strategy	Regret
Print 5,000 books	$11,250
Print 10,000 books	7,500
Print 15,000 books	10,000
Print 20,000 books	15,000

The minimax criterion indicates that the publisher should print 10,000 books because that strategy produces the minimum regret.

Table 4–4 Expected values, using insufficient-reason criterion.

Strategies: Books Printed		Calculation		Expected Value
5,000	$1/4$	($ 3,750 + $3,750 + $ 3,750 + $ 3,750)	=	$3,750.00
10,000	$1/4$	(−1,250 + 7,500 + 7,500 + 7,500)	=	5,312.50
15,000	$1/4$	(−6,250 + 2,500 + 11,250 + 11,250)	=	4,687.50
20,000	$1/4$	(−11,250 − 2,500 + 6,250 + 15,000)	=	1,875.00

Insufficient-reason criterion. The three preceding decision criteria assume that without any previous experience, it is not worthwhile to assign probabilities to the states of nature. The insufficient-reason criterion, however, states that if managers do not know the probabilities of occurrence for the various states of nature, they should assume that all are equally likely to occur. In other words, managers should assign equal probabilities to each state of nature.

Using the insufficient-reason criterion, the publisher would assign a one-in-four ($1/4$) probability to each of the four states of nature (see Table 4–4).

Based on those probabilities, the publisher should print 10,000 books.

Reviewing the choices. The application of the four criteria to the decision faced by the book publisher results in different choices, depending on the orientation of the decision maker:

1. The optimist would print 20,000 books.
2. The pessimist would print 5,000 books.
3. The regretter would print 10,000 books.
4. The insufficient-reasoner would print 10,000 books.

Different criteria result in different decisions. Each decision problem has unique data that lead to unique situations.

One point should be clear. The greater the amount of reliable information, the more likely it is that the manager will make a good decision. Making sure the right information is available at the right time to the right decision maker is the function of a decision support system. The relationship of decision support systems to the decision-making process is the subject of the next chapter.

Selecting an Alternative

A manager selects a strategy to solve a problem and to achieve predetermined objectives. This point is most important. A decision is not an end in itself but only a *means* to an end. A decision also is not an isolated act. Therefore, you should not forget the factors that lead up to the decision. Nor should you ignore the factors that follow the decision, such as implementation and evaluation.

In the development of alternative strategies, it is vital that managers be capable of creative and innovative thinking. Many organizations believe these talents are so important that they train managers in the development of creative thinking.[14]

Often a situation will exist in which two objectives cannot be fully achieved at the same time. If one objective is achieved to the fullest, the other cannot be. For example, a manufacturing firm might have an objective of a high-quality product and an objective of low maintenance costs. Obviously, both objectives cannot be achieved to their fullest at the same time. In all likelihood, an attempt to keep maintenance costs low eventually would influence the quality of the product. The multiple objectives of most organizations complicate the real world of the decision maker.[15]

An organizational objective might also conflict with a societal objective. Society's objective of clean air conflicts with the profitability objectives of some manufacturing firms. Society's objective of equal rights has conflicted with some bank credit practices, specifically credit policies toward women and the poor. In any case, whether one objective conflicts with another objective or with a societal objective, the values of the decision maker will influence the strategy chosen.[16] Such influences on the decision-making process will be discussed later in this chapter.

As you can see, *optimal* solutions often are impossible in managerial planning because you cannot be aware of every possible strategy or the possible consequences of each strategy. Most managers therefore are not optimizers but are instead *satisficers.* They select the strategy that they know meets some minimal, yet *satisfactory,* standard of acceptance.[17]

Implementing the Decision

A planning decision is useless unless the chosen strategy is implemented, and the choice must be implemented effectively to achieve the objectives for which it was made. You could argue that implementation may be more important than the activity of selecting a strategy.

In most situations, people are affected when decisions are implemented. And a decision that has been well thought through can easily be undermined by dissatisfied subordinates. People cannot be manipulated like other resources, so a manager's job is not limited to selecting good solutions. The manager also needs the skills and knowledge necessary to make decisions become acceptable to, and part of the behavior of, the people in the organization. This requires communicating effectively with individuals and groups. Decisions cannot be easily put into action without communication.[18]

[14]Ray Rowan, *The Intuitive Manager* (Boston: Little Brown, 1986).

[15]Shrivastava and Mitroff, "Enhancing Operations Research Utilization: The Role of Decision Makers' Assumptions," *Academy of Management Review,* January 1984, pp. 18–26.

[16]Linda Klebe Trevino, "Ethical Decision Making in Organizations: A Person-Situation Interactionist Model," *Academy of Management Review,* July 1986, pp. 601–17.

[17]See Anna Grandori, "A Prescriptive Contingency View of Organizational Decision Making," *Administrative Science Quarterly,* June 1984, pp. 192–209.

[18]Ronald N. Taylor, *Behavioral Decision Making* (Glenview, Ill.: Scott, Foresman, 1984).

Evaluation and Control

The management function of control involves comparing actual performance with the performance specified in the objectives. If deviations exist, changes or corrections must be made. This is indicated clearly in Figure 4–3. Here again you can see the importance of measurable objectives. When none exist, there is no way to judge performance.

If actual results do not match planned results, then changes must be made in the choice of action or in implementation—or in the original objective if the manager determines that it is unreasonable. Figure 4–3 indicates that if the original objective must be revised, then the entire decision-making process must be reactivated. A manager should never assume that once a decision has been implemented, the objective will be reached. Some system of evaluation and control is necessary.

It is easy to see why some managers believe that *what managers do is make decisions*. The steps in the decision-making process outlined in this chapter are very much like the functions of managers.

INFLUENCES ON INDIVIDUAL DECISION MAKERS

Many important factors affect the decision-making process. Some of them affect only certain phases of the process, but others can affect the entire sequence. Each influence, however, will have an impact and therefore must be understood. Although such influences are numerous, we shall discuss what we believe are the four major ones: the importance of the decision, time pressures, the manager's values, and the manager's propensity for risk.

The Importance of the Decision

The mayor of a city may make two decisions in an afternoon, one extending the school year for children because of days missed during bad weather, the other committing $50 million to constructing an expressway around the city. In each case, the steps in the decision-making process were similar, but the time and techniques used were different. There are numerous yardsticks for measuring the importance of a decision, including the amount of resources involved, the number of people influenced by the decision, and the time required to make the decision. The important point is that managers must allot more time and attention to significant problems. In deciding to extend the school year, the mayor may have considered only a small number of possibilities because the amount of time a public school student must spend in class each year is determined by law. Before deciding to construct an expressway around the city, however, more alternatives were generated, more time and thought were utilized, and more detailed information was required. The importance of the decision in terms of monetary commitments, the number of people affected, and the decision's long-term impact influenced the amount of time and money spent on making the decision.

Time Pressures

A key influence on the quality of decisions is how much time the decision maker has to make the decisions. Unfortunately, managers must make the most of their decisions in time frames established by others. Obviously, when time pressures are significant, managers may be unable to gather enough information. They may not have enough time to consider additional alternatives.[19] Still, managers must deal with this reality.

The Manager's Values

An individual's values become guidelines when he or she confronts a choice. These values are acquired early in life, and they are a basic, often taken-for-granted part of an individual's thoughts. Because our values are basic to us, we are usually unaware of how they influence us. Their influence on the decision-making process, however, is great.

Many experts consider values to be one of the most important influences on human behavior. Values are the likes, dislikes, shoulds, oughts, judgments, and prejudices that determine how we view the world. Once values become part of an individual, they become (often subconsciously) a standard for guiding his actions.

The values of managers underlie much of their behavior. How they approach the management functions of planning, organizing, leading, and controlling reflects their values. The decisions managers make in identifying their objectives and strategies, and how managers interpret society's expectations, also reflect their values. Here are some specific influences of values on the decision-making process:

1. Value judgments are necessary in the development of objectives and the assignment of priorities.
2. In developing alternatives, you must make value judgments about the various possibilities.
3. When you select an alternative, your value judgments will be reflected in your choice.

Types of individual values.   Every individual holds various goals in life and various means to achieve the goals. Recognizing this, psychologists have identified two basic types of values. An *instrumental value* is a belief that a certain way of behaving is applicable in all situations. For example, "Do unto others before they do unto you" and "Always tell the truth" represent instrumental values. They will influence behavior in many situations. A *terminal value* is a long-standing belief that a certain end-state of existence is worth striving for.[20] For example, inner harmony is a terminal value

---

[19]For a related discussion, see Charles R. Schwenk, "Information, Cognitive Biases, and Commitment to a Course of Action," *Academy of Management Review,* April 1986, p. 298–310.

[20]Milton Rokeach, *Beliefs, Attitudes, and Values* (San Francisco: Jossey-Bass, 1968), p. 124.

Table 4–5 Value survey.

Instructions: Study the two lists of values presented below. Then rank the instrumental values in order of importance to you (1 = most important, 18 = least important). Do the same with the list of terminal values.

Instrumental Values	Terminal Values
Rank	Rank
_____ Ambitious (hard-working, aspiring)	_____ A comfortable life (a prosperous life)
_____ Broadminded (open-minded)	_____ An exciting life (a stimulating, active life)
_____ Capable (competent, effective)	_____ A sense of accomplishment (lasting contribution)
_____ Cheerful (lighthearted, joyful)	_____ A world at peace (free of war and conflict)
_____ Clean (neat, tidy)	_____ A world of beauty (beauty of nature and the arts)
_____ Courageous (standing up for your beliefs)	_____ Equality (brotherhood, equal opportunity for all)
_____ Forgiving (willing to pardon others)	_____ Family security (taking care of loved ones)
_____ Helpful (working for the welfare of others)	_____ Freedom (independence, free choice)
_____ Honest (sincere, truthful)	_____ Happiness (contentedness)
_____ Imaginative (daring, creative)	_____ Inner harmony (freedom from inner conflict)
_____ Independent (self-sufficient)	_____ Mature love (sexual and spiritual intimacy)
_____ Intellectual (intelligent, reflective)	_____ National security (protection from attack)
_____ Logical (consistent, rational)	_____ Pleasure (an enjoyable, leisurely life)
_____ Loving (affectionate, tender)	_____ Salvation (saved, eternal life)
_____ Obedient (dutiful, respectful)	_____ Self-respect (self-esteem)
_____ Polite (courteous, well-mannered)	_____ Social recognition (respect, admiration)
_____ Responsible (dependable, reliable)	_____ True friendship (close companionship)
_____ Self-controlled (restrained, self-disciplined)	_____ Wisdom (a mature understanding of life)

Source: Copyright by Milton Rokeach, and published by Halgren Tests, 873 Persimmon Avenue, Sunnyvale, Calif. 94087, 1976.

for many individuals. Others may seek fame or power. In all cases, instrumental values help you achieve terminal values.

To gain insight into your own values, complete Table 4–5. You may be surprised by the results. In most cases, people do not think consciously about their values and rarely arrange them in any kind of order. Future managers, however, should be very aware of their values. It is easy to see that serious conflicts can occur among values. For example, do you value both honesty and obedience in the instrumental value column or happiness and accomplishment in the terminal value column? Someone who seeks high levels of accomplishment may have to forgo some happiness. Examples abound daily in the media of individuals who let obedience get in the way of honesty. Some individuals will have important instrumental values that will not enable them to achieve high-priority terminal values. For example, someone who values independence may find it difficult to also value the security of a family. An individual's values may conflict with those of the organization where he or she works. If you value broad-mindedness (instrumental column), you may have problems working in an organization that values strict adherence to certain dress and behavior codes. To manage effectively, you must understand your own values.

Values of today's young people.   To what extent are the values of today's young people compatible with those of today's managers? Another vital question: "If the values of future managers conflict with those of present managers, will the future managers change their values to conform to the job or will they change the job to conform to their values?"

There is evidence that today's students, like today's managers, stress practical values. Unlike today's managers, however, today's students would rather achieve their ends through their own efforts than through the efforts of others. Perhaps these students will be tomorrow's entrepreneurs and will not seek careers in ongoing organizations.

The values of the younger generation will be reflected in their decisions as managers. The basic functions of management will not change, but the ways in which they are performed may. Depending on value orientations, there will be different outcomes from the process of decision making. However, organizations today seem able to accommodate different values among managers, and there is little reason to believe that they will not be able to do so in the future.

The Manager's Propensity for Risk

Risk taking is a necessity in most decision situations. From personal experience, you are certainly aware that decision makers vary greatly in their propensity to take risks. This aspect of the decision maker's personality has a strong influence on the decision-making process. A manager who is less inclined toward risk taking will establish different objectives, evaluate alternatives differently, and make different choices than will a manager who is more inclined toward risk taking. Understanding this is important because the propensity for risk does not enter the picture only when the time comes to make a choice. It influences the entire decision-making process. One manager will be inclined toward situations in which the risk or uncertainty is low or in which the certainty of the outcome is high. Another, because of a greater propensity for risk, will choose the opposite kinds of situations. In the final section of this chapter, we shall see that decision makers very often are bolder, more innovative, and inclined toward greater risks when they are participating in a group than when they make decisions alone. Many individuals apparently are more willing to accept risk as members of a group.

The following Management Application illustrates clearly the influence of time pressures, the importance of the decision, values, and propensity for risk on individual decision makers.

MANAGEMENT APPLICATION

THE CHALLENGER DISASTER: A TRAGEDY OF MANAGERIAL DECISION MAKING

In the aftermath of the explosion of the space shuttle *Challenger,* investigations were launched to identify possible causes. Unfortunately the cause was identified as a managerial failure and more specifically, a decision-making failure. Top administrators of the National Aeronautics and Space Administration were isolated from critical decision-making issues which investigators believe might have averted the disaster.

For example, on the day of scheduled launch, the chief administrator of NASA was on leave of absence, the No. 2 man was in Washington working on budgeting problems and issues, and the head of the space shuttle program was at Houston mission control but not in direct contact with engineers at the launch site. The associate administrator for the space flight and the person who had the last word on the launch, was at Cape Kennedy but was totally unaware of serious arguments among the engineers responsible for launch operations. At lower levels in the organization there were unprecedented arguments and objections to launching due to unsafe O-rings on the rocket booster. For the first time in the history of the space shuttle program, engineers from the manufacturer of the booster rocket refused to sign off on the launch.

The real management tragedy is that none of the above decisions or information ever reached the management (command) level of NASA. Their much heralded communication system and their management by objectives planning system failed. The critical information that was so necessary was unable to advance upward through the levels of management.

Source: Adapted from Michael Brody, "NASA's Challenge: Ending Isolation at the Top," *Fortune,* May 12, 1986, pp. 26–28, 32.

GROUP DECISION MAKING

The first part of this chapter focused on individuals making decisions. In most organizations, however, a great deal of decision making is achieved through committees, teams, task forces, and other kinds of groups. This is because managers frequently face situations in which they must seek and combine judgments in group meetings. This is especially true for nonprogrammed problems, which are novel, with much uncertainty regarding the outcome. In most organizations, it is unusual to find decisions on such problems being made by one individual on a regular basis. The increased complexity of many of these problems requires specialized knowledge in numerous fields, usually not possessed by one person. This requirement, coupled with the reality that the decisions made must eventually be accepted and implemented by many units throughout the organization, has increased the use of the collective approach to the decision-making process. The result for many managers has been an endless amount of time spent in meetings of committees and other groups. It has been found that many managers spend as much as 80 percent of their working time in committee meetings.

An example of a problem which requires knowledge from numerous specialized fields is the focus of the following Management Application.

MANAGEMENT APPLICATION

A HIGH-RISK DECISION IN A HIGH-RISK MARKET

In the highly competitive wine cooler market, high risk is part of the game. Firms must develop tasty products and spend fortunes promoting them with catchy, memorable, and offbeat promotion campaigns. Then they hope both the decision and implementation of the decision result in success. Thus far, that approach has worked extremely well for California Cooler, Bartles and Jaymes, and House of Seagram.

Obviously attracted by the success of others, Miller Brewing Co. recently made the decision to enter the wine cooler business. The decision involved committing $40 million to a noncarbonated Australian cooler named Matilda Bay.

The decision is high risk because some believe the timing of Miller's decision may not be the best. For the first time since coolers were introduced in 1982, sales growth began slowing in mid-1987, and shipments were also down for the first time. However, the risk for Miller is apparently worth the potential payoff. Americans spent over $1 billion on coolers in 1987 and no one is ready to count out the company that brought us Miller Lite.

Source: Adapted from "Miller Jumps Into a Cooler Cooler Market," *Business Week,* October 26, 1987, pp. 36, 38.

Individual versus Group Decision Making

There has been considerable debate over the relative effectiveness of individual versus group decision making. Groups usually take more time to reach a decision than individuals do, but bringing together individual specialists and experts has its benefits since the mutually reinforcing impact of their interaction results in better decisions.[21] In fact, a great deal of research has shown that consensus decisions with five or more participants are superior to individual decision making, majority vote, and leader decisions.[22] Unfortunately, open discussion has been found to be negatively influenced

---

[21]John P. Wanous and Margaret A. Youtz, "Solution Diversity and the Quality of Group Decisions," *Academy of Management Journal,* March 1986, pp. 149–58.

[22]For some examples of research on group decision making, see Charles Holloman and Harold Henrick, "Adequacy of Group Decisions as a Function of the Decision-Making Process," *Academy of Management Journal,* June 1972, pp. 175–84; Andrew H. Van de Ven and Andre Delbecq, "Nominal versus Interacting Group Processes for Committee Decision-Making Effectiveness," *Academy of Management Journal,* June 1972, pp. 203–12; B. M. Staw, "The Escalation of Commitment to a Course of Action," *Academy of Management Review,* October 1981, pp. 577–88; and David M. Schweiger, William R. Sandburg, and James W. Ragan, "Group Approaches for Improving Strategic Decision Making," *Academy of Management Journal,* March 1986, pp. 51–71.

by such behavioral factors as: (1) the pressure to conform; (2) the influence of a dominant personality type in the group; (3) "status incongruity," as a result of which, lower status participants are inhibited by higher status participants and "go along" even though they believe that their own ideas are superior; and (4) the attempt of certain participants to influence others because these participants are perceived to be expert in the problem area.[23]

Certain decisions appear to be better made by groups, while others appear better suited to individual decision making. Nonprogrammed decisions appear to be better suited to group decision making. Such decisions usually call for pooled talent in arriving at a solution; the decisions are so important that they are usually made by top managers and to a somewhat lesser extent by middle managers.

In terms of the decision-making process itself, the following points concerning group processes for nonprogrammed decisions can be made:

1. In *establishing objectives,* groups are probably superior to individuals because of the greater amount of knowledge available to groups.

2. In *identifying alternatives,* the individual efforts of group members are necessary to ensure a broad search in the various functional areas of the organization.

3. In *evaluating alternatives,* the collective judgment of the group, with its wider range of viewpoints, seems superior to that of the individual decision maker.

4. In *choosing an alternative,* it has been shown that group interaction and the achievement of consensus usually result in the acceptance of more risk than would be accepted by an individual decision maker. In any event, the group decision is more likely to be accepted as a result of the participation of those affected by its consequences.

5. *Implementation* of a decision, whether or not it is made by a group, is usually accomplished by individual managers. Thus, since a group cannot be held responsible, the responsibility for implementation necesssarily rests with the individual manager.

Figure 4–4 summarizes the research on group decision making. It presents the relationship between the probable quality of a decision and the method utilized to reach the decision. It indicates that as we move from "individual" to "consensus," the

---

[23]For examples, see Solomon Asch, "Studies of Independence and Conformity," *Psychological Monographs,* 1956, pp. 68–70; Normal Dalkey and Olaf Helmer, "An Experimental Application of Delphi Method to Use of Experts," *Management Science,* April 1963, pp. 458–67; E. M. Bridges, W. J. Doyle, and D. J. Mahan, "Effects of Hierarchical Differentiation on Group Productivity, Efficiency, and Risk-Taking," *Administrative Science Quarterly,* Fall 1968, pp. 305–39; Victor Vroom, Lester Grant, and Timothy Cotten, "The Consequences of Social Interaction in Group Problem-Solving," *Organizational Behavior and Human Performance,* February 1969, pp. 77–95; P. A. Collaras and L. R. Anderson, "Effect of Perceived Expertise upon Creativity of Members of Brainstorming Groups," *Journal of Applied Psychology,* April 1969, pp. 159–63; Richard A. Guzzo and James A. Waters, "The Expression of Affect and the Performance of Decision-Making Groups," *Journal of Applied Psychology,* February 1982, pp. 67–74; and D. Tjosvold and R. H. G. Field, "Effects of Social Context on Consensus and Majority Vote Decision Making," *Academy of Management Journal,* September 1983, pp. 500–6.

Figure 4–4 Probable relationship between quality of group decision and method utilized.

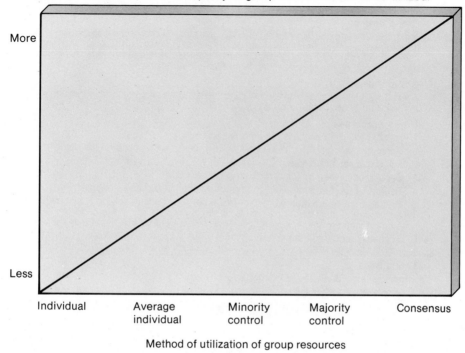

quality of the decision improves. Note also that each successive method involves a higher level of mutual influence by group members. Thus, for a complex problem requiring pooled knowledge, the quality of the decision is likely to be higher as the group moves toward achieving consensus.

Creativity in Group Decision Making

If groups are better suited to nonprogrammed decisions than individuals, then it is important that an atmosphere fostering group creativity be created. In this respect, group decision making may be similar to brainstorming in that discussion must be free flowing and spontaneous. All group members must participate, and the evaluation of individual ideas must be suspended in the beginning to encourage participation. However, a decision must be reached, and this is where group decision making differs from brainstorming. Table 4–6 presents guidelines for developing the permissive atmosphere that is important for creative decision making.[24]

---

[24]Andre L. Delbecq, "The Management of Decision Making within the Firm: Three Strategies for Three Types of Decision Making," *Academy of Management Journal*, December 1967, pp. 334–35.

Table 4–6 Creative group decision making.

Group Structure

The group is composed of heterogeneous, generally competent personnel who bring to bear on the problem diverse frames of reference, representing channels to each relevant body of knowledge (including contact with outside resource personnel who offer expertise not encompassed by the organization), with a leader who facilitates the creative process.

Group Roles

Each individual explores with the entire group all ideas (no matter how intuitively and roughly formed) that bear on the problem.

Group Processes

The problem-solving process is characterized by:

1. Spontaneous communication between members (not focused on the leader).
2. Full participation from each member.
3. Separation of idea generation from idea evaluation.
4. Separation of problem definition from generation of solution strategies.
5. Shifting of roles, so that interaction that mediates problem solving (particularly search activities and clarification by means of constant questioning directed both to individual members and to the whole group) is not the sole responsibility of the leader.
6. Suspension of judgment and avoidance of early concern with solutions, so that the emphasis is on analysis and exploration, rather than on early commitment to solutions.

Group Style

The social-emotional tone of the group is characterized by:

1. A relaxed, nonstressful environment.
2. Ego-supportive interaction, where open give-and-take between members is at the same time courteous.
3. Behavior that is motivated by interest in the problem, rather than concern with short-run payoff.
4. Absence of penalties attached to any espoused idea or position.

Group Norms

1. Are supportive of originality and unusual ideas and allow for eccentricity.
2. Seek behavior that separates source from content in evaluating information and ideas.
3. Stress a nonauthoritarian view, with a realistic view of life and independence of judgment.
4. Support humor and undisciplined exploration of viewpoints.
5. Seek openness in communication, where mature, self-confident individuals offer "crude" ideas to the group for mutual exploration without threat to the individuals for "exposing" themselves.
6. Deliberately avoid giving credence to short-run results or short-run decisiveness.
7. Seek consensus but accept majority rule when consensus is unobtainable.

Techniques for Stimulating Creativity

It seems safe to say that in many instances group decision making is preferable to individual decision making. But we have all heard the statement "A camel is a racehorse designed by a committee." Thus while the necessity and the benefits of group decision making are recognized, numerous problems are also associated with it, some of which have already been noted. Practicing managers are in need of specific techniques that will enable them to increase the benefits from group decision making while reducing the problems associated with it.

We shall examine three techniques that, when properly utilized, have been found to be extremely useful in increasing the creative capability of a group in generating ideas, understanding problems, and reaching better decisions. Increasing the creative capability of a group is especially necessary when individuals from diverse sectors of the organization must pool their judgments in order to create a satisfactory course of action for the organization. The three techniques are known as brainstorming, the Delphi technique, and the nominal group technique.

Brainstorming. In many situations, groups are expected to produce creative or imaginative solutions to organizational problems. In such instances, *brainstorming* has often been found to enhance the creative output of the group. The technique of brainstorming includes a strict series of rules. The purpose of the rules is to promote the generation of ideas while at the same time avoiding the inhibitions of members that are usually caused by face-to-face groups. The basic rules are:

No idea is too ridiculous. Group members are encouraged to state any extreme or outlandish idea.

Each idea presented belongs to the group, not to the person stating it. In this way, it is hoped that group members will utilize and build on the ideas of others.

No idea can be criticized. The purpose of the session is to generate, not evaluate, ideas.

Brainstorming is widely used in advertising and some other fields, where it is apparently effective. In other situations, it has been less successful because there is no evaluation or ranking of the ideas generated. Thus, the group never really concludes the problem-solving process.

The Delphi technique. This technique involves the solicitation and comparison of anonymous judgments on the topic of interest through a set of sequential questionnaires that are interspersed with summarized information and feedback of opinions from earlier responses.[25]

The *Delphi process* retains the advantage of having several judges while removing the biasing effects that might occur during face-to-face interaction. The basic approach has been to collect anonymous judgments by mail questionnaire. For example, the members independently generate their ideas to answer the first questionnaire and return it. The staff members summarize the responses as the group consensus, and feed this summary back along with a second questionnaire for reassessment. Based on this feedback, the respondents independently evaluate their earlier responses. The underlying belief is that the consensus estimate will result in a better decision after several rounds of anonymous group judgment. While it is possible to continue the procedure for several rounds, essentially no significant change occurs after the second round of estimation.

---

[25]Norman Dalkey, *The Delphi Method: An Experimental Study of Group Opinion* (Santa Monica, CA: Rand Corporation, 1969). This is the classic work on the Delphi method.

The Nominal Group Technique (NGT).   NGT has gained increasing recognition in health, social service, education, industry, and government organizations.[26] The term *Nominal Group Technique* was adopted by earlier researchers to refer to processes that bring people together but do not allow them to communicate verbally. Thus, the collection of people is a group "nominally," or "in name only." We shall see, however, that NGT in its present form combines both verbal and nonverbal stages.

Basically, NGT is a structured group meeting that proceeds as follows: A group of individuals (7 to 10) sit around a table but do not speak to one another. Rather, each person writes ideas on a pad of paper. After five minutes, a structured sharing of ideas takes place. Each person around the table presents one idea. A person designated as recorder writes the ideas on a flip chart in full view of the entire group. This continues until all of the participants indicate that they have no further ideas to share. There is still no discussion.

The output of this phase is a list of ideas (usually between 18 and 25). The next phase involves structured discussion in which each idea receives attention before a vote is taken. This is achieved by asking for clarification or stating the degree of support for each idea listed on the flip chart. The next stage involves independent voting in which each participant, in private, selects priorities by ranking or voting. The group decision is the mathematically pooled outcome of the individual votes.

Both the Delphi technique and NGT are relatively new, but each has had an excellent record of successes. Basic differences between them are:

1. Delphi participants are typically anonymous to one another, while NGT participants become acquainted.
2. NGT participants meet face-to-face around a table, while Delphi participants are physically distant and never meet face to face.
3. In the Delphi process, all communication between participants is by way of written questionnaires and feedback from the monitoring staff. In NGT, communication is direct between participants.[27]

Practical considerations, of course, often influence which technique is used. For example, such factors as the number of working hours available, costs, and the physical proximity of participants will influence which technique is selected.

Our discussion here has not been designed to make the reader an expert in the Delphi process or NGT.[28] Our purpose throughout this section has been to indicate the frequency and importance of group decision making in every type of organization.

---

[26]See Andre L. Delbecq, Andrew H. Van de Ven, and David H. Gustafson, *Group Techniques for Program Planning* (Glenview, Ill.: Scott, Foresman, 1975) for an outstanding work devoted entirely to NGT and other group decision-making methods. The discussion here is based on this work.

[27]*Ibid.*, p. 18.

[28]The reader desiring to learn more about each of these techniques is encouraged to consult Delbecq, Van de Ven, and Gustafson, *Group Techniques for Program Planning;* and Frederick C. Miner, Jr., "A Comparative Analysis of Three Diverse Groups' Decision-Making Approaches," *Academy of Management Journal,* March 1979, pp. 81–93.

The three techniques discussed are practical devices whose purpose is to improve the *effectiveness* of group decisions.

Decision making is a common responsibility shared by all executives, regardless of functional area or management level. Every day, managers are required to make decisions that shape the future of their organization as well as their own futures. The quality of these decisions is the yardstick of their managers' effectiveness. Some of these decisions may have a strong impact on the organization's success, while others will be important but less crucial. However, *all* of the decisions will have some effect (positive or negative, large or small) on the organization.

MANAGEMENT SOLUTION

BURGER KING MAKES A MAJOR DECISION

As they entered the last quarter of 1987, Burger King's management decided to end their 11-year relationship with their advertising agency. This one decision meant that it would move its $200 million account from one agency to another. The result of the decision was the largest account switch in the history of advertising. Obviously, the decision had a tremendous positive impact on the new advertising agency and a negative impact on the financial performance of the former agency. The decision is expected to give momentum to the new agency. Because of the size of the account, it is expected to serve as a showcase for the agency, helping the firm attract additional business as well as helping in recruiting creative staff. Hopefully the decision will not have the opposite effect on the losing agency.

As we have seen in this chapter, managers are evaluated and rewarded on the basis of the results of their decisions. In this case Burger King's decision was a response to a problem and resulted from much thought and deliberation.

Source: Adapted from Mark N. Vamos, "N. W. Ayer Bags Itself a Whopper," *Business Week,* October 12, 1987, p. 42.

MANAGEMENT SUMMARY

- ☐ Planning and decision making are two managerial activities that cannot be separated. Every stage of planning involves decision making.
- ☐ The quality of management decisions determines to a large extent the effectiveness of plans.
- ☐ Managers are evaluated and rewarded on the basis of the importance, number, and results of their decisions.
- ☐ Decisions may be classified as programmed or nonprogrammed, depending on the type of problem. Each type requires different kinds

of procedures and applies to very different types of situations.

☐ Decision making is a many phased process. The actual choice is only one phase.

☐ Decisions should be thought of as *means* rather than ends. They are a manager's responses to problems and the results of a process of thought and deliberation.

☐ Different managers may select different alternatives in the same situation. This is because of differences in values and in attitudes toward risk.

☐ Managers spend a great deal of time in group decision making. This is especially true for nonprogrammed decisions. Much evidence exists that, in certain situations, group decisions are superior to individual decisions. However, there are exceptions, and group decision making itself can create problems.

☐ A great deal of nonprogrammed decision making occurs in group situations. Much evidence exists to support the claim that in most instances group decisions are superior to individual decisions. Three relatively new techniques (brainstorming, the Delphi technique, and the Nominal Group Technique) have the purpose of improving the effectiveness of group decisions. The management of collective decision making must be a vital concern for future managers.

REVIEW AND DISCUSSION QUESTIONS

1. What is a decision?

2. We make decisions daily. Describe in detail two programmed decisions you make each day. Why do you consider them to be programmed? Were they ever nonprogrammed? If so, discuss why.

3. Describe what you believe is a nonprogrammed decision that you recently made. Describe the circumstances surrounding the decision and state why you believe it was nonprogrammed. Did this belief influence your decision-making approach? In what ways?

4. Re-examine the decision you described in question 3 and discuss it in terms of the decision-making process outlined in the chapter.

5. Select a major political or business decision with which you are familiar. Evaluate the decision in terms of how good you think it was. Be specific, and state how you determined the quality of the decision.

6. What type of risk taker do you believe you are? Indicate how the characteristic has influenced some decisions that you have made recently.

7. Describe a group decision-making situation in which you were involved. Did any problems develop? Describe them in detail. Was the decision reached by the group different from the one you would have made as an individual? Do you think that the group decision was better? Why?

8. Why are the management function of planning and the process of decision making so closely related?

9. Think of a decision that you or someone you know has made recently. Do you believe that any of the various influences on the decision-making process discussed in the chapter could have affected the outcome? Discuss each influence and indicate how it may have affected the decision.

10. In your opinion, what are the advantages and shortcomings of group decision making?

CASES

4–1 MANAGERS ARE PAID TO MAKE DECISIONS

Bob Wilson is president of Security National Bank (SNB). During the seven years he has been president, the bank has become one of the three largest banks serving metropolitan Rockford. It has been extremely successful, mostly at the expense of competing banks.

On his desk, Wilson has a report from Barbara Stark, the bank's director of marketing. The report focuses on the bank's entry into the first phase of electronic banking: the purchase and installation of automatic tellers (ATs). Wilson is very impressed by the report and has asked Stark to come to his office to discuss the proposal. It is a very positive meeting, with both parties agreeing on the necessity for getting the program started. Stark says:

> Mr. Wilson, most experts believe that before very long every bank in the
> country will be faced with a decision concerning these machines. The
> decision will be either offensive (to install them in order to be the first in
> the market) or defensive (to respond to a competitor that has already
> installed them). I believe that to maintain the growth rate we have
> achieved during your seven years as president, our move should be an
> offensive one.

"I don't think anyone would argue with you on that point, Ms. Stark," Wilson agrees.

Wilson is extremely impressed with the position taken by his director of marketing and is in general agreement with it. He decides to take up Barbara Stark's proposal at the next meeting of the board of directors and to strongly support it. In addition, he sends a copy of the report to Dick Bryan, vice president of branch operations, along with a memo supporting the proposal and asking Bryan for additional ideas that he might have.

Five days later, Bryan asks to see Wilson concerning the report. What he has to say comes as a surprise.

> Mr. Wilson, I have read carefully the report concerning ATs. Let me say
> that I am in total agreement with the philosophy of aggressive, consumer-
> oriented banking that you have instilled into each of us at SNB.
> Certainly, we have been successful. I also agree that the concept of
> electronic banking is the wave of the future and support each of the
> benefits outlined in Ms. Stark's report.
>   I see one potential problem, however, in implementing any decision in
> this direction. It involves the dismissal of several tellers. First, from the
> standpoint of social responsibility, I do not think that this would be very
> responsible, and it might subject us to much criticism in the community. I
> can relate to how each of the tellers might feel, because I remember the
> late 1950s and what my family went through when my father's plant was

being automated. Maybe that experience has biased my thinking in this matter, but I feel it necessary to at least express it.

Second, this decision could create morale problems for the remaining tellers. As you know, I must work through all of these people, the branch managers, and the people in the branches. They are our contact with customers, and as you have said many times. "An unhappy, rude teller is an unhappy, rude bank to the customer." I believe there is a potential problem here that was not addressed in Ms. Stark's report. That is, what will the impact be on our branch managers and our branch personnel when they see their subordinates and peers being replaced by a machine?

Since branch operations is my area, I feel compelled to let my views be known. I know that the decision is not mine to make and that many other factors must be considered. In fact, I can't say I disagree with the concept, but I do know that if we go with ATs, it will have to be implemented through my area.

That evening, Wilson thinks about what Bryan said. It is certainly something he has never considered, and it is good that Bryan brought it to his attention. He tosses around all the benefits, costs, and problems associated with the decision. What position should he now take on the matter at the meeting of the board of directors? "Oh well," he thinks, "I guess this is what I'm paid for, to make decisions like this."

Questions

1. Analyze this decision situation in terms of what you know about the decision-making process and the influences on it.
2. If you were a consultant to the president, what would your advice be? Why?

4–2 GROUP DECISION MAKING AT LONGLEY UNIVERSITY

Tom Madden slipped into his seat at the meeting of the faculty of the College of Business Administration of Longley University. He was 10 minutes late because he had come completely across campus from another meeting that had lasted $1^1/_4$ hours. "Boy!" he thought, "if all of these meetings and committee assignments keep up, I won't have time to do anything else."

"The next item of importance," said the dean, "is consideration of the feasibility report prepared by the assistant dean, Dr. Jackson, for the establishment of our Latin American MBA program."

"What's that?" Tom whispered to his friend Jim Lyon, who was sitting next to him.

"Ah, Professor Madden," winked Lyon as he passed the 86-page report to Tom, "evidently you've not bothered to read this impressive document. Otherwise, you'd know."

"Heck, Jim, I've been out of town for two weeks on a research project, and I've just come from another meeting."

"Well, Tom," chuckled Jim, "the report was circulated only three days ago to, as the dean put it, 'ensure that we have faculty input into where the college is going.' Actually, Tom, I was hoping you had read it because then you could have told me what was in it."

"Dr. Jackson," said the dean, "why don't you present a summary of your excellent report on what I believe is an outstanding opportunity for our college, the establishment of an MBA program in Latin America."

"Hey, Jim," said Tom, "they've got to be kidding. We're not doing what we should be doing with the MBA program we've got here on campus. Why on earth are we thinking about starting another one 3,000 miles away?"

Jim shrugged. "Some friends of the dean's or Jackson's from down there must have asked them, I guess."

While the summary was being given, Tom thumbed through the report. He noted that the college was planning to offer the same program that it offered in the United States. "Certainly," he thought, "their students' needs are different from ours." He also noted that faculty were going to be sent from the United States on one- to three-year appointments. "You would think that whenever possible they would seek local instructors who were familiar with the needs of local industry," Tom thought. He concluded in his own mind, "Actually, why are we even getting involved in this thing in the first place? We don't have the resources."

When Jackson finished the summary, the dean asked, "Are there any questions?"

"I wonder how many people have had the time to read this report in three days and think about it," Tom thought to himself.

"Has anybody thought through this entire concept?" Tom spoke up. "I mean . . . "

"Absolutely, Professor Madden," the dean answered. "Dr. Jackson and I have spent a great deal of time on this project."

"Well, I was just thinking that . . . "

"Now, Professor Madden, surely you don't question the efforts of Dr. Jackson and myself. Had you been here when this meeting started, you would know all about our efforts. Besides, it's getting late and we've got another agenda item to consider today, the safety and security of final examinations prior to their being given."

"No further questions," Tom said.

"Wonderful," said the dean. "then I will report to the president that the faculty of the College of Business Administration unanimously approves the Latin American MBA program. I might add, by the way, that the president is extremely pleased with our method of shared decision making. We have made it work in this college, while other colleges are having trouble arriving at mutually agreed-upon decisions.

"This is a great day for our college. Today we have become a multinational university. We can all be proud."

After the meeting, as Tom headed for the parking lot, he thought, "What a way to make an important decision. I guess I shouldn't complain though, I didn't even read the report. I'd better check my calendar to see what committee meetings I've got the rest of the week. If I've got any more, I'll . . . "

Questions

1. Analyze this case, and outline the factors that influenced the faculty decision in this case—either positively or negatively.

2. Does this case indicate that shared decision making cannot be worthwhile and effective? How could it be made more effective in the College of Business Administration?

3. Do you believe that decision making of this type may be more worthwhile and effective in some types of organizations than in others? Discuss.

EXERCISE

4–1 LOST-AT-SEA DECISION MAKING

Purpose: The purpose of this exercise is to offer you the opportunity to compare individual versus group decision making.

Setting Up the Exercise: You are adrift on a private yacht in the South Pacific. As a consequence of a fire of unknown origin, much of the yacht and its contents have been destroyed. The yacht is now slowly sinking. Your location is unclear because of the destruction of critical navigational equipment and because you and the crew were distracted trying to bring the fire under control. Your best estimate is that you are approximately 1,000 miles south-southwest of the nearest land.

Exhibit 1 contains a list of 15 items that are intact and undamaged after the fire. In addition to these articles, you have a serviceable rubber life raft with oars, large enough to carry yourself, the crew, and all the items listed here. The total contents of all survivors' pockets are a package of cigarettes, several books of matches, and five $1 bills.

1. Working independently and without discussing the problem or the merits of any of the items, your task is to rank the 15 items in terms of their importance to your survival. Under column 1, place the number 1 by the most important item, the number 2 by the second most important, and so on through number 15, the least important. When you are through, *do not discuss* the problem or your rankings of items with anyone.

2. Your instructor will establish teams of four to six students. The task for your team is to rank the 15 items, according to the group's consensus, in the order of importance to your survival. Do not vote or average team members' rankings; try to reach agreement on each item. Base your decision on knowledge, logic, or the experiences of group members. Try to avoid basing the decision on personal preference. Enter the group's ranking in column 2. This process should take between 20 and 30 minutes, or as the instructor designates.

3. When everyone is through, your instructor will read the correct ranking, provided by officers of the U.S. Merchant Marine. Enter the correct rankings in column 3.

4. Compute the accuracy of your individual ranking. For each item, use the absolute value (ignore plus and minus signs) of the difference between column 1 and column 3. Add up these absolute values to get your *individual accuracy index*. Enter it here on the worksheet.

5. Perform the same operation as in Step 4, but use columns 2 and 3 for your group ranking. Adding up the absolute values yields your *group accuracy index*. Enter it on the worksheet.

Exhibit 1 Worksheet.

Items	(1) Individual Ranking	(2) Group Ranking	(3) Ranking Key
Sextant	——	——	——
Shaving mirror	——	——	——
Five-gallon can of water	——	——	——
Mosquito netting	——	——	——
One case of U.S. Army C rations	——	——	——
Maps of the Pacific Ocean	——	——	——
Seat cushion (flotation device approved by the Coast Guard)	——	——	——
Two-gallon can of oil-gas mixture	——	——	——
Small transistor radio	——	——	——
Shark repellent	——	——	——
Twenty square feet of opaque plastic	——	——	——
One quart of 160-proof Puerto Rican rum	——	——	——
Fifteen feet of nylon rope	——	——	——
Two boxes of chocolate bars	——	——	——
Fishing kit	——	——	

Individual accuracy index   ————

Group accuracy index   ————

Averge of group's individual
  accuracy indexes   ————

Lowest individual accuracy index
  (correct ranking)   ————

---

6. Compute the *average* of your group's individual accuracy indexes. Do this by adding up each member's individual accuracy index and dividing the result by the number of group members. Enter it.

7. Identify the *lowest* individual accuracy index in your group. This is the most correct ranking in your group. Enter it on the worksheet.

A Learning Note: This exercise is designed to let you experience group decision making. Think about how discussion, reflection, and the exchange of opinions influenced your final decision.

FIVE

Managing Information Systems

LEARNING OBJECTIVES

After completing Chapter 5, you should be able to:

Define: decision support systems and their importance.

State: the major functions of a decision support system.

Describe: how the types of decisions managers make relate to the types of information they need.

Explain: the differences between decision support systems and management information systems.

Discuss: the organization of decision support systems.

MANAGING INFORMATION TO BETTER MATCH SUPPLY AND DEMAND?

A chain such as Wal-Mart Stores, Inc., can lose a great amount of sales if it should run out of popular garments at the height of a selling season. In many situations the manufacturers cannot produce and deliver more garments fast enough to meet seasonal demand. In such a situation everyone loses, both the retailer and the manufacturer. The problem is especially serious in businesses such as the $55 billion textile industry, which has suffered as retailers have doubled their purchases of inexpensive Asian apparel over the past five years.

Recently, 220 top retail and clothing executives convened to develop industry-standard formats for purchase orders, shipping documents, and other forms. Their goal: to beat Asian rivals by making it easier for retailers to deal with U.S. suppliers. The goal is to move information faster from the retailer's cash register to the textile maker's factory floor. This means that sales data, new orders, shipment information, inventory receipts, and invoices must all flow smoothly in both directions in order to make the quickest turnaround possible.

(The Management Solution to this Management Incident can be found at the end of this chapter.)

As organizations grow in complexity, managers depend more heavily upon various internal and external sources of information. Growing complexity also increases the number of points at which decisions must be made, ranging from individual decision makers at the lowest operating levels to strategic decision makers at the top. Management information systems, designed to provide information to these decision makers, are certainly not new. Many firms have accounting information systems, marketing information systems, customer information files, warehouse information systems, and others. But one very important idea moves beyond the management information system: the decision support system.

THE NEED FOR DECISION SUPPORT SYSTEMS

You know from the last chapter that the quality of a decision depends greatly on understanding the circumstances surrounding an issue and knowing the available alternatives and states of nature. The better the information, the better the resulting decision, because there is less risk and uncertainty. If new, advanced information technology is to support management decision making, organizations must plan now. The need for comprehensive decision support systems has resulted from three factors: (1) the importance of information in decision making,[1] (2) mismanagement of current information,[2] and (3) the increased use of personal computers by individual decision makers.[3]

The Importance of Information in Decision Making

Information is really a fuel that drives organizations. A major purpose of a manager is to convert information into action through the process of decision making. Therefore, a manager and an organization act as an *information-decision system*.

> Information-decision systems should be considered in conjunction with the fundamental managerial functions: planning, organizing, and controlling. If an organization is to implement planning and control, if an organization is tied to communication, and if communication is represented by an information-decision system, then the key to success in planning and controlling any operation lies in the information-decision system.[4]

---

[1]Cornelius H. Sullivan, Jr., "Systems Planning in the Information Age," *Sloan Management Review,* Winter 1985, pp. 3–12.

[2]C. Wood, "Countering Unauthorized Systems Accesses," *Journal of Systems Management,* April 1984, pp. 26–28.

[3]E. W. Robak, "Toward a Microcomputer-Based DSS for Planning Forest Operations," *Interfaces,* September–October 1984, pp. 105–11; W. L. Fuerst and M. P. Martin, "Effective Design and Use of Computer Decision Models," *MIS Quarterly,* March 1984, pp. 17–26.

[4]Richard A. Johnson, Fremont E. Kast, and James E. Rosenzweig, *The Theory and Management of Systems* (New York: McGraw-Hill, 1978), p. 108.

Viewing an organization as an information-decision system points out the importance of only generating information that is necessary for effective decisions. If management converts information into action, then how effective the action is depends on how complete, relevant, and reliable the information is. The effectiveness of an organization is more often than not at the mercy of the information available to its managers.[5]

Mismanagement of Current Information

The ability of organizations to generate information is really not a problem, since most are capable of producing massive amounts of information and data. In fact, the last decade has often been described as the Age of Information. Why then do so many managers complain that they have insufficient or irrelevant information on which to base their everyday decisions? Specifically, most managers' complaints fall into the following categories:

1. There is too much of the wrong kind of information and not enough of the right kind.
2. Information is so scattered throughout the organization that it is difficult to locate answers to simple questions.
3. Vital information is sometimes suppressed by subordinates or by managers in other functional areas.
4. Vital information often arrives long after it is needed.

Historically managers did not have to deal with an overabundance of information. Instead they gathered a bare minimum of information and hoped that their decisions would be reasonably good. In fact, in some business organizations, marketing research came to be recognized as an extremely valuable staff function during the 1930s and 1940s because it provided information for marketing decisions where previously there had been little or none.

Today, by contrast, managers often feel buried by the deluge of information and data that comes across their desks. This deluge of information, much of which is not useful, has led to the mismanagement of current information. More is not always better.

The Increased Use of Personal Computers

Many experts believe that before this decade is over, almost all managers will be sharing their desk space with a personal computer. Personal computers have the capability of increasing both the productivity of managers and the quality of their decisions. First, the capacity of computers to extract, process, and analyze data swiftly

[5]D. Lynch, "MIS: Conceptual Framework, Criticism, and Major Requirements for Success," *Journal of Business Communication*, Winter 1984, pp. 19–31; and Michael Davis and Joseph L. Sardinas, Jr., "Creating the Right Decision Support System—Pitfalls," *Management Accounting*, June 1985, pp. 12, 69.

and accurately is awesome. Second, computers have gotten smaller, faster, and smarter in a shorter period of time than any other technological innovation in history. A common desktop personal computer can solve ordinary arithmetic problems 18 times faster than the world's first large-scale computer (weighing 30 tons) built only 41 years ago. Present-day computers have become extremely inexpensive compared to earlier models. Just 30 years ago, a medium-sized computer cost a quarter of a million dollars. A firm can now buy a desktop computer with three times the memory capacity for less than $1,500. Consequently many firms are now making personal computers widely available to their employees.

The means necessary to produce information are available. Still, managers complain of information losses, delays, and distortions. Apparently many managers have been so concerned about advancing technology and the ready availability of computers that they have overlooked the planning necessary for their effective use. To enable managers to make swift and effective decisions, however, present management information systems must be developed into more effective decision support systems.[6]

MANAGEMENT INFORMATION SYSTEMS (MIS) AND DECISION SUPPORT SYSTEMS (DSS)

Decision support systems have one primary purpose: *to provide the manager with the necessary information for making intelligent decisions.*

The critical point here is that not just any information will do. A system is needed that converts raw data into information that management can actually use. Such systems are known as *decision support systems* (DSS's). They can be described as:

> a wide variety of systems which have the direct objective of supporting managerial decision making. Thus, a *management information system* (MIS) is a DSS if, and only if, it is designed with the primary objective of managerial decision support. A computerized data processing system is *not* a DSS—despite that it may, as a by-product, produce aggregated operating data that are useful to management in making decisions. Only those systems that have the direct and primary objective of supporting managerial decision making are considered DSS's.[7]

Thus, a DSS is a specialized MIS designed to support a manager's skills at all stages of decision making—identifying the problem, choosing the relevant data, picking the approach to be used in making the decision, and evaluating the alternative courses of action. A DSS must produce information in a form managers understand and at a time when such information is needed, and place the information under the managers' direct control. Thus, a DSS is an MIS, but an MIS is not always a DSS; their purposes are different, as shown in the Management Application comparing several systems.

---

[6]See John Deardon, "Will the Computer Change the Job of Top Management?" *Sloan Management Review,* Fall 1983, pp. 57–60.

[7]William R. King, "Developing Useful Management Decision Support Systems," *Management Decision,* Fall 1978, pp. 262–73; and R. W. Blanning, "What Is Happening in DSS?" *Interfaces,* October 1983, pp. 71–80.

MANAGEMENT APPLICATION

COMPARING MIS AND DSS

An MIS at United Services Automobile Association

The United Services Automobile Association, the nation's eighth largest insurer of passenger cars, purchased a $4 million information system that now contains virtually all of the company's written records. When a customer reports an accident, an adjustor can call up the customer's file, check the coverage, and keep track of all the paperwork through the final settlement of the claim. The company figures that it once took five people a day and a half to perform tasks that one person now handles in 20 minutes.

An MIS at Savin Corporation

Savin Corporation has installed a computer terminal in each of its warehouses to keep track of every item in its inventory. The system identifies the quantity on hand, the location and movement of stock, and the status of all orders. The major purposes of this system are to plan shipments, locate single items in inventory, and locate customer records.

A DSS at Crocker National Bank

Crocker National Bank in San Francisco has purchased desktop terminals for most of its top-level executives. Each terminal is tapped into the huge computers that record all bank transactions. The executives are able to make comparisons, analyze problems, and prepare charts and tables in response to simple commands. For example, they can analyze emerging trends in deposits and loans and monitor the influence of various interest rates and loan maturities on the bank.

A DSS at Gould, Inc.

Gould, Inc. has developed a decision support system to help managers retrieve, manipulate, and display information needed for making decisions. The system combines a large visual display and video terminals with a computerized information system. The system is designed solely to help managers make comparisons and analyze problems for decision-making purposes. The DSS instantly prepares tables and color charts in response to simple commands.

In short, an MIS provides information, but a DSS shapes that information to management's needs as shown in the following Management Application.

MANAGEMENT APPLICATION

SELECTING SUPPLIERS AT IBM

International Business Machines Corp. (IBM) operates a manufacturing facility in Poughkeepsie, New York. The plant develops and manufactures processors for the highly competitive international market. The plant's 150-person purchasing department is responsible for buying all production and nonproduction parts from outside suppliers. These parts range from inexpensive screws to relatively expensive frames. Because the cost of purchased parts comprises a large percentage of total product cost, the purchasing manager continually seeks ways to cut costs. Basically, the purchase decision involves selecting specific suppliers to supply specific parts in specific quantities to arrive at specified times.

After an investment of considerable time and money, the purchasing department developed a system that enabled it to make optimal decisions. The system is named the vendor selection system (VSS) because it enables the decision maker to specify the decision variables and constraints and select the optimal combination of suppliers. The system is no more complicated to use than the current popular electronic spreadsheet software and is a good example of an information system dedicated to producing decision-relevant information: a decision support system.

Source: Adapted from P. S. Bender, R. W. Brown, M. H. Isaac, and J. F. Shapiro, "Improving Purchasing Productivity at IBM with a Normative Decision Support System," *Interfaces*, May–June 1987, pp. 106–15.

PROVIDING THE RIGHT INFORMATION FOR THE RIGHT DECISIONS

The preceding chapter discussed how the types of problems faced and the procedures used for dealing with them vary according to a manager's level in the organization. The same factors—level in the organization and the type of decision being made—also affect managerial information requirements. To ensure that the types of information match the types of decisions being made, appropriate information must be directed to the proper decision points.

Types of Decisions and Types of Information

The types of information needed are classified by the types of decisions being made: planning decisions, control decisions, and operations decisions. Decision support systems must generate the right types of information for particular types of decisions.[8] Planning, control, and operations decisions require planning, control, and operations information.

☐ *Planning decisions* are made by top management. These decisions involve formulating objectives for the organization, the amounts and kinds of resources necessary to attain these objectives, and the policies that govern the use of the resources. Much of this *planning information* comes from external sources and relates to such factors as the present and predicted

[8]L. Mann, "User Profiles for Systems Planning and Development," *Journal of Systems Management*, April 1984, pp. 38–40.

state of the economy, availability of resources (nonhuman as well as human), and the political and regulatory environment. Planning information forms the input for nonprogrammed types of decisions made at this top level in the organization.[9]

☐ *Control decisions* are made by middle management to ensure that the organization's performance is consistent with its objectives. *Control information* comes mainly from internal sources (often interdepartmental) and involves such problems as developing budgets and measuring performance of first-line supervisors. The nature of problems faced may be either programmable or nonprogrammable.[10]

☐ *Operations decisions* focus on the day-to-day activities of the organization and how efficiently its resources are being used. *Operations information* comes from routine and necessary sources, such as financial accounting, inventory control, and production scheduling. This information is generated internally; and since it usually relates to specific tasks, it often comes from one designated department. First-line supervisors are the primary users. Since decision making at this level in the organization usually involves programmed types of problems, many problems at the operations level are stated as mathematical models.[11]

Computer-Assisted Decision Making

As we enter the 1990s, computers will be relied on more and more to improve the quality of management decisions. Three important developments are (1) interactive decision making, (2) modeling, and (3) artificial intelligence.

Interactive decision making.   Interactive decision making allows the user to interact with the computer, reading the information it provides, and responding to questions, rather than just feeding in data and waiting for an answer. What actually occurs is a team effort which draws on the strengths of people and computers. Many bank customers are familiar with this type of computer-assisted decision making. The technology used for public-access banking machines—interactive video—has been adopted by some banks and accepted by their customers. The machines are appearing in some bank branches. Mixing video messages, text, and graphics on one screen, they supply customers with bank products and general information, financial modeling capabilities, and transaction processing.

---

[9]Robert Fildes, "Quantitative Forecasting—the State of the Arts," *Journal of the Operations Research Society,* July 1985, pp. 549–80; and Kelvin Cross, "Manufacturing Planning with Computers at Honeywell," *Long Range Planning,* December 1984, pp. 64–75.

[10]John Murdoch, "Forecasting and Inventory Control on Micros," *Journal of the Operations Research Society,* July 1985, pp. 607–8.

[11]John Bowers, "Network Analysis on a Micro," *Journal of the Operations Research Society,* July 1985, pp. 609–12; and A. C. McKay, "Linear Programming Applications on Microcomputers," *Journal of the Operations Research Society,* July 1985, pp. 633–36.

Modeling the decision maker.   In the previous chapter we saw that managers often face the same routine decisions day after day. These were identified as programmed decisions. A branch manager of a bank deciding whether to approve an automobile loan or a college officer deciding whether or not a student qualifies for admission are examples of this kind of routine decision. In such situations it is possible to design a computer model of the decision maker. Such models designed to behave just as the decision maker behaves are increasingly being used for programmed decisions. Many bank lending decisions are now actually made by computer models. Once such a model is constructed and tested for accuracy and reliability, it can actually replace the decision maker. In borderline cases, the model could leave the decision up to the manager.

Artificial intelligence.   The objective of artificial intelligence is to enable computers to process information in the same manner as human beings. This involves developing the capability of the computer to work in the same manner as the human brain would process information, draw analogies, and solve puzzles.[12] In other words, it involves making the computer "think." Since the computer is faster, more reliable, and more objective it hopefully should be able to make more effective decisions. The reader is probably familiar with such programs. Some have been developed to play chess, backgammon, make generalizations, draw inferences, and make analogies. Although actual learning and true creativity are presently beyond the capability of computers, some people believe that one day it will be accomplished.[13]

One important application of artificial intelligence is known as *expert systems*.[14] Expert systems attempt to apply the results of artificial intelligence research to decision problems by imitating the capabilities and judgments of human experts in a particular field. These expert systems perform similarly to the human expert by combining artificial intelligence software with other aspects of a decision support system. Similar to a decision support system, expert systems store and retrieve data, are interactive, manipulate data, and develop models. However, they also diagnose problems, recommend alternative solutions, offer reasons for their diagnoses and recommendations, and even learn from experience by adding information developed in solving similar problems to their current base of knowledge.[15] These exciting systems guide users through problems with a set of logical and orderly questions about the situation and draw conclusions based on the answers it is provided. Its problem-solving capabilities

---

[12]See Shoshana Zuboff, "Technologies That Inform: Implications for Human Resource Management in the Computerized Workplace," in *The Future of MIS*, ed. Richard E. Walton and Paul R. Lawrence (Boston: Harvard Business School Press, 1985), pp. 134–37.

[13]For a complete discussion of artificial intelligence, see Jeffrey Rothfelder, *Minds over Matter: A New Look at Artificial Intelligence* (New York: Simon & Schuster, 1985).

[14]Walter Reitman, "Artificial Intelligence Applications for Business: Getting Acquainted," in *Artificial Intelligence Applications for Business*, ed. Walter Reitman (Norwood, N.J.: Ablex Publishing, 1984), pp. 1–9.

[15]Michael W. Davis, "Anatomy of Decision Support," *Datamation*, June 15, 1985, p. 201.

are guided by a set of programmed rules modeled on the actual reasoning processes of human experts in the field.[16]

We can see that such developments as artificial intelligence and expert systems are applying the capabilities of technology to help solve unstructured, nonprogrammed management decisions. While some business-oriented expert systems software is currently available, the entire area of artificial intelligence is in the early stages of development. How long will it be until artificial intelligence applications are commonplace? There are five characteristics of managerial decision making which will greatly influence the acceptance and use of artificial intelligence and expert systems:[17]

1. The majority of management problems are unstructured.

2. A manager's time and attention are limited resources.

3. Managers have different problem-solving styles.

4. Managers frequently work in groups on both formal and informal bases.[18]

5. Many managers already have access to an array of computer-based tools.

Given what we have read in the previous chapter, it is easy to see that programming management expertise into an expert system will not be an easy task. Different managers facing the same unstructured problem will often solve it in very different ways. We will likely see artificial intelligence and expert systems being applied to structured and possibly partially unstructured problems before they are applied to highly unstructured management problems. An example of the type of development we are likely to see is presented in the following Management Application.

MANAGEMENT APPLICATION

SOFTWARE THAT HELPS MANAGERS "THINK"

Most software manufacturers, like all good marketers, develop products for those individuals who are "heavy users." For software firms, this means that most new programs are aimed at two groups who purchase a lot of software: number crunchers and word processors. Lately, however, this is changing. Most firms are trying to develop a new market—programs that help manipulate information much more creatively.

For example, Lotus Development Corporation has developed a new program, code-named *Agenda* with so-called artificial intelligence features, that is designed to learn from experience. It will let managers feed notes, lists, memos, phone messages, and so on into a computer, labeling the information as they go. Then if they want to call up all the various pieces of information on a particular topic, for example, the company's

---

[16]Robert C. Schank and Peter G. Childers, *The Cognitive Computer: On Language, Learning, and Artificial Intelligence* (Reading, Mass.: Addison-Wesley, 1985), p. 33.

[17]Robert W. Blanning, "Issues in the Design of Expert Systems for Management," *Proceedings of the 1984 National Computer Conference*, pp. 489–95.

[18]See George P. Huber, "Issues in the Design of Group Decision Support Systems," *MIS Quarterly*, September 1984, pp. 195–204.

competitive position, the computer will assemble them instead of making the manager retrieve them from a couple of dozen separate files. A developer of the program says that "things that looked like different, discrete pieces of information actually become coherent and whole." Since Agenda is designed to learn from experience, when a manager enters information into the program, it automatically suggests how to label that data based on similar past entries.

Source: Adapted from "PC Software That Helps You Think," *Business Week*, November 2, 1987, p. 142.

DESIGNING A DECISION SUPPORT SYSTEM

The first step in designing a DSS is to develop a clear understanding of the various information flows that must be dealt with.

Understanding Information Flows

An organization must deal with two broad types of information flows (see Figure 5–1):

External information flows.   These proceed from the organization to its environment and/or from the environment to the organization. The inward flow is referred to as intelligence information and the outward flow as organizational communications.

Intelligence information includes data on the various elements of the organization's operating environment—such as clients, patients, customers, competitors, suppliers, creditors, and the government—for use in evaluating short-run trends in the immediate external environment. It also includes long-run, strategic planning information on the economic environment—such as consumer income trends and spending patterns for a business organization—as well as tracing developments in the social and cultural environment in which the organization operates. This type of information has long-run significance to the organization and aids in long-range strategic planning.

Organizational communications flow outward from the organization to the various components of its external operating environment. Advertising and other promotional efforts are considered organizational communications. Whatever the type of organization, the content of this information flow is controlled by the organization. Although an important information flow, it nevertheless is an *outward* flow, with which we will not be concerned in this book.

Intraorganization flows.   This term means exactly what the name says: information flowing within an organization. To be useful, intelligence information must, along with internally generated information, reach the right manager at the right time. Within every organization, there are *vertical* (both upward and downward) as well as *horizontal* information flows.[19] The rationale of a DSS is that all information flows must become

---

[19]Lawrence W. Foster and David M. Flynn, "Management Information Technology: Its Effects on Organizational Form and Function," *MIS Quarterly*, December 1984, pp. 229–36.

Figure 5–1   Information flows and types of information.

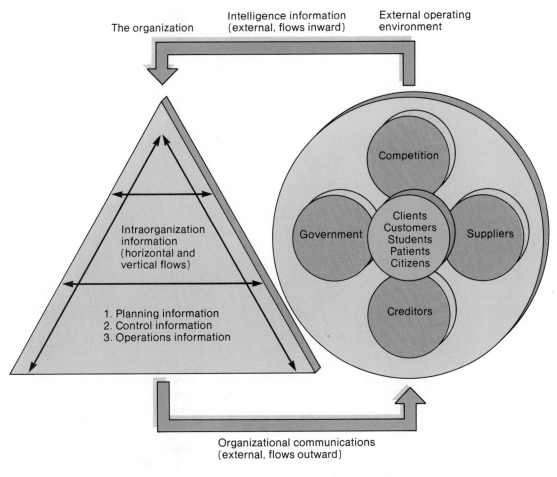

part of a master plan and not be allowed to function without a formal scheme and direction. The objective of the master plan is to circulate information to the proper person at the right time.

The Functions of a Decision Support System

An effective DSS should provide managers with four major services: determination of information needs, information gathering, information processing, and utilization (see Figure 5–2).

Determination of information needs.   At the start, the manager must attempt to answer such questions as: How much information is needed? How, when, and by whom will it be used? In what form is it needed? In other words, the manager begins

Figure 5–2
The functions of
a decision
support system.

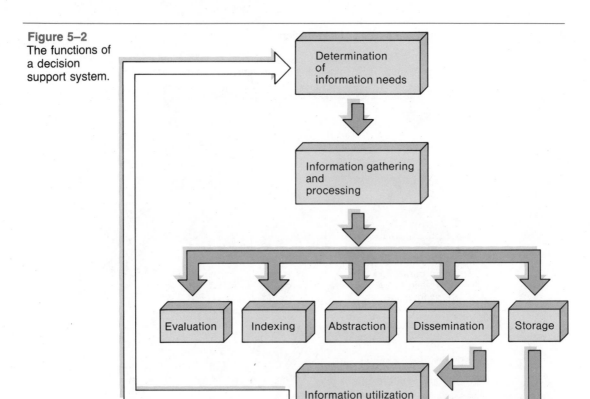

with an examination of the output requirements. Questions helpful for identifying a manager's information needs are presented in Table 5–1. Research and practical experience have demonstrated the need to involve people in changes that affect them. No less is true if a decision support system is being installed: Managers expected to use it should be involved in implementing it.[20] Thus, output requirements are based on answers to such questions as: What information is necessary for planning and controlling operations at different organizational levels? What information is needed to allocate resources? What information is needed to evaluate performance? These types of questions recognize that a different kind of information is needed for formulating organizational objectives than for scheduling production. They also recognize that too much information may actually hinder a manager's performance. The manager must distinguish between "need to know" types of information and "nice to know" types of information. Remember the point we made at the beginning of this chapter: More information does not always mean better decisions.

---

[20]William J. Doll, "Avenues for Top Management Involvement in Successful MIS Development," *MIS Quarterly,* March 1985, pp. 17–36; and Robert I. Mann and Hugh J. Watson, "A Contingency Model for User Involvement in DSS Development," *MIS Quarterly,* March 1984, pp. 27–36.

Table 5–1 Checklist for manager's information needs.*

1. What types of decisions do you make regularly?
2. What types of information do you need to make these decisions?
3. What types of information do you regularly get?
4. What types of information would you like to get that you are not now getting?
5. What information would you want daily? Weekly? Monthly? Yearly?
6. What types of data analysis programs would you like to see made available?

*Source: Adapted from Philip Kotler, *Principles of Marketing*, 3d ed. (Englewood Cliffs, N.J.: Prentice-Hall, 1986).

Determining what information a manager needs for decision making is a useless exercise unless that information can be obtained. For example, any production manager would like to know exactly how many employees are going to show up each day. With that information, the production manager could always accurately schedule the use of part-time and temporary employees. But such information is seldom available. Other information that a manager might need is likely to be found in the minds of experts who have done a particular task for many years but are unable to articulate what it is that they do. For example, Campbell Soup Company recently faced the problem of replacing an employee who was retiring after 44 years with the company. This particular employee knew more about operating the company's huge soup kettles than anyone in the organization. To replace him was next to impossible.[21]

In response to the problem of obtaining information about the kettle operation, Campbell developed an expert system.[22] The system incorporates the latest in decision system technology and includes computer software that simulates the thought processes that the retired employee has used when running the kettles.

Information gathering and processing.   The purpose of this service is to improve the overall quality of the information. It includes five component services: *Evaluation* involves determining how much confidence can be placed in a particular piece of information. Such factors as the credibility of the source and reliability of the data must be determined. *Abstraction* involves editing and reducing incoming information in order to provide the managers only with information relevant to their particular task. Once information has been gathered, the service of *indexing* provides classification for storage and retrieval purposes. *Dissemination* entails getting the right information to the right manager at the right time; indeed, this is the overriding purpose of a DSS. The final information-processing service is that of *storage*. As noted earlier, an organization has no natural memory, so every DSS must provide for storage of information so that it can be used again if needed. Modern electronic information storage equipment has greatly improved the "memory" capabilities of organizations.

---

[21]Emily T. Smith, "Turning an Expert's Skill into Computer Software," *Business Week*, October 7, 1985, pp. 104, 108.

[22]Richard Vedder and Chadwick H. Nestman, "Understanding Expert Systems: A Companion to DSS and MIS," *Industrial Management*, March–April 1985, pp. 1–8.

Information utilization.   How information is used depends greatly on its quality (accuracy), presentation (form), and timeliness. Effective utilization is only possible if the right questions to determine information needs are asked in the beginning and if the system is planned carefully. *The major goal of a DSS is to provide the right information to the right decision maker at the right time.* To this end, timeliness may take precedence over accuracy.[23] If information is not available when it is needed, then its accuracy is not important. In most cases, however, both accuracy and timeliness are critical.

Timeliness is not the same for every manager; it is determined by the nature of the decisions that must be made. For example, a sales manager may find accurate weekly reports of sales for each company product to be adequate, while an investment manager may need accurate information every few minutes.

The following Management Application focuses on matching the information needs of the manager with the capabilities of the information system.

MANAGEMENT APPLICATION

MATCHING MANAGERS' NEEDS WITH SYSTEM CAPABILITIES

Management Level	Managerial Responsibilities	Information Needed	How Information is Used
Top management	Enhance performance, growth, accumulation, and use of resources; survival of total organization	Environmental data and trends, forecasts, summary reports of operations, exception reports on problems	Set organizational objectives, policies, constraints, make decisions on strategic plans and control of total organization
Middle management	Allocate resources to assigned tasks, establish operating plans, control operations	Summaries and exception reports on operating results; relevant actions and decisions of other middle managers	Set operating plans and policies, control procedures, make exception reports, operating summaries, on resource allocations, and decisions related to other middle managers
Lower management	Produce goods or services within budgets, estimate resource requirements, move and store materials	Summary reports of transactions, detailed reports of problems, operating plans and policies, control procedures, actions and decisions of related managers	Create exception and progress reports, identify resource needs, make work schedules

Source: Adapted from Robert G. Murdick, "MIS for MBO," *Journal of Systems Management,* March 1977, pp. 34–40.

[23]Kenneth M. Drange, "Information Systems: Does Efficiency Mean Better Performance?" *Journal of Systems Management,* April 1985, pp. 22–29.

Figure 5–3 The central data bank in a DSS and two-component management information systems.

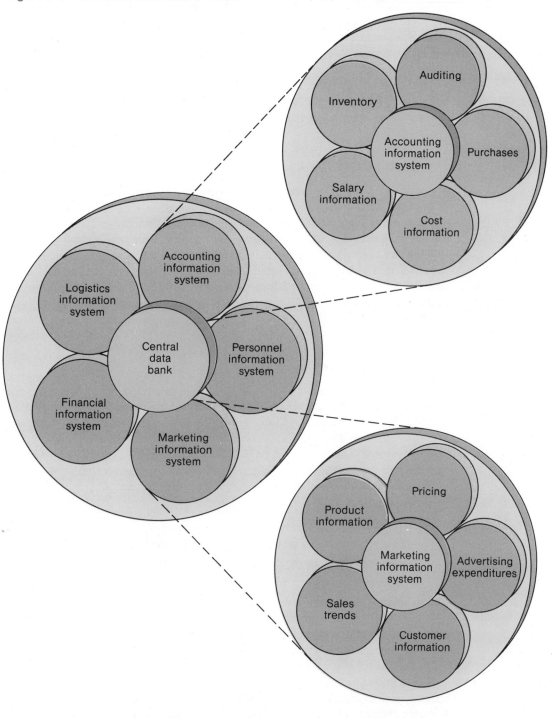

ORGANIZING A DECISION SUPPORT SYSTEM

In most organizations, many different independent information systems exist for different organizational functions. Along with the development of accounting information systems, other line and staff groups in businesses have developed management information systems uniquely suited to their own needs. While management information systems are critical for effective performance within functional areas, what happens when a decision maker requires information from other functional areas? Organizing a DSS means developing a central data bank and an information center, plus viewing information as an important organizational resource.

The Central Data Bank

A central data bank is the core of a decision support system. Information in one area of an organization is made readily available for decision making in other areas through use of a central data bank. Recent developments in computer and communications technology have made such decision support systems both possible and affordable. And the idea is simple: Centralizing information means that sales data would not have to be stored in accounting, marketing, and production but would be available in one central data bank. Since its data can be accessed at will by any decision maker needing it, the central data bank increases both the quality and timeliness of decisions. Figure 5–3 presents the central data bank concept, illustrating two subsystems in more detail.

The Information Center

The information requirements of most managers have greatly changed in the past decade, while the information arrangements within most organizations have remained essentially the same. Because both users and suppliers of information are scattered throughout an organization, some unit is needed to oversee the operation of the central data bank. In fact, a basic weakness in most organizations has been the absence of a central entity—known as the information center—for the gathering and processing of information.

To develop an information center, three tasks are necessary:

1. Dispersed information activities must be identified throughout the organization.
2. These activities must be viewed as parts of a whole.
3. These activities must be brought under the management of a separate, centralized information center.

The information center is a consultant, coordinator, and controller for the functions of a DSS such as determination of information needs, information gathering and processing, and information utilization. In order to justify its existence, it must facilitate improved managerial performance through more as well as better information availability and use.

Many "information-oriented" organizations have developed a separate, centralized, companywide information office. The use of such an office is probably more widespread in highly competitive, volatile consumer-goods industries. However, the need is becoming greater in both private industry and the public sector.[24] This organizational arrangement offers several advantages, such as increased efficiency and more effective use of information, because all computer facilities, knowledge, and storage and re-trieval facilities become available to all other functions in the organization. As the following Management Application illustrates, the information center becomes the organizing unit for decision support systems.

MANAGEMENT APPLICATION

WHAT IS A CIO?

A bank faces a dilemma when it comes to managing information. On one hand it must be centralized for uniformity and control but it must also be decentralized so that business units can stay close to their customers. The inevitable conflict built into this arrangement has led to a new management job in many banks; that is, a senior executive who is in charge of making sure the bank gets maximum return for its investment in technology. The individual must balance the information needs of the various business units with the overall objectives of the bank. The new job is titled *chief information officer.*

This designation of one individual to manage information technology points out just how serious banks are about the importance of having the right information at the right time. Ultimately, the ability of a bank to manage its credit risk and other investment decisions rests on its ability to assimilate information quickly and to react to changes in the financial marketplace. One CIO commented, "The better you're wired, the more complete are your information bases, both external and internal. The better your analysis, the better you can control risk, and your operating and marketing strategies."

The CIO designation is so new in banking that job responsibilities vary from one bank to another. One conclusion is clear, however: the CIO is more of a corporate planner than a glorified head of data processing.

Source: Adapted from Thomas P. Fitch, "The CIO-Banking's New Technology Guru," *ABA Banking Journal,* December 1987, pp. 46–50.

Information as an Organizational Resource

Developing a central data bank and an information center does not guarantee that information will be used widely. A frequent problem in many organizations is that a great deal of information is generated for no real purpose and should be eliminated. The tendency to generate large quantities of information is based on the assumption that a direct relationship exists between the amount of information and the quality of decisions. But as we have seen, the quality rather than the quantity of information is more important for decision making.[25] To promote effective utilization of a DSS is

---

[24]John C. Henderson and David A. Schilling, "Design and Implementation of Decision Support Systems in the Public Sector," *MIS Quarterly,* June 1985, pp. 157–70.

[25]T. Hirouchi and T. Kosaka, "An Effective Database Foundation for Decision Support Systems," *Information and Management,* August 1984, pp. 183–95.

to see information as a basic resource of the organization, just as we do money, materials, personnel, and plant and equipment. Thus, as a basic resource, information:

1. Is vital to the survival of the organization.
2. Can only be used at a cost.
3. Must be at the right place at the right time.
4. Must be used efficiently for an optimal return on its cost to the organization.

Each user of information should consider the cost of the information relative to its utility for decision making. For example, the cost of compiling complete information for a decision must be weighed against the expected value of a decision made with incomplete information.

While the concept of a DSS is relatively new, we have seen in this chapter that it is a reality in small[26] and large[27] organizations. Certainly, one of the major reasons for the increased interest in and the development of DSS has been the growth in information technology. However, the development of DSS is more than technology; its purpose is more effective management decision making.

MANAGEMENT SOLUTION

ELECTRONIC DATA INTERCHANGE MATCHES SUPPLY AND DEMAND

Seminole Manufacturing Co. is doing something about better matching supply and demand. By setting up a new electronic information system, it has cut delivery time of men's slacks to Wal-Mart Stores, Inc., by 50 percent, to 22 days. Now the retailer is better stocked in the 64 size and color combinations of Seminole's slacks, and sales are up 31 percent.

To get these results, Wal-Mart and Seminole have begun using a technique called *electronic data interchange* (*EDI*) which the top U.S. apparel industry executives have moved to adopt. EDI allows specially formatted documents, such as purchase orders, to be sent from one company's computer to another's. This simple improvement has resulted in many advantages. It allows companies to use fewer data-entry employees, thus eliminating human error and avoiding time delays. It also lowers inventory levels, eliminates lost invoices, and improves customer service because suppliers can respond faster to customer needs. Finally, salespeople can spend more time selling since they do not spend their time keeping track of routine orders.

Source: Adapted from "An Electronic Pipeline That's Changing The Way America Does Business," *Business Week*, August 3, 1987, p. 80.

---

[26]Stewart C. Malone, "Computerizing Small Business Information Systems," *Journal of Small Business Management*, April 1985, pp. 10–16.

[27]G. Nigel Gilbert, "Decision Support in Large Organizations," *Data Processing*, May 1985, pp. 28–30.

MANAGEMENT SUMMARY

☐ More comprehensive decision support systems are necessary because the importance of information in decision making, mismanagement of current information, and the use of personal computers by decision makers all are on the rise.

☐ A management information system (MIS) is a decision support system (DSS) if, and only if, it is designed primarily for managerial decision support. Thus, a DSS is an MIS, but an MIS is not necessarily a DSS.

☐ A DSS must be designed to support a manager's skills at all stages of the decision-making process—from identifying and defining problems to evaluating alternative courses of action.

☐ The types as well as sources of information required for management decisions vary by level in the organization. We identified three types of information—planning, control, and operations—based on the types of decisions made.

☐ Designing a DSS involves understanding information flows as well as the functions of such a system. The functions of a DSS are: (1) determination of information needs, (2) information gathering and processing, and (3) information utilization.

☐ Organizing a DSS involves developing a central data bank and an information center, plus viewing information as an important organizational resource.

REVIEW AND DISCUSSION QUESTIONS

1. What reasons account for the growing importance of information in management decision making? Can a manager make a decision without information? Explain.

2. Do you believe that it is easy to mismanage information in contemporary organizations? Why? What personal experiences have you had with organizations that mismanaged information?

3. In your own words, define a decision support system. What are the characteristics of good quality information provided by a DSS?

4. Does the organization level of managers affect their information needs? How? Explain, using examples.

5. What is the major difference between an MIS and a DSS?

6. What kinds of information do you need to make a good decision in the following situations:

    a. Purchasing an automobile.

    b. Operating a stereo equipment store.

    c. Developing a new course in decision support systems at your school.

    d. Getting married.

7. How does planning information differ from control information?

8. Is the study of DSS primarily the study of information technology? Why or why not?

9. You are provided with a great deal of information by your college or university. List as many types of this information as you can. Are you doing an adequate job of managing this information? Why? Can the information be placed in categories such as information for planning or information for control? Explain.

10. Discuss this statement: "In the area of organizational information, more is not always better."

CASE

5–1 MAKING DECISIONS AT LOBO ENTERPRISES

Return on investment (ROI) for Lobo Enterprises had not exceeded 7 percent for the last five years. Late last year, when it became apparent that ROI this time would not even reach 5 percent, top management finally decided that something needed to be done. One of the nation's largest management consulting firms was contracted to examine the company's operations from top to bottom.

Seven weeks later, the consultants submitted their report with numerous suggestions and recommendations. One of the strongest recommendations read as follows:

> Decision makers at the present time are relying on an inefficient, ineffective information system. In fact, Lobo Enterprises does not have anything that resembles an information system. We strongly recommend the design of an information system to include all levels of the organization. Its major goal should be to provide decision makers with relevant, accurate, and timely information for use in making decisions in their specific areas of responsibility.

Lobo's top management agreed with the recommendation and ordered the electronic data processing (EDP) department to work with the consultants in designing a DSS. As part of the initial phase of the project, each decision maker in the organization was asked to think carefully about the information necessary to make decisions related to his or her area of responsibility. Within the next three weeks, each manager was to submit a report relating information needs and the specific types and sources of information utilized on a regular basis.

Two weeks later, Ralph Reeves, the chief purchasing agent for Lobo, had just completed a rough draft of his report. He called in one of his purchasing agents, Scott Reed, and asked him to take the report home for the weekend, read it, and be prepared on Monday to comment on it and make recommendations for changes. Here is Reeves's report:

Information Needs and Sources of Information for the Purchasing Function

To make effective purchasing decisions, an industrial buyer needs a certain amount and quality of information. The information needs include the following:

1. Price of the items.
2. Quantities to be purchased.
3. Number of sources of supply.
4. Urgency of the buy.
5. Complexity of the items.

6. Current market situation relative to the items.

7. Authority over details of the purchase decision.

The buyer will have two specific informational needs: technical and quantitative. The technical needs relate to such things as dimensional prints, engineering specifications, and quality requirements. The quantitative requirements include such things as lot size, estimated prices, and terms of shipment.

A careful analysis of the purchasing task reveals numerous and diverse sources of information. Some of the most important and widely used sources are:

1. Engineering department.

2. Research and development department.

3. Production control.

4. Supplier literature.

5. Trade papers and magazines.

6. Supplier salesmen.

7. Accounting department.

8. Receiving department.

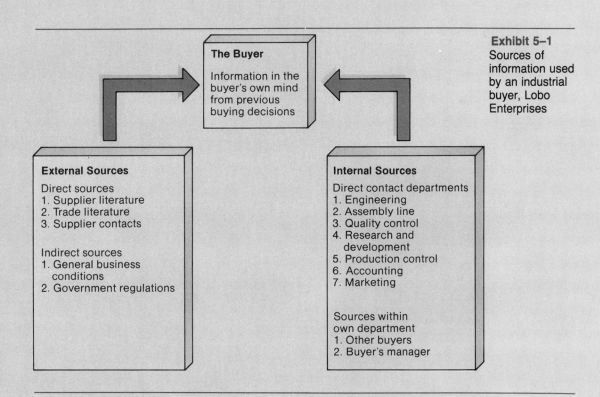

The Buyer

Information in the buyer's own mind from previous buying decisions

External Sources

Direct sources
1. Supplier literature
2. Trade literature
3. Supplier contacts

Indirect sources
1. General business conditions
2. Government regulations

Internal Sources

Direct contact departments
1. Engineering
2. Assembly line
3. Quality control
4. Research and development
5. Production control
6. Accounting
7. Marketing

Sources within own department
1. Other buyers
2. Buyer's manager

Exhibit 5–1
Sources of information used by an industrial buyer, Lobo Enterprises

9. Competitors.
10. Other buyers in the department.
11. Production department.
12. Legal department.

Exhibit 5–1 illustrates more completely the sources of information used by a buyer prior to most procurement decisions. We in the purchasing department believe it clearly illustrates the need for some type of formal systemization of information.

On Monday, Scott Reed brought the report in to Ralph Reeves. "What do you think?" asked Reeves.

"Ralph, it's excellent," Reed said. "I believe you have accurately detailed the information needs and sources for most purchasing decisions. I have no suggestions or recommendations for changes. But one thing did cross my mind as I saw all of our information needs and numerous sources all laid out before my eyes."

"What's that?" asked Reeves.

There was a slight pause before Scott Reed said, "How do we ever make a decision?"

Questions

1. What would be your answer to Scott Reed's question?
2. Could Figure 5–2 be of use to Lobo Enterprises? How?
3. Could the concept of a central data bank be of use to Lobo Enterprises? Why? Illustrate using specific examples.

SIX

Strategic Planning

LEARNING OBJECTIVES

After completing Chapter 6, you should be able to:

Define: in terms meaningful to you the "what" and "why" of strategic planning.

State: why strategic planning has become increasingly important.

Describe: the planning system outlined in the chapter.

Explain: why organizational objectives are necessary for strategic planning.

Discuss: the major considerations in developing an organizational mission.

CAN MCI DO IT OVER AGAIN?

In the mid-1960s an aggressive, young company picked a fight with the biggest company in the world at the time. The upstart was MCI Communications Corporation, and it eventually won the right to compete in the long-distance telephone business against American Telephone and Telegraph. In the process, it became most successful and reaped high profits.

But now it's the late 1980s, and competition is hurting MCI more than it is helping. The company is struggling to redefine its strategy and to regain its entrepreneurial instincts to compete in a world in which the penalty for mistakes is suddenly much higher. The strategic moves that MCI makes in the late 1980s may determine whether it ever again will be a "hot" company.

The company's problems developed quickly.

As competition and the Federal Communications Commission have driven long-distance rates down by more than 30 percent since 1984, MCI has lost most of its price advantage over AT&T. At the same time, slowing growth in the residential phone market means it must look elsewhere to expand.

In 1986, the company lost $448 million, its first deficit in over a decade. Always aware of the threat from hard-charging, third-place U.S. Sprint Communications, MCI must develop a strategy to win big business customers from AT&T if it is going to retain its No. 2 position.

(The Management Solution to this Management Incident can be found at the end of this chapter.)

Chapter 3 examined the four phases of planning and introduced important planning terminology. However, before a production manager, marketing manager, or personnel manager can develop plans for their individual departments, a larger plan—a blueprint—for the entire organization must be developed. Otherwise, on what would the individual departments' plans be based?

In other words, for the various planning activities, there is a larger context that we would like to consider in this chapter. A large business organization usually has several business divisions and several product lines within each division (such as General Electric or Philip Morris). Before any planning can be done by individual divisions or departments, a plan must be developed for the entire organization. Then, objectives and strategies established at the top level provide the planning context for each of the divisions and departments.[1] Finally, divisional and department managers develop their plans within the constraints developed at the higher levels.

THE GROWTH OF STRATEGIC PLANNING

Many of today's most successful business organizations continue to survive because many years ago they offered the right product at the right time; the same can be said for nonprofit and government organizations. Many critical decisions of the past were made without the benefit of strategic thinking or planning. Whether these decisions were based on wisdom or luck is not important. They resulted in momentum that has carried these organizations to where they are today. However, present-day managers increasingly recognize that wisdom and intuition alone are not sufficient to guide the destinies of large organizations in today's ever-changing environment. These managers are turning to strategic planning.[2]

In earlier, less dynamic periods in our society, the planning systems utilized by most organizations extrapolated current-year sales and environmental trends for 5 and 10 years. Based on these, they made plant, product, and investment decisions. In most instances, the decisions were fairly accurate because the factors influencing sales were more predictable and the environment was more stable.

In the years after World War II, many of the factors on which earlier planners counted could no longer be taken for granted. Uncertainty, instability, and changing environments became the rule rather than the exception. Managers faced increased inflation and intensifying foreign competition, technological obsolescence, and changing market and population characteristics.

Because changes are occurring so rapidly, there is increased pressure on top management to respond. In order to respond more accurately, on a more timely schedule, and with a direction or course of action in mind, managers are increasingly turning to the use of strategic planning. *Strategic planning* is a process that involves the review of market conditions; customer needs; competitive strengths and weaknesses; sociopolitical, legal, and economic conditions; technological developments; and the avail-

---

[1]George Schreyogg and Horst Steinman, "Strategic Control: A New Perspective," *Academy of Management Review,* April 1987, pp. 355–65.

[2]L. Rosenberg and C. D. Schewe, "Strategic Planning: Fulfilling the Promise," *Business Horizons,* July–August 1987, pp. 54–63.

Figure 6–1 The strategic planning process.

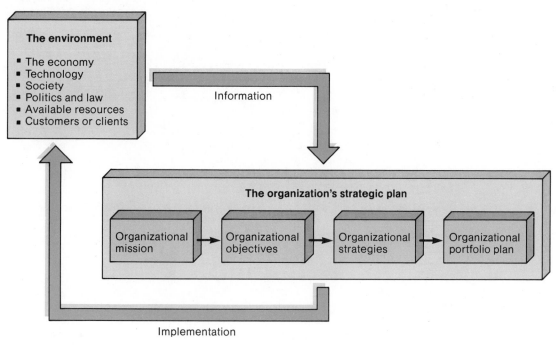

ability of resources that lead to the specific opportunities or threats facing the organization. In practice, *the development of strategic plans involves taking information from the environment and deciding upon an organizational mission and upon objectives, strategies, and a portfolio plan.* The strategic planning process is depicted in Figure 6–1.

As indicated, to develop a unity of purpose across the organization, the strategic planning process must be tied to objectives and goals at all levels of management. At Matsushita, for example, department managers provide three plans every six months: (1) a five-year plan that incorporates technological and environmental changes; (2) a two-year plan that translates strategies into new products; (3) a six-month operating plan, developed by department managers, that addresses monthly projections for production, sales, profits, inventories, quality control, and personnel requirements.

The basic questions that must be answered when an organization decides to examine and restate its mission are "What is our business?" and "What should it be?" While the questions may appear simple, they are in fact such difficult and critical ones that the major responsibility for answering them must be with top management.[3]

---

[3]Lewis W. Walker, "The CEO and Corporate Strategy in the Eighties: Back to Basics," *Interfaces,* January–February 1984, pp. 3–9; and Peter Drucker, *Management: Tasks, Responsibilities, Practices* (New York: Harper & Row, 1974), chap. 7.

Figure 6–2
The environment of the strategic planner.

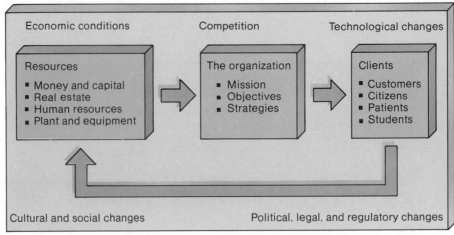

The Environment of Strategic Planning

Figure 6–1 indicates that any strategic planning effort requires an analysis of those factors in the organization's environment which may have an influence on the selection of appropriate objectives and strategies.[4] Also some organizations must survive in more uncertain environments than others.[5] In fact, an important goal of a strategic planner is to anticipate change that is beyond the control of the organization so that change within the organization's control can be initiated. Figure 6–2 presents the major components of the organization's environment. You should note that the components can influence an organization in two important ways. They may act as *constraints* or as *opportunities*. Many of today's high-performing companies, enjoying above-average rates of growth have capitalized on opportunities presented by their environments. These opportunities were identified through strategic planning and enabled the firms to adapt early to environmental shifts.[6] Unfortunately, other firms, such as A&P, Hershey Foods, Montgomery Ward, and Adolph Coors have lost considerable ground during the 1980s because of late adaptation to changes in their environment. These

---

[4]Jane E. Dutton and Edward Ottensmeyer, "Strategic Issues Management: Forms, Functions, and Contexts," *Academy of Management Review,* April 1987, pp. 355–65.

[5]See Lawrence R. Jauch and Kenneth L. Kraft, "Strategic Management of Uncertainty," *Academy of Management Review,* October 1986, pp. 777–90; and Frances J. Milliken, "Three Types of Perceived Uncertainty about the Environment: State, Effect, and Response Uncertainty," *Academy of Management Review,* January 1987, pp. 133–43.

[6]Sidney L. Barton and Paul J. Gordon, "Corporate Strategy: Useful Perspective for the Study of Capital Structure," *Academy of Management Review,* January 1987, pp. 67–75. Also see N. Venkatramen and V. Ramanujam, "Measurement of Business Performance in Strategy Research," *Academy of Management Review,* October 1986, pp. 801–14.

Figure 6–3
Some expected
technological
advances by the
year 2000.

- Undersea farming and mining.
- Mechanical devices to replace human organs.
- Automatic language translators.
- Reliable weather forecasts.
- Controlled affective relationships and sleep.
- Extensive use of robots and machine slaves.
- Centralization of business information and high-speed data processes.
- Human hibernation for fairly extensive time periods.
- Increased mastery of energy.
- New rapid transit systems.

firms simply did not react fast enough, and this ultimately influenced their performance. The shifts may have been social changes, technological changes, competitive moves, or changes in consumer tastes. Whatever the case, the firms did not identify the changes in time and thus could not develop constructive responses.

Economic conditions. The state of the economy affects: (1) the level of demand for the organization's product or services, (2) the cost of its resources, and (3) the opportunities available.

Technological changes. Changes in technology can influence the destiny of an organization. Technology can become a constraint when opportunities exist, but the necessary technology is not available. At the same time, technological innovations can create new industries or vastly alter existing ones. Consider the impact of the personal computer on management education, of electronic funds transfer and automatic tellers on banking, and of synthetic fibers on the apparel and carpeting industries. Technological innovations have vastly altered management education. As a result, instructors have had to learn new ways of teaching, and students have been exposed to new learning methods. Electronic banking has reduced operating costs for bankers and made banking services more widely and conveniently available to customers. To appreciate the pace of technological achievement, examine Figure 6–3. Science and technology will be compelling forces for change in the next decade. In fact, a relatively new field, technological forecasting, attempts to predict what technological developments can occur within a specific period of time with a given level of resource allocation. In some organizations, strategic planners will be forced to stay alert and develop plans to compensate for technological changes. Meanwhile, in other organizations, a prime managerial task will be to instigate changes made possible by improved technology.

Political, legal, and regulatory changes.   Numerous laws legislated by a multitude of authorities make up the political, legal, and regulatory environment that most organizations face. Strategic planners must consider these laws because they may act as constraints as well as opportunities. For example, government action to combat inflation in the mid-1980s hurt the builders of single-unit homes but provided opportunities for apartment builders. The deregulation of the trucking, airline, and banking industries has provided opportunities for some firms in these industries, but others have been unable to compete.

Cultural and social changes.   Change is constant in our society. Strategic planners therefore must be able to identify the changing cultural and social conditions that will influence the organization. Unfortunately, many organizations still have not considered the impact such changes will have or have underestimated their impact. The importance of cultural and social changes to strategic planning can be seen in the impact of Americans' concern for their health on numerous industries (see the Management Application on Procter & Gamble in this chapter). In addition, as we enter the 1990s, society's demand for more socially responsible and ethical behavior from both public and private organizations will have a great impact on strategic planning. These changes, coupled with the more specific problems of equal rights for women and minority groups, make cultural and social change an environmental component that cannot be ignored. Societal values eventually must be reflected in strategic plans.

Competition.   The actions of both domestic and international competitors also have a significant impact on strategic planning. *Intratype competition* is competition between institutions engaged in the same basic activity. Post competes with Kellogg for cereal customers. Ford Motor Co. competes with General Motors Corp. for automobile customers. The Universities of Kentucky and Tennessee compete for undergraduate and graduate students, faculty members, and athletes. *Intertype competition*, meanwhile occurs between institutions engaged in different activities. Kellogg competes with Procter and Gamble for shelf space in supermarkets, hospitals compete with health maintenance organizations for medical practitioners, and recently, some colleges and universities have faced competition from professional teams for high school athletes. The important point here is that all organizations face some type of competition for either resources or clients.

Resources

Our nation's on-again, off-again problems with energy shortages have underscored an important reality: The ability of an organization to compete for and attract resources must be a critical consideration in strategic planning. The availability of resources determines the organization's capacity to respond to threats and opportunities. Depending on the type of organization, some resources will be more critical than others. A publicly supported college, for example, needs alumni backing, plus faculty, students, and the backing of state legislators who influence budget allocations. A hospital needs funds and qualified staff. A business organization needs capital and managerial talent.

The Organization

The organization is, of course, the focal point of the strategic planning process. From a manager's point of view, how well the organization performs depends on two things: (1) how well it integrates and directs the conversion of resources in response to the needs of its clients; and (2) how well it interacts with its environment. The organization's performance is the ultimate purpose of the practice of management.

Examine Figure 6–3 again. Although it does not specify every component of a strategic planner's environment, it does underscore the danger of viewing any organization as an independent entity. Managers can no longer afford the luxury of concentrating solely on the internal functioning of their organizations. Things are changing more rapidly now than ever before. Strategic planning represents management's attempt to anticipate the future and to guard itself against the threat of change.[7]

Clients

Ultimately, how effective any organization is depends on how well it satisfies its clients' needs. For a business organization, the customer plays the pivotal role in decision making. The main clients of a college are prospective students, present students, and the organizations that hire its graduates. Clients are an important influence on strategic planning. The economic and social justification for the existence of an organization is that it serves clients.

THE STRATEGIC PLANNING PROCESS

The output of the strategic planning process is the development of a strategic plan. Figure 6–1 indicates that there are four components to such plans: mission, objectives, strategies, and the portfolio plan. Let us examine each one.

Organizational Mission

The organization's environment supplies the resources that sustain the organization, whether it is a business organization, a college or university, or a governmental agency.

---

[7]See Jay B. Barney, "Types of Competition and the Theory of Strategy: Toward an Integrative Framework," *Academy of Management Review,* October 1986, pp. 791–800; and Jane Dutton and Susan Jackson, "Categorizing Strategic Issues: Links to Organizational Action," *Academy of Management Review,* January 1987, pp. 76–90.

In exchange for these resources, the organization must supply the environment with goods and services at an acceptable price and quality. In other words, every organization exists to accomplish something in the larger environment, and that purpose or mission usually is clear at the start. As time passes, however, the organization expands, the environment changes, and managerial personnel change. And one or more things are likely to occur. First, the original purpose may become irrelevant as the organization expands into new products, new markets, and even new industries. Second, the original mission may remain relevant, but some managers begin to lose interest in it. Finally, changes in the environment may make the original mission inappropriate. The result of any or all of these three conditions is a "drifting" organization, without a clear mission or purpose to guide critical decisions. When this occurs, management must renew the search for purpose or restate the original purpose.

The mission statement should be a long-run vision of what the organization is trying to become—the unique aim that differentiates it from similar organizations. The need is not for a stated purpose (such as "to fulfill all the cosmetic needs of women") that would enable stockholders and managers to feel good or to promote public relations. Rather, the need is for a stated *mission* that provides direction and significance to all members of the organization, regardless of their level.

The following Management Application illustrates the practical use of a clear mission for planning purposes.

MANAGEMENT APPLICATION

MARRIOTT MOVES BACK TOWARD ITS ORIGINAL MISSION

It has been more than 60 years since J. Willard Marriott opened a root beer stand in Washington. His Hot Shoppe chain of restaurants grew to a success and became the foundation of the $5.3 billion Marriott Corporation empire. Recently, however, some observers believe the company has drifted away from the vision of its founder. While the company's earnings in hotels and food service have shown spectacular growth, it has apparently lost ground in its original business—restaurants serving basic meals to budget-conscious families.

Currently, however, Marriott is involved in a deal that could make it No. 1 in the $28 billion family restaurant market. Family restaurants are those that fall between limited-menu, fast-food restaurants and more expensive restaurants. Marriott is negotiating to buy the nation's largest coffee shop chain, privately held Denny's, Inc. Marriott sees growth potential in this part of the restaurant business and believes such an acquisition will increase its market share as well as its leadership position. If they are successful in acquiring Denny's, Marriott will also begin moving back toward the original purpose and mission envisioned by its founder over 60 years ago.

Source: Adapted from "The First Name in Coffee Shops," *Business Week*, June 15, 1987, pp. 35–36.

Developing a statement: key elements. In developing a statement of mission, management must take into account three key elements: the organization's history, its distinctive competencies, and its environment.[8]

1. *History*. Every organization, large or small, profit or nonprofit, has a history of objectives, accomplishments, mistakes, and policies. In formulating a mission, the critical characteristics and events of the past must be considered. It would not make sense for McDonald's to become a chain of gourmet restaurants or for Yale University to become a community college, even if such moves were opportunities for growth in the future.

2. *Distinctive competencies*. While there are many things an organization may be able to do, it should seek to do that which it can do best. Distinctive competencies are the things that an organization does well—so well, in fact, that they are an advantage over similar organizations. Procter & Gamble probably could enter the synthetic fuel business, but such a decision certainly would not take advantage of its major distinctive competence: knowledge of the market for low-priced, repetitively purchased consumer products. No matter how appealing an opportunity may be, the organization must have the competencies to capitalize on it. An opportunity without the competence to capture it is not really an opportunity for the organization.[9]

3. *Environment*. The organization's environment dictates the opportunities, constraints, and threats that must be identified before a mission statement is developed.[10] For example, technological developments in the communications field (such as long-range picture transmission, closed-circuit television, and the television phone) may have a negative impact on business travel and certainly should be considered in the mission statement of a large motel chain.[11]

Characteristics of a mission statement.   Needless to say, it is extremely difficult to write a useful and effective mission statement. It is not unusual for an organization to spend a year or two developing a useful mission. When completed, an effective mission statement will *focus on markets rather than products; it will also be achievable, motivating,* and *specific.*[12]

---

[8]Philip Kotler, *Marketing Management: Analysis, Planning, and Control,* 6th ed. (Englewood Cliffs, N.J.: Prentice-Hall, 1988), chap. 2.

[9]For a study of the relationship between corporate distinctive competencies and firm performance in 185 industrial firms, see M. A. Hitt and R. D. Ireland, "Corporate Distinctive Competence, Strategy and Performance," *Strategic Management Journal,* July–September 1985, pp. 273–93.

[10]See C. Smart and I. Vertinsky, "Strategy and the Environment: A Study of Corporate Responses to Crises," *Strategic Management Journal,* April–June 1984, pp. 199–214. This study of the largest U.S. and Canadian companies examines the relationship between a firm's external environment and its repertoire of strategic responses to cope with crises. For a different view of the environment, see L. Smircich and C. Stubbart, "Strategic Management in an Enacted World," *Academy of Management Review,* October 1985, pp. 724–36.

[11]For a related discussion, see Carl P. Zeithaml and Louis W. Fry, "Contextual and Strategic Differences among Mature Businesses in Four Dynamic Performance Situations," *Academy of Management Journal,* December 1984, pp. 841–60.

[12]Drucker, *Management,* pp. 77–89; Kotler, *Marketing Management,* chap. 2.

1. *Market rather than product focus.* The customers or clients of an organization are critical in determining its mission. Traditionally, many organizations defined their business in terms of what they made ("our business is glass") and, in many cases, named the organization after the product or products (for example, National Cash Register, Harbor View Savings and Loan Association). Often these organizations have found that when products and technologies become obsolete, their mission is no longer relevant and the name of the organization may no longer describe what it does. Thus, a more enduring way of defining the mission is needed. In recent years, a key feature of mission statements has been an *external* rather than *internal* focus. In other words, the mission statement should focus on the broad class of needs that the organization is seeking to satisfy (external focus), not on the physical product or service that the organization is offering at present (internal focus). This has been clearly stated by Peter Drucker:

> A business is not defined by the company's name, statutes, or articles of incorporation. It is defined by the want the customer satisfies when he buys a product or service. To satisfy the customer is the mission and purpose of every business. The question "What is our business?" can, therefore, be answered only by looking at the business from the outside, from the point of view of customer and market.[13]

While Drucker was referring to business organizations, the same necessity exists for both nonprofit and governmental organizations.[14] That necessity is to state the mission in terms of serving a particular group of clients or customers and/or meeting a particular class of need.

2. *Achievable.* While the mission statement should "stretch" the organization toward more effective performance, it should at the same time be realistic and achievable. In other words, it should open a vision of new opportunities but should not lead the organization into unrealistic ventures far beyond its competencies. Examples would be a pen manufacturer stating it is in the communications business or an antique car restorer viewing its mission in terms of transportation.

3. *Motivational.* One of the side (but very important) benefits of a well-defined mission is the guidance it provides employees and managers working either in geographically dispersed units or on independent tasks. A well-defined mission provides a shared sense of purpose *outside* of the various activities taking place within the organization.[15] Therefore, end results (such as sales, patients cared for, reduction in

---

[13]Drucker, *Management,* p. 79.

[14]See Paul C. Nutt, "A Strategic Planning Network for Nonprofit Organizations," *Strategic Management Journal,* January–March 1984, pp. 57–76; and Peter Smith Ring and James L. Perry, "Strategic Management in Public and Private Organizations: Implications of Distinctive Contexts and Constraints," *Academy of Management Review,* April 1985, pp. 276–86.

[15]W. Graham Astley, "Toward an Appreciation of Collective Strategy," *Academy of Management Review,* July 1984, pp. 526–35; and R. K. Bresser and J. E. Harl, "Collective Strategy: Vice or Virtue," *Academy of Management Review,* April 1986, pp. 408–27.

Table 6–1 Some actual mission statements.

Organization	Mission
1. Office equipment manufacturer	We are in the business of problem solving. Our business is to help solve administrative, scientific, and human problems.
2. Credit union	To produce a selected range of quality services to organizations and individuals to fulfill their continuing financial needs.
3. Large conglomerate	Translating new technologies into commercially saleable products.
4. Consumer-products paper company	The development and marketing of inedible products for food stores.
5. State department of health	Administering all provisions of law relating to public health laws and regulations of the state board of health, supervising and assisting county and regional boards and departments of health, and doing all other things reasonably necessary to protect and improve the health of the people.
6. Appliance manufacturer	A willingness to invest in any area of suitable profit and growth potential in which the organization has or can acquire the capabilities.

violent crimes) can be viewed as the result of careful pursuit and accomplishment of the mission and not as the mission itself.

4. *Specific.* As we mentioned earlier, public relations should not be the primary purpose of a statement of mission, which must be specific and provide direction and guidelines to management when it chooses between alternative courses of action. In other words, "to produce the highest quality products at the lowest possible cost" sounds very good, but it does not provide direction for management.

Table 6–1 presents actual mission statements of various types of organizations. While some have been abbreviated, they illustrate clearly the purpose of each as defined by management. Review each one with respect to the four criteria just discussed.

The questions related to the mission statement need to be asked and answered at the inception of an organization and whenever it is experiencing serious problems. However, a successful organization should also ask them from time to time.[16] The reason for this should be clear: Because of the ever-changing environment, even the most successful definition of purpose will sooner or later become obsolete. Thus, the process of periodically addressing the issue will force management to anticipate the impact of environmental changes on the organization's mission, objectives, markets, and products.

Finally, the mission statement of an organization whose strategic planning process is very sophisticated also will include major policies it plans to adhere to in the pursuit of its mission. Such policies establish the ground rules for the organization in its relationships with government, customers or clients, suppliers, distributors, and creditors. An example of such a document is shown in Table 6–2.

---

[16]Drucker, *Management*, p. 87.

Table 6–2 Example of a mission statement and supporting organizational policies.

It is the basic purpose of this organization, in all of its decisions and actions, to attain and maintain the following:

1. A continuous, high level of profits, which places it in the top bracket of industry in its rate of return on invested capital.
2. Steady growth in profits and sales volume, and investment at rates exceeding those of the national economy as a whole.
3. Equitable distribution of the fruits of continuously increasing productivity of management, capital, and labor among stockholders, employees, and the public.
4. Design, production, and marketing, on a worldwide basis, of products and services that are useful and beneficial to its customers, to society, and to mankind.
5. Continuous responsiveness to the needs of its customers and of the public, creating a current product line that is "first in performance" and a steady flow of product improvements, new products, and new services that increase customer satisfaction.
6. A vital, dynamic product line, by continuous addition of new products and businesses and prompt termination of old products and businesses when their economic worth, as measured by their profit performance, becomes substandard.
7. The highest ethical standards in the conduct of all its affairs.
8. An environment in which all employees are enabled, encouraged, and stimulated to perform continuously at their highest potential of output and creativity and to attain the highest possible level of job satisfaction.

Organizational Objectives

In the previous chapter, we saw that a critical phase of planning is the determination of future outcomes that, if achieved, enable the organization to satisfy the expectations of its relevant environment. These desired future outcomes are objectives. Organizational objectives are the end points of an organization's mission and are what it seeks through the ongoing, long-run operations of the organization. The organizational mission is defined into a finer set of specific and achievable organizational objectives.

As with the statement of mission, organizational objectives are more than good intentions. In fact, if formulated properly, they will accomplish the following:

1. They will be capable of being converted into specific actions.
2. They will provide direction. That is, organizational objectives serve as a starting point for more specific and detailed objectives at lower levels in the organization. Each manager will then know how his objectives relate to those at higher levels.
3. They will establish long-run priorities for the organization.
4. They will facilitate management control, because they will serve as standards against which overall organizational performance can be evaluated.

Organizational objectives are necessary in any and all areas that may influence the performance and long-run survival of the organization. These were identified in the previous chapter as profitability, competitiveness, efficiency, and flexibility.

The above objectives are by no means exhaustive. An organization may very well have additional ones. The important point is that management must translate the organizational mission into specific objectives that will support the realization of the

Area of performance	Possible objective
1. Profitability	A continuous, high level of profits, which places us in the top bracket of the industry in rate of return on invested capital.
	Steady growth in profits and sales volume, and investment at rates exceeding those of the national economy.
2. Competitiveness	To make our brands number one in their field in terms of market share.
	To be a leader in introducing new products by spending no less than 7 percent for research and development.
3. Efficiency	To manufacture all products efficiently as measured by the productivity of the work force.
	To protect and maintain all resources—equipment, buildings, inventory, and funds.
4. Flexibility	To identify critical areas of management depth and succession of leadership.
	To respond appropriately whenever possible to societal expectations and environmental needs.

Figure 6–4
Sample strategic objectives.

mission. The objectives may flow directly from the mission or be considered subordinate necessities for carrying out the mission of the organization. Figure 6–4 presents some examples of organizational objectives. Note that they are broad statements that serve as guides and that they are of a continuing nature. They specify the end points of an organization's mission and the results that it seeks in the long run, both externally and internally. Most importantly, however, the objectives in Figure 6–4 are all capable of being converted into specific targets and actions for *operational plans* at lower levels in the organization.

Organizational Strategies

When an organization has formulated its mission and developed its objectives, it knows where it wants to go. The next management task is to develop a "grand design" to get there.[17] This grand design constitutes the organizational strategies. The role of strategy in strategic planning is to identify the general approaches that the organization

---

[17]See Ellen Earle Chaffee, "Three Models of Strategy," *Academy of Management Review,* January 1985, pp. 89–98.

Figure 6–5
Product-market
matrix.

Markets \ Products	Present Products	New Products
Present Customers	Market penetration	Product development
New Customers	Market development	Diversification

will utilize to achieve its organizational objectives. It involves the choice of major directions the organization will take in pursuing its objectives.[18]

Achieving organizational objectives comes about in two ways. They are accomplished by better managing what the organization is presently doing and/or finding new things to do. In choosing either or both of these paths, it then must decide whether to concentrate on present customers, to see new ones, or both. Figure 6–5 presents the available strategic choices. Known as a product-market matrix, it shows the strategic alternatives available to an organization for achieving its objectives. It indicates that an organization can grow in a variety of ways by concentrating on present or new products and on present or new customers.

Market penetration strategies.   These organizational strategies focus on improving the position of the organization's present products with its present customers. For example:

1. A brewer concentrates on getting its present customers to purchase more of its product.
2. A charity seeks ways to increase contributions from present contributors.
3. A bank concentrates on getting present depositors to use additional services.

Such a strategy may involve devising a marketing plan to encourage present customers to purchase more of the product or a production plan to produce the present product more efficiently. In other words, it concentrates on improving the efficiency of various functional areas in the organization.

Market development strategies.   Following this strategy, an organization would seek to find new customers for its present products. For example:

1. A manufacturer of industrial products may decide to develop products for entrance into the consumer market.

---

[18]Ari Ginsberg, "Operationalizing Organizational Strategy: Toward an Integrated Framework," *Academy of Management Review*, July 1984, pp. 548–57.

2. A governmental social service agency may seek individuals and families who have never utilized the agency's services.

3. A manufacturer of children's hair care products decides to enter the adult market because of the declining birthrate.

Product development strategies.   In choosing either of the remaining two strategies, the organization in effect seeks new things to do. With this particular strategy, the new products developed would be directed to present customers. For example:

1. A cigarette manufacturer may decide to offer a low-tar cigarette.

2. A social service agency may offer additional services to present client families.

3. A college or university may develop graduate programs for minority students.

Diversification.   An organization diversifies when it seeks new products for customers it is not serving at present.[19] Some examples include:

1. A discount store purchases a savings and loan association.

2. A cigarette manufacturer diversifies into real estate development.

3. A college or university establishes a corporation to find commercial uses for the results of faculty research efforts.

On what basis does an organization choose one or more strategies? The answer lies in the organization's mission and its distinctive competencies. This underscores the critical role the mission statement plays in the direction(s) the organization takes. Management will select those strategies that capitalize on the organization's distinctive competencies and are consistent with its mission.[20]

The following Management Application illustrates one company's strategic response to environmental change.

MANAGEMENT APPLICATION

NEW GROWTH STRATEGY AT PROCTER & GAMBLE

Procter & Gamble Company, traditionally a supplier of detergent, diapers, and toothpaste has made a strategic decision that health care will be its future area of growth throughout this century and on into the next. Procter & Gamble has spent nearly $2

---

[19]See Jeffrey L. Kerr, "Diversification Strategies and Managerial Rewards: An Empirical Study," *Academy of Management Journal,* March 1985, pp. 155–79, for a study of the relationship between diversification and the design of managerial reward systems in 20 large industrial firms.

[20]N. Venkatramen and J. C. Camillus, "Exploring the Concept of 'Fit' in Strategic Management," *Academy of Management Review,* July 1984, pp. 513–25; and H. Mintzberg and J. A. Waters, "Of Strategies, Deliberate and Emergent," *Strategic Management Journal,* July–September 1985, pp. 257–72.

billion during this decade to buy Norwich Eaton Pharmaceuticals, Richardson-Vicks, and part of G. D. Searle. At present, Procter & Gamble is the largest supplier of over-the-counter health remedies. If previous laboratory research is successful, Procter & Gamble's laboratories may be on the verge of releasing products that could alter American diets and hygiene. America's health awareness is also changing the way the company markets such familiar brands as Pepto-Bismol and Puritan cooking oil. While important questions remain as to how well the company will do, there is no doubt that based on an analysis of its environment and changing American values and priorities, Procter & Gamble has made a strategic decision to pursue a new growth strategy.

Source: Adapted from "Procter & Gamble Goes on a Health Kick," *Business Week*, June 29, 1987, pp. 90–91.

Organizational Portfolio Plan

The final phase of the strategic planning process is the formulation of the organizational portfolio plan. In reality, most organizations at a particular time are a portfolio of businesses. For example, an appliance manufacturer may have several product lines (such as televisions, washers and dryers, refrigerators, stereos) as well as two divisions, (consumer appliances and industrial appliances). A college or university will have numerous schools (e.g., education, business, law, architecture) and several programs within each school. The YMCA has hotels, camps, spas, and schools. Some widely diversified organizations such as Philip Morris are in numerous unrelated businesses, such as cigarettes, land development, industrial paper products, and breweries.

Managing such groups of businesses is made a little easier if resources and cash are plentiful and each group is experiencing growth and profits. Unfortunately, providing larger and larger budgets each year to all businesses is no longer feasible. Many are not experiencing growth, and profits and/or resources (financial and nonfinancial) are becoming more and more scarce. In such a situation, choices must be made; and some method is necessary to help management make the choices. Management must decide which businesses to build, maintain, or eliminate or which new businesses to add. One of the best known and widely used methods to accomplish this is the *business portfolio matrix* developed by the Boston Consulting Group.[21]

The business portfolio matrix.   Obviously, the first step in this approach is to identify the various divisions, product lines, and so forth, that can be considered a business. When identified, these are referred to as *strategic business units* (SBUs) and have the following characteristics:

---

[21]There are other portfolio models; each has its supporters and detractors. The one presented here, while one of the most popular, is also not without critics. The important point is the concept of viewing an organization as a "portfolio" of businesses or activities, each competing for resources. The interested reader should consult Day, *Analysis*, chaps. 5–7; Richard G. Hammermesh and Roderick E. White, "Manage beyond Portfolio Analysis," *Harvard Business Review*, January–February 1984, pp. 103–9; and J. A. Seeger, "Revising the Images of BCG's Growth/Share Matrix," *Strategic Management Journal*, January–March 1984, pp. 93–97.

- ☐ They have a distinct mission.
- ☐ They have their own competitors.
- ☐ They are a single business or collection of related businesses.
- ☐ They can be planned for independently from the other businesses of the total organization.

Thus, depending on the type of organization, an SBU could be a single product, product line, division, a department of business administration, or a state mental health agency. Once the managers have identified and classified all of the SBUs, some means is then necessary to determine how resources should be allocated among the various SBUs. This is the important contribution of the Boston Consulting Group's approach.

Using this approach, the organization would classify all of its SBUs in the business portfolio matrix. (An example is shown in Figure 6–6.) Its basic purpose is to assist management in deciding how much resource support should be budgeted to each SBU.

The business portfolio matrix illustrates two business indicators of great strategic importance. The vertical indicator, *market growth rate,* refers to the annual rate of growth of the market in which the product, division, or department is located. For example, the number of individuals of college age is declining, and the impact on enrollments has been felt. However, enrollments in some fields of study have been increasing. Thus, certain departments in a college would have different market growth rates.

The horizontal indicator, *relative market share,* illustrates an SBU's market share compared to that of the most successful competitor. This indicator ranges from high to low share of the market. As illustrated, four classifications of SBUs can be identified by dividing the business portfolio matrix in the ways indicated:

1. *Stars.* An SBU that has a high share of a high-growth market is considered a star. Examples might include an electronics firm with a high market share of the video recorder market or a university with an outstanding, nationally recognized master's degree program in business administration (enrollments in most business schools are growing, in contrast to declining enrollments across most university departments). Obviously, stars need a great deal of financial resources because of their rapid growth. When growth slows down, they become cash cows and become important generators of cash for the organization.[22]

2. *Cash cows.* An SBU that has a high share of a low-growth market is labeled a cash cow. A bank that has a large share of passbook savings depositors in a community that is not growing or a state university with the largest number of elementary education majors in the state would be examples of such SBUs. They produce a great amount of cash for the organization but, since the market is not growing, do not require a great amount of financial resources for growth and expansion. As a result, the cash they generate can be used by the organization to satisfy current debt and to support other SBUs that are in need of cash.

---

[22]See David A. Aaker and George S. Day, "The Perils of High Growth Markets," *Strategic Management Journal,* October–December 1985, pp. 24–32.

Figure 6–6
Business portfolio matrix.

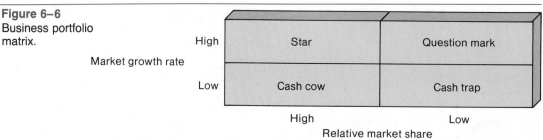

3. *Question marks.* When an SBU has a low share of a high-growth market, the organization must decide whether to spend more financial resources to build it into a star, or to phase it down or eliminate it all together. Elimination was the decision made by General Electric with its computer business and line of vacuum cleaners. Many times, such SBUs require high amounts of resources just to maintain their share, let alone increase it.

4. *Cash traps.* When an SBU has a low share of a low-growth market, it may generate enough cash to maintain itself or may drain money from other SBUs. The only certainty is that cash traps are not great sources of cash. A men's cosmetics firm that still sells a traditional oily liquid hair tonic or the Slavic language department in a college or university are examples of cash traps.

Strategic choices. Thus, depending on whether the SBUs are products, product lines, entire divisions, or departments, an organization may have one star, three cash cows, two question marks, and two cash traps. After classifying each SBU according to the business portfolio matrix, management must then decide which of four alternative strategies should be pursued for each.[23]

1. *Build.* If an organization has an SBU that it believes has the potential to be a star (probably a question mark at present), this would be an appropriate objective. Thus, the organization may even decide to give up short-term profits in order to provide the necessary financial resources to achieve this objective.

2. *Hold.* If an SBU is a very successful cash cow, a key objective would certainly be to hold or preserve the market share so that the organization can take advantage of the very positive cash flow. The opportunity to use cash cow businesses to generate resources for diversification has been pursued by Philip Morris, R. J. Reynolds/Nabisco, and other cigarette manufacturers that have used cash from cigarette businesses to fund diversification into unrelated industries.

3. *Harvest.* This objective is appropriate for all SBUs except those classified as stars. The basic objective is to increase the short-term cash return without too much

---

[23]Stephen C. Burnett, "The Ecology of Building, Harvesting, and Holding Market Share," Report no. 6, *Research in Marketing,* 1983, pp. 1–63. Also see Vijay Govindarajan, "Decentralization, Strategy, and Effectiveness of Strategic Business Units in Multibusiness Organizations," *Academy of Management Review,* October 1986, pp. 844–56.

Figure 6–7   The relationship between the organization's strategic plan and operational plans.

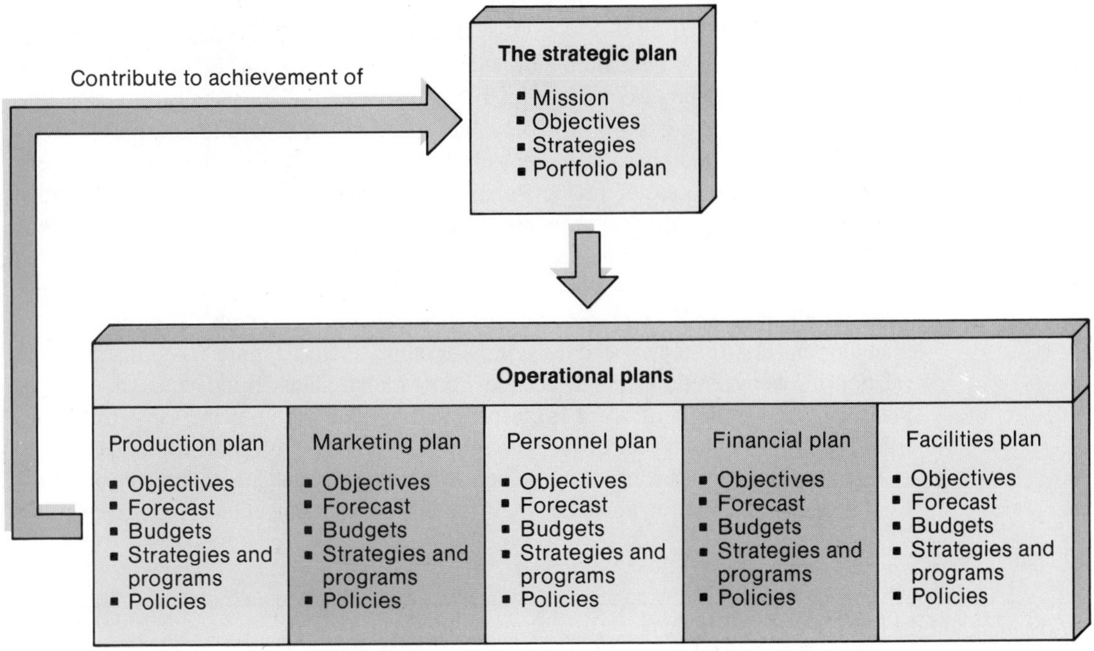

concern for the long-run impact. It is especially worthwhile when more cash is needed for a cash cow whose long-run prospects are not good because of a low market growth rate.

4. *Divest.* Getting rid of SBUs with low shares of low growth markets is often appropriate. Cash traps are particularly suited for this objective.

SBUs will change their positions in the business portfolio matrix. As time goes by, question marks may become stars, stars may become cash cows, and cash cows may become cash traps. In fact, one SBU can move through each category as the market growth rate declines; how quickly these changes occur is influenced by the technology and competitiveness of the industry. This underscores the importance and usefulness of viewing an organization in terms of SBUs, and the necessity of constantly seeking new ventures as well as managing existing ones.[24]

Strategic planning provides direction for an organization's mission, objectives, and strategies, facilitating the development of plans for each of the organization's functional areas. A completed strategic plan guides each area in the direction the organization wishes to go and allows each area to develop objectives, strategies, and programs

---

[24]Anil K. Gupta and V. Govindarajan, "Business Unit Strategy, Managerial Characteristics, and Business Unit Effectiveness at Strategy Implementation," *Academy of Management Journal,* March 1984, pp. 25–41.

consistent with those goals. The relationship between strategic planning and operational planning is an important concern of managers.

Relating the strategic plan and operational plans.   Most managers in an organization will not directly develop the organization's strategic plan. However, they may be involved in this process in two important ways: (1) They usually influence the strategic planning process by providing inputs in the form of information and suggestions relating to their particular areas of responsibility. (2) They must be completely aware of what the process of strategic planning involves as well as the results, because everything their respective departments do, the objectives they establish for their areas of responsibility, should all be derived from the strategic plan.

In well-managed organizations, therefore, there is a direct relationship between strategic planning and the planning done by managers at all levels. The focus of the planning and the time perspectives will, of course, differ. Figure 6–7 illustrates the relationship between the strategic plan and operational plans. It indicates very clearly that all plans should be derived from the strategic plan while at the same time contributing to the achievement of the strategic plan.

Operational plans also help to implement the strategic plan. The importance of effective implementation is illustrated clearly in the following Management Application.

MANAGEMENT APPLICATION

THE IMPORTANT RELATIONSHIP BETWEEN STRATEGY AND IMPLEMENTATION

A few years ago, National Steel Corporation decided to pursue what appeared to be an obvious course: diversify out of the troubled steel business. In the mid-1980's, they tried to sell the business to USX but threats of antitrust problems shot the deal down. They settled for selling half the company to Japan's No. 2 steelmaker, Nippon Kokan, in a joint venture. Previously, they had also purchased First Nationwide Financial Corporation, a business far removed from steel.

In 1985, they attempted to merge with Bergen Brunswig Corporation, which is the second largest distributor of health care products in the country. Drug distribution appealed to the company (now called National Intergroup, Inc.) because it appeared to be everything the steel business wasn't. It does not require a lot of workers or capital, it isn't susceptible to foreign competition, and it doesn't swing wildly with the business cycle. It is also a fast-growing field that will likely expand as the population ages and health care expands. Unfortunately, the deal did not go through and the company was forced to sell First Nationwide to Ford Motor Company for some needed cash.

Management as well as other experts are, however, optimistic. As the firm's chief executive stated, "The strategy has been simple, the execution has been damned complicated."

Source: Adapted from Gregory L. Miles, "The Best-Laid Plans for Howard Love," *Business Week*, August 10, 1987, p 74.

Figure 6–8 Relating organizational objectives and strategies and operational objectives and strategies.

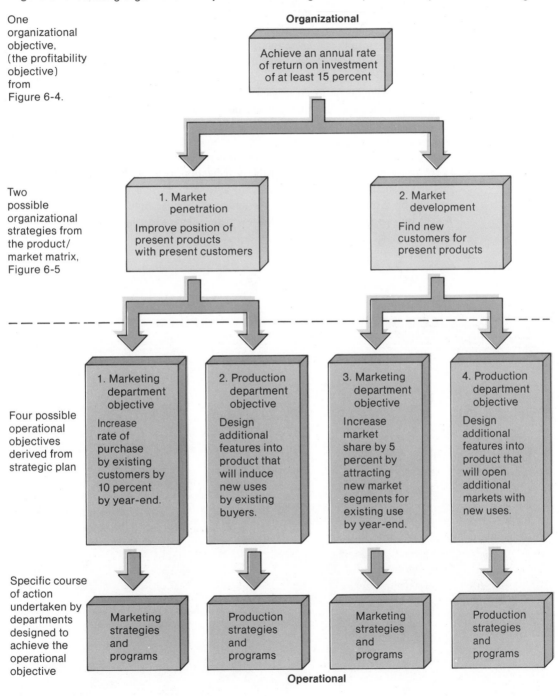

One organizational objective, (the profitability objective) from Figure 6-4.

Organizational

Achieve an annual rate of return on investment of at least 15 percent

Two possible organizational strategies from the product/market matrix, Figure 6-5

1. Market penetration

Improve position of present products with present customers

2. Market development

Find new customers for present products

Four possible operational objectives derived from strategic plan

1. Marketing department objective

Increase rate of purchase by existing customers by 10 percent by year-end.

2. Production department objective

Design additional features into product that will induce new uses by existing buyers.

3. Marketing department objective

Increase market share by 5 percent by attracting new market segments for existing use by year-end.

4. Production department objective

Design additional features into product that will open additional markets with new uses.

Specific course of action undertaken by departments designed to achieve the operational objective

Marketing strategies and programs

Production strategies and programs

Marketing strategies and programs

Production strategies and programs

Operational

Relating Organizational Objectives and Strategies and Operational Objectives and Strategies

If planning is done properly, it will result in a clearly defined blueprint for management action *at all levels* in the organization. Figure 6–8 illustrates the *hierarchy of objectives and strategies,* using only one objective from the strategic plan and two strategies from the strategic plan. In the figure, all objectives are related to other objectives at higher and lower levels in the organization. We have illustrated only four possible operational objectives. Obviously many others could be developed, but our purpose is that the reader clearly understand how objectives and strategies from the strategic plan for the entire organization (above the dotted line) relate to objectives and strategies that are part of operational plans for individual departments (below the dotted line). As we move down from the top of the organization to lower levels in terms of who does the planning, we increase the detail and specificity of the objectives, and we decrease their time span. However, although the scope, time span, and issues confronted by operational plans differ, they are all derived from those in the strategic plan.

MANAGEMENT SOLUTION

MCI'S STRATEGY FOR A COMEBACK

MCI's strategy for the 1980s and beyond includes three parts:

1. *Cut costs*. Since 1986, the company has reduced its work force by 16 percent and cut its internal operating budget by $100 million. It has also cut its capital budget by 12 percent and refinanced some loans which cut interest payments by $15 million per year.

2. *Improve marketing*. The company is cooperating with IBM which owns 17 percent of the company to jointly market packages of computers and long-distance service to big business customers. It is also revising its advertising strategy, aiming more at corporate customers than residential ones.

3. *Attract new business*. To attract business customers from AT&T and stay ahead of No. 3 Sprint, MCI is introducing new computerized network phone service. It is also adding digital transmission lines, which are ideal for computer communications. MCI is also aiming at AT&T's $4 billion 800, or toll-free phone business. Finally, the company has started providing services to Western Europe and Japan.

MANAGEMENT SUMMARY

☐ The rapidly changing world that managers face has made strategic analysis increasingly important. Strategic analysis represents management's attempt to anticipate the future and to guard the organization against the effects of change.

☐ A strategic plan consists of a clearly stated organizational mission, organizational objectives, and organizational strategies.

☐ The organizational mission is a long-term vision of what the organization is trying to become. The basic questions that must be answered are: "What is our business?" and "What should it be?"

☐ Three important considerations in formulating the organizational mission are the organization's environment, its distinctive competencies, and its clients.

☐ Organizational strategies are the general approaches used to achieve the organizational objectives. These strategies include market penetration, market development, product development, and diversification alternatives.

☐ There is a direct relationship between strategic planning and the planning done by an organization's managers. If the organization's strategic plan is properly executed, the scope, range, issues, and time perspectives will differ from department to department. But all of the organization's plans will be derived from the strategic plan and, after a time, will contribute to its achievement.

REVIEW AND DISCUSSION QUESTIONS

1. "Plans are sometimes useless, but the planning process is always indispensable." What does this mean?

2. What is meant by the statement, "Every manager plans"?

3. How can components of the environment act as constraints or opportunities?

4. As the U.S. population ages, what impact will it have on the college you are attending?

5. Provide examples of businesses that have pursued a market development, product development, and/or diversification strategies. In your view, what factors influenced the selection of these strategies?

6. What are some market development strategies that your college might pursue?

7. Choose any organization you are familiar with and develop for it a statement of organizational mission.

8. Suppose Christie Hefner, the chief executive of Playboy Enterprise, Inc., came to you and asked the questions "What is my business?" and "What should it be?" What would your answers be?

9. Why did you choose to attend your present school? Can your reasons be considered distinctive competencies of your school? Can schools have distinctive competencies? What do schools compete with, and for what do schools compete?

10. Someone once quoted a well-known cosmetic executive as saying, "In the factory we make cosmetics; in the drugstore we sell hope." What does this statement indicate about the executive?

CASES

6–1   STRATEGIC PLANNING IN THE STATE GOVERNMENT

Jim Wilkerson recently has been appointed head of a new strategic planning unit in the state's department of transportation. The new section has been asked by the secretary of transportation to help identify and select sites in the state suitable for the construction of two large airports. The state historically has been rural, with many large farms and a large-scale state parks system. However, growth in the state's industrial segment, an influx of population, and the growth in several nearby metropolitan areas in bordering states have necessitated the creation of the new strategic planning unit. At present, the state has only one airport capable of handling commercial jets. Specifically, Jim has been given two objectives:

1. Given the present and future needs for air transportation in the state, identify the two most desirable sites.
2. Consider the impact on the communities involved.

Jim is particularly concerned with the second objective. He is not an ecologist or environmentalist, but he does consider the environmental impact important and also is concerned about preserving the wilderness and wildlife in the state. He believes the best way to ensure that such issues are considered is to conduct public hearings in all of the proposed site areas. Accordingly, for the past three months, his section has actively sought and received much public input into its site studies. Jim knows that many of his peers in the department of transportation do not share his views. Many of them consider the public to be uninformed on such matters and their input to be more emotional than rational. Last Monday, the Commissioner of Transportation asked Jim to come to his office. The following conversation took place:

Commissioner: Jim, I'm glad to see you and want you to know that I think you're getting this new section off to a good start.

Jim: Thank you, Commissioner. I certainly am glad to get the assignment, and I must admit that I truly enjoy the work.

Commissioner: The only problem I see is that you may run short of time.

Jim: Why do you say that?

Commissioner: Jim, while I can't argue with your efforts at public participation, I must say that I believe it just won't work. You need a more objective or rational approach.

Jim: Could you explain what you mean?

Commissioner: When you have been in the business as long as I have, the one thing you learn is that you can't please everybody. Remember, one of us is going to have to defend the proposed sites before the state legislators and other politicians, as well as the general public. How, for example, are you going to tell farmers that the two airports ought to be constructed on farmland instead of wilderness? Or, if it goes the other way, how are you going to explain to the environmentalists and the Department of Parks that the airports should be constructed in the wilderness instead of on farmland? Do you see what I mean, Jim? Are you going to say, "On the basis of public opinion"? What public?

Jim: I can see your point, but surely you see the impact these airports will have on the public? Aren't we here to serve the public?

Commissioner: Again, I ask you: What public? All I know is we need two airport sites that will be accepted. We need a more objective approach that we can lean on instead of an emotion-based recommendation. Can't you crank up some kind of quantitative model? You can work in your environmental factors but also include some economic figures and transportation costs. Believe me, the politicians like numbers. It's hard to argue with numbers, and they can lean on them when the press starts asking questions. Jim, we're not fooling around here. We need to come up with two sites that are acceptable. We've got to be on firm ground, and numbers and economic payoffs can give it to us.

As Jim left the commissioner's office, he was unsure of what to do. The commissioner probably was right in some respects, he thought. He decided to consider all the factors before making his decision. One thing was sure: He had seven possible sites and just two weeks to select the two final ones.

Questions

1. What does this exercise indicate about the process of strategic planning?
2. What is your opinion of the commissioner's advice?
3. Do the values of society influence managerial planning? Should they? Are they influencing Jim? The commissioner?

6–2 CITIBANK'S DIVERSIFICATION STRATEGY

Citibank, a subsidiary of Citicorp, was facing heavy competition in its traditional lines of business. Savings banks, savings and loan associations, credit unions, and brokerage houses were competing effectively with banks by moving into such typical banking activities as interest-bearing checking accounts and by offering higher interest rates for deposits. Because of the squeeze on profit, the bank had to consider other sources of earnings.

Citibank decided to enter the computer services industry, using its considerable expertise and experience in data processing. It identified three distinct business units to be developed:

1. *Systems*. The bank combines its own programs and software with someone else's hardware and markets the system to end-users.
2. *Remote computing*. The bank sells time on its own computers to outside customers.
3. *Software*. The bank sells its software packages to other firms with similar applications.

These three businesses were mutually supportive but were aimed at different customer needs.

The foundation for the move into computer services began in the early 1970s, when Citicorp decided to streamline its own data processing capability. The program moved away from reliance on a central mainframe computer to small minicomputers that could be located near the spot where processing was required. The program encountered numerous problems. But when it was finally going, the effect was to enable one person to handle work that previously would have taken six people.

Many of the products that Citibank now markets were developed as a result of the streamlining program. These products enable other banks to streamline their own "back office" processing and turn a potential cost center into a potential profit center. Citibank not only sells the system but also offers continuing educational and consultative support services. This capability distinguishes Citibank from other suppliers of computer services.

At the present time, Citibank has set its sights on selling computer services to 20 percent of the nation's 50,000 financial institutions. That objective's potential profit of $250 million by 1990 would be equivalent to 10 percent of Citicorp's net income. The diversification into computer services represents an important potential source of earnings to Citicorp.

Citicorp's entry into computer services has met considerable opposition from both banking and computer service competitors. Banking competitors believe that Citicorp's data processing relationships with other banks put it in a better position to acquire them. This concern is particularly telling if laws regulating interstate banking are changed so that banks can branch across state lines. Computer service competitors charge that Citicorp is violating the National Bank Act and the Bank Holding Company Act. These acts limit banks and their holding companies from offering services unrelated to their basic banking business.

Other observers note that some customers might well purchase Citibank's computer services with the expectation that their loan applications would receive more favorable treatment. The bank is in the position of playing two different roles but is able to combine the two roles and thereby confuse the customer. For example, Citibank might "persuade" the customer that it should subscribe to the bank's computer services.

Despite these criticisms, Citibank is now well entrenched in the computer services industry. To reverse its decision to enter the industry would involve a complete overhaul of the company's long-term corporate strategy.

Questions

1. What environmental forces caused Citicorp to move into the computer service industry?

2. Is the computer service business consistent with Citicorp's mission? Its distinctive competence?

3. Where would Citicorp's computer service business show up on a portfolio matrix? Explain.

EXERCISE

6–1   PROTECTING THE ORGANIZATION BY PLANNING

Purpose: The purpose of this exercise is to emphasize the importance of planning in organizations.

Setting Up the Exercise:

1. First, every person in the class should be assigned the same organization from the list below and should answer the following questions.

   a. What events in this organization's environment should be considered in developing short- and long-run plans?

   b. How likely are the events to occur? What is the probability of the events (e.g., a gasoline shortage, a change in government regulations, increased foreign competition, a drastic change in consumer demand)?

   c. How can planning improve the organization's chances of capitalizing on, or adjusting to, the occurrence of the events cited in your answer to question B?

   The organizations for the exercise:

NASA	Bell & Howell
Red Cross	J. C. Penney
R. J. Reynolds/Nabisco	Burger King
Winnebago	Shell Oil
Toyota	Gerber Foods
Procter & Gamble	Crocker National Bank

2. After the members of the class complete the first part of the exercise individually, the instructor will form groups of five to eight students. The groups will each be assigned one of the remaining organizations. Each group will be assigned a different organization. The groups should answer questions A, B, and C and report their answers to the class.

A Learning Note: This exercise will require some out-of-class homework to prepare the answers. It will also show that some organizations need planning more than others because of the forces they must deal with in the environment.

COMPREHENSIVE CASE FOR PART II

NATIONAL LUMBER COMPANY

Frank Jensen was general manager of the Fabricated Components Division of the National Lumber Company. Located in Trenton, New Jersey, the Fabricated Components Division manufactured and sold a line of prefabricated components such as walls, floors, and roofing systems to building contractors on the eastern seaboard. By utilizing the products of the Fabricated Components Division contractors could, under certain circumstances, achieve great economy in construction of their projects.

The Fabricated Components Division was significantly different from the other operations of the National Lumber Company. National Lumber Company manufactured and sold a wide range of lumber products from a series of plants and wholesaling points throughout the United States. The National Lumber Company was a large, successful organization which had been in business for over 75 years. The Fabricated Components Division had been started on an experimental basis, as the management of the National Lumber Company felt that prefabricated components offered real promise in the construction industry, and it wished to be aware of the problems and opportunities in the field. By establishing this division, management felt that valuable experience and insights could be gained and that the National Lumber Company would be in a good position to capitalize on the expected boom in components.

A large modern plant, more than adequate for the expected level of immediate operations, was erected in Trenton. Mr. Jensen had a great deal of experience in the fabricated components business as manager of one of the small independent organizations which were engaged in this type of activity. He was hired for the purpose of supervising the construction of the plant and for heading the operations of Fabricated Components Division after the plant was completed. He was considered to be a very capable administrator by executives of National Lumber Company.

During the first year of operation many diverse things had to be done: building an organization to both manufacture and sell the products, staffing the office force, working at production and control difficulties, and establishing a market for what was basically a new, relatively untested concept in the building industry. Many problems were encountered, but at the end of the first year the Fabricated Components Division had shown a profit of $24,000 on sales of $800,000 and an investment of $500,000.

The second year was, according to Mr. Jensen, a continuation of the "shakedown period." Changes in both the product and the organization were made, additional capital was invested in the plant, and advertising and selling expenditures were increased. The product line seemed to be gaining the approval of many contractors, although competition with the more traditional methods of construction was severe. At the end of the second year the operating statements showed a net loss of $8,000 on sales of $700,000 and a net investment of $600,000.

The third and fourth years of the life of Fabricated Components Division were, in Mr. Jensen's words, "a madhouse." Several new products were introduced, the plant was again expanded, advertising expenditures were increased still more, and a great number of people were added to the organization to handle the increased volume of business. Sales for the third year totaled almost $2 million. However, a net loss of $126,000 was realized. Mr. Jensen stated:

> It was mass confusion and things just got away from us. We had too many things to do and too many people involved. When we lived through the third year without going under, we expected things to go very well from then on, but we had some unexpected problems with some of our people quitting. We also lost a lot of money on a big government order, partly because we didn't have good enough control of our operations. During the fourth year of operations we lost $160,000 on the big job and overall $254,000. But I felt that we were learning through our mistakes and that we still had great potential in this part of the business. We had pretty well perfected our manufacturing operations in Trenton, had added some new equipment and had our organizational problems pretty well worked out.
>
> I was concerned about the increasing pressure I was subjected to from National Lumber, however. Naturally, I didn't expect top management to be overjoyed by our performance. When we started, both they and I knew that we would have some difficult times, but neither of us expected our financial picture to be quite so bleak. Although we were doing some very good work and were by far the most outstanding outfit in this part of the business, we did not seem to be able to make any money.

Pressures from above increased greatly during the fifth year. At one time or another Mr. Jensen was called on by literally every member of the top management of National Lumber, including the chairman of the board of directors. According to Mr. Jensen, these visits were relatively pleasant, but unproductive and prevented him from attending to what he considered at that time to be the most important part of his job—getting sufficient sales so that the large plant could be operated on a profitable basis. Mr. Jensen stated:

> We were like Grand Central Station! I couldn't get anything done, and the constant stream of top-level visitors was upsetting to our plant and office people. They knew that we hadn't yet proved ourselves financially, and all the top brass made them nervous.
>
> Some of our visitors were quite candid. One man told me he had no faith in the basic ideas of our organization and that he stopped by just "to see the rathole we're pouring all our money down." And when I found out many of our visitors were charging the expenses of their visits to our operations and we were getting billed for them through interdivisional charges, I got pretty angry.
>
> But the main thing was that we got little realistic advice or help from these people. Several suggested we "do better," but didn't tell us how we might.
>
> There were several things that I felt they could have done—but I got nowhere. Everyone had a gloomy attitude except me. I knew what our capabilities were and had great hopes. I didn't feel that many people

understood the differences between running an old established business
such as National Lumber and a new, struggling business such as the
Fabricated Components Division.

During the fifth year Mr. Jensen was under considerable pressure from his immediate
superior, Avery Randell, Eastern Regional Manager for the parent company. Mr.
Randell sent Mr. Jensen a "confidential memo" about every other week in which he
commented upon events that had occurred or decisions that Mr. Jensen had made that
did not meet with his approval. Mr. Jensen regularly ignored these memos. He kept
them locked in his desk—to which only he had a key—as he did not want their contents
known to his subordinates for fear of the effect upon their morale. Mr. Randell also
frequently asked Mr. Jensen to have lunch in New York, where Mr. Randell's office
was located, so that he could keep in closer touch with the activities at Fabricated
Components Division. Often Mr. Jensen would decline these invitations, but he did
have lunch with Mr. Randell in New York City about every two weeks. In an effort
to satisfy Mr. Randell's demands for information, Mr. Jensen started to send him a
weekly report on the activities of Fabricated Components Division. The information
that went into this report was carefully screened by Mr. Jensen so that nothing would
upset Mr. Randell or increase his demands on Mr. Jensen's time was included. According to Mr. Jensen, "The sole purpose of these reports was to keep him off my
back."

Mr. Jensen made the following comments about his relationship with Mr. Randell:

> Avery's OK, but he's quite nervous about our operations. His division
> almost runs itself. His people are experienced and well trained, and he
> really doesn't have too much to do. He plays golf a lot and cruises on his
> boat for long weekends, while I'm at the plant seven days a week and
> most evenings. He doesn't know much about what we're trying to do and
> this makes him uncomfortable. We're a thorn in his side and the only
> "disreputable" part of his division financially. He inherited us because
> we're geographically close to him, but he doesn't have much sympathy
> for or understanding of what we're trying to do and the problems we
> face. I keep telling him that I'll take all the blame for our operations, but
> with all the attention we're getting from top management he's very much
> interested in taking part in many of our decisions—even though he
> doesn't know what is going on and is technically incompetent to assist in
> managing Fabricated Components Division. Personally, I like him and
> enjoy his company. Our meetings are very pleasant and we go to some
> very nice places for lunch. Avery does give us some kinds of help, too.
> For example, we've had some minor legal problems which he has gotten
> off our hands. But, in general, he is more of a hindrance than a help. He
> doesn't know enough about our operation to really help us, and the things
> he could do, he doesn't. I've wanted to hire another salesman for a long
> time, but I can't get Avery to approve it. It would cost us about $3,000 a
> month, but we need more sales and a good man would pay for himself in
> no time. But Avery's so upset about our losses that he won't let me hire
> anyone else without his approval, and he won't give it. I would guess
> that I spend 30 percent of my time either dealing with Avery or worrying

about our relationship. I've told him that if I answered all of his memos, I wouldn't have time for anything else. He's been a real problem for me, and it keeps me from doing the really important things. I'd like to hire some kid to do all of that kind of thing so I would have time to run the business.

About two months before the end of the fifth year of operations, a meeting of top management of the National Lumber Company was held in New York to decide the future of Fabricated Components Division. Mr. Jensen was not asked to attend this meeting, which irritated him considerably. He was asked to submit his plans for the next year's operations, as well as several alternative plans and a capital and expense budget for the coming year. He spent a great deal of time preparing this information and submitted alternative plans ranging from considerable expansion of operations to shutting down of the plant completely and going out of business. In the letter submitting this information, he requested that he be permitted to attend the meeting. He received no reply to this request.

Two weeks after the meeting was held, Mr. Jensen had not been informed of what decision, if any, had been made. As he had no information to the contrary, he assumed that operations for the next year would continue about as they had in the past. About three weeks after the meeting, Mr. Jensen began to hear rumors that the Fabricated Components Division would be shut down at the end of the year. These rumors came from sources both within and outside the company. On hearing these rumors, Mr. Jensen called Mr. Randell who told him that, "Things are still undecided, but don't spend any more money than you have to." Mr. Jensen then called the chairman of the board of directors who informed him that the company had decided to shut down the Fabricated Components Division and get out of that part of the business. Shortly thereafter, Mr. Jensen received a letter from the president of National Lumber Company confirming this information. Mr. Jensen then began making plans for closing down the Fabricated Components Division. He felt that a poor decision had been made, but that it would be useless to attempt to have the decision reversed.

During these last few weeks of operation Mr. Jensen was faced with several unique problems:

He was not sure what, if anything, to tell his employees—or what the timing should be. He was not greatly concerned about the 50 men in the plant, for they were skilled workers who could easily find other employment without suffering financial losses. He was especially concerned about the future of the production manager, the sales manager, and the office manager, all of whom had been with him since the start of Fabricated Components Division. Because none of these people had been with the National Lumber Company for very long, they would get little severance pay and though capable people, could well be faced with a period of unemployment until they found other jobs. He wanted to give these people adequate time to find new positions, yet felt that if the news was out, efficiency would drop considerably and the Fabricated Components Division would have an even greater loss than anticipated for its fifth—and last—year of operation.

Mr. Jensen also faced another kind of problem. He still had great faith in the kind of thing that the Fabricated Components Division was doing and had often considered the advantages of operating his own company in this field. When he had learned that the Fabricated Components Division was to be shut down, he had quietly explored the possibilities of buying the business and had found that he could arrange adequate financing without too much difficulty. Much of the equipment was specialized and not readily saleable. He didn't know of anyone—other than himself—who might want to buy the Fabricated Components Division and felt that he could get everything that he needed to operate with at a reasonable price. Thus, if the Fabricated Components Division showed a great loss for this year, this might discourage other prospective buyers, as well as increase National Lumber Company's desire to get out of an unprofitable venture for any kind of recovered investment, thus driving down the price he might have to pay.

Along these same lines, Mr. Jensen was undecided about what action, if any, should be taken regarding several large sales that were in the closing stages. It would be quite easy to defer action on these sales until after he had purchased the operations and thus start on his own with a considerable order file. If the sales were closed now, the customers would probably revert to the conventional construction techniques when they learned that Fabricated Components Division was not going to be in business. Or it was possible that these orders would be farmed out to small independents by National Lumber Company before Mr. Jensen could get operating on his own.

In reflecting upon the history of the Fabricated Components Division, Mr. Jensen observed that this was an excellent example of a good idea that had been defeated because of lack of support and meddling on the part of top management:

> They bought the idea of the Fabricated Components Division in theory but refused, or were literally unable, to recognize the kinds of problems that would arise. When these problems did arise—and almost any new operation faces the same kinds of problems—they wouldn't leave me alone long enough to solve them. Certainly, I must take a great share of the blame for our poor record, but I sincerely believe that if we hadn't had so many visitors and so much attention from top management, we would have had a respectable, if not spectacular, financial success.

Avery Randell made the following comments regarding the Fabricated Components Division:

> Frank Jensen is a very capable man, but we never really got him to operate as a part of the company. He ran the Fabricated Components Division as if it were an independent organization and never really accepted or respected our advice. This past year in particular we had the very definite feeling that Frank wanted no part of us, even though several of our top management people went considerably out of their way to help him. Frank has not yet learned how to live in a relatively large organization and, because of his inability to accommodate the organization, creates a lot of problems for himself and detracts considerably from his excellent technical skills. He probably knows more about prefabricated components than anyone in the country, but, because of his inability to adjust to the organization, he has been an unsuccessful manager for us.

Questions

1. Did the management of National Lumber engage in planning activities when deciding to set up the Fabricated Components Division?

2. Would specific objectives and a strategic analysis have helped in improving the chances of success in the Fabricated Components Division? If so, how?

3. Why was the new division not successful?

PART III

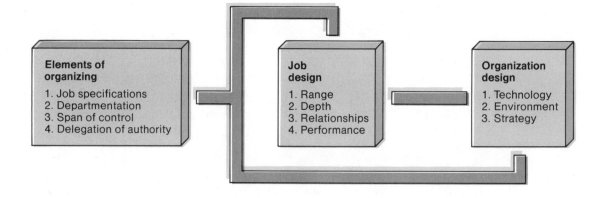

Elements of organizing

1. Job specifications
2. Departmentation
3. Span of control
4. Delegation of authority

Job design

1. Range
2. Depth
3. Relationships
4. Performance

Organization design

1. Technology
2. Environment
3. Strategy

THE ORGANIZING FUNCTION

INTRODUCTION TO PART III

Part III, the organizing function, contains three chapters.

7 **Elements of Organizing**
8 **Job Design**
9 **Organization Design**

The inclusion of the material contained in the three chapters is based on the following rationale:

The organizing function consists of managerial actions and decisions that result in the creation of a stable set of jobs and relationships among jobs. The stability of the set of jobs and job relationships is both a part of the definition of organization structure and an advantage of it. To understand the structure of an organization and the managerial actions and decisions that create it, it is necessary to consider the four elements of all organizations: job specifications, departmentation bases, spans of control, and delegation of authority. Every organization can be described in terms of these four elements and is the result of managerial decisions and actions concerning them. The four *elements of organizing* are the topics of Chapter 7.

The basic building blocks of organization structures are the jobs people perform. The manner in which employees perform their jobs and the expectations they must satisfy are the consequences of managerial decisions and actions. Through techniques of job analysis, managers determine the depth, range, and relationships of jobs. These attributes combine with characteristics of individuals and the work environment to create the conditions determining job performance. In some circumstances, the jobs of individuals are the focus of job redesign efforts as managers attempt to improve job performance and other meaningful job outcomes. The issues associated with *job design* are the topics of Chapter 8.

Jobs are designed in the context of a larger work environment. This environment consists of departments linked together by the authority of different managers. The characteristics of different combinations of departments and delegated authority can be identified and related to different desirable outcomes. For example, highly specialized jobs in homogeneous departments with centralized authority may achieve high levels of production but at the expense of adaptability. At the other extreme are relatively unspecialized jobs in heterogeneous departments with delegated authority; these jobs may achieve high levels of adaptability but at the expense of productivity. These issues of *organization design* are the topics of Chapter 9.

The figure on the facing page depicts the relationships among the key issues of the organizing function. The figure demonstrates that the elements of organizing run through both job and organization design. It also indicates that job design and organization design are themselves related.

SEVEN

Elements of Organizing

LEARNING OBJECTIVES

After completing Chapter 7 you should be able to:

Define: what is meant by the term *organizing*.

State: the four key decisions of organizing and the three dimensions of organization structures.

Describe: the effects of the span of control on the shape of the organization.

Explain: why the choice of departmental basis is such a crucial management decision.

Discuss: the importance of the distinction between line and staff departments.

RESTRUCTURING AT MOTOROLA

Competitive pressures from home and abroad have forced many business firms to consider ways to cut costs, and eliminate waste. At the same time that firms sought ways to cut costs, they were also looking for ways to increase the flow of innovative ideas. Many firms responded to these twin challenges in the 1980s by reducing the levels of management and increasing the spans of control. These flatter structures had the advantage of reducing costs by eliminating managerial jobs (and salaries) and increasing the flow of ideas by giving individuals more authority to make decisions. Many reports of the positive results of these restructuring efforts filled the popular press.

Some of the more notable success stories included Ford Motor Company's acknowledgement that its 12 layers of management should be reduced and brought more in line with Toyota's 7 layers, and Xerox Corporation's reduction in middle management. Even those firms with records of efficient operations announced that they were attempting to do better by reducing the number of managers in their organizations. Dana Corporation, for example, as an acknowledged efficiency leader, announced its intention to reduce its five levels of management to four. These success stories came to the attention of top management of Motorola, Inc., who instructed the company's human resource professionals to evaluate potential gains through "flattening" the structure.

Motorola's top management was particularly concerned with how any efforts to reduce managerial personnel would affect the company's long-standing commitment to certain values. The company enjoyed the reputation of treating employees with respect and dignity including "protecting" employees who had served the company well in the past. Any effort to restructure so as to eliminate managerial jobs would have to be consistent with the company's reputation. Top management was also concerned with how managers themselves would respond to efforts to reduce managerial jobs. Wouldn't they see such efforts as threats, particularly if it meant reducing personnel in their own departments?

(The Management Solution to this Management Incident can be found at the end of this chapter.)

The organizing function of management naturally and logically follows the planning function. As we have seen, managers decide what they want to accomplish in the way of profit, return on investment, patient care, students graduated, or whatever performance measures are appropriate objectives for the type of institution they are managing. But before these objectives can be accomplished, somebody must do some work. Not only must people do some work, they must do the right work. And that brings us to the organizing function, because it is through the organizing function that managers decide how the strategy and planned objectives will be accomplished.[1] In a practical sense the organizing function involves managers in decisions which result in a system of specialized, coordinated jobs.

Another purpose of the organizing function is to achieve coordinated effort through the design of a structure of task and authority relationships.[2] The two key words are design and structure. Design, in this context, implies that managers make a conscious effort to predetermine the way employees do their work. Structure refers to relatively stable relationships and processes of the organization. Organizational structure is considered by many to be "the anatomy of the organization, providing a foundation within which the organization functions."[3] Thus, the structure of an organization, similar to the anatomy of a living organism, can be viewed as a framework. The idea of structure as a framework "focuses on the differentiation of positions, formulation of rules and procedures, and prescriptions of authority."[4] Thus, the purpose of structure is to regulate, or at least reduce, uncertainty in the behavior of individual employees.

From a managerial perspective, an effective organizational structure accomplishes several purposes. First it makes clear who is supposed to do a particular job or perform a task. In other words the organization structure clarifies who is responsible. Second, it clarifies who is accountable to whom. It indicates who is in charge, who has the authority. Third, it clarifies the channels of communication. Communications flow between defined jobs and the principle of "need to know" determines who should be included in the channel. Finally, an effective organization structure will enable managers to allocate resources to the objectives defined in the planning process.

When viewed in rather abstract terms, the organizing function is the process of breaking down an overall task into individual jobs and then putting them back together in units, or departments. A certain amount of authority is delegated to managers of each unit, or department. In this chapter we will describe the elements of organizational structure.

---

[1]Danny Miller, "The Genesis of Configuration," *Academy of Management Review,* October 1987, pp. 691–92.

[2]George P. Huber and Reuben R. McDaniel, "The Decision-Making Paradigm of Organizational Design," *Management Science,* May 1986, p. 573.

[3]Dan R. Dalton, William D. Todor, Michael J. Spendolini, Gordon J. Fielding, and Lyman W. Porter, "Organization Structure and Performance: A Critical Review," *Academy of Management Review,* January 1980, p. 49.

[4]Stewart Ranson, Bob Hinings, and Royston Greenwood, "The Structuring of Organizational Structures," *Administrative Science Quarterly,* March 1980, p. 2.

ORGANIZATIONAL STRUCTURE

We will introduce the concept of organizational structure by describing the typical experience of an individual taking her first job. Most readers will have work experience that they can relate to the discussion. More than likely, you have worked for a company, or perhaps a church, governmental agency, or summer camp. Perhaps you are now employed. One of the first things your boss told you was what your job would involve—what machines you should use, what you should produce, including how many and how often you should produce. For example, if you were employed as a bank teller, you were told how to deal with each type of customer transaction such as deposits, withdrawals, check cashing, and even loan payments. Each type of transaction required a slightly different method, and you were taught those methods.

You also quickly learned which other people you had to work with to complete your job satisfactorily. For example, you were perhaps required to secure the approval of another person before you could cash a check for someone who was not a customer of the bank. In this instance, you were acting on orders or directives that defined how much authority you had to complete a transaction. In any setting, an individual's job is specified in terms of basic tasks and authority to complete those tasks.

You also quickly found out another piece of important information; that is, just what your boss expected of you. Your boss is the individual who supervises your work to see that you do it properly and within the bounds of your authority. But perhaps more importantly, your boss has authority over you. He has the right to tell you what to do, and to evaluate that work. If the boss is pleased with your performance, then you know that you have a good chance to continue working and even to get pay raises and promotions.

Another important piece of information is the names of others under your supervisor. These other people are the members of your department or unit or group. You may even attend a meeting of your co-workers during which the boss introduces you. Chances are, all of your co-workers' jobs are more or less similar. If you are a teller, your boss is the head teller. Some of your co-workers may have more tasks than others and more freedom (authority) to do those tasks. As you distinguish between responsibilities of peers, you probably will discover that differences are the result of the longer experience and greater skill of those co-workers. You also may find out (or suspect) that those co-workers make more money than you do.

If you continue to work in the bank, you will discover that people in your department come and go. Some will get fired; some will be promoted to other jobs. But as quickly as one person leaves a job, another person usually will be hired to fill it. Thus, you begin to realize that the work goes on despite the comings and goings of different people. It may even be that your boss—the head teller—changes. Your original boss may be promoted, or may retire, or may quit to take another job. But soon, another person will take the job. Perhaps a teller in your department has been promoted. These experiences should cause you to understand that the bank has created ways to avoid dependence on people. It has devised, in effect, a system of jobs, departments, and authority which enables the work to be done irrespective of the people who are employed at the time. That system and its parts are the bank's organizational structure.

Figure 7–1 Security Bank: organizational chart.

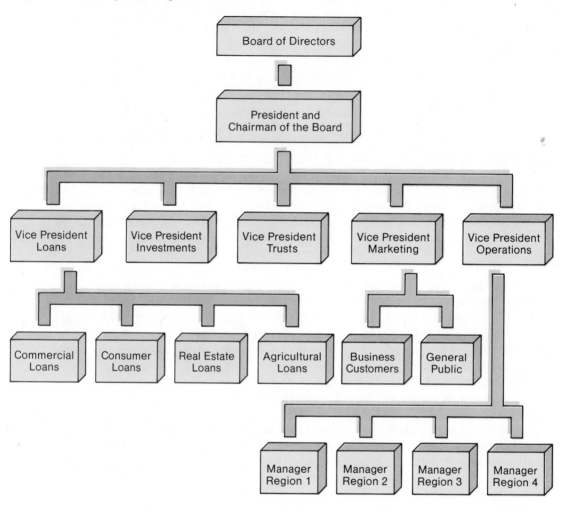

As you gain experience in your job, and as you become more familiar with what goes on in the bank, you begin to see that the bank consists of numerous jobs and departments. You also discover that your boss has a boss who in turn has a boss. You may even be curious enough to ask someone about how the bank is run. When you first began your job you may have been given a bank publication, such as its annual report. There, you likely would see an organization chart. Figure 7–1 is a facsimile of a bank's organization chart.

An organizational chart shows jobs and departments and is the most tangible depiction of an organizational structure. Reporting relationships and channels of communication are indicated by the solid lines connecting the positions. Now you see the whole complicated picture. What does the chart really show? What concepts enable you to understand it? Why is the bank organized in the way it is and not in some other way? Why were you hired? How could the organization be changed? This chapter and those which follow will present ideas that will enable you to answer questions such as these.

FOUR DECISIONS WHICH DETERMINE ORGANIZATIONAL STRUCTURE

Managers responsible for designing a specific system of tasks and authority must make many decisions, but the four primary ones are:

1. *Job design.* The fundamental building blocks of organization structures are jobs. Managers must specify what each of these jobs will do and get done. Thus job design is the first managerial decision of the organizing function. A job is assigned to an individual and it consists of specialized tasks and objectives of the organization. The necessity to specify jobs arises because the overall task cannot be done by one person. It is apparent that the bank depicted in Figure 7–1 consists of numerous individuals doing different jobs. Some individuals take deposits and cash checks, others make loans, administer trusts, and invest funds. Each individual's job is the result of a managerial decision which specifies what the individual must do to contribute to the bank's overall tasks and objectives. Thus the jobs of individuals are specialized components.

2. *Departmentation.* The next step in structuring an organization is to decide how to group the jobs. They must be grouped to achieve coordination. Once the jobs have been grouped, a manager can be assigned the responsibility of coordinating each group. It is unlikely that one individual could coordinate all the jobs at Security Bank. There would simply be too much work for one person to perform effectively, thus we see departments for loans, investments, trusts, marketing, and operations. When managers make decisions about how to group the individual jobs, they create departments. Departmentation is the second element of organizational structure.

3. *Span of control.* The third decision involves how many jobs should be included in each department. Span of control refers to the number of jobs that the department manager will be responsible for coordinating. As we will see, that number will vary from manager to manager, from a few to many. The number of workers who report to a manager determines his or her span of control.

4. *Delegation of authority.* Once managers establish a span of control, they must decide how much authority individuals should have to do their jobs. In this context, authority is the right to make decisions without having to obtain approval from a supervisor. Some managers will be granted greater authority than others; few managers are ever satisfied that they have enough authority to match their responsibilities. In managerial terms, defining the authority of jobs is called *delegation*.

The design of an organization structure varies depending on the outcomes of each of the four decisions. Conceptually, the choices for each of the decisions vary along a continuum as shown below:

		Specialization	
Job design	High		Low

		Basis	
Departmentation	Homogeneous		Heterogeneous

		Number	
Span of control	Few		Many

		Delegation	
Authority	Centralized		Decentralized

The structures of organizations tend toward one or the other ends of the continuums. An organization that employs people to do highly specialized jobs will also group jobs according to common and homogeneous functions, and the managers will have narrow spans of control and little authority. Organizations that utilize low specialization will have heterogeneous departments, wide spans of control, and decentralized authority. Exactly where along the continuum a particular organization finds itself has implications for its performance, but also for employee attitudes and perceptions.[5]

JOB DESIGN

The most important element of an organization structure are the jobs that people perform. And management's most important organizing responsibility is to design jobs that enable people to perform the right tasks. Although we can think about jobs in a number of different ways, the usual way is in terms of specialization. In fact, the ability to divide overall tasks into smaller and specialized tasks is the chief advantage of organized effort.[6] All organizations consist of specialized jobs, people doing different tasks.

A major managerial decision is to determine the extent to which jobs will be specialized. Historically we have seen that managers will tend to divide jobs into rather narrow specialties because of the advantages of division of labor. Two such advantages are:

[5]Greg R. Oldham and J. Richard Hackman, "Relationship between Organizational Structure and Employee Reactions: Comparing Alternative Frameworks," *Administrative Science Quarterly,* March 1981, pp. 66–83.

[6]Richard E. Kopelman, "Job Redesign and Productivity: A Review of the Literature," *National Productivity Review,* Summer 1985, p. 239.

1. If a job consists of few tasks, you can quickly train replacements for personnel who are terminated, transferred, or otherwise absent. The minimum training effort results in a lower training cost.

2. When a job entails only a limited number of tasks, the employee can become highly proficient in performing those tasks. This proficiency can result in a better quality of output.

The benefits of specialization are largely economic and technical, and they usually apply to nonmanagerial jobs. But similar economic and technical benefits can be gained through specialization in managerial positions, as well.

The gains derived from narrow divisions of labor can be calculated in purely economic terms. Frederick W. Taylor, the leading proponent of scientific management demonstrated that as the job is divided into ever smaller elements, additional output is obtained.[7] However, more people and capital must be employed to do the smaller jobs. At some point, the costs of specialization (labor and capital) begin to outweigh the increased efficiency of specialization (output), and the cost per unit of output begins to rise.

Specialization, or division, of labor at the job level is measured in relative terms. One job can be more or less specialized than another. In making comparisons of degrees of specialization, it is useful to identify five aspects that differentiate jobs:

1. *Work pace*—the more control the individual has over how fast she must work, the less specialized the job.

2. *Job repetitiveness*—the greater the number of tasks to perform, the less specialized the job.

3. *Skill requirements*—the more skilled the job holder must be, the less specialized the job.

4. *Methods specification*—the more latitude the job holder has in using methods and tools, the less specialized the job.

5. *Required attention*—the more mental attention a job requires, the less specialized it is.

If you now re-examine the job specification continuum, you can identify the specific characteristics of jobs that are relatively high or low in specialization.

Specialization

High	Low
1. No control over pace	1. Control over pace
2. Repetitive	2. Varied
3. Low skill requirements	3. High skill requirements
4. Specified methods	4. Unspecified methods
5. No required attention	5. Required attention

---

[7]Frederick W. Taylor, *Principles of Scientific Management* (New York: Harper & Row, 1911).

Figure 7–2 Security Bank: partial organizational chart, functional departmentation.

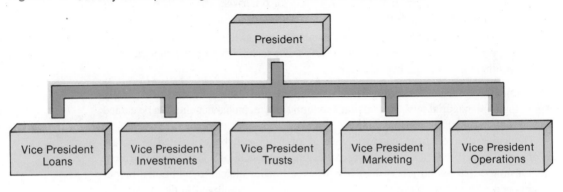

The principle of specialization of labor has been the traditional guideline for managers when determining the content of individual jobs.[8] In recent years, management's attention has been directed to alternative ways of designing jobs that focus on teams doing the work rather than on individuals doing the work. The following Management Application reports a growing sentiment in the auto industry toward applying principles of teamwork to jobs.

MANAGEMENT APPLICATION

TEAMWORK VERSUS INDIVIDUAL WORK IN THE AUTO INDUSTRY

During the summer of 1987 the United Autoworkers and the auto industry were preparing for a round of contract talks. The auto industry leaders were anxious to discuss with union leaders the potential of teamwork to increase productivity, product quality, and competitiveness. The traditional way to make cars was based on the ideas of scientific management, first popularized by Frederick W. Taylor some 85 years ago. According to Taylor, the jobs of making cars should be reduced to small, repetitive, and specialized tasks requiring little individual initiative and decision making. Over time these specialized jobs have been incorporated in bargaining agreements and have become rigid and inflexible. Rigid job classifications and the accompanying work rules hamper the ability of the auto industry to utilize modern technology and to be competitive with foreign automakers.

The team approach to carmaking is more flexible and would enable the automakers to respond quickly to market changes. The basic elements are teams consisting of from 5 to 20 individuals who already work next to each other. But rather than doing only one job, team members learn several jobs. Work can then be organized as needed with different individuals doing different jobs as they are required. As the number of different jobs is reduced, the number of different job classifications and work rules is reduced.

---

[8]David A. Buchanan, *The Development of Job Design Theories* (Farnborough, England: Saxon House, 1979).

Figure 7–3 Business firm: partial organizational chart, functional departmentation.

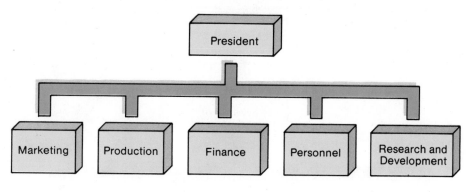

The reduction in work rules provides management with the flexibility to achieve higher levels of productivity and quality. As the bargaining sessions neared, the automakers and the union were deliberating what they had at stake in the traditional way of making cars and what they would concede and demand to move to the team approach.

Source: Adapted from "Detroit vs. the UAW: At Odds over Teamwork," *Business Week,* August 24, 1987, pp. 54–55.

COMBINING JOBS: DEPARTMENTATION

The process of combining jobs into groups is termed *departmentation*. A manager must have a basis, or rationale, for combining jobs. Numerous bases for departmentation exist.[9] The more important ones are explained in the discussions below.

Functional Departmentation

Jobs can be grouped according to the functions of the organization. A business firm includes such functions as production, marketing, finance, accounting, and personnel. A hospital consists of such functions as surgery, psychiatry, housekeeping, pharmacy, personnel, and nursing.[10] The functions of Security Bank are the basis for the departments at the very top of its organization chart, as shown in Figure 7–2. Within each of the five departments, individuals perform specialized jobs in the areas of loans, investments, trusts, marketing, and operations. A partial organization chart for a manufacturing firm is shown in Figure 7–3. It reflects the basic functions required to manufacture and sell a product.

---

[9]Mariann Jelinek, "Organization Structure: The Basic Conformations," in *Organization by Design,* ed. Mariann Jelinek, Joseph A. Litterer, and Raymond E. Miles (Plano, Tex.: Business Publications Inc., 1981), pp. 293–302.

[10]Peggy Leatt and Rodney Schneck, "Criteria for Grouping Nursing Subunits in Hospitals," *Academy of Management Journal,* March 1984, pp. 150–64.

Figure 7–4 Security Bank: partial organizational chart, territorial departmentation.

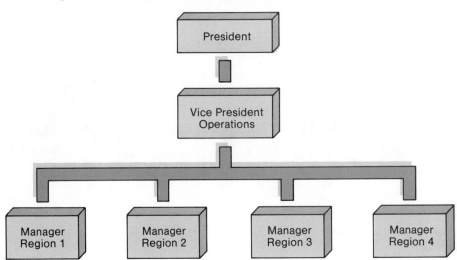

An important advantage of functional departmentation is that it makes use of the benefits of specialization. That is, you may logically set up departments that consist of experts in particular fields such as production or accounting. By having departments of specialists, a manager creates at least theoretically, the most efficient unit possible.

A major disadvantage of the functional arrangement, however, appears when specialists, working with and encouraging one another in their respective areas of expertise and interest, let the organizational objectives take a back seat to departmental objectives. Accountants may see only their problems, and not those of production or marketing or the total organization. In other words, identification with the department and its objectives is often stronger than identification with the organization and its objectives.[11]

Territorial Departmentation

Another commonly used departmental basis is built around geography. All activities in a geographic area are assigned to a particular manager. This individual is in charge of all operations in that geographic area. The operations department of the Security Bank is subdivided into four geographic regions, each served by a branch bank. Figure 7–4 depicts that part of the Security Bank that is organized according to territorial bases. If you were a teller in a branch bank in Region 1, your boss likely would report to the manager of that geographical area.

---

[11]Henry Tosi, *Theories of Organization* (New York: John Wiley & Sons, 1984).

A business firm that is dispersed geographically often will use territory as a departmentation basis. The territorial basis frequently is used by firms whose operations are similar from region to region. Chain stores, railroads, airlines, bakeries, and dairies all are typical organizations that establish departments along territorial lines.

An advantage often associated with territorial departmentation is that it provides a training ground for new managers. The company can place managers out in territories, then assess their progress. The experience managers gain away from headquarters can provide invaluable insights into how the organization's products or services are accepted in the field. The territorial basis also enables the firm to develop local market areas and adjust more quickly to local customers' needs.

The disadvantages of territorial departmentation include: difficulties in maintaining consistent adherence to company policy and practices, duplication of effort, and the necessity of having a relatively large number of managers. Companies that use territory as a primary basis for departmentation often need a large headquarters staff to control the dispersed operations.

Product Departmentation

In many large, diversified companies, activities and personnel are grouped on the basis of product. As a firm grows, coordinating its various functional departments becomes more difficult, and product departmentation can ease coordination problems. This form of organization allows personnel to develop total expertise in researching, manufacturing, and distributing one product line. Concentrating authority, responsibility, and accountability in a specific product department allows top management to better coordinate its activities. The need for coordinating production, engineering, sales, and service cannot be overestimated. Figure 7–5 is a partial organization chart that represents a large electrical products company.

Within each of these product groups, you find production and marketing personnel. Since group executives coordinate the sales, manufacture, and distribution of a product, they become overseers of a profit center. This is the manner in which profit responsibility is exacted from product organizational arrangements. Managers establish profit goals at the beginning of a time period and then compare the actual profit with the planned profit. This approach is used in the Buick, Cadillac, Chevrolet, Pontiac, and Oldsmobile divisions of General Motors. Product-based organizations can also be found in health care as well as in business.[12]

The disadvantages of product-based organizations stem from the need to create relatively independent divisions. Each division must have all the resources and types of jobs necessary to be in business. Each division also must have accountants, lawyers, engineers, market researchers, and scientists assigned to it. Therefore, the product-based organization runs the danger of duplication of effort among its divisions.

Product-based departmentation is used in our example, the Security Bank. The vice president of the loan department is responsible for four units—commercial loans,

---

[12]Dennis J. Patterson and Kent A. Thompson, "Product-line Management: Organization Makes the Difference," *Healthcare Financial Management*, February 1987, pp. 66–77.

Figure 7–5 Business firm: partial organizational chart, product departmentation.

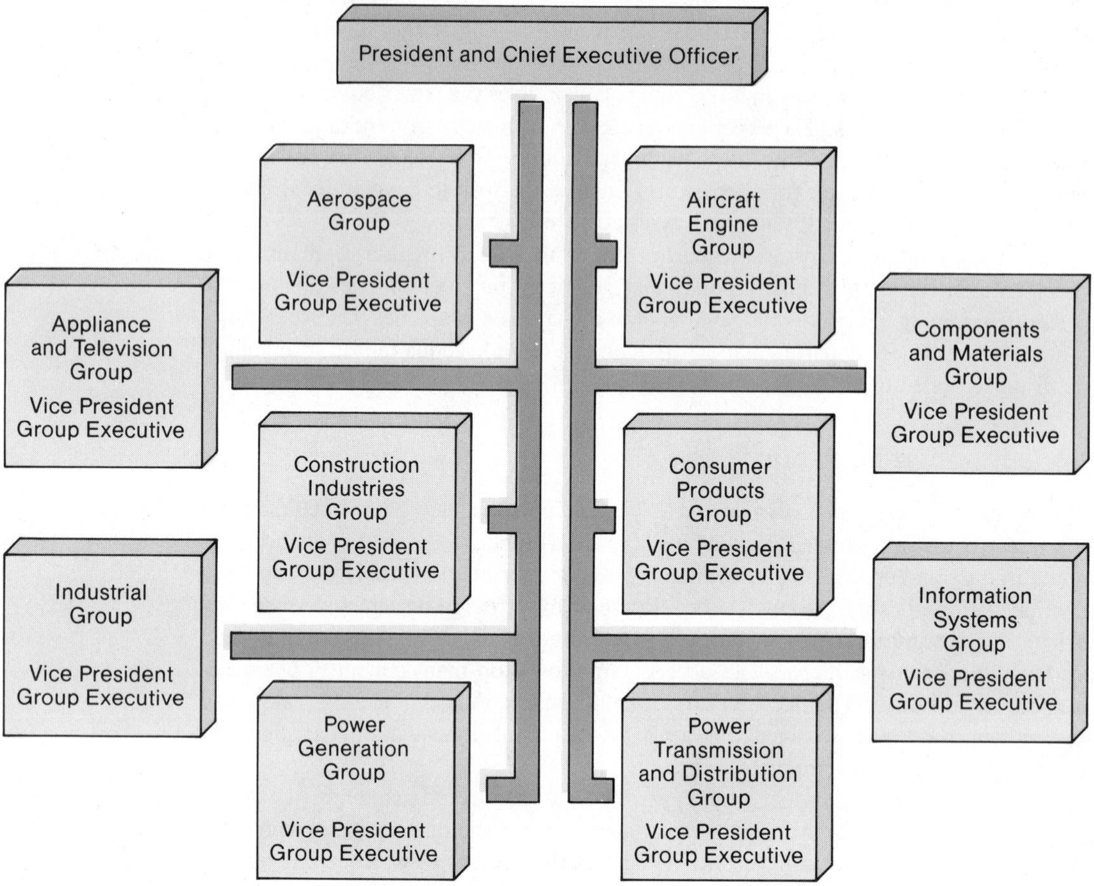

consumer loans, real estate loans, and agricultural loans. The partial organization chart is shown in Figure 7–6.

Customer Departmentation

Customer-oriented departments are found frequently in educational institutions. Some educational institutions have regular (day and night) courses and extension courses. In some instances, a professor will be affiliated solely with the regular students or the extension students. In fact, the titles of some faculty positions often specifically mention the extension division. Some department stores also are departmentalized to some degree on a customer basis. They have such groupings as university shops, menswear, and boys' clothing.

Figure 7–6   Security Bank: partial organizational chart, product departmentation.

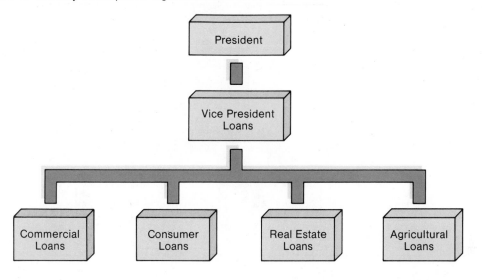

The advantages and disadvantages of customer- or client-based organizations are identical to those of product organizations. Figure 7–7 depicts the manner in which Security Bank uses customers as the basis for organizing its marketing function. The bank's management believes that marketing and promotional efforts differ enough for business and nonbusiness customers so that specialization along those two lines is justified. The emergence of the service sector as a major source of business activity has encouraged managers to consider customer contact as a basis for organizing.[13]

Multiple Bases for Departmentation

The methods cited above for dividing work are not exhaustive; there are many other ways to combine jobs into departments. Furthermore, most large organizations are composed of departments using different bases. For example, at the upper levels of management, the vice presidents reporting to the president may represent different product groups. At the level directly below the vice presidents, the managers may be part of a particular function. At the next level in the organization, there may be a number of different technical classifications. This multiple division of work in organizational design is illustrated in Figure 7–8. The figure's business example can be compared to the banking example in Figure 7–1.

The principle of departmentation specifies the general purpose to be followed when grouping activities. But the basis actually chosen is a matter of balancing advantages

---

[13]Richard B. Chase and David A. Tansik, "The Customer Contact Model for Organization Design," *Management Science*, September 1983, pp. 1037–50.

Figure 7–7
Security Bank:
partial
organizational
chart, customer
departmentation.

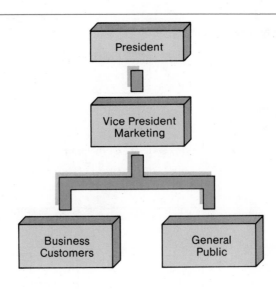

against disadvantages. For example, the advantage of departmentalizing on the basis of customers or products is that it can bring together under the control of a single manager all the resources necessary to make the product for the customers. In addition, specifying objectives is made considerably easier when the emphasis is on the final product. At the same time, this ease of objective identification and measurement can encourage individual departments to pursue their own goals at the expense of company objectives. A second disadvantage of product and customer departmentation is that the task of coordinating the activities tends to be more complex. Reporting to the unit manager are the managers of the various functions (production, marketing, and personnel, for example) whose diverse but interdependent activities must be coordinated.

Departmentation based on functional operations has certain advantages and disadvantages. The primary advantage is that such departmentation centers on specific skills and training, and activities assigned to the departments emphasize the skills that individual members bring to the job. Because of the similarity of the subordinates' jobs, the task of coordinating the activities of functional departments is considerably less complex than that of coordinating the activities of product departments. But functional departments have disadvantages as well. The principal one is that they cannot provide managers sufficient job depth to make their jobs challenging. Since creating functional departments involves breaking up a natural work flow and assigning parts of that flow to each department, every department manager must work very hard to coordinate the work of his section with the work of all the other departments.

SPAN OF CONTROL

The determination of appropriate bases for departmentation establishes the *kinds* of jobs that will be grouped together—but not the *number* of jobs to be included in a

Figure 7–8 Business firm: organizational chart.

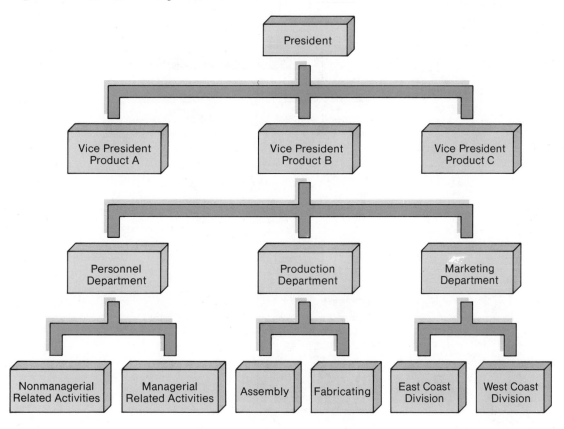

specific group. That involves the issue of *span of control*. Generally, a span of control comes down to the decision of *how many people a manager can effectively oversee;* that is, will the organization be more effective if the manager's span of control is relatively large or small?[14]

Consider, for instance, the impact of different spans of control. In Figure 7–9 you see a graphic comparison of two structures, each with 24 nonmanagerial employees to be managed. In the first case, the maximum span of control is 12, and there are two levels of management and three managers (a president and two supervisors). In the second case, the maximum span of control is four, and there are three levels of management and nine managers (a president, two department heads, and six supervisors).

The exact number of jobs (and people) reporting to a manager cannot be stated in

_____

[14]William G. Ouchi and John B. Dowling, "Defining the Span of Control," *Administrative Science Quarterly,* September 1974, pp. 357–65.

Figure 7–9
Wide and narrow
spans of control.

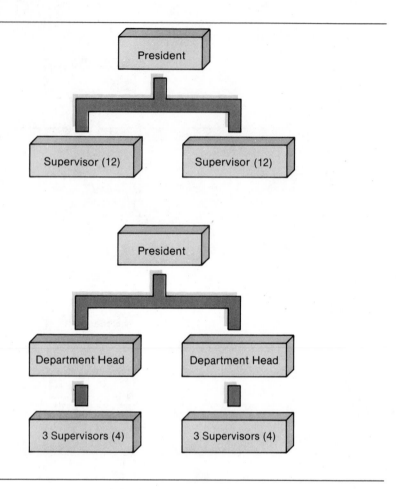

specific terms for all managers in all organizations. Rather, the only feasible approach to determining optimal span of control is to weigh the relative importance of a number of factors.[15] Those factors include the following:

1. *The competence of both the manager and the subordinates.* The more competent they are, the wider the span of control can be.

2. *The degree of interaction that is required among the units to be supervised.* The more the required interaction, the narrower the span of control must be.

3. *The extent to which the manager must carry out nonmanagerial tasks.* The more technical and job-related work the manager has to do, the less

---

[15]Robert D. Dewar and Donald P. Simet, "A Level-Specific Prediction of Spans of Control Examining the Effects of Size, Technology, and Specialization," *Academy of Management Journal,* March 1981, pp. 5–24.

time is available to supervise others, and thus, the narrower the span of control must be.

4. *The relative similarity or dissimilarity of the jobs being supervised.* The more similar the jobs, the wider the span of control can be; the less similar the jobs, the narrower it must be.

5. *The extent of standardized procedures.* The more routine the jobs of subordinates are, and the greater the degree to which each job is performed by standardized methods, the wider the span of control can be.

6. *The degree of physical dispersion.* If all the people to be assigned to a manager are located in one area, and within eyesight, the manager can supervise relatively more people than one whose people are dispersed throughout the plant or countryside at different locations.

Many studies have attempted to determine the exact relationships between these factors and the span of control. One recent review of these studies notes that they are, by and large, inconclusive. The actual spans of control in organizations are the result of the interplay of events and personalities unique to the particular organization.[16]

DELEGATION OF AUTHORITY

Delegation of authority is the final issue managers must consider when designing an organizational structure. In practical terms, the issue concerns the relative benefits of decentralization; that is, delegation of authority to the lowest possible level in the managerial hierarchy. The concept of decentralization does not refer to geographic dispersion of the organization's operating units; rather, it refers to the delegated right of managers to make decisions without approval by higher management. Let us evaluate some of the arguments for decentralization.

The Advantages of Decentralized Authority

First, some experts believe that decentralization encourages the development of professional managers. As decision-making authority is pushed down in the organization, managers must adapt and prove themselves if they are to advance. That is, they must become generalists who know something about the numerous job-related factors that they must cope with in the decentralized arrangement.

Managers in a decentralized structure often have to adapt and to deal with difficult decisions, so they are trained for promotion into positions of greater authority and responsibility. In a decentralized structure, managers can be readily compared with their peers on the basis of actual decision-making performance, not personality. In effect, the decentralized arrangement can lead to a more equitable performance appraisal program and to a more satisfied group of managers. You should recall from Chapter 2, however, that it is extremely difficult to develop specific performance criteria for most managers.

---

[16]David D. Van Fleet, "Span of Management Research and Issues," *Academy of Management Journal,* September 1983, pp. 546–52.

The decentralized arrangement also can lead to a competitive climate within the organization. The managers are motivated to contribute in this competitive atmosphere, since they are compared with their peers on various performance measures.

In the decentralized pattern, managers likewise can exercise more autonomy and satisfy their desires to participate in problem solving. This freedom can lead to managerial creativity and ingenuity, which contribute to the flexibility and profitability of the organization. These advantages are cited by the president of Domino's Pizza in the following Management Application.

MANAGEMENT APPLICATION

DECENTRALIZATION OF DOMINO'S PIZZA

According to the president of Domino's Pizza Distribution Corporation, the advantages of decentralized authority far exceed the disadvantages. The company is headquartered in Ann Arbor, Michigan, and had in 1987 nearly 4,000 Domino's Pizza Stores. Almost 95 percent of the stores buy their food supplies and equipment from the Distribution Company even though only the 35 percent that are company owned are required to do so. But the president believes that the reason that all the others count on the Distribution Company for supplies is its reputation for reliability. The worst sin in the company is to force a store to close because it has inadequate supplies to meet customer demand.

The Distribution Company's profits increased from a negative $330,000 in 1978 to $13.7 million in 1986. This record of success reflects the benefits of decentralization as practiced at Domino's. All employees of the Distribution Company are given sufficient autonomy to achieve specific goals consistent with the company's mission. To reinforce its commitment to decentralization, the company insists that employees be willing to use their own minds to solve problems. There are no formal job titles except that each employee is referred to as a *team member*. But beyond that, the company places little importance on job titles and encourages employees to refer to themselves in whatever terms reflect their duties. Individuals must assume a large amount of responsibility and can count on very little hand-holding from headquarters. The company motto: "Do anything to get the job done" accounts for its record of reliable delivery.

Source: Adapted from Donald J. Vlcek, Jr., "Decentralization: What Works and What Doesn't," *Journal of Business Strategy*, Fall 1987, pp. 71–74.

Decentralization has disadvantages and they must be weighed against the advantages. The advantages are not without drawbacks, and most advocates of decentralization recognize that if an organization shifts from centralized to decentralized authority, certain costs may be incurred. These are some of the costs:

1. Managers must be trained to handle decision making, and this may require expensive formal training programs.

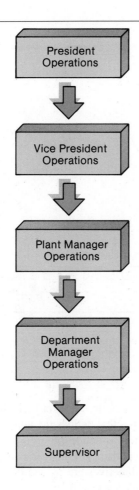

Figure 7–10
Chain of
command.

2. Since many managers have worked in centralized organizations, it is uncomfortable for them to delegate authority in a decentralized arrangement. Their attitudes are difficult to alter, and attempts often lead to resistance.
3. Accounting and performance appraisal systems must be made compatible with the decentralized arrangement, and this can be costly. Administrative costs are incurred because new or altered accounting and performance appraisal systems must be tested, implemented, and evaluated.

These are, of course, only some of the costs of decentralizing. As with most issues, there is no definite, clear-cut answer to whether decentralization is better for an organization. But one prerequisite for successful decentralization is thorough consideration of each organization factor (e.g., work force requirements, size, and control mechanisms).

Figure 7–11
Communication
bridge.

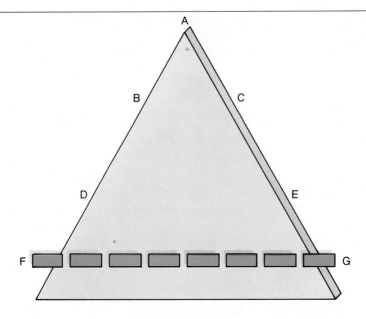

The Chain of Command and Authority

One result of delegated authority is the creation of a chain of command. The chain of command is the formal channel that defines the authority, responsibility, and communication relationships from top to bottom in an organization. Figure 7–10 depicts the chain of command for a hypothetical managerial hierarchy. In theory, the chain should be followed whenever directives are passed downward or whenever communications are passed upward and downward.

At the same time, there must be means to bypass the formal chain when conditions warrant. Consequently, a subordinate often is empowered to communicate directly with a peer outside the chain. However, the appropriate superiors must indicate beforehand the circumstances under which the crossovers will be permitted. Figure 7–11 shows a bridge between F and G (the dashed line) which D and E have approved. In special circumstances, F and G may communicate directly without going through channels, yet both would be accountable only to their respective superiors—in this case, D and E.

The Line-Staff Distinction

In examining organizational structure, you must be careful to distinguish between line and staff. The definitions for line and staff are endless. Perhaps the most concise and least confusing approach is to view line as deriving from operational activities in a direct sense; that is, creating, financing, and distributing a good or service. Staff, meanwhile, is an advisory and facilitative function for the line. The crux of this view

Figure 7–12 A line and staff design (partial organizational chart).

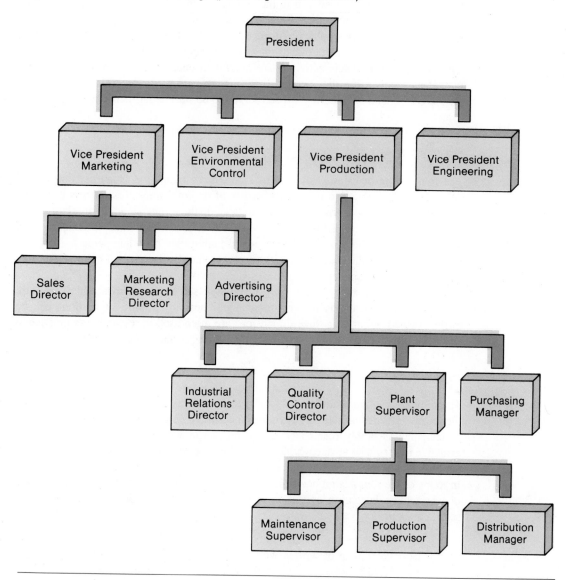

of line and staff is the degree to which the function contributes directly to the attainment of organizational objectives. The line function contributes directly to the accomplishment of the major objectives of the organization, and the staff function contributes to their accomplishment indirectly. Figure 7–12 illustrates a line and staff organization design of a hypothetical firm. If you assume that the organization depicted in Figure 7–12 is a manufacturing firm, you should be able to differentiate between line and staff positions. Using the criterion that the line function contributes directly to the firm's objective should lead you to the conclusion that the marketing and production departments perform activities directly related to the attainment of a most important organizational objective—placing an acceptable product on the market. You also can see that the activities of the managers of environmental control and engineering are advisory in nature. Their activities are helpful in enabling the firm to produce and market its product, but they do not directly contribute to the process. Thus environmental control and engineering are considered to be staff departments in this particular firm.

DIMENSIONS OF STRUCTURE

The four design decisions (division of labor, departmentation, span of control, and delegation of authority) result in a structure of organizations. Researchers and practitioners of management have attempted to develop their understanding of relationships between structures and performance, attitudes, satisfaction, and other variables thought to be important. The development of understanding has been hampered not only by the complexity of the relationships themselves, but also by the difficulty of defining and measuring the concept of organizational structure.

Although universal agreement on a common set of dimensions which measure differences in structure is neither possible nor desirable, some suggestions can be made. At the present time three dimensions are often used in research and practice to describe structure. They are formalization, centralization, and complexity.[17]

Formalization

The dimension of formalization refers to the extent to which expectations regarding the means and ends of work are specified and written. An organization structure which is described as highly formalized would be one in which rules and procedures are available to prescribe what each individual should be doing. Such organizations would have written standard operating procedures, specified directives, and explicit policy. In terms of the four design decisions, formalization is the result of high specialization of labor, high delegation of authority, the use of functional departments, and wide spans of control.[18]

1. High specialization of labor such as in the auto industry, is amenable to the development of written work rules and procedures. The jobs are so specialized as to leave little to the discretion of the job holder.

2. Functional departments are made up of jobs which have great similarities. This basis brings together jobs which make up an occupation such as

---

[17]Richard S. Blackburn, "Dimensions of Structure: A Review and Reappraisal," *Academy of Management Review,* January 1982, pp. 59–66.

[18]See Peter H. Grinyer and Masoud Yasai-Ardekani, "Dimensions of Organizational Structure: A Critical Replication," *Academy of Management Journal,* September 1980, pp. 405–21, for discussion of formalization in relation to centralization.

accountants, engineers, machinists, and the like. Because of the similarity of the jobs and the rather straightforward nature of the department's activities, management can develop written documents to govern the department's activities.

3. Wide spans of control discourage one-on-one supervision. There are simply too many subordinates for managers to keep up with on a one-to-one basis. Consequently, managers will require written reports to inform them.

4. High delegation of authority creates the need to have checks on its use. Consequently, the organization will write guidelines for decision making and will insist upon reports which describe the use of authority.

Although formalization is defined in terms of the existence of written rules and procedures, it is important to understand how they are viewed by the employees. Some organizations may have all the appearances of formalization, complete with thick manuals of rules, procedures and policies, but employees do not perceive them as affecting their behavior. Thus, even though rules and procedures exist, they must be enforced if they are to affect behavior.[19]

Centralization

Centralization refers to the location of decision-making authority in the hierarchy of the organization. More specifically, the concept refers to the delegation of authority among the jobs in the organization. Typically, researchers and practitioners think of centralization in terms of (1) decision making and (2) control. But despite the apparent simplicity of the concept, it can be complex.

The complexity of the concept derives from three sources: First, people at the same level can have different decision-making authority. Second, not all decisions are of equal importance in organizations. For example, a typical management practice is to delegate authority to make routine operating decisions (i.e., decentralization), but to retain authority to make strategic decisions (i.e., centralization). Third, individuals may not perceive that they really have authority even though their job descriptions include it. Thus, objectively they have authority, but subjectively they do not.[20]

The relationships between centralization and the four design decisions are generally as follows:

1. The higher the specialization of labor, the greater the centralization. This relationship holds because highly specialized jobs do not require the discretion which authority provides.

2. The greater the use of functional departments, the greater the centralization. The use of functional departments requires that the

---

[19]Eric J. Walton, "The Comparison of Measures of Organization Structure," *Academy of Management Review,* January 1981, pp. 155–60.

[20]Jeffrey D. Ford, "Institutional versus Questionnaire Measures of Organizational Structure," *Academy of Management Journal,* September 1979, pp. 601–10.

activities of the several interrelated departments be coordinated. Consequently, authority to coordinate them will be retained in top management.

3. The wider the spans of control, the greater the centralization. Wide spans of control are associated with relatively specialized jobs which as we have seen have little need for authority.

4. The less authority is delegated, the greater the centralization. By definition of the terms, centralization involves retaining authority in the top-management jobs, rather than delegating it to lower levels in the organization.

Complexity

Complexity is the direct outgrowth of dividing work and creating departments. Specifically the concept refers to the number of distinctly different job titles, or occupational groupings, and the number of distinctly different units, or departments. The fundamental idea is that organizations with a great many different kinds and types of jobs and units create more complicated managerial and organizational problems than those with fewer jobs and departments.

Complexity, then, relates to differences among jobs and units. It, therefore, is not surprising that differentiation is often used synonymously with complexity. Moreover, it has become standard practice to use the term *horizontal differentiation* to refer to the number of different units at the same level;[21] *vertical differentiation* refers to the number of levels in the organization. The relationships between complexity (horizontal and vertical differentiation) and the four design decisions are generally as follows:

1. The greater the specialization of labor, the greater the complexity. Specialization is the process of creating different jobs and thus more complexity. Specialization of labor contributes primarily to horizontal differentiation.

2. The greater the use of territorial, customer, and product bases, the greater the complexity. These bases involve the creation of self-sustaining units that operate much like freestanding organizations. Consequently there must be considerable delegation of authority and consequently considerable complexity.[22]

3. Narrow spans of control are associated with high complexity. This relationship holds because narrow spans are necessary when the jobs to be supervised are quite different from one another. A supervisor can manage more people in a simple organization than in a complex organization. The apparently simple matter of span of control can have profound effects on organizational and individual behavior. Hence, we should expect the controversy which surrounds it.

---

[21]Richard L. Daft and Patricia J. Bradshaw, "The Process of Horizontal Differentiation: Two Models," *Administrative Science Quarterly,* September 1980, pp. 441–56.

[22]Dennis S. Mileti, Doug A. Timmer, and David F. Gillespie, "Intra- and Interorganizational Determinants of Decentralization," *Pacific Sociological Review,* April 1982, pp. 163–83.

Table 7–1 The relationship between organizing decisions and organization dimensions.

High formalization is the result of:	1. High specialization. 2. Functional departments. 3. Wide spans of control. 4. Delegated authority.
High centralization is the result of:	1. High specialization. 2. Functional departments. 3. Wide spans of control. 4. Centralized authority.
High complexity is the result of:	1. High specialization. 2. Territorial, customer and product departments. 3. Narrow spans of control. 4. Delegated authority.

4. The greater the delegation of authority, the greater the complexity of the organization. Delegation of authority is typically associated with a lengthy chain of command; that is, with a relatively large number of managerial levels. Thus delegation of authority contributes to vertical differentiation.

The discussion of the relationships between dimensions of organizational structure and the four design decisions are summarized in Table 7–1. The table notes only the causes of high formalization, centralization, and complexity. However the relationships are symmetrical: the causes of low formalization, centralization, and complexity are the opposite of those shown in Table 7–1.

Organizations differ in their degree of formalization, centralization, and complexity. The important managerial issue is the relationship between these dimensions and individual, group, and organizational performance.[23]

MANAGEMENT SOLUTION

MOTOROLA REORGANIZES

Motorola assigned the task of considering appropriate solutions to the human resources unit. The human resource professionals devised the following strategy for dealing with the necessity to cut costs and, at the same time, to adhere to people-first values.

The strategy consisted of five steps involving the managers and human resource professionals in joint activities:

Step 1: Data gathering. Each top manager drew an organization chart showing every re-

Continued

[23]Gregory S. Whitney, "Organizational Analysis: Its Application to Performance Improvement," *National Productivity Review,* Spring 1987, pp. 168–76.

Concluded

porting relationship down to the direct-labor level. These hand-drawn charts were to show what really went on in the unit as distinct from what was supposed to go on.

Step 2: Analysis. Human resource professionals analyzed the charts and identified issues for discussion with the managers. The analysis indicated instances of too many managerial levels, too narrow spans of control, and overlapping responsibilities.

Step 3: Discussion. The analyses of the human resource professionals were presented to managers for discussion. The managers were given opportunities to explain and clarify the relationships shown on the charts.

Step 4: Goals negotiation. As discussions between managers and the human resources staff revealed problems, managers were asked to propose solutions. In those instances when managers disagreed with the staff, they were challenged to present their own analyses and solutions.

Step 5: Implementation and tracking. As the changes in organization structure were im-

plemented, the resultant cost savings were documented. The sources of these savings were salaries of managers not replaced upon retirement or transfer. A second source of savings was the replacement of a manager with a nonmanager at a lower salary.

Thus through elimination of some jobs and redefinition of others, Motorola succeeded in its efforts to reduce costs by restructuring its organization. The restructuring has caused Motorola's managers to constantly ask themselves whether they each can effectively direct one more employee. They ask: "If I manage five, why not six?" The results of the restructuring in economic terms is impressive, with the annual savings in excess of $4.3 million in the first year. Other results included improved vertical communications, more effective managerial selection and training, and greater participation in decision making by all employees.

Source: Adapted from Phil Nienstedt and Richard Wintermantel, "Motorola Restructures to Improve Productivity," *Management Review*, January 1987, pp. 47–49.

MANAGEMENT SUMMARY

☐ The organizing function includes action steps that managers take to determine which jobs and which authority relationships are necessary to implement plans and policies.

☐ The four primary decisions that managers make when performing the organizing function are job design, departmentation bases, spans of control, and delegated authority. Conceptually, these decisions are different, but in practice they are highly interrelated.

☐ Job design involves deciding the appropriate tasks and authority to be assigned to each job and job holder.

☐ Departmentation involves deciding the bases to use in grouping jobs that are to be directed by a manager. The bases typically used are function, territory, customer, and product.

☐ The number of individuals who report to a manager determines her span of control. Deciding the appropriate span is a key organizing decision, and although there are

□ no precise rules, managers can follow guidelines to determine optimal spans.

□ The delegation of authority involves providing job holders with the right, or the freedom, to make decisions without approval by higher management. The relative advantages of centralization versus decentralization must be weighed, however.

□ All organization structures can be described in terms of three dimensions: formalization, centralization, and complexity. The decisions that managers make regarding job design, departmentation, spans of control, and delegation of authority determine the dimensions for a particular organization.

REVIEW AND DISCUSSION QUESTIONS

1. What are primary purposes of organizational structure?

2. Assume that the management of a large company has completed its review of progress toward annual profit objectives. The review indicates that the company is significantly below its target profit. Explain how the causes of the poor performance might be traced to the organizational structure.

3. From your own work experience, what important information is not shown in the Security Bank organization chart (Figure 7–1)?

4. Use the four elements of organizational structure to describe your college or university.

5. Why is it necessary to create staff positions in organizations? Do these positions reduce the authority of line managers? Explain.

6. Summarize the advantages and disadvantages of decentralization. Describe a situation where decentralization is highly effective.

7. Use the three dimensions of organization structure to compare and contrast two organizations that you know about.

8. How is a functional-base organization most effective in obtaining the advantages of specialization of labor?

9. What factors other than structure contribute to organization performance? Explain.

10. Evaluate Motorola's solution to the problem associated with excessive numbers of managers and managerial layers.

CASES

7–1 DECENTRALIZATION AT CURTICE-BURNS, INC.

Curtice-Burns, Inc., consists of seven food manufacturing divisions with sales in excess of $270 million. The company grew primarily through acquisitions of food companies which then became divisions of the company. The management philosophy at Curtice-Burns, Inc., emphasizes decentralization and autonomy. Each division is completely responsible for its own business—with the exception of major capital investments. To underscore the importance of decentralization, the company has a headquarters staff of only 12 people.

President and CEO Hugh Cumming is committed to decentralization and can readily identify the advantages and disadvantages of the approach. The primary advantage is the clearly defined responsibility of each division's CEO for that division's performance. A CEO whose division's performance is below planned performance cannot blame headquarters for meddling in division matters. Instead, he alone makes all the strategic and operational decisions.

A second advantage derives from the company's incentive plan. Because of the cyclical nature of the food business, Curtice-Burns does not tie its incentive plan to the performance of a single division. Rather, the plan is based upon overall corporate results and allocated to the divisions on the basis of payroll. The incentive plan creates positive peer pressure because a poorly performing division will reduce the bonus for all divisions.

Decentralization stimulates and sustains the entrepreneurial spirit so often found in small business, but often missing in large corporations. All the top-management personnel began their careers in small business, and they tend to continue to manage entrepreneurially. For example, when one division decided it was time to get into the natural potato chip business, it did so in less than a month. By contrast, Pepsico's Frito-Lay Division took 15 months to bring out the product.

The decentralized concept is not without difficulties. For example, the emphasis on divisional marketing of regional brands does little to promote the visibility of Curtice-Burns stock. Consequently, the stock sells at prices lower than what the company's board of directors thinks is appropriate. Investors simply are not familiar with Curtice-Burns.

A second disadvantage of decentralization is the inherent duplication of functions such as accounting, sales, and marketing. A corollary problem is that some divisions (acquired companies) are too small to operate independently. Small divisions often cannot provide the full range of functional support required to operate as an independent unit.

A third problem is difficult to define. But it relates to the managerial question of knowing when headquarters should assist or even overrule a division decision. Constant interference in division affairs obviously ruins the concept, but total disregard is likewise ruinous. Striking a balance between the two extremes is a problem only because it is a matter of managerial judgment.

Cumming believes the advantages of decentralization outweigh its disadvantages. In fact, he sees the practice as the primary cause for the company's steady growth.

Questions

1. Evaluate Curtice-Burns, Inc.'s policy of decentralization.
2. What specific company strategies facilitate the use of decentralized authority?
3. At what point should Cumming consider centralizing certain functions? What functions are most likely to be centralized when and if that point is reached?

7–2 ORGANIZATION STRUCTURE OF SAXE REALTY COMPANY, SAN FRANCISCO

Saxe Realty Company, Inc., located in the San Francisco Bay area, was founded in 1938 by Jules and Marion Saxe. For most of its history, the company was a single-office agency run by its founders. But over time, the company grew in size and sales revenue. Company revenue increased from $1 million in 1973 to more than $10 million in 1979, and rather than a single office, the company had six branches located in the San Francisco and Marin County area.

The firm grew for many reasons. An important reason was the founders' ability to do certain things very well. They knew how to select locations, time moves, and design offices. They recruited and hired people with above-average ability and trained them to be effective salespersons. The rewards of growth were enjoyed by the Saxe family and employees of their firm. But with growth came problems.

The problems stemmed from the mismatch between the firm's organization structure, management practices, and the requirements of a large firm compared to a small one. In the early days, Saxe Realty could handle its business matters in simple and informal ways. After all, it was a family corporation and family members ran it as a family, not as a business.

Some of the problems which surfaced with growth included the absence of clearly defined roles and areas of responsibility. People held certain jobs because of family relationships, rather than skills. Important decisions were made by relatively few people who often were not knowledgeable of all available information. The firm, moreover, had no strategic plan; it responded and reacted to opportunities rather than being proactive. In a sense, the firm's success had simply outgrown its organization. Changes were necessary.

Saxe consequently had to make many changes in its operations and organization structure. The overriding consideration of all the changes was to move Saxe away from an "entrepreneurial-style" firm to a "professionally managed" one. Moreover, the change itself involved a process of preparation and implementation. Significant changes do not just come about; they must be planned and managed. But only the end results of the change are of interest here.

The organization structure which Saxe adopted relies upon geography as the basis for departmentation. There is a central office, and the branch offices report to that central office. Geographic departmentation encourages decentralization, one of the outcomes sought by Saxe's top management. Branch managers are responsible for the day-to-day activities of their branch offices. The central office maintains overall direction through planning and controlling processes. For example, each branch office participates in the annual planning process during which objectives for each branch are developed. These objectives are then the targets and the responsibility of branch managers.

Saxe's top management developed formal descriptions for all key positions. These descriptions defined the responsibilities of each job with special attention to avoiding overlap and duplication of effort. The company's experience during its entrepreneurial stage was that things often were not done because everyone assumed that someone else was doing them. In other instances, several people would assume responsibility for a task when it required the attention of only one person. Thus a key consideration in the new organization structure was to define explicitly and formally the work expected from each individual job.

Finally, the new structure provides for reporting channels from each branch associate to the chief executive officer. The chain of command is the channel for progress reports on planned objectives, financial and sales reports, and other informational needs. In comparison to the previous organization, the chain of command is much more explicit and formal. Individuals are encouraged to go through channels.

The entire change at Saxe was both extensive and time consuming. Nearly every aspect of the firm's operations was affected. And the changes will take two years or more to be fully implemented.

Questions:

1. Draw an organization chart which depicts the structure being implemented at Saxe.

2. What alternative structures could Saxe have implemented, and what would be the advantages of each in comparison to the one Saxe implemented?

3. What are the relationships between the planning function and the organizing function as depicted in the Saxe case?

Adapted from Clay E. Duncan and Eric G. Flamholtz, "Making the Transition from Entrepreneurship to a Professionally Managed Company," *Management Review*, January 1982, pp. 57–62.

EXERCISES

7-1 DESIGNING THE NEW VENTURE

Purpose: The purpose of this exercise is to provide students with first-hand experience in organizing a new business venture.

Setting Up the Exercise: A few years ago, George Ballas got so frustrated trying to keep his lawn neatly trimmed around the roots of oak trees that he developed what is now called the Weed Eater. The original Weed Eater was made from a popcorn can that had holes in it and was threaded with nylon fishing line. Weed Eater sales in 1972 totaled $568,000; but by 1978, sales were in excess of $100 million. There are now 20 or so similar devices on the market.

Two brothers from Pittsburgh, George and Jim Gammons, are starting a new venture called Lawn Trimmers, Inc. They are attempting to develop an organization that makes a profit by selling Lawn Trimmers that do not wear out for over 2,000 trimming applications. The Weed Eater and similar products often have breaks in the nylon lines that require the user to turn off the trimmer and readjust the line. The Gammons brothers have developed a new type of cutting fabric that is not physically harmful and cuts for over 2,000 applications.

In order to sell the Lawn Trimmers, the Gammons brothers will have to market their products through retail establishments. They will make the products in their shop in Pittsburgh and ship them to the retail establishments. The profits will come entirely from the sales of the Lawn Trimmers to retail establishments. The price of the product is already set, and it appears that there will be sufficient market demand to sell at least 6,000 Lawn Trimmers annually.

1. The instructor will set up teams of five to eight students to serve as organizational design experts who will provide the Gammons brothers with the best structure for their new venture. The groups should meet and establish a design that would be feasible for the Gammonses at this stage in their venture.

2. Each group should select a spokesperson to make a short presentation of the group's organizational design for the Gammonses.

3. The class should compare the various designs and discuss why there are similarities and differences in what is presented.

A Learning Note: This exercise will show that organizational design necessitates making assumptions about the market, competition, labor resources, scheduling, and profit margins, to name just a few areas. There is no one best design that should be regarded as a final answer.

EIGHT

Job Design

LEARNING OBJECTIVES

After completing Chapter 8, you should be able to:

Define: what is meant by the term, *job design*.

State: how jobs differ in range, depth, and relationships.

Describe: how managers can undertake job analysis.

Explain: why perceived job content is important.

Discuss: ways managers can change both the range and the depth of jobs to increase performance.

VW OBTAINS EMPLOYEE LOYALTY THROUGH JOB DESIGN

Volkswagen's growth from a one-car company located in Wolfsburg, West Germany, to a multinational automaker challenged its management to find ways to retain one of its important strengths, employee loyalty and commitment. VW's management must be constantly alert to cost and quality control opportunities because of its heavy reliance on foreign markets. In these markets VW's cars must compete directly with Japanese cars which have long had the edge in both cost and quality and American cars which are quickly regaining their reputation for reliability and economy. The opportunities for obtaining lower production costs and higher quality often means automation and modernization which can eliminate the jobs of production workers.

West Germany sells nearly one third of everything it makes in the world market. The country is even more dependent on foreign markets than Japan which sells 17 percent of its production overseas. Thus it is in the national interest for major industrial firms such as VW to remain competitive in world markets. All West German companies with multinational business must spend great sums on research and technology for both product development and production systems. For example, VW lost money in both 1982 and 1983, yet it made record investments in innovative and highly automated auto assembly lines. Today as a consequence of that investment, robots weld, paint, install batteries and tires on autos produced at the world's largest car factory. These improvements meant a loss of nearly 20 percent of the jobs formerly done by autoworkers.

VW's management recognized that its high-tech policy ran the danger of inciting its workers to retaliation in the form of strikes and walkouts. Similar circumstances had produced precisely those results in other European countries and in the United States. How then to avoid those unhappy and costly outcomes was the issue to be confronted.

(The Management Solution to this Management Incident can be found at the end of this chapter).

Jobs are the building blocks of organizational structures. Job design refers to the process by which managers determine individual job tasks and authority. Apart from the very practical issues associated with job design, that is, issues which relate to effectiveness in economic, political, and monetary terms, job designs have social and psychological implications. Jobs can be sources of psychological stress and even mental and physical impairment. On a more positive note, jobs can provide income, meaningful life experiences, self-esteem, esteem from others, regulation of our lives, and association with others. The performance of organizations and people depends upon how well management is able to design jobs.

In recent years the issue of designing jobs has gone beyond the determination of the most efficient way to perform tasks. The concept of quality of work life is now widely used to refer to "the degree to which members of work organizations are able to satisfy important personal needs through their experiences in organizations."[1] The emphasis on satisfaction of personal needs does not imply de-emphasis of organizational needs. Instead, contemporary managers are finding that when personal needs of employees are satisfied, the performance of the organization itself is enhanced.[2]

Job design and redesign techniques, attempt (1) to identify the most important needs of employees and the organization and (2) to remove obstacles in the workplace which frustrate those needs. Managers hope that the results are jobs which (*a*) fulfill important individual needs and (*b*) contribute to individual and organizational performance. The remainder of this chapter reviews selected job design techniques that facilitate the achievement of personal and organizational performance.

JOB ANALYSIS

Job analysis is the process of determining the tasks that make up the job and the skills, abilities, and responsibilities that are required of an individual in order to successfully accomplish the job. The information for obtaining the facts about a job is contained in what are called a *job description* and a *job specification*. These terms are used to describe the information for nonmanagerial jobs. When discussing managerial jobs, we use the terms *position description* and *position specification*. The relationship between job analysis, job description, and job specification is presented in Figure 8–1.

Job analysis provides information that can be used by every manager within the organization. For example, to recruit and select effectively, it is necessary to match qualified personnel with job requirements. The relevant set of job information is provided by the job description and the job specification. Another use of job information is to establish proper rates of pay. In order to have an equitable pay system, it is necessary to have a complete job description. An example of a job description and a job specification for a project general manager is provided in Figure 8–2.

---

[1]J. Richard Hackman and J. Lloyd Suttle, eds., *Improving Life at Work* (Santa Monica, Calif.: Goodyear Publishing, 1977), p. 4.

[2]Richard E. Kopelman, *Managing Productivity in Organizations: A Practical, People-Oriented Perspective* (New York: McGraw-Hill, 1986).

Figure 8–1 Job analysis components.

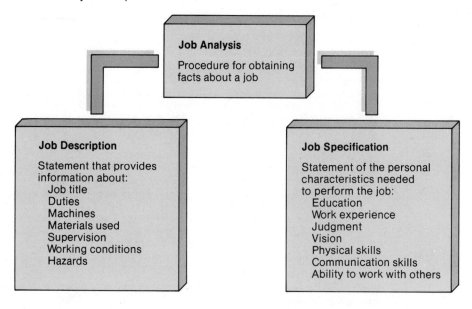

*Terms used primarily for nonmanagerial jobs. For managerial jobs, *position description* and *position specification* are the usual terms.

Performing an informative and accurate analysis of managerial jobs is no easy task. The duties of managers, such as those presented in the job description for the project general manager in Figure 8–2, are difficult to spell out. However, because of the range and types of managerial behaviors and duties, there must be a careful analysis of each managerial job. Suggested steps for gathering relevant information on managerial or nonmanagerial jobs include the following:

1. Accumulate systematic observations, reports, or records of many job behaviors of individuals carrying out the job.

2. Analyze these job behaviors and group them in sets; define the behaviors in the various sets.

3. Try to observe the job behaviors of job occupants, using the various sets developed in step 2.

4. Modify the behaviors, definitions, and sets after making new observations. By gathering information in this manner, better and more meaningful job descriptions can be created.

A good job analysis can provide the basic information needed for the recruitment and placement of people. Particular circumstances and laws affect the recruitment and placement of personnel. For organizations with low turnover that promote and transfer from within, external recruitment is rarely used. However, in high-turnover situations, external recruitment is essential. The company image also influences recruitment.

Figure 8–2
Job description and job specification.

Classification: Manager   Power Division (Eastern Base)

Title: Project General Manager

Summary: Manages engineering, procurement, operations, and construction of single-responsibility power project.

Specific duties:
1. Establishes with Owner and Power Division, Engineering, Operations, and Construction the basic criteria for project plan and schedules.
2. Reviews project status to measure performance and minimize delays.
3. Continually monitors project to identify and resolve potential or real problem areas.
4. Administers contract and coordinates contract changes.
5. Reviews and issues progress reports to Owner and Division management.
6. Reviews and issues Engineering and Construction change notices.
7. Reviews and issues estimates and cash flow schedules to provide financial information to Owner.
8 Arranges and conducts project status meetings with Owner, Engineering, Procurement, and Construction management.
9. Prepares Project Management Office procedures.
10. Performs other duties as assigned.

Supervisory responsibilities:
Directly supervises four or more project coordinators; indirectly supervises three or more project team leaders.

Desirable qualifications:
College degree in Engineering with 10 or more years of related experience or equivalent and professional registration in Illinois; with knowledge of power plant design and construction, planning and scheduling, cost engineering, procurement, estimating, and utility practices and requirements.

Companies such as Alcoa, Tenneco, Rockwell, TRW, and General Mills have such good reputations in the labor market that they have a steady flow of qualified job applicants who can perform the duties specified in the job descriptions.

Job analysis is the process of decision making which translates task, human, and technological factors into job designs. Either managers or personnel specialists undertake the process, and a number of approaches exist to assist them. Two of the more widely used approaches are functional job analysis (FJA) and position analysis questionnaire (PAQ).

Functional Job Analysis

Functional job analysis focuses attention on task and technological factors. FJA directs attention to the following four aspects of each job or class of jobs:

1. What the worker does in relation to data, people, and jobs.
2. What methods and techniques the worker uses.

3. What machines, tools, and equipment the worker uses.

4. What materials, products, subject matter, or services the worker produces.

The first three aspects relate to job activities. The fourth aspect relates to job performance. FJA provides descriptions of jobs which can be the bases for classifying jobs according to any one of the four dimensions. In addition to defining what activities, methods, and machines make up the job, FJA also defines what the individual doing the job should produce. FJA can, therefore, be the basis for defining standards of performance.

FJA is the most popular and widely used of the job analysis methods.[3] In addition, it is the basis for the most extensive available list of occupational titles.[4]

Position Analysis Questionnaire

The position analysis questionnaire takes into account human as well as task and technological factors. PAQ has been the object of considerable attention by researchers and practitioners alike who believe that accurate job analysis must take human factors into account.[5] PAQ analysis attempts to identify the following six job aspects:

1. Information sources critical to job performance.

2. Information processing and decision making critical to job performance.

3. Physical activity and dexterity required of the job.

4. Interpersonal relationships required of the job.

5. Physical working conditions and the reactions of individuals to those conditions.

6. Other job characteristics such as work schedules and work responsibilities.

It is important to note that FJA and PAQ overlap considerably. Each attempts to identify job activities that are necessary given the task to be done and the technology to do it with. But PAQ includes the additional consideration of the individual's psychological responses to the job and its environment. Thus PAQ attempts to acknowledge that job designs should combine the effects of all three factors.

Numerous methods exist to perform job analysis, and different methods can give

---

[3]Marc J. Wallace, Jr., N. Fredric Crandall, and Charles H. Fay, *Administering Human Resources* (New York: Random House, 1982), p. 196; and Roger J. Plachy, "Writing Job Descriptions that Get Results," *Personnel,* October 1987, pp. 56–63.

[4]U.S. Department of Labor, *Dictionary of Occupational Title,* 4th ed., (Washington, D.C.: U.S. Government Printing Office, 1977).

[5]E. J. McCormick, *Job Analysis: Methods and Applications* (New York: AMACOM, 1979); and E. J. McCormick, P. R. Jeanneret, and R. C. Mecham, "A Study of Job Characteristics and Job Dimensions as Based on the Position Analysis Questionnaire (PAQ)," *Journal of Applied Psychology,* August 1972, pp. 347–68.

different answers to important questions such as "How much is the job worth?"[6] Thus the selection of the method for performing job analysis is not trivial and is one of the most important decisions to be made in job design. As we noted, PAQ and FJA appear to be two of the most popular ones in practice. A recent survey of the opinions of expert job analysts bears out the popularity of PAQ and FJA.[7]

Job Analysis in Different Settings

People perform their jobs in a variety of settings. It is not possible to discuss them all. We will, instead, discuss two significant job settings—the factory and the office.

Jobs in the factory.   Job analysis began in the factory. Industrialization created the setting in which individuals perform many hundreds of specialized jobs. The earliest attempts to do job analysis followed the ideas advanced by the proponents of scientific management. They were industrial engineers who, at the turn of the 20th century, began to devise ways to analyze industrial jobs.

The major theme of scientific management is that objective analyses of facts and data collected in the workplace could provide the bases for determining the one best way to design work.[8] F. W. Taylor stated the essence of scientific management as follows:

> First: Develop a science for each element of a man's work which replaces the old rule-of-thumb method.
>
> Second: Scientifically select and then train, teach, and develop the workman, whereas in the past he chose his own work and trained himself as best he could.
>
> Third: Heartily cooperate with the men so as to ensure all of the work being done in accordance with the principles of the science which has been developed.
>
> Fourth: There is almost an equal division of the work and the responsibility between the management and the workmen. The management takes over all work for which they are better fitted than the workmen, while in the past, almost all of the work and the greater part of the responsibility were thrown upon the men.[9]

---

[6]Robert M. Madigan and David J. Hoover, "Effects of Alternative Job Evaluation Methods on Decisions Involving Pay Equity," *Academy of Management Journal,* March 1986, pp. 84–100; and Edward H. Lawler III, "What's Wrong with Point-Factor Job Evaluation," *Personnel,* January 1987, pp. 38–44.

[7]Edward L. Levine, Ronald A. Ash, Hardy Hall, and Frank Sistrunk, "Evaluation of Job Analysis Methods by Experienced Job Analysis," *Academy of Management Journal,* June 1983, pp. 339–48.

[8]The literature of scientific management is voluminous. The original works and the subsequent criticisms and interpretations would make a large volume. Of special significance are the works of the principal authors including: Frederick W. Taylor, *Principles of Scientific Management* (New York: Harper & Row, 1911); Harrington Emerson, *The Twelve Principles of Efficiency* (New York: The Engineering Magazine, 1913); Henry L. Gantt, *Industrial Leadership* (New Haven, Conn.: Yale University Press, 1916); Frank B. Gilbreth, *Motion Study* (New York: Van Nostrand Rheinhold, 1911); and Lillian M. Gilbreth, *The Psychology of Management* (New York: Sturgis & Walton, 1914).

[9]Taylor, *Principles of Scientific Management,* pp. 36–37.

These four principles express the theme of scientific management methods. Management should determine the best way for each job and then train people to do the job according to that method.

Scientific management produced many techniques in current use. Motion and time study, work simplification, and standard methods are at the core of job analysis in factory settings. Functional job analysis reflects the scientific management philosophy in that it excludes consideration of the human factor.

Jobs in the office. In the short space of time since the advent of scientific management, the American economy has shifted from factory-oriented to office-oriented work. The fastest growing segment of jobs is secretarial, clerical, and information workers. The growth of these jobs is the result of technological breakthroughs in both settings.

Technological breakthroughs in automation, robotics, and computer-assisted manufacturing have reduced the need for industrial jobs. But that same technology has increased the need for office jobs. The modern office is not a mere extension of the traditional factory. The modern office reflects the new computer technology. Its most striking feature is the replacement of paper with some electronic medium, usually a visual display terminal (VDT). One individual interacts with the VDT to do a variety and quantity of tasks which in earlier times would have required many individuals. A significant aspect of job analysis in modern offices is the creation of work modules, interrelated tasks that can be assigned to a single individual.

In recent times, managers and researchers have found that human factors must be given special attention when analyzing jobs in the electronic office. VDT operators report that they suffer visual and postural problems such as headaches, burning eyes, and shoulder and backaches.[10] The sources of these problems seem to be in the design of the workplace particularly the interaction between the individual and the VDT.

Job analysis in the office must pay particular attention to human factors. The tendency is to overemphasize the technological factor—in this case, the computer— and to analyze jobs only as an extension of the technology. As was true of job analysis in factories, it is simply easier to deal with the relatively fixed nature of tasks and technology than to deal with the variable human nature.[11]

JOB DESIGNS

Job designs are the results of job analysis. They specify three characteristics of jobs: range, depth, and relationships.

---

[10]Barbara S. Brown, Key Dismukes, and Edward J. Rinalducci, "Video Display Terminals and Vision of Workers: Summary and Review of a Symposium," *Behavior and Information Technology*, April–June 1982, pp. 121–40; and John Storey, "The Management of New Office Technology," *Journal of Management Studies*, January 1987, pp. 43–62.

[11]David A. Buchanon and David Boddy, "Advanced Technology and the Quality of Working Life: The Effects of Word Processing on Video Typists," *Journal of Occupational Psychology*, March 1982, pp. 1–11; and Walter B. Kleeman, "The Future of the Office," *Environment and Behavior*, September 1982, pp. 593–610.

Range and Depth

The range of a job refers to the number of tasks a job holder performs. The individual who performs eight tasks to complete a job has a wider job range than a person performing four tasks. In most instances, the greater the number of tasks performed the longer it takes to complete the job.

A second job characteristic is depth, the amount of discretion an individual has, to decide job activities and job outcomes. In many instances job depth relates to personal influence as well as delegated authority. Thus, an employee with the same job title and at the same organizational level as another employee may possess more, less, or the same amount of job depth because of personal influence.

Job range and depth distinguish one job from another not only within the same organization, but also among different organizations. To illustrate how jobs differ in range and depth, Figure 8–3 depicts the differences for selected jobs of business firms, hospitals, and universities. For example, business research scientists, hospital chiefs of surgery, and university presidents generally have high job range and significant depth. Research scientists perform a large number of tasks and are usually not closely supervised. Chiefs of surgery have significant job range in that they oversee and counsel on many diverse surgical matters. In addition, they are not supervised closely, and they have the authority to influence hospital surgery policies and procedures.

University presidents have a large number of tasks to perform. They speak to alumni groups, politicians, community representatives, and students. They develop, with the consultation of others, policies on admissions, fund raising, and adult education. They can alter the faculty recruitment philosophy and thus alter the course of the entire institution. For example, a university president may want to build an institution that is noted for high-quality classroom instruction and for providing excellent services to the community. This thrust may lead to recruiting and selecting professors who want to concentrate on these two specific goals. In contrast, another president may want to foster outstanding research and high-quality classroom instruction. Of course, another president may attempt to develop an institution that is noted for instruction, research, and service. The critical point is that university presidents have sufficient depth to alter the course of a university's direction.

Examples of jobs which have high depth and low range are packaging machine mechanics, anesthesiologists, and faculty members. Mechanics perform the limited tasks that pertain to repairing and maintaining packaging machines. But they can decide how breakdowns on the package machine are to be repaired. The discretion means that the mechanics have relatively high job depth.

Anesthesiologists also perform a limited number of tasks. They are concerned with the rather restricted task of administering anesthetics to surgical patients. However, they can decide the type of anesthetic to be administered in a particular situation, decisions indicative of high job depth. University professors specifically engaged in classroom instruction have relatively low job range. Teaching involves comparatively more tasks than the work of the anesthesiologist, yet fewer tasks than that of the business research scientist. However, professors' job depth is greater than that of graduate student instructors. This follows from the fact that they determine how they will conduct the class, what materials will be presented, and the standards to be used

Figure 8–3   Job depth and range.

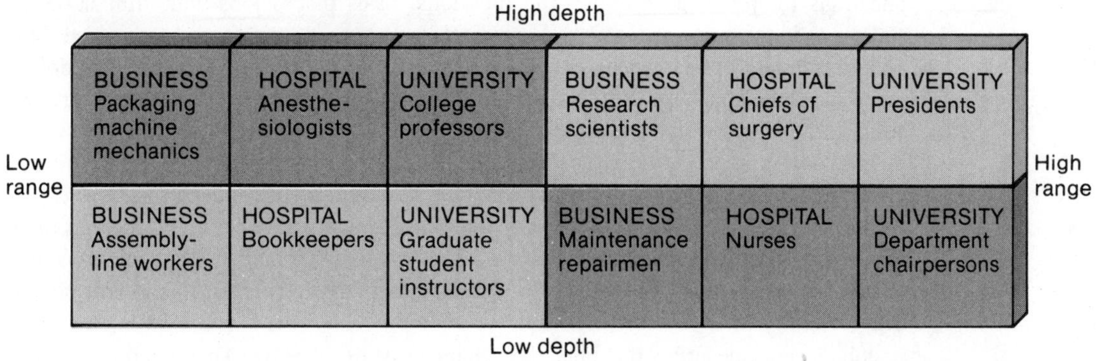

High depth

BUSINESS Packaging machine mechanics	HOSPITAL Anesthe-siologists	UNIVERSITY College professors	BUSINESS Research scientists	HOSPITAL Chiefs of surgery	UNIVERSITY Presidents
BUSINESS Assembly-line workers	HOSPITAL Bookkeepers	UNIVERSITY Graduate student instructors	BUSINESS Maintenance repairmen	HOSPITAL Nurses	UNIVERSITY Department chairpersons

Low range

High range

Low depth

in evaluating students. Graduate students typically do not have complete freedom in the choice of class materials and procedures. Professors decide these matters for them.

Highly specialized jobs are those which have few tasks to accomplish by prescribed means. Such jobs are quite routine; they also tend to be controlled by specified rules and procedures (low depth). A highly despecialized job (high range) has many tasks to accomplish within the framework of discretion over means and ends (high depth). Within an organization there typically are great differences among jobs in both range and depth. Although there are no precise equations which managers can use to decide job range and depth, they can follow this guideline: Given the economic and technical requirements of the organization's mission, goals, and objectives, what is the optimal point along the continuum of range and depth for each job?

Job Relationships

Job relationships are determined by managers' decisions regarding departmentation bases and spans of control. The resulting groups become the responsibility of a manager to coordinate toward organization purposes. These decisions also determine the nature and extent of job holders' interpersonal relationships, individually and within groups. Group performance is affected in part by group cohesiveness. And the degree of group cohesiveness depends upon the quality and kind of interpersonal relationships of job holders assigned to a group.

The wider the span of control, the larger the group, and consequently the more difficult it is to establish friendship and interest relationships. Simply, people in larger groups are less likely to communicate (and interact sufficiently to form interpersonal ties) than people in smaller groups. Without the opportunity to communicate, people will be unable to establish cohesive work groups. Thus, an important source of satisfaction may be lost for individuals who seek to fulfill social and esteem needs through relationships with co-workers.

The basis for departmentation which management selects also has important implications for job relationships. The functional basis places jobs with similar depth and range in the same groups, while product, territory, and customer bases place jobs with dissimilar depth and range. Thus in functional departments, people will be doing much the same specialty. Product, territory, and customer departments, however, are comprised of jobs which are quite different and heterogeneous. Individuals who work in heterogeneous departments experience feelings of dissatisfaction, stress, and involvement more intensely than those in homogeneous, functional departments. People with homogeneous backgrounds, skills, and training have more common interests than those with heterogeneous ones. Thus it is easier for them to establish social relationships which are satisfying with less stress, but also less involvement in the department's activities.

Job designs describe the objective characteristics of jobs. That is, through job analysis techniques such as FJA and PAQ, managers can describe jobs in terms of required activities to produce a specified outcome. But there is yet another factor to be considered before we can understand the relationship between jobs and performance: perceived job content.

PERCEIVED JOB CONTENT

Perceived job content refers to aspects of a job which define its general nature as perceived by the job holder as influenced by the social setting. It is important to distinguish between the objective properties and the subjective properties of a job as reflected in the perceptions of people who perform them. Managers cannot understand the causes of job performance without consideration of individual differences such as personality, needs, and span of attention. Thus if managers desire to increase job performance by changing job content, they can change job design, individual perceptions, or social settings. These factors are the causes of job content.

Individuals perceive and describe their jobs using many different adjectives. These adjectives describe aspects of the job's range, depth, and relationship and are termed *job characteristics*. Figure 8–4 defines selected job characteristics. Terms such as *variety, task identity,* and *feedback* are perceptions of job range. *Autonomy* is the perception of job depth; and *dealing with others* and *friendship opportunities* reflect perceptions of job relationships. Employees sharing similar perceptions, job designs, and social settings should report similar job characteristics. Employees with different perceptions, however, will perceive different job characteristics of the same job. For example, an individual with a high need for social belonging would perceive "friendship opportunities" differently than another individual with a low need for social belonging.[12]

Jobs can be designed so as to provide high levels of any or all of the important job characteristics. Many organizations have devised ways to increase employees' perceptions as illustrated in the following Management Application.

---

[12]Ramon J. Aldag, Steve H. Barr, and Arthur P. Brief, "Measurement of Perceived Task Characteristics," *Psychological Bulletin,* November 1981, pp. 415–31.

Figure 8–4 Selected job characteristics.

- **Variety.** The degree to which a job requires employees to perform a wide range of operations in their work and/or the degree to which employees must use a variety of equipment and procedures in their work.
- **Autonomy.** The extent to which employees have a major say in scheduling their work, selecting the equipment they will use, and deciding on procedures to be followed.
- **Task identity.** The extent to which employees do an entire or whole piece of work and can clearly identify with the results of their efforts.
- **Feedback.** The degree to which employees, as they are working, receive information that reveals how well they are performing on the job.
- **Dealing with others.** The degree to which a job requires employees to deal with other people to complete their work.
- **Friendship opportunities.** The degree to which a job allows employees to talk with one another on the job and to establish informal relationships with other employees at work.

MANAGEMENT APPLICATION

ROHM & HAAS BAYPORT'S JOB DESIGN

Rohm & Haas Bayport was founded in 1981 to produce specialty chemicals. The plant is located in LaPorte, Texas, and its 67 employees play active roles in management because their jobs are designed with that activity in mind. The company's philosophy is to provide autonomy and responsibility in each individual's job and, consequently, to enable employees to feel a sense of "ownership" of key decisions and actions. Every person in the organization is trained to be and to act like a manager. The 46 process engineer technicians and 15 engineers and chemists report to one of the two manufacturing unit managers who in turn report to the executive team.

The technicians make operating decisions among themselves while working in teams of four to seven people. The company has no shift foremen or line supervisors in the usual sense of these positions. Rather, the technicians are expected to be self-managed. Team members rotate jobs with other team members every 4 to 12 weeks to provide task variety and cross-training. They are also trained to do routine maintenance and repairs of their equipment and not to depend on a separate maintenance unit for that support. The company's idea is to give individuals almost complete control of the conditions that govern work pace and quality. They evaluate each other's performance and interview applicants for positions. The job designs at Rohm & Haas Bayport contribute to individual performance according to company spokespersons.

Source: Adapted from Don Nichols, "Taking Participative Management to the Limit," *Management Review*, August 1987, pp. 28–32.

Differences in social settings of work also affect perceptions of job content. Examples of social setting differences include leadership style[13] and what other people say about the job.[14] As has been pointed out by more than one expert, how one perceives a job is greatly affected by what other people say about it. Thus if one's friends state their jobs are boring, one is likely to state that her job is also boring. If the individual perceives the job as boring, job performance will no doubt suffer. Job content, then, results from the interaction of many factors in the work situation.

JOB PERFORMANCE

The purpose of job design is to encourage job performance. Job performance includes a number of outcomes. In this section we will discuss performance outcomes that have value to the organization and to the individual.

Objective Outcomes

Quantity and quality of output, absenteeism, tardiness, and turnover are objective outcomes that can be measured in quantitative terms. For each job, implicit or explicit standards exist for each of these objective outcomes. Industrial engineering studies establish standards for daily quantity, and quality control specialists establish tolerance limits for acceptable quality. These aspects of job performance account for characteristics of the product, client, or service for which the job holder is responsible. But job performance includes other outcomes.

Personal Behavior Outcomes

The job holder reacts to the work itself and also reacts by either attending regularly or by being absent, by staying with the job or by quitting. Moreover, physiological and health-related problems can ensue as a consequence of job performance. Stress related to job performance can contribute to physical and mental impairment; accidents and occupationally related disease can also ensue.

Intrinsic and Extrinsic Outcomes

Job outcomes include intrinsic and extrinsic work outcomes. The distinction between intrinsic and extrinsic outcomes is important for understanding the reactions of people to their jobs. In a general sense, intrinsic outcomes are objects or events which follow from the worker's own efforts, not requiring the involvement of any other person.

---

[13]Ricky W. Griffin, "Supervisory Behavior as a Source of Perceived Task Scope," *Journal of Occupational Psychology,* September 1981, pp. 175–82.

[14]Joe Thomas and Ricky W. Griffin, "The Social Information Processing Model of Task Design: A Review of the Literature," *Academy of Management Review,* October 1983, pp. 672–82; Ricky W. Griffin, "Objective and Subjective Sources of Information in Task Redesign: A Field Experiment," *Administrative Science Quarterly,* June 1983, pp. 184–200; and Jeffrey Pfeffer, "A Partial Test of the Social Information-Processing Model of Job Attitudes," *Human Relations,* July 1980, pp. 457–76.

More simply, it is an outcome clearly related to action on the worker's part. Such outcomes typically are thought to be solely in the province of professional and technical jobs; yet all jobs potentially have opportunities for intrinsic outcomes. Such outcomes involve feelings of responsibility, challenge, and recognition; the outcomes result from such job characteristics as variety, autonomy, identity, and significance.[15]

Extrinsic outcomes, however, are objects or events which follow from the workers' own efforts in conjunction with other factors or persons not directly involved in the job itself. Pay, working conditions, co-workers, and even supervision are objects in the workplace which are potentially job outcomes, but which are not a fundamental part of the work. Dealing with others and friendship interactions are sources of extrinsic outcomes.

Job Satisfaction Outcome

Job satisfaction depends on the levels of intrinsic and extrinsic outcomes and how the job holder views those outcomes. These outcomes have different values for different people. For some people, responsible and challenging work may have neutral or even negative values. For other people, such work outcomes may have high positive values. People differ in the importance they attach to job outcomes. Those differences alone would account for different levels of job satisfaction for essentially the same job tasks.

Another important individual difference is job involvement.[16] People differ in the extent that: (1) work is a central life interest; (2) they actively participate in work; (3) they perceive work as central to self-esteem; and (4) they perceive work as consistent with self-concept. Persons who are not involved in their work cannot be expected to realize the same satisfaction as those who are. This variable accounts for the fact that two workers could report different levels of satisfaction for the same performance levels. A final individual difference is the perceived equity of the outcome in terms of what the job holder considers a fair reward. If the outcomes are perceived to be unfair in relation to those of others in similar jobs requiring similar effort, the job holder will experience dissatisfaction and seek means to restore the equity, either by seeking greater rewards (primarily extrinsic) or by reducing effort.

Thus we see that job performance includes many potential outcomes. Some are of primary value to the organization—the objective outcomes, for example. Other outcomes are of primary importance to the individual—job satisfaction. Job performance is, without doubt, a complex variable that depends upon the interplay of numerous factors. Nevertheless, managers have at their disposal a number of approaches to guide their job design and redesign decisions. The next section reviews the most important of these approaches.

---

[15]Hugh J. Arnold, "Task Performance, Perceived Competence, and Attributed Causes of Performance as Determinates of Intrinsic Motivation," *Academy of Management Journal,* December 1985, pp. 876–88.

[16]S. D. Saleh and James Hosek, "Job Involvement: Concepts and Measurements," *Academy of Management Journal,* June 1976, pp. 213–24.

REDESIGNING JOB RANGE: JOB ROTATION AND JOB ENLARGEMENT

The earliest attempts to redesign jobs date to the scientific management area. The efforts at that time emphasized efficiency criteria. In so doing, the individual tasks which comprise a job are limited, uniform, and repetitive. This practice leads to narrow job range, and consequently, reported high levels of job discontent, turnover, absenteeism, and dissatisfaction. Accordingly, strategies were devised which resulted in wider job range through increasing the required activities of jobs. Two of these approaches are job rotation and job enlargement.

Job Rotation

Managers of organizations such as Western Electric, Ford, Bethlehem Steel, and TRW Systems have utilized different forms of the job rotation strategy. This practice involves rotating an individual from one job to another. In so doing, the individual is expected to complete more job activities since each job includes different tasks. Job rotation involves increasing the range of jobs and the perception of variety in the job content. Increasing task variety should increase the intrinsic value associated with job satisfaction. However, the practice of job rotation does not change the basic characteristics of the assigned jobs. Critics state that this approach involves nothing more than having people perform several boring and monotonous jobs rather than one. An alternative strategy is job enlargement.

Job Enlargement

The pioneering Walker and Guest study[17] was concerned with the social and psychological problems associated with mass production jobs in automobile assembly plants. They found that many workers were dissatisfied with their highly specialized jobs. In particular, they disliked mechanical pacing, repetitiveness of operations, and a lack of a sense of accomplishment. Walker and Guest also found a positive relationship between job range and job satisfaction. The findings of this research gave early support for motivation theories which predict that increases in job range will increase job satisfaction and other, objective, job outcomes. Job enlargement strategies focus upon the opposite of dividing work—they are a form of despecialization or increasing the number of tasks which an employee performs. For example, a job is designed such that the individual performs six tasks instead of three.

Although in many instances an enlarged job requires a longer training period, job satisfaction usually increases because boredom is reduced. The implication, of course, is that the job enlargement will lead to improvement in other performance outcomes.

The concept and practice of job enlargement have become considerably more sophisticated. In recent years effective job enlargement involves more than simply in-

[17]Arthur N. Turner and Paul R. Lawrence, *Industrial Jobs and the Worker: An Investigation of Response to Task Attributes* (Cambridge, Mass.: Harvard University Press, 1965).

creasing task variety. In addition, it is necessary to redesign certain other aspects of job range, including providing the worker-paced (rather than machine-paced) control.[18] Each of these changes involves balancing the gains and losses of varying degrees of division of labor.

Some employees cannot cope with enlarged jobs because they cannot comprehend complexity; moreover, they may not have an attention span sufficiently long to stay with and complete an enlarged set of tasks. However, if employees are known to be amenable to job enlargement and if they have the required ability, then job enlargement should increase satisfaction and product quality and decrease absenteeism and turnover. These gains are not without costs, including the likelihood that employees will demand larger salaries in exchange for their performance of enlarged jobs. Yet these costs must be borne if management desires to implement the redesign strategy which enlarges job depth and job enrichment. Job enlargement is a necessary precondition for job enrichment.

REDESIGNING JOB DEPTH: JOB ENRICHMENT

The impetus for redesigning job depth was provided by Herzberg's two-factor theory of motivation.[19] The basis of his theory is that factors which meet individuals' need for psychological growth, especially responsibility, job challenge, and achievement must be characteristic of their jobs. The application of his theory is termed *job enrichment*. The implementation of job enrichment is realized through direct changes in job depth. Managers can provide employees with greater opportunities to exercise discretion by making the following changes:

1. *Direct feedback:* The evaluation of performance should be timely and direct.
2. *New learning:* A good job enables people to feel that they are growing. All jobs should provide opportunities to learn.
3. *Scheduling:* People should be able to schedule some part of their own work.
4. *Uniqueness:* Each job should have some unique qualities or features.
5. *Control over resources:* Individuals should have some control over their job tasks.
6. *Personal accountability:* People should be provided with an opportunity to be accountable for the job.

As defined by the executive in charge of a pioneering job enrichment program at Texas Instruments (TI), job enrichment is a process which (1) encourages employees to behave like managers in managing their jobs, and (2) redesigns the job to make

---

[18]Kae H. Chung and Monica F. Ross, "Differences in Motivational Properties between Job Enlargement and Job Enrichment," *Academy of Management Review*, January 1977, pp. 114–15.

[19]Frederick Herzberg, "The Wise Old Turk," *Harvard Business Review*, September–October 1974, pp. 70–80.

such behavior feasible.[20] The process as implemented at TI is continuous and pervades the entire organization. Every one of the jobs at TI is viewed as subject to analysis to determine if it can be enriched to include managerial activities, and thereby made more meaningful. Moreover, as the jobs of nonmanagerial personnel are redesigned to include greater depth, the jobs of managers must be redesigned. The redesigned managerial jobs emphasize training and counseling of subordinates and de-emphasize control and direction. An application of job enrichment in a nonmanufacturing setting is illustrated in the following Management Application.

MANAGEMENT APPLICATION

JOB ENRICHMENT AT CITIBANK

Citibank extensively changed the ways its employees did their work. According to George E. Seegers, a bank vice president, a customer survey indicated that the bank scored very low on "customer service." Upon examining the causes of the problem, the bank management concluded that the reason was that its employees didn't "feel like somebody." They were dissatisfied with their rather mundane jobs created in part by the decision of the bank, some time ago, to introduce automatic teller machines. Building on the idea that everybody wants to feel like somebody, the bank undertook extensive changes designed to recognize the individuality of employees as well as customers. Among the many changes implemented were the following:

Encouraging communications between the functional departments: operations, marketing and servicing.

Decentralizing operations so that one person could handle an entire transaction from the time it comes into the bank until it leaves.

Putting the employees who do the job in direct contact with the customers and the computers.

Asking the people who do the job what is boring and/or troublesome before automating.

Undertaking considerable training and education for the entire work force.

These changes in job design were done over a two-year period. The changes were accompanied by training sessions which taught the new skills. It was also necessary to develop new attitudes among the management personnel including the attitude that employee opinions are valuable and desirable inputs into decisions.

Source: Adapted from Roy W. Walters, "The Citibank Project: Improving Productivity through Work Design," in *How to Manage Change Effectively*, ed. Donald L. Kirkpatrick (San Francisco: Jossey-Bass, 1985), pp. 195–208.

As the theory and practice of job enrichment have evolved, managers have become aware that successful applications require numerous changes in the way work is done.

---

[20]M. Scott Myers, *Every Employee a Manager* (New York: McGraw-Hill, 1970), p. xii.

Some of the more important changes include delegating greater authority to workers to participate in decisions, to set their own goals, and to evaluate their (and their work groups') performance. Job enrichment also involves changing the nature and style of managers' behavior. Managers must be willing and able to delegate authority. Given the ability of employees to carry out enriched jobs and the willingness of managers to delegate authority, gains in performance can be expected. These positive outcomes are the result of increasing employees' beliefs that efforts lead to performance, that performance leads to intrinsic and extrinsic rewards, and that these rewards have power to satisfy needs. These significant changes in managerial jobs when coupled with changes in nonmanagerial jobs suggest the importance of a supportive work environment as a prerequisite for successful job enrichment efforts.[21]

Job enrichment and job enlargement are not competing strategies. Job enlargement but not job enrichment may be compatible with the needs, values, and abilities of some individuals. Yet job enrichment, when appropriate, necessarily involves job enlargement. A promising new approach to job redesign which attempts to integrate the two approaches is the job characteristic model devised by Hackman, Oldham, Janson, and Purdy.[22]

REDESIGNING JOB RANGE AND DEPTH: JOB CHARACTERISTICS MODEL

The job characteristics model attempts to account for the interrelationships among: (1) certain job characteristics, (2) psychological states associated with motivation, satisfaction, and performance, (3) job outcomes, and (4) growth need strength. Figure 8–5 describes the relationships among these variables. Although variety, identity, significance, autonomy, and feedback do not completely describe perceived job content, they, according to this model, sufficiently describe those aspects which management can manipulate to bring about gains in productivity. You can measure how important these job characteristics are to you by completing the Job Design Preference form in Table 8-1.

The steps which management can take to increase the core dimensions include combining task elements, assigning whole pieces of work (i.e., work modules), allowing discretion in selection of work methods, permitting self-paced control, and opening feedback channels. These actions increase task variety, identity, and significance; consequently the "experienced meaningfulness of work" psychological state is increased. By permitting employee participation and self-evaluation and creating autonomous work groups, the feedback and autonomy dimensions are increased along

---

[21]Gerald R. Ferris and David C. Gilmore, "The Moderating Role of Work Context in Job Design Research: A Test of Competing Models," *Academy of Management Journal*, December 1984, pp. 885–92; and Edwin A. Locke and Richard L. Somers, "The Effects of Goal Emphasis on Performance on a Complex Task," *Journal of Management Studies*, July 1987, pp. 405–12.

[22]J. Richard Hackman, Greg Oldham, Robert Janson, and Kenneth Purdy, "New Strategy for Job Enrichment," *California Management Review*, Summer 1975, pp. 57–71; and J. Richard Hackman and Greg Oldham, "Development of the Job Diagnostic Survey," *Journal of Applied Psychology*, April 1975, pp. 159–70.

Figure 8–5 The job characteristics model.

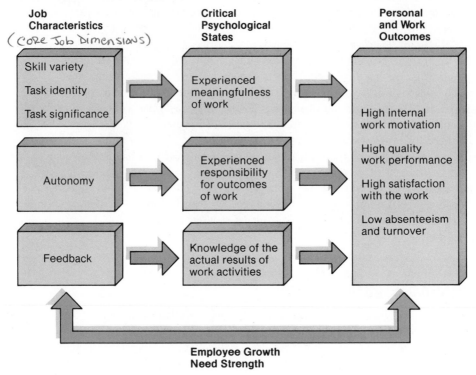

Source: J. Richard Hackman and Greg R. Oldham, "Development of the Job Diagnostic Survey," *Journal of Applied Psychology,* vol. 60 (1975), pp. 159–70.

with the psychological states "experienced responsibility" and "knowledge of actual results."

The positive benefits of these redesign efforts are moderated by individual differences in the strength of employees' growth needs. That is, employees with strong needs for accomplishment, learning, and challenge will respond more positively than those with relatively weak growth needs. Employees forced to participate in job redesign programs but who lack either the need strength or the ability to perform redesigned jobs may experience stress, anxiety, adjustment problems, erratic performance, turnover, and absenteeism.

The available research on the interrelationships between perceived job content and performance are meager. One recent survey of 30 actual applications of job redesign strategies confirms that failures are as frequent as successes.[23] It is apparent, however, that managers must cope with significant problems in matching employee needs and

---

[23]Richard E. Kopelman, "Job Redesign and Productivity: A Review of the Evidence," *National Productivity Review,* Summer 1985, pp. 237–61.

Table 8–1 Assessment of preferred job characteristics.

The Job Design Preferences form is presented below. Please read it carefully, and complete it after considering each of the characteristics listed. Due to space limitations, not all job design characteristics are included. Use only the ones on the form.

Job Design Preferences

A. Your Job Design Preferences

Decide which of the following characteristics is most important to you. Place a *1* in front of the most important characteristic. Then decide which characteristic is the second most important to you and place a *2* in front of it. Continue numbering the items in order of importance until the least important is ranked *10*. There are no right answers, since individuals differ in their job design preferences.

___ Variety in tasks
___ Feedback on performance from doing the job
___ Autonomy
___ Working as a team
___ Responsibility
___ Developing friendships on the job
___ Task identity
___ Task significance
___ Having the resources to perform well
___ Feedback on performance from others (e.g., the manager, co-workers)

B. Others' Job Design Preferences

In section A, you have listed your job design preferences. Now number the items as you think others would rank them. Consider others in your course, class, or program who also are completing this exercise. Rank the factors from 1 (most important) to 10 (least important).

___ Variety in tasks
___ Feedback on performance from doing the job
___ Autonomy
___ Working as a team
___ Responsibility
___ Developing friendships on the job
___ Task identity
___ Task significance
___ Having the resources to perform well
___ Feedback on performance from others (e.g., the manager, co-workers)

---

differences and organizational needs.[24] The problems associated with job redesign are several including:

1. The program is time consuming and costly.

2. Unless lower level needs are satisfied, people will not respond to opportunities to satisfy upper level needs. And even though our society has been rather successful in providing food and shelter, these needs

---

[24]William E. Zierden, "Congruence in the Work Situation: Effects of Growth Needs, Management Style, and Job Structure on Job-Related Satisfactions," *Journal of Occupational Behavior*, October 1980, pp. 297–310.

regain importance when the economy moves through periods of recession and inflation.

3. Job redesign programs are intended to satisfy needs typically not satisfied in the workplace. As workers are told to expect higher order need satisfaction, they may raise their expectations beyond that which is possible. Dissatisfaction with the program's unachievable aims may displace dissatisfaction with the jobs.

4. Finally job redesign may be resisted by labor unions who see the effort as an attempt to get more work with the same pay.

Practical efforts to improve productivity and satisfaction through implementation of job redesign strategy have emphasized autonomy and feedback. Relatively less emphasis has been placed on identity, significance, and variety.[25] Apparently it is easier to provide individuals with greater responsibility for the total task and increased feedback than to change the essential nature of the task itself. To provide identity, significance, and variety often requires enlarging the task to the point of losing the benefits of work simplification and standardization. But within the economic constraints imposed by the logic of specialization, it is possible to design work so as to give individuals complete responsibility for its completion to the end and at the same time to provide supportive managerial monitoring.

These and other problems account for many failed efforts to achieve satisfactory results with job redesign efforts. Despite the instances of failure, organizations continue to search for ways to improve job designs. The following Management Application describes an instance of providing challenge to employees through job design by defining job objectives that stretch the individual's capabilities.

MANAGEMENT APPLICATION

"STRETCH" OBJECTIVES IN JOB DESIGN

DePuy is a 700-employee division of Boehringer Mannheim Corporation. The corporation is a high-tech, growth-oriented producer of medical devices. The DePuy Division's culture encourages an informal, participative management style. Employees generally like to work for the company. In the mid-1980s, the division's management saw the need to review its performance in light of information that indicated the next several years would be difficult ones for the company. In fact DePuy's management sensed the need to encourage every employee to make a stronger commitment to specific results that would contribute to the firm's performance. Management made the decision to redesign jobs to include objectives that would stretch the ability of each individual to achieve them.

The job descriptions were revised to include not only regular job duties and performance standards, but also to include a "stretch dimension." This addition was to be objectives that would be written into the job description. The objectives would be included only after discussions between each individual and manager and would have

---

[25]Kopelman, "Job Design and Productivity," p. 253.

to be judged as truly innovative and creative. The success of DePuy in developing these job designs no doubt reflects the confidence of employees in company management and as well as commitment to the company's well-being.

Source: Adapted from B. Taylor Seward, "Revitalizing MBO: The Stretch Dimension," *Management Review*, October 1987, pp. 16–19.

In general, the conclusion that one reaches, when considering the experience of job redesign approaches, is that they are relatively successful in increasing quality of output, but not quantity. This conclusion pertains, however, only if the reward system already satisfies lower-level needs. If it presently does not satisfy lower-level needs, employees cannot be expected to experience upper-level need satisfaction (intrinsic rewards) through enriched jobs. Since a primary source of organizational effectiveness is job performance, managers should design jobs according to the best available knowledge. At present, the strategies for designing and redesigning jobs have evolved from scientific management approaches to work design with emphasis on quality of work-life issues in the context of rapidly changing technology.

MANAGEMENT SOLUTION

VW SHARES DECISION MAKING

The opportunity to share and to take responsibility for important decisions is a key job characteristic. VW's management builds into the job of each production worker the expectation that the job holder will share with management the responsibility for important decisions. In part the practice is required by a law that requires all major firms to give half the votes on their supervisory boards to labor representatives. But the law only provides the opportunity to involve employees in decision making. Many companies are unable to take advantage of the opportunity. VW on the other hand has integrated the practice of sharing power throughout the organization by making responsibility for decision making an element of job performance for managers and workers alike.

The attitude of management toward the work force disavows blind obedience to the directives of managers. Rather management pays careful attention to the social aspects of company decisions and in particular the impact of these decisions on the work force. Consequently the idea that workers should be responsible not only for their jobs but for the future of the company is a natural outcome. Job designs which include the provision that job holders recognize their contribution to and responsibility for the organization's general welfare makes sense in Volkswagen. Through this practice the company has developed and maintained a stable and loyal work force.

Source: Adapted from Dennis Phillips, "How VW Builds Worker Loyalty Worldwide," *Management Review*, June 1987, pp. 37–40

MANAGEMENT SUMMARY

☐ Job design involves managerial decisions and actions which specify job depth, range, and relationships to satisfy organizational requirements as well as the social and personal requirements of the job holders.

☐ Contemporary managers must consider the issue of quality of work life when designing jobs. The issue reflects society's concern for work experiences which contribute to the personal growth and development of employees.

☐ Strategies for increasing the potential of jobs to satisfy the social and personal requirements of job holders have gone through an evolutionary process. Initial efforts were directed toward job enlargement. This strategy produced some gains in job satisfaction but did not change primary motivators such as responsibility, achievement, and autonomy.

☐ During the 1960s, job enrichment became a widely recognized strategy for improving quality of work-life factors. This strategy is based upon Herzberg's motivation theory and involves increasing the depth of jobs through greater delegation of authority to job holders. Despite some major successes, job enrichment is not universally applicable because it does not consider individual differences.

☐ Individual differences are now recognized as crucial variables to consider when designing jobs. Experience, needs, values, and perceptions of equity are some of the individual differences which influence the reactions of job holders to their jobs. When individual differences are combined with environmental, situational, and managerial differences, job design decisions become increasingly complex.

☐ The most recently developed strategy of job design emphasizes the importance of core job characteristics as perceived by job holders. Although measurements of individual differences remain a problem, managers should be encouraged to examine ways to increase positive perceptions of variety, identity, significance, autonomy, and feedback. By doing so, the potential for high-quality work performance and high-job satisfaction is increased given that job holders possess relatively high-growth need strength.

☐ Many organizations including Volvo, Saab, General Motors, and General Foods have attempted job redesign with varying degrees of success. The current state of research knowledge is inadequate for making broad generalizations regarding the exact causes of success and failure in application to determine the applicability of job redesign in their organizations.

DISCUSSION AND REVIEW QUESTIONS

1. Explain the difficulties that management would encounter in attempting to redesign existing jobs as compared to designing new jobs.

2. Explain why it is impossible for a job analysis to identify every possible job relationship that an individual will encounter on a job.

3. Evaluate the approach that VW takes to encourage employee loyalty. Is the approach appropriate only in European countries that legislate employee participation in decision making?

4. What are the characteristics of individuals who would respond favorably to job enlargement, but not to job enrichment?

5. To what extreme can an individual firm redesign jobs to include motivational factors? Are there economic, social, and legal limits?

6. Explain the relationships between feedback as a job content factor and personal goal setting. Is personal goal setting possible without feedback? Explain.

7. What specific core dimensions of jobs could be changed to increase employees' perceptions of challenge and intrinsic satisfaction?

8. Which of the core dimensions do you now value most highly? Explain and list them in rank order of importance to you.

9. In your own work experience have managers been concerned with developing challenging jobs? How do your experiences compare to the practice of devising stretch objectives?

10. What are the important differences between the jobs of technicians and the jobs of assemblers? Do these differences have an effect on the success of efforts to redesign jobs so as to improve performance of the two types of jobs?

CASES

8–1 JOB REDESIGN IN AN INSURANCE COMPANY

The executive staff of a relatively small life insurance company was considering a proposal to install an electronic data processing system. The proposal to install the equipment was presented by the assistant to the president, John Skully. He had been charged with studying the feasibility of the equipment after a management consultant had recommended a complete overhaul of the jobs within the company.

The management consultant had been engaged by the company to diagnose the causes of high turnover and absenteeism. After reviewing the situation and speaking with groups of employees, the consultant had recommended that the organization structure be changed from a functional to a client basis. The change in departmental basis would enable management to redesign jobs to reduce the human costs associated with highly specialized tasks.

The present organization included separate departments to issue policies, collect premiums, change beneficiaries, and process loan applications. Employees in these departments had complained that their jobs were boring, insignificant, and monotonous. They had stated that the only reason they stayed with the company was because they liked the small-company atmosphere. They felt that management had a genuine interest in their welfare but that the trivial nature of their jobs contradicted that feeling. As one employee said, "This company is small enough to know almost everybody. But the job I do is so boring that I wonder why they even need me to do it." This and similar comments had led the consultant to believe that the jobs must be altered to provide greater motivation. But he also recognized that work redesign opportunities were limited by the organization structure. He had recommended therefore that the company change to a client basis. In such a structure, each employee would handle every transaction related to a particular policyholder.

When the consultant had presented his views to the members of the executive staff, they had been very much interested in his recommendation and agreed that it was well-founded. They had noted, however, that a small company must pay particular attention to efficiency in handling transactions. The functional basis enabled the organization to achieve the degree of specialization necessary for efficient operations. The manager of internal operations stated: "If we move away from specialization, the rate of efficiency must go down because we will lose the benefit of specialized effort. The only way we can justify redesigning the jobs as suggested by the consultant is to maintain our efficiency; otherwise, there won't be any jobs to redesign, because we will be out of business."

The internal operations manager had explained to the executive staff that despite excessive absenteeism and turnover, he was able to maintain acceptable productivity. The narrow range and depth of the jobs reduced training time to a minimum. It was also possible to hire temporary help to meet peak loads and to fill in for absent employees. "Moreover," he said, "changing the jobs our people do means that we must change the jobs our managers do. They are experts in their own functional areas, but we have never attempted to train them to oversee more than two operations."

A majority of the executive staff had believed that the consultant's recommendations should be seriously considered. At that point, the group had directed John Skully to evaluate the potential of electronic data processing (EDP) as a means of obtaining efficient operations in combination with the redesigned jobs. He had completed the study and presented his report to the executive staff.

"The bottom line," Skully said, "is that EDP will enable us to maintain our present efficiency, but with the redesigned jobs, we will not obtain any greater gains. If my analysis is correct, we will have to absorb the cost of the equipment out of earnings, because there will be no cost savings. So it comes down to what price we are willing and able to pay for improving the satisfaction of our employees."

Questions

1. What core characteristics of the employees' jobs will be changed if the consultant's recommendations are accepted? Explain.

2. What alternative redesign strategies should be considered? For example, job enrichment and job enlargement are possible alternatives. What are the relevant considerations for these and other designs in the context of this company?

3. What would be your decision in this case? What should management be willing to pay for employees satisfaction? Defend your answer.

8–2 WORK DESIGN AT GENERAL FOODS

General Foods (GF) is a multibillion-dollar company with more than 55,000 employees. The corporation has hundreds of manufacturing, sales, and research offices and facilities located throughout the world. The size and diversity of GF creates both opportunities and problems for its managers. One of the more recent problems they were confronting eventually faces all organizations, business and nonbusiness, large and small: dealing with the effects of computer technology on employees' jobs. Organizations no longer can ignore the fact that many jobs simply were not designed with computer technology in mind. And no jobs have been affected more by computers than those of office workers.

Most organizations began to feel the effects of computers on the jobs of office workers in the 1970s with the advent of word processing. This application of computer technology to secretarial/clerical activities has since brought about great changes in the depth, range, and relationship of office jobs. In some organizations, managers have handled the transition simply by replacing the typewriters with video display terminals on the desks of office workers and providing training in word processing technology. After all, the managers have reasoned, the only difference between typing and word processing is the visual medium—paper versus video screen. General Foods took a different—and what its management considers a more enlightened—approach to the problem. It believed that the appropriate approach recognized the fundamental changes required in the job designs of office workers and required a complete redesign of those jobs.

A fundamental aspect of GF's approach to job redesign was the full participation of all employees whose jobs were involved. Within this framework of participation, a Work-Design Process (as GF refers to it) has evolved which has other definite features. The process begins with a study of the administrative work of a unit to determine how jobs can be redesigned to increase productivity and job satisfaction. This study is undertaken only after the manager of the unit requests it. No units can be compelled to undergo the Work-Design Process. But once requested, the study begins with the formation of a study team.

The study team is made up of a specialist from the corporate personnel unit and members of the unit whose work is the focus of the study. Included are managers, professionals, secretaries, and clerks from representative parts of the unit. From this group, a project leader is selected to work with the corporate work-design specialist. This group then begins a study of the unit's work, using the following five steps.

1. The group studies and charts the flow of work within the unit as well as between the unit and other units in the corporation.

2. The group studies and charts the flow of work between managers and their secretaries and other clerical support personnel.

3. The group describes how work is presently organized and assigned in the unit.

4. The group describes how work is presently accomplished in the unit.

5. The group describes how people feel about the way work is organized, assigned, and accomplished.

The completion of these five steps can take as long as five months and chew up considerable time and money. Depending on the scope of the study team's recommendation for change, implementation can take anywhere from two to six months. Thus, GF gave significant commitment to the Work-Design Process.

Because work-design studies are time-consuming, costly, and disruptive, GF has since worked to find critical success factors. Successful work-redesign efforts have certain characteristics that distinguish them from unsuccessful ones. By recognizing the success factors, companies can avoid undertakings that are doomed from the beginning. After several good and bad experiences, GF believes that four critical success factors are necessary:

1. Each unit must be treated as a unique group with its own problems.

2. Each study team must set clear, unambiguous objectives in advance of the study.

3. The employees in the unit must be regarded as the real experts on what their jobs are all about and how they are best done.

4. The unit's managers must fully support and be fully committed to the need for the recommended changes.

Although the Work-Design Process evolved in response to developments in automated office technology, GF's work-design staff believed that it incorporated features worthy of general applications.

Questions

1. From your general knowledge or interviews with an office staff, compare the jobs of a secretary and a word processor in terms of depth, range, and relationships.

2. Based on the analysis above, evaluate GF's Work-Design Process. Are there significant differences between the two jobs, and do these differences require such an elaborate process?

3. Evaluate the four critical success factors in terms of their general applicability to other organizations.

Source: Adapted from Pat Smith, "How Work Design Teams Introduced New Technology to General Foods Offices" *Management Review*, November 1984, pp. 38–41.

EXERCISE

8-1 YOUR JOB PREFERENCES COMPARED TO OTHERS

Purpose: This exercise identifies what makes a job attractive or unattractive to you. Preferences of employees, if known, could be used as information by managers to develop and restructure jobs that are more attractive, rewarding, and generally more fulfilling. It is this type of information that would permit a manager to create a positive motivational atmosphere for subordinates.

Setting Up the Exercise:

1. Think about your present job (if you have one) or the type of job you would like. Decide which of the following job factors is most important to you. Place a *1* in front of it. Then decide which is the second most important to you and place a *2* in front of it. Keep ranking the items in order of importance until the least important job factor is ranked *14*. Individuals differ in the order in which these job factors are ranked. What is your present preference?

   _____ Advancement (opportunity for promotion).

   _____ Pay (income received for working).

   _____ Fringe benefits (vacation period, insurance, recreation facilities).

   _____ Schedule (hours worked, starting time).

   _____ Location (geographic area: Midwest, South, West, East, Southwest).

   _____ Supervisor (a fair, influential boss).

   _____ Feedback (receiving prompt, meaningful, and accurate feedback on job performance).

   _____ Security (steady work, assurance of a future).

   _____ Challenge (interesting and stimulating work).

   _____ Working conditions (comfortable and clean work area).

   _____ Co-workers (colleagues who are friendly, interesting).

   _____ The organization (working for a company you are proud of).

   _____ Responsibility (having responsibility to complete important job).

   _____ Training and development opportunities (the ability to receive training and development in the organization or through external sources).

2. Now rank the job factors as you think other members of your class would rank them. Look around and think how the average person in your class would rank the job factors.

_____ Advancement

_____ Pay

_____ Fringe benefits

_____ Schedule

_____ Location

_____ Supervisor

_____ Feedback

_____ Security

_____ Challenge

_____ Working conditions

_____ Co-workers

_____ The organization

_____ Responsibility

_____ Training and development opportunities

3. The instructor will form four-to-six-person groups to discuss the _individual_ and _other_ rankings. Each group should calculate averages for both rankings. What does this show? The members of the group should discuss these average scores.

4. The average individual and average other rankings should be placed on the board or flip chart and discussed by the entire class.

A Learning Note: Individuals consider different factors important. Can a manager realistically respond to a wide range of different preferences among subordinates?

NINE

Organization Design

LEARNING OBJECTIVES

After completing Chapter 9, you should be able to:

Define: what is meant by organizational design.

State: the two extreme types of organization design.

Describe: the basic conclusions of contingency theory of organization design.

Explain: why technology, environment, and strategy are important contingency variables.

Discuss: the advantages of the matrix form of organization.

MANAGEMENT INCIDENT

FEDERAL EXPRESS STRIVES FOR A LEAN ORGANIZATION

Federal Express specializes in transporting high-priority business goods and documents throughout the United States and abroad. It employs 42,000 individuals and operates facilities in more than 300 U.S. cities and 15 foreign cities. The company has stated that one of its key strategic objectives is to maintain a lean organization structure. This objective reflects CEO Frederick W. Smith's concern that an organization can get out of control in a fast-growth environment such as the one in which Federal Express competes. The responsibility for maintaining the lean organization is delegated to all line managers who receive support from the organization's planning department, located in the personnel department. To develop strategies that would achieve the objective, it was necessary to first define exactly what was meant by the term *lean organization*.

After an extensive review of managerial literature, the organizational planning department manager found that the concept usually included three dimensions: the number of managerial levels, the span of control, and certain work force statistics that related the number of managers to types of nonmanagerial employees. When these dimensions are applied to Federal Express, it is found that the maximum number of managerial levels is five. The manager of corporate planning believes that five levels of management is

well within the limits implied by lean organization. The average span of control for all managers in Federal Express is 1 to 12. The average span is calculated by dividing the number of nonmanagement employees by the number of managers and 12 is the quotient. But since it is an average, certain managers in the company will have more or less than 12. The planning department manager believes the span of control is consistent with a lean organization. The manager also believes that its work force statistics are consistent and cites as evidence its 2.1 staff officers per $1 million in sales compared to an average of 5 for other service organizations.

Federal Express management believes that it has established the correct definition of a lean organization. The many studies undertaken in the corporate planning department indicate that the organization has achieved and maintained just such an organization structure, despite the pressures of growth to add staff and managers. As it looks to the future, the management wants to be sure that it has policies which perpetuate and reinforce the objective of remaining a lean organization.

(The Management Solution to this Management Incident can be found at the end of this chapter.)

Organization design is the specific structure of task and authority relationships that managers explicitly decide is optimal to achieve performance objectives. As noted in Chapter 8, organization structures vary in terms of four elements: task specialization, departmental bases, spans of control, and delegation of authority. The initial managerial decision is to determine the specific arrangement of these four elements. Thus, the concept of organization design implies conscious and proactive managerial action to create and maintain the optimal structure of jobs and job relationships. Thus, organization design is both a process (designing, selecting, deciding) and a result (design, structure, arrangement).[1]

This chapter reviews contemporary theory and practice of organization design. Despite the importance of organization design to the attainment of performance objectives, not a great deal is known about how design and performance are related. It is understood that organization designs are different, and that different designs are appropriate in different situations. But the exact nature of the optimal fit between a design and a situation is but little known, much less understood.

ALTERNATIVE ORGANIZATION DESIGNS

Alternative organization designs tend to reflect differences in the four elements or organization structures. At one extreme are organization designs which have high specialization of labor, homogeneous departments, narrow spans of control, and centralized authority. Designs having these extreme characteristics are referred to as *bureaucratic, classical, formalistic, mechanistic,* and *System-1.* All of these terms describe essentially the same organizational design. Throughout the following discussion, the term *System-1* will describe this design thus avoiding the value-laden connotations of the other terms.

Organization designs at the opposite extreme have low specialization of labor, heterogeneous departments, wide spans of control, and decentralized authority. Terms which identify this extreme design include *nonbureaucratic, behavioral, informalistic, organic,* and *System-4.* System-4 will be used in the following discussion to identify this design. Figure 9–1 summarizes the important characteristics of these two extreme types. In reality, organizations will be somewhere between these extremes and contain characteristics of both extremes. In addition, the units within an organization can differ one from the other in the degree to which they reflect characteristics of System-1 and System-4 designs.

SYSTEM–1 ORGANIZATION DESIGN

The earliest writers, those of the classical approach to management, made forceful arguments for the superiority of System-1 organization design in comparison to any alternative design. According to their reasoning, System-1 organizations are natural extensions of specialization of labor to the institutional level. The use of System-1

---

[1]Ralph H. Kilmann, Louis R. Pondy, and Dennis P. Slevin, "Directions of Research on Organization Design," in *The Management of Organization Design: Research and Methodology*, ed. Ralph H. Kilmann, Louis R. Pondy, and Dennis P. Slevin (New York: Elsevier North-Holland, 1976). p. 1.

Figure 9–1   System-1 and System-4 organizational designs.

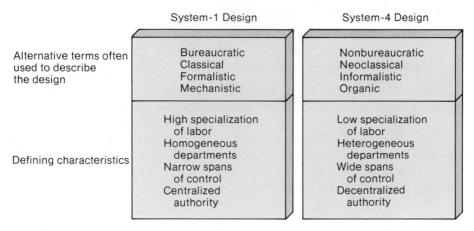

organization was widespread during the late 1800s at the height of the Industrial Revolution. A primary social, and therefore managerial, concern was efficient use of resources and maximum production. From these times, two different, yet compatible, sets of ideas emerged. One set of ideas has come to be associated with bureaucracy as an ideal type of organization. The other set of ideas are those of the classical approach.

Bureaucracy

Bureaucracy refers to the form of organization first described in the literature of public administration as government by bureaus; that is, nonelected civil servants. However, it is more usually associated with negative consequences of large organizations such as red tape, unexplained delays, and general frustration. But its more important meaning is to describe an organization design which is "superior to any other form in precision, in stability, in the stringency of its discipline, and its reliability. It thus makes possible a high degree of calculability of results for the heads of the organization and for those acting in relation to it."[2]

The characteristics of the ideal-type bureaucracy are as follows:

1. It has a clear division of labor, with each job well defined, understood, and routine.

2. Each manager has a clearly defined relationship with other managers and subordinates which follows a formal hierarchy.

---

[2]Max Weber, *The Theory of Social and Economical Organization,* trans. A. M. Henderson and Talcott Parsons (New York: Oxford University Press, 1947), p. 334.

3. Specific rules, policies, and procedures guide behaviors of employees in relation to each other and to clients.

4. Impersonal application of rules, policies, discipline, and rewards minimizes the possibility of favoritism.

5. Managers use rigid and equitable criteria to screen and select from among candidates for jobs in the organization.

The desired effect of the ideal type is to de-emphasize the idiosyncrasies of human behavior and to emphasize the predictability of machines and mechanical behavior.

As summarized by Max Weber, the bureaucratic design compares to other designs "as does the machine with nonmechanical modes of production."[3] Weber based this conclusion on extensive analyses of the Prussian civil service and military organizations. He believed that the advantages of bureaucracy were applicable in any context, whether government, military, or business.

Classical Organization Design

The classical approach to organization design refers to ideas that were expressed in the early 1900s. These ideas propose that the design of organization structures, that is, the process of design, should be guided by certain principles of organization.[4] Thus, managers who are guided by these principles would design a certain type of organization structure; that is, a classical design.

The classical design's most important principles of organization are:

1. *Specialization of labor.* Work should be divided and subdivided to the highest possible degree consistent with economic efficiency.

2. *Unity of direction.* Jobs should be grouped according to function or process; that is, like jobs should be grouped.

3. *Centralization of authority.* Accountability for the use of authority is retained at the executive or top-management level.

4. *Authority and responsibility.* A job holder must have authority commensurate with job responsibility.

5. *Unity of command.* Each job holder should report to one, and only one, supervisor.

The application of these principles results in organizations in which jobs are highly specialized, departments are based upon function, spans of control are narrow, and authority is centralized. Such organizations tend to be relatively "tall," with several layers of management through which communications and directions must pass. Taken together, bureaucratic and classical design theories describe the essential features of

---

[3]Max Weber, *From Max Weber: Essays in Sociology,* trans. H. H. Gerth and C. W. Mills (New York: Oxford University Press, 1946), p. 214.

[4]See Henri Fayol, *General and Industrial Management,* trans. C. Storrs (London: Pitman Publishing, 1949), pp. 19–42, for the original statement of classical principles.

System-1 organizations. According to this point of view, properly managed System-1 organizations are means for obtaining maximum efficiency and production.

The five classical principles of organization and characteristics of the ideal type are comparable. Regardless of whether a manager follows the classical principles or the bureaucratic characteristics, the results will be the same. The organization structure will emphasize specialization of labor and centralized authority.

SYSTEM-4 ORGANIZATION DESIGN

System-4 organizations are the exact opposite of System-1. System-4 organizations feature relatively despecialized jobs, heterogeneous departments, wide spans of control, and decentralized authority. The support for the application of the System-4 design derives from two perspectives. One perspective notes the inherent flaws of the System-1 design. A second perspective notes its limitations in particular settings.

The Inherent Flaws of System-1 Organizations

The inherent flaws of System-1 designs were first noted in the famous Hawthorne studies, a series of experiments carried out at the Western Electric plant in Hawthorne, Illinois.[5] These studies were the bases for the contention that extensive specialization of labor and centralized authority underestimates the complexity of employees. Rather than being a passive and inert being, dumbly performing assigned tasks, the average employee is a complex, multifaceted person who seeks more than monetary rewards from work. The researchers at the Hawthorne plant found that workers were members of friendship groups which defined the level of output considered fair and equitable. These groups seemed to exert far greater influence on employees than their managers, even though the groups had no authority to back up their influence.

Subsequent studies supported the conclusions of the Hawthorne studies. For example, one study focused on the relationship between rules and procedures and job behavior.[6] The study found instances where the effect of rules was to cause employees to follow them in robotlike fashion and to be unable to cope with instances not covered by the rules. The rules encouraged conforming rather than problem-solving behavior. A later study supported the idea that the primary effect of rules was to define minimal, rather than optimal, levels of behavior.[7]

Other writers take the position that the System-4 organization is more compatible with the needs of individuals and that System-1 designs create inherent conflict. For example, Chris Argyris believes that System-1 organizations suppress the development and growth of employees.[8] The domination of subordinates through the use of rules and hierarchy can cause subordinates to become passive, dependent, and noncreative.

---

[5]Fritz J. Roethlisberger and W. H. Dickson, *Management and the Worker* (Cambridge, Mass.: Harvard University Press, 1939).

[6]Robert K. Merton, "Bureaucratic Structure and Personality," *Social Forces,* 1940, p. 560–68.

[7]Alvin W. Gouldner, *Patterns of Industrial Bureaucracy* (New York: The Free Press, 1954).

[8]Chris Argyris, *Personality and Organization* (New York: Harper & Row, 1975).

Such conditions are not congruent with the human needs for autonomy, self-expression, accomplishment, and advancement. Consequently, the organization forfeits a considerable portion of its human resources through the use of System-1.

The Limitations of System-1 Organizations in Contemporary Situations

A considerable body of evidence supports the idea that System-1 designs are not compatible with contemporary society. As noted earlier, System-1 designs gained in popularity during the early periods of industrialization and economic development (the late 1800s and early 1900s). That period of relative stable and predictable change gave way to one of instability and uncertainty. Advanced technology in communications, transportation, manufacturing processes, and medicine creates the necessity for organizations to be adaptable and flexible so that new ways of doing work can be quickly utilized.

A leading advocate of System-4 design is Rensis Likert.[9] After considerable study, Likert proposed that in contemporary society, System-4 organizations utilize human and technical resources more fully than System-1. The System-4 design emphasizes the importance of decentralized authority and nondirective, participative management behavior. Relatively wide spans of control and heterogeneous departments facilitate the interaction of multiple and diverse points of view. Consequently, as circumstance and technology change, the organization is able to respond because of the diverse perspectives that can be brought to bear on any issue or problem that it confronts. Thus, advocates of System-4 organization design believe that it is universally applicable. But more important, they believe that it is the best way to organize in modern society. System-4 is therefore seen as the superior alternative in comparison to System-1.

CONTINGENCY ORGANIZATION DESIGN

An important alternative point of view, termed the *contingency approach,* is that either System-1 or System-4 can be the best way to organize depending upon the nature of such underlying factors as the organization's strategy, environment, and technology. The contingency approach to organization design is based on the idea that different organization designs facilitate different purposes. System-1 organizations are relatively more efficient and productive, but relatively less adaptive and flexible, than System-4 organizations. A particular organization, whether a business firm, government agency, hospital or university, or a particular unit within an organization should be structured depending upon whether it must be relatively (1) efficient and productive, or (2) adaptive and flexible. The critical issue then becomes to determine the circumstances which create the necessity to be relatively efficient and productive or adaptive and flexible.

---

[9]Rensis Likert, *New Patterns of Management* (New York: McGraw-Hill, 1961); and Rensis Likert, *The Human Organization* (New York: McGraw-Hill, 1967).

The researchers and practitioners who have contributed to the ideas of contingency design have suggested a number of circumstances, or variables, which influence the design decision. Among these variables are age of the organization, size of the organization, form of ownership, technology, environmental uncertainty, strategic choice, member (employee) needs, and current fashion.[10] There is evidence that older organizations, those that have been around a while, are more complex, formalized, and centralized than those of younger years. Also, researchers have noted the tendency of large organizations to be designed more along System-1 than System-4 prescriptions.

No attempt will be made here to discuss all the evidence related to each of these variables. Rather, the three which have the most apparent implications for management will be analyzed. They are technology, environment, and strategic choice.

Technology

The concept of technology can be narrowly defined as "the manufacturing, as distinct from administrative or distributive, processes employed by manufacturing firms to convert inputs into outputs."[11] Alternatively, it can be broadly defined as "the types and patterns of activity, equipment and material, and knowledge or experience used to perform tasks."[12] Regardless of how one defines the concept, whether narrowly or broadly, it is obvious that performing any kind of work, whether making cars, shoes, or computers or serving clients, patients, customers, or students involves technology. The technology can be machines or it can be knowledge.

The interest in the relationship between technology and structure was stimulated by the studies of Joan Woodward.[13] In one study Woodward classified technologies as unit, mass, or process production. Unit production referred to production to meet a customer's specific order. Here the product is developed after an order is received. The manufacture of custom-made shirts is an example of unit production technology. Mass production refers to the production of large quantities, such as on an assembly line. Zenith Corp. uses a mass-production technology to make television picture tubes. Process production refers to producing materials or goods on the basis of weight or volume. Processing 3 million barrels of oil or producing vats of paint at Sherwin-Williams are examples of production in this category.

Woodward found that a strong relationship existed between performance and both

[10]W. Alan Randolph and Gregory G. Dess, "The Congruence Perspective of Organization Design: A Conceptual Model and Multivariate Research Approach," *Academy of Management Review,* January 1984, pp. 114–27.

[11]Charles Perrow, "A Framework for the Comparative Analysis Organizations," *American Sociological Review,* April 1967, p. 195. See Michael Withey, Richard L. Daft, and William H. Cooper, "Measurements of Perrow's Work-Unit Technology: An Empirical Assessment and a New Scale," *Academy of Management Journal,* March 1983, pp. 45–63.

[12]Denise M. Rousseau, "Assessment of Technology in Organizations: Closed versus Open Systems Approaches," *Academy of Management Review,* October 1979, p. 531.

[13]Joan Woodward, *Industrial Organization: Theory and Practice* (London: Oxford University Press, 1965). A recent study based on Woodward's research is reported in Frank M. Hull and Paul D. Collins, "High-Technology Batch Production: Woodward's Missing Type," *Academy of Management Journal,* December 1987, pp. 786–97.

organizational design and technology. The highest performing organizations with unit and process technologies had System-4 characteristics. However, the highest performing organizations with mass-production technologies had the characteristics of System-1 structures. The effects of unit and process manufacturing technology are jobs with low specialization, high depth, and range. These jobs are best organized in a structure with relatively low complexity, formalization, and centralization. The rationale is that employees must have considerable latitude, discretion, and freedom of choice in the use of such technologies. Mass production, on the other hand, requires no such latitude on the part of employees and, accordingly, a System-1 organization design "fits" the situation.

Woodward's research findings are evidence that managers must consider the effects of technology on organization design. She encouraged managers to consider the role that technology plays in influencing work behavior and to recognize that appropriate design decisions require consideration of technological complexities. Woodward's research has resulted in a number of principles that suggest how technology influences organizational design. They are:

1. The more complex the technology—going from a unit system to a more process system—the greater are the number of managerial personnel and the levels of management.

2. The more complex the technology, the larger is the number of clerical and administrative personnel.

3. The span of control of first-line managers increases from unit production systems to mass-production systems and then decreases from mass-production systems to process production systems.

The successful firms in each technology category seem to employ the design characteristics suggested by the three principles. The idea that an organization design must be compatible with the technology it uses to achieve optimal performance is termed organization *fit*. An effective organization fits its technological requirements as suggested by the following Management Application.

MANAGEMENT APPLICATION

HONEYWELL'S SYSTEM-4 STRUCTURE

Honeywell, Inc.'s Defense and Marine Systems Groups (DMSG) is opening a new plant in Joliet, Illinois. The organizational design of the new plant will have many of the features of a System-4 structure to permit the company to cope with the demands of complex technology. A major characteristic of the plant will be jobs which have relatively wide range and depth. All employees will participate in policy formulation and goal setting. There will be no time clocks and no status hierarchy. Jobs will be loosely defined and employees will be encouraged to take on any task that they are competent to complete. Information and communications will flow throughout the organization to assure that individuals are involved fully in the plant's activities and decisions. Many task groups will exist to involve individuals from across specialties. In some instances quality circles will be used, in other instances task forces and committees will be used. The exact form of Honeywell's interpretation of the System-4 design varies from plant to plant, and from unit to unit within each plant, but the Joliet plant is a milestone in the company's experience with it.

Source: Adapted from Rosabeth Moss Kanter and John D. Buck, "Reorganizing Part of Honeywell: From Strategy to Structure," *Organizational Dynamics*, Winter 1985, pp. 4–25.

The publication and dissemination of Woodward's research stimulated a great number of follow-up studies. These studies have examined the relationship between technology and structure in a variety of settings using various definitions and measurements. As should be expected, there is inconsistency in the research findings. It is intuitively appealing to expect that routine technology, such as mass-production techniques, is most efficiently used in organizations adhering to System-1 design. Likewise, nonroutine technology, such as unit and process techniques, should be compatible with System-4 design. Yet to demonstrate the validity of what seems obvious is often a difficult research and practical task.

The problem of verifying the exact relationship has been complicated by inconsistency: (1) in definition and measurement of the two key concepts—technology and structure—and (2) in selection of the level of analysis—individual, group and organizational. To go into the details of these rather technical issues is beyond the scope of the present discussion. But it is important to acknowledge the conclusions drawn from a recent survey of the technology—structure literature. According to Fry's extensive review, routine technology (mass production, assembly lines, for example) is associated with System-1 design, while nonroutine technology (unit, small batch, and process) is associated with System-4 design.[14]

Environment

Every organization must operate within an environment. There are competitors, suppliers, customers, creditors, and the government, each making demands on the organization. Each of these external forces can have an effect on the organization's design.

The environment can be stable; that is, one in which there is little unpredictable change. In a stable environment, customer tastes remain relatively unchanged. New technology is rare, and the need for innovative research to stay ahead of competition is minimal. There has been little change in the environments affecting the manufacturers of accordions, zippers, and book covers.

Another type of environment is referred to as changing. There are changes in the

---

[14]Louis W. Fry, "Technology-Structure Research: Three Critical Issues," *Academy of Management Journal*, September 1982, pp. 532–52.

competition's strategy and in market demands, advertising, personnel practices, and technology. The changes are rather frequent and somewhat expected. Automobile manufacturers operate in a changing environment.

A turbulent environment exists when changes are unexpected and unpredictable. New competitive strategies, new laws, and new technology can create a turbulent condition. Electronic firms such as IBM, Hewlett-Packard, and Honeywell face unexpected environmental forces.

Matching an organizational design to the environment would require accurate managerial assessment of the environmental forces. Are they stable, changing, or turbulent? A group interested in organizational design studied 20 English and Scottish firms. Through analysis of interview responses, the researchers concluded that two types of organizational systems exist which they labeled *mechanistic and organic*.[15] Mechanistic structures had the same characteristics as System-1 designs; organic structures had the characteristics of System-4 designs.

After completing its study, the group concluded the System-1 structures were optimal in stable environments. However, System-4 structures were most suited to turbulent environments. Stable, placid environments are no cause for unexpected events that employees must deal with. Consequently, their jobs can be designed to include minimal depth and range and maximal specialization. But changing, turbulent environments create unexpected events and circumstances that cannot be anticipated. Jobs must be designed so as to give the employees considerable range and depth. The compatible organization design for such jobs is low in complexity, formalism, and centralization—System-4.

Following the lead of the English study group, an American team initially studied 10 companies. These companies were in three industries—plastics, consumer foods, and standardized containers. The team was concerned about how to design departments in organizations faced with distinct environments.[16] Unlike other analysts of organization design, these researchers believed that the organization design decision could be made less complicated if managers consider it in terms of parts of the organization.

The American team proposed that organizations should be designed with an emphasis on the different subunits, or departments of the organization. Those departments which face highly uncertain and turbulent environments should follow System-4 design prescriptions; that is, they should be relatively despecialized, informal, and decentralized. On the other hand, a department which faces certain and predictable environments should follow System-1 design ideas and be specialized, formalized, and centralized. The contingency viewpoint is reflected in the researchers' conclusion that "the internal functioning of organizations must be consistent with the organization task, technology, or external environment, and the needs of its members if the organization is to be effective."[17]

---

[15]Tom Burns and G. M. Stalker, *The Management of Innovation* (London: Tavistock Publications, 1961).

[16]Paul R. Lawrence and Jay W. Lorsch, *Organization and Environment* (Homewood, Ill.: Richard D. Irwin, 1967).

[17]Ian C. MacMillan and Patricia E. Jones, "Designing Organizations to Compete," *Journal of Business Strategy,* Spring 1984, pp. 11–26; and Balaji S. Chakravarthy and Peter Lorange, "Managing Strategic Adaptation: Options in Administrative System Design," *Interfaces,* January/February 1984, pp. 34–46.

Environmental characteristics such as uncertainty, change, turbulence, and volatility affect the design of organizational subunits by defining the characteristics of the jobs. The managerial implications of this effect relate to the possibility of having a diverse range of organizational designs among departments within the same organization.

For example, a manufacturing firm typically must deal with three critical subenvironments. One subenvironment consists of the market for its products. This subenvironment is the source of pressure to compete for customers through pricing, promotion, product development, and other marketing activities. The dominant characteristic of the market subenvironment can be highly uncertain to highly certain. The degree of certainty would be influenced by (1) the reliability of available information on customer preferences and competitors' actions, and (2) the rate of change in those preferences and actions. A relatively certain market subenvironment is one for which reliable information exists regarding stable customer preferences and competitors' actions. An uncertain market subenvironment would be the opposite: unreliable information and changing preferences and actions. Firms in plastics and computer manufacturing face relatively uncertain market subenvironments. Public utilities and container manufacturers face relatively certain market environments.

The environmental contingent model specifies that the organization design of departments fits the demands of the departments' subenvironment. Accordingly, the organization design of the marketing departments which face uncertain environments would take on characteristics of the System-4 approach. Those which face certain environments would organize according to the System-1 approach. Thus, there is no best way to organize a marketing department. Most manufacturing firms face two other important subenvironments in addition to the market subenvironment. The technical-economic subenvironment refers to the external sources of information and resources which are required in the production of the firm's product. This subenvironment can be certain or uncertain depending upon knowledge and rates of change in the technology of production, sources, types, and supplies of human, physical, and natural resources. Production departments must be organized to reflect the state of this subenvironment.

The third subenvironment is the scientific knowledge and know-how that firms relate to through their research and development departments. Research and development units are typically closer to System-4 structures than any other departments because of the somewhat higher degrees of uncertainty in the scientific subenvironment compared to market and technical-economic subenvironments. After all, the fundamental characteristic of research is to reveal the unknown. But in some industries, the scientific subenvironment can be relatively stable and certain in comparison to those of other industries. For example, the container industry scientific subenvironment is far less uncertain than that of the personal computer industry.

The process of designing the organization structure on a department-by-department basis can result in considerable diversity of designs within the same organization. The environmental perspective emphasizes the fitting of departments to subenvironments and then designing methods to coordinate the departments toward organizational objectives. The methods can range from strict applications of rules and procedures to the use of cross-departmental groups and individuals.

An organization which consists of departments predominately designed along System-1 lines could achieve interdepartmental coordination through rules, procedures, and policy. But organization made up of departments designed according to System-4 guidelines could achieve coordinated effort only through cross-departmental teams and individuals.

Strategic Choice

As noted in our discussion of the planning function, strategy involves the selection of missions and objectives and appropriate courses of action to achieve these objectives. Logically, several courses of action could be identified for any given objective, and for each alternative strategy, an alternative organization design exists. Thus, the specific organization design should follow from a specified strategy.

Porter's views.   As one of the most influential writers in the field of corporate strategy, Porter states that corporations can adopt one of three general (generic) strategies: (1) cost leadership, (2) differentiation, and (3) focus.[18]

Cost leadership implies that the firm will outstrip its competition by being the low-cost producer. It will build efficient-scale facilities, pursue cost control policies, avoid marginal customers, and generally be cost conscious in all areas of the business. In other words, the firm will emphasize efficiency and productivity. With lower costs, the firm can afford lower prices and with lower prices, generate larger sales volume. Two firms which have achieved notable success by striving for cost leadership are Briggs and Stratton and Lincoln Electric.

The organization design that facilitates overall cost leadership must be one that encourages efficiency and productivity. The System-1 design with its emphasis on specialization, formalization, and centralization fits this strategy.

Differentiation involves the firm in creating products that consumers perceive to be unique. The perception of uniqueness (differentiation) can be based upon a variety of factors, such as brand image, product features, customer service, and dealer network. To be effective, differentiation requires creativity, basic research skill, strong marketing, and a reputation for quality. Firms such as Mercedes, Jenn-Air, Coleman, and Caterpillar have successfully pursued differentiation. Differentiation strategy does not imply that cost control is ignored, only that it is not the primary strategic consideration. The emphasis on differentiation requires flexible response to changing customer preferences and perceptions. The organization design which facilitates the strategy would tend toward System-4 characteristics which encourage the freedom of action required by the differentiation strategy.

Focus, the third general strategy, involves achieving either cost leadership or differentiation or both in a particular segment of the market. Rather than compete throughout the market, the firm focuses on one segment. For example, Porter Paint attempts to serve the needs of the professional painter rather than the do-it-yourself segment. Thus, the focus strategy implies a trade-off between market share and profitability. The compatible organization design implies a mix of both System-1 and System-4 characteristics because the firm can attempt both cost leadership and differentiation aimed at its segment.

---

[18]Michael E. Porter, *Competitive Strategy* (New York: The Free Press, 1980), pp. 34–46.

Chandler's views. The contemporary impetus for the idea that structure should reflect strategy is the work of Chandler.[19] After a study of the history of the 70 largest firms in the United States, Chandler concluded that organization structures follow the growth strategies of firms. He also found that growth strategies tended to follow a certain pattern. In their initial stage, firms are typically plants, sales offices, or warehouses in a single industry, in a single location, and perform a single function such as manufacturing, sales, or warehousing. But they grow if successful, and their growth follows a fairly standard path through four stages as follows:

1. *Volume expansion*. Firms manufacture, sell, or distribute more of their product or service to existing customers.

2. *Geographic expansion*. Firms continue to do what they have been doing but in a larger geographic area by means of field units.

3. *Vertical integration*. Firms either buy or create other functions. For example, manufacturers integrate backward by acquiring or creating sources of supply or forward by acquiring or creating sales and distribution functions.

4. *Product diversification*. Firms become involved in new industries either through merger, acquisition, or creation (product development).

As a firm moves through each stage, it must change its organization structure. Initially, System-1 design is appropriate because volume expansion of a single product or service in a single industry stresses low unit cost (efficiency) and maximum resource utilization (production), with relatively low concern for response to change and uncertainty. But as the firm moves through the steps of geographic expansion and, ultimately, to product diversification, it becomes increasingly concerned with adaptability and flexibility because it faces diverse and complex environments. Thus, the organization structures of highly diversified firms are characterized by product-based divisions and departments, decentralized authority, and relatively wide spans of control. The following Management Application describes one company's efforts to maintain flexibility through its policy of decentralization.

MANAGEMENT APPLICATION

APOGEE ENTERPRISE'S POLICY OF DECENTRALIZATION

Apogee Enterprise, a leading manufacturer of glass, windows, and curtain walls, has annual sales in excess of $300 million, 150 profit centers, 13 operating units, and four divisions. The company manages this complex organization with a headquarters staff of only 11 people. Its philosophy and practice emphasize decentralization and the delegation of authority. Each division and operating unit handles its own staff functions such as public relations, legal affairs, and human resources. The idea is to develop

---

[19]Alfred D. Chandler, *Strategy and Structure* (Cambridge, Mass.: MIT Press, 1962). Robert E. Hoskisson, "Multidivisional Structure and Performance: The Contingency of Diversification Strategy," *Academy of Management Journal*, December 1987, pp. 625–44, reports a recent study of the relationship between strategy and structure.

the attitudes of profit center managers that they are managing their own businesses and that they should act independently of headquarters.

To add to the sense of independence, Apogee strives to break down any unit that gets excessively large. The development of smaller units from larger ones provides further opportunities for individuals to become managers of their own units and to think in entrepreneurial terms. Apogee also strives to create among its nonmanagers the sense of ownership by matching the contributions of peak performers with equal amounts of stock. This and other benefit plans have enabled 35 percent of Apogee's employees to become owners of the firm. The employees are encouraged to be loyal not only to their individual units, but also to Apogee.

Source: Adapted from Anthony J. Rutigliano, "Apogee Lets Managers Grow Their Own Businesses," *Management Review*, September 1987, pp. 28–33.

The increasing utilization of divisional forms of organization among companies that have diversified into related and unrelated products is borne out by recent studies. Rumelt's 1974 study of Fortune 500 firms found an inexorable movement toward product-based divisional forms of organization.[20] But there is some question whether such divisional structures always follow System-4 design principles.[21] There is no doubt that organizations such as Philip Morris, which consists of divisions producing and marketing products as diverse as beer and cigarettes, are more complex than General Motors, whose divisions produce and market different models of trucks and automobiles.

The idea that organization design should change to reflect the organization's strategic choice implies growth-oriented strategy. It also implies that managers will know the need for changing the structure. This orientation to change and knowing is termed a *process approach* to organization design. A process approach places its emphasis on how and why an organization moves from one design to another. Implicit in the strategic choice approach is the assumption that managers know that they should alter the organization design as they change the firm's strategy from volume expansion to product diversification.

But the same could be said for other approaches to organization design. Both the technology and uncertainty approaches assume that managers can know what design to use in a particular situation. The simpler one-best approaches also recognize the importance of competent managers. Nevertheless, the proponents of contingency approaches often present their ideas without giving explicit attention to the role of the organization's management, particularly the cognitive and psychological traits of managers.

---

[20]R. P. Rumelt, *Strategy, Structure, and Economic Performance* (Cambridge, Mass.: Division of Research, Graduate School of Business Administration, Harvard University, 1974).

[21]Peter H. Grinyer and Masoud Yasai-Ardekani, "Dimensions of Organizational Structure: A Critical Replication," *Academy of Management Journal*, September 1980, pp. 405–21.

Figure 9–2 A matrix design.

Projects, products	Functions President			
	VP Manufacturing	VP Marketing	VP Engineering	VP Finance
Project or Product A				
Project or Product B				
Project or Product C				
Project or Product D				
Project or Product E				

MATRIX ORGANIZATION DESIGN

An emerging organization design, termed *matrix organization,* attempts to maximize the strengths and minimize the weaknesses of both the System-1 and System-4 designs. In practical terms, the matrix design combines functional and product departmental bases.[22] Companies such as American Cyanamid, Avco, Carborundum, Caterpillar Tractor, Hughes Aircraft, ITT, Monsanto Chemical, National Cash Register, Prudential Insurance, TRW, and Texas Instruments are only a few of the users of matrix organization. Public sector users include public health and social service agencies.[23] Although the exact meaning of matrix organization is not well established, the most typical meaning sees it as a balanced compromise between functional and product organization, between departmentalization by process and by purpose.[24]

The matrix organizational design achieves the desired balance by superimposing, or overlaying, a horizontal structure of authority, influence, and communication on the vertical structure. The arrangement can be described as in Figure 9–2, where personnel assigned in each cell belong not only to the functional department, but also to a particular product or project. For example, manufacturing, marketing, engineering,

---

[22]Jay R. Galbraith and Robert K. Kazanjian, "Organizing to Implement Strategies of Diversity and Globalization: The Role of Matrix Organizations," *Human Resource Management,* Spring 1986, pp. 37–54; and Diane Krusko and Robert R. Cangemi, "The Utilization of Project Management in the Pharmaceutical Industry," *Journal of the Society of Research Administrators,* Summer 1987, pp. 17–24.

[23]Kenneth Knight, "Matrix Organization: A Review," *Journal of Management Studies,* May 1976, p. 111.

[24]Ibid., p. 114.

and finance specialists will be assigned to work on one or more projects or products A, B, C, D, and E. As a consequence, personnel will report to two managers, one in their functional department and one in the project or product unit. The existence of a dual authority system is a distinguishing characteristic of matrix organization.

Matrix structures are found in organizations which require responses to rapid change in two or more environments, such as technology and markets, which face uncertainties that generate high information-processing requirements, and which must deal with financial and human resources constraints.[25] Managers confronting these circumstances must obtain certain advantages which are most likely to be realized with matrix organization.[26]

Advantages of Matrix Organization

A number of advantages can be associated with the matrix design. Some of the more important ones are given below:

Efficient use of resources.   Matrix organization facilitates the utilization of highly specialized staff and equipment. Each project, or product unit can share the specialized resource with other units, rather than duplicating it to provide independent coverage for each. This advantage is particularly so when projects require less than the full-time efforts of the specialist. For example, a project may require only half a computer scientist's time. Rather than having several underutilized computer scientists assigned to each project, the organization can keep fewer of them fully utilized by shifting them from project to project.

Flexibility in conditions of change and uncertainty.   Timely response to change requires information and communication channels which efficiently get the information to the right people at the right time. Matrix structures encourage constant interaction among project unit and functional department members. Information is channeled vertically and horizontally as people exchange technical knowledge. The result is a quicker response to competitive conditions, technological breakthroughs, and other environmental conditions.

Technical excellence.   Technical specialists interact with other specialists while assigned to a project. These interactions encourage cross-fertilization of ideas such as when a computer scientist must discuss the pros and cons of electronic data processing with a financial accounting expert. Each specialist must be able to listen, understand, and respond to the views of the other. At the same time, specialists maintain ongoing contact with members of their own discipline because they are also members of a functional department.

---

[25]Paul R. Lawrence, Harvey F. Kolodny, and Stanley M. Davis, "The Human Side of the Matrix," *Organizational Dynamics,* September 1977, p. 47.

[26]The following discussion is based upon Knight, "Matrix Organization," pp. 109–21.

Freeing top management for long-range planning.   An initial stimulus for the development of matrix organizations is that top management increasingly becomes involved with day-to-day operations. Environmental changes tend to create problems with cross-functional and product departments that cannot be resolved by the lower-level managers. For example, when competitive conditions create the need to develop new products at faster than previous rates, the existing procedures become bogged down. Top management is then called upon to settle conflicts among the functional managers. Matrix organization makes it possible for top management to delegate ongoing decision making, thus providing more time for long-range planning.

Improving motivation and commitment.   Project and product groups are comprised of individuals with specialized knowledge. Management assigns to them, on the basis of their expertise, responsibility for specific aspects of the work. Consequently, decision making within the group tends to be more participative and democratic than in hierarchical settings. The opportunity to participate in key decisions fosters high levels of motivation and commitment, particularly for individuals with acknowledged professional orientations.

Providing opportunities for personal development.   Members of matrix organizations are provided considerable opportunity to develop their skills and knowledge. They are placed in groups consisting of individuals representing diverse parts of the organization. They must, therefore, come to appreciate the different points of view expressed by these individuals; each group member becomes more aware of the total organization. Moreover, they have opportunities to learn something of other specialties. Engineers develop knowledge of financial issues; accountants learn about marketing. The experience broadens each specialist's knowledge not only of the organization, but of other scientific and technical disciplines.

Different Forms of Matrix Organization

Matrix organization forms can be depicted as existing in the middle of a continuum which has System-1 organizations at one extreme and System-4 organizations at the other. Organizations can move from System-1 to matrix forms or from System-4 to matrix forms. Ordinarily the process of moving to matrix organization is evolutionary. That is, as the present structure proves incapable of dealing with rapid technological and market changes, management attempts to cope by establishing procedures and positions which are outside the normal routine. This evolutionary process consists of the following steps:

Task force.   When a competitor develops a new product that quickly captures the market, a rapid response is necessary. Yet, in a System-1 organization, new-product development is often too time consuming because of the necessity to coordinate the various units that must be involved. A convenient approach is to create a task force of individuals from each functional department and charge it with the responsibility to expedite the process. The task force achieves its objective and dissolves, as members return to their primary assignments.

Figure 9–3 Fully evolved matrix organization.

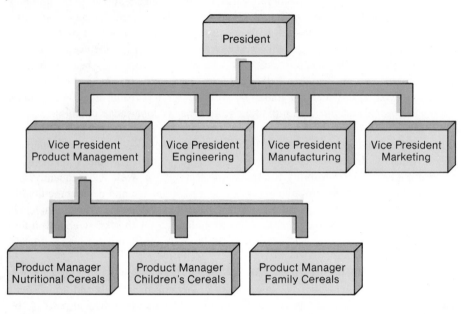

Teams.   If the product or technological breakthrough generates a family of products that move through successive stages of new and improved product development, the temporary task force concept is ineffective. A typical next step is to create permanent teams which consist of representatives from each functional department. The teams meet regularly to resolve interdepartmental issues and to achieve coordination. When not involved with issues associated with new-product development, the team members work on their regular assignments.

Product managers.   If the technological breakthrough persists such that new-product development becomes a way of life, top management will create the roles of product managers. In a sense, product managers chair the teams, but they now are permanent positions. Ordinarily they report to top management, but they have no formal authority over the team members. They must rely upon their expertise and interpersonal skill to influence the team members. Companies such as General Foods, DuPont, and IBM make considerable use of the product management concept.

Product management departments.   The final step in the evolution to matrix organization is the creation of product management departments. Figure 9–3 depicts the organization which has a product manager reporting to top management and with subproduct managers for each product line. In some instances, the subproduct managers are selected from specific functional departments and would continue to report directly to their functional managers. There is considerable diversity in the application of matrix organization, yet the essential feature is the creation of overlapping authority and the existence of dual authority.

Exactly where along the continuum an organization stops in the evolution depends upon factors in the situation. Specifically and primarily important are the rates of change in technological and product developments. The resultant uncertainty and information required to deal with the uncertainty varies.

Despite the many advantages of matrix organizations including the various forms it can take to adapt to an organization's specific circumstances and needs, not all the reports are success stories. The following Management Application describes an attempt to discover the truth of reports that many organizations were abandoning the matrix structures.

MANAGEMENT APPLICATION

IS THE MATRIX STRUCTURE PASSÉ?

Organizations of all kinds implemented matrix-type structures during the 1970s. Yet by the 1980s reports circulated in the business literature that these same firms were abandoning it. Texas Instruments, Medtronic, and Xerox had been prominent proponents but were reported to be phasing out the matrix. The most damaging criticisms of matrix structures were that they stifled the very activity that they were to encourage; that is, product and service development. The creation of dual reporting, authority, and evaluation systems and channels also required the creation of considerable paperwork and controls to maintain accountability. However, the only evidence that matrix organizations are ineffective is anecdotal, and no informed information has been available until recently.

Two researchers sought to document the extent to which matrix organizations had failed to live up to their promise. They decided to concentrate their study in firms that had to rely on product development for survival. They sent questionnaires to over 500 managers who were involved in the development of new products and services. The industries represented in the study included pharmaceutical, aerospace, computer and data processing products, telecommunications, and medical instruments. Over three fourths of the respondents indicated that their companies had used the matrix organization for product development projects, and 89 percent of them stated that they would probably or definitely use the matrix design again. Those who responded that they would not use it again reported that project and functional leaders were unable to coordinate their interrelated activities. But the vast majority of respondents believed that matrix structures are effective, particularly when the project leader is given sufficient authority to complete the job, including authority over all assigned functional personnel. Thus in contrast to anecdotal information, this evidence indicates the enduring popularity of matrix structures.

Source: Adapted from Erik W. Larson and David H. Gobeli, "Matrix Management: Contradictions and Insights," *California Management Review*, Summer 1987, pp. 126–38.

Managerial decision making plays a key role in organizational design.[27] In fact, much of what has been stated in this chapter can be summarized in the idea that structure follows technology, environmental demands, and strategy. Maximum performance is achieved when structure fits the relevant contingencies. Managerial strategy involves the choice of what products and services the organization will supply to specific customers and markets. Thus managers who decide to supply a single product to a specific set of customers can be expected to design a far simpler organizational structure than a manager of a highly diversified company serving multiple markets with multiple products and services.[28]

Organizational design remains an important issue in the management of organizational behavior and effectiveness. As the decade of the 1980s comes to an end and as the 1990s loom, organizational design will become even more important. As is apparent, strategies which have been successful in the past will prove ineffectual in the face of the new international competition, technological change, and the shifting patterns of industrial development. As organizations experiment with new strategies, they will be forced to experiment with new organizational designs. These designs will bear closer resemblance to System-4 than to System-1 designs.[29]

MANAGEMENT SOLUTION

FEDERAL EXPRESS IMPLEMENTS ITS STRATEGY

The challenge to maintain a lean organization is formidable in a growth-oriented firm. Federal Express responded to that challenge by implementing a number of techniques and practices. Some of these include:

1. The company developed an awareness campaign consisting of presentations at staff meetings, articles in the employee newsletter, and the creation of a logo featuring a belt-tightening organization.

2. It communicates with other, like-minded firms to share information on policies and techniques that worked for them in efforts to maintain a lean organization.

3. Federal Express has created performance evaluation systems which reward both managerial and nonmanagerial employees for ideas which contribute to a lean organization.

4. The company has implemented a process for reviewing all requests for additional staff and managerial

Continued

---

[27]James W. Frederickson, "The Strategic Decision Process and Organizational Structure," *Academy of Management Review,* April 1986, pp. 280–97.

[28]Jay R. Galbraith and Daniel A. Nathanson, *Strategy Implementation: The Role of Structure and Process* (St. Paul, Minn.: West Publishing, 1978).

[29]Raymond E. Miles and Charles C. Snow, "Organizations: New Concepts for New Forms," *California Management Review,* Spring 1986, pp. 62–73.

MANAGEMENT SOLUTION

Concluded

positions. The process involves stringent and detailed analysis of all alternatives to an additional position including combining tasks, technology, and external contracting.

In addition to these proven practices, Federal Express is considering other, somewhat nontraditional techniques including the following:

1. The company is examining the applicability of self-managed work groups which together would do many of the tasks of first-line management such as scheduling, training, and performance appraisal. One of the effects of self-managed work groups includes making possible even wider spans of control because fewer managers are required.

2. Group incentives are being evaluated as a way to make bonuses available to members of high-performing groups. Since the bonus would be paid to the group to be distributed on a per-person basis, this technique would encourage groups to forgo hiring additional personnel because

that would dilute each individual's share.

3. The company is turning to scientific management practices to discover sources of productivity increases in the work flow processes. Work simplification has the effect of reducing the demand for additional employees.

4. The company is considering hiring temporary employees to staff short-term functions in new departments with the understanding that the employee will be reassigned at a definite future date. Through this variation of sunset laws, all new positions in new departments must be justified.

Federal Express balances its commitment to a lean organization against its commitment to avoiding layoffs. Thus the effort to achieve the objective of a lean organization must be ongoing and constant with every personnel action seen as an opportunity to further the end.

Source: Adapted from William Wagel, "Keeping the Organization Lean at Federal Express," *Personnel*, March 1987, pp. 4–12.

MANAGEMENT SUMMARY

☐ The bureaucratic design offered by Weber, the classical suggestions of Fayol (System-1), and the participative theme offered by Likert and Argyris (System-4) are all one best-way designs. In some situations, these designs are

probably excellent, but they are rather inflexible, and changes in the situation often render them inadequate.

☐ The contingency design approach borrows

from other design approaches and introduces more emphasis on technology, strategy, and environment than the one best-way designs.

☐ The ideas of mechanistic and organic systems, differentiation and integration, and technology have provided the bases for contingency organizational design decision making among managers.

☐ The matrix form of organization design enables managers in some situations to obtain the advantages of both System-1 and System-4 designs. Although the matrix design has certain specific advantages, there are still problems associated with it, such as unfamiliarity, conflict, and lack of structure for some individuals.

☐ If performance is the crucial determinant of managerial competence, then awareness of organizational design alternatives and the ability to make changes must be included in the manager's tool kit. The manager needs knowledge, energy, and a willingness to make changes to put the optimal design in place. After it is in place, fine tuning, total revamping, or starting over again may soon become realities. The best managers are able to make these adjustments when they are needed.

REVIEW AND DISCUSSION QUESTIONS

1. Define the term *organizational design* to distinguish it from the term *organizational structure*. Why is it important to distinguish between the two terms?

2. What are the practical and theoretical bases for the belief that there is one best way to design an organizational structure? After reviewing the evidence, explain your own beliefs on this matter.

3. Compare and contrast the characteristics of an ideal-type bureaucracy and the principles of classical organization design theory. Will the application of these two theories result in the same organization design regardless of the setting? Explain.

4. Describe the inherent flaws in System-1 organization design and discuss the extent to which these flaws persist in contemporary American society.

5. Are the behavioralists as narrow in their design approaches as the classicists or Weber? Explain.

6. Some believe that Argyris's concern about having the organization help people grow psychologically is misguided. They state that an organization in the profit sector is an economic institution and not a counseling center. What do you think?

7. Why is the matrix organizational design so popular in organizations with a technical and research orientation?

8. Is a focus on technology more important than a focus on organizational strategy in the contingency design approach?

9. Are you a System 1- or a System 4-oriented person? Why is this type of self-knowledge important for a manager?

10. Explain why and how the matrix form of organization is able to deliver its several advantages when nonmatrix forms are apparently unable to do so.

CASES

9–1 ORGANIZATION DESIGN AT GENERAL MOTORS

General Motors was the only U.S. auto manufacturer with a clearly identified strategy to compete in the world market. The strategy was formulated in the 1970s in response to worldwide consumer demand for fuel-efficient, quality automobiles. The most important part of GM's strategy was to replace its entire line of cars with smaller ones. Most of them would have front-wheel drive and compete in the world market. The company planned to introduce a new product every six months beginning with the subcompact J car in May 1981.

The innovativeness of GM's strategy is all the more striking when compared to its history and reputation. Throughout its earlier years, GM was not known as an innovator or a risk taker. Its advantage was in manufacturing technology, through which it reduced unit costs of production by spreading machinery and tooling expenses over larger volume. That strategy was so successful that GM's return on equity averaged almost 20 percent per year during the 1950s and 1960s. The company apparently did not need to innovate to maintain profitability. Consequently, it acquired a reputation as a "lumbering organization" most recently popularized in former GM Group Executive, John Z. DeLorean's book, *On a Clear Day You Can See General Motors*.

The idea of GM as a lumbering, or perhaps slumbering, giant doesn't seem to square with its recent history. Yet observers close to the scene at GM believe that the popular view of the company has always been a false one. Although product innovation has not been a focus of change, the company has, in fact, been through numerous and significant changes. The mobilization of the company during World War II is a striking example of significant change.

In addition, GM's organization structure changes frequently. Since 1977, it has added vice presidents for consumer relations and service, for quality and reliability, and for technical operations. These changes reflect the company's adaptation to growing concerns for consumers, quality, and technology as important strategic factors during the 1980s.

Probably the most important source of structural change is the almost constant shifting balance between decentralized operations and centralized controls. As a divisionalized structure, GM's operating divisions must have considerable autonomy to make key decisions. Yet that same autonomy must be counterbalanced by accountability to corporate headquarters. In practice, the optimal balance is never achieved. Consequently, a continual state of flux exists as divisions and headquarters negotiate the terms of the balance.

Recently, a major thrust of GM's production strategy has been to achieve greater economies of scale and flexibility in assembly operations. That emphasis caused the company to centralize all vehicle assembly operations into one assembly division. As a result, Chevrolet, for example, no longer assembles its own cars. But the car divisions are granted greater freedom to modify components that will give their cars distinctive handling and ride qualities. Research and development also is being decentralized into the car divisions to reinforce the importance of dealing with specific problems at the operating level.

The formal organization structure is not the only source of flux. Inherent in the way that GM makes decisions is its committee system, but in recent years, these formal committees meet to confirm and communicate decisions that have been made in the informal system consisting of lunch meetings and other casual settings. It is in sessions such as these that decisions as important as the one to downsize the 1977 big cars are reached. The informal system simply works faster and is more responsive to circumstances requiring immediate action. The formal system of regular committees coexists with the informal system, but its purpose is to inform, not to deliberate.

Thus, the organizational structure facilitates strategic redirection of GM's resources. The structure is far too complex to be simply described, but it does seem to encourage change in the midst of stability and informality along with formality.

Questions

1. How can an organization be both stable and dynamic as is suggested in the case?

2. How does GM's organizational structure enable it to achieve its corporate strategy?

3. What does the GM case suggest about the existence of "pure" types, such as bureaucratic, mechanistic, or organic, of organizations in the real world?

Source: This case is adapted from Charles G. Burck, "How GM Stays Ahead," *Fortune*, March 9, 1981, pp. 43–56.

9–2 ORGANIZING FOR INNOVATION AT RAYTHEON COMPANY

Raytheon Company depends upon innovation for survival. The company competes in the highly technical and volatile electronic-based product industry. Its business with the government includes missile systems, radar, and underwater surveillance products which account for more than half of its $7 billion annual sales. The other half comes from business groups including such well-known consumer products as Amana appliances, Speed Queen laundry products, and Caloric cooking appliances. In this environment the importance of developing new products and new technology becomes crucial to the firm's very survival and it is imperative to design an organization that facilitates new product development. Typically, firms create research and development (R&D) units to do product and process development research and, Raytheon uses this organizational form but supplements it with a centralized, corporate-level, New Products Center.

The New Products Center (NPC) is a 35-person group located at a corporate headquarters in Burlington, Massachusetts. Since its formation in 1969, it has participated in the early development of 39 products which have become mainstays in the firm's product line. The NPC stands alone and works with all the divisions and subsidiaries of the company including those R&D units that are parts of the divisions and subsidiaries. The company also uses other ways to initiate and sustain innovation including external consultants as well as internal and external ventures groups. The NPC plays the special role in this configuration of approaches to innovation because it views the entire organization as both a source of clients and a source of resources. All the expertise in all the divisional R&D groups can be made available to the NPC during the course of developing new products.

The NPC serves as a way to cross functional and divisional boundaries so as to tap all the skills and abilities in Raytheon. The primary goal of the NPC is to develop profitable products. New products are worthless if they do not generate profits, no matter how brilliant or interesting the underlying idea. Thus the bottom-line criterion for evaluating the performance of the NPC is its contribution to profit. Its basic operating procedure is to develop the first functioning model of a new product that can then be turned over to the appropriate product or business center. If the product is successful, it will extend the product line and will be manufactured with existing facilities and distributed through existing channels.

The center is staffed by both generalists and specialists. The generalists are capable of working on a variety of products and fields simultaneously. Three major categories of specialists in Raytheon's NPC focus on: (1) computer applications for electronic controls, (2) materials design and development, and (3) product engineering which transfers the product manufacturing responsibility to a product or business group. However, even the ablest of research and technical talent will go untapped if a satisfactory relationship with the client group is not established. In Raytheon every organizational unit is a potential client group of NPC, and the development of satisfactory working relationships requires mutual trust. A satisfactory working relationship includes agreement on which market to target with what product, the scale of company investment, the role of each person involved, and who will get credit for success and blame for failure. These are important issues that must be negotiated before the real work of developing the product can begin.

The internal operations, organization, staffing, and interpersonal skills are critical to the success of the NPC. But its place in the overall organizational structure is also critical. In recognition of the possibility that the center could be the first victim of hard times when revenues and cash flows require retrenchment, Raytheon funds the center's $3 million annual cost entirely out of the executive office resources. This practice means that no operating division or group will be assessed any cost for using the center's resources for product development. In addition, the director of the center reports to the CEO thus emphasizing the support of top management for the center's importance. Raytheon's experience with its NPC indicates that it is one approach to organizing for innovation that other firms could adopt.

Questions

1. Evaluate Raytheon's approach to organizing for innovation. What alternatives come to mind? Would any of these alternatives be appropriate for Raytheon to consider?

2. Based upon what you know about the way organizational subunits should be organized so as to fit its environmental demands, how should the NPC be structured? What would be the important characteristics of the organizational structure?

3. How would you evaluate the effectiveness of the NPC and how would you know whether and to what degree the unit's organizational structure contributes to its effectiveness?

Source: Adapted from George Freedman, "Raytheon's New Product Development Center," *Management Review*, December 1986, pp. 40–45.

COMPREHENSIVE CASE

CHANDLER'S RESTAURANT

In discussing the kitchen as a status system, we have only incidentally taken into account the fact that the kitchen is part of a communication and supply system, which operates to get the food from the range onto the customer's table. Looking at it this way will bring to light other problems.

Where the restaurant is small and the kitchen is on the same floor as the dining room, waitresses are in direct contact with cooks. This does not eliminate friction, but at least everybody is in a position to know what everybody else is doing, and the problems of communication and coordination are relatively simple.

When the restaurant is large, there are more people whose activities must be coordinated, and when the restaurant operates on several floors, the coordination must be accomplished through people who are not generally in face-to-face contact with each other. These factors add tremendously to the difficulty of achieving smooth coordination.

The cooks feel that they work under pressure—and under a pressure whose origins they cannot see or anticipate.

As one of them said,

> It's mostly the uncertainty of the job that gets me down, I think. I mean, you never know how much work you're going to have to do. You never know in advance if you're going to have to make more. I think that's what a lot of 'em don't like around here. That uncertainty is hard on your nerves.

For a cook, the ideal situation is one in which she always has a sufficient supply of food prepared ahead so that she is never asked for something she does not have on hand. As one of them said, "You have to keep ahead or you get all excited and upset."

Life would be simpler for the cook if she were free to prepare just as much food as she wanted to. But the large and efficiently operated restaurant plans production on the basis of very careful estimates of the volume of business to be expected. Low food costs depend in part upon minimizing waste or leftover food. This means that production must be scheduled so as to run only a little ahead of customer demand. The cook therefore works within a narrow margin of error. She can't get too far ahead, and that means that on extra-busy days, she is certain sometimes to lose her lead or even to drop behind.

When the cook drops behind, all the pressures from customer to waitress to service pantry to runner descend upon her, for no one between her and the customer can do his job unless she produces the goods. From this point of view, timing and coordination are key problems of the organization. Proper timing and good coordination must be achieved in organizations or else efficiency is dissipated in personal frictions.

While these statements apply to every step in the process of production and service, let us look here at the first steps—the relations of cooks to kitchen runners to the service pantry.

When the restaurant operates on different floors, the relations must be carried on in part through mechanical means of communication. There are three common channels of this nature, and all have their drawbacks. Use of a public address system adds considerably to the noise of the kitchen and service pantries. This teleautograph (in which orders written on the machine on one floor are automatically recorded on the kitchen machine) is quiet but sometimes unintelligible. Orders written in a hurry and in abbreviated form are sometimes misinterpreted so that sliced ham arrives when sliced toms (tomatoes) were ordered. Besides, neither of those channels operates easily for two-way communication. It is difficult to carry on a conversation over the public address system, and, while kitchen runners can write their replies to orders on the teleautograph, this hardly makes for full and free expression. The telephone provides two-way communication, but most kitchens are so noisy that it is difficult to hear phone conversations. And in some restaurants, there is only one telephone circuit for the whole house, so when kitchen and pantry runners are using it, no one else can put in a call.

The problems that come up with such communication systems can best be illustrated by looking at a particular restaurant, Chandler's, where teleautograph and phone were used.

A kitchen supervisor was in charge of Chandler's kitchen, and pantry supervisors were in charge of each pantry under the kitchen supervisor's general supervision. There was also an assistant supervisor working in the kitchen.

The supplying function was carried on in the kitchen by two or three runners (depending upon the employment situation) and by a runner on each of the service-pantry floors. Food was sent up by automatic elevator.

The kitchen runners were supposed to pick up their orders from storage bins, iceboxes, or directly from the cooks. When the order was in preparation, the cook or salad girl was supposed to say how long it would be before it was ready, and the runner would relay this information by teleautograph to the service pantries. When the cooking or salad making had not been begun, the runner had no authority to tell the cook to hurry the order. Before each meal, the cook was given an open order (a minimum and maximum amount) on each item by the kitchen supervisor. She worked steadily until she had produced the minimum, and, from then on, she gauged her production according to the demands that came to her from the runner. That is, if the item was going out fast, she would keep producing as fast as she could until she had produced the maximum. Beyond this point she could not go without authorization from her supervisor. Ideally, the supervisor and cook would confer before the maximum had been reached in order to see whether it was necessary to set a new figure, but this did not always happen.

While the runner could not order the cook to go beyond her maximum, his demands directly influenced her behavior up to that point. He originated action for her.

That was at the base of his troubles. Among kitchen employees, the cooks have the highest status. In Chandler's, runners had a low status, just above potwashers and sweepers. The jobs were filled by inexperienced employees, women or men who, if they performed well, were advanced to something of higher status. Their wages were considerably lower than the cooks', and the cooks also had a great advantage in seniority. In this particular case, the age difference was important too. The runners were a young man, a teenaged boy, and a young woman, while the cooks were middle-aged women.

The runners would have been in a more secure position if they had been in close touch with a supervisor, but here the communication was sporadic and ineffective. The supervisor was inclined to let the runners fend for themselves.

When the runners put pressure on them, the cooks often reacted so as to put the runners in their place. For example, we observed incidents like this one. One runner (Ruth) asked another to get some salmon salad from the salad girl. The second runner found that the salad girl had no more on hand.

> "They want me to get some more of that salmon salad," he said. "Could you make it, please?"
> "Who told you that?" she asked.
> "Ruth did."
> "You can tell Ruth that I don't take no orders from her. I have a boss, and I don't take no orders from nobody else. You can just tell her that."

Now it may have been that the salad girl had made her maximum and could not go on without authorization from her supervisor, but the runner had no way of knowing that this was the case. He put his request to her politely, and she could have responded in kind by saying she was sorry that she could not make more without consulting the supervisor. Instead she responded aggressively, as if she felt a need to make it clear that no mere runner was going to originate action for her.

Even when they complied with the runner's requests, the cooks sometimes behaved so as to make it appear as if it were really they who originated the action. They always liked to make it clear that they had authority over the foods after they had been prepared, and that they could determine what should be done with them. While this was a general reaction, the salad girl was most explicit in such cases.

A runner went to look for some boiled eggs. The salad girl was not present at the moment, so he could not ask her, but after he had gotten the eggs from the icebox, he saw that she was back at her station. He showed her the pan of eggs, asking, "What about that?"

> "I don't like that," she said belligerently. "You have no business taking them eggs out of the icebox without asking."
> "Well, I'm asking you now."
> "I have to know how much there is. That's why I want you to tell me. . . . Go on, you might as well take them now that you have them."

On other occasions when he asked her for salad, she would say:

> "Why don't you people look in the icebox once in a while?"

In such a case, whatever the runner did was wrong. The salad girl's behavior was irrational, of course, but it did serve a function for her. Behaving in this way, she was able to originate action for the runner instead of being in the inferior position of responding to his actions.

The runners also had difficulty in getting information out of the cooks. When there was a demand from the service pantries, and the food could not be sent up immediately, the runners were always supposed to give an estimate as to when they could furnish the item. This information they were expected to get from the cooks. The cooks sometimes flatly refused to give a time and were generally reluctant to make an estimate. When they did give a time, they nearly always ran considerably beyond it.

Incidentally, time seems to be used as a weapon in the restaurant. It is well known that customers feel and complain that they wait for a table or for service far longer than they actually do. Waitresses, as we observed them, estimated their waiting time on orders as much as 50 to 100 percent more than the actual time. While they were not conscious of what they were doing, they could express impatience with the service-pantry girls more eloquently by saying, "I've been waiting 20 minutes for that order," than by giving the time as 10 minutes. In the front of the house, time is used to put pressure on people. In the back of the house, the cooks try to use time to take pressure off themselves. They say that an item will be done "right away," which does not tell when it will be done but announces that they have the situation well in hand and that nobody should bother them about it. Giving a short time tends to have the same effect. It reassures the runner, who reassures the service pantries. When the time runs out, the pantry runners begin again to demand action, but it may take a few minutes before the pressure gets back to the cooks, and by that time the item may really be ready for delivery. Furthermore, the cook's refusal to give a time turns the pressure back on runners and other parts of the house—a result that they are not able to accomplish in any other way.

In the case of some of the inexperienced cooks, it may be that they simply did not know how to estimate cooking time, but that would hardly explain the persistent failure of all the cooks to cooperate with the runners in this matter.

The management was quite aware of this problem but had no real solution to offer. One of the pantry supervisors instructed a kitchen runner in this way:

> "You have to give us a time on everything that is going to be delayed. That is the only way we can keep things going upstairs. On our blackboards we list all of our foods and how long it will take to get them, and most of the time we have to list them 'indefinite.' That shouldn't be. We should always have a definite time, so the waitress can tell the guest how long he will have to wait for his order. We can't tell the guest we're out of a certain food item on the menu and that we don't know how long it will take to replace it. They'll ask what kind of a restaurant we're running."
>
> The runner thought that over and then went on to question the supervisor. "But sometimes we can't get that information from the cooks . . . They won't tell us, or maybe they don't know."
>
> "Then you should always ask the food-production manager. She'll tell you, or she'll get the cook to tell you."
>
> "But the cooks would think we had squealed."
>
> "No, they wouldn't. And if they did, all right, it's the only way

they'll ever learn. They've got to learn that, because we must always
have a time on all delayed foods."

"Yes, surely we couldn't tell on them if they refused to give the
information."

"Yes, you could. You have to. They'll have to learn it somehow."

The efficiency of this system depended upon building up a cooperative relationship
between cooks and runners. For runners to try to get action by appealing to the boss
to put pressure on the cooks is hardly the way to build up such a relationship. It is
clear that, considering their low status in relation to the cooks, runners are not in a
position to take the lead in smoothing out human-relations difficulties.

Some of the runner's problems arise from failure to achieve efficient coordination
and communication between floors. For example, on one occasion, one of the upstairs
floors put in a rush order for a pan of rice. With some difficulty, the kitchen runner
was able to fill the order. Then, 15 minutes later, the pan came back to the kitchen
again, still almost full, but apparently no more was needed for the meal. The cooks
gathered around the elevator to give vent to their feelings. This proved, they said,
that the rice had not been needed after all. Those people upstairs just didn't know
what they were doing. After the meal was over, the kitchen runner went up to check
with the pantry runner. The pantry man explained, "I ran out of creole, and there
wasn't going to be any more, so I had no use for any more rice."

This was a perfectly reasonable explanation, but it did not reach the cooks. As a
rule, the cooks had little idea of what was going on upstairs. Sometimes there would
be an urgent call for some food item along toward the end of the meal-time, and it
would be supplied only after a considerable delay. By the time it reached the service
pantries, there would no longer be a demand for it, and the supply would shortly be
sent back. This would always upset the cooks. They would then stand around and
vow that next time they would not take it seriously when the upstairs people were
clamoring for action.

"In the service pantries," one of the cooks said, "they just don't care how much
they ask for. That guy, Joe [pantry runner], just hoards the stuff up there. He can't
always be out of it like he claims. He just hoards it."

A kitchen runner made this comment:

> Joe will order something and right away he'll order it again. He just
> keeps calling for more. Once or twice I went upstairs, and I saw he had
> plenty of stuff up there. He just hoards it up there, and he has to send a
> lot of stuff downstairs. He wastes a lot of stuff. After I caught on to the
> way he works, I just made it a rule when he called for stuff and the first
> floor was calling for stuff at the same time, I divided it between them.

On the other hand, when Joe was rushed and found that he was not getting quick
action on his orders, his tendency was to make his orders larger, repeat the orders
before any supply had come up, and mark all his orders *rush*. When this did not bring
results, he would call the kitchen on the phone. If all else failed, he would sometimes
run down into the kitchen himself to see if he could snatch what he needed.

This kind of behavior built up confusion and resentment in the kitchen. When orders
were repeated, the kitchen runners could not tell whether additional supply was needed

or whether the pantry runners were just getting impatient. When everything was marked rush, there was no way of telling how badly anybody needed anything. But most serious of all was the reaction when the pantry runner invaded the kitchen.

One of them told us of such an incident:

> One of the cooks got mad at me the other day. I went down there to get this item, and boy, did she get mad at me for coming down there. But I got to do *something*! The waitresses and the pantry girls keep on yelling at me to get it for them. Well, I finally got it, or somehow it got sent upstairs. Boy, she was sure mad at me, though.

Apparently the cooks resented the presence of any upstairs supply man in the kitchen, but they were particularly incensed about Joe, the runner they all suspected of hoarding food.

One of them made this comment:

> That guy would try to come down in the kitchen and tell us what to do. But not me. No sir. He came down here one day and tried to tell me what to do. He said to me, "We're going to be very busy today," I just looked at him. "Yeah?" I said, "Who are you? Go on upstairs. Go on. Mind your own business." Can you beat that! "We're going to be very busy today!" He never came down and told me anything again. "Who are you?" I asked him. That's all I had to say to him.

Here the runner's remark did not have any effect upon the work of the cook, but the implication was that he was in a superior position, and she reacted strongly against him for that reason. None of the cooks enjoy having the kitchen runners originate action for them, but, since it occurs regularly, they make some adjustment to it. They are not accustomed to any sort of relationship with the pantry runners, so when they come down to add to the pressure and confusion of the kitchen, the cooks feel free to slap them down.

It was not only the pantry runners who invaded the kitchen. The pantry supervisors spent a great deal of time and energy running up and down. When an upstairs supervisor comes after supplies, the kitchen reaction is the same as that to the pantry runners—except that the supervisor cannot be slapped down. Instead, the employees gripe to each other.

As one kitchen runner said,

> I wish she would quit that. I wonder what she thinks she's doing, running down here and picking up things we're waiting for. Now like just a minute ago, did you see that? She went off with peaches and plums, and we'd never have known about it if I hadn't seen her. Now couldn't she have just stepped over here and told us? . . . She sure gets mad a lot, doesn't she? She's always griping. I mean, she's probably a nice person, but she's hard to get along with at work—she sure is!

There were other pantry supervisors whose presence in the kitchen did not cause such a disturbance. The workers would say that so-and-so was really all right. Nevertheless, whenever a pantry supervisor dashed into the kitchen for supplies, it was a sign to everybody that something was wrong—that somebody was worried—and thus it added to the tension in the atmosphere and disturbed the human relations of the regular supply system, such as they were.

In this situation, the kitchen runner was the man in the middle. One of the service-pantry girls we interviewed put it this way:

> Oh, we certainly are busy up here. We don't stop even for a moment. I
> think this is the busiest place around here. It's bad when we can't get
> those foods, though. We get delayed by those supply people down stairs
> all the time. I could shoot those runners. We can be just as busy up
> here—but down there it's always slow motion. It seems like they just
> don't care at all. They always take all the time in the world.

On the other hand, the cooks blamed the inefficiency of the runners for many of their troubles. They felt that the runners were constantly sending up duplicate orders just through failure to consult each other on the progress of their work. Actually, according to our observation, this happened very rarely, but whenever a runner was caught in the act, this was taken as proof that duplication was common practice. The failure of the runners to coordinate their work efficiently did annoy the cooks in another way, as they were sometimes asked for the same order within a few seconds by two different runners. However, while this added to the nervous tension, it did not directly affect the flow of supplies.

Such were the problems of supply in one restaurant where we were able to give them close attention. However, as it stands, this account is likely to give a false impression. The reader may picture the restaurant as a series of armed camps, each one in constant battle with its neighbor. He may also get the impression that food reaches customers only intermittently and after long delays.

To us it seemed that the restaurant was doing a remarkable job of production and service, and yet, in view of the frictions we observed, it is only natural to ask whether it would not be possible to organize the human relations for better teamwork and greater efficiency.

According to one point of view, no basic improvement is possible because "you can't change human nature."

But is it all just personalities and personal inefficiency? What has been the situation in other restaurants of this type (operating on several floors) and in other periods of time?

Unfortunately, we have no studies for other time periods, but we do have the testimony of several supervisors who have had previous experience in restaurants facing similar problems, and who have shown themselves, in the course of study, to be shrewd observers of behavior in their own organizations. Their story is that the friction and incoordination we observed were not simply a war time phenomenon. While increased business and inexperienced help made the problem much more acute, the friction came at the same places in the organization—between the same categories of people. The job of the kitchen runner, apparently, has always been a "hot spot" in such an organization.

This, then is not primarily a personality problem. It is a problem in organization design. When the organization operates so as to stimulate conflict between people holding certain positions within it, then we can expect trouble.

Questions

1. What kind of organizational problems existed at Chandler's Restaurant?

2. Are differences in status of cooks, runners, potwashers, and sweepers related to their positions in the organizational hierarchy? Explain.

3. What is the likely perceived job content for a cook working at Chandler's Restaurant?

Source: This case was prepared by William F. Whyte and is reprinted here by permission of the author.

PART IV

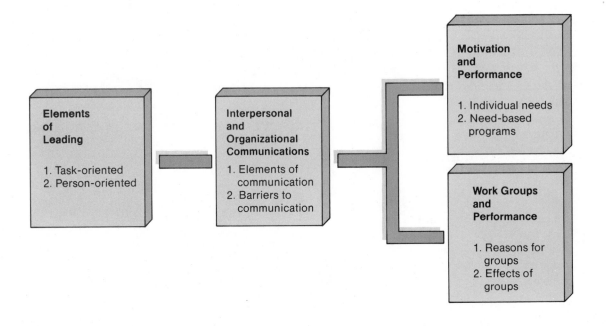

Elements of Leading

1. Task-oriented
2. Person-oriented

Interpersonal and Organizational Communications

1. Elements of communication
2. Barriers to communication

Motivation and Performance

1. Individual needs
2. Need-based programs

Work Groups and Performance

1. Reasons for groups
2. Effects of groups

THE LEADING FUNCTION

INTRODUCTION TO PART IV

Part IV, the leading function, contains four chapters.

The inclusion of the material contained in the four chapters is based on the following rationale:

The leading function is defined as the attempt of managers to influence the behavior of individuals and groups through interpersonal and organizational communication. The *elements of leading,* presented in Chapter 10, consist of task- and person-oriented influence. Effective leadership is contingent upon the leader's personality, the needs of individuals and groups, and factors in the situation itself. Numerous theories identify the circumstances in which a particular kind of influence attempt will be effective.

Leaders *exercise influence through communications,* and while the most apparent communication channels are interpersonal ones, more formal organizational channels such as memorandums, written directives, and policies are also important. Chapter 11 reviews some of the more important ideas on communication from the perspective of the leading function.

Finally, Chapters 12 and 13 present relevant information on the objects of leadership influence—individuals and groups. Chapter 12 describes theory and practice in the use of *motivation to influence individual performance.* Methods such as job enrichment, behavior modification, and pay programs are presented. Chapter 13 deals with the positive and negative *effects of work groups on performance objectives.*

The figure on the facing page depicts the four aspects of the leading function.

TEN

Elements of Leading

LEARNING OBJECTIVES

After completing Chapter 10, you should be able to:

Define: what is meant by the term *leadership*.

State: the three general approaches to the study of leadership.

Describe: the two primary functions of leadership.

Explain: why leadership is a necessary management function.

Discuss: why the maturity level of followers would be expected to change over time.

A LEADER WHO ADMITS HE WAS COMPLACENT

An Wang, Ph.D., is the 67-year-old founder, CEO, and chairperson of Wang Laboratories, Inc. In the early 1980s, after a long period of breathtaking growth—between 3 and 40 percent a year—Wang Labs began to fade. The leaders simply failed to foresee the personal computer revolution. While its competitors were offering desktop machines that could both edit text and crunch numbers, under Dr. Wang's direction, the company was still selling word processors that were only good for creating documents. The company didn't recognize the opportunities available in personal computers and just kept plodding along.

The result was a tremendous slump in sales and a loss of over $109 million in one quarter. It was the first loss for Wang Labs in more than 10 years. Dr. Wang believes that as a leader he failed to sense a shifting market. He had handed over the company to a five-member executive committee. After the large losses, he took sole control again.

(The Management Solution to this Management Incident can be found at the end of this chapter.)

Leadership is an important and necessary skill for achieving individual, group, and organizational performance. Managers, whether they are chief executive officers like An Wang of Wang Laboratories or first-level supervisors, influence attitudes and expectations that encourage or discourage performance, secure or alienate employee commitment, reward or penalize achievement. Despite the growth of large, impersonal organizations, people still relate to leaders. We see this in our everyday lives, and we make judgments about the leaders of our business, governmental, and educational organizations. Leadership does make a difference.

This chapter reviews some of the current theories and ideas about leadership. Efforts to analyze effective leadership have focused on three general areas: (1) *the personal characteristics of leaders,* (2) *the behavior of leaders,* and (3) *the situations in which leaders are found.* Despite the extensive research into leadership, it is impossible to state that there is one best way to lead. Rather, the contingency view of leadership suggests that the best way to lead varies with each situation. That is, good leadership in one situation may, when practiced in another situation, result in chaos, nonperformance, and unfulfilled goals.

Leadership involves other people; therefore, where there are leaders, there must be followers.[1] Leadership can arise in any situation where people have combined their efforts to accomplish a task. Thus, leaders may or may not be managers. Within the organization, informal groups develop, and within those groups are people who influence the behavior of other group members. Such people are the *informal leaders.* Individuals who influence the behavior of their assigned groups are the *formal leaders* of organizations. Our emphasis in this chapter is formal leadership; that is, managers who must exhibit leadership behavior.

Leading and being a manager are not necessarily the same. A manager is a person formally recognized in the organization's hierarchy. He is expected to plan, organize, control, and make effective decisions. It is correct to state that a good manager is always a good leader, but a good leader is not necessarily a good manager. The key difference between leadership and management has been given an outstanding description:

> Leadership is a part of management but not all of it. . . . Leadership is
> the ability to persuade others to seek defined objectives enthusiastically. It
> is the human factor which binds a group together and motivates it toward
> goals. Management activities such as planning, organizing, and decision
> making are dormant cocoons until the leader triggers the power of
> motivation in people and guides them toward goals.[2]

Leadership is not an easy term to define precisely. We define *leadership* as the ability to influence through communication the activities of others, individually or as a group, toward the accomplishment of worthwhile, meaningful, and challenging goals. First, this definition indicates that one cannot be a leader unless there are people (e.g., co-workers, followers) to be led. Second, leadership involves the practice of influence

---

[1]John P. Kotter, *The Leadership Factor* (New York: The Free Press, 1988).

[2]Keith Davis, *Human Relations at Work* (New York: McGraw-Hill, 1967), pp. 96–97.

skills. The use of these skills has a purpose, to accomplish goals. Finally, an objective of leadership is to bring about influence so that important goals are achieved. The following Management Application presents in a general way a few straightforward statements about what a leader does in influencing followers.

MANAGEMENT APPLICATION

EXPERT TIPS ABOUT THE WORK OF LEADERS

Warren Bennis has for decades presented some straightforward comments and insights about leadership. (These insights provide value for considering what can be done in organizations to improve the flow of talented leaders into key decision-making positions.) Unfortunately, Bennis is somewhat pessimistic about the pool of leaders we have waiting to take over and make crucial decisions. There doesn't seem to be any Washington, Jefferson, Adams, Truman, Roosevelt, and Lincoln type of leaders in politics. Likewise, the handful of business leaders, such as Lee Iacocca, Armand Hammer, and Victor Kiam, are too few for accomplishing what is needed to enhance the nation's standard of living, quality of life, and image among Third World developing nations.

Bennis suggests that a leader, like anyone else, is the sum of all his experiences, but unlike others, amounts to more than the sum because he makes more of the experience. A leader doesn't just practice his profession or vocation, he masters it. He adapts, imagines, reverses, connects, compares, rejects, incubates, and plans. Roosevelt, Truman, and Eisenhower mastered the presidency. Carter and Nixon were mastered by it.

Lao Tzu said, to lead, one must follow. The leader must have virtue and vision, and some abiding passion, but she must also understand and be understood by followers. This is advice that applies to organizations. It indicates that there is no leadership without followers. Leaders chart the course and guide followers to accomplish goals. Truman was able to do this. Iacocca has succeeded in doing this, and some others in politics and business have not been successful. Being willing to chart the course and guide takes a very special kind of courage to lead. As you continue reading in this chapter, think about the challenges a leader faces and the gratification that results from knowing that one has been able to influence the activities of others.

Source: Adapted from Warren Bennis, "The Dreamless Society," *New Management,* Winter 1988, pp. 17–24.

THE CORE OF LEADERSHIP: INFLUENCE

The exercise of influence is the essence of leadership behavior. However, there has been only limited research on the methods leaders use in attempts to influence the behavior of others. For example, Henry Mintzberg's classic study of what managers do on the job fails to describe the influence tactics used.[3] Furthermore, French and

---

[3]Henry Mintzberg, *The Nature of Managerial Work* (Englewood Cliffs, N.J.: Prentice-Hall, 1980).

Raven propose that social power is used to influence others.[4] They state that the bases of power include rewards, coercion, legitimate power, referent power, and expertise. Their social power explanation, however, fails to outline all the strategies used by managers.

Seven influence strategies have been proposed as particularly vital for practicing leadership roles.[5] These strategies are:

- Reason—Using facts and data to develop a logically sound argument.
- Friendliness—Using supportiveness, flattery, and the creation of goodwill.
- Coalition—Mobilizing others in the organization.
- Bargaining—Negotiating through the use of benefits or favors.
- Assertiveness—Using a direct and forceful approach.
- Higher Authority—Gaining the support of higher levels in the hierarchy to add weight to the requests.
- Sanctions—Using rewards and punishment.

A study of 360 first- and second-level managers in the United States, Great Britain, and Australia assessed their personal influence strategies.[6] The most popular methods used with subordinates were reason and assertiveness, while the least-used methods were higher authority and sanctions. The study also determined that managers with the power to control resources use a greater variety of influence strategies. This study suggests that using influence is a fundamental activity in organizations. Leaders apparently need to learn a variety of influence strategies; they cannot rely solely on the traditional strategy of exercising the power they possess by virtue of their position in the formal hierarchy or informal group.

FUNCTIONS OF LEADERS

Leadership involves simultaneous attention to (1) the tasks to be accomplished by groups and individuals and (2) the needs and expectations of groups and individuals. Leaders exercise influence through *communication* to specify the individual and group task-related activities required to achieve effective performance. At the same time, leaders exercise influence to maintain their groups' ability to work as units and also to support the specific needs of individuals. Performance criteria such as turnover, absenteeism, grievances, and job satisfaction are achieved through effective leadership. Many organizations have developed programs to aid individuals in becoming effective leaders. The following Management Application points out some of the steps taken by General Electric and IBM.

---

[4]John R. P. French and Bertram Raven, "The Basis of Social Power," in *Studies in Social Power,* ed. D. Cartwright (Ann Arbor: University of Michigan Press, 1959), pp. 150–167.

[5]David Kipnis, Stuart M. Schmidt, Chris Swaffin-Smith, and Ian Wilkinson, "Patterns of Managerial Influence: Shotgun Managers, Tacticians, and Bystanders," *Organizational Dynamics,* Winter 1984, pp. 58–67.

[6]Ibid.

MANAGEMENT APPLICATION

GROWING LEADERSHIP TALENT AT GE AND IBM

A managing director of a large South Korean corporation attended a management development program at General Electric's headquarters in Fairfield, Connecticut. After observing and discussing the program in detail, the visitor asked what was the real secret for developing effective leaders—he wanted the magic formula. Of course, there is nothing magical about grooming leaders.

General Electric carefully trains its managerial talent throughout their careers. Each of the 80,000 salaried employees is given an annual performance review. Whenever there is an opening among the 500 or so top GE jobs, an internal candidate search is conducted. To keep this talent flowing, GE has instituted a five-stage, on-the-job education and training program. The stages are: (1) a corporate leadership program for new college hires, with an advanced version three years later; (2) a one-week, new-manager course; (3) senior-level functional courses; (4) a sequence of three executive programs, each four weeks long, for those with the highest potential; and (5) workshops for officers, focusing on critical GE issues. This course involves hard work, and no magic is involved.

The IBM strategy is to develop individuals with leadership potential to have a general view. It is believed that the first 10 years are the most important time in a person's development. Thus, IBM asks managers to identify high potential people; that is, those who can be leaders and top-level executives. These fast trackers are expected to move from job to job and test their range and potential every 18 to 24 months.

Fast trackers are rotated between line and staff duty. Several hundred people are selected annually to serve as administrative assistants for a year or so. Job assignments, including task forces, are coupled with educational training, both inside and outside the company. For new IBM managers there is a week of basic management training. Then six months later, the new manager attends a second class in his function. Middle managers attend a one-week school, emphasizing involvement in problem-solving exercises. Then about five years later, they return to school.

IBM executives receive some type of educational training every three years. Each manager from executives down to the new first-line supervisor has an opportunity to learn more, develop skills, and review her potential. The development of leaders is what IBM pays attention to so that talented people are always available.

Source: Adapted from James Braham, "Cultivating Tomorrow's Execs," *Industry Week,* July 27, 1987, pp. 34–38.

A manager in specific situations may not recognize that effective leadership requires attention to *tasks* and *people*. No doubt, in time experienced managers develop a particular style that reflects their own ideas and perspectives on the relative importance of tasks and people.

Thus, leadership consists of attempting to influence others. These attempts are directed toward two separate yet related types of functions: (1) task-oriented, and (2) person-oriented. Task-oriented functions are achieved by specifying work activities and work goals of the group as a whole and of each member of the group. Person-oriented functions require leaders to maintain group processes and to support individuals' needs and aspirations. Successful influence attempts result in performance gains such as higher quality, lower costs, lower absenteeism, and fewer grievances.

APPROACHES TO STUDYING LEADERSHIP IN ORGANIZATIONS

Leadership has been one of the most studied topics in management, yet the conclusions reached have been contradictory, exaggerated, and controversial. Part of the problem lies in the definitions, measurement, and theory used to study leadership. The three main approaches at the center of the debate surrounding leadership are as follows:

1. *The leader trait approach*—attributes performance differences among employees to the individual characteristics (traits) of leaders.
2. *The leader behavior approach*—attributes performance differences to the behaviors and style of leaders.
3. *The situational contingency approach*—the leader's behavior and style in combination with situational factors are the key reason for performance differences.

Over the years each of these main approaches have been refined and various dimensions have been added, but they still remain the primary basis for leadership theory, research, and application discussions.

Leader Trait Approach

We observe good leaders such as Sam Walton of Wal-Mart, Debbi Fields of Mrs. Fields' Cookies, and Warren Phillips of Dow-Jones. So it is natural to ask whether the secret of leadership is to be found in the individual characteristics of leaders. Are there differences between leaders and nonleaders in terms of personality traits, physical characteristics, motives, and needs?

Many people believe that effective leadership has roots in a particular personality trait. Some even assume that unless one possesses that trait, he is doomed to failure as a leader. The search for people with this trait often is frustrating, confusing, and difficult.

Winston Churchill had leadership traits. He was a good manager first. He could identify problems, weigh alternatives, and make decisions. He sent people into action during World War II when many didn't want to go. And here is where a distinction between leadership and managership could be seen. For the people who perceived Churchill as correct in his assessment and his plan, he was both a manager *and* a leader. But for the dissenters, he was only their manager until the moment they could agree that what was good for England also was good for them as individuals.

Some organizations today continue to search for talented people who possess traits associated with good leaders and good managers. They need these multitalented, creative, inspirational individuals to point the way for and influence others. Just as was true with Winston Churchill, leadership is in the eye of the beholder.

The systematic study of the personal characteristics and traits of leaders began as a consequence of the need for military officers during World War I. Many business and governmental organizations also began researching the characteristics that distinguished their most effective from the less effective managers.

The studies that attempt to identify these traits have produced a lengthy list. They are grouped into six categories:

1. *Physical characteristics*—age, height, weight.
2. *Background characteristics*—education, social class or status, mobility, experience.
3. *Intelligence*—ability, judgment, knowledge.
4. *Personality*—aggressiveness, alertness, dominance, decisiveness, enthusiasm, extroversion, independence, self-confidence, authoritarianism.
5. *Task-related characteristics*—achievement need, responsibility, initiative, persistence.
6. *Social characteristics*—supervisory ability, cooperativeness, popularity, prestige, tact, diplomacy.

Even today, some executives involved in the recruitment and selection of managers believe that the *trait theory* is valid. However, the comparison of leaders by various physical, personality, and intelligence traits has resulted in little agreement.

Physical Traits.   Some advocates of the trait theory contend that the physical stature of a person affects ability to influence followers. For example, an extensive review of 12 leadership investigations showed that 9 of the studies found leaders to be taller than followers; 2 found them to be shorter; and 1 concluded that height was not the most important factor.[7] Other physical traits that have been studied with no conclusive results include weight, physique, and personal appearance.

Personality.   A number of studies have found several personality factors to be related in some, but not all, cases of effective leadership.[8] These studies have found that leaders with the drive to act independently and with self-assurance (e.g., with confidence in their leadership skills) are successful in achieving task and group performance.

One study suggests that successful leaders may be more perceptive than unsuccessful leaders.[9] Accordingly, effective leaders are more proficient in differentiating their best from their poorest followers than are the less effective leaders. The leaders of high-performing groups maintain greater psychological distance between themselves and their followers than do the leaders of less effective groups.

---

[7]Ralph Stogdill, "Personal Factors Associated with Leadership," *Journal of Applied Psychology,* January 1948, pp. 35–71.

[8]Edwin E. Ghiselli, "Managerial Talent," *American Psychologist,* October 1963, pp. 631–41.

[9]Fred Fiedler, "The Leader's Psychological Distance and Group Effectiveness," in *Group Dynamics,* ed. Dorwin Cartwright and Alvin Zander (New York: Harper & Row, 1968), pp. 586–605.

Intelligence.   After surveying the literature, one scholar concluded that leadership ability is associated with the judgment and verbal facility of the person.[10] Another researcher concluded that within a certain range, one's intelligence is an accurate predictor of managerial success.[11] Above and below this range, the chances of successful leadership decrease significantly. However, the leader's intelligence should be close to that of the followers. The leader who is too smart or not smart enough may lose the followers' respect.

Ghiselli's Leadership Trait Studies.   Edwin E. Ghiselli, an important student of leadership, has studied eight personality traits and five motivational traits.[12] The traits he studied are:

> *Personality traits:*
>   Intelligence.
>   Initiative.
>   Supervisory ability.
>   Self-assurance.
>   Affinity for the working class.
>   Decisiveness.
>   Masculinity-femininity.
>   Maturity.
> *Motivational traits:*
>   Need for job security.
>   Need for financial reward.
>   Need for power over others.
>   Need for self-actualization.
>   Need for occupational achievement.

Ghiselli's research findings suggest the relative importance of the traits as noted in Figure 10–1.

The Center for Creative Leadership Study.   The Center for Creative Leadership is a nonprofit research and educational institution located in Greensboro, North Carolina. It is interested in studying and understanding the practice of leadership. Two of the Center's researchers, Morgan McCall and Michael Lombardo, working with an associate, Ann Morrison, sought to compare traits of 21 derailed executives—successful people who were expected to be promoted, but who reached a plateau, were fired, or were forced to retire early—with those of 20 "arrivers," who made it all the way to the top.[13]

---

[10]Stogdill, "Personal Factors," pp. 40–42.

[11]Ghiselli, "Managerial Talent," pp. 633–35.

[12]Edwin E. Ghiselli, *Explorations in Management Talent* (Pacific Palisades, Calif.: Goodyear Publishing, 1971).

[13]Morgan W. McCall, Jr. and Michael M. Lombardo, "What Makes a Top Executive?" *Psychology Today,* February 1983, pp. 26–31.

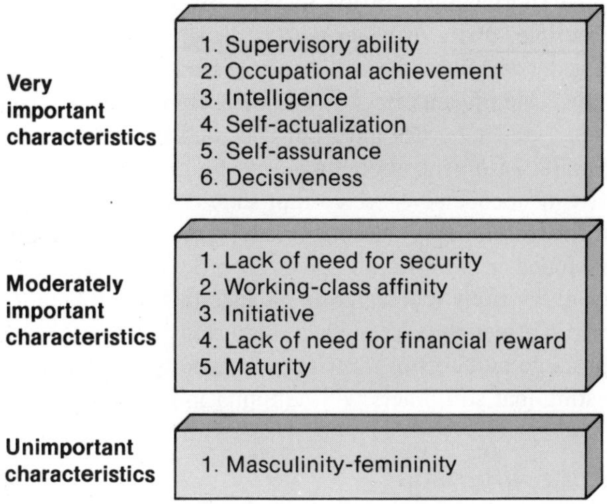

Very important characteristics	1. Supervisory ability 2. Occupational achievement 3. Intelligence 4. Self-actualization 5. Self-assurance 6. Decisiveness
Moderately important characteristics	1. Lack of need for security 2. Working-class affinity 3. Initiative 4. Lack of need for financial reward 5. Maturity
Unimportant characteristics	1. Masculinity-femininity

Figure 10–1
The relative importance of leader characteristics and effective leadership.

The derailed executives' flaws merged into a list of 10 traits:

1. Insensitive to others; abrasive; intimidating, bullying style.
2. Cold; aloof; arrogant.
3. Betrayal of trust.
4. Overly ambitious; thinking of next job; playing politics.
5. Specific performance problems with the business.
6. Overmanaging; unable to delegate or build a team.
7. Unable to staff effectively.
8. Unable to think strategically.
9. Unable to adapt to boss with different style.
10. Overdependent on advocate or mentor.

None of the derailed executives had all the trait flaws cited. The arrivers appeared to possess more ability to get along with all types of people. They either possessed or developed the skills required to be outspoken without offending people. They were seen as being direct and diplomatic.

The Center for Creative Leadership researchers suggest, however, that no one—the arrivers or the derailed executives—can possess every skill and trait needed to fit every situation. A leader is human like everyone else and therefore possesses strengths and weaknesses. But if there is one trait that seems to be associated with success, it is the ability to get along with people. Exactly how this ability can become a part of a leaders's repertoire remains a mystery, however. There is no foolproof, step-by-step training program or procedure that can assure the exact amount of this elusive ability in each situation.

There are some shortcomings in the method of employing a trait approach and assuming, for example, that a manager who is decisive, self-assured, and intelligent will be an effective leader. First, the trait theory of leadership ignores the subordinates. The followers have a significant effect on the job accomplished by the leader. Second, except for Ghiselli, trait theorists have not specified the relative importance of the various traits. Should an organization attempt to find managers who are confident or managers who act independently—which trait should be weighted more? Third, most of the trait-based research relies on small study samples. For example, only 41 executives were included in the McCall and Lombardo study. Fourth, the evidence is inconsistent. For every study that supports the idea that a particular trait is positively related to leadership effectiveness, another study finds a negative or no relationship. Finally, although large numbers of traits already have been uncovered, the list grows annually, suggesting that still others will be found in the future.

Leader Behavior Approach

The disappointing results of the search for leadership traits have led to a somewhat different line of thought. Rather than focusing on the *characteristics* of effective leaders, an alternative is to focus on their *behavior*. The question of *behavioral leadership theories* then becomes: What do effective leaders *do* that ineffective ones *do not do?* For example, are effective leaders democratic rather than autocratic, permissive rather than directive, person-oriented rather than task-oriented? Or are effective leaders characterized by some balance of these behaviors? This line of questioning is based on the reasoning shown in Figure 10–2.

Terms such as *permissive-directive, democratic-autocratic, and person-oriented–production-oriented* are nearly synonymous. Generally, these terms refer to whether the leader's behavior reflects *primary* concern for the work or for the people who are doing the work. We noted earlier that the essence of leadership is getting work done through others. One point of view holds that the best way to lead is to be task-oriented.

Task-Oriented Leadership.   Scientific management techniques such as time and motion study, work simplification, and piece-rate incentive pay plans emphasize the need for leaders to plan each worker's job tasks and job outcomes. The leader is assumed to be the most competent individual in planning and organizing the work of subordinates. According to a major proponent of scientific management:

> The work of every workman is fully planned out by the management at least one day in advance, and each man receives . . . complete written instructions, describing in detail the task which he is to accomplish, as well as the means to be used in doing the work.[14]

To ensure that each task is performed according to the plan, the worker is paid on an incentive basis. The performance standards are stated in terms of quantity and quality of output, and the worker is paid for each unit of acceptable quality.

---

[14]Frederick W. Taylor, *Scientific Management* (New York: Harper & Row, 1911), p. 39.

Figure 10–2 Behavior of effective leaders.

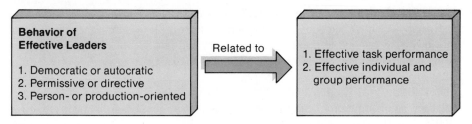

The terms used to refer to leader behaviors that are concerned primarily with task goods and activities (in other words, the task function of leadership) include *directive, production-oriented, autocratic,* and *initiating structure.* Each of these terms is used in contemporary management and leadership literature. Although the origins of task-oriented leadership can be found in literature first published some 70 years ago, some modern leaders still believe that task-oriented behavior is the most effective for obtaining performance.

Person-Oriented Leadership. Rensis Likert is a pioneer in the development of the idea that the behaviors of the most effective leaders are person oriented. Likert and his associates at the University of Michigan have conducted studies in various organizational settings such as industrial, governmental, educational, and health care. These studies have led Likert to conclude that the most effective leaders focus on the human aspects of their groups. They attempt to build effective teamwork through supportive, considerate, and nonpunitive *employee-centered* behavior. Such leaders were found to be more effective than those who emphasized *task-centered* behavior; that is, leaders who specifically detailed the work of subordinates, closely supervised them, and rewarded them only with financial incentives.[15]

The idea that effective leaders are person-oriented is an outgrowth of the behavioral approach to management, particularly the human relations branch. The concept that people seek a wide array of satisfactions through work is at the core of many management practices. It is not surprising that it should also be the underpinning of a popular point of view regarding leadership.

Thus, it would seem that we are left with the choice that the effective leader is *either* task oriented *or* person oriented, *but not both.* And if this is the case, then aspiring leaders need only a narrow range of skills. If the most effective leaders are task oriented, then leaders need only be skilled in the technical aspects of planning and organizing the work of others. But if the most effective leaders are person oriented, then human relations and interpersonal skills are required. But what if both points of

[15]Rensis Likert, "Management Styles and the Human Component," *Management Review,* October 1977, pp. 23–28; 43–45.

view are correct? Some believe that effective leaders are equally task and person oriented in their behavior toward subordinates.

The idea that the one best way to lead effectively requires a balance between task- and person-oriented behavior has considerable appeal. Two approaches to studying this idea have become well known in the theory and practice of leadership. The first is the *two-dimensional theory,* and the second is the *managerial grid* theory.

Two-Dimensional Theory.   One of the most significant investigations of leadership has been an ongoing program at Ohio State University that began immediately after World War II. The researchers associated with this program have produced many studies of leadership effectiveness. The two key concepts in the two-dimensional theory are *initiating structure* and *consideration.* Initiating structure refers to task-oriented behavior in which the leader organizes and defines the relationships in the group, establishes patterns and channels of communications, and directs the work methods. Consideration refers to person-oriented behavior in which the leader exhibits friendship, trust, respect, and warmth toward subordinates.

Generally, the behaviors of leaders who emphasize initiating structure fall into a consistent pattern. They tend to insist that subordinates follow rigid structures in work methods; they insist on being informed; they push their subordinates for greater effort; they decide in detail what shall be done and how it shall be done. Considerate leaders express appreciation for jobs well done, stress the importance of high morale, treat everyone as equals, and are friendly and approachable.

One study of the relationship between initiating structure and consideration and leadership effectiveness focused on first-level management—supervisors in a manufacturing facility. The measures of leadership effectiveness included proficiency ratings made by top management, absenteeism, accident rates, grievances, and turnover. The study found that supervisors of line departments (production) scored high on proficiency ratings if they also scored high on initiating structure and low on consideration. However, supervisors of staff departments were most proficient when they scored low on initiating structure and high on consideration. Subsequent studies tended to conclude that supervisors who score high on both dimensions generally are more effective than those who score low.[16]

Managerial Grid Theory.   One highly publicized leadership behavior model, developed by Robert Blake and Jane Mouton, is called the *managerial grid.* According to the proponents of this theory, leaders are most effective when they achieve a high and balanced concern for both people *and* task.[17] This idea is shown in Figure 10–3. Each leader, according to the model, can be rated somewhere along each of the axes from 1 to 9 depending on her orientation.

Although there are 81 possible positions in the grid, attention is drawn to five of them:

---

[16]Edwin A. Fleishman and James G. Hunt, eds., *Current Developments in the Study of Leadership* (Carbondale: Southern Illinois University Press, 1973), pp. 1–37.

[17]Robert S. Blake and Jane S. Mouton, *The Managerial Grid* (Houston: Gulf Publishing, 1964).

Figure 10–3

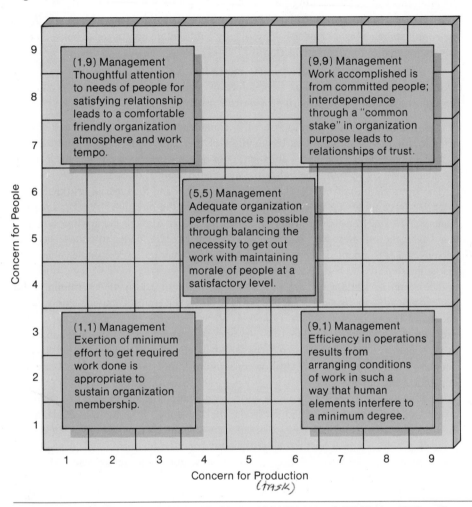

Source: Robert R. Blake and Jane S. Mouton, *The Managerial Grid* (Houston: Gulf Publishing, 1964), p. 10.

1. *The 9, 1 leader* is primarily concerned for production and only minimally concerned for people. This type of leader, categorized under the term *task management*, believes that the primary leadership responsibility is to see that the work is completed.

2. *The 1, 9 leader* is primarily concerned for people and only incidentally concerned for production. This leader, who practices *country club management*, believes that a supervisor's major responsibility is to establish harmonious relationships among subordinates and to provide a secure and pleasant work atmosphere.

3. *The 1, 1 leader*, under the classification of *impoverished management*, is concerned neither for production nor people. This leader would attempt to stay out of the

way and not become involved in the conflict between the necessity for production and the attainment of good working relationships.

4. *The 5, 5 leader* reflects a middle-ground position and thus practices *middle-of-the-road management*. A leader so described would seek to compromise between high production and employee satisfaction.

5. *The 9, 9 leader's* behavior is the most effective—it is the one best way. This style, termed *team management,* is practiced by leaders who achieve high production through the effective use of participation and involvement of people and their ideas.

Team Builder

The managerial grid is used to assess the actual leadership styles of men and women prior to *training*. An important assumption of this approach is that people can be trained to become 9, 9 leaders. Thus a 1, 9 or a 9, 1 leader can change and become more effective by learning the behaviors associated with 9, 9 leadership.

The significant contribution of the two-dimensional and managerial grid theories is that they force us to seek more complete answers to the question "What is effective leadership?" The trait theory simply requires the leader to have the appropriate characteristics; the one-best-way behavior theories require the leader to choose between person- and task-oriented behavior. But the answer may be more complex than even that suggested by the balanced 9, 9 approach.

The study of leadership behavior is a step in the direction of determining what leaders actually do in their leadership roles. However, most behavior-based explanations of leadership fail to specify how a follower's behavior affects a leader.[18] For example, a hard-working, productive computer programmer may cause her supervisor to be supportive or people-oriented, rather than the other way around. Perhaps the interaction between leaders and followers is more important than influence attempts initiated by the leader.

Another weakness in the behavior-based explanations is the failure to include an analysis of the situation in which the leader must perform. Like the trait explanation, the behavior models neglect the type of situation—routine, crisis, novel. What is good leadership behavior in a hostile merger situation may be far from ideal in a situation that requires teamwork to beat back a main competitor in the marketplace.

Charismatic Leadership.   Steven Jobs when he was at Apple Computer, Lee Iacocca at Chrysler, and Vince Lombardi when he coached the Green Bay Packers football team are used as examples of leaders with charisma. A charismatic leader is a person who by force of his personal abilities and style is capable of having a profound and extraordinary effect on followers.[19] The charismatic leadership view combines both traits and behaviors to describe this type of leader.

What Jobs, Iacocca, and Lombardi were able to do because of their energy, self-

---

[18]Henry P. Sims, Jr. and Charles C. Manz, "Observing Leader Verbal Behavior: Toward Reciprocal Determinism in Leadership Theory," *Journal of Applied Psychology,* May 1984, pp. 222–32.

[19]Robert J. House, "Research Contrasting the Behavior and the Effect of Reputed Charismatic Visions Reported by Non-Charismatic Leaders." Paper presented at the annual meeting of the Administrative Science Association of Canada, Montreal, 1985.

confidence, and dominating personalities was to project a conviction in the moral rightness of their beliefs.[20] Charismatic leaders generate excitement and increase the expectations of followers through their visions of the future. Research by Howell suggests that charismatic leadership is a function of what followers perceive. Some fortunate individuals are born with this gift, but most charismatic leaders apparently learn it and use it with great success.[21]

Some theorists propose that charisma is distributed throughout the organization. We usually only read about world-class leaders.[22] However, there are executives, middle-level managers, salespersons, and truck drivers that possess charisma. In management it is difficult to be a successor to a charismatic leader. The following Management Application spells out some recommendations for following a charismatic leader.

MANAGEMENT APPLICATION

RECOMMENDATIONS FOR FOLLOWING IN THE FOOTSTEPS OF A CHARISMATIC LEADER

When Chairperson John Reed of Citibank announced that the bank would be putting aside a $3 billion reserve fund to cover future loan losses, it was a significant announcement on two fronts. First, it was letting the financial community know that Citicorp would be taking a hard line on its Third World loans. Second, John Reed was now exerting his leadership agenda and style. He had finally emerged from the shadow of his charismatic predecessor Walter Wriston.

Many leaders find themselves taking over from a charismatic leader who was bigger, more forceful, and more dynamic than life. How can a successor carve out his or her leadership identity? There are a few pointers to consider.

- ☐ Keep a low profile for a while, so that the luster of the predecessor can grow a little dimmer.
- ☐ Develop your own style. Do not attempt to be the other person.
- ☐ Use what you can from the prior regime. Some of the predecessor's programs may be fine and may fit your objectives. Rather than reject them out of hand, use what you can.
- ☐ Discreetly assemble your own team. Part of establishing your own style means building your own loyal team.

---

[20]Kimberly B. Boal and John M. Bryson, "Charismatic Leadership: A Phenomenological and Structural Approach," in *Energy Leadership Vistas,* ed. J. G. Hunt, B. R. Billiga, H. P. Dachler, and C. A. Schriesheim (Lexington, Mass.: Lexington Books, 1988), pp. 11–28.

[21]J. M. Howell, "A Laboratory Study of Charismatic Leadership." Paper presented at the annual meeting of The Academy of Management, San Diego, 1985.

[22]B. M. Bass, *Leadership and Performance: Beyond Expectations* (New York: The Free Press, 1985).

☐ Remain respectful. Do not belittle the previous regime's contributions. Show respect so that you do not look like a small-minded, insecure complainer.

Each leader is different. Following in the footsteps of a charismatic leader is difficult, but it is not impossible. After all, most of us are not charismatic leaders.

Source: Adapted from Mortimer R. Feinberg and Bruce Serlen, "Charismatic Leader's Act Is Tough to Follow," *The Wall Street Journal*, September 14, 1987, p. 20.

Through interviews with 90 reputedly charismatic leaders, researchers identified a set of behavior strategies used by these individuals as follows:

1. *Focusing attention* on specific issues of concern, concentrating on analysis, problem solving, and action.
2. *Communicating* with empathy and sensitivity.
3. *Demonstrating consistency* and trustworthiness by one's behavior, being honest, sticking with a decision, and following through on decisions.
4. *Expressing active concern for people* including one's self, thus modeling self-regard, and reinforcing feelings of self-worth in others.[23]

Notice that the first two behaviors are task oriented and the latter two are people oriented. Much more theoretical work and research is needed to explore a more complete picture of charismatic leadership behaviors and traits, but the initial set of findings is interesting.[24] The initial findings also indicate that charismatic leaders are not all born which suggests that individuals may be trained or developed in management programs to use charismatic leadership behaviors.

CHECK YOUR OWN LEADERSHIP BEHAVIORS AND STYLE

You may wish, at this point, to assess your own leadership style. The following questionnaire is based on a two-dimensional leadership theory and, specifically, the managerial grid. By completing the questionnaire and scoring your answers, you can get a fairly good idea of your leadership-style tendencies at this point.

The Task-People (T-P) Leadership Questionnaire

The following items describe aspects of leadership behavior. Respond to each item according to the way you would be most likely to act if you were the leader of a work

---

[23]W. G. Bennis and B. Nanns, *Leaders* (New York: Harper & Row, 1985); and M. Sashkin, *Trainer Guide: Leader Behavior Questionnaire* (Bryn Mawr, Pa.: Organizational Design and Development, 1985).

[24]Jay A. Conger and Rabindra N. Kanungo, "Toward a Behavioral Theory of Charismatic Leadership in Organizational Settings," *Academy of Management Review,* October 1987, pp. 637–47.

work group. Circle whether you would be most likely to behave in the described way: always (A), frequently (F), occasionally (O), seldom (S), or never (N).

A F O S N	1.	Most likely act as the spokesman of the group.
A F O S N	2.	Encourage overtime work.
A F O S N	3.	Allow members complete freedom in their work.
A F O S N	4.	Encourage the use of uniform procedures.
A F O S N	5.	Permit the members to use their own judgment in solving problems.
A F O S N	6.	Stress being ahead of competing groups.
A F O S N	7.	Speak as a representative of the group.
A F O S N	8.	Needle members for greater effort.
A F O S N	9.	Try out my ideas in the group.
A F O S N	10.	Let the members do their work the way they think best.
A F O S N	11.	Be working hard for a promotion.
A F O S N	12.	Tolerate postponement and uncertainty.
A F O S N	13.	Speak for the group if there were visitors present.
A F O S N	14.	Keep the work moving at a rapid pace.
A F O S N	15.	Turn the members loose on a job and let them go to it.
A F O S N	16.	Settle conflicts when they occur in the group.
A F O S N	17.	Get swamped by details.
A F O S N	18.	Represent the group at outside meetings.
A F O S N	19.	Be reluctant to allow the members any freedom of action.
A F O S N	20.	Decide what should be done and how it should be done.
A F O S N	21.	Push for increased production.
A F O S N	22.	Let some members have authority that I could keep.
A F O S N	23.	Things would usually turn out as I had predicted.
A F O S N	24.	Allow the group a high degree of initiative.
A F O S N	25.	Assign group members to particular tasks.
A F O S N	26.	Be willing to make changes.
A F O S N	27.	Ask the members to work harder.
A F O S N	28.	Trust the group members to exercise good judgment.
A F O S N	29.	Schedule the work to be done.
A F O S N	30.	Refuse to explain my actions.
A F O S N	31.	Persuade others that my ideas are to their advantage.
A F O S N	32.	Permit the group to set its own pace.
A F O S N	33.	Urge the group to beat its previous record.
A F O S N	34.	Act without consulting the group.
A F O S N	35.	Ask that group members follow standard rules and regulations.

T _____   P _____

Scoring the T-P questionnaire.   To score your responses, follow these directions:

1. Circle the item number for items 8, 12, 17, 18, 19, 30, 34, and 35.

2. Write the number 1 in front of a *circled item number* if you responded S (seldom) or N (never) to that item.

3. Also write a number 1 in front of *item numbers not circled* if you responded A (always) or F (frequently).

4. Circle the number 1s you have written in front of the following items: 3, 5, 8, 10, 15, 18, 19, 22, 24, 26, 28, 30, 32, 34, and 35.

5. *Count the circled number 1s.* This is your score for concern for people. Record the score in the blank following the letter *P*.

6. *Count the uncircled number 1s.* This is your score for concern for task. Record this number in the blank following the letter *T*.

Shared leadership results from balancing concern for task and concern for people.

Task-orientation	Shared leadership	Person-orientation
High productivity	High morale and productivity	High morale

T: Concern for task

20
15
10
5

High

Medium

Low

P: Concern for people

15
10
5

The T-P leadership-style profile sheet.   To determine your style of leadership, mark your score on the concern-for-task dimension (T) on the left-hand arrow shown above. Next, move to the right-hand arrow and mark your score on the concern-for-people dimension (P). Draw a straight line that intersects the P and T scores. The point at which that line crosses the shared leadership arrow indicates the extent to which you have a balanced concern for tasks and people.

Situational Leadership

An increasing number of managers are prone to believe that the practice of leadership is too complex to be represented by unique traits *or* behaviors. Rather, a current idea is that effective leadership behavior depends on the situation. But even this idea is not now fully settled. One variation of the idea assumes that leaders must change behaviors to meet situational needs. A second variation assumes that leaders' behaviors are difficult to alter and that the situation itself must be changed to make it compatible with the leaders' behavior.

The situational theory of leadership is considerably more complex than either the trait or the behavioral approach. As indicated in Figure 10–4, effective leadership depends on the interaction of the leader's personal characteristics, the leader's behavior,

Figure 10–4   The situational approach to effective leadership.

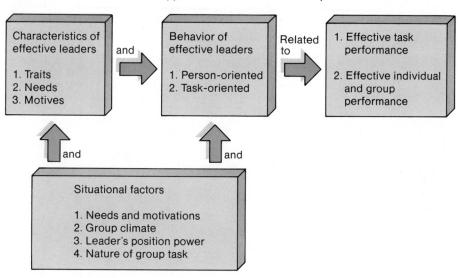

and factors in the leadership situation. In a sense, the situational approach is based on the idea that effective leadership cannot be defined by any one factor. This approach does not deny the importance of the leader's characteristics or behavior. Rather, it states that *both* must be taken into account and considered in the context of the situation.

Leadership Flexibility: Fit the Style to the Situation.   A recurring theme in leadership theory and practice is the concept of *participation* by subordinates in decision making. This theme originated in the writings of the behavioral approach to management, and it has held a prominent place in the thinking of managers for the last 40 years. The fundamental idea is shown in Figure 10–5.[25]

At the extremes of this continuum are boss-centered leadership and subordinate-centered leadership. Between these extremes are five points representing various combinations of managerial authority and subordinate freedom. One of the extreme positions, boss-centered leadership, represents a manager who simply makes a decision and announces it.

The subordinate-centered leader permits subordinates to participate fully in decision making. Within prescribed limits, the subordinates act as partners with the leader.

The proponents of participative management believe that the difficulty is not so much in convincing people that they must change their behavior as the situation changes, but in teaching leaders how to recognize the need for the change. A number

---

[25]Robert Tannenbaum and Warren H. Schmidt, "How to Choose a Leadership Pattern," *Harvard Business Review,* May–June 1973, pp. 162–80.

Figure 10–5 Continuum of leadership behavior.

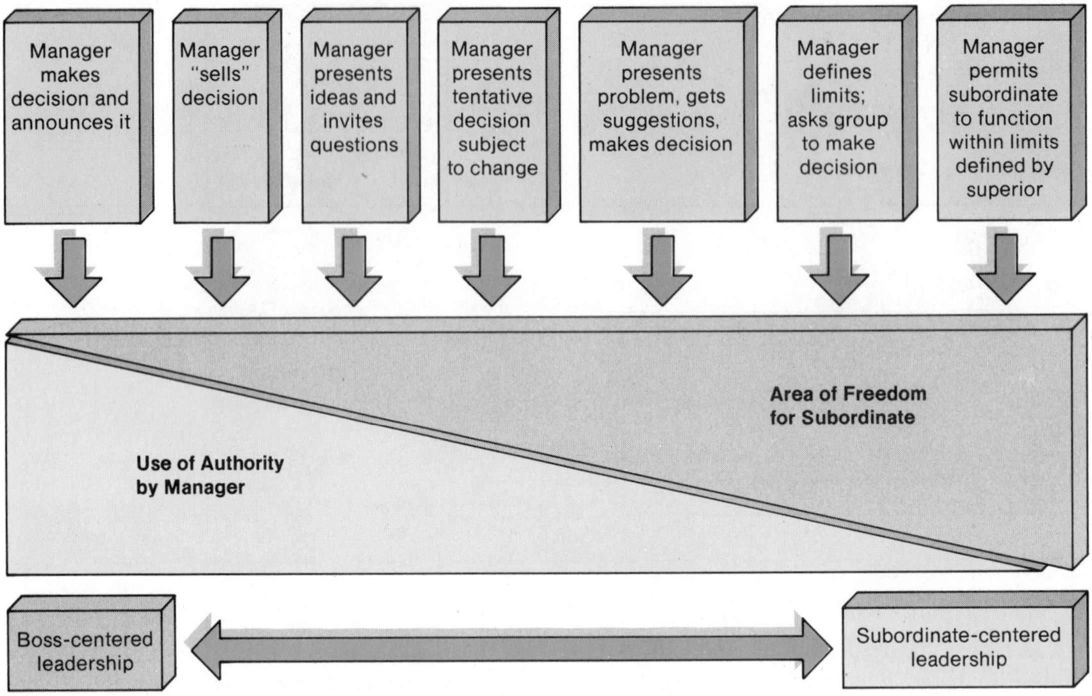

of guidelines have been proposed to help leaders identify situations which lend themselves to participative decision making.

Whether a leader should make the decision and announce it (boss-centered) or share the problem with subordinates and seek group consensus (subordinate-centered) depends on the interaction of factors related to the problem and to the subordinates. Factors related to the *problem* are:[26]

1. The likelihood that one solution to the problem is more effective than another.
2. The extent to which the leader has sufficient information to make a high-quality decision.
3. The extent to which alternative solutions are known with some certainty.

Factors related to *subordinates* are:

1. The likelihood that effective implementation of the solution depends on subordinates accepting it as appropriate.

---

[26]Victor Vroom and Arthur Jago, "Decision Making as a Social Process: Normative and Descriptive Models of Leader Behavior," *Decision Sciences*, 1974, pp. 743–70.

2. The likelihood that if the leader makes the decision, the subordinates will accept it.

3. The extent to which subordinates recognize and accept the organizational objectives to be attained by the solution.

4. The likelihood that conflict among subordinates will result if the preferred solution is adopted.

In a practical sense, combining these seven factors creates different situations. At one extreme are situations for which a number of solutions exist, none of which require acceptance by subordinates for effective implementation. The manager should make the decision and announce it. On the other hand, participation is warranted to the extent that only one solution is likely and its consequences are not known with certainty *and* subordinates have relevant information *and* their acceptance is necessary for implementation. The effective leader changes style whenever the situation demands it. That is, the leader is flexible enough to be relatively task-centered or employee-centered as situations change.

Leadership Flexibility: Fit the Style to the Maturity Level of Followers.   Paul Hersey and Kenneth H. Blanchard have developed a situational theory of leadership. They call it the *life cycle theory*.[27] This explanation is based on the belief that the most effective leadership style varies with the maturity of followers. *Maturity* is viewed as consisting of two components—job-related maturity and psychological maturity. Job-related maturity refers to the ability to perform a task. Psychological maturity refers to a person's willingness to perform a job. Four distinct levels of maturity exist:

M1: Person is unwilling and unable to perform the job.

M2: Person is unable but willing to perform the job.

M3: Person is able but unwilling to perform the job.

M4: Person is able and willing to perform the job.

The life-cycle theory suggests that as the individual matures, the leadership style will change. There are four leadership styles presented in Figure 10–6. When an employee is first brought into an organization, he or she is considered immature (M1). Therefore, a high task-low relationship style of leadership (telling) is most appropriate to learn the new job. After the employee has learned the job, a high task-high relationship style (selling) is most appropriate.

In the third phase, the employee has now matured (M3) to the point of seeking responsibility and taking the initiative to do the job. The leader would provide emotional support, but should not overdirect and initiate structure in terms of task completion (participating style).

Finally, as the follower becomes confident, experienced, and self-motivated, the leader can practice a low task-low relationship style (delegating). A fully matured person (M4) expects to be able to operate with a minimum amount of influence from a leader. This can be considered a situation in which the follower's maturity and self-

---

[27]Paul Hersey and Kenneth H. Blanchard, *Management of Organizational Behavior* (Englewood Cliffs, N.J.: Prentice-Hall, 1979).

Figure 10–6 Life-cycle theory of leadership.

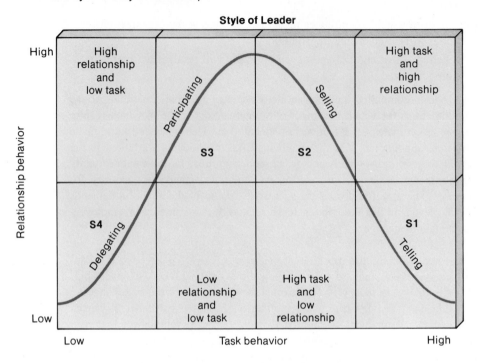

Source: From Paul Hersey and Kenneth H. Blanchard, *Management of Organizational Behavior* (Englewood Cliffs, N.J.: Prentice-Hall, 1982), p. 152. Used by permission.

direction area substitute for leadership.[28] A person with a high level of skill, experience, and self-motivation does not need a leader to structure the job.

There are some exceptions to the life-cycle theory. For example, when faced with a crisis situation involving filling an important order, a leader may find it necessary to be very task oriented [e.g., use telling style (S1) even when the followers are very

---

[28]Steven Kerr and John M. Jermier, "Substitutes for Leadership: Their Meaning and Measurement," *Organizational Behavior and Human Performance,* December 1978, pp. 375–403.

mature (M4)]. However, using the high task-low relationship leadership style over an extended period of time will likely result in a backlash from the followers. A mature follower wants to be treated in a particular way.

The main points of Hersey and Blanchard's life-cycle theory are set out in terms of a parent-child relationship. When the child is young, the parents must protect him and must structure everything. When the child enters school, there must still be structure, but there must also be high-relationship behavior. As the child moves through high school and early adulthood, the parents typically provide less structure and high emotional support. Finally, as the child leaves home and begins to establish roots elsewhere, parents provide less and less structure and emotional support.

The life-cycle theory has intuitive appeal. However, the theory assumes that leaders are perceptive enough to accurately pinpoint maturity levels. The theory also assumes that followers will agree with a leader's assessment of their maturity level. Using the parent-child example, we know how much disagreement can occur in determining maturity levels.

Also, the life-cycle theory assumes that a leader is flexible enough to move through four phases or back and forth. Is this amount of flexibility possible? Hersey and Blanchard think so, but research evidence to support their views is quite limited. In fact, the validity of measurement instruments and the relationship of the model to performance has not been carefully investigated by independent researchers. In one of few tests of the theory, Vecchio studied 303 high school teachers. He found that the leadership style—maturity mix for the S1–M1 condition was supported. On the other hand, the theory was unable to predict the best leadership style for high maturity and moderate maturity employees.[29]

Finally, the mix of followers is constantly changing. Can any leader hope to be astute enough to be able to assess the mix, determine the appropriate leadership style, and behave accordingly?

Despite some shortcomings, the life-cycle theory has generated interest among practicing managers. It calls attention to the need to be flexible. Leadership is, after all, a dynamic process that requires flexibility. Also, the life-cycle theory illustrates the interactive nature of leadership. That is, a leader can influence followers, but followers, because of their maturity level, can also influence leadership behavior.

Leadership Inflexibility: Fit the Situation to the Leader's Style.   Using a considerable body of research evidence, Fred E. Fiedler has developed an important contribution to the situational theory of leadership.[30] He identifies three important *situational factors* or *dimensions* that he believes influence the leader's effectiveness. The dimensions are the following:

1. *Leader-member relations*. This refers to the degree of confidence the subordinates have in the leader. It also includes the loyalty shown to the leader and the leader's attractiveness.

---

[29]Robert P. Vecchio, "Situational Leadership Theory: An Examination of a Prescription Theory," *Journal of Applied Psychology,* August 1987, pp. 444–51.

[30]Fred E. Fiedler and Martin M. Chemers, *Leadership and Effective Management* (Glenview, Ill.: Scott, Foresman, 1974).

2. *Task structure*. This refers to the degree to which the subordinates' jobs are routine rather than nonroutine.

3. *Position power*. This refers to the power inherent in the leadership position. It includes the rewards and punishments typically associated with the position, the leader's official authority (based on ranking in the managerial hierarchy), and the support that the leader receives from superiors and the overall organization.

Fiedler has obtained data which relate leadership style to the three-dimensional measures of different situations. Fiedler's measure of leadership style distinguishes between leaders who tend to be permissive and considerate and foster good interpersonal relations among group members and leaders who tend to be directive, controlling, and more oriented toward task than people. Fiedler suggests that leaders who are directive and leaders who are permissive can function best in certain types of situations. Instead of stating that a leader must adopt this or that style, Fiedler identifies the type of leader who functions best in a given situation. According to Fiedler, we should not talk simply about good leaders or poor leaders. A leader who achieves effectiveness in one situation may not be effective in another. The implication of this logic is that managers should think about the situation in which a particular leader (subordinate manager) performs well or badly. Fiedler assumes that managers can enhance subordinates' effectiveness if they carefully choose situations that are favorable to the subordinates' styles.[31]

Table 10–1 presents some of Fiedler's findings about the relationship of the three dimensions to leadership style for such groups as bomber crews, management groups, high school basketball teams, and steel mill crews. A review of Table 10–1 indicates a relationship between effective task performance and directive leadership under conditions 1, 2, 3, and 8, and a relationship between effective task performance and permissive leadership under conditions 4 and 5. These results indicate that, in certain situations, a particular leadership style achieves the best results.

An example of an effective leader under condition 1 could be the following:

> A well-liked head nurse in a university medical center is in charge of getting the nursing team ready for open-heart surgery. The tasks to be performed by the head nurse are very tightly structured. There is no room for error or indecision, and the duties of everyone on the nursing team are clearly specified. The head nurse has complete power to correct any personnel or performance problems within the nursing team.

An example of a leader who is working under condition 5 would be the following:

> A recent college graduate's first job assignment was to supervise 18 technicians in a manufacturing plant in Chicago. Most of the technicians had little education past the eighth grade and had worked for more than 10 years in the plant. They generally believed that college kids were either wise guys or good people, but they took their time deciding.

---

[31]Fred E. Fiedler and Joseph E. Garcia, *New Approaches to Effective Leadership* (New York: John Wiley & Sons, 1987).

Table 10–1 Summary of Fiedler's situational variables and their preferred leadership styles.

| Condition | Group Situation | | | Leadership Style Correlating with Performance |
	Leader-Member Relations	Task Structure	Position Power	
1	Good	Structured	Strong	Directive
2	Good	Structured	Weak	Directive
3	Good	Unstructured	Strong	Directive
4	Good	Unstructured	Weak	Permissive
5	Moderately poor	Structured	Strong	Permissive
6	Moderately poor	Structured	Weak	No data
7	Moderately poor	Unstructured	Strong	No relationship found
8	Moderately poor	Unstructured	Weak	Directive

Because they were genuine experts on their job, a formal leader had very little control over sequencing or structuring the job. The job was structured by the experts, and the manager actually concentrated on paperwork, not technical work.

Although Fiedler and associates cite extensive research to support the theory, critics suggest that the theory has measurement problems and that a limited number of situational variables are incorporated. The measures Fiedler uses to assess a person's preferred leadership style are claimed to be unreliable and unstable. There is also the criticism that the theory fails to specify what an effective leader actually does in various situations.[32]

Some pragmatic procedures for improving a leader's relations, task structure, and position power are as follows:

☐ Leader-member relations could be improved by restructuring the leader's group of subordinates so that the group is more compatible in terms of background, educational level, technical expertise, or ethnic origin.

☐ The task structure can be modified either in the structured or the nonstructured direction. A task can be made more structured by spelling out the jobs in greater detail. A task can be made less structured by providing only general directions for the work that is to be accomplished.

☐ Leader position power can be modified in a number of ways. A leader can be given a higher rank in the organization or more authority to do the job. In addition, a leader's reward power can be increased if the organization delegates authority to evaluate the performance of subordinates.

[32]Terence R. Mitchell and James R. Larson, Jr., *People in Organizations* (New York: McGraw-Hill, 1987), p. 452.

Figure 10–7   A framework for combining leadership approaches.

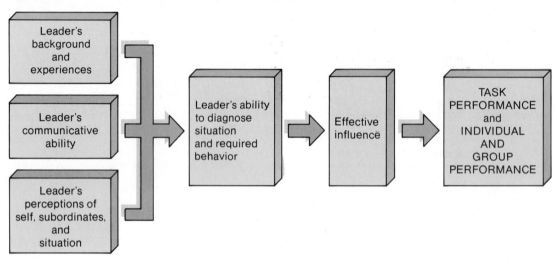

Combining the Leadership Approaches

A framework for understanding and integrating contemporary leadership theory is proposed in Figure 10–7. The framework emphasizes the effect of the *leader's background and experiences* on (1) the *leader's qualities,* such as communicative ability, self-awareness, and confidence; and (2) the *leader's perceptions* of subordinates, the situation, and self. The interaction of all these factors is important in determining the *leader's ability* to *influence* others. The manner in which these variables interact and the proportionate weight of each are not known with certainty, but there is no doubt of their importance.

The leader should consider a number of important organizational and environmental variables, as illustrated in Figure 10–7. In the context of the leadership framework, the effective leader influences followers in such a manner that high productivity, high group morale, low absenteeism and turnover, and the development of followers are achieved. Figure 10–7 specifies only three personal qualities which contribute significantly to a leader's ability to influence others. The three qualities are suited for most leadership styles and are especially compatible with the situational, or contingency, theory of leadership.

One of the most important factors in the situational approach to leadership centers on leader self-awareness. Leaders should be aware of the impact of their behaviors on those they lead, even though they cannot predict accurately in every situation how those behaviors will affect followers. Leaders should attempt to learn more about their influence on others.

Every leader must be able to communicate with followers. The leader who fails to communicate with followers may become ineffective as an influencer of others. As noted earlier, Winston Churchill was a great leader who had excellent skills as a communicator. The following chapter examines in detail the problems and potential of communications.

Apparently, an important ability of effective leaders is that they understand themselves, their subordinates, and their situations. They must understand the causes and effects of individual motivation and behavior and group dynamics and behavior. Leadership training programs should stress diagnostic and adaptability skills. It should not be concluded that managers can be easily trained to diagnose work situations accurately and to develop appropriate leadership abilities. Rather, patience is essential if leaders are to become flexible enough to change their leadership styles.

MANAGEMENT SOLUTION

PUTTING WANG BACK ON THE ROAD TO SUCCESS

The $109 million loss had a major impact on Dr. Wang. He took over and began a brutal nonstop work schedule. He met with customers and employees. He also gave his regional managers autonomy to make major decisions without checking first with headquarters. Dr. Wang has a reputation of being generous and humane with his employees, providing such benefits as stock options, subsidies for tuition and child care, liberal health care, and other options. The setback, however, caused him to eliminate more than 2,600 jobs. Hard times meant that hard decisions were needed, and Dr. Wang didn't hesitate to do what was necessary to improve Wang Labs' posture in the market.

Now Wang Labs is back on its feet. It has earned a modest profit in the last quarter. Dr. Wang again has withdrawn from day-to-day management, and following a Chinese tradition, bequeathed the business to his eldest son, Frederick. Still today the shadow of Dr. Wang, the driven leader who is considered a visionary by employees, is present at Wang Labs. Fred Wang under the guidance of his father has set a challenging goal of turning the firm into a $5 billion company. Presently, Wang's sales annually are in the $3 billion range. This challenging goal is the type that was established by Dr. Wang in 1964 when he invented a desktop calculator for scientists and engineers. The Wang family believes that sound leadership can encourage employees to meet such challenging goals.

Source: Adapted from Corie Brown, "How the Doctor's Son Is Getting Wang Back on Its Feet," *Business Week*, January 25, 1988, pp. 84–86.

MANAGEMENT SUMMARY

□ Leadership is the ability to influence followers toward the accomplishment of worthwhile, meaningful, and challenging goals.

□ The trait approach to leadership relates personal characteristics and effective leadership. Despite much study and effort, no conclusive results are available to guide managers in selecting future leaders.

□   The idea that effective leaders behave differently from ineffective leaders has led to inconclusive results. An important issue is whether an individual can shift between person-oriented behavior and task-oriented behavior.

□   More attention is being paid to the charismatic leader or those individuals who because of their energy, self-confidence, and dominating personality project a conviction in the moral rightness of their beliefs.

□   The situational approaches to leadership are more complex than the trait and behavior approaches. The complexity arises from the necessity to consider the interactions of the leader, behavior, and situation.

□   The situational approaches are based on two different assumptions about leadership flexibility. One approach assumes that leaders can and must change their behavior to fit the situation. The other assumes that leaders cannot change their behavior but must change the situation.

□   The most important conclusion to be made from leadership theory is that managers must understand their own abilities and their impact on others.

REVIEW AND DISCUSSION QUESTIONS

1.   Do you believe that a manager can be effective if she is not considered by subordinates to be a leader? Explain.

2.   Can leadership concepts be applied in the classroom setting? That is, can the teaching styles of your professors be described as person oriented and task oriented? Are these distinctions useful for analyzing why some professors are more effective than others? Explain.

3.   Leadership obviously is one factor that contributes to the performance of a group or an organization. What other factors can you think of, and how important are they in comparison to leadership?

4.   It is often said that leaders are born, not trained. In light of what you have studied about the trait theory of leadership, how would you respond to that statement?

5.   "Person-oriented leadership is OK if you are only interested in employee satisfaction, but if you want to get the job done, then task-oriented leadership is the only way." Evaluate this quotation.

6.   What is your reaction to the idea that an effective leader must be able to shift from person orientation to task orientation as the situation dictates? Do you believe that you can be flexible in your behavior? Explain.

7.   Describe in practical terms the ways in which a manager's job can be altered to fit his or her leadership style.

8.   In how many of the eight situations described in Fiedler's theory have you had work experience? Describe in detail one of those experiences and determine whether the manager was using the "appropriate" style.

9.   What does maturing mean in job and in psychological terms?

10.   Evaluate the strengths and shortcomings of the Managerial Grid theory of leadership. Can you think of situations where a 9, 1 leader or a 1, 9 leader may be more effective than a 9, 9 leader? Explain.

CASES

10–1 LEADER TRAITS, BEHAVIORS, AND SITUATIONS

The superstars of industry all have a particular leadership style that is recognized by others. These leaders reach the top of their profession because of different traits, behaviors, and situational factors. The following is a brief list of a few of the recognized superstars and some explanation about why they are considered the *best*.

John S. Reed (Chairperson and CEO, Citicorp)

John Reed (see the Managerial Application in the chapter) is called one of the true geniuses in the business world. He thinks ahead in 10- to 15-year blocks of time and seems to have an amazing ability to forecast what the future holds. His unique characteristics are patience, stamina, and courage to make tough decisions. He increased Citicorp's bad debt reserves by $3 billion, acknowledging the riskiness of Third World loans. This took decisive leadership according to experts in the field.

Kenneth H. Olsen (President and Director, Digital Equipment Corporation (DEC))

Mr. Olsen formed the firm in 1957. He has never appointed a CEO since he runs the company. He believed in what he was doing and conveyed this feeling to his employees. He works hard and long and stays with an idea from start to finish. Being persistent and exercising control are behaviors that have made Ken Olsen a tough market competitor for IBM.

D. Wayne Calloway (Chairperson and CEO, PepsiCo., Inc.)

Wayne Calloway is considered to be an aggressive and competitive leader. These are behaviors he believes are needed in the soft drink war zone. On the other hand, he is an exceptional manager of people. Although he is a hard driver, people like to be around him because he likes people. He values being able to help people develop by giving them challenging assignments.

Charles F. Knight (Chairperson and CEO, Emerson Electric Co.)

Mr. Knight is viewed as a strategic thinker and an incredibly disciplined manager. One of his important characteristics is the ability to ask tough questions. He asks these questions to stimulate thinking, planning, and teamwork. In a staid industry, Mr. Knight has been able to encourage innovative thinking by subordinates. He has also helped develop managers who, when and if they leave Emerson, are considered disciplined and competent individuals who are well respected.

Donald E. Petersen (Chairperson and CEO, Ford Motor Co.)

Donald Petersen in 1988 was riding a wave that has placed him in a position to be considered a hero in the U.S. auto industry. Ford Motor was in terrible shape until

Mr. Petersen came along. His style, his work ethic, and his energy helped make the difference. He is a technical expert who loves cars. He has pressed hard to have Ford produce only high-quality cars and trucks. If they are not the very tops in quality, customers should not buy them. His enthusiasm for quality is so contagious the workers on the floor of Ford assembly plants are talking up quality. The role model for quality at Ford is Donald E. Petersen.

Questions

1. Develop a list of traits and behaviors that these leaders appear to possess and use in their organizations.

2. Which leader appears to be the most task oriented? Which is the most people oriented?

3. Do these leaders display any charismatic leadership qualities? Explain.

Source: Adapted from James Braham, "America's Best CEOs," *Industry Week,* August 10, 1987, pp. 37–42.

10–2 CHANGING A LEADERSHIP STYLE

The thermocoupling research group was a subunit of the nuclear engineering department of a large corporation. The group contained 20 persons, most of whom had or were working toward Ph.D.s. The organization of the group was well defined, and the manager had insisted on following the formal rules and procedures of the company whenever problems occurred.

The group was currently working on a project to develop coupling units that would withstand the wear, tear, and temperature changes of space travel. The manager was Marianne Newley, a 35-year-old Ph.D. physicist. The 19 other employees in the group were assigned to three sections: analysis, experimental, and testing and quality control. The section leaders were Marla Beeler, Allen Samuels, and Jason Martin.

Marianne was known around the company as a competent, but often abrasive, manager. She worked long hours and was assigned difficult projects because of her record of doing excellent work. Subordinates, however, often complained about her lack of concern for them and about her obsession with finishing the job on time and within the allocated budget.

Marianne's superior, Mark Neeley, was aware of the complaints and wanted Marianne to reconsider her leadership style. He called her into his office and asked her to attend a three-week leadership training program. The training program covered the managerial grid theory of leadership. The bulk of the training focused on self-diagnosis through the managerial grid and discussions of leadership behavior and effectiveness.

Marianne attended the training program just before her present assignment in the thermocoupling group. Twelve of the group's members had worked with her on other projects and were aware of her task-oriented behavior. After attending the training course, Marianne's style became somewhat more people-oriented. She asked for more advice from subordinates, and she also encouraged them to voice complaints about her methods of running the project. In the past, she would never ask subordinates for advice and she would become angry when subordinates questioned her decisions. She still insisted, however, that the rules and policies regarding work hours, time off, and bid preparation be followed exactly as stated in the company operating manual.

The individuals who had worked for Marianne previously were puzzled by her sudden change of behavior. They were skeptical about accepting her suggestion that they voice their complaints. One of the section leaders, Marla Beeler, visited with Mark Neeley and informed him that the group was disorganized because of Marianne's behavior. The conversation between them proceeded as follows:

Mark: Hi, Marla. Can I help you with anything?

Marla: I sure hope so. Mark, we just do not know what to do in our project group. Marianne is completely different than before, and her attitudes toward us seem strange.

Mark: What do you mean, strange?

Marla: Well, she is asking for advice, and in six years, this has never happened.

Mark: Perhaps the training program she attended is paying off.

Marla: Come on, Mark. We think it is the quiet before the storm, and we are not buying any of it. You just cannot teach or train a person so rapidly.

Mark: Are you familiar with the managerial grid and the power of this technique?

Marla: The behavioralists have really brainwashed you. The grid is something I studied in college. I know it is not as powerful as you believe. You just can't change a leader's style with a broad-brush approach.

This meeting with Marla puzzled Mark, and he re-examined what was said in the conversation. He then called in Marianne, and their discussion proceeded as follows:

Mark: Marianne, how are things going?

Marianne: Fine, I'm on schedule and rounding the turn for home on the project.

Mark: How was the training program?

Marianne: Interesting, but not very challenging. They talked about leadership and the "mystery zone" of effective leadership behavior. I found out that my predominant style is 9, 1. I ended up a 6, 5 after the program. However, when I'm pressed, I may become 100, 1.

Mark: Do you feel any differently about your subordinates now?

Marianne: No, except I know that they expect me to be more employee-centered after attending the training program. Thus, I have made some gradual changes in my style. If they work, who knows, I may change permanently.

Mark: What do you mean?

Marianne: My group is superintelligent, and they know that you do not change overnight. You just do not become a 9, 9 without a long period of trial and error. In fact, 9, 9 would be a disaster in my group.

Mark was taken aback once again. He had learned a lot about leadership style just by discussing the topic with two intelligent and articulate people.

Questions

1. Do you believe that any change in Marianne's leadership style has occurred?
2. What does Marianne mean when she states, "In fact, 9, 9 would be a disaster in my group"?
3. Should Marianne have been sent to the training program in the first place? Why?

ELEVEN

Interpersonal and Organizational Communications

LEARNING OBJECTIVES

After completing Chapter 11, you should be able to:

Define: the basic elements of the communications process.

State: what is meant by the term nonverbal communication and its importance in organizational communication.

Describe: the major obstacles to effective communication and how a manager can minimize these barriers.

Explain: the three formal communication flows found in organizations.

Discuss: the important psychological variables that affect interpersonal communications.

COMMUNICATING IN CRISIS: THE TYLENOL TRAGEDY

In September 1982, Johnson & Johnson Co. was enjoying several years of impressive growth and profits. Its stock price had more than doubled in the last two years. Tylenol, its most successful product, had captured 35 percent of the analgesic market. The pain reliever accounted for $450 million in sales annually, more than the top four leading competing products combined. Tylenol also provided 20 percent of Johnson & Johnson's profits.

As Johnson & Johnson grew, it maintained a closed-door communications policy with the press. This cold-shouldered approach was evident in a comment by Joseph Chiesa, president of the division which makes Tylenol, "We maintain a strict policy not to talk to reporters about anything."

However, on September 30, 1982, a tragedy unprecedented in the U.S. consumer products industry struck the company and called into question its closed-mouth approach to communications. On that day, the first of seven consumers in Chicago died from cyanide poisoning from Tylenol capsules.

J&J Chairman James E. Burke immediately convened a special task force comprised of himself, J&J President Donald Clare, and five other top-level executives. The task force quickly worked to devise a plan designed to avert any further loss of life and, if possible, save the Tylenol brand.

(The Management Solution to this Management Incident can be found at the end of this chapter.)

Communicating and communication are vital aspects of the managerial function of leading. Without communications, managers cannot *influence* individuals and groups to attain performance objectives. Effective communication is at the very heart of managerial performance, but behind that simple declaration lie many complex issues and factors. A framework for understanding communications is presented in the following section of this textbook. Then, organizational communication is explored, followed by consideration of some of the problems associated with interpersonal communications. The chapter concludes with a discussion of the causes and cures of communication breakdowns.

In Chapter 2, we described Henry Mintzberg's assumptions and research, which views the manager's job in terms of three primary managerial roles.[1] Communication is at the core of each of these roles. For example:

1. The manager's *interpersonal* roles require constant communication between managers and subordinates, customers, suppliers, peers, and superiors. The Mintzberg research indicates that managers spend about 45 percent of their contact time with peers, about 45 percent with people outside their work unit, and about 10 percent with superiors.

2. In the *informational* roles, managers seek information from all their contacts that may affect their job performance and goal accomplishment. Managers also send information to others inside and outside their unit and the organization.

3. The manager's *decisional* roles involve using information, contacts, and relationships to allocate limited resources, solve conflict-laden situations, and initiate problem-solving solutions. Once a decision is made by a manager, it must be communicated clearly to others.

The roles introduced and discussed by Mintzberg indicate that managers rarely get to do their thinking and contemplating alone. Interacting and orally communicating with others are major activities of managers. Studies indicate that managers spend from 60 to 80 percent of their time at work involved with oral communications.[2]

A FRAMEWORK FOR UNDERSTANDING COMMUNICATIONS

Communication is defined as *the transmission of mutual understanding through the use of symbols*. If mutual understanding does *not* result from the transmission of symbols, there is no communication. Figure 11–1 reflects the definition and identifies the important elements of communication.

As shown in Figure 11–1, the process of communication can be broken down into basic elements: the *communicator, encoding,* the *message,* the *medium, decoding,* the *receiver, noise,* the *feedback.* In simple terms, an individual or a group of individuals

---

[1]Henry Mintzberg, *The Nature of Managerial Work* (New York: Harper & Row, 1973).

[2]Walter Kiechel III, "The Big Presentation," *Fortune,* July 26, 1982, pp. 98–100; and Henry Mintzberg, "The Manager's Job: Folklore and Fact," *Harvard Business Review,* July–August 1975, pp. 49–61.

Figure 11–1 A model of the communication process.

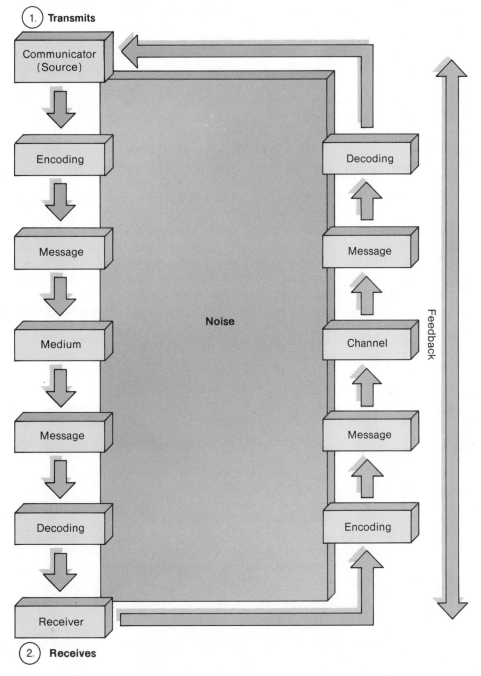

(the communicator) has an idea, message, or understanding to transmit to another individual or group of individuals (the receiver). To transmit the idea, the communicator first must translate it into a language (encoding) and send the message by verbal, nonverbal, or written means (the medium). The message is received through the senses of the receiver and translated (decoded) into a message received. Occasionally, noise enters the communication picture. That is, some form of interference occurs at some point in the process. Communication interference must be reduced or eliminated so that an understanding between the sender and receiver can result. By a nod of the head, a facial expression, or action, the receiver acknowledges whether understanding has been achieved (feedback). Let us examine each element more closely.

The Communicator

Communicators in an organization can be managers, nonmanagers, departments, or the organization itself. Managers communicate with other managers, subordinates, supervisors, clients, customers, and parties outside the organization. Nonmanagers likewise communicate with managers and nonmanagers, clients, customers, and external parties. People in sales departments communicate with people in production departments, and engineering personnel communicate with product design teams. Communications within the organization are important means for coordinating the work of separate departments. And more and more organizations communicate with employees, unions, the public, and government. Each of these communicators has a message, an idea, or information to transmit to someone or some group.

Encoding

The communicator's message must be translated into a language which reflects the idea; that is, the message must be encoded. The reader of spy novels is familiar with the scene in which the enemy (or friendly) agent has a message to send to headquarters. To prevent opposing agents from obtaining the message and understanding it, the agent transmits the message in *code,* a language presumably known only by the agent and headquarters. In situations less dramatic and intriguing, encoding usually is the selection of language specific to the purpose of the communicator's message. The encoding action produces the communicable message.

A manager usually relies on languages, words, symbols, or gestures that portray his thoughts and feelings. By encoding, the manager translates his thoughts and feelings into a code that subordinates are able to understand.

The Message

The result of the encoding process is the *message.* The purpose of the communicator is expressed in the form of the message—either verbal or nonverbal. Managers have numerous purposes for communicating, such as to have others understand their ideas, to understand the ideas of others, to gain acceptance of themselves or their ideas, and to produce action. The message, then, is what the individual hopes to communicate, and the exact form that the message takes depends to a great extent on the medium used to carry it. Decisions relating to the two—message and medium—are inseparable.

The Medium

The *medium* is the carrier of the intended message. Organizations provide information to their members by a variety of means, including face-to-face communication, telephone, group meetings, computers, memos, policy statements, reward systems, bulletin boards, production schedules, company publications, and sales forecasts.

Unintended messages can be sent by silence or inaction on a particular issue as well as by decisions on which goals and objectives are *not* to be pursued and which methods are *not* to be utilized. Finally, such nonverbal media as facial expressions, tone of voice, and body movements also can communicate an unintended or intended message.

Decoding

Decoding refers to the process by which receivers *translate* the message into terms meaningful to them. If headquarters uses the same code book that the agent used in preparing the coded message, then the message it receives will be the same as what was sent. But if the code is known only to the agent, then no common understanding can be reached. In a business organization, if the message that the chief executive receives from the accounting department includes many technical terms that are known to accountants but not to nonaccountants, no communication occurs. An often-cited complaint in organizations with staff specialists is that they cannot communicate. Each staff group has a language and symbols that persons outside the group cannot decode.

The Receiver

Communication requires a *receiver* who must be taken into account when a communicator attempts to transmit information. "Telling isn't teaching" if the teacher uses language that the student cannot understand (cannot decode). Engineers cannot expect to communicate to nonengineers if the symbols they use are beyond the receivers' training and ability to comprehend. Effective communication requires that the communicator anticipate the receiver's decoding ability. Effective communication is receiver oriented, not sender oriented.

Noise

Noise is any element or condition that disturbs or interferes with the effective sending and receiving of communication. Disturbances or interferences can occur at any point in the communication process. A manager may not be able to express himself well; a subordinate may be bored and not pay attention to what a manager says; memos may be poorly reproduced and thus hard to read; or an electrical power surge may shut down the organization's computer. These are all examples of noise. They disturb and interfere with the regular flow of information. Managers must take action whenever possible to reduce or eliminate noise.

Feedback

Feedback enables the communicator to determine if the message has been received and if it has produced the intended response. *One-way* communication processes do not allow receiver-to-communicator feedback. *Two-way* communication processes, however, do.[3] For the manager, communication feedback may come in many ways. In face-to-face situations, *direct* feedback is possible through verbal exchanges as well as through subtle means such as facial expressions that indicate discontent or misunderstanding. In addition, communication breakdowns may be indicated by *indirect* means, such as declines in productivity, the poor quality of production, increased absenteeism or turnover, and conflict or a lack of coordination between units.

ORGANIZATIONAL COMMUNICATION: FORMAL CHANNELS

Managers must provide for communication in three distinct directions: downward, upward, and horizontal. These three formal channels of communication and a few examples for each direction flow are provided in Figure 11–2. Since these three directions summarize the paths that official communications travel in an organization, let us briefly examine each of them. The manager who understands and examines the formal flow of communication is better able to appreciate the barriers to effective organizational communication, as well as the means for overcoming them.

Downward Communication

Downward communication flows from individuals in higher levels of the organization to those at lower levels. The most common forms of downward communication are job instructions, official memos, policy statements, procedures, posters, manuals, and company publications. In many organizations, downward communication often is both inadequate and inaccurate, and employees typically receive such tremendous amounts of downward communication that they selectively decide which messages to fully receive, which to partially receive, and which to disregard.

Many organizations understand how this *individual selectivity* influences which messages are received, and they work to improve the downward communication flow. For example, Philips Industries, a British firm, communicates downward with members of its seven unions through annual conferences of management and labor. The principal purpose of the conferences is to allow the firm to give a "state-of-the-company" report to the union leadership. The focus of the report is the broad economic problems facing Philips. The communication of ideas and views between the management and union officials is carried on without reference to salaries and contracts. The proceedings of

---

[3] "A GM Plant with a Hot Line between Workers and Buyers," *Business Week,* June 11, 1984, p. 165.

Figure 11–2 Formal organizational channels of communication.

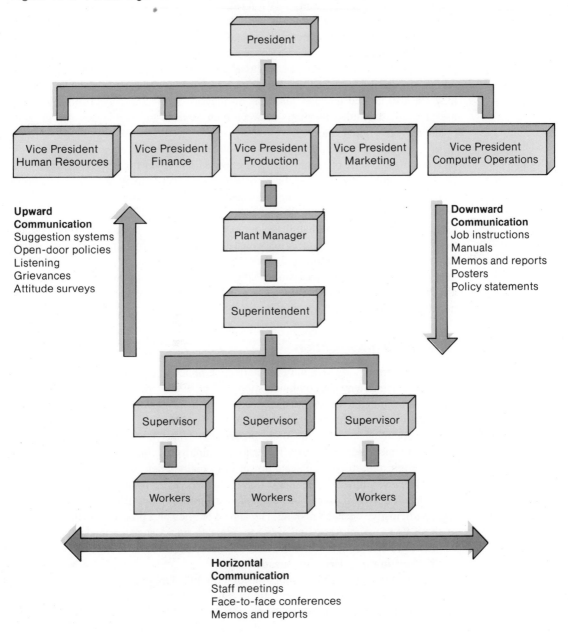

the conference are videotaped and made available to all personnel in the 25 Philips plants in the United Kingdom.

An American company, Pitney-Bowes, Inc., also has made special efforts to develop effective downward communications. One of its most successful practices is its annual "job holders' meeting." These employees' meetings serve much the same purpose as stockholders' meetings: persons who attend get a face-to-face management accounting on the progress of the business. The employees not only hear from management, but they are also invited to raise questions on matters of specific concern to them. The use of open, scheduled meetings between management and employees is a growing practice in the United States.

In large organizations, the process of communicating with employees typically is undertaken by a staff of communication experts. The usual function of the staff is to produce a publication aimed at these three purposes: (1) to explain the organization's plans and programs as they are implemented; (2) to answer complaints and criticisms; and (3) to defend the status quo and those who are responsible for it. The medium usually selected to accomplish these purposes is a periodic publication. The publication's intended messages are those which present the organization's side of issues. Large organizations are more and more viewed with distrust and suspicion. Although they may not always be successful in convincing the general public that their actions are public-minded, it has become increasingly necessary for them to try to win and maintain the support of their employees.

Upward Communication

A high-performing organization needs effective *upward communication* as much as it needs effective downward communication. Effective upward communication—getting messages from employees to management—is difficult to achieve, especially in larger organizations. Some studies suggest that of the three formal communication channels, upward communication is the most ineffective. Upper-level managers often don't respond to messages sent from lower-level employees, and lower-level employees often are reluctant to communicate upward especially when the message contains bad news.[4] However, upward communication is often necessary for sound decision making.

Widely used upward communication devices include suggestion boxes, group meetings, participative decision making, and appeal or grievance procedures. In the absence of these flows, employees find ways to adapt to nonexistent or inadequate upward communication channels, as evidenced by the emergence of underground employee publications in many large organizations.

The practices of ESCO Corporation of Portland, Oregon, reveal one company's commitment to upward communications. Employees in this company who wish to communicate directly with top management—whether to express complaints, suggestions, questions, compliments, or comments—simply dial a listed telephone number

---

[4]Allan D. Frank, "Trends in Communication: Who Talks to Whom?" *Personnel,* December 1985, pp. 41–47.

and state their views. The calls are recorded, transcribed, and reviewed by ESCO's vice president of industrial relations in charge of personnel. The vice president forwards the transcriptions to the appropriate department managers for reply and action. If callers give their names, they receive a written answer; if they choose to be anonymous, the answers are posted on the bulletin board. No call is unanswered, and each call is answered within 48 hours.

Effective upward communications are important because they provide employees with opportunities to be heard. Top management must depend on subordinates for vital information, so the information received from suggestion systems, open-door discussions, attitude surveys, and participative decision meetings can provide valuable insight into the thoughts, feelings, and opinions of employees to which managers then can respond. Current problems can be corrected and future difficulties can be headed off.

Horizontal Communication

Often overlooked in the design of most organizations is provision for the formal *horizontal* flow of communication. When the supervisor of the accounting department communicates with the director of marketing concerning advertising budget expenditures, the flow of communication is horizontal. Although vertical (upward and downward) communication flows are the primary considerations in organizational design, effective organizations also need *horizontal communication*. Horizontal communication—for example, between production and sales in a business organization and between different departments within a hospital—is necessary for the coordination of diverse organizational functions.

Managers who recognize the need for horizontal communication can appoint committees of representatives from the departments. One plant manager routinely meets each Monday at 7:30 A.M. with each department head to go over the upcoming week's work schedule, to review progress toward objectives, and to anticipate any problems that will require the attention of more than one department. The use of routinely scheduled staff meetings can facilitate horizontal communication. The more interdependent the work of the departments, the greater is the need to formalize horizontal communication. Of the three formal communication channels, horizontal communication tends to be the most effective. Messages are often sent and accurately received, and feedback is frequently obtained.[5]

An organization's formal structure (see Figure 11–2) can have impacts on its flow of communication. The three basic patterns of formal communication—upward, downward, and horizontal—are spelled out by the relationships depicted in an organization chart. However, communication involves people as well as structure. Managers and employees tend to adapt and modify the formal channels to suit their needs, goals, and time. In some cases, *informal* channels emerge to supplant the formal channels.

---

[5]Ibid., p. 42.

Figure 11–3   Sociogram: Informal communication patterns on technical aspects of the job.

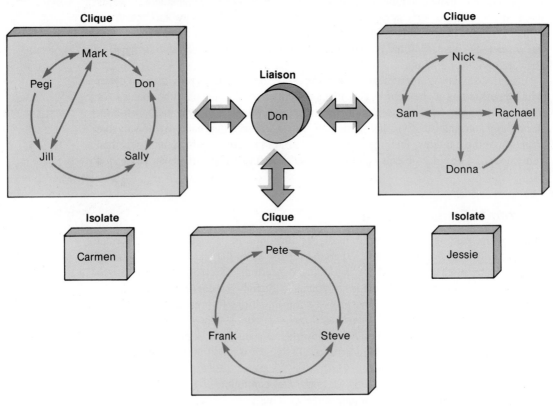

ORGANIZATIONAL COMMUNICATION: INFORMAL CHANNELS

Research suggests that communications do not flow randomly within organizations, nor do they necessarily follow the formal pathways published in an organizational chart.[6] The study of informal pathways has been helped by a method known as sociometry. In sociometry, members of a group or unit are asked about the other members with whom they communicate. Then a diagram of these patterns, known as a *sociogram,* is drawn showing the pathways used for communication.

An example of a sociogram is shown in Figure 11–3. It was developed after asking members of a department to list whom they communicate with on technical job-related problems, issues, or concerns. Some of the connections shown in Figure 11–3 have arrowheads on one end, indicating that that person passes information on to another

[6]K. M. Watson, "An Analysis of Communication Patterns: A Method for Discriminating Leader and Subordinate Roles," *Academy of Management Journal,* June 1982, pp. 107–22.

person, while others have arrowheads at both ends, suggesting that that person gives and receives information. By constructing sociograms such as the one in Figure 11–3, the patterns of informal communications can be graphically represented. This can provide a manager with insights into the informal patterns as well as the formal patterns that control the flow of communications within a department.

The sociogram shows that three close-knit *cliques* tend to communicate on a regular basis. These cliques have formed because of common interests, physical proximity, or similar jobs. On the other hand, Carmen and Jessie are revealed as *isolates* who communicate with no one on technical matters. Being an isolate may indicate such things as having different goals from others in the unit or being disaffected from the job.

The sociogram also singles out a *liaison* person, Don, who is not a member of a clique, but is at the center of information flow. Don has contact with the three cliques and serves as a liaison who ties the unit together on technical matters. Liaisons have been referred to as "the 'cement' that holds the structural 'bricks' of an organization together; when the liaisons are removed, a system tends to fall apart into isolated cliques."[7]

The Grapevine

An informal communication pathway that is recognized as a part of organizational life is called the *grapevine*. The use of the term *grapevine* is said to have originated during the Civil War, when telegraph lines were strung loosely between trees and soldiers said the wires resembled a grapevine. Messages that were difficult to decipher were said to have come through "the grapevine."

Today's grapevine cuts across formal channels of communication. Through it passes an assortment of facts, opinions, suspicions, and rumors that typically do not move through the formal channels. Research suggests (1) organizations have several grapevine systems, (2) information traveling in a grapevine does not follow an orderly path, and (3) organizationally related grapevine information is about 75 percent accurate.[8] The patterns of grapevine communication are shown in Figure 11–4. The cluster pattern, in which only select individuals repeat what they hear, is the pattern most commonly found in organizations.

The Rumor

The grapevine is so much a part of organizational life that it is somewhat futile for management to attempt to eliminate it as an informal channel. However, a manager must recognize that a grapevine can be troublesome if it serves as a constant source

---

[7]E. M. Rogers and R. Agarwala-Rogers, *Communication in Organizations* (New York: The Free Press, 1976).

[8]Keith Davis, *Human Behavior at Work: Organizational Behavior* (New York: McGraw-Hill, 1981); and O. W. Baskin and C. E. Aronoff, *Interpersonal Communication in Organizations* (Santa Monica, Calif.: Goodyear Publishing, 1980).

Figure 11–4 Grapevine patterns.

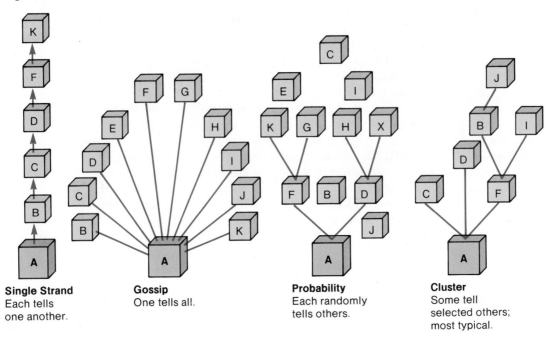

Single Strand
Each tells
one another.

Gossip
One tells all.

Probability
Each randomly
tells others.

Cluster
Some tell
selected others;
most typical.

Source: Keith Davis, *Human Behavior at Work: Organizational Behavior,* 6th ed. (New York: McGraw-Hill, 1981), p. 339. Used with permission.

of rumors. Rumors are an everyday part of business and management; it is estimated that over 33 million rumors are generated in U.S. businesses every day.[9]

A rumor can be defined as an unverified belief that is in general circulation inside the organization (an internal rumor) or in the organization's external environment (an external rumor).[10] A rumor has three components. The *target* is the object of the rumor. For example, in the late 1970s, McDonald's was the object of the rumor that it put red worms in its hamburger meat to boost the protein content. (This rumor and McDonald's response to the problem is profiled in Case 11–1 at the end of this chapter.) The *allegation* is the rumor's point about the target (putting worms in the hamburger meat). The rumor has a *source,* the communicator of the rumor. Often, individuals will attribute a rumor to a prestigious or authoritative source to give the rumor more credibility.[11]

---

[9]Robert Levy, "Tilting at the Rumor Mill," *Dun's Review,* December 1981, pp. 52–54.

[10]R. L. Rosnow, "Psychology in Rumor Reconsidered," *Psychological Bulletin,* May 1980, pp. 578–91.

[11]Frederick Koenig, *Rumor in the Marketplace* (Dover, Mass.: Auburn House Publishing, 1985).

Some rumors that travel through the company grapevine or outside the organization are true; however, sometimes they are not. Regardless of their validity, rumors tend to flourish if their content is entertaining, important, and ambiguous. Entertaining rumors have staying power because people find them interesting. For example, the rumor in the late 1970s that Life Savers Bubble Yum chewing gum was infected with spider eggs was logically nonsensical. However, the rumor's entertainment value gave the rumor much clout (Life Savers spent over $100,000 in advertisements to squelch the story).

Important rumors have staying power because their information concerns people. For example, rumors run rampant in a company shortly after it has been acquired by another firm. Many rumors are believed because the information is important to the acquired work force. Employees seek information to reduce their uncertainty and anxiety about their jobs and the future of the company. Ambiguous rumors have staying power because their lack of clarity makes it difficult to quickly refute and dismiss the rumor.[12]

Grapevines, rumors, and gossip are deeply ingrained in organizational life, so managers must be tuned in and listening to what is being said. Falsified facts traveling through the rumor mill can be corrected by feeding accurate information to primary communicators or liaison individuals. Also, informal communication systems such as the grapevine can be used by managers to benefit programs, policies, or plans. The grapevine can provide yet another albeit weak communication vehicle to keep the work force informed about job-related matters.

INTERPERSONAL COMMUNICATION

One type of communication travels from individual to individual in face-to-face and group settings. Such flows are termed *interpersonal communications,* and the forms vary from direct verbal orders to casual, nonverbal expression. Interpersonal communication is the primary means of managerial communication; on a typical day, over three fourths of a manager's communications occur via face-to-face interactions.[13]

The problems that can arise when managers attempt to communicate with other people can be traced to *perceptual* and *interpersonal style differences*. Each manager perceives the world in terms of her background, experiences, personality, frame of reference, and attitude. The primary manner in which managers relate to and learn from the environment (including people in that environment) is through information received and transmitted. The way managers receive and transmit information partly depends on how they relate to themselves and others. A number of studies suggest that some differences in interpersonal communication styles may also be due to gender. The following Management Application tests your understanding of some communication differences between male and female managers.

---

[12]Roy Rowan, "Where Did that Rumor Come From?" *Fortune,* August 13, 1979, pp. 130ff.

[13]Fred Luthans and Janet K. Larsen, "How Managers Really Communicate," *Human Relations*, 39, no. 2 (1986), pp. 161–78.

MANAGEMENT APPLICATION

GENDER DIFFERENCES IN COMMUNICATION

Do men and women differ in the ways they communicate? To test your understanding of male/female differences in communication, read the following 10 questions and check the responses which you believe are correct. Your instructor will provide the answers to this quiz which are based on results of communication research. The quiz was developed by Professors Hazel Rozema and John Gray.

		True	False
1.	In an open discussion, men usually talk more than women.	____	____
2.	In discussions, men usually try more than women to keep the conversation going.	____	____
3.	Men use more personal space when communicating than do women.	____	____
4.	In discussions, a man is more apt to interrupt women than men.	____	____
5.	Women are better at interpreting nonverbal cues than are men.	____	____
6.	Women use more polite communication tactics than do men.	____	____
7.	Women tend to initiate more conversations in the workplace than do men.	____	____
8.	When communicating, women are more likely to reveal personal information about themselves than are men.	____	____
9.	Women managers communicate with more emotion and drama than do male managers.	____	____
10.	Male and female subordinates are likely to see their female managers as better communicators than their male managers.	____	____

Source: Adapted from Hazel J. Rozema and John W. Gray, "How Wide Is Your Communication Gender Gap?" *Personnel Journal*, July 1987, pp. 98ff.

Interpersonal Styles

Interpersonal styles differ among individuals, and understanding these differences is important for managerial and organizational performance. *Interpersonal style refers to the way in which an individual prefers to relate to others.* The fact that much of the relationships among people involve communication indicates the importance of interpersonal style.[14]

Information is held by you and by others. But you or they may not have all the necessary facts. The different combinations of knowing and not knowing information are shown in Figure 11–5. The figure identifies four regions, or combinations, of information known and unknown by self and others.

---

[14]This discussion is based on Jay Hall, "Communication Revisited," *California Management Review,* Fall 1973, pp. 56–67.

Figure 11–5 Interpersonal styles and communication.

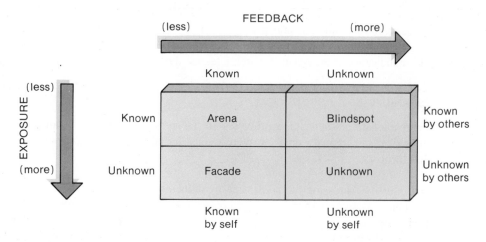

The arena.   The region most conducive to effective interpersonal relationships and communications is termed the *arena*. In this setting, all the information necessary to carry on effective communication is known to both the sender (self) and the receivers (others). As expressed in the current cliché, each party to the communication knows where the other comes from. In practical terms, if a communication attempt is in the arena region, the parties to the communication share identical feelings, data, assumptions, and skills which bear on the attempt.

The blind spot.   When relevant information is known to others but not to you, a *blind spot* results. In this context, a person (self) is at a disadvantage when communicating with others because he cannot know the others' feelings, sentiments, and perceptions. Consequently, interpersonal relationships and communications suffer.

When one party is unable to know her true feelings or sentiments about an issue, she may be unable to perceive accurately the information received from others. The idea of *selective perception* is related to blind-spot problems, since an individual experiencing a blind spot likely will be unable to receive and decode information properly. The greater the blind spot, the smaller the arena, and vice versa.

The facade.   When information is known to the self but unknown to others, the person (self) may resort to superficial communications; that is, he may present a *facade*. A facade is a false front. The facade area is particularly damaging when a subordinate "knows" and an immediate supervisor "does not know." The facade, like the blind spot, diminishes the arena and reduces the possibility of effective communication.

The unknown.   If neither party knows the relevant feelings, sentiments, and information, each party is functioning in the unknown region. Such a situation often is stated as "I can't understand them, and they don't understand me." In this predicament, interpersonal communications are sure to suffer. The unknown factor often occurs in organizations when individuals in differing technical areas must coordinate their activities through communications.

Thus, we see that the larger the areas affected by blind spots, facades, and unknowns, the smaller the arena. But how can we reduce those areas and enlarge the arena?

Exposure and Feedback

Interpersonal communication problems are the results of unsound relationships. An individual can improve unsound relationships by adopting two strategies—exposure and feedback.

Exposure. Increasing the arena area by reducing the facade area requires that one be open and honest in sharing information with others. The unwillingness of companies to discuss salary matters is an example of inadequate exposure. The process that the self uses to increase the information known to others is termed *exposure* because it leaves one in a vulnerable position. Exposing one's true feelings and sentiments is a ploy that involves some risk.

Feedback. When the self does not know or understand, more effective communications can be developed through feedback from those who do know. Thus, the blind spot can be reduced with a corresponding increase in the arena. Whether feedback is possible depends on the individual's willingness to hear it or the willingness of others to give it. Thus, the individual is less able to control the provision of feedback than the provision of exposure. Obtaining feedback is dependent on the active cooperation of others, while exposure requires the active behavior of the individual and passive listening by others.

MANAGEMENT STYLES AND INTERPERSONAL STYLES

The day-to-day activities of managers require effective interpersonal communications. Managers provide *information* (which must be *understood*); they give *commands* and *instructions* (which must be *obeyed* and *learned*); they make *efforts to influence* and *persuade* (which must be *accepted* and *acted upon*). Thus, the way managers communicate, both as senders and receivers, is crucial for effective performance.

Managers theoretically can use both exposure and feedback to enlarge the area of common understanding, the arena. As a practical matter, however, such is not the case. Managers differ in their ability and willingness to use exposure and feedback. At least four different managerial styles can be identified:

Type A

Managers who use neither exposure nor feedback are said to have a Type A style. The unknown region predominates in this style because the manager is unwilling to enlarge the area of her own knowledge or the knowledge of others. Such managers exhibit anxiety and hostility and give the appearance of aloofness and coldness toward others. If an organization has a large number of Type A managers in key positions, then you could expect to find poor and ineffective interpersonal communications and a loss of individual creativity. Type A managers often display the characteristics of autocratic leaders.

Type B

Some managers desire some degree of satisfying relationships with their subordinates, but because of their personalities and attitudes, they are unable to open up and express their feelings and sentiments. Consequently, they cannot use exposure and must rely on feedback. The facade is the predominant feature of interpersonal relationships when managers overuse feedback to the exclusion of exposure. The subordinates are likely to distrust such managers because they realize that these managers are holding back their own ideas and opinions. Type B behavior often is displayed by managers who desire to practice some form of permissive leadership.

Type C

Managers who value their own ideas and opinions, but not the ideas and opinions of others, will use exposure at the expense of feedback. The consequence of this style is the perpetuation and enlargement of the blind spot. Subordinates will soon realize that such managers are not particularly interested in communicating, only in telling. Consequently, Type C managers usually have subordinates who are hostile, insecure, and resentful. Subordinates soon learn that such managers are mainly interested in maintaining their own sense of importance and prestige.

Type D

The most effective interpersonal communication style is one which uses a balance of exposure and feedback. Managers who are secure in their positions will feel free to expose their own feelings and to obtain feedback from others. To the extent that the manager practices Type D behavior successfully, the arena region becomes larger, and communication becomes more effective. A Type D style of communicating can increase the level of trust between a manager and subordinate. When the communication concerns the subordinate's job, performance, and the organization, open communication can make the subordinate more knowledgeable and comfortable about his place in the organization.[15]

To summarize, the importance of interpersonal styles in determining the effectiveness of interpersonal communication should not be underestimated. The primary force in determining the effectiveness of interpersonal communication is the attitude of managers toward exposure and feedback. The most effective approach is that of the Type D manager. Type A, B, and C managers resort to behaviors detrimental to the effectiveness of communication and to organizational performance.

---

[15]Everett T. Suters, "Show and Tell," *Inc.*, April 1987, pp. 111–12.

NONVERBAL INTERPERSONAL COMMUNICATION

Communication that is nonverbal can occur in any face-to-face interaction between individuals. A manager's nonverbal behavior may communicate a stronger message than information presented in a memo, policy statement, or conversation.[16] *Nonverbal communication* is present in the vocal cues, facial expressions, posture, or spatial orientation of a sender.

Communicating nonverbally involves the sending and receiving of messages by some medium other than verbal or written. One researcher has found that only 7 percent of a message's impact comes from its verbal content. The rest of the impact is nonverbal—38 percent from vocal inflection and content, and 55 percent from facial content.[17] When a sender's communication is contradictory (the nonverbal message contradicts the verbal message), the receiver places more weight on the nonverbal content of the overall communication.[18]

The vocal part of a message pertains to how it is transmitted. A message can be transmitted loudly or softly, quickly or slowly, with controlled or uncontrolled inflection, or with a high or low pitch. The method of transmission adds meaning to the receiver who assesses these cues. For example, suppose a manager who is usually calm and collected delivers a high-pitched, uncontrolled message to his subordinates. The subordinates are likely to infer from the message that the manager is under heavy pressure. This interpretation may cause them to listen more attentively, since it is not normal for the manager to seem so troubled.

Body expressions are another important source of nonverbal communication. Ekman and Friesen have classified body language into five types of expression.[19] *Emblems* are gestures that are much like sign language (the hitchhiker's thumb, the OK sign with thumb and forefinger, the "V" sign for victory). These movements quickly convey an understood word or phrase. *Illustrators* are gestures that illustrate what is being said (a raised forefinger to indicate the first point of a sender's position, extended hands to illustrate the size of an object). *Regulators* are movements that regulate a conversation. For example, an upraised palm from the receiver tells a sender to slow down, an arched eyebrow can convey a request for the sender to clarify what has been said, and a nod of the head indicates understanding. Emblems, illustrators, and regulators are consciously used by individuals in communication.

Two other types of body expressions, *adapters* and *affect displays,* are often subconsciously communicated and can reveal much about a sender and receiver's feelings and attitudes. *Adapters* are expressions used to adjust psychologically to the interpersonal climate of a particular situation.[20] Usually learned early in life, adapters are frequently used to deal with stress in an interpersonal situation. Drumming fingers on

---

[16]Dale A. Level, Jr. and William P. Galle, Jr. *Managerial Communications* (Plano, Tex.: Business Publications, 1988).

[17]Albert Mehrabian, *Silent Messages* (Belmont, Calif.: Wadsworth, 1971).

[18]John Keltner, *Interpersonal Speech—Communication* (Belmont, Calif.: Wadsworth, 1970).

[19]Paul Ekman and W. V. Friesen, *Unmasking the Face* (Englewood Cliffs, N.J.: Prentice-Hall, 1975).

[20]Level and Galle, *Managerial Communications,* p. 66.

a table, tugging a strand of hair, or jiggling a leg or foot are all ways of releasing some degree of stress.

Affect displays are usually subconscious expressions that directly communicate an individual's emotions. Most affect displays are facial expressions which are a particularly important communicator of a person's feelings. There is a long-held assumption that a person's emotions are mirrored in her face and that these emotions can be "read" with a great deal of accuracy. For example, many communications experts agree that a smile communicates friendship, affection, and a desire to be helpful. Infrequent eye contact conveys dislike and an ill-at-ease feeling about the subject being discussed.

Affect displays are also expressed in body positions. For example, a "closed posture" (arms folded across the chest, legs crossed) communicates defensiveness and often dislike. Interestingly, body positions can visibly convey a high degree of rapport between the sender and receiver. Communications researchers have found that when rapport exists, the two individuals mirror each other's movements—shifting body position, dropping a hand or making some other movement at the same time. If a rapport is abruptly ended in a conversation, the "mirror" is quickly broken.[21]

The image that a person projects through body language and overall appearance is a concern of many employees in organizations. Dress is particularly important in business. Many organizations implement dress codes to communicate a particular employee and company image to customers and other constituents. The power of dress as a communicator is illustrated in a study of more than 10,000 female managers and their styles of dress. The study found a strong relationship between a woman's style of dress and her rate of promotion and pay. Specifically, women whose attire was viewed by their bosses as "extremely feminine" received fewer promotions and were paid lower salaries than did women whose dress was viewed as professional, conservative, and even dull. The women whose dress was too feminine were viewed by their superiors as incompetent, fragile, unsure of themselves, unprofessional, and not serious about their jobs.[22]

Reading an individual's body language and assessing messages about dress can be a challenging exercise because it involves subjectively evaluating nonverbal communication cues. The messages conveyed by nonverbal communication can also greatly differ across international environments which is discussed in the following Management Application.

MANAGEMENT APPLICATION

WHEN A NOD "YES" MEANS "NO"

Most communication experts agree that understanding the nonverbal messages body language sends can be challenging. However, the task is even more difficult for U.S. managers traveling abroad because there is no universal agreement on the meaning

---

[21]Michael B. McCaskey, "The Hidden Messages Managers Send," *Harvard Business Review*, November–December 1979, pp. 135–48.

[22]Kathleen A. Hughes, "Businesswomen's Broader Latitude in Dress Codes Goes Just So Far," *The Wall Street Journal*, September 1, 1987, p. 27.

of the different moves and gestures of body language. A shake of the head in the United States can mean something quite different in another country. And the translations vary widely across nations.

A few examples will be discussed here.

Winking. In the United States, winking your eye conveys friendship or sharing a joke. In many other countries, especially Australia, it conveys rudeness.

Nodding your head. A nod means yes in the United States and most other countries. In Greece and Bulgaria, it means no.

Grasping an earlobe. Tugging an earlobe says "I repent" or signals insincerity in India; it communicates appreciation in Brazil.

Raising your eyebrows. Lifting an eyebrow means yes or "I agree" in Tonga, and "pay me" in Peru.

Tapping your nose. Tapping your nose with a finger conveys a friendly warning in Italy and confidentiality and secrecy in Great Britain.

Folding your arms across your chest. This movement communicates arrogance and pride in Finland and disrespect in Fiji.

Tapping your elbow. In The Netherlands, tapping means the individual of interest is unreliable; in Columbia, it means the person is stingy.

The fingers circle (the OK sign). The sign in the United States means OK; it signals "money" in France and "worthless" in Japan. The gesture is obscene in Brazil and considered very rude in Greece and the Soviet Union.

Waving. Perfectly acceptable as a greeting or farewell in the United States, but waving is considered a grave insult in Greece and Nigeria.

Circling the ear with the forefinger. It means "crazy" in most European countries; in The Netherlands, it means "you have a phone call."

Because of the international differences in the interpretation of body language, more companies include classes in deciphering nonverbal communication as a part of the managers' training for overseas assignments. This is particularly the case for managers with assignments in Japan. There, over 95 percent of interpersonal communication is nonverbal.

Source: Adapted from Roger E. Axtell (ed.) and the Parker Pen Co. (producer), *Do's and Taboos around the World* (Elmsford, N.Y.:The Benjamin Co., 1985).

One other important but often overlooked element of nonverbal communication is *proxemics* which is defined as an individual's use of space when interpersonally communicating with others. According to Edward Hall, a prominent researcher of proxemics, people have four zones of informal space which are spatial distances they maintain when interacting with others: the intimate zone (from physical contact to 18 inches); the personal zone (from 1.5 to 4 feet); the social zone (from over 4 to 12 feet); and the public zone (more than 12 feet).[23] For Americans, supervisor-subordinate relationships begin in the social zone and progress to the personal zone after mutual trust has been developed.[24] An individual's personal and intimate zones comprise a "private bubble" of space and is considered to be private territory not to be entered by others unless invited.

Proxemics affects interpersonal communication when the proxemic behavior of the sender and receiver differs. For example assume, like most Americans, that you communicate standing in the social zone while interacting at a social gathering such as a cocktail party. However, in the South American culture, a personal-zone distance is considered more natural in such situations. You are talking with a South American businessperson at a cocktail party who is assuming a personal-zone distance. How would you feel? Typically in such a situation, an individual feels so uncomfortable with the person standing "too close" that any verbal communication is not heard. Conflicts in proxemic behavior often create a substantial barrier to effective communication. Such conflicts can also influence each individual's perceptions of the other (you may view the South American as pushy and aggressive; he may see you as cold and impolite).

WHY COMMUNICATIONS BREAK DOWN

A manager has no greater responsibility than to develop effective communications. However, communications often break down for various reasons. Problems occur both in formal *organizational communications,* such as public relations press releases, and in interpersonal communications. In general, managers should recognize that a breakdown can occur whenever any one of the elements of communication—sender, encoding, medium, decoding, receiver, or feedback—is defective.

Conflicting Frames of Reference

Individuals can interpret the same communication differently, depending on their previous experiences. This type of communication breakdown is related to the *encoding* and *decoding* elements. When the receiver and sender use the same encoding and decoding language, they can achieve common understanding. But each of us is unique in background and experience. Words can take on different meanings for different people. In terms of interpersonal communication, the arena area is relatively small when compared to blind spots, facades, and unknown area. To the extent that individuals have distinctly different *frames of reference,* communications among these individuals will be difficult to achieve.

One result of different frames of reference is that communications become distorted. For example, teenagers have different experiences than do their parents (the oft-cited generation gap); district sales managers have different perceptions than do salespersons.

---

[23]Edward Hall, *The Hidden Dimension* (Garden City, N.Y.: Doubleday Publishing, 1966).

[24]Phillip L. Hunsaker, "Communicating Better: There's No Proxy for Proxemics," *Business,* March–April 1980, pp. 41–48.

In an organization, the *jobs* that people perform will create barriers and distortions in communications. For example, a pricing problem will be viewed differently by the marketing manager than by the plant manager. An efficiency problem in a hospital will be viewed by the nursing staff from its frame of reference and its experiences, and this may result in interpretations that differ from those of the staff physicians.

Different *levels* in the organization will also have different frames of reference. First-line supervisors have frames of reference that differ in many respects from those of vice presidents. As a result, the needs, values, attitudes, and expectations of these two groups will differ, and this often will result in unintentional distortions of the communications between them. Neither group is wrong nor right. In any situation, individuals will choose that part of their own past experiences which relates to their current experiences and helps them form conclusions and judgments. Unfortunately, such incongruities in encoding and decoding can result in barriers to effective communication.

Selective Perception

Selective perception occurs when people block out new information, especially if it conflicts with what they believe. Thus, when people receive information, they are apt to hear only those words that reaffirm their beliefs. Information that conflicts with preconceived notions either is not noted or is distorted to confirm their preconceptions.

For example, a notice may be sent to all operating departments that costs must be reduced if the organization is to earn a profit. Such a communication may not achieve its desired effect because it conflicts with the "reality" of the receivers. Operating employees may ignore or be amused by the notice in light of the large salaries, travel allowances, and expense accounts of some managers. Whether these expenditures are justified is irrelevant; what is important is that such preconceptions result in breakdowns in communication. In other words, if people hear only what they want to hear, they cannot be disappointed.

Value Judgments

In every communication situation, receivers make *value judgments* by assigning an overall worth to a message prior to receiving the entire communication. Such value judgments may be based on the receiver's evaluation of the communicator, the receiver's previous experiences with the communicator, or the message's anticipated meaning. Thus, a hospital administrator may pay little attention to a memorandum from a nursing team leader because "he's always complaining about something." An employee may consider a merit evaluation meeting with the supervisor as going through the motions because she perceives the supervisor as being more concerned about administrative matters than performance.

Status Differences

Every employee has a particular status in an organization which is determined by such factors as position, title, pay, office size, and other factors. Communication is often hindered when *status differences* exist between communicators. For example, subordinates are usually reluctant to be open and honest in their communications with supervisors who have higher status and more power. Few are willing to provide their bosses with frank feedback concerning their decisions or actions because of concern about their supervisors' reactions.[25] As a result, many managers don't receive needed accurate feedback; what little feedback they receive is *filtered*. The information is manipulated by the sender to be perceived as positive by the receiver. Filtering occurs at all levels of the organization.

The problem of isolation from accurate feedback is particularly acute at the top levels of the organization. There, an executive of a company of 20,000 employees or so may have direct relationships with only 10 or 15 individuals. The personality of highly successful executives further discourages honest feedback. An executive demeanor of total confidence and command doesn't easily invite criticism from subordinates. An abrasive style with subordinates has the same effect.[26] Upper-level executives also often encounter another communication barrier: their comments to subordinates often take on an exaggerated importance. For example, one executive once casually wondered aloud how a proposed law would affect the company, knowing that the bill stood little chance of being passed. Later, he discovered that his subordinates had responded to the casual remark with a thorough, costly—and ultimately useless—analysis of the bill's impact. From then on, the executive was cautious with his comments.[27]

Some organizations are de-emphasizing status and power differences to encourage more open supervisor-subordinate communication. At Honda Motors Co. in Marysville, Ohio, for example, visible differences in status and power have been intentionally avoided. There is no executive cafeteria, washroom, or special parking spaces, and executives work in open offices with no frills. Management believes that these actions reduce communication barriers between managers of all levels and their subordinates.

Source Credibility

Source credibility refers to the trust, confidence, and faith that the receiver has in the words and actions of the communicator. The level of credibility that the receiver assigns to the communicator, in turn, directly affects how the receiver views and reacts to the words, ideas, and actions of the communicator.

Thus, how subordinates view a communication from their manager is affected by their evaluations of the manager. The degree of credibility they attach to the communication is heavily influenced by their previous experiences with the manager. Hospital medical staff members who view the hospital administrator as less than honest, manipulative, and not to be trusted are apt to assign inaccurate motives to any communication from the administrator. Union leaders who view managers as exploiters

---

[25]Frank, "Trends in Communication," p. 45.

[26]Robert E. Kaplan, Wilfred H. Drath, and Joan R. Kofodimos, "Why Some Managers Don't Get the Message," *Across the Board,* September 1985, pp. 63–69.

[27]William Hennefrund, "Fear of Feedback," *Association Management,* March 1986, pp. 80–83.

and managers who view union leaders as inherent enemies are unlikely to engage in much real communication.

Time Pressures

The pressure of time is an important barrier to communication. An obvious problem is that managers do not have the time to communicate frequently with every subordinate. *Time pressures* often can lead to serious problems. *Short-circuiting* is a failure of the formally prescribed communication system often resulting from time pressures. It means simply that someone who normally would be included has been left out of the formal channel of communication.

For example, a salesperson who needs a rush order for a very important customer goes directly to the production manager with the request, since the production manager owes the salesperson a favor. Other members of the sales force get word of this and become upset over this preferential treatment and report it to the sales manager. Obviously, the sales manager knows nothing of the deal, since she has been short-circuited. However, in some cases, going through formal channels is extremely costly or impossible from a practical standpoint. Consider the impact on a hospital patient if a nurse had to report a malfunction in some critical life-support equipment in an intensive care unit to the nursing team leader, who in turn had to report it to the hospital engineer, who would then have instructed a staff engineer to make the repair.

Communication Overload

In decision making, one of the necessary conditions for effective decisions is the presence of *information*. In fact, because of advances in communication technology, difficulties may arise not from the absence of information but from *excessive* information. The last decade has often been described as the Information Era or the Age of Information. Managers often are deluged by information and data. They cannot absorb or adequately respond to all of the messages directed to them. They screen out the majority of messages, which in effect means that these messages are never decoded. Thus, the area of organizational communication is one in which "more" is not always "better."

Semantic Problems

Communication is the transmission of *information* and *understanding* through the use of *common symbols*. Actually, we cannot transmit understanding. Usually we can only transmit information in the form of words, which are the common symbols. Unfortunately, the same words may mean entirely different things to different people. The understanding is in the receiver, not in the words.

When a plant manager announces that a budget increase is necessary for the growth of the plant, the manager may have in mind the necessity for new equipment, and expanded parts inventory, and more personnel. To the existing personnel, however, growth may be perceived as excess funds that can be used for wage and salary increases.

Again, because different groups use words differently, communication often can be impeded. This is especially true with abstract or technical terms or phrases. A *cost-benefit study* would have meaning to persons involved in the administration of the hospital but probably would mean very little to the staff physicians. In fact, it might even be scorned by the latter. Such concepts as *trusts, profits,* and *Treasury bills* may have concrete meaning to bank executives but little or no meaning to bank tellers. Thus, because words mean different things to different people, it is possible for a communicator to speak the same language as a receiver but still not transmit *understanding*.

Occupational, professional, and social groups often develop words and phrases that have meaning only to group members. Such special language can serve many useful purposes. It can provide group members with feelings of belonging, cohesiveness, and, in many cases, self-esteem. Special languages also can facilitate effective communication *within* the group. The use of in-group language can, however, result in severe *semantic problems* and communication breakdowns when outsiders or other groups are involved. Technical and staff groups often use such language in an organization, not for the purpose of transmitting information and understanding, but to communicate a mystique about the group or its function.

The following Management Application looks at popular lingo used in a number of prominent companies.

MANAGEMENT APPLICATION

BUSINESS LINGO

Over time, almost every organization develops a lingo—words and phrases for people, situations, events, and things—in short, a language that is distinctly the company's own. Some examples are as follows:

IBM. At Big Blue, a "hipo" is someone with high potential and is quickly moving up through the organizational hierarchy. An "alpo" is an employee with low potential. When people disagree, they "nonconcur." Someone who nonconcurs frequently but for constructive reasons is a "wild duck."

Walt Disney. At Walt Disney, all employees are called "cast members." They're "on stage" when they're working and "off stage" when at lunch or taking a break. When the company treats guests for lunch or throws a party or other functions for employees, the treat is "on the mouse." Any situation or event that's positive is a "good Mickey." Anything less is a "bad Mickey."

Newsweek. Employees at *Newsweek* call each issue's leading national story the *violin* so named because the story reflects the tone of the news. The top editors are called *Wallendas,* named after the legendary aerial acrobatic troupe, The Flying Wallendas. The reason: their jobs are hectic, responsibilities are immense and job security is nonexistent. The *Wallendas* work in their offices, the *Wallendatorium.*

Other companies sport imaginative lingos. At McDonald's, dedicated employees have "ketchup in their veins." At Eastman Kodak, committed, hard-working employees "work for the great yellow father." And when employees at Prudential Life Insurance

Co. of America throw a birthday party for a colleague or celebrate some other occasion, they have a *desk* for the employee. The term comes from the company's tradition of decorating an employee's desk on special occasions. Although today the parties are held in conference rooms, the event is still called a *desk*.

Lingo serves a purpose in an organization, according to communication experts. It makes the organization more distinctive and unique, and it tends to build employees' identity with and commitment to the company. It is also an efficient way to communicate inside the organization. But for associates outside the company, lingo can sometimes hinder communication when the outsiders don't know the jargon.

Source: Adapted from Michael W. Miller, "At Many Firms, Employees Speak a Language That's All Their Own," *The Wall Street Journal*, December 29, 1987, p. 15.

Poor Listening Skills

Effective interpersonal communication requires that each participant not only hear the words that are said but understand their meaning. This task requires the ability to listen—to focus on the speaker, block out distractions, and carefully comprehend the communicator's message. Although listening is a key requirement for effective communication, most individuals listen at only a 25 percent level of efficiency.[28]

Several factors hinder effective listening. Perhaps the primary obstacle is an individual's free time while listening. On average, an individual speaks about 125 words a minute but listens at a rate that is more than three times as fast (from 400 to 600 words a minute). As a result, 75 percent of listening time is free time—that is, time to become mentally sidetracked by any number of distractions.[29] The physical surroundings, the speaker's appearance, his mention of a controversial concept or idea, or a problem nagging at the listener—can all compete for a listener's attention.[30]

Because of the recognized importance of listening, a growing number of companies are conducting training workshops in listening skills. Sperry Corporation has launched perhaps the most publicized training program where all of its employees have received listening materials and over one fourth have completed listening skills–based training.

HOW COMMUNICATIONS CAN BE IMPROVED

Managers striving to become better communicators must accomplish two separate tasks. First, they must improve their messages—the information they wish to transmit. Second, they must improve their own *understanding* of what other people are trying to communicate to them; they must become better encoders and decoders. *They must*

---

[28]Sheperd Walker, "Listening Skills for Managers," in *The Handbook of Executive Communication*, ed. John Louis DeGaetani (Homewood, Ill.: Dow Jones-Irwin, 1986), p. 651.

[29]Cynthia Hamilton and Brian H. Kleiner, "Steps to Better Listening," *Personnel Journal*, February 1987, pp. 20–21.

[30]Walter Kiechel III, "Learn How to Listen," *Fortune*, August 17, 1987, pp. 107–8.

Figure 11–6 Ten commandments for effective listening.

1. **Stop talking!** You cannot listen if you are talking.
   Polonius (Hamlet): "Give every man thine ear, but few thy voice."

2. **Put the talker at ease.** Help him feel that he is free to talk.
   This is often called a permissive environment.

3. **Show him that you want to listen.** Look and act interested. Do not read your mail
   while he talks. Listen to understand rather than to oppose.

4. **Remove distractions.** Don't doodle, tap, or shuffle papers.
   Will it be quieter if you shut the door?

5. **Empathize with him.** Try to put yourself in his place so that you can
   see his point of view.

6. **Be patient.** Allow plenty of time. Do not interrupt him.
   Don't start for the door or walk away.

7. **Hold your temper.** An angry man gets the wrong meaning from words.

8. **Go easy on argument and criticism.** This puts him on the defensive.
   He may "clam up" or get angry. Do not argue; even if you win, you lose.

9. **Ask questions.** This encourages him and shows you are listening.
   It helps to develop points further.

10. **Stop talking!** This is first and last, because all other commandments
    depend on it. You just can't do a good listening job while you are talking.

    Nature gave man two ears but only one tongue, which is a gentle hint
    that he should listen more than he talks.

Source: Keith Davis, *Human Behavior at Work* (New York: McGraw-Hill, 1972), p. 396. Reprinted by permission.

strive not only to be understood but also to understand. The techniques discussed here will help managers to accomplish these two important tasks.

Effective Listening

To *understand,* managers first must *listen.* One way to encourage someone to express true feelings, desires, and emotions is to listen. Just listening is not enough, of course. You must listen with understanding. Figure 11–6 provides a list of the "Ten Commandments for Effective Listening."

No communications occur until managers make the *decision to listen.* The above guidelines are useless unless one realizes that effective communication involves understanding as well as being understood.

Following Up

Following up involves assuming that you are misunderstood. Whenever possible, you should attempt to determine whether your intended meaning was actually received.

As we have seen, meaning often is in the mind of the receiver. An accounting unit leader in a government office communicates notices of openings in other agencies to the accounting staff members. Although this action may be understood among longtime employees as a friendly gesture, a new employee might interpret it as an evaluation of poor performance and a suggestion to leave.

Regulating Information Flow

Regulating the flow of communications ensures an optimum flow of information to managers, and reduces the likelihood of communication overload. Both the quality and quantity of communications should be regulated. The idea is based on the *exception principle* of management, which states that only significant deviations from policies and procedures should be brought to the attention of managers.

Certain types of organizational designs are more amenable to the exception principle than are other types. Certainly, in an organization with an emphasis on free-flowing communication, the principle would not apply. However, in a more structured organization, it likely would prove useful.

Utilizing Feedback

Feedback is an important element in effective two-way communication. It provides a channel for receiver response. Through feedback, the communicator can determine whether the message has been received and if it has produced the intended response.

In face-to-face communication, direct feedback is possible. In downward communication, however, inaccuracies often occur because there is insufficient opportunity for feedback from receivers. Thus, distributing a memorandum on an important policy statement to all employees does not guarantee that communication has occurred. One might expect feedback in the form of upward communication to be encouraged more in System-4 organizations. But the mechanisms discussed earlier that can encourage upward communication are found in many different organizational designs. An organization needs effective upward communication if its downward communication is to have any chance of being effective. The point is that developing and supporting feedback involves far more than following up on communications.

Empathy

Empathy is the ability to put oneself in the other person's role and to assume the viewpoints and emotions of that person. This involves being a listener rather than a talker. Empathy requires communicators to place themselves in the receivers' positions and anticipate how the message is likely to be decoded.

It is vital that a manager understand and appreciate the process of decoding. Decoding involves perceptions, and the message will be filtered through the perceptions of the receiver. For vice presidents to communicate effectively with supervisors, for faculty to communicate effectively with students, and for government administrators to communicate effectively with minority groups, empathy is often an important ingredient. Empathy can reduce many of the barriers to effective communication that have been discussed above. The greater the gap between the experiences and background of the communicator and the receiver, the greater is the effort that must be made to find a common ground of understanding—ground on which there are overlapping fields of experience.

Simplifying Language

Complex language has been identified as a major barrier to effective communication. Students often suffer when their instructors use technical jargon that transforms simple concepts into complex puzzles.

Schools are not the only places, however, where complex language is used. Government agencies are known for their often incomprehensible communications. We have noted instances in which professional people attempt to use their in-group language to communicate with individuals outside their group. Managers must remember that effective communication involves transmitting *understanding* as well as information. If the receiver does not understand, then there has been no communication. In fact, many of the techniques discussed in this section work solely to promote understanding. Managers must encode messages in words, appeals, and symbols that are meaningful to the receiver.

In conclusion, it would be hard to find an aspect of a manager's job that does not involve communication. If all members of the organization had a common point of view, communicating would be easy. Unfortunately, each member comes to the organization with a distinct personality, background, experience, and frame of reference. The structure of the organization itself influences status relationships and the distance (levels) between individuals, and these in turn influence the ability of individuals to communicate.

In this chapter, we have tried to convey the basic elements in the process of communication and what it takes to communicate effectively. These elements are necessary whether the communication is face-to-face or written and whether it occurs vertically or horizontally within an organization. Several common communication barriers exist, and there are several ways to remove them. Often, however, there is insufficient time to utilize many of the techniques for improving communications, and such skills as empathy and effective listening are not easy to develop. Communicating is a matter of transmitting and receiving, and managers must be effective at both. They must understand as well as be understood.

MANAGEMENT SOLUTION

JOHNSON & JOHNSON'S OPEN COMMUNICATION STRATEGY

Over the few weeks following the consumer deaths, Burke's committee launched a strategy that included several actions. The company immediately suspended all Tylenol advertising and stopped the production of Tylenol capsules.

Continued

MANAGEMENT SOLUTION

Concluded

Within one week after the first loss of life, Johnson & Johnson pulled all Tylenol capsules—about 31 million bottles—off the retail shelves. Tylenol's market share dropped 87 percent in two weeks. Working with the Food and Drug Administration, the company tested eight million bottles (and discovered that eight bottles and about 75 capsules had been poisoned). Based on an examination of the poisoned capsules, the FDA concluded that the capsules were most likely tampered with after the bottles were placed on the retail shelf, an opinion Johnson & Johnson publicized. The company also posted a $100,000 reward for information leading to the arrest of the poisoner.

A key element of J&J's actions was an open, proactive communication strategy with the press and the public. The company launched a nationwide campaign via the press and published notices to alert consumers to stop taking Tylenol capsules. The company established a 24-hour, toll-free hotline to answer inquiries from the public. Over 350,000 calls were received in October through December. Every one of the some 3,000 letters from consumers was answered. Over 2 million mailgrams were sent to medical professionals and retailers concerning the Tylenol recall and other developments. Johnson & Johnson also kept its work force informed via letter updates and videotaped special reports. Through these mechanisms, Johnson & Johnson asked employees for help; they responded by manning the hotline as volunteers.

Once closed-mouthed to the press, Johnson & Johnson's senior executives accepted every media request for a newspaper interview or a television appearance. Chairman Burke was the company's primary spokesman, appearing on "Donahue" and "60 Minutes" which filmed one of the task force's twice-daily strategy sessions.

Advertising was a particularly important communications tool, especially after Johnson & Johnson decided to reintroduce Tylenol capsules in tamper-resistant packaging. In late October, the company launched a $2 million TV campaign which ran a commercial featuring Dr. Thomas Gates, the company's medical director. He urged consumers to maintain their trust in Tylenol and announced the product's future return in tamper-resistant packaging.

Three weeks later, the company held a video news briefing televised from New York to 30 cities nationwide via satellite. By means of a two-way audio hookup, Chairman Burke answered questions from reporters across the 30 locations concerning Tylenol's return to market. Newspaper advertising was also effective in explaining to consumers tamper-resistant packaging (a first in the consumer-products industry) and later in offering coupons for free bottles of the tamper-resistant Tylenol which debuted January 1.

By the crisis' end in early 1983, more than 125,000 media reports had been produced about the story. Johnson & Johnson lost $100 million in Tylenol recall and testing costs. However, its response to the crisis stopped any further loss of life. It also changed forever the packaging of tamperable consumer products. And by spring of 1983, Johnson & Johnson's Tylenol had regained 80 percent of its lost market share.

Source: Adapted from Marion K. Pinsdorf, *Communicating When Your Company Is under Siege* (Lexington, Mass.: D.C. Heath, 1987); and Rebecca Fannin, "Tylenol: Diary of an Amazing Comeback," *Marketing & Media Decisions*, Spring 1983, pp. 129ff.

MANAGEMENT SUMMARY

- Communication is the process of achieving common understanding. For managerial purposes, it is undertaken to achieve an effect.

- The elements of communication are the sender, encoding, the message, the medium, decoding, the receiver, noise, and feedback. All of these elements must be in harmony if communication is to achieve understanding and effect.

- A crucial factor in determining the effectiveness of formal communications in an organization is the way in which the organization is structured.

- Rumors are an everyday part of organizational life. Regardless of their validity, rumors tend to flourish when they are viewed by the receiver as important, entertaining, and ambiguous.

- Such psychological factors as perception, personality, and interpersonal style are critical in determining the effectiveness of interpersonal communications.

- Nonverbal communication is an important source of information about people's thoughts and feelings. The voice, body expressions, style of dress, and proxemics are all important mechanisms of nonverbal communication.

- The extent to which individuals share understanding depends on their use of feedback and exposure. Balanced use of both is the most effective approach.

- Communication barriers can be identified in organizations and in people. Effective managers can remove or at least minimize these barriers by developing effective listening skills and empathy, by following up on their communications, regulating information flow, using feedback, and simplifying their language.

REVIEW AND DISCUSSION QUESTIONS

1. Explain why no communication occurs if the manager does not achieve the purpose or effect that he desired after sending a message.

2. Several studies indicate that managers are poor listeners. As one subordinate commented, "The boss doesn't listen; she argues." What factors in the workplace hinder a manager's ability to listen?

3. Explain the relationship between organizational structure and communication flows within the organization.

4. As a chief communications officer within an organization, what strategies would you implement to stop damaging rumors you've identified in the organization?

5. Which barriers to communication are most controllable by managers? Explain.

6. What, if anything, can managers do to remove barriers to communication that are beyond their control?

7. Of the "Ten Commandments for Effective Listening," which commandment do you believe is the most difficult to successfully obey? Explain.

8. Do you tend to be a Type A, B, C, or D person when you engage in interpersonal

communications? Are you content to be
what you think you are? If not, how could
you change?

9. How would you apply the concept of
proxemics in designing an office that
facilitates open, effective communication?

10. In your experience, which communication
element has often been the cause of
your failures to communicate? What
can you do to improve your ability to
communicate?

CASES

11-1 A CAN OF WORMS FOR MCDONALD'S

In the summer of 1978, a rumor began circulating in the Southeast that McDonald's was putting red worms in its hamburger meat to boost its protein content. Although the rumor was untrue, it quickly spread from Chattanooga to Atlanta and north to Ohio and Indiana. By the time it reached the northern states, the rumor was clearly cutting into the sales of McDonald's franchises.

McDonald's was already rumor weary. In the preceding months, the company had finally succeeded in squelching the absurd rumor that Ray Kroc, McDonald's president, was making financial donations to the Church of Satan. Now the company was faced with the challenge of devising a strategy to debunk the worm story.

McDonald's decided to repeat their Satan rumor strategy and deal with the rumor locally. Company officials identified the areas where the rumor was running rampant. In these areas, the company distributed McDonald's materials about its food content and letters from the secretary of agriculture that assured customers that the hamburger served was wholesome, properly identified, and in compliance with standards prescribed by the food safety and quality regulations.

Franchise owners in these areas followed a three-part strategy: First, distribute an illustrated materials kit on McDonald's beef to customers. Second, if this action doesn't work, run local ads on the company's high quality of food. Third, as a last resort, contact the press for coverage on food quality. In working with franchise owners, McDonald's stressed one unbreakable rule: Never mention the word *worm*.

Despite the efforts by franchises in the affected areas, sales plummeted. McDonald's research found that although most consumers believed the rumor was ridiculous, they were beginning to go elsewhere for fast food. Meanwhile, the rumor was catching fire. Over 75 percent of the populations of Atlanta and Cincinnati had heard the rumor; in Atlanta, many believed it was true.

In November, McDonald's decided to go public and attack the rumor nationwide. At a press conference in Atlanta, the company denied it used "protein additives" in its hamburger meat. Shortly thereafter, McDonald's ran a nationwide ad campaign with color photos of its hamburgers and copy stressing its 100 percent U.S. government inspected beef.

A few weeks later, the rumor faded away. However, some observers questioned McDonald's strategy. Some observers asserted that McDonald's should have gone public sooner. Others argued that they should not have gone public at all.

Questions

1. What are the pros and cons of going public with a rumor and denying it in a nationally publicized press conference?

2. In your opinion, did McDonald's follow the best strategy? What other options could they have chosen?

3. In your opinion, why do obviously illogical rumors about a company often have staying power and are so difficult to squelch?

Source: This case is adapted from Frederick Koenig, *Rumor in the Marketplace* (Dover, Mass.: Auburn Publishing, 1985).

11–2 GET THE JOB DONE

Jack Forrester, 35, is a bloodstock agent in the thoroughbred horse industry. As bloodstock agent, he locates and brings together buyers and sellers of thoroughbred horses and breeding rights. He has achieved tremendous success through his hard work and his knowledge of thoroughbred bloodlines. He started his business five years ago, and he now employs eight other agents, three secretaries, an office manager, and me. Jack hired me four months ago and told me that I was the "assistant office manager." I thought that was (and is) a grand job title, even though no one ever told me what I was supposed to do. But the pay is great for a part-time job (I am a junior in college), and I am learning a lot about an interesting industry. I am also learning a lot about people.

I stood by the door of Forrester's office. Forrester was on the phone, and before I could knock, he motioned for me to come in and sit down. His desk was covered by numerous reports, memos, horse sale catalogs, telephone messages, and racing results. Other reminders on bits of paper were taped to the wall, and a "to do" list with at least 10 entries was taped to the base of the telephone. Evidently these were things that he had "to do" immediately. While talking on the phone, he added another item to this list.

As he continued the phone conversation, he was shaking his head and signing letters at the same time. Finally, he put his hand over the phone and said to me, "This is Robinson in Florida on that two-year-old filly deal. All the tests on her are not in yet, but he insists on giving me every detail on the entire test procedure. The guy is going to drive me nuts."

Turning his attention back to the phone, Forrester removed his hand and resumed talking. "Right, Robbie, OK. . . . Great. . . . OK. . . . Sure. . . . Call me back on that. . . . Terrific. . . . Bye."

Forrester hung up the phone with a sigh of relief and looked at me. "Do you know what I like about you, Tinsley?" I didn't have time to answer, nor did he, because the phone rang again. "Yeah. . . . Fine. . . . Terrific. . . . Count me in. . . . Bye." At this point, his secretary looked in and said, "John Towne of Winthrop Farms is on hold. It sounds urgent."

Forrester shook his head again and went back to the telephone. After a few minutes of conversation, he put his hand over the receiver and called to his secretary. "Get Johnson and Burke in here, fast." Johnson was the office manager, and Burke was an agent. They arrived as he hung up the phone.

"Burke," he said, "you know that deal you put together for the syndication of that three-year-old, Ol' Blue? Well, they don't like it. Put this information into it and tell me what effect the changes will have on us. When you get it finished, bring it to me so I can call Towne back." Burke left.

"Johnson, I want all of the training fees, jockey expenses, and all other expenses on that horse. Don't give them to me by the month like you did last time. I need totals in all categories, and for crying out loud, this time break out the 'other' category a little better. I looked real bad last week when Towne asked me what the $6,300 in 'other expense' was for. I want all the information at my fingertips in case we've got to go to war with these people." Johnson left.

"Now Tinsley, what did you need me for?"

"Just sign this bill of sale," I said. "No reason to spend a lot of time on it. It's for the sale of that yearling you asked me to take care of."

"That's what I like about you, Tinsley," he said as he leaned back in his chair and signed the bill of sale. "When I give you a job, you listen, and then you do it right the first time, and then you tell me when it's done. You don't tell me how you did it, the problems you're having doing it, who you met while doing it, and every other Mickey Mouse detail. If the rest of the people around here had that ability, I might be able to get some work done. I think I got more work done five years ago when I had nobody working for me."

As I left his office, I didn't have time to thank him because the phone began ringing.

Questions

1. Explain why Forrester communicates as he does with his employees.
2. Identify barriers to communication in the interactions described in the case.
3. What kinds of personalities, needs, and motivations must people have to work effectively with Forrester?

EXERCISE

11–1 PERCEPTUAL DIFFERENCES

Purpose: To illustrate how people perceive the same situation differently through the process of selective perception.

Setting Up the Exercise: The instructor will divide the class into groups of four students each. Then, complete the following activities:

1. As individuals, complete the following quiz. Do not talk to your group members until everyone in the class has finished.

Quiz: The Robbery

The lights in a store had just been turned off by a businessman when a man appeared and demanded money. The owner opened a cash register. The contents of the cash register were scooped up, and the man sped away. A member of the police force was notified promptly.

Answer the following questions about the story by circling T for true, F for false, or ? for unknown.

1.	A man appeared after the owner turned off his store lights.	T F ?
2.	The robber was a man.	T F ?
3.	The man who appeared did not demand money.	T F ?
4.	The man who opened the cash register was the owner.	T F ?
5.	The store owner scooped up the contents of the cash register and ran away.	T F ?
6.	Someone opened a cash register.	T F ?
7.	After the man who demanded money scooped up the contents of the cash register, he ran away.	T F ?
8.	While the cash register contained money, the story does not state how much.	T F ?
9.	The robber demanded money of the owner.	T F ?
10.	A businessman had just turned off the lights when a man appeared in the store.	T F ?
11.	It was broad daylight when the man appeared.	T F ?
12.	The man who appeared opened the cash register.	T F ?
13.	No one demanded money.	T F ?
14.	The story concerns a series of events in which only three persons are referred to: the owner of the store, a man who demanded money, and a member of the police force.	T F ?
15.	The following events occurred: someone demanded money, a cash register was opened, its contents were scooped up, and a man dashed out of the store.	T F ?

Source: William V. Haney, *Communication and Interpersonal Relations: Text and Cases* (Homewood, Ill.: Richard D. Irwin, 1979), pp. 250–51.

---

2. Your instructor will provide the answers to the 15 questions. Score your responses.

3. As a group, discuss your members' responses. Focus your discussion on the following questions:

a. Why did perceptions differ across members? What factors could account for these differences?

b. Many people don't perform very well with this quiz. Why? What other factors beyond selective perception can adversely affect performance?

A Learning Note: This exercise aptly demonstrates the wide variety of perceptual differences among people when considering a situation where little factual information is provided. The exercise should also indicate that most people selectively perceive the information they are comfortable with in analyzing the situation. Many will also subconsciously fill in gaps of information with assumptions they suppose are facts.

TWELVE

Motivation and Performance

LEARNING OBJECTIVES

After completing Chapter 12, you should be able to:

Define: the meaning of motivation.

State: why individuals react differently to being frustrated or blocked in satisfying their needs.

Describe: why money is not always a motivator of employee behavior in organizations.

Explain: the different kinds of quality of work life programs that managers are now using in organizations.

Discuss: how reinforcement theory principles can be applied by a manager to influence behavior.

MORALE AT DIAMOND INTERNATIONAL'S EGG CARTON PLANT IS DOWN

Diamond International Corporation has an egg carton plant in Palmer, Massachusetts. Management had a meeting with the Paperworkers Union representative about 14 major grievances. At least the union considered the grievances to be major. The meeting pointed out morale problems. A recently conducted survey showed that 65 percent of the workers felt that management did not treat them respectfully, 56 percent approached their work with pessimism, and 79 percent felt they weren't rewarded for a job well done. These are considered to be serious morale problems that management needs to address and to show genuine concern about.

The Palmer plant is important to Diamond's success in a competitive egg carton market. The plant employs 300 people, of whom 254 are hourly workers represented by the Paperworkers Union. Issues were discussed at the meeting that suggested management was not being viewed in positive terms by the hourly employees, and this was affecting attendance and productivity. Continuation of a no-corrective action stance by management would jeopardize Diamond's favorable market image.

(The Management Solution to this Management Incident can be found at the end of this chapter.)

Motivation is a general term used to describe the process of starting, directing, and maintaining physical and psychological activities. It is a broad concept that embraces such internal mechanisms as *(a)* preference for one activity over another, *(b)* enthusiasm and vigor of a person's responses, and *(c)* persistence of organized patterns of action toward relevant goals.[1] The word *motivation* comes from the Latin *movere* "to move."

No manager has ever "seen" motivation, just as no manager has ever seen thinking, perceiving, or learning. All that a manager sees are changes in behavior. To explain or justify these observed changes, managers make inferences about underlying psychological processes—inferences that are formalized in the concept of motivation. Thus, in a formal sense motivation is defined as "all those inner striving conditions described as needs, drives, desires, motives, and so forth. It is an inner state that activates or moves."

Instead of using a formal interpretation of motivation to accomplish the job of managing other employees, a manager observes behavior and makes inferences about motivation. If an employee displays the following type of behavior, she is considered to be motivated:

- ☐ Is regularly present on the job.
- ☐ Puts forth her best effort.
- ☐ Is always working at performing the job.
- ☐ Is directing her efforts toward the accomplishment of meaningful goals.

In essence, managers observe presence, effort, persistence, and goal-orientation, and make inferences about whether or not an employee is motivated.

MOTIVATION AND BEHAVIOR

All behavior is in some way motivated. People have reasons for doing what they do or for behaving in the manner that they do. Thus, human behavior is directed toward certain goals and objectives. Such goal-directed behavior revolves around the desire for *need satisfaction*. A *need* is a physiological, psychological, or sociological want or desire that can be satisfied by reaching a desired goal.

Motivation

An unsatisfied need, drive, desire, or motive initiates motivation as shown in Figure 12–1. An unsatisfied need, drive, desire, or motive causes tension (physical, psychological, or sociological) within the individual, leading him to engage in some kind of behavior (to seek a means) to satisfy the need and thereby reduce the tension. Note that this activity is directed toward a goal; arrival at the goal satisfies the need. For example, a thirsty person needs water, is driven by thirst, and is motivated by a desire for water in order to satisfy the need. Depending on how well the goal is accomplished, the inner state is modified as shown by the feedback loop. Thus, motivation begins

---

[1] Philip G. Zimbardo, *Psychology and Life* (Glenview, Ill.: Scott, Foresman, 1985), pp. 263–65.

Figure 12–1 A model of the motivation process.

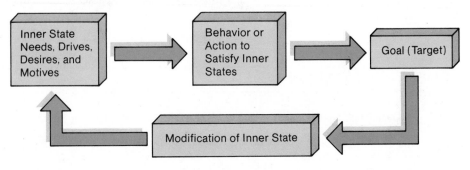

with an unsatisfied inner state condition and ends with movement to release that unsatisfied condition, with goal-directed behavior as a part of the process.

Motivation and Performance

In reviewing the general motivation model shown in Figure 12–1, it is important to point out that motivation and performance are distinct concepts. Managers are concerned about employees accomplishing significant work goals; that is, output, quality, cost containment. The successful accomplishment of these work goals is the result of a number of factors such as the effort, time, and commitment of the employee. There is also the employee ability factor, as well as the type of support and guidance provided by the manager.[2] It is important for a manager to note that some of the factors that result in accomplished goals are internal, a part of the employee's makeup or characteristics. However, other factors are external to the employee.

Since both internal and external factors interact in accomplishment of goals, it is important for the manager to not reach incorrect or incomplete conclusions about motivation. A manager, for example, may notice a drop in performance and react by increasing the incentive pay for producing each unit. The manager's reaction is an attempt to increase the employee's motivation level and to show the employee how interested the manager is in performance. However, the drop in performance may be due to not feeling well, to having problems at home, or to believing that management doesn't trust him and is now closely monitoring every activity.

Managerial mistakes in diagnosing what are thought to be motivational (inner-state) problems are common in work settings. Other factors interact with motivation to determine if job performance goals will be accomplished. The employees' abilities, outside work activities, available resources, working conditions, and the style of management are important factors to consider when diagnosing what is thought to be a motivation problem.

---

[2]Craig C. Pender, *Work Motivation* (Glenview, Ill.: Scott, Foresman, 1984), pp. 10–13.

Some organizations believe that outside speakers can inspire employees in terms of motivation. The following Management Application discusses some of these speakers.

MANAGEMENT APPLICATION

SERMONS FROM THE EVANGELISTS OF MOTIVATION

Zig Ziglar is called a *motivational speaker*. He talks about being motivated, tells jokes about being motivated and, above all, attempts to convince people that the key to motivation is themselves. He believes that his job is to "fit people with new glasses," so they can really see what they can accomplish in life.

For his performance Ziglar is paid about $10,000 a speech. He is already booked up to give speeches to managers, top executives, professional associations, and college groups for the next two years. Ziglar has been called an "evangelist of inspiration." His messages are positive and this is what clients such as Ford, General Motors, IBM, DuPont, and Scott Paper want their managers to hear. The demand for Ziglar's type of motivational message is growing, and other speakers are joining his ranks.

Denis Waitley often appears with Ziglar but has a quieter, softer style. He preaches the importance of basic virtues in managing people in an organization—integrity, goal setting, positive thinking. He has a Ph.D. in human behavior and has a client list that includes Mutual of New York, Shearson Lehman, Upjohn, and some Bell companies.

Tom Peters, the best selling author of *In Search of Excellence,* is another motivational speaker in high demand. His message is: America's big corporations are poorly managed, and if they want to compete they will have to "give the customer what he wants—quality, quality, quality." He makes about 250 appearances a year. Peters doesn't like to be called a motivational speaker, because he feels that so-called motivational speakers are not effective.

There are some loud critics of the motivational "evangelist." One executive claims that American industry is so desperate to increase productivity it will do anything, even use what he refers to as "witchcraft." Critics claim that these speakers are using intimidation and fear, which have negative effects that will be detrimental to motivation in the long run.

There are, however, organizations like DuPont which believe that the motivational speeches are a positive force for change. After listening to motivational speeches, DuPont workers seem more willing to communicate, to start their own projects, and to take charge.

Presently there is no research evidence available that indicates whether motivational speeches by Ziglar, Waitley, Peters, or anyone else have a lasting positive effect on employees in terms of morale, self-confidence, or performance. It is doubtful that needs, motives, and desires can be changed by listening to a single speech if other changes in the workplace do not occur. Despite the lack of supportive research data, the $10,000 per speech fee is being paid by thousands of firms for the top-notch evangelists of motivation.

Source: Adapted from Jeremy Main, "Merchants of Inspiration," *Fortune,* July 6, 1987, pp. 69–74.

Individual Needs and Motivation

Over the years, a number of concepts have been studied by psychologists that have represented the energetic force which constitutes human motivation. The most commonly used concept in theories of work motivation is *needs*. It is important to note again that *needs* are internal and they cannot be observed directly.

Needs may be classified in different ways. Many of the early management theorists regarded monetary incentives as the prime motivating means. These writers were influenced by the classical economists of the 18th and 19th centuries, who emphasized the rational pursuit of economic objectives and believed that economic behavior was characterized by rational economic calculations. Today, some behavioral scientists and managers hold that while money obviously is an important motivator, people seek to satisfy needs that are other than purely economic. In fact, Sigmund Freud was the first to state that much of a person's behavior may be influenced by needs of which she is not aware.

Most behavioral scientists now agree that human beings are motivated by the desire to satisfy many needs. But there is a wide difference of opinion as to what those needs and their relative importance are. Abraham Maslow, a clinical psychologist, developed a widely publicized theory of motivation called the *need hierarchy*.

Maslow's need hierarchy is widely accepted today in management theory and practice, because it seems to make sense and is easy to understand.[3] This theory of motivation is based on two important assumptions:

1. Each person's needs depend on what he already has. Only needs not yet satisfied can influence behavior. A satisfied need cannot influence behavior.

2. Needs are arranged in a hierarchy of importance. Once one need is satisfied, another emerges and demands satisfaction.

Maslow believed five levels of needs exist. These levels are (1) physiological, (2) safety, (3) social, (4) esteem, and (5) self-actualization.[4] He placed them in a framework he called the *hierarchy of needs*. This is presented in Figure 12–2.

Maslow stated that if all of a person's needs are unsatisfied at a particular time, the most basic needs will be more pressing than the others. Needs at a lower level must be satisfied before higher-level needs come into play, and only when they are sufficiently satisfied do the next needs in line become significant. Let us briefly examine each need level.

The unsatisfied needs are displayed on the left of Figure 12–2. Some areas that managers can influence for each of the five need categories are presented in Figure 12–2. Managers can have a significant impact in helping employees satisfy needs in each of Maslow's categories.

---

[3]F. Tuzzolino and B. R. Armandi, "A Need Hierarchy Framework for Assessing Corporate Social Responsibility," *Academy of Management Review*, January 1981, pp. 21–28.

[4]Abraham H. Maslow, *Motivation and Personality* (New York: Harper & Row, 1954), pp. 93–98.

Figure 12–2 Maslow's need hierarchy and management influence example.

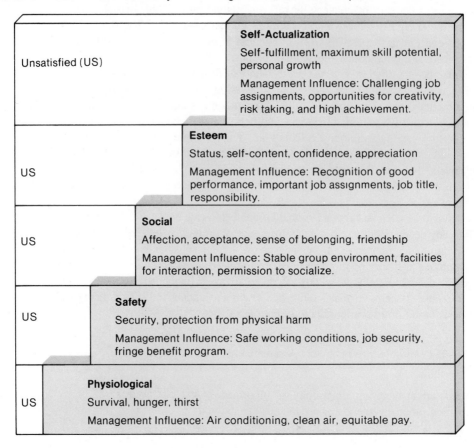

Unsatisfied (US)

Self-Actualization

Self-fulfillment, maximum skill potential, personal growth

Management Influence: Challenging job assignments, opportunities for creativity, risk taking, and high achievement.

US

Esteem

Status, self-content, confidence, appreciation

Management Influence: Recognition of good performance, important job assignments, job title, responsibility.

US

Social

Affection, acceptance, sense of belonging, friendship

Management Influence: Stable group environment, facilities for interaction, permission to socialize.

US

Safety

Security, protection from physical harm

Management Influence: Safe working conditions, job security, fringe benefit program.

US

Physiological

Survival, hunger, thirst

Management Influence: Air conditioning, clean air, equitable pay.

Physiological needs. This category consists of the basic needs of the human body, such as food, water, and sex. *Physiological needs* will dominate when all needs are unsatisfied. In such a case, no other needs will serve as a basis for motivation. As Maslow states, "A person who is lacking food, safety, love, and esteem would probably hunger for food more strongly than for anything else."[5] Organizational factors that might satisfy physiological needs include enough pay to permit an employee to survive and working conditions that permit a healthy environment.

Safety needs. *Safety needs* include protection from physical harm, ill health, economic disaster, and the unexpected. From a managerial standpoint, safety needs manifest themselves in attempts to ensure job security and to move toward greater financial support.

[5]Ibid., p. 82.

Social needs. *Social needs* are related to the social nature of people and to their need for companionship. This level in the hierarchy is the point of departure from the physical or quasi-physical needs of the two previous levels. Nonsatisfaction in this level of needs may affect the mental health of the individual. Organizational conditions that help to satisfy these needs include encouraging team building, providing supportive supervision practices, and permitting co-workers the opportunity to interact socially on the job.

Esteem needs. *Esteem needs* comprise both the awareness of one's importance to others (self-esteem) and the actual esteem of others. The satisfaction of esteem needs leads to self-confidence and prestige. Organizations can support the satisfaction of these needs by recognizing good performance and permitting employees to work autonomously to complete challenging and meaningful job tasks.

Self-actualization needs. Maslow defines these needs as the "desire to become more and more what one is, to become everything one is capable of becoming."[6] The satisfaction of *self-actualization needs* enables the individual to realize fully the potentialities of his talents and capabilities. Maslow assumes that the satisfaction of self-actualization needs is possible only after the satisfaction of all other needs. Moreover, he proposes that the satisfaction of self-actualization needs will tend to *increase* the strength of those needs. Thus, when people are able to attain a state of self-actualization, they will tend to be motivated by increased opportunities to satisfy that level of needs. Organizations can help employees satisfy self-actualization needs by encouraging creativity, allowing risk-taking decision making, and supporting workers in their efforts to develop their skills.

Most managers and nonmanagers believe that Maslow's needs hierarchy explanation of motivation is accurate, concise, and informative. There is, however, little evidence to support the claim of accuracy. In fact, there is some evidence available that fails to support a need hierarchy explanation.[7]

The motivation quiz in Table 12–1 will help provide you with some knowledge about your present state of need satisfaction. Take a few minutes and determine which of Maslow's needs are the most and least satisfied. Why is a particular need unsatisfied at this point in your life? (Scoring instructions are at the end of this chapter, p. 402)

ACHIEVEMENT MOTIVATION THEORY

David McClelland, a psychologist, has been studying the conditions under which people develop a motive to achieve, and its impact on behavior.[8] The term *achievement* is used to mean both a need and a motive. McClelland and his colleagues devised a

---

[6]Ibid., p. 92.

[7]J. Ranschenberger, N. Schmitt, and J. E. Hunter, "A Test of the Need Hierarchy Concept by a Markov Model of Change in Need Strength," *Administrative Science Quarterly*, 1980, pp. 654–70.

[8]D. C. McClelland, "Some Social Consequences of Achievement Motivation," in *Nebraska Symposium on Motivation*, M. R. Jones, ed. (Lincoln: University of Nebraska Press); and D. C. McClelland, *The Achievement Society* (Princeton, N.J.: Van Nostrand, 1975).

Table 12–1

Motivation Quiz

Directions: The following statements have seven possible responses:

Strongly agree +3	Agree +2	Slightly agree +1	Don't know 0	Slightly disagree −1	Disagree −2	Strongly disagree −3

Please mark one of the seven responses by circling the number that fits your opinion. For example, if you "Strongly agree," circle the number "+3." Complete every item.

1. Special wage increases should be given to employees who do their jobs very well.   +3 +2 +1 0 −1 −2 −3
2. Better job descriptions would help employees to know exactly what is expected of them.   +3 +2 +1 0 −1 −2 −3
3. Employees need to be reminded that their jobs are dependent on the company's ability to compete effectively.   +3 +2 +1 0 −1 −2 −3
4. A supervisor should give a good deal of attention to the physical working conditions of his employees.   +3 +2 +1 0 −1 −2 −3
5. The supervisor ought to strive to develop a friendly working atmosphere among her people.   +3 +2 +1 0 −1 −2 −3
6. Individual recognition for above-standard performance means a lot to employees.   +3 +2 +1 0 −1 −2 −3
7. Indifferent supervision can often bruise feelings.   +3 +2 +1 0 −1 −2 −3
8. Employees want to feel that their real skills and capacities are put to use on their jobs.   +3 +2 +1 0 −1 −2 −3
9. The company retirement benefits and stock programs are important factors in keeping employees on their jobs.   +3 +2 +1 0 −1 −2 −3
10. Almost every job can be made more stimulating and challenging.   +3 +2 +1 0 −1 −2 −3
11. Many employees want to give their best in everything they do.   +3 +2 +1 0 −1 −2 −3
12. Management could show more interest in the employees by sponsoring after-hours social events.   +3 +2 +1 0 −1 −2 −3
13. Pride in one's work is actually an important reward.   +3 +2 +1 0 −1 −2 −3
14. Employees want to be able to think of themselves as "the best" at their own jobs.   +3 +2 +1 0 −1 −2 −3
15. The quality of the relationships in the informal work group is quite important.   +3 +2 +1 0 −1 −2 −3
16. Individual incentive bonuses would improve the performance of employees.   +3 +2 +1 0 −1 −2 −3
17. Visibility with upper management is important to employees.   +3 +2 +1 0 −1 −2 −3
18. Employees generally like to schedule their own work and to make job-related decisions with a minimum of supervision. +3 +2 +1 0 −1 −2 −3
19. Job security is important to employees.   +3 +2 +1 0 −1 −2 −3
20. Having good equipment to work with is important to employees.   +3 +2 +1 0 −1 −2 −3

Source: This survey was developed by University Associates, La Jolla, California, 1973.

way to measure the strength of a need and then looked for relationships between strength of needs in different societies, conditions that had fostered the needs, and the results of needs in work organizations.

Subjects were shown pictures and asked to make up stories about them, that is, to describe what was happening in the picture and what the probable outcome would be. McClelland assumed that what a person perceived and reported in the pictures (called the *Thematic Apperception Test* [TAT]) reflected her values, interests, and motives. McClelland stated, "If you want to find out what's on a person's mind, don't ask him, because he can't always tell you. Study his fantasies and dreams. If you do this over a period of time, you will discover the themes to which his mind returns again and again. And these themes can be used to explain his actions . . ."[9]

From subjects' responses to a series of pictures, McClelland calculated scores for three human needs—need for achievement, need for affiliation, and need for power. The need for achievement was designated as n Ach. For example, one picture was of a boy holding a violin. Table 12–2 provides hypothetical stories prepared by a person who scored high on need for achievement and one who scored low on need for achievement.

Self-motivated need achievers like to set their own goals. Goals that they set are moderately difficult, but are not impossible to achieve. Also, those with high needs for achievement like to receive feedback on their performance.[10]

The need for affiliation (n Aff) is the desire to work and to be with other people. There is a high need to socially interact, to support others, and to be concerned with the development and growth of others. The n Aff is similar to Maslow's social need.

The need for power (n Pow) refers to the desire to have impact, to be influential, and to have control over others. McClelland proposes that there are two "faces of power"—one positive and one negative. The positive face emphasizes a concern for helping others achieve goals. The negative face is aimed at personal gain; it is designed to create a dominance over others.

McClelland's research suggests that these three needs have implications for job selection, placement, motivation, and training. For example, individuals can increase their achievement motivation when they are taught how to set goals that stretch their skills. Also, a person who has a high n Aff and a low n Pow and is given an assignment where power must be used will have a difficult time succeeding.[11]

A problem with McClelland's theory rests in measuring the needs. The TAT is a projective device that is prone to error and subjective bias by raters who interpret the stories written. There is also the problem of the writing ability of subjects. One subject may have a flair for writing, while another may write in a stilted and ponderous manner. The person's writing skills will influence how the stories are rated.

---

[9]D. C. McClelland, *Motivational Trends in Society* (Morristown, N.J.: General Learning Press, 1971), p. 5.

[10]D. C. McClelland, "Motive Dispositions: The Merits of Operant and Respondent Measures," in *Review of Personality and Journal Psychology,* L. Wheeler, ed. (Beverly Hills, Calif.: Sage Publications, 1980), pp. 10–41.

[11]D. C. McClelland and D. H. Burnham, "Power Is the Great Motivator," *Harvard Business Review,* March–April 1976, pp. 100–10.

Table 12–2   Examples of n Ach stories.

High n Ach Story	Low n Ach Story
The boy just completed a long, daily violin lesson. He is happy with his improvement and thinks that his daily practice is well worth the hard work. He knows that to become a top, concert violinist by the time he turns 19, he will have to practice when his friends are partying, playing baseball, dating, and attending musical concerts. He wants to be the best and is willing to pay whatever the price it takes.	Jim is simply holding his Dad's violin. He likes the music it makes, but feels that his Dad spends too many hours playing the instrument. If only he could play without having to practice like his Dad. It seemed that practicing was boring and would take away valuable time from his friends and his girlfriend. Maybe there are other instruments that are easier to learn to play. Then again, maybe he should be a good listener of music performed by others.

NONSATISFACTION OF NEEDS

As noted previously, unsatisfied needs produce tensions within an individual. When an individual is unable to satisfy needs (and thereby reduce the tension), *frustration* results. The reactions to frustration vary from person to person. Some people react in a positive manner (constructive behavior), while others react negatively (defensive behavior).

Constructive Behavior

You may be familiar with the constructive behavior in which people engage when their attempts to satisfy needs have been frustrated. An assembly line worker whose attempts to satisfy esteem needs have been frustrated because of the nature of the job may seek esteem off the job. She may, for example, run for election to leadership posts in civic organizations. In order to satisfy frustrated social and belonging needs, a worker may conform to the norms and values of a group which bowls on weekends. Each of these is an example of constructive adaptive behavior which individuals employ to reduce frustration and satisfy needs.

Defensive Behavior

Individuals who are blocked in attempts to satisfy their needs may exhibit *defensive behavior* instead of constructive behavior. We all employ defensive behavior in one way or another because it performs an important protective function in our attempts to cope with frustration. In most cases, defensive behavior does not handicap the individual to any great degree. Ordinarily, however, it is not adequate for the task of protecting the self. As a result, adults whose behavior is continually dominated by defensive behavior have great difficulty in adapting to the responsibilities of work and social relationships.

What happens when needs are not satisfied is difficult to understand but worth considering. Some general patterns of defensive behavior have been identified, and some of the more common ones are discussed below.

Withdrawal.   One obvious way to avoid frustration is to withdraw from or avoid situations which will prove frustrating. The withdrawal may be physical (leaving the scene), but more likely it will be expressed as apathy. Workers whose jobs provide little need satisfaction may withdraw, and this will be reflected by excessive absences, latenesses, or turnover.

Aggression.   A common reaction to frustration is aggression. In some cases, this may take the form of a direct attack on the source of the frustration. Unfortunately, aggression is often directed toward another object or party unrelated to the cause of the frustration. For example, a supervisor may direct aggression toward a subordinate production worker who, in turn, may direct aggression toward a spouse.

Substitution.   This occurs when the individual puts something in the place of the original object. An employee whose attempts to win a promotion have been frustrated may substitute that desire with achieving leadership status in a management-resisting work group.

Compensation.   When a person goes overboard in one area or activity to make up for deficiencies in another, the defense mechanism known as *compensation* is being evoked. A manager whose personality is disagreeable may compensate with attempts to practice good "human relations" with subordinates.

Every person relies to some extent on defense mechanisms. However, subordinates' overreliance on defensive behavior can be minimized if managerial decisions provide conditions that encourage constructive behavior. In addition, a manager who understands defensive behavior will have greater empathy with those who use it and will realize that such behavior may not be a true indication of the person's actual character.

THE TWO-FACTOR THEORY OF MOTIVATION

Frederick Herzberg advanced a theory of motivation based on a study of need satisfactions and on the reported motivational effects of those satisfactions on 200 engineers and accountants. His approach is termed the *two-factor theory of motivation.*[12]

Herzberg asked the subjects of his study to think of times when they felt especially good and especially bad about their jobs. Each subject was then asked to describe the conditions that caused those feelings. Significantly, the subjects *identified different work conditions for each of the feelings.* For example, if managerial recognition for doing an excellent job led to good feelings about the job, the lack of managerial recognition was seldom indicated as a cause of bad feelings.

Based on this research, Herzberg reached the following two conclusions:

1.   Although employees are dissatisfied by the absence of some job conditions, the presence of those conditions does not cause strong motivation. Herzberg called such conditions *maintenance factors,* since they are necessary to maintain a minimum level

---

[12]See Frederick Herzberg, B. Mausner, and B. Snyderman, *The Motivation to Work* (New York: John Wiley & Sons, 1959).

of need satisfaction. He also noted that these have often been perceived by managers as factors which can motivate subordinates, but that they are, in fact, more potent as dissatisfiers when they are absent. He concluded that there were 10 maintenance factors, namely:

a. Company policy and administration.
b. Technical supervision.
c. Interpersonal relations with supervisor.
d. Interpersonal relations with peers.
e. Interpersonal relations with subordinates.
f. Salary.
g. Job security.
h. Personal life.
i. Work conditions.
j. Status.

2. Some job factors, which Herzberg calls *motivators,* cause high levels of motivation and job satisfaction when present. However, the absence of these factors does not prove highly dissatisfying. Herzberg described six of these motivational factors:

a. Achievement.
b. Recognition.
c. Advancement.
d. The work itself.
e. The possibility of personal growth.
f. Responsibility.

Prior to Herzberg's research, managers viewed job satisfaction and dissatisfaction at opposite ends of the same continuum, as shown in Figure 12–3. Herzberg's research findings introduced the notion of two continuums. If employees are not satisfied, they indicate no satisfaction, and not dissatisfaction.

The motivational factors are job centered. They relate directly to the job itself; that is, the individual's job performance, the job responsibilities, and the growth and recognition obtained from the job. The maintenance factors are peripheral to the job and are more related to the external environment of work. The distinction between motivational and maintenance factors is similar to the distinction between *intrinsic* and *extrinsic* rewards. Intrinsic rewards are part of the job and occur when the employee performs the work; the work itself is rewarding. Extrinsic rewards are external rewards (e.g., receiving a paycheck) that have meaning or value after the work has been performed or away from the workplace. They provide little, if any, satisfaction when the work is being performed.

Since conducting the original study, Herzberg has cited numerous replications supporting his position.[13] These studies were conducted with professional women,

---

[13]Frederick Herzberg, *Work and the Nature of Man* (Cleveland: World Publishing, 1966).

Figure 12–3 Contrasting views of satisfaction—dissatisfaction.

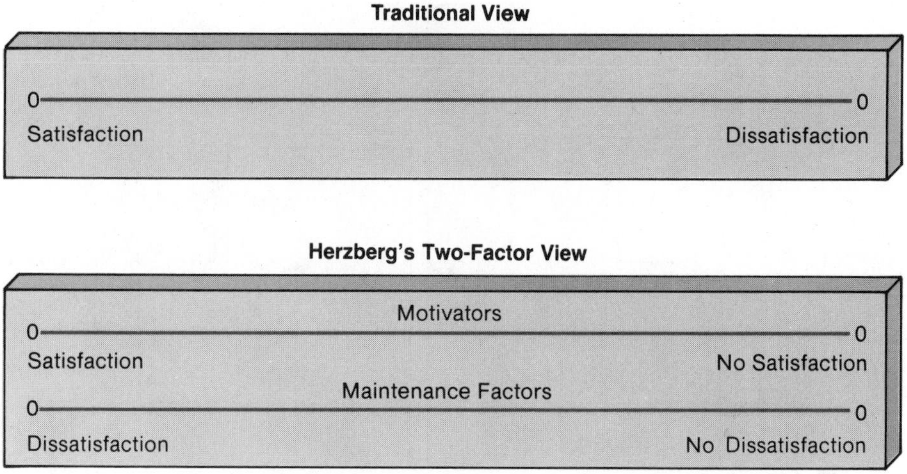

hospital maintenance personnel, agricultural administrators, nurses, food handlers, manufacturing supervisors, engineers, scientists, military officers, managers ready for retirement, teachers, technicians, and assemblers. Some of the studies were conducted in cultural settings beyond the United States, in Finland, Hungary, the Soviet Union, and Yugoslavia.

Herzberg reports that American, Japanese, and Italian employees are motivated by similar job motivations. In fact about 80 percent of the factors that are intrinsic to the job result in satisfying job experiences for workers across these different cultures.[14] He has concluded that there are more commonalities among workers throughout the world than was originally assumed in studying motivation. Employees in Italy, like those in the United States, are motivated by their own inherent need to succeed at a challenging task. The manager in Rome or Chicago needs to provide opportunities for employees to achieve so they will become motivated.

Herzberg's theory of motivation has generated quite a bit of controversy. Three main criticisms have been directed at it and its accompanying research. Doubts have been raised about the Herzberg methodology (his use of the structured interview to collect information). Other researchers have used other methods and have failed to replicate his findings.[15] Thus, there is a possibility that his results may have been influenced by the method used to collect the information.

Some claim that the two sets of job factors uncovered by Herzberg are not inde-

---

[14]Frederick Herzberg, "Workers Needs: The Same around the World," *Industry Week*, September 21, 1987, pp. 29–32.

[15]R. House and L. Wigdor, "Herzberg's Dual Factor Theory of Job Satisfaction and Motivation," *Personnel Psychology*, Winter 1967, pp. 369–89.

Figure 12–4   A comparison of the Maslow and Herzberg models.

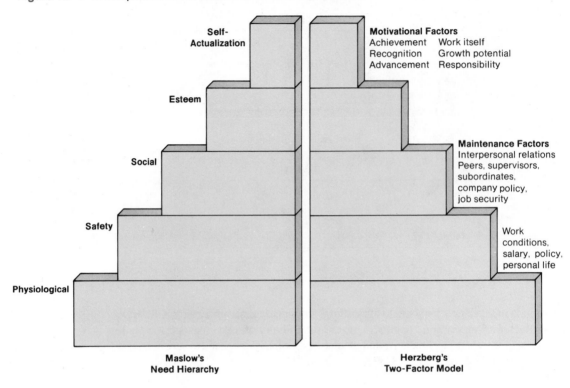

pendent. Some individuals are motivated by salary, while other individuals are not at all motivated by advancement opportunities. In fact, some individuals perceive advancement as something to avoid. Sex differences also have been found. Some female workers report that interpersonal relations are important motivators.

A third criticism is that Herzberg proposed a theory of motivation based on the responses of engineers and accountants.[16] Can such a theory be generalized to non-professionals and less-educated employees? Any theory based on such a limited sample, engineers and accountants, should be considered cautiously.

Despite some criticisms, Herzberg's theory of motivation has stimulated discussion and further research into motivation. Herzberg has looked at and discussed motivation in terms that managers understand. He has done so without loading his discussion with the psychological terminology that managers typically gloss over and ignore.

Maslow and Herzberg: Similarities.   There is much similarity between Herzberg's and Maslow's models. A close examination of Herzberg's ideas indicates that what

---

[16]L. K. Waters and C. W. Waters, "An Empirical Test of Five Versions of the Two-Factor Theory of Job Satisfaction," *Organizational Behavior and Human Performance*, February 1972, pp. 18–24.

he actually was saying is that some employees may have achieved a level of social and economic progress in our society such that the higher-level needs of Maslow (esteem and self-actualization) are the primary motivators. However, these employees still must satisfy their lower-level needs to maintain their present state. Thus, money might still be a motivator for nonmanagement workers (particularly those at a minimum wage level) and for some managerial employees. Herzberg's model adds to the need hierarchy model because it distinguishes between the two groups of motivational and maintenance factors and points out that the motivational factors often are derived from the job itself. Figure 12–4 compares the two models.

THE EXPECTANCY THEORY OF MOTIVATION

A theory of motivation developed by Victor H. Vroom expands on the work of Maslow and Herzberg.[17] Vroom's expectancy theory views motivation as a process governing choices. Thus, an individual who has a particular goal must practice a certain behavior to achieve it. She will weigh the likelihood that various behaviors will achieve the desired goal, and if a certain behavior seems to be more successful than others, that behavior likely will be the one the goal-seeker selects.

In the *expectancy motivation model,* motivation, or the force to perform, is defined as expectancy times instrumentality times valence, or $M = E \times I \times V$. The theory proposes three determinants of motivation:

1. *The expectancy that individual effort will result in performance.* Employees generally are motivated to exert effort if they believe their effort will be reflected in high performance.

2. *The expectancy that performance will result in reward.* Employees are motivated if they believe performance will lead to desired rewards. The employee considers whether performance is *instrumental* in achieving rewards.

3. *The valence of rewards.* Valence refers to an employee's preference for rewards he believes will result from performing well. A manager who provides rewards that have low valence (are not highly preferred) is not likely to see that rewards bring much improvement in performance.

Expectancies are probabilities calculated by a person's thought processes. If a person decides that if she works hard, she will be a high performer, expectancy is likely to be close to 1.00, or certainty. On the other hand, if a person decides that no matter how hard she works, there is little likelihood that she will be a high performer, expectancy will be close to 0.

Whether or not high performance is associated with desired outcomes is determined by examining what is called *instrumentality* in the expectancy theory. Instrumentalities are correlations or indicators of association which range from -1.00 to $+1.00$. If a

---

[17]Victor H. Vroom, *Work and Motivation* (New York: John Wiley & Sons, 1964).

person sees no association between high performance and an outcome such as a merit pay increase, the instrumentality is 0. On the other hand, if a person believes high performance is always associated with a merit pay increase, the instrumentality is +1.00. Since instrumentality is an indicator of association or correlation, it can range from −1.00 to +1.00.

Valences are the values an individual attaches to work outcomes, such as a merit pay increase, a promotion, a transfer to a new group, more job responsibility, or having a longer work day. If one desires an outcome, it has a positive valence; if one does not prefer an outcome, it has a negative valence; if one is indifferent to a particular outcome, it is considered to have a zero valence.

Expectancy theory predicts that motivation to work will be high if:

1. *Expectancy is high*—The employee feels that high performance can be attained.

2. *Instrumentality is high*—The employee associates high performance with a desired (positive valence) outcome such as a merit pay increase.

3. *Valence is high*—the employee has a high preference for a merit pay increase.

Since $M = E \times I \times V$, all three components in the equation must be high to achieve optimal motivation. A zero for expectancy, instrumentality, or valence means that there is no motivation. Figure 12–5 illustrates a general and a work-related example of the expectancy theory.

An important contribution of the expectancy theory is that it explains how the *goals* of individuals influence their *effort* and that the behavior individuals select depends on their assessment of whether it will successfully lead to the goal. For example, members of an organization may not all place the same value on such job factors as a bonus, management recognition, or co-worker friendship. Vroom believes that what is important is the perception and value that the individual places on certain goals. Suppose that one individual places a high value on a bonus and perceives high performance as instrumental in reaching that goal. Accordingly, this individual will strive toward superior performance in order to achieve the bonus. However, another individual may value relationships with co-workers. The individual, therefore, is not likely to emphasize superior performance to achieve the goal. Think of expectancy theory in terms of student motivations, where one student has the goal of an A grade and another the goal of a C grade in a particular course. How might their respective efforts and behaviors in the course vary?

Research studies of expectancy theory usually involve asking employees to estimate the expectancy they have of being an outstanding, good, or average performer.[18] In addition, the employees are asked to estimate the association (instrumentality) of performance and outcomes (pay, promotion). They also are asked to rate or rank the valence of outcomes. Their responses then are combined to determine the degree of effort (motivation) expended.

---

[18]Hugh J. Arnold, "A Test of the Multiplicative Hypothesis of Expectancy-Valence Theories of Work Motivation," *Academy of Management Journal*, March 1981, pp. 128–41.

Figure 12–5 Expectancy theory from a manager's perspective.

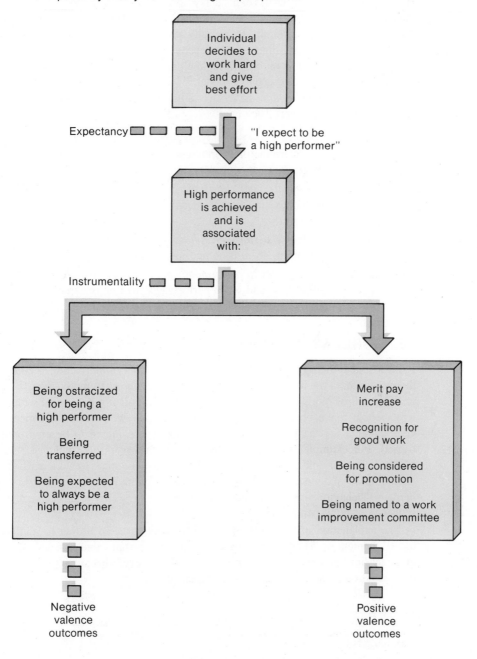

For the most part, empirical studies provide some support for the expectancy theory.[19] However, many factors besides expectancy, instrumentality, and valence may influence the amount of effort expended on the job, and accurately measuring the factors in the expectancy theory is difficult. Is it really possible to have people report on their expectancies, instrumentalities, and valences? How can their answers be measured? These questions have not yet been completely resolved by researchers who have tested various portions of the expectancy model.[20]

The expectancy theory does have several important practical implications managers should consider, however. They can:

1. *Determine what outcomes employees prefer.* Communicating with employees to determine their preferences is important for developing reward packages that can stimulate motivation.

2. *Define, communicate, and clarify the level of performance that is desired.* An employee needs realistic and meaningful performance goals before she can exert proper effort.

3. *Establish attainable performance goals.* Setting impossible goals will create frustration and confusion and lower motivation.

4. *Link desired outcomes to performance goal achievement.* A manager should spell out how and when performance will be rewarded. Every effort should be made to link performance and rewards.

REINFORCEMENT THEORY

Reinforcement theory is another widely discussed theory of motivation. Reinforcement theory considers the use of positive or negative reinforcers to motivate or to create an environment of motivation. This theory of motivation is not concerned with needs or why people make choices. Instead, it is concerned with the environment and its consequences for the person; that is, behavior is considered to be environmentally caused. For example, suppose Jeff Wilkins, a hard-working employee, is given a $1,000 bonus for doing a good job. In the future, Jeff continues to work hard, expecting another bonus payment. Why does Jeff continue to work hard? When Jeff first worked hard, his behavior was reinforced by a $1,000 bonus. This reinforcement is a consequence of good performance.

The explanation of why Jeff continued to work hard, according to reinforcement theory, centers on Thorndike's law of effect, which states that behavior that results in a pleasing outcome will likely be repeated; however, behavior that results in an unpleasant outcome is not likely to be repeated.[21]

---

[19]John P. Wanous, Thomas L. Keon, and Janina C. Latack, "Expectancy Theory and Occupational/Organizational Choices: A Review and Test," *Organizational Behavior and Human Performance,* August 1983, pp. 66–86.

[20]T. R. Mitchell, "Expectancy Models of Job Satisfaction, Occupational Preference, and Effort: A Theoretical, Methodological, and Empirical Appraisal," *Psychological Bulletin,* December 1974, pp. 1053–77.

[21]E. L. Thorndike, *Animal Intelligence* (New York: Macmillan, 1911), p. 244.

Figure 12–6 Four types of reinforcement available to managers: Illustration.

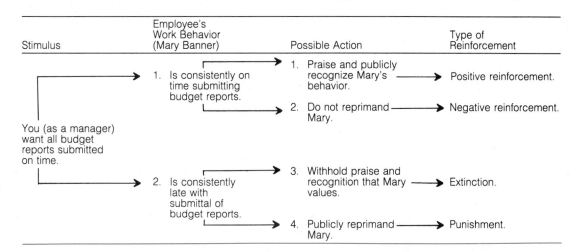

Stimulus	Employee's Work Behavior (Mary Banner)	Possible Action	Type of Reinforcement
You (as a manager) want all budget reports submitted on time.	1. Is consistently on time submitting budget reports.	1. Praise and publicly recognize Mary's behavior.	Positive reinforcement.
		2. Do not reprimand Mary.	Negative reinforcement.
	2. Is consistently late with submittal of budget reports.	3. Withhold praise and recognition that Mary values.	Extinction.
		4. Publicly reprimand Mary.	Punishment.

Operant conditioning is a powerful tool used for changing employee behavior. The term *operant conditioning* in the management literature applies to controlling work behavior by manipulating the consequences. It is based on the research work of psychologist B. F. Skinner and is built on two principles: (1) Thorndike's law of effect and (2) properly scheduled rewards influence individual behaviors.[22] *Behavior modification* is the contemporary term used to describe techniques for applying the principles of operant conditioning to the control of individual behavior.

Suppose you are a manager and your employee Mary Banner is always late with required budget reports. There are four types of reinforcement that you could use. First, you could focus on reinforcing the desired behavior (which, in this example, is preparing budget reports on time). You could use positive or negative reinforcement. Positive reinforcement would include rewards such as praise, recognition, or a pay bonus. Negative reinforcement also focuses on reinforcing the desired behavior. However, instead of providing a positive reward, the reward is that the employee avoids some negative consequence. Thus, Mary would complete the report on time to avoid the negative consequence of being reprimanded by her manager.

Alternatively, the manager might focus on reducing the tardiness of submitting the budget report by use of two other reinforcements: extinction or punishment. Through the use of extinction (withholding positive reinforcement), Mary might unlearn her bad habit of submitting late reports. Another method that reduces the frequency of undesired behavior is called *punishment*. In this case, punishment could involve the public reprimand of Mary by the manager for submitting a late report. These four types of reinforcement that can be applied by a manager are presented in Figure 12–6.

---

[22]B. F. Skinner, *Science and Human Behavior* (New York: Macmillan, 1953); and B. F. Skinner, *Contingencies of Reinforcement* (New York: Appleton-Century-Crofts, 1969).

A few pointers on what managers can do to help motivate employees are spelled out in the following Management Application.

MANAGEMENT APPLICATION

SOME MANAGEMENT POINTS ON HOW TO MOTIVATE

Everyone has suggestions about how to motivate employees to perform the tasks required of them. *Executive Productivity* advisory board member Robert Half, who is president of the world's largest recruiting organization, offers some "how to motivate your employees" advice.

☐ *Humanize the work environment.* Respect the need to treat each employee as an individual.

☐ *Publicize both short- and long-term company goals.* Encourage personal and departmental goal setting.

☐ *Promote from within.* It's great for morale and simplifies hiring procedures.

☐ *Use incentive programs.* If you're creative enough, you won't have to rely on expensive financial bonuses.

☐ *Establish appropriate deadlines.* Every project should have a deadline.

☐ *Be liberal with praise.* It's almost impossible to overpraise and easy to underpraise.

☐ *Be consistent in your own work and in your relations with others.*

☐ *Show a personal interest in the people who work for you.* Relations are always smoother between people who know each other on a personal basis than between people who merely want something from each other.

☐ *Admit mistakes.* People will respect you for it and will be less likely to hide their own mistakes.

☐ *Don't "whitewash" unpleasant assignments.* Prepare subordinates for them well in advance and offer what support you can.

Source: Adapted from "28 Ways to Make Employees More Happy and Productive," *Executive Productivity*, July 1987, p. 2.

MANAGERIAL APPROACHES FOR IMPROVING MOTIVATION

A number of approaches can help managers motivate workers to perform more effectively. Two approaches, however, have been especially effective: linking pay to job performance, and quality of work-life programs.

Pay and Job Performance

Pay often can be used to motivate employee performance.[23] But a pay plan also must (1) create the belief that good performance leads to high levels of pay, (2) minimize

---

[23]Richard I. Henderson, *Compensation Management* (Reston, Va.: Reston Publishing, 1983), pp. 487–88.

the negative consequences of good performance (in which the better you do, the more they give you to do), and (3) create conditions in which rewards other than pay are seen to be related to good performance. These three conditions follow from the expectancy theory of motivation, which states that individuals will be motivated to seek goals they value and can attain.

Relating pay to performance. Managers use numerous methods in their attempts to relate pay to performance. One survey of personnel practices reported high dissatisfaction with pay plans.[24] Many pay plans are disliked because they are implemented poorly or because they are not well suited for a particular job.

There is some interest in moving more to what is called *knowledge-based pay* which is also called *skill-based pay*.[25] In a knowledge-based system workers are paid at a rate based on the knowledge or skill they possess. There is still not much research evidence that can provide guidelines for managers interested in such a program for employees. Thus, more traditional and incentive pay plans are still the most popular pay systems especially for blue-collar workers.

Incentive pay plans can be rated on three separate criteria. First, each plan can be rated in terms of its effectiveness in creating the perception that pay is tied to performance. Second, pay plans can be evaluated in terms of their success in minimizing negative side effects, such as disruptive competition, conflict, and grievances. Third, each plan can be rated in terms of whether it contributes to the perception that important rewards other than pay (e.g., feelings of esteem and increased responsibility) result from high performance.[26]

Table 12–3 summarizes the relative effectiveness of different types of pay plans in terms of the three criteria. The six basic plans are straight salary on (1) individual, (2) group, and (3) organizationwide bases, and salary plus bonus on (4) individual, (5) group, and (6) organizationwide bases. Moreover, salary and salary-plus-bonus plans can be based on different performance measures. For example, an individual's salary or salary-plus-bonus plan can be based upon his productivity, cost-effectiveness, or superior's rating. Similar performance measures are applicable to group-based salary and salary-plus-bonus plans. Organizationwide salary and salary-plus-bonus plans can be based on productivity and cost-effectiveness, but also upon profits. Thus, when these three performance measures are linked to the six basic pay plans, 18 different variations are possible. Each of these 18 variations can range from very effective ($+3$) to very ineffective (-3) in relation to each of the three criteria, as summarized in Table 12–2.

The most effective plan for producing the perception that pay is in fact related to performance is the individual salary plus bonus based upon productivity. However, this same plan is least effective in minimizing negative side effects. Highly productive employees often are ostracized by their fellow employees for being rate-busters. Thus,

---

[24]Frederick S. Hills, K. Dow Scott, Steven E. Markham, and Michael J. Vest, "Merit Pay: Just or Unjust Desserts," *Personnel Administrator*, September 1987, pp. 53–59.

[25]Henry Tosi and Lisa Tosi, "What Managers Need to Know about Knowledge-Based Pay," *Organizational Dynamics*, Winter 1986, pp. 52–54.

[26]Jeffrey Kerr and John W. Slocum, Jr., "Managing Corporate Culture through Reward Systems," *Academy of Management Executive*, May 1987, pp. 99–107.

Table 12–3   Ratings of selected pay-incentive plans.

Type of Plan	Performance Measure	Tie Pay to Performance	Minimize Negative Side Effects	Tie Other Rewards to Performance
Salary				
1. Individual plan	Productivity	+2	0	0
	Cost effectiveness	+1	0	0
	Superiors' rating	+1	0	+1
2. Group	Productivity	+1	0	+1
	Cost effectiveness	+1	0	+1
	Superiors' rating	+1	0	+1
3. Organizationwide	Productivity	+1	0	+1
	Cost effectiveness	+1	0	+1
	Profits	0	0	+1
Bonus				
4. Individual plan	Productivity	+3	−2	0
	Cost effectiveness	+2	−1	0
	Superiors' rating	+2	−1	+1
5. Group	Productivity	+2	0	+1
	Cost effectiveness	+2	0	+1
	Superiors' rating	+2	0	+1
6. Organizationwide	Productivity	+2	0	+1
	Cost effectiveness	+2	0	+1
	Profits	+1	0	+1

Source: Edward E. Lawler III, *Pay and Organizational Effectiveness* (New York: McGraw-Hill, 1971), pp. 164–65.

as is the case of many other managerial practices, the alternative that is most effective for one purpose is least effective for other purposes. Clearly, the choice of pay plan involves compromise, and the direction of the decision will be affected by factors specific to a situation, including the relative ease of developing valid performance measures.[27]

In many situations, it is difficult to develop valid, equitable, and acceptable measures of performance. Therefore, it is hard to relate pay to performance. For example, measures of college teaching effectiveness are quite controversial. No widely accepted, objective performance measurement technique exists, although subjective peer or student evaluations are often used.

In other situations, too much emphasis may be placed on objective measures of performance. If objective measures only are used in determining pay increases, the employee may emphasize only these and disregard others that are also important. Management must balance its objective and subjective performance evaluations. The manner in which performance and pay are perceived by employees certainly influences what is called the *culture* of the organization. The culture of a firm influences the values, beliefs, and attitudes a person has about pay.[28]

[27]*Lincoln's Incentive System and Approach to Manufacturing* (Cleveland, Ohio: The Lincoln Electric Company, 1983).

[28]Maryann Mrowca, "Ohio Firm Relies on Incentive-Pay System to Motivate Workers and Maintain Profits," *The Wall Street Journal*, August 12, 1983, p. 17.

Another important issue involved in tying pay to performance is that of amounts. Motivating high performers may cost a lot of money. A company that cannot afford large increases may not want to use pay to motivate exceptional performance. Moreover, some individuals are not motivated by even large increases in pay. Management should determine what value employees place on pay before tying pay increases to improved performance.

In summary, before using pay to motivate performance, management should consider a number of issues. They are:

1. Methods of measuring individual job performance.
2. The subjective-objective criteria for evaluating job performance.
3. The size of pay rewards for high performers.
4. The preferences of the employees.

A premier pay plan: Lincoln Electric Co. A profit sharing plan developed by James E. Lincoln of the Lincoln Electric Co. of Cleveland, Ohio, is considered one of the nation's most outstanding incentive compensation plans.[29] The principal features of the plan are as follows:

☐ If an employee has at least two years of service, he is guaranteed 30 hours of work for 50 weeks a year. No rate of pay is guaranteed and workers must be willing to transfer from one job to another and work overtime when needed.

☐ Standard job evaluation procedures set the base wage rate.

☐ The majority of employees are paid on a piecework incentive plan.

☐ All employees may participate in the firm's suggestion system—with the exception of department heads and members of the engineering and time study departments. Employee suggestions that result in improvements are considered during merit ratings.

☐ Twice a year, a merit rating program appraises the work performance of each employee.[30]

☐ Each employee can purchase from 10 to 25 shares of company stock annually. About 25 percent of Lincoln's employees together own 45 percent of the stock.

☐ All profits from the business are split three ways: (a) with the corporation; (b) with the shareholders, who receive approximately 6–8 percent dividends based on the book value of the two types of company stock; and (c) with the employees, who receive all remaining profits.[31]

The Lincoln system has helped create a work-oriented culture. There is no room for the "I don't care" or "I'm not going to give a good effort" worker. The success

[29]"Lincoln Electric's Past Enhances Its Future," *Management Review,* January 1984, pp. 40–41.

[30]John M. Ivancevich and William F. Glueck, *Foundations of Personnel/Human Resource Management* (Plano, Tex.: Business Publications, Inc., 1989), pp. 441–42.

[31]Ibid.

of the plan depends on all the workers pitching in and making a positive contribution. In 1987, the company's 1,800 production employees received on average an $18,773 bonus and $26,442 in earnings.[32]

Quality of Work Life Programs

Quality of work life (QWL) is defined as an attempt through a formal program to integrate employee needs and well-being with the intention of improved productivity, greater worker involvement, and higher levels of job satisfaction. It is an attempt to better personalize the workplace by improving the quality of a person's daily existence on the job. A combination of factors has led to this increased interest in improving the quality of work life. Managerial concern about productivity, government regulations such as Title VII of the Civil Rights Act, The Occupational Safety and Health Act (1970), and the Fair Labor Standards Act of 1963, and increased competition for personnel has encouraged companies to pay more attention to the QWL.

Programs for QWL improvements range from those requiring minor changes in the organization to those requiring extensive modifications in structure, personnel, and the utilization of resources. Three types of QWL programs are quality circles, employee stock ownership plans, and the use of alternative work schedules.

Quality circles.   Faced with sluggish productivity, an increasingly competitive work market, and inflation, some managers have discovered and experimented with quality circles (QCs). Quality circles are small groups of workers (7 to 12) who meet regularly (weekly in most cases) with their supervisor as the circle leader to solve work-related problems (e.g., quality, quantity, cost).

QCs give the employee opportunity for involvement, social-need satisfaction, participation in work improvement, challenge, and opportunity for growth. They are, in essence, vehicles for providing employees with opportunities to satisfy lower- and upper-level needs as stated by Maslow, through the motivators described in Herzberg's theory. Participation in QCs provides the vital Herzberg-type motivators to even the lowest-level employee. Members assume responsibility to identify and analyze problems in their work areas.

Although in most cases, QCs meet for only about an hour a week, this meeting carries over into the rest of the week. Circle activities are carried to breaks and lunchtimes. Also, members continue to think about the points raised in the meetings. Frequently, circle members meet on their own time to complete QC assignments such as comparing their own circle's progress to that of other QCs.

The QC provides employees with an opportunity to be a part of a team seeking common goals. Matching the worker's needs to company goals can be accomplished in a QC. Organizational goals can be reached while personal needs keep the process moving forward. However, like any managerial program with motivational overtones, QCs have some risks. QCs are *not* the answer to all motivational problems.

The Japanese popularized the use of QCs. A report by the Japanese Union of Scientists and Engineers indicates that 100,000 QCs are now registered in the country.

---

[32]Bruce G. Posner, "Right from the Start," *Inc.*, August 1988, pp. 95–96.

Toyo Kogyo, maker of the Mazda, alone has 1,800 QCs.[33] A concern, however, is whether a method of motivation which works in Japan can work in the United States or Canada. Japan differs in many important ways from the United States or Canada. For example, Japan has a homogeneous culture that treats organizational life as an extension of family life. This, of course, is not the case in plants, offices, and construction projects in Detroit, Chicago, Los Angeles, Toronto, and elsewhere in North America. Today in the United States and Canada, QC users include General Electric, RCA Corp., Control Data Corp., Westinghouse Electric Corporation, General Motors, IBM, General Mills, Inc., and Ford Motor Co.

Culture is certainly a powerful consideration. However, managers must also determine whether labor and management are willing to work together in QCs. Instead of initiating the Japanese style of QCs, it seems more realistic to develop an American-style QC, a Canadian-style QC, and so forth. The appropriate QC style must be developed by labor and management through a cooperative team effort. If such cooperation is not possible, then QCs, no matter how they are designed, have little chance of being successful in motivating participants.[34]

The American aerospace industry has used QCs successfully. This industry is concerned with quality because one small error can have a devastating effect on human lives. There is also a history of labor-management cooperation in the aerospace industry. The results of QCs in the industry have been positive—higher productivity and morale. The industry is well suited for QCs.

On the other hand, in the auto industry, the use of QCs has been much more difficult. For years, the labor-management relationship has been antagonistic. This relationship is difficult to overcome through the use of QCs. The common good, common interest, and common goals are extremely difficult to accomplish if labor and management are not inclined to cooperate and work together.

Another potential problem with QCs is managerial resistance. QCs encourage people to voice opinions, make suggestions, and display their ideas about work. This practice theoretically reduces the "administrative distance" between worker and manager. The result is that some managers feel threatened by what they perceive as a loss of power, status, prestige, and authority. They may consciously or subconsciously hinder the work and processes of the QC.

Still another potential area of difficulty is the role of the QC leader. In organizations, leadership roles are taken by managers and supervisors. However, in the QC, the leader is not in an authority position. She is instead a facilitator, a discussion leader who helps the group reach solutions. The leader who attempts to autocratically enforce his viewpoints quickly loses the respect, cooperation, and attention of the QC members. Many managers have a difficult time making the transition from a legitimate authority position in the formal hierarchy to the role of a facilitator in a QC.

The introduction of, and research into, QCs in American and Canadian industry undoubtedly will continue into the 1990s. Whether or not QCs can work as well in

---

[33]Ron Zemke, "What's Good for Japan May Not Be Best for Your Training Department," *Training/HRD*, October 1981, p. 62.

[34]Edward E. Lawler III and Susan A. Mohrman, "Quality Circles: After the Honeymoon," *Organizational Dynamics*, Spring 1987, pp. 42–54.

North America as they have in Japan remains to be tested in the next few years. But they are worth a look from managers and organizations willing to allow employees to participate in job-related problem solving. If management doesn't support a participative orientation, it is likely that QCs are not likely to be effective.[35]

Employee stock ownership plans (ESOPs). Ever since 1974, when Congress enacted the first of a series of tax measures designed to encourage ESOPs, the number of employee-owned (or partially owned) companies has grown to more than 8,000, and the number of employees owning stock has jumped from 250,000 to more than 8 million.[36]

Employee owners publish the *Milwaukee Journal,* sell home improvement products at Lowe's Companies, produce roller bearings at the Hyatt Roller Bearing Plant, and drive cabs for Denver Yellow Cabs.

Worker ownership is a democratic ideal that was created in the 1950s by a lawyer, Louis Kelso. He was able to convince Senator Russell Long to provide the idea with appropriate statutory legitimation plus a number of special tax incentives.[37] The 1986 tax reform act has made ESOPs even more agreeable in terms of tax deduction incentives.

Rosen and Quarrey studied 45 ESOP companies, looking at data for each during the five years before it instituted the plan and then five years after. Five comparison companies for every ESOP were selected from *Dun & Bradstreet* in terms of business type, size, and location. Sales and employment growth were closely monitored. The data were clear in showing that some companies did better after setting up ESOPs.

Further analysis of attitude data indicated that workers enjoyed participating in decision making, were enthusiastic about owning a part of the company, and had better morale after the ESOP was established.

Clearly not all organizations can or should establish ESOPs. There must be further research on what ESOPs can and cannot do in terms of productivity, morale, and QWL.[38] In some cases employees in ESOP who feel that they can share ideas, opinions, and creativity with their organizations apparently are self-motivated to work hard and long hours.

Alternative work schedules. Each year an increasing number of organizations are adopting alternative work schedules; that is, a work schedule that is not a traditional 8:00 A.M. to 5:00 P.M. schedule. Employee preferences, management flexibility, the growing number of single-parent families, and the anxiety of traveling to and from work during peak traffic times are reasons why alternative work schedules are growing in popularity.

At the turn of the 20th century, the average workweek was about 60 hours long. Today the workweek average is around 38 to 40 hours weekly. About 20 percent of the work

---

[35]David A. Garvin, "Quality Problems, Policies, and Attitudes in the United States and Japan: An Exploratory Study," *Academy of Management Journal,* December 1986, pp. 653–73.

[36]Corey Rosen and Michael Quarrey, "How Well Is Employee Ownership Working?" *Harvard Business Review,* September–October 1987, pp. 126–28, 132.

[37]J. Lawrence French, "Employee Perspective on Stock Ownership: Financial Investment or Mechanism of Control?" *Academy of Management Review,* July 1987, pp. 427–35.

[38]Rosen and Quarrey, "How Well is Employee Ownership Working?" p. 128.

force uses shift schedules; that is, one week a worker works from 7:00 A.M. to 3:00 P.M.; the next week from 3:00 P.M. to 11:00 P.M.; and the next week from 11:00 P.M. to 7:00 A.M. This type of shift schedule is difficult for employees in terms of sleeping patterns, eating habits, and family relations and interactions. A popular alternative to the standard schedule or a shift schedule is the flextime arrangement. Flextime is a schedule that gives an employee some choices as to when he will work. There is a *core* time when the employee must be at work and a *flexible* time when the employee chooses the remaining work time. The core time may be from 10:00 A.M. to 2:00 P.M. For this four-hour period the worker must be present. The worker then must schedule another five hours of work around the core. One person may elect to work from 8:00 A.M. to 5:00 P.M.; another may decide to work from 10:00 A.M. to 7:00 P.M.; and still another may decide to work from 5:00 A.M. to 2:00 P.M. Each of the employees works nine hours and each is present during the *core* time.

Another alternative is to work a "compressed" workweek.[39] Instead of working a five-day schedule, the employee may elect to extend the workday and work only four days, 11 hours a day.

Some banks and related establishments use *permanent part-time* employees; that is, part-time help is used on a regular basis for, say, four hours a day, five days a week (1:00 P.M. to 5:00 P.M.).[40] Another form of part-time employment is called *job sharing*. In such a schedule two employees divide a full-time job. Each person may work half the job or one person may work 60 percent of the hours and the other works the remaining 40 percent of the time.

There are also firms that permit work-at-home schedules. By using computer terminals linked to mainframes in the main office or plant, work information can be exchanged. The employee's home is called an *electronic cottage*.[41]

Each of these alternative work arrangements has some potential motivational value. Workers are given more freedom of choice to make decisions about their work schedule. This permits employees electing one of these alternative options the opportunity to decide when to conduct personal business and how to spend their workday.

MANAGEMENT SOLUTION

THE 100 CLUB HAS A MOTIVATIONAL IMPACT

The management at the Palmer plant decided to install what was called the 100 Club. The 100 Club program stressed attendance, punctuality, safety, achievement of goals, and support among the hourly employees. The number 100 stands

Continued

---

[39]J. C. Latack and L. W. Foster, "Implementation of Compressed Work Schedules: Participation and Job Redesign as Critical Factors for Employee Acceptance," *Personnel Psychology*, Spring 1985, pp. 75–89.

[40]S. R. Sacco, "Are In-House Temporaries Really an Option?" *Personnel Administrator*, May 1985, pp. 20–24.

[41]D. Kroll, "Telecommuting: A Revealing Peak inside Some of Industry's First Electronic Cottages," *Management Review*, November 1984, pp. 18–23.

MANAGEMENT SOLUTION

Concluded

for points. An employee earns 25 points for a year of perfect attendance, 20 points for a year without sustaining a lost-time injury. For each day or partial day of absence, the company deducts five points. A worker also earns points for group participation, individual achievements, suggestions, and community service such as participation in blood drives, the United Way, or Little League. Thus, points can be added for work and nonwork-related achievements. Management considers achievement to be extremely important in self-motivation.

What does a worker receive for earning 100 points? A jacket—a nylon and cotton jacket with the Diamond logo and the words "The 100 Club." Is this really what they get? Yes and it seems to be important to the workers. The workers like the recognition and the tangible item that shows they achieved a goal, 100 points.

Skeptics predicted that the 100 Club program would be a novelty at first and then wither away. The plant's first-year productivity increased by 14.7 percent, and smaller but significant gains have been achieved for three years.

The lesson of the Palmer example is that recognition is important to employees. They don't want to be numbers, faceless employees, pawns. Recognition helps satisfy the type of needs Maslow described and Herzberg referred to as *motivators*. The Palmer experiment has spread to other Diamond International plants with similar success. Productivity and morale have improved with the help of an attractive nylon and cotton jacket.

Source: Adapted from Daniel C. Boyle, "The 100 Club," *Harvard Business Review*, March–April 1987, pp. 26–27.

MANAGEMENT SUMMARY

☐ Motivation is not something that can be seen. All that a manager can observe are changes in behavior. From these changes a manager makes inferences about motivation or what we define as "all those inner striving conditions described as needs, drives, desires, motives, etc. . . . ."

☐ Maslow proposed that each person has a hierarchy of five needs—physiological, safety, social, esteem, and self-actualization. Needs at the lower level must be adequately satisfied before high-level needs emerge and play a role in shaping behavior.

☐ McClelland studied the conditions under which people develop a motive to achieve and its impact on behavior. He identified three important needs—achievement, affiliation, and power.

☐ When a person is blocked from satisfying needs, a variety of constructive or defensive behaviors can occur—the choice in dealing with need satisfaction.

☐ Herzberg proposes a two-factor theory of motivation. One set of job conditions called the maintenance factors is needed to maintain a minimum level of satisfaction. On the other hand, motivational factors result in higher levels of motivation and job satisfaction.

☐ Vroom suggested an expectancy theory of motivation; that is, an individual engages in deciding what type of behavior is likely to result in her being able to achieve desired goals.

☐ The reinforcement theory of motivation uses positive or negative reinforcers to help motivate individuals. B. F. Skinner's

application of behavior modification utilizes reinforcement theory to influence individual behavior.

☐ Job enrichment, pay for performance, and quality of work life programs are formal, organizationally initiated programs designed to create a positive work environment to motivate employees. Each of these programs have had some research conducted on their effectiveness, as well as their limitations.

REVIEW AND DISCUSSION QUESTIONS

1. Quality of work life (QWL) programs sound interesting and attractive. Why, however, are QWL programs not used in more organizations than they are currently used to improve motivation?

2. What is the problem with a manager concluding that motivation and performance are the same or are similar concepts?

3. The manager of a fast-food restaurant was overheard saying, "I believe that money is the best of all possible motivators. You can say what you please about all the other nonsense, but when it comes right down to it, if you give a guy a raise, you'll motivate him. That's all there is to it." In light of what we have discussed in this chapter, advise this restaurant manager.

4. Think of a situation from your personal experience in which two individuals reacted differently to frustration. Discuss each situation and the reactions of the two individuals. Can you give a possible explanation of why they reacted differently?

5. Some critics of job enrichment and behavior modification programs state that most of the declared successes are based on short-term results. These critics contend that a proper evaluation over a longer

period of time would show negative results for these programs. Comment.

6. Since motivation can't be seen, is it difficult to measure? What kind of problems would exist if a person attempted to use the Thematic Apperception Test (TAT) to assess the motivation levels of a group of subordinates?

7. This chapter emphasizes that managers must be familiar with the fundamental needs of people in order to motivate employees successfully. Select two individuals with whom you are well acquainted. Do they differ, in your opinion, with respect to the strength of various needs? Discuss these differences and indicate how they could affect behavior. If you were attempting to motivate those persons, would you use different approaches for each? Why?

8. Can a student's "job" be enriched? Assume that your professor has asked you to consult with her about applying the two-factor motivation theory in your class. You are to answer these questions for your teacher: (1) Can you apply this approach to the classroom? Why or why not? (2) If so, differentiate between maintenance and

motivational factors and develop a list of motivational factors your professor can use to enrich the student's job.

9. Assume that you have just read that the *goals* of individuals influence their *effort* and that the behavior they select depends on their assessment of the probability that the behavior will lead to the goal. What is your goal in this management course? Is it influencing your effort? Do you suppose that another person in your class might have a different goal? Is his effort (behavior) different from yours? Could this information be of any value to your professor?

10. What is the difference between intrinsic and extrinsic rewards? What types of rewards are used in job enrichment, pay, behavior-modification, and quality circle programs?

CASES

12–1 MOTIVATING DIFFERENT INDIVIDUALS

Below are brief descriptions of several individuals. Assume that you are their manager. Select from the following the strategy you feel would be most likely to motivate each person to improve performance. Explain the reasons for your selections.

- a. An individual incentive plan.
- b. Recognition for achievement.
- c. A salary increase.
- d. The threat of demotion or discharge.
- e. Additional status (e.g., a bigger office, a title, carpeting in the office, a secretary).
- f. A group profit sharing plan.
- g. Job enrichment.
- h. Additional fringe benefits.
- i. More participation in management decisions.
- j. More freedom of action (i.e., less supervision).

1. Jim Hammer is a marketing representative for a large pharmaceutical firm. His job involves calling on physicians to promote the firm's line of prescription drugs. He is 31 years old, married, has one child, and holds a college degree in business administration. He has been with the firm five years and earns $27,300 annually.

2. Barbara Oldeck is the head pediatrics nurse at a large public hospital. She is 24 years old, married, has two children, and is currently pursuing a master's degree. She has a reputation among staff physicians as an extremely competent nurse. Her yearly salary is $19,300.

3. John Ekard is vice president of operations for one of the nation's largest fast-food franchisers. He is 49 years old, divorced, and has three children—two attend college, and one is married. He has been with the company for nine years, and he earns a salary of $82,500 per year. He is among a group of top-level executives in the company who share in company profits through a bonus system.

4. Dave Noe is a part-time employee for a large supermarket chain. He is 26 years old and an Air Force veteran, and he worked for the firm before entering the Air Force and has worked for it since being discharged. He is a highly valued employee, and he earns approximately $6.40 per hour. He attends a local university and at present is completing the final 15 hours for a degree in business administration.

5. Marie Glass is assistant director of market development for a new space industry firm. She is 32 years old, single, bright, witty, and energetic. She exemplifies the "new woman." Her annual salary is $30,000. She has just completed her master's degree.

12–2 FIRESTONE, HALLMARK, PACIFIC BELL, AND OTHER PROGRAMS IMPARTING JOB SECURITY

Job security has become a major concern of employees. The new labor contracts signed by Ford and the United Autoworkers, and General Motors and the United Autoworkers, have job security clauses that protect employees. Allegis, Firestone, and Owens-Illinois, however, have laid off employees to cut costs and raise profits. Trimming people has become the "quick fix" preference for the cost and profit paradox.

There are a number of solutions being attempted to slow down the charge to use the quick fix or what some call the *quick ugly hook*. Hallmark's Kansas City plant, which employs 1,000 people, has deliberately begun operating an alternative work schedule that uses three work shifts. Hallmark also is shifting work from plant to plant to even out operating loads. Some employees have been rotating from manufacturing to office to cafeteria jobs. Hallmark has also instituted a training program to teach new skills. The cross-training opportunities have been well received.

Pacific Bell has postponed layoffs and has traded cost reductions for employment security. A critical element in the new labor contract links compensation to the success of the business, measured by service levels and profits. Employees can boost their pay to 9 percent over the life of the three-year contract if the company meets or exceeds its profit goals. Eliminated in the contract are potentially costly benefits not tied to the company's performance such as a cost-of-living allowance.

Management believes that with the employment security agreement, Pacific Bell can now invest in, and derive the most from, the new technology it needs. The workers are more likely to participate enthusiastically in changes rather than to block suggestions and drag their feet. Moving workers, retraining workers, and involving workers in the changes needed to cut costs, improve service, and offer services at a reasonable price, are all needed to adhere to the employment security contract requirements.

There are some who believe, instead of setting up employment security in contracts, employees should have a personal responsibility to protect their skills. The employee should have full responsibility for her own career such as keeping skills up to date, taking jobs that will broaden skills, planning for retirement, and seizing opportunities for growth and advancement. At a minimum, the person is going to have to engage in motivation, career, and life planning—figuring out what motivates her, where she is now, where she wants to be, and how to get there. This criticism suggests that Hallmark and Pacific Bell's programs are too paternalistic.

This new personal responsibility for everything from job security to retirement has occurred because of the changes in organizational reality—global competition, take-overs, deregulation, new technologies and skill requirements—and the promise of more change to come. Ignoring these changes will leave organizations unprepared to cope and will cause individuals to become obsolete and expendable.

Instead of being responsible for employment security, organizations should be doing more homework and should be more creative in developing equitable pay systems. Yes, the new thinking is that pay is important to most people, especially in terms of equity. People want to be paid what they feel is an equitable amount for performing.

There will be some firms that follow the massive layoff strategy. Others will adopt a Hallmark and Pacific Bell stance and will offer forms of employment security. Still others will declare that security is the employees' responsibility. Only time will tell which of these approaches is best in terms of motivation, costs, and profits.

Questions

1. Demographics point to labor shortages in the next few years. Which of the three security approaches described in the case seem best in a labor shortage market?

2. What are the advantages to an organization of using an "employee is responsible" strategy?

3. In terms of the motivation theories discussed in the chapter, how could the Hallmark and Pacific Bell approaches impart individual motivation?

Source: This case is adapted from Bill Saporito, "Cutting Costs without Cutting People," *Fortune,* May 25, 1987, pp. 26–32; and Walter Kiechel III, "Your New Employment Contract," *Fortune,* July 6, 1987, pp. 109–10.

EXERCISE

12–1 RANKING MOTIVATORS

Purpose: The purpose of this exercise is to compare the importance of various individual motivational factors among several people so that an awareness of differences and similarities is brought into focus.

Setting Up the Exercise:

1. Individually complete the ranking priority form shown below, using Exhibit 12–1. The 12 factors in Exhibit 12–1 were identified by Herzberg in developing his two-factor theory of motivation.

2. After the ranking has been individually completed, the instructor will form groups of four to six students to discuss their rankings.

3. Each group will appoint a spokesperson to report to the entire class on how individual rankings differed in his group.

A Learning Note: This exercise will illustrate that there are major individual differences in motivational preferences. The difficulties faced by managers in addressing such individual differences should become clear.

Priority of Motivation Factors
(most influential first)

1. _____

2. _____

3. _____

4. _____

5. _____

6. _____

7. _____

8. _____

9. _____

10. _____

11. _____

12. _____

Exhibit 12–1   Motivation Factors

Rate the following factors in the order of their actual or assumed (if not currently working) influence on your job performance.

Factors	Description
Recognition	Recognition could be from anyone—a superior, another individual in management, a peer, the general public. Could be either positive or negative recognition.
Achievement	Successful completion of a job, solutions to problems, seeing the results of one's work. Includes its opposite, failure, and the absence of achievement.
Possibility of growth	The potential of moving up in the organization or enlarging skills and responsibilities. Objective evidence that the possibilities for personal growth are increased or decreased.
Advancement	An actual change in status or position within the company.
Salary	Events in which compensation plays the dominant role. Could be increases or unfulfilled expectations for increases.
Interpersonal relations	Events in which interaction with a superior, subordinates, or peers is the major factor.
Responsibility	Factors relating to the assignment of responsibility and authority or the lack thereof.
Company policy and administration	Covers adequacy or inadequacy of company organization and management. Also covers harmfulness or beneficial effects of company policies, usually personnel policies.
Working conditions	Physical conditions for work, the facilities available for doing work. Adequacy or inadequacy of ventilation, lighting, tools, space, and other environmental factors.
Work itself	The actual doing of the job or task as a source of good or bad feelings whether it is routine, creative, and so forth.
Status	Having a secretary in a new position, flying first class while on company work, being assigned a "prestige" parking spot, and so forth, or the deprivation of such status items.
Security	Objective signs of the presence or absence of security, such as tenure and company stability or instability.

Scoring instructions for the motivation quiz in Table 12–1

1. Transfer the numbers you circled in Table 12–1 to the appropriate places in the chart below.

Statement number	Score		Statement number	Score
10	_____		2	_____
11	_____		3	_____
13	_____		9	_____
18	_____		19	_____
Total (self-actualization needs)	_____		Total (safety needs)	_____

Statement number	Score		Statement number	Score
6	_____		1	_____
8	_____		4	_____
14	_____		16	_____
17	_____		20	_____
Total (esteem needs)	_____		Total (physiological needs)	_____

Statement number	Score
5	_____
7	_____
12	_____
15	_____
Total (social needs)	_____

2. Record your total scores in the chart below by marking an X in each row next to the number of your total score for that area of needs motivation.

	-12	-10	-8	-6	-4	-2	0	$+2$	$+4$	$+6$	$+8$	$+10$	$+12$
Self-actualization													
Esteem													
Social													
Safety													
Physical													

Low use   High use

Once you have completed this chart, you can see the relative strength of each of these needs. Which need is your most deficient? Why? How do you plan to satisfy this need?

THIRTEEN

Work Groups

LEARNING OBJECTIVES

After completing Chapter 13, you should be able to:

Define: the work group from a manager's perspective.

State: the reasons why groups are formed within organizations.

Describe: the difference between formal and informal groups.

Explain: how work groups can apply pressure to an individual and cause him to conform.

Discuss: management strategies that can be implemented to deal with intergroup conflict.

INDIVIDUAL CONFLICT CAN INFECT THE GROUP

Problems are inevitable in business. Machines stop working properly, people with special talents quit, unions attempt to organize workers, orders are lost to competitors, workers loaf and cause more work to fall on their co-workers. Such problems produce conflicts between individuals or groups.

If an order was lost, was it because the salesperson goofed, because the last order was delivered late, or because product quality has slipped? Members of the sales force, the distribution unit, and quality control team all would probably disagree. But if the company is to retain the customer, the problem must be solved.

Dealing with conflict lies at the heart of managing. As a result, confrontation—facing issues about which there is disagreement—is an unavoidable fact of life in an organization. Andrew Grove, president of Intel Corporation, recalls a challenge he faced at the beginning of his management career. Two of his subordinates, one in charge of manufacturing and the other in charge of quality assurance, disliked each other. The manufacturing manager would complain that the quality manager didn't know what he was doing. Soon after, the quality manager would say the same thing about the manufacturing manager. Serving as a referee, Grove would become frustrated and angry as he listened to one person's story and then the other's. These two formal group leaders took a lot of Grove's time and also were pitting their separate work groups against each other. Since the individual conflict was spreading to the groups, it had to be stopped.

(The Management Solution to this Management Incident can be found at the end of this chapter.)

This chapter is concerned with the issues of managing work groups and group processes in organizations. Managers and researchers have paid special attention to the group processes that affect individuals and organizations. Thus, any presentation of management would be incomplete if it did not include a framework for understanding the nature and characteristics of work groups. We define a *work group* as follows: A *collection of interacting employees (managerial or nonmanagerial) who share certain norms and are striving toward member need satisfaction through the attainment of group goals.*

The purposes of this chapter are to give you (1) a classification of the different types of groups, (2) some knowledge about the reasons for the formation and development of groups, (3) an understanding of some characteristics of groups, and (4) some insights into the outcomes of group membership.

Students often ask why work groups should be studied in a management text. Many different answers could apply. Two of the more relevant responses are:

1. The formation of work groups is inevitable in and throughout organizations. Thus, it is in management's interest to understand what happens within and among work groups.

2. Work groups strongly influence the behavior and performance of their members. Understanding the influences exerted by such groups requires a systematic analysis.

A MANAGERIAL MODEL OF GROUP FACTORS

Figure 13–1 depicts a general model of group factors a manager can use to gain some understanding of group dynamics and outcomes. The model indicates that two types of groups, formal and informal, exist in organizations. These groups either are formed by management or naturally evolve. All groups emerge, however, because they help satisfy individual needs and because of physical proximity.

A group, once it evolves or is formed, begins a specific pattern of development. Like individuals, over time groups become more efficient and more productive.[1] As a group develops, it begins to exhibit various typical characteristics such as norms, cohesiveness, and political maneuvering. The characteristics, their intensity, clarity, and frequency all culminate in a unique group personality.

A group's existence also has tangible consequences, called *outcomes*. They include performance, the number of units produced or services provided, and for individual members, satisfaction arising from group affiliation.

According to our model in Figure 13–1, group outcomes are influenced by individual needs and proximity, the type of group, the stage of group development, and the personality of the group, which is built up by its characteristics. These outcomes provide standards by which management can assess group effectiveness. The remainder of this chapter is devoted to understanding each of the group elements portrayed in the framework in Figure 13–1.

---

[1]Robert R. Blake, Jane S. Mouton, and Robert L. Allen, *Spectacular Teamwork* (New York: John Wiley & Sons, 1987).

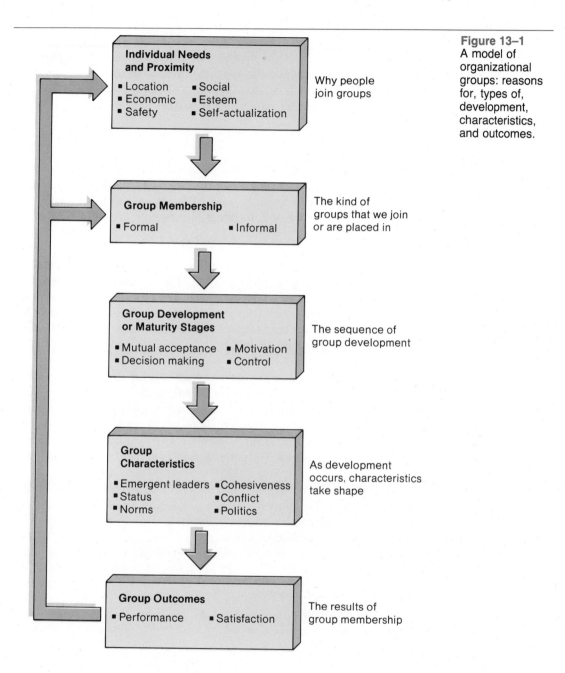

Figure 13–1
A model of organizational groups: reasons for, types of, development, characteristics, and outcomes.

CLASSIFICATION OF GROUPS

Managers and nonmanagers belong to a number of different groups within organizations, and individual memberships in groups often overlap. In some instances, individuals are members of a group because of their position in the organization. But through contacts they make in the group, they may also see some members informally.

Formal Work Groups

All employees are members of at least one group based on their positions in the organization. These *formal groups* are the departments, units, project teams, and so on, that the organization forms to do the work. The demands and processes of the organization lead to the formation of these groups. Two specific types of formal groups are *command* and *task* groups.

The command group.   The *command group* is specified by the organizational hierarchy, usually outlined on the organization chart. The subordinates who report directly to a supervisor make up a command group. The relationship between a department manager and his three supervisors in a machine shop for instance, is indicated in the organization chart. As the span of control of the department manager increases, the size of the command group also increases.

The task group.   A number of employees who work together to complete a specific project or job are considered a *task group*. A manufacturing or office work process that requires a great deal of interdependence is an example of a task group. For example, suppose that three office clerks are required: (1) to secure the file of an automobile accident claim; (2) to check the accuracy of the claim by contacting the persons involved; and (3) to type the claim, obtain the signatures of those involved, and refile the claim.

The activation of the file and the things that must be done before the claim is refiled constitute required tasks. The process creates a situation in which three clerks must communicate and coordinate with each other if the file is to be handled properly. Their interactions facilitate the formation of a task group.

Committees are very common in organizations. Committees actually are task groups established for such purposes as:

- ☐ Exchanging views and information.
- ☐ Recommending actions.
- ☐ Generating ideas.
- ☐ Making decisions.

Committees can achieve all of these purposes. However, a group may have difficulty coming to decisions. Managers typically attempt to keep a committee's size relatively small, since size affects the quality of a group's decisions. Increasing a committee's size tends to limit the extent to which its members want to or can communicate, and members tend to feel threatened and less willing to actively participate. The perceived threat can lead to increased stress and conflict. Stress and conflicts are outcomes that do not facilitate the generation of good committee decisions.

The *committee chairperson* is expected to provide proper direction. Ordinarily, successful committees have chairpersons who understand group processes. Such chairpersons see that the committee's objectives and purposes remain clear. They encourage committee members to participate and know how to move the committee toward its objectives.

A committee chairperson must walk a fine line. A chairperson who is too nondirective may lose the members' respect. On the other hand, a chairperson who exerts tight control may alienate the members and not receive the group's acceptance.

Managerial experience on committees has led to some guidelines that can aid committee chairpersons. Some of these are:

1. Be a careful listener, and keep an open mind.
2. Allow each member to voice opinions; do not place your opinion above those of others.
3. Get everyone involved in the committee's activities.
4. Display an active interest in the purpose of the committee and in the ideas of its members.
5. Help the committee focus on the task at hand and on the progress being made.

Committee members also must be responsible for creating an atmosphere of cooperation within the group. Management experience indicates that in cooperative groups, as distinguished from competitive groups, one finds:

1. Stronger motivation to accomplish the task.
2. More effective communication.
3. More ideas generated.
4. More membership satisfaction.
5. More group performance.

Thus, when cooperation prevails, the results are generally positive. Communication, satisfaction, and productivity all tend to be more positive in a cooperative committee. Both the committee's chairperson and its members are important determinants of cooperative committee efforts.

Informal Work Groups

Whenever employees associate on a fairly regular basis, groups tend to form, and their activities may differ from those required by the organization. The *informal groups* are natural groupings of people in the workplace. They do not arise as a result of deliberate design but evolve naturally. The evolution of informal groups follows a path in response to the common interests, needs, or attractions of members. Informal groups often

Figure 13–2 Informal-formal group types.

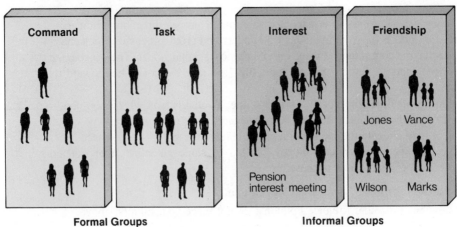

Formal Groups

Created by organization
to accomplish
performance goals

Informal Groups

Created to satisfy
needs of employees

develop within formal groups because of certain values or needs which members find that they have in common. The informal group is not sanctioned by management, and its membership usually cuts across a number of formal groups. Two types of informal work groups are *interest* and *friendship* groups.

The interest group.   Groups often form because their members share a common interest in some particular job-related event or possible outcome. This type of group can be viewed as an *interest group,* since the members have joined together to achieve some objective, such as an equitable pension payment. The members of the group may or may not be members of the same command or task group.

The friendship group.   In the workplace, drawn together by common characteristics such as age, ethnic background, political sentiment, or family structure, employees often form *friendship groups*. These groups frequently extend their interaction and communication to off-the-job activities. For example, the members become friends in the workplace, then bowl together, or attend sporting events together, or take their families on picnics together.

The formation of informal groups in an organization does not signal anything especially good or bad about management practices. The informal groups evolve naturally in response to the needs, interests, or characteristics of the members. Few, if any, organizations have no informal groups. Therefore, if you look only at the formal groupings in an organization chart, you are likely to have only a partial view of the important group memberships of employees.

Figure 13–2 classifies groups on the basis of formality, informality, and type. Many individuals are members of several or all of these groups at the same time. Not all groups can be neatly placed on a formal-informal continuum, however.

THE FORMATION OF WORK GROUPS

By going to work for an organization, you are actually joining a group. Once individuals become members of the organization, they are placed in, or volunteer for, various group memberships. They also join or create informal groups, because of common interests and characteristics. These and other reasons for group formation suggest that common *location* and *attitudes* strongly influence people to join formal groups and join or establish informal groups.

Location

When people are in close proximity, they tend to interact and communicate. Some degree of interaction and communication is necessary for group formation, particularly informal groups.

In organizations, a typical practice is to position workers with similar occupations *together*. For example, in the construction of a home, the bricklayers perform their jobs side by side. The same situation exists in offices, where clerks or secretaries are located next to one another.

Economic Reasons

In some cases, work groups form because individuals believe that they can gain economic benefits on their jobs if they band together. For example, individuals working at different stations on an assembly line may be paid on a group-incentive basis. Whatever the particular group produces determines the wages of each member. Since the workers all want to increase their wages, they will interact and communicate with one another. By working as a group instead of as individuals, they may actually obtain higher economic benefits.

Another example of how the economic motive affects the formation of informal work groups is a nonunion organization formed by workers to bring pressure on management for more economic benefits. The group members have a common interest—increased economic benefits—which leads to group affiliation.

Sociopsychological Reasons

Workers in organizations also are motivated to form work groups so that needs other than economic can be more satisfied. The safety, social, esteem, and self-actualization needs singled out by Maslow can be satisfied to some degree by work groups.

Safety. Work groups can protect members from management pressures such as demands for better quality and quantity of production, insistence that employees punch the clock on time, and recommendations for changes in individual work area layouts. By being members of a group, individual employees can openly discuss these management demands with other workers. Without the group to lean on, individuals often assume that they are alone against management and the entire organization. The interactions and communications that exist among members of a work group serve as a buffer to management demands.

Social.   Employees often join work groups because of their need for affiliation. The basis of affiliation ranges from wanting to interact with and enjoy other employees to more complex desires for group support of the self-image. A management atmosphere that does not permit interaction and communication deprives employees of a sense of belonging.

Esteem.   Some employees are attracted to a work group because they gain prestige by being in it. A particular group in an organization may be viewed by employees as a top-notch work group. Consequently, membership in the elite group bestows prestige on the members. This prestige is conferred on the members by other employees (nonmembers), which leads to more gratification of the esteem need. By sharing in the activities of a high-prestige work group, the individual identifies more closely with the group. This form of identification is valued highly by some employees.

Self-actualization.   The desire of individuals to grow and develop psychologically on the job constitutes the self-actualization need. Employees often believe that rigid job requirements and rules prevent them from satisfying this need sufficiently. One reaction is to join a work group, which can be a vehicle for communicating among friends about the use of a job-related skill. The jargon utilized and the skill employed are appreciated by the knowledgeable group members. This appreciation can lead to the feeling of accomplishing a worthwhile task. This feeling, and similar feelings of being creative and skillful, often help satisfy the self-actualization need.

THE DEVELOPMENT OF WORK GROUPS

Once a group is established as a part of the formal hierarchy or is initiated by its members, it begins to mature and develop into a distinct unit. The development of groups is related to learning—learning to work together and learning to accept and trust each other. A group that has reached maturity is characterized by openness and realism. A mature group is one in which:

1. Individual differences are accepted.
2. Conflict is over real issues, rather than emotional issues.
3. Decisions are made through rational discussion. There is no forcing decisions on members.
4. The members are aware of the group's processes.

There are four phases in what is called the *maturation* of a group. The following account of a four-phase group development process points out clearly some of the problems and frustrations inherent in group development.[2]

First Phase: Mutual Acceptance

Employees often are hampered by their mistrust: mistrust of each other, of the organization, and of their superiors. They fear they do not have the necessary training or skill to perform the job or compete with others. These insecurities motivate employees to seek out others in the same predicament so they can express their feelings openly. A group is born, and the mistrust subsides. After an initial period of uneasiness, in which they get to know one another, individuals typically begin to accept each other. In some groups, however, members never accept each other.

Second Phase: Decision Making

During this phase, you see the emergence of open communication and expression of thoughts concerning the job or an important issue. Problem solving and decision making are undertaken. The members trust one another's viewpoints and beliefs; they develop strategies to make the job easier and to help one another perform more effectively.

Third Phase: Motivation

The group has reached maturity, and the problems of its members are clear. It accepts that it is better for members of the group to cooperate rather than compete. Such group solidarity makes the job more rewarding both economically and sociopsychologically.

Fourth Phase: Control

The group has organized itself successfully, and its members are contributing according to their abilities and interests. The group exercises sanctions, when control is needed to bring members into line with the group's norms.

The structures and processes found in work groups develop over a period of time. The motivation of group members and the control of their behavior do not occur overnight. Through observing, listening, and working with a group, however, a manager can acquire some awareness about the stage of the group's development. An awareness of the group's stage of development allows the manager to better understand and cope with the group's behavior and performance.

---

[2]The discussion of the development of groups is based largely on Bernard Bass, *Organizational Psychology* (Boston: Allyn & Bacon, 1965), pp. 197–98. A number of alterations were made by the authors. Also see J. Stephen Heiner and Eugene Jacobson, "A Model of Task Group Development in Complex Organizations and a Strategy of Implementation," *Academy of Management Review,* October 1976, pp. 98–111.

Teamwork in Japanese firms is an example of what can occur in a fully matured group. The following Management Application highlights some group practices within Japanese work groups.

MANAGEMENT APPLICATION

JAPANESE TEAMWORK LESSONS THAT WARRANT SOME CONSIDERATION

Working together is so ingrained in the Japanese society that it spills over into work organizations. A major difference between the Japanese and American worker is that the Japanese is above all else a team player. Certainly there are imperfections in the Japanese system such as the manner in which women are paid, life-long employment agreements in a firm's struggling to survive, and forced early retirement for many highly productive middle-aged individuals. However, the teamwork approach is not considered an imperfection.

A few lessons about Japanese teamwork that provide a message and some insight for Westerners interested in Japanese management methods are these:

1. *It is important to work with your colleagues.* Unlike their American counterparts, every decision is discussed within the team. Each member adds his insight and works hard to make the best decision.

2. *Do not make a quick decision.* Team members must be in agreement which means decision making is slow. Since each alternative is carefully considered and debated, the process is slow.

3. *A performance mistake by a team member is a mistake by all members.* Mistakes and failures as well as successes are shared. If there is a mistake, the team must work together to correct errors. Through sharing, the group's spirit, mission, and culture become important parts of each member's life.

4. *Work with total devotion.* Anything less than complete dedication is considered an insult to the entire team. Being a "social loafer" is simply not permitted.

5. *Listen to others and avoid confrontation.* Nothing takes away more from production than not listening. You can always learn something. If you do not like what you hear, do not confront the person. Confrontation exacerbates rather than solves problems within and between groups.

These teamwork lessons work well in Japan. Whether they could work in Toronto, Canada; Baltimore, Maryland; or Portland, Oregon, is debatable. However, before they are discarded it might be useful to consider them on a case-by-case or a situation-by-situation basis. It's time to observe, listen, and experiment to see what really can and what can't work.

Source: Adapted from Milton Pierce, "Lessons from the Japanese," *New Management,* Fall 1987, pp. 23–26.

Figure 13–3 Characteristics of group development.

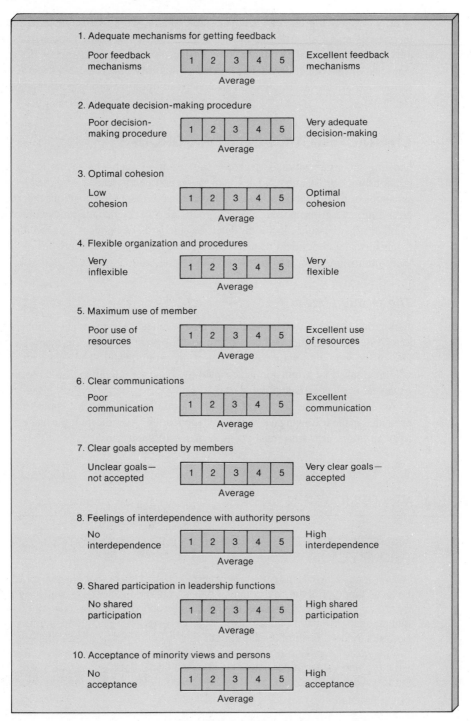

Source: Edgar H. Schein, *Process Consultation,* Copyright © 1969, Addison-Wesley Publishing Company, Inc., Chapter 6, p. 62. Reprinted with permission.

A fully developed group can handle complex tasks, work as a stable unit, and tolerate the viewpoints of all group members. Figure 13–3 covers 10 characteristics of group development proposed by Schein.[3] The 10 questions focus on characteristics a manager can seek when evaluating a group's level of maturity. Once these questions are asked and answered, managers then can take steps to optimize group performance or commitment.

CHARACTERISTICS OF WORK GROUPS

Creating an organizational structure can result in such characteristics as specified relationships among subordinates, superiors, and peers; leaders assigned to positions; standards of performance; a status rank order according to the positions that individuals are filling; and group politics. Work groups also have characteristics similar to those of other organizations, including leaders, standards of conduct, reward and sanction mechanisms, and political maneuvering. These and other characteristics of groups and work groups are discussed below.

The Group Leader

As a group attempts to complete some objective and the individual members begin to know one another, the members begin to fill one or more of the many group roles. One of the most important roles is that of the group leader. The leader emerges from within an informal group and is accepted by the group members. In the formal group, however, the leader is appointed.

An example of the important role that group leaders play in Apple Computers is presented in the following Management Application. As indicated, the leader is referred to as an impresario who must perform many different activities.

MANAGEMENT APPLICATION

MANAGING CREATIVITY: APPLE COMPUTER'S HISTORY OF GROUP LEADERS

Steven Jobs, currently the president of Next, Inc., and the cofounder of Apple Computer, believes that one of the reasons for Apple's tremendous success was the role played by group leaders. Jobs was fired from Apple by John Sculley because of philosophical differences. However, Sculley, like Jobs, believes that the group leaders' role was powerful in the growth of the firm because it encouraged and fed creativity.

The wizards working on Apple products were all extremely creative. They disliked structure and valued autonomy. This is exactly what Jobs encouraged. Apple's group leaders were like impresarios. They had to deal cleverly with the creative styles and

---

[3]Edgar H. Schein, *Process Consultation* (Reading, Mass.: Addison-Wesley Publishing, 1969), p. 62.

temperaments of the wizards in the group. It was important for group leaders to coach, listen, cajole, stroke, and scold. These behaviors were more important than establishing a management structure; that is, a set of task requirements, and a time to start and finish the work. The group impresario had to bring the talents of self-centered, highly motivated, and intelligent artists together.

The group artists wanted recognition, resources, and latitude. Only a strong-willed group leader could deliver these factors. Managing the creative talents of the Apple groups is different than managing a typical work group. Consensus, control, timely feedback, and certainty were simply not possible at Apple when Jobs was in charge. Instinct, autonomy, debate, and uncertainty were the order of the day.

The falling out between Sculley and Jobs was not caused by the way groups of creative artists or "knowledge" workers were managed. They both believe that Apple's success has a lot to do with how group leaders worked with the engineers and the research and development experts. The traditional management approach of structure, efficiency, and punctuality wasn't correct for Apple. Someday, perhaps, the impresario-type group leader will be discussed and observed more than the traditional group leader.

Source: Adapted from John Sculley, *Odyssey: Pepsi to Apple . . . A Journey of Adventure, Ideas and the Future* (New York: Harper & Row, 1987).

Leaders in formal groups are followed and obeyed because employees perceive them as possessing the power and influence to reward them or punish them if they do not comply with requests. The formal leaders possess the power to regulate the formal rewards of the work group members.

The informal leader emerges from within the group and serves a number of functions. First, any group of individuals without a plan or some coordination becomes an ineffective unit. Its members are not directed toward the accomplishment of goals, and this can lead to a breakdown in group effectiveness. The leader initiates action and provides direction. If there are differences of opinion on a group-related matter, the leader attempts to settle the differences and to move the group toward accomplishing its goals.

Second, some individual must communicate the group's beliefs about policies, the job, the organization, the supervision, and other related matters to nonmembers.[4] The nonmembers could include members of other groups, supervisory personnel, and the union. In effect, the group leader communicates the values of the group.

The characteristics of informal group leaders can be summarized as follows:

1. The leadership role is filled by an individual who possesses the attributes that members perceive as being critical for satisfying their needs.
2. The leader embodies the values of the group and is able to perceive those values, organize them into an intelligible philosophy, and verbalize them to nonmembers.

---

[4]Ben Heirs, "Managing a Thinking Team," *Industry Week,* November 2, 1987, pp. 109–11.

3. The leader is able to receive and interpret communication relevant to the group and to effectively communicate important information to group members.

In most groups, leaders perform two specific roles. A leader who performs the *task role* typically concentrates on accomplishing the desired goals, such as providing a number of units within quality and cost standards or delivering a product to a customer by 5 P.M. or setting up a grievance meeting time and place with management. The task role requires the leader to accomplish something specific of importance to the membership.

Leaders of groups also perform a *supportive or maintenance role*, which involves personally helping members, listening to their problems, and encouraging group cohesiveness. While the task role is job oriented, the supportive role is people oriented. Both orientations are important for accomplishing group performance and satisfaction. In some groups, one person performs both roles. In other groups, two individuals perform the roles.

Group Status

Status is the rank, respect, or social position that an individual has in a group. Managers have relative status that depends upon their positions in the hierarchy; that is, the top managers of the firm have more status than middle managers, and the middle managers have more status than lower-level managers. The top-level positions have more authority, responsibility, power, and influence—and thus are accorded more status.

A similar status system develops in groups. For many different reasons, members are accorded status by their groups. Individuals in leadership roles possess status because of their roles. Consequently, they are ranked highly in the group-status hierarchy.

Other factors influence the status systems of groups. Many groups consider the seniority of a member to be important. A worker having more seniority is often thought of as being "organizationally intelligent," which means that she knows how to adapt to the demands of supervisors, subordinates, or peers. This ability to adjust is an important status factor with group members.

The skill of an individual in performing a job is another factor related to status. An individual with expertise in the technical aspects of the job is given a high status ranking in some groups. This type of status does not mean that the individual actually utilizes the skill to perform more effectively, but simply that the group members admire this skill.

Group Norms and Compliance

A *group norm* is an implicit or explicit agreement among the group members as to how they should behave. The more a person complies with norms, the more the person accepts the group's standards of behavior.

Work groups can utilize norms to bring about acceptable job performance. The following are examples of production-related norms: (1) disagree with management in its effort to change the wage structure; (2) present a united front to resist the directives of the new college graduate assigned to the group's work area; (3) don't produce above the group leader's level of production; (4) help members of the group to achieve an acceptable production level if they are having difficulty and if you have time; and (5) don't allow the union steward to convince you to vote for his favorite union presidential candidate in the upcoming election.

Three specific social processes bring about compliance with group norms, namely, *group pressure, group review and enforcement,* and *personalization of the norms.*

Group pressure.   The pressure to adhere to a specific group norm can bring conformity to the behavior of the group's membership. Conformity occurs when a person complies with a group's wishes because of the pressure it applies or fear of future group pressure. Complying to group pressure does not mean the person agrees with the group's wishes.

Group review and enforcement.   If group members, either veterans or newcomers, are not complying with generally accepted norms, a number of different approaches may be employed. One soft approach is a discussion between respected leaders and the noncomformists. If discussion does not prove effective, more rigorous corrective action is used, such as private and public scolding by the members. The ultimate enforcement is to ostracize the deviating members.

Personalization of norms.   Behavioral patterns are influenced significantly by values. Values, in turn, are influenced by the events occurring around individuals; values are learned and become personalized. For example, the norm of a work group may be to treat college graduates *and* persons who did not go to college equally. This norm may be accepted by a group member as morally and ethically correct. Prior to group affiliation, the member may have displayed little interest in whether an individual attended college. However, based on a feeling of fairness, the member personalizes this group-learned norm, and it becomes a standard of her behavior.

The group norms can either be positive or negative as far as a manager is concerned. However, both types of norms typically are encountered when compliance is the issue of concern. Figure 13–4 illustrates some examples of work conditions for which norms often are established by groups. Positive and negative norms are presented to portray what managers often must face.

Group Cohesiveness

Cohesiveness refers to the extent that group members are attracted to each other and to the group values. It is the pressure on the individual member to remain active in the group and to resist leaving it.[5]

All characteristics of groups are influenced in some degree by *group cohesiveness.*

---

[5]This definition is based on the group cohesiveness concept presented by Stanley E. Seashore, *Group Cohesiveness in the Industrial Work Group* (Ann Arbor: University of Michigan, Institute for Social Research, 1954).

Figure 13–4 Positive and negative group norms.

Condition	Positive Group Norm	Negative Group Norm
Performance Output	Members work hard to produce at optimal skill levels.	Members work just hard enough to get by.
Quality	Members take pride in producing quality products.	Members pay enough attention to quality to keep management minimally happy.
Absenteeism	Members pride themselves on being present.	Members not interested in good attendance.
Supervisor relations	Members respect supervisors and are honest in their interactions.	Members distrust management and hold back vital information.
Honesty	Members are against stealing and slowdowns.	Members encourage some pilferage and slow down the line when everyone seems tired.
Wages/salaries	Members expect a fair day's pay for a good day's work.	Members expect to be taken care of despite a lack of effort—the "organization owes me" attitude.

For example, the greater the attraction within the group, the more likely its members will adhere closely to a group norm such as a production level.[6]

Some of the conditions that can enhance or reduce cohesiveness are presented in Figure 13–5.

The size of the work group.   It is important that group members interact and communicate. If a group is so large that members do not know one another, it is unlikely that the group will be cohesive. Managers have learned that an inverse relationship exists between group size and group cohesiveness.[7] As the size of a group increases, its cohesiveness decreases.

---

[6]Marvin E. Shaw, *Group Dynamics—The Psychology of Small Group Behavior* (New York: McGraw-Hill, 1981), p. 64.

[7]Ibid., pp. 90–95, Also see Robert C. Cummins and Donald C. King, "The Interaction of Group Size and Task Structure in an Industrial Organization," *Personnel Psychology,* Spring 1973, pp. 87–94.

Figure 13–5 Factors contributing to group cohesiveness.

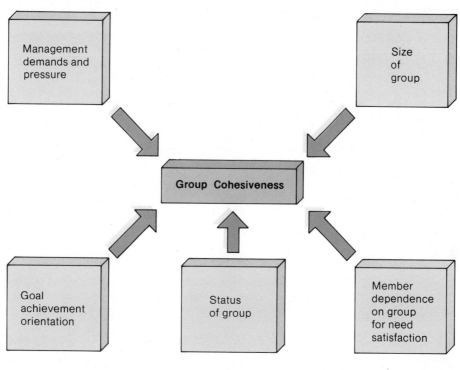

The dependence of the members on the work group. The greater the individual's dependency on the group, the stronger will be his attraction for it. Individuals join groups because the groups can help them satisfy economic and sociopsychological needs. A group that is able to satisfy a significant portion of an individual's needs will be attractive to that individual. Group processes such as interaction with co-workers and overall friendship make the group a key factor in the individual's life. Thus, what the group stands for, its norms, and its membership are bonds that tie the individual to the group.

The achievement of goals. The attainment of some set of group-established goals (e.g., better production than another group) influences the group's members. For example, if a work group attains a highly desired rating for completing a task, then the value of belonging to that group is enhanced. Its members feel pride in being part of a group that has achieved a superior performance.

Work groups that have successfully attained goals are likely to be highly cohesive units. The members tend to be more attracted toward one another because they have worked together in the past and their efforts have resulted in achieving goals. Thus, success and cohesiveness are interrelated: Success in goal achievement encourages cohesiveness, and cohesive work groups are more likely to attain goals. Managers

Figure 13–6 Cohesiveness and goal similarities: Similarity between group and organization performance goals.

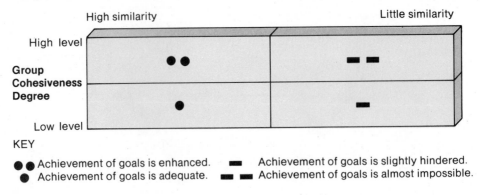

know, however, that although group cohesiveness can lead to the achievement of goals, cohesiveness can prove detrimental when group and organization goals are incompatible.

Managers clearly must recognize that they will have a difficult job if a group is highly cohesive but has performance goals that differ from those of the organization. On the other hand, a cohesive group whose goals are similar to those of management can be a very enjoyable unit to manage. The possible relationships between cohesiveness and goal similarities are illustrated in Figure 13–6. The ideal situation occurs when the highly cohesive group's goals are similar to those of the organization, which is shown as the ●● cell in Figure 13–6.

The status of the group. In an organizational setting, groups typically are ranked in a status hierarchy. A status hierarchy may develop among groups for many different reasons, including the following:

1. The group is rated higher than another group in overall performance; this rating measures success in an organization.
2. To become a member of the group, individuals must display a high level of skill.
3. The work being done by the group is dangerous, or financially more rewarding, or more challenging, than other work.
4. The group is less closely supervised than other groups.
5. In the past, members of the group have been considered for promotion more often than members of other groups.

These are only some of the criteria that affect the status hierarchy of groups. Generally, the higher a group ranks in the intergroup status hierarchy, the greater its cohesiveness. However, the higher-status groups appear attractive only to some nonmembers. In-

Figure 13–7 Identifying symptoms of groupthink.

- **Illusions of group invulnerability.** Members of the group feel it is basically beyond criticism or attack.

- **Rationalizing unpleasant and disconfirming data.** Refusal to accept contradictory data or to consider alternatives thoroughly.

- **Belief in inherent group morality.** Members of the group feel it is "right" and above any reproach by outsiders.

- **Stereotyping competitors as weak, evil, and stupid.** Refusal to look realistically at other groups.

- **Applying direct pressure to deviants to conform to group wishes.** Refusal to tolerate a member who suggests the group may be wrong.

- **Self-censorship by members.** Refusal by members to communicate personal concerns to the group as a whole.

- **Illusions of unanimity.** Accepting consensus prematurely, without testing its completeness.

- **Mind guarding.** Members of the group protect the group from hearing disturbing ideas or viewpoints from outsiders.

Source: Irving Janis, *Victims of Groupthink* (Boston: Houghton Mifflin, 1972).

dividuals outside the group may not want to become members of a high-status group because membership entails close adherence to group norms.

Management demands and pressure.   Another agent for group cohesiveness is management demands and pressure. In many organizations, management has a significant impact on group cohesiveness. The members of groups tend to stick together when they are pressured by superiors to conform to some organizational norm.

The group cohesiveness attributed to managerial demands may be either a short-run or long-run phenomenon. In some cases, a loosely knit group (low in cohesiveness) may interpret a company policy statement as a threat to the job security of its members. Consequently, the group may become a more cohesive and unified whole to withstand the perceived management threat. After the danger is past (i.e., the policy statement is rescinded), the group may drift back toward low cohesiveness. In other cases, the cohesiveness may be a longer-lasting phenomenon.

When groups are characterized by high conformity and cohesiveness, a phenomenon called *groupthink* might occur.[8] Groupthink exists when a group believes that it is invincible, rationalizes away criticisms, believes that everyone should comply with a group norm, and is characterized by unanimity among its members. Figure 13–7

---

[8]Irving L. Janis, *Victims of Groupthink: A Psychological Study of Foreign Policy Decisions and Fiascos* (Boston: Houghton Mifflin, 1972); and Irving L. Janis and Leon Mann, *Decision Making: A Psychological Analysis of Conflict, Choice, and Commitment* (New York: Macmillan, 1977).

identifies a number of symptoms of groupthink, which must be overcome if group effectiveness is to be restored.

Irving L. Janis uses the meetings of President John F. Kennedy and his team of advisers in 1961, planning the Bay of Pigs invasion, to illustrate how groupthink blocked any chance for the mission's success. The advisers approved a plan that would meet with total failure. There was no critical thinking, listening to minority opinions, or realistic analysis of the facts in the invasion planning sessions. Instead, a rationalized plan supported by the cohesive membership of the group was proposed and acted upon by a force of about 1,400 ill-trained, poorly equipped Cuban exiles.

Several managerial actions can minimize the groupthink phenomenon. Preventive actions include:

- ☐ Assigning the role of critical evaluator to all members of the group. Critical thinking should be encouraged, supported, and rewarded.

- ☐ Encouraging members to be impartial and to engage in open interaction instead of sticking with predetermined preferences.

- ☐ Establishing subgroups to work on problem issues and to then share with the total group the proposed solutions.

- ☐ Including outside experts in group discussions and permitting them to challenge the views expressed by members.

- ☐ Having at least one group member play the devil's advocate and challenge the majority position.

- ☐ Developing an analysis of how the group's decision will affect other groups. Discuss the consequences of the group's proposal so that changes can be made before action is taken.

- ☐ Holding a "second chance" meeting at which every group member expresses any doubts about the decision.

These preventive actions do have disadvantages.[9] For instance, the open dialogue, debate, and exchange of ideas is likely to lead to prolonged delays in decision making. Can a manager afford the time in a crisis situation? A crisis may require quick communications, quick discussions, and group meetings with time deadlines.[10] Bringing in outside experts also can create problems. Although experts have much to offer, their use increases the risk of security leakage.

Intergroup Conflict

Conflict occurs when one party perceives that another party has frustrated, or is about to frustrate, the accomplishment of a goal. Conflict is not limited to interacting groups; it also occurs within groups, between individuals, and between organizations. We will focus here on *intergroup conflict* within organizations. Therefore, we will not be

---

[9]Clarence W. VonBergen, Jr., and Raymond J. Kirk, "Groupthink: When Too Many Heads Spoil the Decision," *Management Review,* March 1978, pp. 44–49.

[10]Sally Bell, "Companies Lack Crisis Plans," *Dallas Times Herald,* August 5, 1984, p. 8.

focusing on interorganizational groups composed of members representing a parent organization (e.g., Union Carbide) and community constituencies (e.g., environmental group).[11]

One way to view conflict is to consider it as a sequence of episodes.[12] The sequence is as follows:

☐ *Latent conflict*—This is the time when the conditions for conflict exist: two groups competing for scarce resources, for example.

☐ *Perceived conflict*—This is the time when group members realize that there is conflict between groups.

☐ *Felt conflict*—This occurs when members involved feel tense or anxious.

☐ *Manifest conflict*—This exists when behaviors clearly demonstrate that one group is attempting to frustrate another group.

☐ *Conflict aftermath*—This is the situation after the conflict is minimized or eliminated.

Since conflict can progress to the manifest stage, it can have dysfunctional consequences for organizations and individuals. Conflict can arouse emotions and anxiety, lower satisfaction, and decrease performance. Managers must solve the conflict and get groups once again working cooperatively toward the accomplishment of organizational and individual goals. If the groups are working on interdependent tasks (i.e., Department A's output flows to Department B, and Department B's output flows to Department C), coordination of the groups and the effectiveness with which they work together are crucial managerial issues. The relationships among groups can become so antagonistic and disruptive that the entire flow of production is slowed or even stopped. Yet, cooperation is not always the most desirable result of group interaction. For example, two groups may cooperate because they both oppose the introduction of new equipment being installed to improve cost control. In this instance, the cooperation of the groups can make the trial period of testing the new equipment a bad experience for management.

There are many reasons for conflict among groups. Some of the more important ones relate to limited resources, communication problems, differences in interests and goals, different perceptions and attitudes, and lack of clarity about responsibilities.

Limited resources. Groups that possess an abundance of materials, money, and time usually are effective. However, when a number of groups are competing for limited resources, conflict often results. The competition for equipment dollars or merit increase money or new positions can become fierce.

Communication problems. Groups often become very involved with their own areas of responsibility. They tend to develop their own unique vocabulary. Paying attention

[11]Janice H. Schopler, "Interorganizational Groups: Origins, Structure, and Outcomes," *Academy of Management Review,* October 1987, pp. 702–13.

[12]Louis R. Pondy, "Organization Conflict: Concepts and Models," *Administrative Science Quarterly,* September 1967, pp. 296–320.

to an area of responsibility is a worthy endeavor, but it can result in communication problems. The receiver of information should be considered when a group communicates an idea, a proposal, or a decision. Misinformed receivers often become irritated and then hostile.

Different interests and goals.   A group of young workers may want management to do something about an inadequate promotion system. However, older workers may accuse management of ignoring improvements in the company pension plan. Management recognizes the two different goals but believes the pension issue is the more pressing and addresses it first. The groups want management to solve both problems, but this may not be currently possible. Thus, one group, that of the young workers, may become hostile because it feels it has been ignored.

Different perceptions and attitudes.   Individuals perceive things differently. The groups to which they belong also can have different perceptions. Groups tend to evaluate in terms of their backgrounds, norms, and experiences. Since each of these can differ, there is likely to be conflict among groups. Most groups tend to overvalue their own worth and position and to undervalue the worth and position of other groups.

Lack of clarity.   Job clarity involves knowing what others expect in terms of task accomplishment. Yet, in many cases, it is difficult to specify who is responsible for a certain task. For example: Who is responsible for the loss of a talented management trainee—the personnel department or the training department? Who is responsible for the increased sales revenue—marketing or research and development? The inability to pinpoint positive and negative contributions causes groups to compete for control over the activities that are more easily associated with specific effort.

These causes of conflict are among the more common ones that need to be managed. The management of intergroup conflict involves determining strategies to minimize such causes.

Management reaction to disruptive intergroup conflict can take many different forms.[13] But management usually will first try to minimize the conflict indirectly, and if this fails, become directly involved.

Managing intergroup conflict indirectly.   Initially, managers often avoid direct approaches to solving conflict among groups. Unfortunately, *avoidance* does not always minimize the problem. Matters get worse because nothing is being done, and the groups become more antagonistic and hostile.

Another indirect strategy is to encourage the groups to meet and discuss their differences and to work out a solution without management involvement. This strategy can take the form of bargaining, persuasion, or working on a problem together.

Bargaining involves having the groups agree about what each will get and give to

---

[13]Alan Filley, *Interpersonal Conflict Resolution* (Glenview, Ill.: Scott, Foresman, 1975); and Louis Pondy, "Organizational Conflict: Concepts and Models," *Administrative Science Quarterly*, September 1972, pp. 296–320.

the other. For example, one group may agree to give another group quick turnaround time on the repairs of needed equipment if the second group agrees to bring complaints about the quality of repairs to it before going to management. Bargaining between two groups is successful if both groups are better off (or at least no worse off) after an agreement has been reached.

Persuasion involves having the groups find areas of common interest. The groups attempt to find points of agreement and to show how these are important to each of the groups in attaining organizational goals. Persuasion is possible if clashes between group leaders do not exist.

A problem can be an obstacle to a goal. For groups to minimize their conflicts through *problem solving,* they must agree at least generally on the goal. If there is agreement, then the groups can propose alternative solutions that satisfy all parties involved. For example, one group may want the company to relocate the plant to a suburban area and the other group may want better working conditions. If both parties agree that a common goal is to maintain their jobs, then building a new facility in an area that does not have a high tax rate may be a good solution.

Managing intergroup conflict directly.   To improve intergroup relations, greater integration or collaboration among groups must occur. Various strategies can be used effectively to increase integration. Management can use *domination* to minimize conflict by exercising its authority and requiring that a problem be solved by a specific date. If management uses authority, the groups may join together to resist domination. Management thus becomes a common enemy, and the groups forget their differences in order to deal with their opponent.

Another direct approach is to *remove* the *key figures* in the conflict. If a conflict arises because of personality differences between two individuals, removing them is a possible solution. This approach has three problems. First, the key figures who are to be removed may be leaders of the groups. Removing them could make the groups more antagonistic and lead to greater conflict. Second, it is difficult to pinpoint accurately whether the individuals in conflict are at odds because of personal animosities or because they represent their groups. Third, removal may create martyrs. The causes of the removed leaders may be remembered and fought for, even though the leaders themselves are gone.

Management also can establish a task force with representatives from groups in conflict to work on problems. The task force will develop ideas and procedures for improving group interaction to be presented to their groups.[14]

A final direct strategy to minimize conflict is to find *superordinate goals*. These are goals desired by two or more groups that can only be accomplished through the cooperation of the groups. When conflicting groups have to cooperate to accomplish a goal, conflict can be minimized. For example, a companywide profit-sharing plan may encourage groups to work together. If company profits are distributed among employees at the end of the year, conflict among groups can reduce the amount of

---

[14]Joseph E. McCann and Diane L. Ferry, "An Approach for Assessing and Managing Inter-Unit Interdependence," *Academy of Management Review,* January 1979, pp. 113–19.

profits that each employee receives. Thus, the superordinate goal, generating profit, may take precedence over group conflict.

Group Politics

Political maneuvering to obtain limited resources is an increasingly common group characteristic. Since organizations typically work with scarce resources, *group politics* is a problem that managers become involved with on a regular basis.

Group politics exists when the behavior of the group is specifically self-serving. When a group acts to enhance its own position, regardless of the costs of the action, it acts politically. Often, self-serving group behavior creates such strained group relationships, that both organizational and group performances suffer. When a situation becomes an "us" versus "them" or a "my group" versus "your group" controversy, there are self-serving overtones. Through their actions and their dealings with groups, managers set the tone for the political maneuvering that emerges.[15]

Two types of managerial behaviors can create the atmosphere for group politics— offensive and defensive. *Offensive political behavior* by a group manager includes power building, exploiting or calling attention to the weaknesses of others, and sabotaging the work of others.

Defensive political behavior by a group manager can mean maneuvering in response to others. Placing the blame on another group, covering up mistakes, or even working hard to direct attention away from weaknesses are examples of defensive political behavior.

By example, managers often can create the environment for the degree and kind of politics in organizations. Subordinates look to managers for direction. When managers use political maneuvers, subordinates tend to imitate this action. Managers can modify such behavior by examining their political tendencies:

☐ Is this action only self-serving?

☐ Will this action hurt another group or person?

☐ Will organizational performance be improved by this action?

Confronting these questions can help managers become more aware of the political impact of their behavior. When the behavior initiated by a manager involves working together with other groups, organizational performance can be enhanced.

GROUP OUTCOMES: PERFORMANCE AND SATISFACTION

The purpose of group membership is to achieve group performance. There has been too little emphasis placed on group performance in the United States. One reason may be the exaggeration of the role and value of rugged individuals in American business. The following Management Application discusses how history has influenced our thinking about individual versus group performance.

---

[15]Kenwyn K. Smith and David N. Barg, *Paradoxes of Group Life* (San Francisco: Jossey-Bass, 1987).

MANAGEMENT APPLICATION

THE NEW ERA OF GROUP PERFORMANCE: HAS IT ARRIVED?

Some experts believe that if America is to win in the new global competition, a greater emphasis must be placed on team performance. The story of the successful maverick inventors and the dynamic charismatic leaders is not enough. Recently, one of America's oldest enterprises announced that it was changing the way to assign its personnel: the U.S. Army discarded a system that assigned soldiers to their units individually in favor of a system that keeps teams of soldiers together for their entire tours of duty. An army spokesperson explained, "We discovered that individuals perform better when they are part of a stable group. They are more reliable. They also take responsibility for the success of the overall operation."

Another view of the emphasis on teamwork is Bellsouth's advertisement. It states, "Bellsouth is not a bunch of individuals out for themselves. We're a team."

The American mythology has for years emphasized the fighters, fanatics, and rugged individuals. This is what Horatio Alger captured in the late 1800s in his 135 books written about the American hero. Alger's vision of America was different than what companies face today. There is still a need for rugged individuals, bright inventors, aggressive entrepreneurs—the hero in Alger's stories. However, there is a need for teamwork. Several years ago, when General Motors reached agreement on a contract with the United Autoworkers there was a sense of a new kind of labor-management relationship. This emphasis on teamwork is becoming more important in today's global work.

If the United States is to compete effectively, there must be more concern with group performance. This will require toning down the myths surrounding Alger-type heroes and more recognition of teamwork. The teams that can blend talent and that emphasize teamwork are more likely to compete effectively in a global marketplace. What we need to hear more about is how teams improved the product, services, and morale in such firms as IBM, Corning-Glass Works, Gillette, Alcon, Teledyne, Motorola, Sara Lee, and Kimberly-Clark. These are excellent performing organizations who have been able to use individual talents, while at the same time integrating individuals into high performing work teams.

Source: Adapted from Robert B. Reich, "Entrepreneurship Reconsidered: The Team as Hero," *Harvard Business Review*, May–June 1987, pp. 77–83.

In recent years, social psychologists have increased their efforts to understand group performance. Some contributors to group performance are: (1) *perceived freedom to participate*, (2) *perceived goal attainment*, and (3) *status consensus*.

Perceived Freedom to Participate

A group member's perception of freedom to participate influences his need satisfaction and performance. Work group members who perceive themselves as active participants report that they are more satisfied, whereas those who perceive their freedom to participate as insignificant are typically the least-satisfied members in a work group.

Figure 13–8   Checklist for learning about groups.

Area of Concern	Questions to Answer
1. Activities	Who does what job in the group?
2. Interactions	Who initiates contact? How frequently? On what issues?
3. Norms	What are the task and the behavioral norms? How clear are the norms to the members?
4. Leaders	Who are the informal leaders?
5. Status	What is the status order?
6. Cohesiveness	How cohesive is the group? On what issues is its cohesiveness greatest?
7. Group politics	How much political maneuvering goes on in the group?
8. Performance	How does the group's performance compare to that of other groups? Has its performance fluctuated? When?

The freedom-to-participate phenomenon is related to the entire spectrum of economic and sociopsychological needs. For example, their perceived ability to participate may lead individuals to believe that they are valued members of the group. This assumption can lead to the satisfaction of social, esteem, and self-actualization needs which in turn leads to high levels of performance.

Perceived Goal Attainment

Perceiving that you are progressing toward the attainment of desired goals is an important factor in the performance of group members. Members of groups that have clearly progressed toward results indicate higher levels of satisfaction than members of groups that have not progressed adequately. Goal attainment is effective performance.

At IBM, a technique called *process quality management* (PQM) uses teamwork and goal setting to achieve good group performance.[16] First, an IBM project team develops a clear understanding of the group's mission. Then the team decides on critical success targets or goals—what the team must accomplish to achieve its mission. Consensus on these targets is vital. IBM's European manufacturing arm used PQM goals when it launched a series of changes in continuous-flow manufacturing. The

---

[16]Maurice Hardaker and Bryan K. Ward, "How to Make a Team Work," *Harvard Business Review*, November–December 1987, pp. 112–20.

spirit and morale of the group was so high that problems were overcome, commitment increased, and cost outcomes and quality improved. Reaching the established goals helped increase the cohesiveness experienced by the PQM team.

Status Consensus

Status consensus is defined as agreement about the relative status of all group members. Suppose a person has a high rank or worth because he has a valued characteristic such as education, but is not experienced to perform a group role. In that case, a lack of status consensus or *status incongruence* would exist. A recent college graduate might face status incongruence if she is placed in a position to lead a group of experienced technicians. This lack of consensus between education and experience for the position would create an uncomfortable work atmosphere. According to formal organization procedures, the leader has authority and the responsibility to direct the group. However, the experienced workers likely would not trust the untested opinions and ideas of the new, inexperienced leader. The result might be covertly slowing down performance or even sabotaging the young leader's directives. In any event, a lack of status consensus within a group can cause decreased performance and less satisfaction.

Managers must work with groups and know how they function and perform. Managers who understand groups are better able to turn inevitable group characteristics into positive forces to accomplish desirable performance objectives. Without a solid understanding of group structure, processes, development, and consequences, the manager is placed at an uncomfortable disadvantage. Figure 13–8 presents guidelines that managers can use to learn more about their groups.

MANAGEMENT SOLUTION

THE USE OF CONFRONTATION AND DOMINATION IN CONFLICT RESOLUTION

As the chapter indicates, conflict is inevitable in all organizations. Limited resources, communication problems, and different interests, goals, perceptions, and attitudes, are sources of conflict managers must deal with every day. The management challenge faced by Andrew Grove could be attacked indirectly or directly. Grove decided to meet it with a direct attack.

The next time the manufacturing manager came in to complain about the quality assurance manager, Grove raised his hand and said, "Stop." He then said, "Let's get the other person in here." When he appeared, Grove said to the manufacturing manager in his office, "Now tell me what you were going to say." Grove confronted the conflict directly by using a domination approach. The confrontation between the two managers was tense and embarrassing. However, after a few direct confrontation ses-

Continued

MANAGEMENT SOLUTION

Concluded

sions, both managers learned to deal with each other instead of bringing the problem to Grove, the boss. Grove didn't become an enemy. Instead, he used his position to insist on the resolution of an interpersonal conflict that also was affecting the group members the two managers represented.

The response selected by Grove had a pos-

itive ending. He elected to confront the warring managers instead of avoiding the problem. Sometimes the hardest part of a manager's job is concluding that confrontation is the best way to attack a problem.

Source: Adapted from Andrew S. Grove, "How to Make Confrontation Work for You," *Fortune*, July 23, 1984, pp. 73–75.

MANAGEMENT SUMMARY

☐ Managers must deal with formal and informal groups. Even in the most efficiently managed organizations informal groups will emerge.

☐ Groups are formed to satisfy needs— organizational, economic, and sociopsychological.

☐ Groups develop over a period of time and because of interaction. This suggests that if a mature group is what a manager wants, then the group will have to be kept together.

☐ The different types of groups that managers are involved with as members or leaders include task, command, friendship, and interest groups. Each of these types satisfies some set of needs of the group members.

☐ Group characteristics include emergent leaders, norms, cohesiveness, status, and politics. These are areas that managers must learn about through careful observation.

☐ Group cohesiveness and conformity may result in groupthink—everyone goes along with the group because it is all-powerful.

☐ Group politics can have a negative impact on performance. Providing a good model that minimizes political maneuvering is one procedure a manager can adopt to minimize the dysfunctions of group politics.

☐ To improve the ability to work effectively with groups, it is important for the manager to observe and to ask the right questions.

REVIEW AND DISCUSSION QUESTIONS

1. Explain how a group can exercise control over its members.

2. A manager stated that if he were doing a good job of managing, no informal groups would be formed by subordinates. Do you agree? Explain.

3. Why is it better for managers to try indirect methods of resolving intergroup conflict before becoming directly involved?

4. Why has teamwork become a more recognized concept in the past few years?

5. Why would it be difficult for a group leader to blend the talents of a group of creative individuals?

6. Is the mutual acceptance phase of a group's development the point at which the group exercises control most effectively?

7. Why is proximity a factor that can encourage the formation of groups?

8. Should a manager be excited about having a highly cohesive group of subordinates?

9. Why is self-serving group behavior usually viewed as group politics?

10. Why is being a good listener an important requirement for serving as the chairperson of a committee?

CASES

13–1 THE WORK TEAM APPROACH AT TEXAS INSTRUMENTS

Any chief executive in organizations from small job shops to large firms regularly faces problems that defy easy or quick answers. How can our market share be increased? What foreign markets should we enter? Should we buy a company that is for sale? How can productivity and individual performance be improved? The chief executive can turn to old standbys such as hiring a management consultant or appointing a committee to study the problem. Or she can do what more and more firms are doing: set up short-term task forces or work teams to come to grips with the broad and important problems.

Task forces are groups of people who typically focus on a single issue rather than a laundry list of issues. On the other hand, a *work team* is a group of workers who spring into action when a need arises. But the team is not disbanded like a task force is once a problem has been solved.

At Texas Instruments (TI), work teams are considered the best way to solve work-related problems. More than two-thirds of TI's 60,000 plus employees worldwide participate in work teams. TI feels that task forces can't be assembled fast enough to deal with problems requiring quick response. TI wanted something more permanent. Thus, workers are grouped, based on work area, into work teams.

After study and deliberation, the work teams at TI have drastically changed a number of work procedures. For example, TI workers now use hair dryers instead of paper towels to dry silicon components (which reduces the drying time to about one tenth of what it had been). Work teams also came up with a new drill device and developed a computerized communication network that managers and employees can use to exchange technical information.

The TI work teams are given credit for increasing the company's productivity by 15 percent. In addition, TI's management believes that the work teams break down barriers of mistrust between workers and management. Also, more workers think about and work at problem solving. These problem-solving concerns are job related and meaningful to the workers. There is also at TI a feeling of being in on things and taking pride in helping the team do something.

Under the TI work team approach, the choice of solutions is left to the workers—for example, a TI plant in Malaysia was experiencing excessive scrap rates and a work team came up with a solution. The team responsible for production now affixes labels bearing the team name on parts shipped to customers. The team feels pride in seeing its tag on products being shipped to customers.

Most managers at TI believe that work teams are good for morale, productivity, and cost control. However, a few critics believe that work teams are taking away the need for managers. What will happen if the work teams become even more effective? Some feel that many managers will have to be terminated. If the work team idea works too well, management morale and attitudes may become serious problems at TI.

Questions

1. Are the TI work teams a formal or informal group?
2. What type of group measures of performance can be used at TI?
3. Do you see any possibilities for work team intergroup conflict at TI? Explain.

Source: Adapted from Tom Peters, *Thriving on Chaos* (New York: Alfred A. Knopf, 1987); and Michael A. Verespej, "Mission Extraordinary? Call for a Task Force," *Industry Week*, October 19, 1981, pp. 66–72.

13–2 THE UNDERPERFORMING GROUP

Dan Vance recently was transferred to the company's largest plant. Dan wanted to do the best job possible, and he thought about the kind of strategy that was needed to start off on the right foot. During his first two months on the job, he observed the work of his 12 subordinates and took notes on how they worked together, who the informal leaders were, and how task oriented they were. He decided that the average group production level of 4,100 units per week was lower than it could be if the group was motivated properly. Dan also noticed that the output of the individual group members ranged from 338 units to 347 units per week. That is, the highest performer produced 347 units and the lowest performer produced 338 units. Everyone else was producing an amount between these two figures.

After the observation period and some careful analysis, Dan believed that the way to increase production was to work through the two informal leaders of the group, Randy Bice and Chet Galic. He called Randy and Chet into his office to discuss the group and its production output. Both of them expressed the opinion that the group was at its limit of endurance and performance. Dan, in a tactful manner, disagreed and expressed the opinion that if the group were inclined to do so, it could increase the average group output by at least 1,000 units a week. He pointed out the following production levels of the six groups working in the manufacturing department.

Group Leaders	Average Group Weekly Output
Bruce	4,900
Tony	6,100
Marcus	5,300
Tyrone	4,800
Julio	4,900
Dan	4,100

Dan also hinted that the skills and abilities of the members of the other groups were no better than those of the members in his group.

Randy and Chet seemed surprised about the figures. They did not commit the group to a higher production level, but they did state that they wanted to check a few things and to meet with Dan in about a week.

Questions

1. What do you think Randy and Chet were going to check?
2. How do you rate Dan's approach to this situation?
3. What could be the next step for Dan to take?

EXERCISE

13–1 GROUP BRAINSTORMING IN ACTION

Purpose: The purpose of this exercise is to provide experience in group brainstorming—to learn to use and pool the ideas, good and bad, of group members.

Setting Up the Exercise: The rules for the group brainstorming session are:

- ☐ Each group member is to contribute at least two ideas. The ideas must be written on a sheet of paper.
- ☐ The instructor (or group leader) will write each idea on a chalkboard or flip chart.
- ☐ Every idea will be recorded, no matter how unrealistic.
- ☐ While ideas are being recorded, there must be NO evaluation by other group members. This is an important part of brainstorming, the freedom to simply "say it like it is" and have no fear of being evaluated.

1.   The instructor will form groups of six to eight persons. A group leader will be elected. The leader serves mainly as a recorder of ideas. He should also contribute ideas.

2.   The groups will brainstorm and develop solutions to the following problem:

> The midwest region of the United States is becoming known as the "rust bowl" of America. Steelworkers and autoworkers have been losing their jobs. Today, there are only 260,000 steelworkers in the United States, while in 1977 there were 460,000. Most of the job loss has occurred in the "rust bowl" states—Illinois, Michigan, Ohio, Indiana, and Pennsylvania. The dire prediction is that those who have lost their jobs will never again work in steel mills or auto plants. The jobs are lost forever. Assume that this prediction is basically correct. Using a brainstorming method, develop some solutions that labor, management, and government can take to ease the social, emotional, and psychological pain of job-loss victims. What should and can be done?

3.   Each group member independently is to develop two solutions for the job-loss problem. After about 20 minutes, begin recording the solutions.

4.   Discuss the brainstorming procedure in the group. What would be the next step to take once brainstorming is completed, if it were being done in an organization?

A Learning Note: This exercise will indicate that it is rather difficult to brainstorm. The technique sounds easy, but it is difficult to accomplish. Group members will find that during the brainstorming, it is difficult to refrain from evaluating the quality of each idea.

COMPREHENSIVE CASE

13–1 WORK GROUP OWNERSHIP OF AN IMPROVED TOOL

The Whirlwind Aircraft Corporation was a leader in its field and especially noted for its development of the modern supercharger. Work in connection with the supercharger called for special skill and ability. Every detail had to be perfect to satisfy the exacting requirements of the aircraft industry.

In 1941 (before Pearl Harbor), Lathe Department 15–D was turning out three types of impeller, each contoured to within 0.002 inch and machined to a mirrorlike finish. The impellers were made from an aluminum alloy and finished on a cam-back lathe.

The work was carried on in four shifts, two men on each. The personnel in the finishing section were as follows:

1. *First Shift*—7 A.M. to 3 P.M. Sunday and Monday off.
   a. Jean Latour, master mechanic, French Canadian, 45 years of age. Latour had set up the job and trained the men who worked with him on the first shift.
   b. Pierre DuFresne, master mechanic, French Canadian, 36 years of age. Both these men had trained the workers needed for the other shifts.

2. *Second Shift*—3 P.M. to 11 P.M. Friday and Saturday off.
   a. Albert Durand, master mechanic, French Canadian, 32 years of age; trained by Latour and using his lathe.
   b. Robert Benet, master mechanic, French Canadian, 31 years of age; trained by DuFresne and using his lathe.

3. *Third Shift*—11 P.M. to 7 A.M. Tuesday and Wednesday off.
   a. Philippe Doret, master mechanic, French Canadian, 31 years of age; trained by Latour and using his lathe.
   b. Henri Barbet, master mechanic, French Canadian, 30 years of age; trained by DuFresne and using his lathe.

4. *Stagger Shift*—Monday, 7 A.M. to 3 P.M.; Tuesday, 11 P.M. to 7 A.M.; Wednesday, 11 P.M. to 7 A.M.; Thursday, off; Friday, 3 P.M. to 11 P.M.; Saturday, 3 P.M. to 11 P.M.; Sunday, off.
   a. George MacNair, master mechanic, Scotsman, 32 years of age, trained by Latour and using his lathe.
   b. William Reader, master mechanic, English, 30 years of age; trained by DuFresne and using his lathe.

Owing to various factors (such as the small number of workers involved, the preponderance of one nationality, and the fact that Latour and DuFresne had trained the other workers), these eight men considered themselves as members of one work group. Such a feeling of solidarity is unusual among workers on different shifts, despite the fact that they use the same machines.

The men received a base rate of $1.03 an hour and worked on incentive. Each man usually turned out 22 units a shift, thus earning an average of $1.19 an hour. Management supplied Rex 95 High-Speed Tool-Bits, which workers ground to suit themselves. Two tools were used: one square bit with a slight radius for recess cutting, the other bit with a 45-degree angle for chamfering and smooth finish. When used, both tools were set close together, the worker adjusting the lathe from one operation to the other. The difficulty with this setup was that during the rotation of the lathe, the aluminum waste would melt and fuse between the two toolbits. Periodically, the lathe had to be stopped so the toolbits could be freed from the welded aluminum and reground.

At the request of the supervisor of Lathe Department 15–D, the methods department had been working on the tool problem. Up to the time of this case, no solution had been found. To make a first-hand study of the difficulty, the methods department had recently assigned one of its staff, Mr. MacBride, to investigate the problem in the lathe department itself. MacBride's working hours covered parts of both the first and second shifts. MacBride was a young man, 26 years of age, and a newcomer to the methods department. For the three months prior to this assignment, he had held the post of "suggestion man," a position which enabled newcomers to the methods department to familiarize themselves with the plant setup. The job consisted in collecting, from boxes in departments throughout the plant, suggestions submitted by employees and making a preliminary evaluation of these ideas. The current assignment of studying the tool situation in Lathe Department 15–D, with a view to cutting costs, was his first special task. He devoted himself to this problem with greal zeal but did not succeed in winning the confidence of the workers. In pursuance of their usual philosophy, "Keep your mouth shut if you see anyone with a suit on," they volunteered no information and took the stance that, since the methods man had been given this assignment, it was up to him to carry it out.

While MacBride was working on this problem, Pierre DuFresne hit upon a solution. One day he successfully contrived a tool which combined the two bits into one. This eliminated the space between the two toolbits, which in the past had caught the molten aluminum waste and allowed it to become welded to the cutting edges. The new toolbit had two advantages: It eliminated the frequent machine stoppage for cleaning and regrinding the old-type tools, and it enabled the operator to run the lathe at a higher speed. These advantages made it possible for the operator to increase his efficiency 50 percent.

DuFresne tried to make copies of the new tool but was unable to do so. Apparently the new development had been a lucky accident during grinding which he could not duplicate. After several unsuccessful attempts, he took the new tool to his former teacher, Jean Latour. The latter succeeded in making a drawing and turning out duplicate toolbits on a small grinding wheel in the shop. At first, the two men decided to keep the new tool to themselves. Later, however, they shared the improvement with their fellow workers on the second shift. Similarly, it was passed on to the other shifts. But all these men kept the new development a closely guarded secret as far as "outsiders" were concerned. At the end of the shift, each locked the improved toolbit securely in his toolchest.

Both DuFresne, the originator of the new tool, and Latour, its draftsman and designer, decided not to submit the idea as a suggestion but to keep it as the property of their group. Why was this decision made? The answer lies partly in the attitude of Latour and DuFresne toward other features of company work life and toward their group.

According to an information bulletin issued by the company, the purpose of the suggestion system was to "provide an orderly method of submitting and considering ideas and recommendations of employees to management; to provide a means for recognizing and rewarding individual ingenuity; and to promote cooperation." Awards for accepted suggestions were made in the following manner: "After checking the savings and expense involved in an adopted suggestion, [the suggestion committee] determined the amount of the award to be paid, based upon the savings predicted upon a year's use of the suggestion. It is the intention of the committee . . . to be liberal in the awards, which are expected to adequately compensate for the interest shown in presenting suggestions." In pursuance of this policy, it was customary to grant the suggestor an award equivalent to the savings of an entire month.

Both DuFresne and Latour considered an award based on one month's saving inadequate. They also argued that such awards were really taken out of the workers' pockets. Their reasoning was as follows: All awards for adopted suggestions were paid out of undistributed profits. Since the company also had a profit sharing plan, the money was taken from a fund that would be given to the workers anyway, which merely meant robbing Peter to pay Paul. In any case, the payment was not likely to be large and probably would be less than they could accumulate if increased incentive payments could be maintained over an extended period without discovery. Thus, there was little in favor of submitting the new tool as a suggestion.

Latour and DuFresne also felt that there were definite hazards to the group if their secret were disclosed. They feared that once the tool became company property, its efficiency might lead to the layoff of some members in their group, or at least make work less tolerable by leading to an increased quota at a lower price per unit. They also feared that there might be a change in scheduled work assignments. For instance, the lathe department worked on three different types of impeller. One type was a routine job and, aside from the difficulty caused by the old-type tool, presented no problem. For certain technical reasons, the other two types were more difficult to make. Even Latour, an exceptionally skilled craftsman, had sometimes found it hard to make the expected quota before the new tool was developed. Unless the work was carefully balanced by scheduling easier and more difficult types, some of the operators were unable to make standard time.

The decision to keep the tool for their own group was in keeping with Latour's work philosophy. He had a strong feeling of loyalty to his own group and had demonstrated this in the past by offering for their use several improvements of his own. For example, he made available to all workers in his group a set of special gauge blocks which were used in aligning work of lathes. To protect himself in case mistakes were traced to these gauges, he wrote on them: "Personnel *(sic)* Property—Do not use. Jean Latour."

Through informal agreement with their fellow workers, Latour and DuFresne "pegged production" at an efficiency rate that in their opinion would not arouse management's suspicion or lead to a restudy of the job, with possible cutting of the rate. This enabled them to earn an extra 10 percent incentive earnings. The other 40 percent in additional efficiency was used as follows: The operators established a reputation for a high degree of accuracy and finish. They set a record for no spoilage and were able to apply the time gained on the easier type of impeller to work on the other types which required greater care and more expert workmanship.

The foreman of the lathe department learned about the new tool soon after it was put into use but was satisfied to let the men handle the situation in their own way. He reasoned that at little expense he was able to get out production of high quality. There was no defective work, and the men were contented.

MacBride was left in a very unsatisfactory position. He had not succeeded in working out a solution of his own. Like the foreman, he got wind of the fact that the men had devised a new tool. He urged them to submit a drawing of it through the suggestion system, but they did not take this advice, and the men made it plain that they did not care to discuss with him the reasons for this position.

Having no success in his direct contact with the workers, MacBride appealed to the foreman, asking him to secure a copy of the new tool. The foreman replied that the men would certainly decline to give him a copy and would resent as an injustice any effort on his part to force them to submit a drawing. Instead, he suggested that MacBride should persuade DuFresne to show him the tool. This MacBride attempted to do, but met with no success in his efforts to ingratiate himself with DuFresne. When he persisted in his attempts, DuFresne decided to throw him off the track. He left in his lathe a toolbit which was an unsuccessful copy of the original discovery. At shift change, MacBride was delighted to find what he supposed to be the improved tool. He hastily copied it and submitted a drawing to the tool department. When a tool was made up according to these specifications, it naturally failed to do what was expected of it. The workers, when they heard of this through the "grapevine," were delighted. DuFresne did not hesitate to crow over MacBride, pointing out that his underhanded methods had met with their just reward.

The foreman did not take any official notice of the conflict between DuFresne and MacBride. Then MacBride complained to the foreman that DuFresne was openly boasting of his trick and ridiculing him before other workers. The foreman talked to DuFresne, but the latter insisted that his ruse had been justified as a means of self-protection.

When he was rebuffed by DuFresne, the foreman felt that he had lost control of the situation. He no longer could conceal from himself that he was confronted by a more complex situation than what initially he had defined as a "tool problem." His attention was drawn to the fact that the state of affairs in his department was a tangle of several interrelated problems. Each problem urgently called for a decision that involved understanding and practical judgment. But having for so long failed to see the situation as a whole, he now found himself in a dilemma.

He wished to keep the goodwill of the work group, but he could not countenance the continued friction between DuFresne and MacBride. Certainly, he could not openly abet his operators in obstructing the work of a methods man. His superintendent would now certainly hear of it and would be displeased to learn that a foreman had failed to tell him of such an important technical improvement. Furthermore, he knew that the aircraft industry was expanding at this time and that the demand for impellers had increased to such an extent that management was planning to set up an entire new plant unit devoted to this product.

Questions

1. In your opinion, what were the causes of the high degree of group cohesion in Lathe Department 15–D?
2. If you were the manager (foreman), how would you get the improved tool from the group?
3. Was the lathe department a motivated group? Explain.

Source: From *Personnel Administration: A Point of View and a Method*, 1956 ed. by Pigors & Myers. Copyright © McGraw-Hill Book Company, 1956. Used with permission of McGraw-Hill Book Company.

PART V

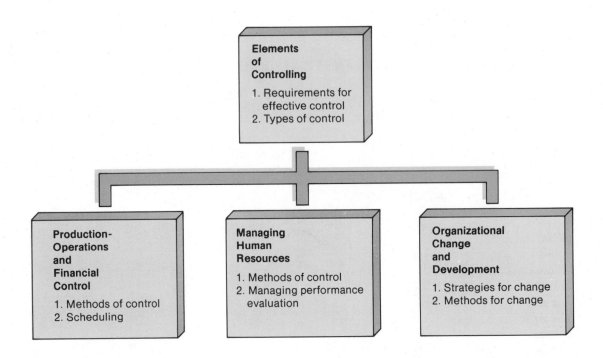

Elements of Controlling

1. Requirements for effective control
2. Types of control

Production-Operations and Financial Control

1. Methods of control
2. Scheduling

Managing Human Resources

1. Methods of control
2. Managing performance evaluation

Organizational Change and Development

1. Strategies for change
2. Methods for change

THE CONTROLLING FUNCTION

INTRODUCTION TO PART V

Part V, The controlling function, contains four chapters.

The inclusion of the material contained in the four chapters is based on the following rationale:

The controlling function involves comparing actual results with planned results and, consequently, *making changes* in individual and group behavior, in financial and technical processes and, often, in the organization itself. Consequently, the essential feature of managerial control is *change*.

The four chapters comprising Part V cover various aspects of the activities of managerial control. Chapter 14 presents the *elements of controlling* with emphasis on requirements for effective control and types of control. Chapter 15 presents control in the context of *production and operations activities*. The focus of management in controlling production and operations includes the material, machines, and financial resources necessary to achieve the objectives of the organization. Chapter 16 stresses control from the perspective of *human resource performance*. The focus of the discussion in that chapter is the work performance of employees and the extent to which their actual performances are consistent with performance standards. The last chapter, Chapter 17, examines the problems and potentials associated with actions to *change the total organization*. Here, the focus is not on any one aspect of the organization, its human and nonhuman resources, but on the entity itself. Managers must at times consider the possibility that results can be achieved only after significant change in the total organization.

The figure on the facing page depicts the four aspects of the controlling function.

FOURTEEN

Elements of Controlling

LEARNING OBJECTIVES

After completing Chapter 14, you should be able to:

Define: the concept of managerial control.

State: the necessary conditions for effective control.

Describe: the steps in developing an integrated quality control system.

Explain: the role of information in managerial control decisions.

Discuss: the eight dimensions of quality.

HARD TIMES AT XEROX CORPORATION

When David Kearns assumed the CEO position at Xerox Corp. in 1982, he confronted a major challenge: how to turn around a hot growth company that had suddenly gone cold. For years, Xerox had enjoyed booming profits and sales growth largely through its exclusive world rights to the xerographic process. Xerox produced copier machines that changed the way people work.

However, by the late 1970s, many companies were licensing the xerographic technology, and Xerox's exclusive patent was expiring. The companies were providing tough competition. The Japanese focused on the low-volume, low-cost segment of the copier market and were producing higher quality copiers than those offered by Xerox. The copiers were also lower priced; the Japanese had developed superior product design, manufacturing processes, and cost control techniques that substantially lowered manufacturing costs.

Meanwhile, Xerox Corp. had become highly bureaucratic and complacent. The company acquired several high-technology companies in the 1970s to provide new product ideas, but Xerox's slow-moving bureaucracy prevented several good ideas from being translated into competitive products.

By 1980, the company suddenly found that the Japanese had more than a 40 percent cost advantage in copiers and that its market share in copiers had severely declined. CEO Kearns believed Xerox faced two challenges: regain its lost market share and rejuvenate the company's sinking employee morale.

(The Management Solution to this Management Incident can be found at the end of this chapter.)

The *controlling function* consists of *actions and decisions managers undertake to ensure that actual results are consistent with desired results.* The key to effective *controlling* is to plan for specific results. Unless managers decide in advance what level of performance they want, they will have no basis for judging actual performance. As described in earlier chapters, when managers plan, they establish the ways and means to achieve objectives. These objectives are the targets, the desired results, that management expects the organization to achieve.

After planning, managers must deploy their organizations' resources to achieve results. And although resources can be allocated and activities can be planned, managers must recognize that unforeseen events such as fuel shortages, strikes, machine breakdowns, competitive actions, and governmental influence can sidetrack the organization from its initial plans. Thus, managers must be prepared and able to redirect their organization's activities toward accomplishing the original objectives. To do this, managers must understand the concept of *necessary conditions for control*.

NECESSARY CONDITIONS FOR CONTROL

Effective control requires three basic conditions: (1) *standards* that reflect the ideal outcomes, (2) *information* that indicates deviations between actual and standard results, and (3) *corrective action* for any deviations between actual and standard results. The logic is evident: Without standards, there can be no way of knowing the situation; and without provision for action to correct deviations, the entire control process becomes a pointless exercise.

Standards

Standards are derived from objectives and have many of the same characteristics. Like objectives, standards are targets; to be effective, they must be stated clearly and be related logically to objectives. Standards are the criteria that enable managers to evaluate future, current, or past actions. They are measured in a variety of ways, including physical, monetary, quantitative, and qualitative terms. The various forms standards take depend on *what* is being measured and on *the managerial level responsible* for taking corrective action.

As a manager moves up in the organization, the standards for which he is accountable become more abstract, and the causes for deviations become more difficult to identify. Chief executive officers gauge the success of their organizations against standards such as "service to the public," "quality health care," and "customer satisfaction." These abstract criteria have no obvious method of measurement. But managers at the top of an organization are not the only ones who must deal with difficult-to-measure standards. For example, managers of staff units that provide service to line units also have problems determining standards to guide their units' actions.

Information

Information that reports actual performance and permits appraisal of that performance against standards is necessary. Such information is most easily acquired for activities that produce specific results. For example, production and sales activities have easily identifiable end products for which information is readily obtainable. The performance of legal departments, research and development units, or personnel departments is more difficult to evaluate, however, because the outputs of these units are difficult to measure.

Corrective Action

Corrective actions depend on the discovery of deviations and the ability to take necessary action. The people responsible for taking the corrective action must know (1) that they are indeed responsible and (2) that they have the assigned authority to take those steps. The jobs and position descriptions must include specific statements clearly delineating these two requirements. Otherwise, the control function likely will fall short of its potential contribution to organizational performance. Responsibilities that fall between the jobs of two individuals are undesirable, but sometimes unavoidable. Managers who work in organizations facing uncertain and unpredictable environments often confront unanticipated situations—the kinds not stated in job descriptions.

The essential elements of management control are diagrammed in Figure 14–1. The control function involves implementing *methods* that will provide answers to three basic questions: (1) What are the planned and expected results? (2) By what means can the actual results be compared to the planned results? (3) What corrective action is appropriate from which authorized person?

THREE TYPES OF CONTROL METHODS

Control methods can be classified according to their foci. Three different types of control methods are identified in Figure 14–2.

Precontrol

Precontrol methods increase the possibility that future actual results will compare favorably with planned results. Policies are important precontrol methods since they define appropriate future action. Other precontrol methods involve human, capital, and financial resources.

Precontrol of *human resources* depends on job requirements. Job requirements predetermine the skills needed by the job holders. How specific the skills must be will depend on the nature of the task. At the shop level, for example, the skills needed may include specific physical attributes and degrees of manual dexterity. On the other hand, the job requirements for management and staff personnel can be more difficult to define with concrete measurements. Chapter 16 discusses this problem in more detail.[1]

---

[1]Precontrol of human resources is one element of personnel management. See George T. Milkovich and John W. Boudreau, *Personnel/Human Resource Management: A Diagnostic Approach* (Plano, Tex.: Business Publications, 1988); and Herbert G. Heneman III, Donald P. Schwab, John A. Fossum, and Lee D. Dyer, *Personnel Human Resource Management* (Homewood, Ill.: Richard D. Irwin, 1980).

Figure 14–1 Management control.

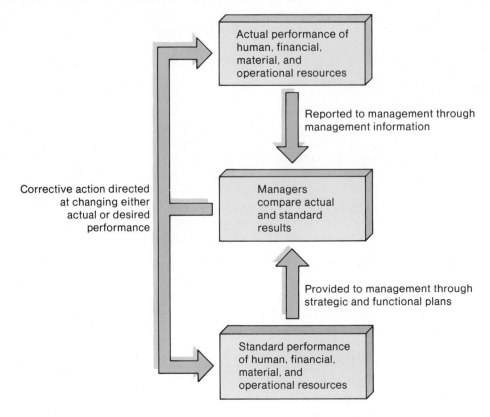

The acquisition of *capital* reflects the need to replace existing equipment or to expand the firm's productive capacity. Capital acquisitions can be precontrolled by establishing criteria of potential profitability that must be met before the acquisitions are authorized. Decisions involving the commitment of present funds in exchange for future funds are termed *investment decisions*. Control methods that screen investment proposals are derived from financial analysis, as will be shown in Chapter 15.

Adequate *financial* resources must be available to ensure the payment of obligations arising from current operations. Materials must be purchased, wages paid, and interest charges and due dates met. Budgets—particularly cash and working capital budgets—are the principal means for precontrolling the availability and cost of financial resources. These budgets anticipate the ebb and flow of business activity when materials are purchased, finished goods are produced, goods are sold, and cash is received. This cycle of activity, the operating cycle, results in a problem of *timing* the availability of cash to meet the obligations. As inventories of finished goods increase, material, labor, and other expenses are incurred and paid, and the supply of cash decreases. As

Figure 14–2   Three types of control methods.

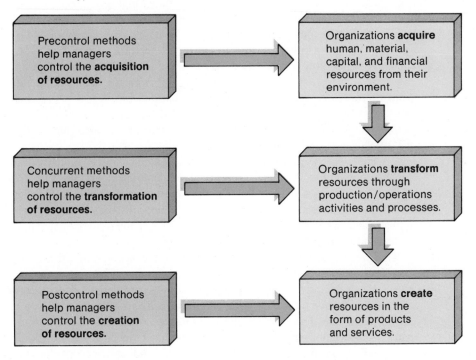

inventory is sold, the supply of cash increases. Precontrol of cash requires that funds be available during the period of inventory buildup, and that cash be used wisely during periods of abundance. Chapter 15 discusses some of the more widely used financial control methods.

Concurrent Control

Concurrent control consists primarily of actions by supervisors who direct the work of their subordinates. *Direction* refers to the acts managers undertake (1) to instruct subordinates in the proper methods and procedures and (2) to oversee the work of subordinates to ensure that it is done properly. Direction follows the formal chain of command, since the responsibility of each manager is to interpret for subordinates the orders received from higher echelons. The relative importance of direction depends almost entirely on the nature of the tasks performed by subordinates. The manager of an assembly line that produces a component part requiring relatively simple manual operations may seldom engage in direction. On the other hand, the manager of a research and development unit must devote considerable time to direction. Research work is inherently more complex and varied than manual work and requires more interpretation and instruction.

Directing is the primary activity of the first-line supervisor, but every manager in an organization engages at some time in directing employees.[2] As a manager moves up the hierarchy, however, the relative importance of directing diminishes and other responsibilities become more important.

Other factors also determine differences in the form of direction. For example, direction is basically a process of *interpersonal communication,* so the *amount* and *clarity* of information are important factors. Subordinates must receive sufficient information to carry out the task, and they must understand that information. On the other hand, too much information and too much detail can be damaging. The manager's mode and tone of voice used in delivering the information also can greatly influence the effectiveness of direction.

Effective direction depends on effective communication. A directive must be reasonable, intelligible, appropriately worded, and consistent with the overall objectives of the organization. The subordinate rather than the manager will decide whether these criteria have been met. Many managers have assumed that their directives were straightforward and to the point, and then discovered that their subordinates had failed to understand them or had refused to accept them as legitimate.

The process of direction involves not only the *manner* in which directives are communicated but also the *manner* of the person who directs.[3] A supervisor may be autocratic or democratic, permissive or directive, considerate or inconsiderate. Each of these could have different impacts on the effectiveness of direction as a concurrent control technique. Direction involves day-to-day overseeing of the work of subordinates. As deviations from standards are identified, managers must take immediate corrective action by coaching their subordinates and showing them how to perform their assigned tasks appropriately.

Using the authority of position to achieve concurrent control has become increasingly difficult. Rapidly changing markets and technology often force managers to use decision-making approaches outside the formal chain of command. These approaches bring together employees with the expertise to solve the problem or to make the decision. In such settings, influence, not authority, is the appropriate way to manage.

Postcontrol

Postcontrol employs *historical* outcomes as bases for correcting *future* actions. For example, a firm's financial statements can be used to evaluate the acceptability of historical results and to determine if changes should be made in future resource acquisitions or operational activities. Four postcontrol methods are widely used in business: financial statement analysis, standard cost analysis, employee performance evaluation, and quality control. Subsequent chapters will give greater attention to the first three control methods; the following discussion provides basic descriptions of these methods.

---

[2]Lawrence L. Steinmetz and H. Ralph Todd, Jr., *First-Line Management,* 3d ed. (Plano, Tex.: Business Publications, 1986).

[3]Cortland Cammann and David Nadler, "Fit Control Systems to Your Managerial Style," *Harvard Business Review,* January–February 1976, pp. 65–72.

A firm's accounting system is a principal source of information from which managers can evaluate historical results. Periodically, managers receive *financial statements* which usually include a balance sheet, an income statement, and a sources-and-uses-of-funds statement. These statements summarize and classify the effects of transactions in terms of assets, liabilities, equity, revenues, and expenses—the principal components of the firm's financial structure.[4]

Standard cost accounting systems are a major contribution of scientific management. A standard cost system provides information that enables management to compare actual costs with predetermined (standard) costs. Management then can take appropriate corrective action or assign others the authority to take action. The first uses of standard cost accounting were concerned with manufacturing costs. In recent years, however, standard cost accounting has been applied to selling expenses and general and administrative expenses.[5]

The most difficult postcontrol method is *performance evaluation*. Yet good performance evaluation is important, because people are the most crucial resource in any organization. Effective business firms, hospitals, universities, and governments must have people who are effectively performing their assigned duties. Evaluating performance can be very difficult, however, because the standards for performance seldom are objective and straightforward. Furthermore, many managerial and nonmanagerial jobs do not produce outputs that can be counted, weighed, and evaluated in objective terms.

Each control method, whether precontrol, concurrent control, or postcontrol, requires the same three fundamental elements: *standards, information,* and *corrective action*. Of the three, information is the element most critical for effective control. Managers act on the basis of information—reports, documents, position papers, and analyses. Without information, standards could not be set, and corrective action could not be taken.

AN INTEGRATED CONTROL SYSTEM

Precontrol, concurrent, and postcontrol methods are not mutually exclusive. Rather, they usually are combined into an integrated control system. Such a control system must provide for standards, information, and corrective action at every point, from input to process to output. An example of an integrated control system is described below. It involves efforts to control the *quality* of a product or service.

Managers desire manufacturing processes that produce output with no defects. But for many reasons, 100 percent, defect-free goods usually are impossible to create. The quality of raw materials varies; machines operate imperfectly; employees have different levels of skills. Thus, managers know defects will be produced. Today, quality has

---

[4]See Burton A. Kolb and Richard DeMong, *Principles of Financial Management* (Plano, Tex.: Business Publications, 1988); George Foster, *Financial Statement Analysis* (Englewood Cliffs, N.J.: Prentice-Hall, 1978); and Diane Harrington and Brent D. Wilson, *Corporate Financial Analysis* (Plano, Tex.: Business Publications, 1986).

[5]See Ralph H. Garrison, *Managerial Accounting: Concepts for Planning, Control, Decision Making* (Plano, Tex.: Business Publications, 1988).

become an increasingly important control issue. Although quality perfection is not possible, a growing number of companies are working to substantially improve the quality of the goods and services they produce.[6]

Quality Is Important

Quality has always been an important aspect of business management. High-quality products lead to customer goodwill and satisfaction. These, in turn, create repeat sales, loyal customers and clients, and testimonials to prospective customers or clients. Today, many organizations are elevating the importance of quality to a key element of their business strategy. The focus on meeting quality objectives is not limited to the production department. Top management considers quality improvement and high-quality standards to be vital corporate objectives. They—and in many cases employees companywide—are becoming actively involved in finding ways to improve quality.[7]

This energized focus on quality is due, in part, to three factors:

Customers want quality.   Recent surveys on customer quality preferences indicate that consumers highly value quality and are willing to pay more to receive it. For example, a Gallup poll for the American Society of Quality Control found that consumers typically are willing to pay one third more for a high-quality car ($13,581 rather than $10,000). They would pay over 50 percent more for a high rather than an average-quality dishwasher ($464 versus $300), and they would accept double the price for a solid rather than average-quality pair of shoes ($47 versus $20).[8] At the same time, however, recent studies indicate that consumers are displeased with the quality of U.S. products and services. One survey found that almost half of American consumers feel that quality has declined in the late 1970s and early 1980s; over one fourth believe that U.S. businesses cannot reliably produce quality goods and services.

Quality is linked to organizational performance.   According to recent research, high quality has a profound impact on organization performance. The Strategic Planning Institute of Cambridge, Massachusetts, has studied the performance of over 2,600 businesses for several years. Its finding: companies with the highest quality earn the highest profits. In this study, quality was defined as a consumer's perception of a company's quality compared to its competitors. Specifically, the study found that companies that rated in the top-third group on quality earned twice as much profit as

---

[6]Several excellent books are available on quality control and approaches to quality improvement. Especially noteworthy are: W. Edwards Deming, *Quality, Productivity, and Competitive Position* (Cambridge, Mass.: MIT Press, 1982); J. M. Juran, Frank M. Gryna, Jr., and R. S. Bingham, Jr., eds., *Quality Control Handbook* (New York: McGraw-Hill, 1974); A. V. Feigenbaum, *Total Quality Control* (New York: McGraw-Hill, 1983); and Richard J. Schonberger, *World Class Manufacturing: The Lessons of Simplicity Applied* (New York: The Free Press, 1986), pp. 123–43.

[7]For some interesting examples of quality improvement efforts by U.S. businesses, see Otis Port, "The Push for Quality," *Business Week,* June 8, 1987, pp. 130ff.

[8]The Gallup Organization, *Consumer Perceptions Concerning the Quality of American Products and Services,* 1985, as cited in Tom Peters, *Thriving on Chaos* (New York: Alfred A. Knopf, 1987).

those in the bottom-third group. The researchers concluded that quality pays—for the company and the consumer.[9]

International competitors are besting American quality. Japan, South Korea, Taiwan, and a host of other international competitors have established superior product quality as a chief strategy for competing abroad. So far, they have achieved exceptional quality in several key American markets, quality that has been difficult for American businesses to surpass. Their superior quality is a major factor behind permanent market share losses that U.S. businesses have sustained in the automobile, steel, and other markets. Japanese businesses have been exceptionally successful in their drive for superior quality. Dr. W. Edwards Deming, considered by many to be the father of Japan's quality achievements, is profiled in the following Management Application.

MANAGEMENT APPLICATION

DR. DEMING'S QUEST FOR QUALITY

In the post-World War II years, Japan had a worldwide reputation for producing shoddy goods. In 1950, a group of Japanese leaders invited Dr. W. Edwards Deming, a statistician with the U.S. Department of Agriculture, to teach Japanese managers and engineers how to improve their product quality. Dr. Deming accepted the invitation and for several years lectured in Japan, teaching his approach to quality control. His message: establish quality as a top-corporate objective. Approach quality control, not by inspection at the end of the production line, but by building quality into the manufacturing process. Make quality everyone's responsibility. Japan listened and trained tens of thousands of managers, workers, and engineers in Dr. Deming's procedures.

Today, many consider Dr. Deming to be the father of Japan's quality achievements. After years of obscurity in the United States, the tall, 85-year-old quality control expert is in high demand. Campbell's Soup, General Motors, the U.S. government, and many other companies have paid up to $10,000 a day for his services and approach to quality improvement.

At the core of Dr. Deming's approach is statistical process quality control. In this approach, quality is built into the manufacturing process by studying each point in the process, identifying problem areas, and then correcting them one by one. The approach requires sophisticated statistical analysis. Companies also apply Dr. Deming's approach beyond manufacturing to other processes such as administrative, R&D, and even sales jobs.

Dr. Deming's plan also includes his 14 principles for management. Among them are: Stop using traditional quality control goals of certain percentages of defective goods as acceptable because such thinking hampers quality improvement. Reduce the number of materials suppliers and focus on developing long-term relationships with good ones. Eliminate quota-based output standards for employees because they neglect quality. Work to eliminate fear in the organization—workers' fear of telling man-

[9]Strategic Planning Institute, "Product Quality," No. 4 (*Pimsletter*, 1985), p. 4.

agement that something is wrong. In Dr. Deming's view, fear is a key obstacle to quality and productivity.

Clients find that Dr. Deming is a demanding taskmaster. He believes that more than 90 percent of a company's quality problems are caused by management, not workers, and he has lectured management sternly on their shortcomings. Dr. Deming is selective about his clients; he will accept a company's request for help only if he deals directly with top management. Dr. Deming also requires that a company produce results within three years after contracting his services or he will drop the client. (Though he lives modestly, Dr. Deming prefers to be chauffered in a Lincoln Town Car on trips equipped with a refrigerator full of his favorite treat: vanilla ice cream.)

However, his approach to improved quality and quality control, works. At Ford Motor, executives call Dr. Deming "the guru" and attribute the company's recent top-quality ratings in the U.S. auto industry to his principles. And every year in Japan, the Japanese Union of Scientists and Engineers awards the nation's highest honor in industry to the company that has made the greatest strides in quality. They call the award *The Deming Prize.*

Source: Adapted from Barbara Ross, "W. Edwards Deming: Shogun of Quality Control," *Magazine for Financial Executives*, February 1986, pp. 25–31; and Jeremy Main, "Under the Spell of Quality Gurus," *Fortune*, August 18, 1986, pp. 31ff.

These three developments have sent a message to American businesses: superior quality is prized by consumers who are quite willing to pay for it. Exceptional quality benefits the company and the consumer, and quality is the new standard for domestic and international competition. As a result, more companies are working to boost quality and are asking: How can quality improvements be achieved, and how can controls effectively maintain quality improvements?

The Quality Concept

Quality has often been defined as the *perception of excellence.*[10] Although many may evaluate quality, the customer is the key perceiver of quality because his or her purchase decision determines the success of the organization's product or service, and often the fate of the organization itself.

A consumer's perception of a product/service's "excellence" is generally based on the degree to which the product or service meets his specifications and requirements. Specifically, a consumer perceives "excellence" by evaluating one or more dimensions of quality which are summarized in Table 14–1. In judging the quality of a Sony television set, for example, a prospective buyer may examine *performance*, how well the TV set performs its primary function. (Is the picture sharp, the color vivid, the sound clear?) The set's extra *features* such as automatic fine tuning may be evaluated. The rate of repair or *reliability* may be a factor as well as *serviceability*, the convenience

---

[10]Tom Peters, *Thriving on Chaos*, p. 82.

Table 14–1 Dimensions of quality.

Dimension	Example
Performance: The product/service's primary operating characteristics	Sony TV's richness of color, clarity of sound.
Features: Secondary, "extra" characteristics	Hyatt Regency's complimentary breakfasts.
Reliability: Consistent performance within a specific period	Honda Accura's rate of repair in the first year of purchase.
Conformance: Degree to which design and characteristics meet specific standards	An Apple Computer's compatibility with IBM software.
Durability: The length of a product/service's useful life	Average 17-year life of Kirby vacuum cleaners.
Serviceability: The speed, courtesy, competence and ease of repair	Caterpillar Tractor's worldwide guarantee of 48-hour delivery of replacement parts.
Aesthetics: The looks, taste, feel, sound, smell of a product/service	Flavor, texture of Baskin-Robbins ice cream.
Perceived quality Quality conveyed via marketing, brand name, reputation	Bose's reputation in stereo speakers.

Source: David A. Garvin, "Competing on the Eight Dimensions of Quality," *Harvard Business Review*, November–December 1987, pp. 101–9.

and quality of repair should a breakdown occur. *Conformance,* for example the set's compatibility with a VCR of another brand, may be assessed. *Durability,* the typical life span of the set, may also be examined as well as the visual appeal of its design (*aesthetics*). Sony's reputation for product quality may also influence the consumer's evaluation of the set's overall quality (*perceived quality*).[11]

Two points are noteworthy concerning a consumer's "perception of excellence" or quality. First, consumers emphasize different dimensions of quality when judging a product or service. For example, some prospective car buyers value *performance* above all; others may be more influenced by the car's appearance (*aesthetics*). Because of these differences in consumer preferences, a company may choose to emphasize one or a few dimensions of quality rather than compete on all eight dimensions. For example, Tandem Computers emphasizes superior reliability in its computer systems. The company achieved exceptional reliability by designing and building dual processors into its computers. If one processor fails (which would shut down most computers),

---

[11]David A. Garvin, "Competing on the Eight Dimensions of Quality," *Harvard Business Review*, November–December 1987, pp. 101–9.

Figure 14–3 The price/quality relationship.

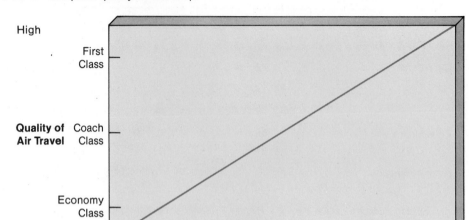

work automatically shifts to the second processor and no operations time is lost. This quality feature has provided tremendous sales growth for Tandem.[12]

Second, perceiving "excellence" can be highly subjective. Some dimensions such as *reliability* or *durability* can be quantified by simply reviewing the product's records. However, other dimensions such as *aesthetics* depend on personal likes and dislikes which are highly subjective. Differences in preferences and the subjectivity of perceptions underscore the need for organizations to obtain accurate market information concerning consumer perceptions and preferences.[13]

One other important element of the quality concept concerns the relationship between quality and price. In many cases, the relationship between a product's or service's quality and price is positive and linear, as shown in Figure 14–3.[14] If quality increases, so will the price (given that price reflects the cost of providing the product or service). This relationship is particularly strong when an organization produces a product or service that rates highly on all eight dimensions of quality. However, sometimes a higher level of quality does not result in a higher price when improving quality actually reduces the *cost of quality*.

---

[12]Ibid., p. 108. Also see Brian O'Reilly, "How Jimmy Treybig Turned Tough," *Fortune*, May 25, 1987, pp. 102–4.

[13]Ibid., p. 107.

[14]Everette E. Adam, Jr., James C. Hershauer, and William A. Ruch, *Productivity and Quality* (Englewood Cliffs, N.J.: Prentice-Hall, 1981).

Figure 14–4 The funnel principle: quality costs as a function of time.

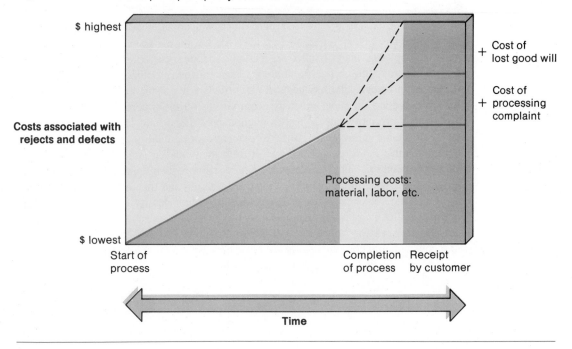

To understand this relationship, it is first necessary to understand the concept of cost of quality and its component parts. An organization's cost of quality is the total expense involved in ensuring that a product or service meets established quality standards. The cost of quality is comprised of three types of costs. *Prevention costs* are the costs of preventing product or service defects—the precontrol aspect of quality control. Examples of prevention costs are the expenses of effective employee training, re-engineering the product's manufacturing process, or working with suppliers to ensure that materials are of high quality. *Appraisal costs* are all expenses involved in directly evaluating quality such as the costs of quality inspection and testing. *Failure costs* occur once a defect is produced and identified. If the defect is found before the product leaves the plant, the failure costs are *internal* (e.g., the costs of scrapped material or of reworking the defective part or product). If the defect is found by the customer, *external failure costs* are incurred (the costs of recalled products, customer complaints, and a damaged product image).[15]

These three components' costs comprise a different proportion of the total cost of quality largely because they are incurred at different points of the production process. Figure 14–4 represents what is often referred to as the quality *funnel principle*. Ac-

---

[15]Jack Campanella and Frank J. Corcoran, "Principles of Quality Costs," *Quality Progress*, April 1983, pp. 16–22.

cording to the principle, the nearer to the start of the production process, the lower the cost of quality. Such is the case because, as the product or service progresses through the process, more resources are invested such as labor, time, and materials. The greater the amount of resources invested, the higher the cost of rejection (and quality). Applying this principle, prevention costs are incurred primarily at the beginning of the production process and are the least expensive component (5 to 10 percent of total quality costs). Failure costs are incurred mostly at the end of the process and thereafter and are the most expensive component (65 to 75 percent). Appraisal costs are incurred primarily during the production process and are larger than prevention but smaller than failure costs (20 to 25 percent of total quality costs).[16]

Importantly, many companies are shifting their quality control emphasis to prevention (precontrol). They are increasing prevention costs of quality by focusing more on such preventive mechanisms as employee training and the design of the manufacturing process. Over time, this increase in prevention quality costs produces larger returns. Quality is improved. Appraisal costs are reduced because improved prevention reduces the need for inspection and testing activities. Above all, failure costs—the most costly quality component—are reduced because the service or product is produced right the first time. Overall quality costs decline.

FACTORS AFFECTING QUALITY

Quality depends on a number of factors: policy, information, engineering and design, materials, equipment, people, and field support. An integrated quality control system must focus on these factors.

Policy.   Management establishes policies concerning product quality. These policies specify the standards or levels of quality to be achieved in a product or service; they can be an important precontrol and concurrent control means for ensuring quality.

Management considers three factors in determining its policy for quality: the product or service's market, its competition, and image. An evaluation of the market provides an indication of customer expectations of quality and the price they are willing to pay for it. Quality expectations and price, for example, widely differ in the luxury car (Mercedes) and economy car markets within the auto industry. Quality levels provided by the competition also affect policy because the company's products or services must be competitive qualitywise to succeed in the marketplace.

Besides considering the market and competition, management must also consider the organization's image. Long-term interests may be damaged by making a product of quality inconsistent with the firm's image. For example, marketing a low-priced Porsche or a new and low-priced Baskin-Robbins ice cream flavor might create a backlash from regular customers. Customer images of these products (and their loyalty) may be tarnished if they associate a lower-priced product or service with lower quality.

---

[16]Quality cost estimates are from A. V. Feigenbaum, *Total Quality Control* (New York: McGraw-Hill, 1983), pp. 112–13.

Information.   Information plays a vital role in setting policy and ensuring that quality standards are achieved. Concerning policy, accurate information must be obtained about customer preferences and expectations and about competitor quality standards and costs. *Competitive benchmarking,* discussed in this chapter's Management Incident Solution, is one effective approach to obtaining valuable information about a competitor's quality standards and costs.[17] Also, new computer technology is enabling organizations to quickly obtain and evaluate information about the quality of products while they are being produced.

Engineering and design.   Once management has formulated a policy concerning quality, it is the engineer or designer who must translate the policy into an actual product or service. The engineer/designer must create a product that will appeal to customers and that can be produced at a reasonable cost and provide competitive quality.

Materials.   A growing number of organizations are realizing that a finished product is only as good as materials used to produce it. In this regard, many manufacturing companies are implementing a new precontrol strategy with material suppliers. They are reducing their number of suppliers, for example, weeding out the lower-quality vendors and focusing on developing effective, long-term relationships with the better ones. Ford, General Motors, and Chrysler use this approach. Chrysler, for example, has cut its parts and materials suppliers from 2,700 in 1985 to less than 2,000 (under 1,500 is the goal by 1991). It has also set new standards for materials quality.[18]

Equipment.   The ability of equipment, tools, and machinery to accurately and reliably produce desired outputs is important, especially in manufacturing industries. If the equipment can meet acceptable tolerances, at competitive costs and quality, an organization will have the opportunity to compete in the marketplace.

People.   While materials, design, and equipment are important ingredients to quality, the employee is the vital contributor to quality. Working individually, or as teams, employees take the ingredients and process them into a final product or service of quality. Management must train employees not only in the specialized knowledge of producing a quality product or service but in an *attitude* of quality. As the following

---

[17]For more information on competitive benchmarking, see Bernard Taylor, "Corporate Planning for the 1990s: The New Frontiers," *Long Range Planning,* December 1986, pp. 13–18; William F. Glavin, "Competitive Benchmarking—A Technique Utilized by Xerox Corp to Revitalize Itself to a Modern Competitive Position," *Review of Business,* Winter 1984, pp. 9–12; and Harris Guilmette and Carlene Reinhart, "Competitive Benchmarking: A New Concept for Training," *Training and Development Journal,* February 1984, pp. 70–71.

[18]For a closer look at efforts by U.S. auto manufacturers to boost materials and product quality, see Alex Taylor III, "Lee Iacocca's Production Whiz," *Fortune,* June 22, 1987, pp. 36ff; William J. Hampton, "Why Image Counts: A Tale of Two Industries," *Business Week,* June 8, 1987, pp. 138–39; and James B. Treece, "Can Ford Stay on Top?" *Business Week,* September 28, 1987, pp. 78ff.

Management Application indicates, effective training is particularly important in service organizations where in many ways, the quality of the employee is the quality of service.

MANAGEMENT APPLICATION

THE SERVICE WINNERS

Fortune magazine recently reviewed quality ratings for service companies by consumer and other groups to answer the question: Who provides the best service in the United States? They found some answers: L. L. Bean was judged as tops among catalog merchants, American Airlines offers the best airlines service, and Liz Claiborne provides the best sales service for retailers in the clothing industry. *Fortune* also found that service winners share the same formula for service success. The formula relies heavily on a precontrol approach to quality control. Winners:

Selectively recruit and keep good people.   Singapore Airlines (judged the best servicer among international airlines) hires less than 2 percent of the women who apply for female flight attendant jobs. Delta Airlines (rated as receiving the fewest complaints per passenger) is even more selective; it hires less than 50 of more than 20,000 people who apply for a flight attendant job each month. High-service performers also strive to keep the people they hire. That can be difficult in industries where turnover is high and workers are young and unskilled. Wedgmans, a 38-supermarket chain in New York, solved this problem by providing tuition scholarships to high performers who want to go to college and to keep working at Wedgmans. These student employees provide the best service in the supermarket industry.

Thoroughly train employees in quality service.   Merck was judged as providing the best sales service to doctors and pharmacists in the pharmaceutical industry. Its strategy: provide new salespersons with 11 months of intense sales training including coursework in medicine with strict testing, and headquarters and in-the-field training in sales presentation. A salesperson also regularly attends medical classes as long as he sells for Merck.

Motivate and reward for quality performance.   Service winners recognize that training is useless if employees aren't motivated to provide top service. Companies motivate in a number of imaginative ways. Embassy Suites Hotels, judged as tops in the hotel industry, sets goals for each of its hotels. Every day, each hotel posts in the employee lounge its average room rate, occupancy rate, and estimated profits and customer comments from the previous day. If the hotel meets its goals, every employee can receive a bonus of more than $100 each month. American Express, judged the best in the credit card industry, provides up to $1,000 in cash awards to certified Great Performers.

Aggressively monitor quality performance.   Service winners highly value feedback on service performance to maintain high standards and take corrective action when needed. To receive feedback, they make a special effort to obtain customer opinions about service quality. Boston's Fidelity Investors, judged the best among discount brokers, surveys 3,000 customers every day about the service their brokers have provided.

Embassy Suites surveys over 6,000 of its customers every day about the hotel's quality. Companies also evaluate service themselves. American Express regularly sends a six-member team to its departments to evaluate service performance.

Source: Adapted from Bro Uttal, "Companies that Serve You Best," *Fortune,* December 7, 1987, pp. 98ff.

Field support.   Often, the field support provided by the supplier determines a product's quality image (*perceived quality*). IBM, General Electric, and Sears Roebuck have reputations for providing strong field support for their products. This is not to say that the products of these firms are necessarily the best in their industries. Many customers select IBM computers, General Electric refrigerators, and Sears Roebuck dishwashers because the field support of these firms is considered excellent.

DEVELOPING A QUALITY CONTROL SYSTEM

A system to reduce the chances that poor quality output will get to the customer involves the following five steps which are shown in Figure 14–5:[19]

Step 1. Develop quality characteristics.   The first step in establishing a quality control system is to define the quality characteristics desired by the customer or client. Examining customer preferences, technical specifications, marketing department suggestions, and competitive products provides quality-characteristic information. As previously noted, the preferences of the customer—the key perceiver of quality—are especially important. These preferences will greatly influence the dimensions of quality an organization will choose to emphasize, and the level of quality to be achieved for each dimension.

Step 2. Establish quality standards.   Once the quality characteristics have been defined, the next step is to determine the desired quality standards. These standards quantify the specific quality requirements for the organization's output. Quality standards serve as the reference point for comparing what is "ideal" to what actually "is."

In many organizations, quality standards are coupled with objectives concerning the organization's cost of quality. Often, the objective is to reduce the failure costs of quality (both internal and external). These costs comprise from 15 to 40 percent of a company's sales.[20] Tennant Co., of Minneapolis, confronted substantial quality problems in the maintenance equipment it produces for industrial floors. The company's failure costs of quality averaged 17 percent of sales. Tennant launched a companywide program to reduce the failure costs to less than 9 percent of sales in four years. It

---

[19]David Bain, *The Productivity Prescription: The Manager's Guide to Improving Productivity and Profits* (New York: McGraw-Hill, 1982), pp.119–27.

[20]Tom Peters, *Thriving on Chaos,* p. 74.

plans to further cut failure costs to less than 3 percent by 1990.[21] DuPont's polymer products department faced a similar problem; internal and external failure costs were running $400 billion each year, about double the department's yearly profits. The department launched a quality campaign designed to reduce failure costs by 10 percent each year.[22]

Step 3. Develop a quality review program.

Management must establish methods for quality review and decide where the reviews will be conducted, by whom, when they will occur, and how the review will be reported and analyzed by managers.

One important management decision involves determining how many products will be checked for quality. Will all products be inspected, or will there be a representative sampling? Representative sampling is less costly than inspecting all products manufactured. But inspecting only a sample, not every product, for quality creates: (1) the risk that a greater number of low-quality products will get into the hands of customers; (2) more likelihood that customer goodwill will be tarnished; and (3) the need to decide what constitutes an acceptable number of defects or low-quality products.

Representative sampling in manufacturing firms can take one of many forms. Some organizations use a *random spot check*. A number of products (e.g., cars, generators, computers) are randomly selected from a sample and are inspected for quality. When a formal random spot check is used, the results can be meaningful and can provide adequate control. Other forms of sampling plans using statistical analysis also are available.[23] In each case, the decision about which plan to use will involve making inferences about the entire production based on samples. Representative sampling, however, means that defective products occasionally will slip through the quality check network.

Toyota, Mitsubishi, and many other Japanese manufacturers do not rely on representative sampling; instead, they train their workers to inspect each product while they are working on it on the assembly line. Employee responsibility for quality control is one of several key characteristics of the Japanese approach to quality control. The following Management Application summarizes the characteristics of this highly successful strategy.

MANAGEMENT APPLICATION

JAPAN'S APPROACH TO QUALITY

Many Japanese experts assert that the real source of Japan's extraordinary industrial success lies in its approach to quality. A discussion of its quality goals and techniques

---

[21]Ed Bean, "Cause of Quality Control Problems Might Be Managers—Not Workers," *The Wall Street Journal,* April 10, 1985, p. 31.

[22]Thomas C. Gibson, "The Total Quality Management Resource," *Quality Progress,* November 1987, pp. 62–66.

[23]For more complete discussions, see Richard J. Schonberger and Edward M. Knod, Jr., *Operations Management: Serving the Customer* (Plano, Tex.: Business Publications, 1988); and J. M. Juran, Frank M. Gryna, Jr., and R. S. Bingham, Jr., eds., *Quality Control Handbook* (New York: McGraw-Hill, 1974).

could fill volumes; however, the following are some of the primary strategies used by Japanese manufacturers to achieve superior quality in the products they produce.

Production responsibility for quality.   In the typical U.S. manufacturing plant, the quality control department directly supervises quality control and is responsible for product quality inspection. In Japan, the production department is responsible for product quality and is viewed as the real quality expert. The Japanese believe that this responsibility brings the task of quality closer to the production managers and employees.

Process quality control.   Quality control is implemented throughout production by the workers who are responsible for checking for quality at their particular points in the production process. The workers are the quality inspectors.

Line stops.   Each worker on the assembly line has the authority to stop the production line to correct quality problems. In many Japanese plants, each worker is stationed by a three-light signal (much like a traffic light). If he spots a problem, he presses a button and a yellow light flashes. If he stops the line, the red light flashes, signaling to all the location of the problem on the line. The entire production line stops and all efforts focus on solving the problem. When it is solved, the green light flashes and the line continues.

100 percent check.   Many Japanese firms check every completed product. Random spot checks are not used to inspect finished goods.

Correcting one's errors.   If a Japanese worker makes bad parts, she fixes them, often on her own time. Consequently, the number of reworked parts is very small.

No-crisis atmosphere.   The Japanese believe that poor quality is a natural product of a hectic production schedule. Therefore, they maintain a no-crisis atmosphere by developing production schedules at least one day in advance and sticking to them. No rush orders are allowed. Machines are also scheduled at less than capacity. These strategies make line stops feasible.

Housekeeping.   Most Japanese plants are spotless, and the workers do the housekeeping chores. The Japanese believe that a neat and clean work environment promotes quality work. The Japanese workers check, maintain and repair their own machines every day.

Easy-to-see quality.   To emphasize the importance of quality, Japanese plants keep quality very visible on the plant floor via large, colorful display boards located throughout the plant. These boards display important quality factors, how they're measured, the latest measurements, and the results of current quality improvement projects. Quality testing equipment is prominently displayed in glass cases.

Just-in-time inventory control.   A key contributor to quality, this concept minimizes inventory on the plant floor and reduces manufacturing problems and costs. JIT will be described in detail in Chapter 15.

Source: Adapted from Richard J. Schonberger, *Japanese Manufacturing Techniques: Nine Hidden Lessons in Simplicity* (New York: The Free Press, 1982).

Step 4: Build quality commitment.   A spirit and commitment to quality among all employees is essential to an effective quality control system. Building this commitment requires four actions by management:

Communicate the need for quality.   Effective quality control systems require a communication program designed to demonstrate to employees the importance of quality to the consumer, the company, and ultimately its work force. These programs use videotapes, seminars, and discussions to illustrate the impact of quality on organizational sales and profits, and on compensation and benefits for the work force.

Train employees in the skills and knowledge of quality.   Inadequate training can be a major barrier to quality; the Tennant Co. found that poor training was a primary source of its quality problems. Management had not effectively trained assembly workers to correctly install certain product parts. The company's engineers were not instructed in the latest technology concerning relevant circuitry. To avoid these problems, companies focus training on providing the skills and abilities needed to achieve the organization's quality standards. And training is not limited to nonsupervisory employees. At Tennant Co., every manager completed at least five courses in quality control during the initial years of the company's quality campaign.

Secure employment involvement in quality.   Some organizations such as Toyota and DuPont train employees in problem-solving techniques and skills and encourage them to use what they've learned in identifying and solving quality-related problems. One indicator of employee involvement in quality at Toyota is the number of suggestions employees provide management concerning productivity and quality. Once averaging about 5,000 ideas a year in the early 1960s, Toyota employees now provide about 1.9 million ideas each year (about 32 per worker). Management implements over 5,000 ideas each day.[24]

Reward for quality.   Management boosts employee motivation and involvement in the quality effort by rewarding them for their contributions to meeting and especially surpassing quality standards. To motivate managers, Ford Motor Co. includes quality objectives as part of its executive compensation plan. In 1986, for example, Ford based 40 to 65 percent of a manager's annual bonus on contributions to quality. IBM extends rewards for quality to its suppliers. IBM pays premiums for materials that exceed a certain quality standard; IBM also penalizes suppliers for materials of lesser quality via reductions in the prices it pays for those materials.[25]

Step 5: Design and use a quality measurement and reporting system.   To control and improve product or service quality, management requires information in the form of quality measurements and progress reports.

Measures of inputs entering the process are important indicators of how good, questionable, or poor these inputs are. Input measures prepare management for possible process and output problems.

Measures of quality at the point of processing are also valuable. Concurrent control

[24]Benjamin Tregoe, "Productivity in America: How to Get It Back," *Management Review,* February 1983, pp. 23–28, 41–45; and Tom Peters, *Thriving on Chaos,* p. 72.

[25]Peters, *Thriving on Chaos,* p. 75.

Figure 14–5 The five key actions to develop a quality control system.

Action	Purpose
1. Develop quality characteristics.	Quality control systems must assure that products deliver what customers expect.
2. Establish quality standards.	Standards of quality must pertain to customer defined characteristics.
3. Develop quality review program.	Quality control is realized only through the implementation of specific procedures.
4. Build quality commitment.	Employees make the product— their commitment is necessary to achieve quality standards.
5. Design reporting system.	Product quality information must be channeled to employees who can take corrective action.

information can indicate the need to alter, regulate, or shut down the process. And making these changes or decisions could prevent faulty outputs from reaching customers or clients.

The final outputs must be checked and the results reported. Measures taken prior to shipment can result in last-minute corrections. Measures and reports from customers or clients also can provide crucial data.

Without a measurement and reporting system, critical quality problems can be overlooked. The consequence of such faulty control can mean the loss of customers or clients. When customers or clients perceive that quality meets their expectations, the image of the product or service is enhanced. It is these perceptions that the five-step quality program attempts to influence.

TOTAL QUALITY CONTROL

In response to competitive pressures, a growing number of organizations are adopting a unique philosophy concerning quality termed *total quality control* (TQC). Hewlett-Packard, IBM, Milliken & Co., and other companies who have adopted this philosophy generally follow three principles concerning quality. First, the objective of quality control is to achieve a constant and continual improvement in quality. Meeting the same quality standards year after year is not sufficient. Instead, the goal is to provide more and better quality for customers. Second, the focus of quality improvement and quality control extends beyond the actual product or service that an organization provides. The focus of quality is on every process in the organization. Accounting systems, product promotion activities, R&D processes, and virtually all other activities in the organization are the focus of quality improvement. Third, employees bear a major responsibility for quality improvement. Quality becomes an integral element of every job in the organization.

Implementing total quality control involves the same five-step approach to establishing a quality control system. However, the breadth of the quality focus and the challenge of continual improvement requires extra efforts. For example, an integral part of the TQC system is the *quality audit,* a careful study of every factor that affects quality in an activity or process. Audits are conducted in every department and division to identify existing and potential contributors to quality problems and to discover new ways to further improve quality.[26]

Like the traditional quality control system, employee training is emphasized. However, because employees are key participants in quality improvement efforts, training focuses on problem-solving skills and techniques such as data collection methods, statistical analysis, and group brainstorming. The CEO and the top-management team are often the first to receive training in quality concepts and quality control. Employees put their newly acquired skills to work in project teams in their divisions. These teams tackle specific assignments such as improving customer service and the manufacturing work flow or making the performance of a certain job more efficient. Team members come from the division's various departments. Projects of wider scope are handled by cross-functional teams with representatives from the organization's different divisions.[27]

To help implement and maintain total quality control, an organization often creates a staff of managers trained in TQC principles and techniques. Staff members direct employee training in problem-solving techniques, coordinate quality audits, assist in the development of quality standards and measurements and perform other functions in the TQC effort. Total quality control councils or committees are also often created at the division and top-management level to oversee the organizationwide TQC effort.

Corning Glass Works, an industrial glass manufacturer, is one company that has successfully implemented a total quality control system. In the mid-1980s, Corning's international competitors were making substantial gains in product quality. To keep its competitive edge, Corning launched the total quality management system to improve quality in every company operation and to involve all of its 28,000 employees in the effort.

Some of Corning's objectives in the TQC effort are to identify the key quality "errors" in every department and reduce those errors by 90 percent, to manufacture new products that equal or beat the competition in quality, and to substantially reduce the company's failure cost of quality (its total cost is estimated to be 20 to 30 percent of sales). The deadline for these objectives is 1991.

Employee training is a major element of Corning's system. To provide effective training, Corning established the Corning Quality Institute which is staffed by 10 veteran employees specially trained in quality concepts and techniques. Every salaried employee has completed courses in quality awareness and skills at the Institute. Corning also trained 150 local line employees as instructors. These trainers have provided

---

[26]John H. Farrow, "Quality Audits: An Invitation to Management," *Quality Progress,* January 1987, pp. 11–13.

[27]Harry W. Kenworthy, "Total Quality Concept: A Proven Path to Success," *Quality Progress,* July 1986, pp. 21–24.

quality training to more than 12,000 production and maintenance people in Corning's plants worldwide. Training has focused on overall quality awareness and on statistics, problem-solving skills, communications, and group dynamics.

To provide employees the opportunity to use the skills they've acquired, Corning organized quality improvement teams in every department. Some of the teams are cross-functional; for example, the customer financial services and information services departments formed a joint corrective action team to find ways to reduce computer-processing costs of accounts receivable. These efforts help to achieve quality implementation goals. All departments—and all employees—have quality goals. Corning also received valuable ideas and suggestions from responses to the "99 Questions," Corning's worldwide employee survey conducted to identify barriers to total quality.

Corning appointed a top-level executive as director of quality to head the quality system and created a quality council staffed by representatives from each division to monitor the overall effort. To date, Corning has substantially reduced its cost of quality and boosted product quality.[28]

MANAGEMENT SOLUTION

KEARNS LAUNCHES "LEADERSHIP THROUGH QUALITY"

Xerox's new CEO launched the "Leadership through quality" program to boost product quality and reduce manufacturing costs. The campaign is comprised of three elements: competitive benchmarking, employee involvement, and a quality improvement program. Competitive benchmarking is a particularly effective element of the campaign.

Competitive benchmarking is a cost analysis technique used to obtain important information on competitor costs and to set tougher standards for cost control. In the technique, Xerox targets a competitor who is clearly producing copiers at a lower cost. Xerox purchases one of the copiers, and product analysts take the copier apart in the Xerox lab, piece by piece. Their objective is to determine the cost of designing and producing each part. In doing so, Xerox can estimate a competitor's total production costs for the copier. They then set the estimated cost as their new standard for cost control.

Xerox has applied competitive benchmarking to other types of costs. For example, Xerox analysts pinpointed Kodak's handling and distribution costs by purchasing a number of Kodak copiers and then tracing where they were shipped from and examining how the copiers were packed.

Xerox has also benchmarked noncompetitors. For example, management at its Logistics and Distribution unit were intrigued by the warehouse system of L. L. Bean, the outdoor sport-

Continued

---

[28]James R. Houghton, " 'The Old Way of Doing Things Is Gone'," *Quality Progress*, September 1986, pp. 15–18; Nancy Karabatsos, " 'The Chairman Doesn't Blink'," *Quality Progress*, March 1987, pp. 19–24; William H. Wagel, "Corning Zeroes in on Total Quality," *Personnel*, July 1987, pp. 4–9; and Barbara Buell, "Smashing the Country Club Image at Corning Glass," *Business Week*, May 5, 1986, pp. 92, 95.

MANAGEMENT SOLUTION

Concluded

ing goods retailer. L. L. Bean's warehouse system was reputed to be one of the best in the business (and was the first to be designed entirely by quality circles). The system handles products with size characteristics similar to Xerox parts and supplies; the system also has similar service levels. A Xerox benchmark team visited the warehouse in Freeport, Maine, carefully studied its design and operations and came back with some valuable ways to modernize its warehouse operations.

Xerox also achieved some substantial boosts in product quality via its employee involvement and quality improvement programs. After sending several employees to observe quality circle operations in Japan, Xerox established circles throughout the company. Circle-generated ideas have reduced operating costs by several million dollars. Xerox has also stressed process quality

control where employees check quality during the production process. Competitive benchmarking has also boosted quality in helping Xerox determine competitors' quality standards; Xerox has worked to meet if not beat these standards. The company has also focused on reducing its costs of quality.

To date, the "Leadership through Quality" campaign has produced results. Xerox estimates that the campaign has saved many millions of dollars in the copier and information systems business. Kearns has stopped the erosion of Xerox's market share and, with these kinds of results, morale has improved.

Source: Adapted from Irving J. DeToro, "Strategic Planning for Quality at Xerox," *Quality Progress,* April 1987, pp. 16–20; and Frances Gaither Tucker, Seymour M. Zivan, and Robert C. Camp, "How to Measure Yourself against the Best," *Harvard Business Review,* January–February, 1987, pp. 8–10.

MANAGEMENT SUMMARY

- ☐ Effective control depends on managerial decisions and actions to correct deviations between actual and planned results.

- ☐ The three necessary elements of control are predetermined standards, information, and corrective action.

- ☐ Precontrol methods and systems depend on information about characteristics and qualities of inputs—materials, capital, financial, and human resources. The foci of corrective action are the inputs themselves.

- ☐ Concurrent control methods and systems depend on information about ongoing

activities and operations. The foci of corrective action can be activities and operations or the inputs, depending on the causes of the deviations between actual and desired performance.

- ☐ Postcontrol methods and systems use the information that measures the characteristics and qualities of actual results and performance. They take corrective action activities, operations, and inputs.

- ☐ A growing number of companies are focusing on developing a superior quality control system because they are realizing: customers want quality, quality affects organizational performance, and high quality is the new standard for domestic and international competition.

☐ Consumers evaluate quality using eight dimensions: performance, features, reliability, conformance, durability, serviceability, aesthetics, and perceived quality.

☐ Developing an integrated quality control system requires defining quality characteristics and standards, developing a

quality review program, building a commitment to quality among employees, and designing a quality measurement and reporting system.

☐ Advocates of a total quality control philosophy assert that companies should continually strive to improve quality in all operations of the organization, and that employees should be a key source of quality improvements.

REVIEW AND DISCUSSION QUESTIONS

1. Explain why predetermined standards are necessary for effective managerial control. Does the fact that management has set standards for crucial aspects of the organization guarantee that control will be effective? Why or why not?

2. Discuss how the college or university you attend controls the teaching performance of the faculty. Organize your answer in terms of the three types of control.

3. The chapter notes that six factors influence the quality of an organization's output. In your opinion, which factor is most important in affecting quality? Explain.

4. Why are the standards that a CEO uses more ambiguous than the standards used by first-level managers?

5. In what ways does planning information differ from controlling information? Can both types of information be provided by an integrated management information system? Explain.

6. Many managers assert that providing superior quality requires high manufacturing costs. However, some research indicates that companies with the best quality earn the highest profits. Are these two statements contradictory? If so, resolve the contradiction.

7. What are the shortcomings of using statistical sampling in monitoring the quality of products or services?

8. In your opinion, what are the individual characteristics required to provide employees with effective direction? Explain.

9. Explain why control is a pointless exercise if it is impossible to take corrective action.

10. Developing an integrated quality control system is a complex, challenging, and time-consuming task. Of the five steps involved in developing the system, which step do you believe is the most challenging for management? Explain.

CASES

14–1 MRS. FIELDS' RECIPE FOR EFFECTIVE COMPANY CONTROL

Nowadays, the cookie business is big business. David's Cookies, Blue Chip Cookies, The Original Great Chocolate Chip Cookie, and dozens of regional and local cookie shops are hotly competing for a share of the growing retail cookie market. Currently, the leader of the pack is Mrs. Fields Cookies of Park City, Utah. The company is owned and operated by a young husband-and-wife team, Randy and Debbi Fields.

Sample some cookies at a Mrs. Fields store, and you'll see one obvious reason why Mrs. Fields shops are tops. The cookies are always fresh, warm, and tasty and the service is friendly. The company sells a "feel-good feeling," says Debbi Fields, the company's CEO.

However, successfully producing and selling this feeling with a consistent quality product and service can be very difficult—especially when your 500 stores and about 4,500 employees are located in 37 states and five foreign countries. An effective control system is a must. The Fieldses have developed a unique computerized approach to management and operations control. At the core of the control system is a computer network that links every store with corporate headquarters.

To illustrate how the control system works, consider Richard Lui, manager of the Pier 39 shop in San Francisco. Each morning, Richard begins his day at the shop by calling up the Day Planner program on his personal computer terminal. The computer asks for the day of the week, the type of day (holiday, school day, sale day), and the day's sales projection which is based on last year's sales adjusted for growth. Richard inputs the information (it's a Thursday holiday, for example), and the computer responds by telling what must be done *hour-by-hour* to meet the sales goal—how many customers are needed every hour, how much must be sold by the hour, how many batches of cookie mix must be made, and so on. The computer's advice is generated from an analysis of the sales levels and hour-by-hour fluctuations that the shop experienced on the three previous Thursday holidays.

Richard will input sales information each hour into the computer system; in many Mrs. Fields stores, cash registers automatically do the task. The computer uses the information to update its early morning suggestions. For example, the computer may detect that while the customer count is fine, the per-sales amount is a bit low. The computer will then offer some suggestions such as having the sales crew boost its suggestive selling.

The computer is a control tool in other areas. For instance, it helps schedule the store's staff. Richard inputs the projected sales levels for the coming two weeks, and the computer responds with a work schedule showing Richard how many employees with what type of skills will be needed to work at what hours. The schedule is calculated using the performance time standards set by Debbi Fields for tasks (e.g., mixing, baking). Mrs. Fields uses her past experience in running her first shop to set the standards. If she took an average five minutes to prepare the cookie dough, for example, then five minutes becomes the standard.

The computer also helps Richard interview job applicants. When a prospect comes in for an interview, Richard sits the candidate down by the computer and calls up the interview program. He asks the applicant questions provided by the computer and inputs the responses. The computer then projects how well the applicant will perform on the job. The computer makes its prediction based on answers given by past applicants who were hired and their subsequent job performance.

The computer helps with other tasks such as personnel administration (the personnel manual is available on the computer) and equipment maintenance. If a machine isn't working, the computer will offer several suggestions on how to fix it before calling the repairman. When service is needed, the computer processes the work order to headquarters. The computer also generates the inventory supply orders which are based on sales projections and weekly inventory reports. Richard only checks the orders to be sure they're correct before sending them electronically to headquarters.

The computer is especially useful in one key area—communications between the 500 store managers and Debbi Fields. Whenever Richard Lui has a message for Debbi, he calls up the FormMail program on his computer, types the communication and sends it electronically to headquarters. It reaches Debbi's desk by the next morning; she or her staff will be in personal contact with him within 48 hours. Richard also telephones headquarters every day for any recorded messages from Debbi.

Although the computer system sounds intimidatingly high tech, it isn't. All of the shop computers are basic PCs, and the software is menu driven and quite simple to run.

All information provided hourly by shop managers is fed into the company's data base at headquarters. There, the controller staff checks how the shops are doing—Did they meet their daily sales goals last week, or are there any inventory discrepancies? The controllers handle any problems by working directly with the shop manager.

Debbi and Randy Fields believe that the computerized control system provides several advantages. The system provides the Fields with direct control of its 500 stores and 4,500 employees. The Fieldses believe that close contact with store managers is essential to maintaining the company's high-quality standards. Debbi's presence is felt in each shop via her frequent computer and telephone communications with shop management and in the computer-provided goals, scheduling, and suggestions which all reflect her experience and preferences.

By computerizing many administrative tasks, the system has kept the size of the corporate staff to a minimum; it also frees store managers from much time-consuming paperwork and administrative tasks. In Randy Fields' view, if a computer can conceivably perform a task, it should—which frees managers to manage people, not paperwork. His plan is to continue to computerize as many such tasks as possible.

Questions

1. Besides the advantages, do you see any shortcomings in the Fields's computerized approach to control? If so, what are they?

2. Is one type of control (precontrol, concurrent, postcontrol) emphasized in the computerized control system? Explain.

3. Would this approach to control be useful in all types of companies and industries? Explain.

Source: This case is adapted from Tom Richman, "Mrs. Fields's Secret Ingredient," *Inc.*, October 1987, pp. 64ff.

14–2 HAIR, INC.

Janet Hoover and Rob Hundley opened their first hair design shop 10 years ago. With two other haircutters, the two of them began what was to become a very successful organization.

Both Jan and Rob keep up to date on the latest hairstyling techniques. They attend international schools and seminars on hair design and transmit the knowledge they acquire to their employees through training sessions. Every new employee must be trained by Jan or Rob. HAIR, Inc., promotes quality delivery of the latest in hairstyling. Modern music is played in their shops, and their haircutters are dressed in the latest fashions to promote the image that HAIR, Inc., represents the latest in hair fashions.

HAIR, Inc., appeals equally to men and women and to all age-groups. Occasionally, a visiting rock star or other celebrity will patronize HAIR, Inc. Because of this, HAIR, Inc., has become very popular with teenagers who come to get their hair styled but also hoping to see a current rock star.

HAIR, Inc., has been so successful that there are now HAIR, Inc., shops in five major cities. This expansion has caused Jan and Rob some concern. Their concern centers on maintaining effective performance with a growing number of employees.

After considerable thought, they decided that they were going to have to become more concerned about managing the performance of their business. Both Jan and Rob had been reading a great deal in their trade publications about effective management, and more recently they had been reading about the importance of maintaining control.

Jan and Rob knew that they could not develop a standardized performance control system for the entire organization because different employees specialized in different activities, for example, cutting and styling, coloring, permanents, hairpieces. In addition, some employees were classified as apprentice cutters and others as master cutters. Jan and Rob therefore concluded that their first step should be to try to identify performance criteria that they should expect and incorporate these criteria in a control document. They would then begin training sessions on the philosophy and process of management control with groups of employees. This would be followed by sessions with each employee during which the level of expected performance on each criteria would be set for each employee.

The performance control document shown in Exhibit 14–1 is a first draft that Rob developed. After examining Rob's form, Jan observed that quantity of work completed should certainly be an expected result and an important performance variable. Being

Exhibit 14–1

HAIR, Inc. Performance Form Name _____				

Responsibility
  Cut and style _____
  Coloring _____
  Permanents _____
  Hairpieces _____
  Apprentice ____ Master ____
	Minimum Daily Performance	*Average Daily Performance*	*Maximum Possible Performance*	*Actual Performance*

Expected quantity				

quantitative, this criterion was easy to measure. However, in their business, customer satisfaction was absolutely critical. In fact, HAIR, Inc., had a policy that a customer who for any reason was not satisfied with the work could return and have additional work done free of charge. Jan noted that most people's self-image was closely tied to their appearance and that poorly performed hairstyling, hair coloring, and permanents could be extremely upsetting if they did not make people look as they thought they should look or as they wished to look.

Thus, Jan suggested a *qualitative* performance criterion that would focus on the result of customer satisfaction. She believed that such a criterion could be measured by the percentage of jobs that were acceptable to the customer when completed. For example, a minimum expected level of performance might be to have 90 percent of all cuts and styles acceptable to the customer; an average expected level might be 98 percent. This, she believed, would enable her and Rob to monitor performance toward achieving their objective of customer satisfaction. "In addition," she said, "a qualitative objective will help the employees focus on how they perform their work and not solely on the quantity of their output." With these ideas in mind, Jan developed the version of Rob's performance form shown in Exhibit 14–2.

Exhibit 14–2

HAIR, Inc. Performance Form Name _____				

Responsibility
  Cut and style _____
  Coloring _____
  Permanents _____
  Hairpieces _____
  Apprentice ____ Master ____
	Minimum Daily Performance	*Average Daily Performance*	*Maximum Possible Performance*	*Actual Performance*

Results expected (quantity)				
Results expected (quality)				

Questions

1. Why do the problems faced by HAIR, Inc., appear to lend themselves to the application of management control practice?

2. What is your opinion of Jan's and Rob's potential as managers? State your reasons.

3. Are Jan and Rob implementing precontrol, concurrent, or feedback control methods? Explain.

EXERCISE

14–1 A CONTROL SYSTEM PROFILE

Purpose: This activity is designed to enhance students' understanding of the purpose, makeup, and operation of actual control systems in organizations.

Setting Up the Exercise: The instructor will divide the class into groups comprised of four students each. Each group should complete the following project:

1. Select a control system which you would like to learn more about. The choices are numerous: budgeting, capital investment, performance appraisal, inventory control, quality control, and employee selection are all control systems that function in the typical organization. Identify an organization in your local community or in your college administration. There are several control systems on campus that are appropriate to study, such as student applicant selection.

2. Interview the individual who manages the respective control system. Your objective is to develop a written profile of the system. The interview should last approximately 30 minutes. Some suggested questions:
   a. What are the objectives of the control system?
   b. How are standards set and information collected to determine whether standards have been met?
   c. How has the control system changed over the years? What factors led to the changes?
   d. In what ways have you fine-tuned the system to meet your organization's particular needs and constraints?
   e. What are the challenges in implementing and managing the system?

3. Prepare a five-page written report on your findings. The paper should focus on presenting an overall profile of the objectives, makeup, and function of the system. You should also address how the system has evolved over the years and how the system is designed to meet the system's particular needs. Be sure to include any system problems you identified and suggest solutions.

A Learning Note: This exercise illustrates that control systems can widely differ across organizations because of each organization's particular needs and characteristics. Control systems are also quite fluid; they often are altered to accommodate particular circumstances and changes in the organization's processes.

FIFTEEN

Production-Operations and Financial Control

LEARNING OBJECTIVES

After completing Chapter 15, you should be able to:

Define: the necessary conditions for effective *internal* control of financial resources and assets.

State: the methods managers can use to precontrol the quality and quantity of financial and production resources.

Describe: the principles of *just-in-time inventory management* and the challenges inherent in implementing the concept.

Explain: the meaning of the key ratios used to evaluate a company's liquidity, profitability, and solvency.

Discuss: the uses and mechanics of the PERT and linear programming models for concurrent operations control.

HARLEY-DAVIDSON: NO LONGER KING OF THE ROAD

Like Levi jeans and Coca-Cola, for years a Harley-Davidson motorcycle was a product that symbolized a part of American culture. Big, powerful, and very durable, the Harley bike dominated the king-size segment of the motorcycle industry from the 1950s through the 1970s with the company generating over $300 million yearly in sales.

However, by the late 1970s, the road to impressive sales and profits had suddenly become quite bumpy. Like many highly successful companies, Harley-Davidson had become complacent. The company had let its product line age with no new technological advancements. Harley offered only two different engines and two chassis while competitors had dozens of models. In 1969, Harley was acquired by AMF, a major manufacturing conglomerate, which was not willing to invest the millions in funds needed to redesign Harley's product line.

Manufacturing operations were plagued by several control problems. Though inventory costs were high, parts shortages were constant, causing frequent shutdowns of the production line. Over 30 percent of the cycles that came off the production line were missing parts; the manufacturing floor was littered with scores of cycles needing rework. Scrap and rework costs were high while product quality plummeted.

Meanwhile, the Japanese motorcycle makers Honda, Yamaha, and Kawasaki had targeted the large-size end of the cycle market. In a short time, the Japanese dealt Harley their now familiar one-two punch: higher quality at a lower price (the Japanese maintained operating costs that were 30 percent lower than Harley's). By the early 1980s, Harley-Davidson was reeling from the blow. Its market share had fallen to 9 percent, and it was dealt staggering financial losses. The company's future was in serious question.

(The Management Solution to this Management Incident can be found at the end of this chapter.)

Managerial control of production-operations and financial activities is critical to organizational performance. Although modern organizations must undertake numerous activities, their ultimate fates depend in large part on how well managers allocate financial and productive resources. All other organizational activities, such as engineering, personnel, marketing, and research and development support and depend on the primary activity of producing goods and services.

This chapter examines several methods managers use to control productive and financial resources. The presentation is organized around the three basic types of control: precontrol, concurrent control, and postcontrol. The primary focus of the discussion is on the three necessary conditions for effective control: standards, information, and corrective action. Production-operations controls are presented first, followed by financial controls.

PRODUCTION-OPERATIONS CONTROL

All organizations produce outputs, whether those outputs are goods, services, or ideas. The outputs are obtained by transforming certain basic inputs—namely, materials, capital, and human resources—through *production*, or *operations*, processes. Manufacturing, publishing, and construction firms, for example, produce tangible, physical outputs. Such transformation processes are known as *production*. Other organizations, such as retailers, wholesalers, banks, railroads, universities, newspapers, and television stations, produce intangible outputs—services and ideas. The transformation process in such organizations is referred to as *operations*.

As noted in Chapter 14, control methods can be discussed in terms of the focus of their corrective action. Accordingly, production-operations control methods can be described as focusing on inputs (precontrol), transformation (concurrent control), or outputs (postcontrol).

Precontrol of Inputs

Operations management involves acquiring resources and allocating them among the resources' competing users. Precontrol methods, meanwhile, focus specifically on the acquisition of resources. The three major types of resources are human resources, capital, and materials. Precontrol requires predetermining standards for the quantity and *quality* of resources. Precontrol of human resources is presented in Chapter 16. In this chapter, precontrol of materials and capital is discussed.

Precontrol of materials quantity. Production managers make two key materials control decisions: (1) how *many* of each lot or batch of materials to order; and (2) how *often* to order each lot or batch. In resolving inventory problems, the manager initially must identify the cost factors that affect the choices being considered.

First are the *ordering costs,* incurred each time material is ordered from a supplier. These are the clerical and administrative costs per order, and they include the costs of placing the materials into inventory.

Second, *carrying costs* are incurred whenever items are held in inventory. These include the interest on money invested in inventory and the cost of storage space, rent,

Figure 15–1 The relationship between ordering costs and carrying costs.

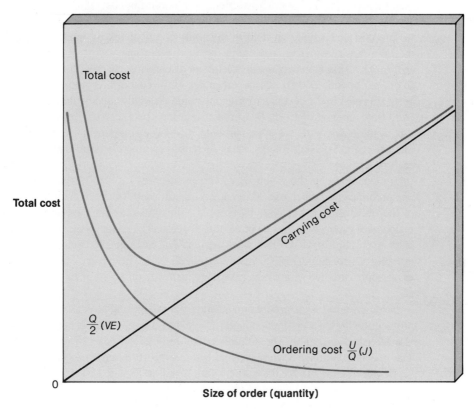

obsolescence, taxes, protection, and insurance on losses due to theft, fire, and deterioration. Carrying costs usually are expressed as an annual figure and as a percentage of the average inventory.

To minimize inventory costs, a manager must minimize both ordering and carrying costs. These two costs are related to each other in opposing directions, as shown in Figure 15–1. That is, as ordering costs decrease, carrying costs increase. As the size of each order increases, the number of orders and the cost of ordering decreases. Yet, since larger quantities are being ordered and placed in inventory, the cost of carrying the inventory increases.

The number of orders for a given time period is equal to usage for the period (U) divided by the size of each order (Q), or U/Q. The total ordering cost per period (week, month, or year) equals the cost of ordering each lot (J) *multiplied by the number of orders per period,* or

$$\frac{U}{Q}(J)$$

You can see that as the order size (Q) increases, fewer orders are required to meet the usage (U) for a period. Consequently, the ordering cost component will decrease. This is demonstrated by the downward-sloping ordering cost curve in Figure 15–1.

The cost of carrying an item in inventory is calculated by multiplying the cost of the item (V) by a percentage figure (ordinarily the firm's cost of borrowing money) (E), or VE. This is management's estimate of carrying charges, taxes, insurance, and so on, per period, expressed as a percentage of the cost of inventory. The total carrying costs are equal to the cost of carrying one item (VE) multiplied by the average inventory $Q/2$. Note, in Figure 15–1, that unlike ordering costs, carrying costs increase as the size of the order increases. One particularly volatile component of carrying cost is the interest charge. Rising interest rates increase carrying cost and decrease the size of each order.

An example can show you why average inventory is $Q/2$. Assume that an organization orders and receives 500 items, and that it uses 100 each week. At the midpoint of the first week, it has 450. Figure 15–2 illustrates the number in inventory at the midpoint of each week, over a period of five weeks. Thus, an average of 250 (1,250 ÷ 5) parts is on hand over the five-week period. The average (250) also can be found by utilizing the formula $Q/2$, in this case, 500/2. Note, however, that the formula $Q/2$, as an approximation of average inventory, depends on how constant the rate of usage is.

Now assume that a production manager is attempting to solve an order quantity problem involving a component part. The yearly usage, which is constant for the part, is established as 1,000. The administrative and clerical costs of each order are $40. The manager estimates insurance and taxes to be 10 percent per year. The cost of a single part is $20. Thus, the variables involved are: usage (U) = 1,000; order costs (J) = $40; insurance and taxes (E) = 10 percent; cost of the item (V) = $20.

Referring to Figure 15–1, you can see that the minimum total inventory cost is at the intersection of the carrying cost and the ordering cost. Total cost decreases as the size of the order increases—up to the intersection. Then it increases beyond the intersection. Thus, to solve for the point where the two lines intersect, we set the carrying cost and the ordering cost equal to each other:

$$\frac{Q}{2}\,(VE) = \frac{U}{Q}\,(J)$$

solving for Q yields:

$$Q(VE) = \frac{2UJ}{Q}$$

$$Q^2(VE) = 2\ UJ$$

$$Q^2 = \frac{2UJ}{VE}$$

$$Q = \sqrt{\frac{2UJ}{VE}}$$

Figure 15–2
Average inventory analysis.

Week	Number in inventory at midpoint of week
1	450
2	350
3	250
4	150
5	50
	1,250

The final equation is commonly referred to as the *economic order quantity* (EOQ) formula and can be used to solve the inventory problem previously outlined. Using the data in the problem, you can determine the economic order quantity where $U = 1,000$, $J = \$40$, $E = 10$ percent, and $V = \$20$.

$$Q = \sqrt{\frac{2(1,000)(\$40)}{(\$20)(0.10)}}$$

$$Q = \sqrt{\frac{\$80,000}{\$2}}$$

$$Q = \sqrt{\$40,000}$$

$$Q = 200$$

The EOQ formula reveals that placing five lots of 200 each will be the least costly option.

The EOQ model here illustrates ordering an item in a job, lot, or batch manufacturing setting. A retail establishment, however, could also use the EOQ approach. In fact, the general approach of the model could be applied wherever an organization must purchase, or manufacture, a resource to hold in inventory.

However, in using the EOQ technique, it is important to understand the model's limitations. Perhaps the most serious shortcoming is the assumption of certainty in two of the formula's variables—unit demand (U) and cost (V). The demand for the unit is assumed to be known and constant, unchanging over a period of time. However, many factors can vary the demand for a unit, in particular the demand for the finished product of which the unit is a part. Changing economic conditions, changes in a competitor's product price, or many other circumstances can influence product demand which can affect unit demand. The model also assumes that the price of a unit is constant. However, often suppliers provide price discounts when units are ordered in large quantities. This factor can influence inventory order decisions.

The model also assumes certainty concerning the time to order inventory. It assumes that the correct time is known. However, such problems as transportation delays and other requisition factors can vary the time required for the supplier to deliver the unit.

For example, the New United Motor Manufacturing Inc. (NUMMI) has built in an extra lead time for its inventory deliveries. NUMMI is a General Motors/Toyota joint venture which produces cars near San Francisco. Most of the parts are shipped overseas from the Port of Nagoya, Japan. The main delivery problem is periodic, severe sea storms that slow the ships' delivery times. In this case, time required for delivery is often uncertain. Consequently, NUMMI carries some extra inventory in case of delivery delays. NUMMI is profiled in Case 15–1 at the end of this chapter.

Because of these limitations, the EOQ model should be used with caution in situations where demand fluctuates, quantity price discounts apply, and delivery time requirements are erratic. In these cases, the model at best provides an approximation of the amount of inventory to order.[1]

Regardless of the technique used to determine the size and frequency of inventory orders, traditionally most manufacturers have used multiple suppliers when purchasing materials. However, as the following Management Application notes, tradition is changing.

MANAGEMENT APPLICATION

THE REWARDS OF SINGLE SOURCING

A traditional rule in purchasing materials is to buy from several suppliers. This practice avoids overdependency on one supplier. If a supplier encounters quality or production problems (i.e., the plant burns down, the production crew goes on strike, the vendor has a supplies shortage), the purchaser has other suppliers to draw upon. Buying from multiple suppliers also maintains a balance of power between the buyer and seller; supply contracts are therefore more reasonable.

However, today an increasing number of companies are implementing single-source strategies. They are picking one supplier for each type of needed materials and focusing on developing a long-term relationship with the single vendor. This trend is particularly notable in the auto industry. At Ford Motor and General Motors, over 98 percent of the purchased materials and parts are single sourced. For instance, all steering wheels for a particular model are provided by one supplier. This strategy sharply contrasts with the dominant practice in the 1970s of buying each type of part or material from two or three different suppliers.

Why the shift to single sourcing in the 1980s? Experts point to five advantages that the new practice provides:

Consistency in materials.   A single vendor makes one part one way which results in a high degree of consistency in the parts produced. Multiple vendors may meet part specifications; however, parts across vendors aren't identical and variations can hinder product quality. One vendor provides part-to-part consistency.

Overall quality improvements.   A growing number of purchasers are requiring that suppliers meet higher quality standards (which reduces the purchasers' need to inspect

---

[1]Roger G. Schroeder, *Operations Management: Decision Making in the Operations Function* (New York: McGraw-Hill, 1981).

incoming materials). With single sourcing, a purchaser can work more easily with a supplier to boost materials quality. With a guaranteed larger volume of purchases, a supplier is more willing to invest in production equipment that boosts materials quality.

Flexible production scheduling.   A purchaser can more easily coordinate production schedules with one supplier. Many purchaser-supplier partnerships maintain "vendor capacity scheduling" where the purchaser can reserve a specified number of the vendor's machines for production of needed parts. The purchaser then schedules the vendor's machines to produce the parts when the purchaser needs them.

Speedier product development.   Often newly designed parts are needed when a purchaser develops a new product. A single-supplier/purchaser relationship facilitates joint efforts between the two parties to quickly design parts that meet the new product's specifications.

Lower administrative costs.   Fewer suppliers mean fewer suppliers' contracts, less time in contract negotiations, fewer visits with suppliers, and less paperwork.

However, despite its advantages, single sourcing requires putting all one's eggs in one basket, supplierwise. Therefore, purchasers take extra care in selecting the one supplier for each part or material.

Source: Adapted from John H. Sheridan, "Betting on a Single Source," *Industry Week*, February 1, 1988, pp. 31 ff.

Precontrol of capital.   Several methods in widespread practice are discussed in this section. Each method for precontrolling capital involves formulating a standard that must be met before capital equipment can be purchased.

The *payback method* is the simplest and apparently the most widely used standard for precontrol of capital. This approach calculates the number of years necessary for the proposed capital acquisition to repay its original cost out of future cash earnings. For example, a manager is considering a machine that would reduce labor costs by $8,000 per year for each of the four years of its estimated life. The cost of the machine is $16,000, and the tax rate is 50 percent. The additional after tax cash inflow, from which the machine cost must be paid, is calculated as follows:

Additional cash inflow before taxes		$8,000
(labor cost savings)		
Less additional taxes:		
Additional income	$8,000	
Less depreciation ($16,000 ÷ 4)	4,000	
Additional taxable income	$4,000	
Tax rate	0.5	
Additional tax payment		2,000
Additional cash inflow after taxes		$6,000

After the additional taxes are deducted from the labor savings, the payback period can be calculated as follows:

$$\frac{\$16,000}{\$6,000} = 2.67 \text{ years}$$

The proposed machine will repay its original cost in $2^2/_3$ years. If the standard requires a payback of at most three years, the machine would be deemed an appropriate investment. An effect of economic uncertainty is the tendency of managers to shorten the required payback period.

The payback method suffers many limitations as a standard for evaluating capital resources. It does not enable a company to accurately compare the profitability of one project with another. For instance, suppose in the preceding example that a payback period has been calculated for a second machine (machine B). The payback period for machine B is two years while the payback for the first machine (A) is 2.67 years. Machine B seems to be a clearly better investment than machine A. However, machine B has a useful life of two years which is half the useful life of machine A. Thus, a purchase of two machine Bs is needed to provide the same length of service as one machine A. In this case, machine A is likely the better investment. The payback method ignores this important information.[2]

Another factor which the method fails to consider is the time value of money. It does not recognize that a dollar received today is worth more than a dollar obtained at a future date. Other methods can be employed which include these important considerations.

Despite its several limitations, the payback method is useful as an initial screening tool to eliminate investment projects that cannot pay for themselves within a reasonable period of time. The payback criteria for evaluating potential investments is very useful to companies that have little cash. For them, an investment with a lower return over time but a shorter payback period may be preferred because they need a faster return on their cash investment.[3]

The *simple rate of return on investment* produces a measure of profitability which is consistent with methods ordinarily employed in accounting. Using the above example, the calculations would be as follows:

Additional gross income		$8,000
Less depreciation ($16,000 ÷ 4)	$4,000	
Less taxes	2,000	
Total additional expenses		6,000
Additional net income after taxes		$2,000

The simple rate of return is the ratio of the additional net income to the original cost:

$$\frac{\$2,000}{\$16,000} = 12.5\%$$

[2]Ray H. Garrison, *Managerial Accounting: Concepts for Planning, Control, Decision Making* (Plano, Tex.: Business Publications, 1988), p. 715.

[3]Ibid., p. 716.

The calculated simple rate of return then must be compared to some standard of minimum acceptability, and the decision to accept or reject depends on that comparison.

Measuring the simple rate of return is a process that has the advantage of being easily understood. However, like the payback method, simple rate of return does not consider the time value of money. A project with a high, simple rate of return that provides most of its cash flows in later years is viewed as superior to a project with a lower simple rate of return that provides most of the cash flows much sooner. Considering the time value of money, the project with the lower-but-faster simple return may be the better investment.[4]

The *discounted rate of return* measures profitability while taking into account the time value of money. It can be used as a standard for screening potential capital acquisitions. This method is similar to the payback method, since it considers only cash inflows and outflows. The method is widely used because it is regarded as the "correct" method for calculating the rate of return. Based on the example above, calculating the discounted rate of return is as follows:

$$\$16,000 = \frac{\$6,000}{(1 + r)} + \frac{\$6,000}{(1 + r)^2} + \frac{\$6,000}{(1 + r)^3} + \frac{\$6,000}{(1 + r)^4}$$
$$r = 18\%$$

The discounted rate of return (r) is 18 percent. This means that a $16,000 investment that repays $6,000 in cash at the end of each of four years yields a return of 18 percent.

The rationale of the method can be understood by thinking of the $6,000 inflows as cash payments received by the firm. In exchange for each of these four payments of $6,000, the firm must pay $16,000. The rate of return, 18 percent, is the factor equating future cash inflows with the present cash outflow.

Whether managers are controlling materials or capital, the decision is essentially go or no-go. If the standard is met, the decision is go; if the standard is not met, the decision is no-go. But new technology has become so advanced and far-reaching that a decision to invest or not to invest can be severely handicapped. As noted in the following Management Application, companies must develop additional criteria to help them screen investment alternatives.[5]

MANAGEMENT APPLICATION

INVESTING IN NEW TECHNOLOGY

American companies often experience difficulty in deciding to invest in new manufacturing technologies. The stumbling block is that traditional financial analysis is based

---

[4]Ibid., p. 720.

[5]For an insightful profile of one company's approach to making investment decisions for its many diversified businesses, see Richard J. Marshuetz, "How American Can Allocates Capital," *Harvard Business Review,* January–February 1985, pp. 82–91. A discussion of the use of the discounted rate of return technique in evaluating high-risk projects appears in the same issue: James E. Hodder and Henry E. Riggs, "Pitfalls in Evaluating Risky Projects," pp. 128–135.

on criteria not easily applied to advanced technology. The usual criteria include *return on investment,* which is based on labor cost savings resulting from new technology. But the savings in new technology are not so much in labor as they are in the more difficult to measure areas of material quality and overhead. The rate of return often fails to measure fully the benefits of new technology, and this discourages managers from adopting the new advances.

One company which has moved full steam ahead, however, is General Electric Co.'s dishwasher manufacturing plant in Louisville, Kentucky. The company recognized that modern technology can be used only if its systemwide implications are evaluated. Consequently, it integrated the product design and manufacturing process by altering the product design to the point of changing the dishwasher tub design.

With automation, the tubs now are touched by human hands only once. Prior to automation, tubs were touched 17 times. Scrap and rework costs have dropped 40 percent, and quality has improved 25 percent. The product redesign reduced the number of parts and subassemblies from 5,600 to 600. All in all, GE's adoption of advanced manufacturing technology has produced phenomenal gains. But these gains were not readily foreseen at the outset of the changeover.

Source: Adapted from Frank T. Curtin, "New Costing Methods Needed for Manufacturing Technology," *Management Review,* April 1984, pp. 29, 33–34.

Concurrent Control of Operations

Operations decisions based on concurrent control methods determine how much and when outputs will be produced. These decisions typically are termed *production scheduling,* and two general types of models can be used, *network models* and *linear programming models.* These two methods typically are used by production schedulers who prepare production schedules that line managers implement.

Network models.   Managers can use network models to combine and schedule resources or to control activities so plans are carried out as stated. Such models are especially suited for, but not restricted to, nonroutine projects, which are conducted a few times at most. In such projects, some type of coordination is needed to ensure that priority tasks are completed on time. Also needed is an approximation of how long the entire project will take. In summary, some method is needed to avoid unnecessary conflicts and delays. It should help keep track of all the events and activities on a specific project—and their interrelationships. Network models provide the means to achieve these goals. One widely used network model is the *Program Evaluation and Review Technique (PERT).*

PERT (and its variations) probably is one of the most widely used production management methods. After the Special Projects Office of the U.S. Navy introduced it on the Polaris missile project in 1958, PERT was widely credited with helping to reduce by two years the time for the completion of the missile's engineering and development programs. By identifying the longest path through all of the necessary project tasks, PERT enabled the program managers to concentrate their efforts on these tasks, since they affected vitally the total project time. During the last two decades, PERT has spread rapidly throughout the defense and space industries. Today, almost every major government military agency involved in the space program utilizes PERT and other network models in planning and controlling their work on government contracts.

The aerospace business faces peculiar problems, but one-of-a-kind development work is an important element in many other kinds of organizations and industries, as well. In addition to helping develop space vehicles and put astronauts on the moon, PERT also has been utilized successfully in:

1. Constructing new plants, buildings, and hospitals.
2. Designing new automobiles.
3. Coordinating the numerous activities (production, marketing, etc.) involved in introducing new products.
4. Planning sales campaigns.
5. Planning logistic and distribution systems.
6. Coordinating the installation of large-scale computer systems.
7. Coordinating ship construction and aircraft repairs.

Beyond its engineering applications, PERT also has been used successfully in coordinating the numerous activities necessary to complete mergers between large organizations. It has assisted economic planning in under-developed countries, and in smaller applications, has helped coordinate and plan all the tasks necessary to organize large-scale conventions and meetings.

PERT networks are developed around two key concepts: activities and events. An *activity* is the work necessary to complete a particular event. An *event* is an accomplishment at a particular point in time. In PERT networks, an event is designated by a circle, and an activity is designated by an arrow connecting two circles. This is shown in Figure 15–3.

In Figure 15–3, two events are connected by one activity. The events are assigned numbers, and the activity is designated with an arrow. Each of the two events occurs at a specific point in time. Event 1 could represent "project begun," and Event 2 could represent "project completed." The arrow connecting the two events, meanwhile, represents the activity—the actual work done—and the time necessary to complete it. Thus, the two events in Figure 15–3 designate the beginning and the end of the activity. The activity takes the time, not the event.

In constructing a PERT network, events and activities must be identified with enough precision that the manager can monitor accomplishment as the project proceeds. Four basic phases are needed when constructing a PERT network:

1. Define each activity to be done.
2. Estimate how long each activity will take.
3. Construct the network.
4. Find the critical path—that is, the longest path in time—from the beginning event to the ending event.

Figure 15–3
The basic
elements of a
simple PERT
network.

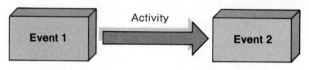

Consists of two events linked by one activity

All events and activities must be sequenced in the network under a strict set of logical rules (e.g., no event can be considered complete until all preceding events have been completed). The rules should allow for the determination of the critical path.

The paramount variable in a PERT network is time—the basic measure of how long a project will take. Estimating the time each activity requires can be extremely difficult, however, since managers may not have similar experiences to compare.

Estimating activity time requirements is a technique for dealing specifically with uncertainty in making the job estimates. For example, assume you are trying to estimate how long it will take you to complete a term project for your management class. You know that one activity will be to collect certain information. If all goes well and you do not encounter any obstacles, you believe you can complete this activity in eight weeks. However, if you encounter obstacles (dates, parties, illness, materials not available in the library), the chances are greater that this activity will take much longer. Thus, you can estimate a variety of potential completion times for this part of your term project.

For projects using PERT, *three time estimates are required for each activity.* Each time estimate should be made by the individual or group most closely connected with, and responsible for, the particular activity. The three estimates needed are:

1. *Optimistic Time (a).* This is the time in which the project can be completed if everything goes exceptionally well and no obstacles or problems are encountered.

2. *Most Likely Time (m).* This is the most realistic estimate of how long an activity might take. It is the average time you would expect to take if the activity were repeated often.

3. *Pessimistic Time (b).* This is the time that would be required if everything went wrong and numerous obstacles and problems were encountered. A PERT network of eight events is depicted in Figure 15–4. The three time estimates for each activity also are indicated.

Obviously, it would be extremely difficult to deal simultaneously with the optimistic time, the most likely time, and the pessimistic time. Fortunately, a method has been developed to arrive at one time estimate. An *expected time (t_e),* can be estimated satisfactorily for each activity by using the following formula:

$$\text{Expected time } (t_e) = \frac{a + 4m + b}{6}$$

Figure 15–4 PERT network.

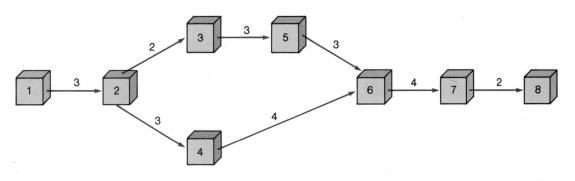

Figure 15–5 depicts the network outlined in Figure 15-4 after the expected time (t_e) has been calculated for each activity. The sequence along the path 1, 2, 3, 5, 6, 7, 8 takes 17 weeks, while the sequence along the path 1, 2, 4, 6, 7, 8 takes 16 weeks. The critical path, then, is the one which takes the longest time (17 weeks).

A major advantage of the Program Evaluation and Review Technique is that the planning involved in constructing the network contributes significantly to the *concurrent control* of the project. The construction of the network is a very demanding but beneficial task that forces the manager to visualize the number and kinds of necessary activities and their sequences.

Effectively used, PERT can be a valuable control device. It provides time schedules for each activity and permits networks to be revised if unforeseen difficulties occur. Resources can be shifted, and activities can be rescheduled with a minimum of delay in the completion of the project.

In a project where subcontractors are used, the need to meet scheduled dates can be stressed by showing the subcontractors the negative effects any deal would have on the entire project. The subcontractors must know that it is vital for them to meet their scheduled delivery dates. For example, the Polaris missile project involved some 250 prime contractors and almost 10,000 subcontractors. The failure of any subcontractor to deliver a piece of hardware on schedule could have stalled the entire project.[6]

Linear programming models. These types of production scheduling models are extremely useful for maximizing an objective, such as profits, or minimizing an objective, such as costs. Linear programming models can help determine what the future values of certain variables affecting the outcome should be to achieve the objective. The manager has some control over these variables.

---

[6]Computer software is increasingly being used to facilitate PERT tasks. Discussion of computerized PERT can be found in Mitchell H. Goldstein, "Project Management Systems," *National Productivity Review,* Summer 1986, pp. 290–92; Mickey Williamson, "Project Management Software," *Computerworld,* December 8, 1986, pp. 55ff; and "Critical Path Management for Project Planners," *ComputerData (Canada),* August 1986, p. 24.

Figure 15–5 Expected time (t_e) for each activity.

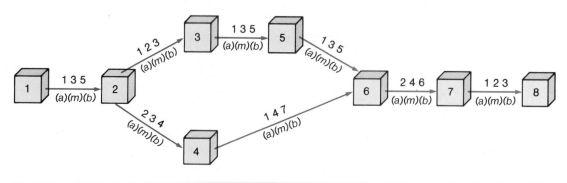

The models are called *linear* because the mathematical equations employed to describe the particular systems under study, as well as the objectives to be achieved, are in the form of linear relations between the variables. A linear relationship between two or more variables is one that is directly and precisely proportional.

Linear programming models are used in a variety of situations in which numerous activities compete for limited resources. Managers must find the optimum way to allocate the limited resources, given an objective and any relevant constraints. A complete discussion of the mathematics involved in linear programming models is beyond the purposes of this text. Here, the emphasis is placed on the applications of these models for concurrent control in production-operations management.[7]

Product-mix problems arise when managers must determine the levels for a number of production activities for the planning period. For example, managers face a problem of this nature if a firm manufactures two products and both must go through the same three production processes. The two products compete for time in the three production processes. So the task of the linear project model in this case would be to find a way to produce enough of each product to maximize the firm's profits.

Feed-mix problems confront large farming organizations that purchase and mix together several types of grains for different purposes. Each grain may contain varying amounts of several nutritional elements. For one situation, the production manager must blend the different grains to produce a mixture for feeding livestock. The mixture must meet the minimal nutritional requirements at the lowest possible cost. Linear programming can be used to allocate the various grains (each containing different

---

[7]For some excellent case profiles of specific uses of linear programming, see Godelieve Vanderstraeten and Michel Bergeron, "Automatic Assignment of Aircraft to Gates of a Terminal," *Computers & Industrial Engineering* 14, no. 1 (1988), pp. 15–25; Thomas O. Davenport and H. David Sherman, "Measuring Branch Profitability," *Bankers Magazine,* September–October 1987, pp. 34–38; Eugene W. Grant, Jr., and Fred N. Hendron, Jr., "An Application of Linear Programming to Hospital Resource Allocation," *Journal of Health Care Marketing,* September 1987, pp. 69–72; and Heikki Rinne, Michael Geurts, and Kelly J. Patrick, "An Approach to Allocating Space to Departments in a Retail Store," *International Journal of Retailing (UK)* 2, no. 2 (1987), pp. 27–41.

amounts of the nutritional elements) in such a way that the resulting mixture will meet the nutritional and diet specifications at minimum cost.

Fluid-blending problems are variations of the feed-mix problem. In this case, the manager seeks to blend fluids such as molten metals, chemicals, and crude oil into finished products. Steel, chemical, and oil companies make wide use of linear programming models for problems of this type. Computing the right mixture of octane requirements in the blending of different gasolines is an example of such a problem in the oil industry.

Transportation problems arise when manufacturers and large retail chains face the following situation: Given a number of sources of supply (e.g., warehouses) and a number of destinations (e.g., customers), and given the cost of shipping a product from each source to each destination, how does one select the routes that will minimize total shipping costs? You can imagine the complexity of the problem if the firm has many warehouses in different parts of the country and thousands of geographically dispersed customers. Linear programming provides a means for arriving at the optimum shipping program.

Advertising media-mix problems have the following characteristics: Given an advertising budget, how can the budgeted funds be allocated over the various advertising media to achieve maximum exposure of the product or service? A number of media (e.g., five magazines) may be competing for a limited advertising budget. Linear programming is widely used in many advertising agencies to solve problems of this type.

Although the above examples represent the most common applications, linear programming has proven its worth in handling many other practical problems. For example, Grant Hospital in Chicago uses linear programming to determine the optimal schedule for its staff of 300 nurses. Before the hospital adopted the technique, the scheduling task required over 20 hours of work each month. The job of ensuring that the schedule placed the right number of nurses with the right abilities in every ward and on every shift was complicated, especially when vacations and unexpected absences must be considered. Linear programming provides a solution in four hours and saves the hospital $80,000 a month because of improved scheduling efficiency. The hospital no longer must hire temporary nurses and schedule overtime.[8]

In British Columbia, water resource experts use linear programming to regulate water levels of lakes controlled by dams. The experts found that more electricity is generated by a dam when the lake behind it is full; however, when the lake overflows due to rain, much generating power is lost. Linear programming boosted electricity generation from dams by 5 percent by telling when and how to open and close the walls of the dam.[9]

In these and most other uses of linear programming, a computer is used to construct the linear programming model. It performs the computations and manipulations and provides a solution that maximizes or minimizes the stated objective within the given

---

[8]William M. Bulkeley, "The Right Mix: New Software Makes the Choice Much Easier," *The Wall Street Journal,* March 27, 1987, p. 24.

[9]Ibid., p. 24.

constraints. Human judgment and creativity are necessary before and after the model has solved the problem. For example, once a solution has been selected, the manager may alter or add a constraint, or change the objective. The computer then can provide a new solution.

Although a computer greatly speeds the linear programming task, some highly complex problems have defied a fast and useful solution. However, a breakthrough in linear programming has occurred which promises to further expand the uses of the technique. This advancement is discussed in the following Management Application.

MANAGEMENT APPLICATION

A BREAKTHROUGH IN LINEAR PROGRAMMING

To date, linear programming has been used to solve a myriad of business problems. However, some problems have been viewed as too complex for the technique to handle efficiently even on a mainframe computer. These problems involve literally thousands of variables (and constraints) with the values of many variables changing over time. Days, even months of computer time are needed to obtain a solution. Consequently, businesses won't use linear programming for these problems because by the time a solution is obtained, values of some variables have changed, rendering the solution useless.

However, a 29-year-old researcher has developed a new technique in linear programming that can solve the most complex problems and do so much faster than the current linear programming method on the fastest computers. Narendra K. Karmarkar of AT&T's Bell Laboratories has developed an algorithm which is a set of computational rules that fills some 20 printed pages. In tests of Karmarkar's technique to date, the algorithm is slightly faster than current linear programming on moderately complex problems. However, when solving the most complex problems, the technique is at least 50 to 100 times faster than traditional linear programming.

For example, AT&T has one problem that had defied a fast solution. The problem: find the most cost-effective way to organize the telephone network that links more than 20 Far East countries along the Pacific Ocean brim. The time span of cost-effectiveness is the next 10 years. Solving this problem requires forecasting the future telephone demand for every pair of switching points in the network. The problem requires 42,000 variables and weeks of computer time to solve. However, with Karmarkar's technique, the problem was solved in less than four minutes.

AT&T used Karmarkar's algorithm to tackle another, even more mind-boggling challenge: to determine the most cost-effective way to organize AT&T's domestic long-distance network, a problem involving 800,000 variables and requiring almost a year of computer time. Karmarkar's approach provided a solution in less than one hour. The solution enabled AT&T to increase the network's capacity by about 10 percent which saved the company millions of dollars.

So far, results such as these indicate that Karmarkar's algorithm is a major breakthrough in linear programming and in business problem solving. However, some linear programming experts are skeptical, in part because Bell Laboratories has kept many of the technical details about the algorithm to itself. The company has not provided scientists with instructions on how to translate the algorithm into digital computer codes. Bell Labs wants to first develop commercial software based on the new technique. Scientists do know that the algorithm does not change the basic principles of linear programming concerning variables and constraints; it simply provides a faster way to find the best solution within the constraints.

However, if the technique fulfills its promise, it could revolutionize complex business decision making and save businesses millions of dollars. Problems previously viewed as too complex to tackle would become solvable. Others would be solved much more efficiently. Officials at American Airlines, for example, assert that Karmarkar's technique would enable them to quickly establish emergency schedules for its several hundred planes and thousands of flights when major storms upend the normal schedule. Before, full-scale emergency scheduling wasn't possible because a linear programming solution took hours. However, with the new technique, optimal revised schedules can be done within minutes.

The technique may well place this type of problem-solving power in the hands of small businesses if software for minicomputers is developed. Observers expect Bell Laboratories to develop the software in the near future.

Source: Adapted from William G. Wild, Jr., and Otis Port, "The Startling Discovery Bell Labs Kept in the Shadows," *Business Week,* September 21, 1987, pp. 69ff; and David Stipp, "AT&T Problem-Solving Math Procedure Passes Early Tests of Its Practical Value," *The Wall Street Journal,* May 3, 1985, p. 23.

Just-In-Time Inventory Management

So far, discussion has focused on operations techniques that exclusively involve either precontrol or concurrent control activities. One unique and relatively new approach to operations control combines precontrol and concurrent control activities. Called *just-in-time inventory management (JIT),* this approach is designed to minimize the amount of inventory in a way that not only cuts inventory costs but also boosts plant productivity and product quality. Well over 100 major U.S. manufacturers (such as Campbell's Soup Co., General Motors, and Motorola) and a growing number of small businesses have implemented JIT in their factories.[10]

JIT was developed in the 1960s by Toyota managers who considered inventory to be "the root of all evil."[11] In their view, excessive inventory produces four problems. It clearly increases carrying costs. Perhaps more important, excessive inventory hides problems in the production process and reduces product quality and plant productivity.

These relationships can be understood by reviewing Figure 15–6 which depicts the path that inventory follows in a production process. In the conventional path, materials first arrive at a plant at the delivery dock and are placed in the materials storeroom.

---

[10]Steven P. Galante, "Small Manufacturers Shifting to 'Just-In-Time' Techniques," *The Wall Street Journal,* December 21, 1987, p. 21; and Richard J. Schonberger, *World Class Manufacturing: The Lessons of Simplicity Applied* (New York: The Free Press, 1986).

[11]Robert H. Hayes, "Why Japanese Factories Work," *Harvard Business Review,* July-August 1981, pp. 57–66.

Figure 15–6 Path of inventory through a production process.

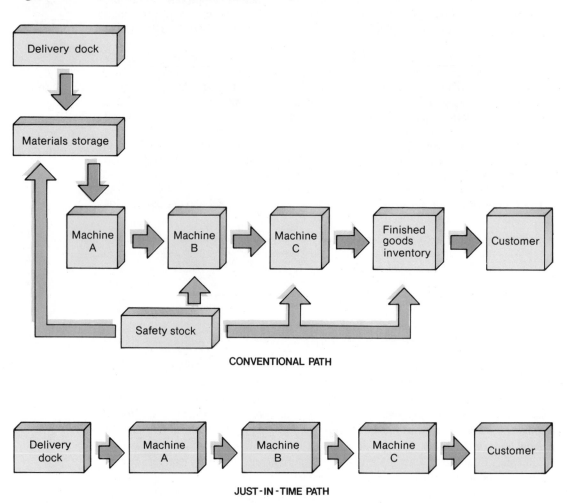

Enough materials are ordered to cover immediate needs at machine A, the first step in the production process. However, additional materials, *safety stock,* are kept in storage for use in case suppliers experience a sudden shortage and can't deliver the needed materials, or their deliveries are late. Safety stock provides machine A the materials it needs in these situations. However, this excess inventory also incurs the costs of rent (for the additional floor space it fills), insurance, labor to handle materials accounting chores, spoilage, and other factors.

Needed materials proceed to machine A where they are processed (as work-in-process inventory) and then proceed to machine B, machine C, and as finished products to finished goods inventory before delivery to the customer. Safety stocks are maintained at each of these three points so that when a production problem occurs, work can still continue uninterrupted or the product can meet customer delivery dates. However, at each point, carrying costs of unused inventory accumulate.

Safety stocks create another problem. Because they ensure that production is not interrupted by a breakdown in the process, safety stocks slow the speed at which problems are solved. For example, when machine A breaks down, work at machine B will continue using safety stock. Employees at machine A aren't motivated to fix the problem as quickly as possible; after all, the production process continues unabated. This tendency lowers plant productivity because machine A is down and some workers must stand idly by while the machine is repaired, incurring unproductive labor costs. The plant's capacity also declines. With safety stocks, problems in the production process also tend to be neglected because their perceived costs are insignificant.

In conventional inventory management and production, materials typically are ordered and processed in large lots or batches. Large lot production reduces setup time, the downtime required to make equipment adjustments to ready machines for a new batch of production. The larger each lot, the fewer setups required, and setup costs are reduced. However, large lot production also hinders product quality. For example, suppose a problem with machine A is producing defects in a batch of 1,000 units being processed by the machine. After machine A processes all of the lot's units, the lot proceeds to machine B. By the time 1,000 units reach machine B and the problem is detected, 1,000 units are wasted or must be reworked. In small lot production (e.g., a lot of 50 units), the lot travels more quickly through the production process. Defects discovered at machine B will cost 50 rather than 1,000 units.

Just-in-time inventory management is designed to alleviate these problems using the following principles:[12]

Provide inventory (raw materials, work-in-process, finished goods) exactly when needed and no sooner. Raw materials are received from suppliers just-in-time for use at machine A. No inventory stands waiting in materials storage. (In many plants using JIT, there is no materials storeroom; suppliers deliver materials directly to machine A.) Work-in-process inventory from machine A arrives exactly when needed at machine B, machine B's finished work is provided just-in-time for machine C, and so on. Finished goods inventory storage is eliminated. No inventory stands waiting anywhere for any purpose.

Eliminate safety stocks. With this action, any problem in a machine shuts the production line down. All attention focuses on eliminating the problem. Consequently, production problems are solved more quickly.

Order materials and produce in small lots. The precontrol of materials involves ordering in small quantities. Concurrent manufacturing control involves scheduling production in small lots. In small lot production, a unit proceeds more quickly through the production process. If machine A produces a defect in the unit, it is more quickly detected at machine B and solved before more units are wasted.

---

[12]Richard J. Schonberger, *Japanese Manufacturing Techniques: Nine Hidden Lessons in Simplicity* (New York: The Free Press, 1982).

Maintain a stable production schedule.   Just-in-time requires a continuous flowing, even, and stable production process. Concurrent production control must provide careful, advance scheduling to give suppliers sufficient notice concerning delivery times and to ensure a smooth, virtual nonstop production flow. Emergencies and expediting orders don't fit in the system.

Train employees to inspect quality while working on the product.   This action is not a core principle of JIT; however, many companies adopt the principle because this concurrent quality control is very compatible with the JIT concept.[13]

At first glance, JIT appears to pose two problems. The concept boosts setup costs because small lot production requires more setups. JIT also increases ordering costs because if materials are purchased in small quantities, more orders are required. The concept alleviates these problems with two additional principles:

Reduce setup times.   Given the greater number of setups, production downtime per setup must be reduced. Many companies have achieved reductions by finding faster ways to make machine adjustments, by altering the plant floor layout, and by making machine design changes. In the early 1970s, Toyota launched a companywide campaign to reduce setup times. One effort focused on cutting the time (one hour) required to ready 800-ton presses that form car fenders and hoods for a new lot of production. Over five years, Toyota reduced the setup time to 12 minutes. (A comparable U.S. competitor takes six hours to achieve the same setup.) Toyota is now working to achieve "single setups" (under 10 minutes) and in some cases "one-touch setups" (under one minute).[14]

Reduce order costs.   This principle involves reducing the number of suppliers and focusing on developing long-term relationships with high-quality vendors. Suppliers should also be located close to the plant to reduce transport time (and thus lower order costs). Nearly 80 percent of Toyota's 220 suppliers are located within one hour of Toyota's plants.

Many American companies have found that developing effective supplier relationships under JIT requirements is the most challenging aspect of JIT implementation. Demands on suppliers are considerable; they must deliver high-quality materials many times, on time. Daily, even hourly deliveries are not uncommon. Under the JIT concept, late or defective materials can shut down the production process as there are no safety stocks to cushion the effects of these problems.

In developing JIT-based supplier relationships, companies such as Xerox and Harley-Davidson have initially made the mistake of viewing JIT as a way to push their

---

[13]For an excellent comparative discussion of JIT and other systems designed to boost manufacturing efficiency, see Sumer C. Aggarwal, "MRP, JIT, OPT, FMS?" *Harvard Business Review,* September–October 1985, pp. 8ff.

[14]Schonberger, *Japanese Manufacturing Techniques* p. 20; and Harris Jack Shapiro and Teresa Cosenza, *Reviving Industry in America: Japanese Influences on Manufacturing and the Service Sector* (Cambridge, Mass.: Ballinger Publishing, 1987).

inventory onto the supplier. The supplier holds the manufacturer's raw materials and incurs the carrying costs. However, this strategy fails over the long term because the vendor simply increases materials costs to cover the extra carrying charges.[15]

Companies that have successfully implemented JIT usually follow three steps in developing relationships with suppliers. They first communicate the technique's benefits for themselves and supplier (the supplier benefits from a stable, long-term purchasing relationship). They train the supplier in JIT concepts; many companies encourage suppliers to adopt JIT in their own operations and help them implement the concept to reap the same benefits in productivity, costs, and quality. They also help the supplier find ways to simplify its own production process to make frequent deliveries easier.[16]

Omark Industries is one company that has successfully implemented JIT.[17] The firm manufactures equipment for the forest products industry. In 1981, Omark's president observed the concept at work in one of Japan's auto manufacturing plants. Returning to Omark, the president headed a corporate team that presented two-day seminars on JIT at each of the company's 21 plants. From there, small groups of managers and employees were formed at each plant to read, study, and discuss Toyota's manual on JIT, chapter by chapter.

Once the study period was completed, Omark's Zero Inventory Production System (ZIPS) was launched. ZIPS teams were established in each plant to devise ways to implement JIT concepts. In Omark's chain saw manufacturing plant in Portland, Oregon, teams were staffed with employees who had received a week's worth of training in ZIPS and quality control. They were further cross-trained in several jobs to boost the production process' flexibility. These teams worked on ways to lower inventory. Machine tooling was changed, some machines were redesigned, and the plant's layout was altered to speed the setup and production process. In the early stages of ZIPS, the plant arbitrarily took one week's supply of safety stock off the factory floor and found that the production process ran more smoothly. With little inventory to cushion the effects of production problems and employees trained in quality inspection, quality problems in materials and the production process became very evident; employees found defects that had previously gone undetected.

Special efforts were made to share production information with suppliers and help them implement ZIPS in their materials production plants. After one year of ZIPS management, the Portland plant had cut finished goods inventory by 50 percent, reduced work-in-process inventory by 50 percent, and reduced manufacturing costs by 6 percent. About one third of the plant's floor space was cleared of inventory along with half of the 100,000 square feet of space in the materials warehouse. Overall, Omark

---

[15]Dexter Hutchins, "Having a Hard Time with Just-In-Time," *Fortune,* June 9, 1986, pp. 64ff.

[16]Nicholas J. Pennucci, "Just-In-Time for a Change," *Quality Progress,* November 1987, pp. 67–68.

[17]For other profiles of successful JIT implementation, see Ira P. Krepchin, "How One Company is Approaching JIT," *Modern Materials Handling,* January 1988, pp. 101–4; Elisabeth Ryan Sullivan, "AT&T Invests in Training Factory Workers," *Manufacturing Week,* January 11, 1988, p. 18; and "Brunswick's Dramatic Turnaround," *Journal of Business Strategy,* January–February 1988, pp. 4–7.

invested $200,000 to implement ZIPS across its plants. In return, the company saves $7 million annually in inventory carrying costs.[18]

JIT is a powerful tool for lowering inventory costs and investment, cutting labor costs, and boosting product quality, plant capacity, and productivity. By eliminating delays in the production process, JIT makes a company's production more flexible. Because the process is quicker, the company can more swiftly respond to customer demand for product variations.[19] However, it is a challenging concept to implement. Consequently, many companies first establish JIT on a small scale before making a plantwide commitment to the concept. For example, Hewlett-Packard's Computer Systems Division first implemented JIT in the last two steps of the production process before implementing the concept back through the factory to the first step in the process.[20] JIT works best in companies where inventory and product demand can be accurately forecasted, the production processes are repetitive, and high-quality suppliers are located nearby.[21]

Postcontrol of Outputs

Effective production-operations control requires managers to establish standards for the finished good or service. Precontrol and concurrent control procedures increase the chances that high-quality, efficiently produced outputs will result. But the real test must be based on analysis of the output. If the output fails to meet acceptable standards, production managers can pinpoint causes in the inputs or the transformation process. Two techniques widely used for postcontrol of outputs are *standard cost analysis* and *statistical quality control*. Statistical quality control was discussed in Chapter 14 in the context of an integrated control system. Consequently we will not discuss it here.

Standard cost analysis.   The three elements of manufacturing costs are direct labor, direct materials, and overhead. For each of these, an estimate must be made of the element's cost per unit of output. For example, the direct labor cost per unit of output consists of the standard usage of labor and the standard price of labor. The standard usage is derived from time studies that determine the expected output per worker-hour. The standard price of labor, meanwhile, is determined by the salary schedule appropriate for the kind of work necessary to produce the output. A similar determination is made for direct materials. Thus, the standard labor and standard materials costs might be as follows:

[18]Shapiro and Consenza, *Reviving Industry in America,* pp. 43–50; and Craig R. Waters, "Why Everybody's Talking about Just-In-Time," *Inc.,* March 1984, pp. 77ff.

[19]Bruce D. Henderson, "The Logic of Kanban," *The Journal of Business Strategy,* Winter 1986, pp. 6–12; and Kimball H. Hannah, "Just-In-Time: Meeting the Competitive Challenge," *Production and Inventory Management,* 1987 (third quarter), pp. 1–3.

[20]Richard C. Walleigh, "What's Your Excuse for Not Using JIT?" *Harvard Business Review,* March–April 1986, pp. 38ff.

[21]Waters, "Why Everybody's Talking about Just-In-Time," 1984; and Walleigh, "What's Your Excuse for Not Using JIT?" 1986.

Standard labor usage per unit	2 hours
Standard wage rate per hour	$ 6.00
Standard labor cost (2 × $6.00)	$12.00
Standard material usage per unit	6 pounds
Standard material price per pound	$ 0.30
Standard material cost (6 × $0.30)	$ 1.80

The accounting information system produces data enabling the manager to compare incurred costs with standard costs. For example, if 200 units of output were produced during the period covered by the report, the standard labor cost is $2,400 (200 × $12.00) and the standard material cost is $360 (200 × $1.80). Assume that the actual payroll cost for that same period was $2,700 and that the actual material cost was $400. That is, there was an *unfavorable labor variance* of $300 and an *unfavorable material variance of $40*. Assuming that the standards are correct, the manager must analyze the variances and fix the responsibility for restoring the balance between standard and actual costs.

It is obvious that if the actual labor cost exceeds the *standard cost,* the reason for the difference will be found in labor usage and labor wage rates. Either the actual labor usage exceeded the standard labor usage or the actual wage rates exceeded the standard wage rates, or both. Suppose the accountant reports that the actual payroll consisted of 450 hours at an average hourly wage rate of $6. The questions management must resolve are now narrowed to two: What happened during the period to cause output per worker-hour to go down (it should require 400 worker-hours to produce 200 units of output)?

Similar analyses must be made to discover the causes for the unfavorable material variance. The first step is to discover the relationships between the actual usage and the standard usage and between the actual price and the standard price. As with the labor usage, the manager may find that the actual material usage exceeded the material usage specified by the standard. He may also find that the actual price exceeds the standard price. Once the cause has been isolated, the analysis must determine what corrective action to take.

Cost accounting systems are essential in controlling manufacturing costs. However, as the following Management Application discusses, cost accounting systems in many companies are outdated and provide distorted numbers, especially concerning the true production costs of a company's different products.[22]

MANAGEMENT APPLICATION

THE COSTS OF FLAWED ACCOUNTING

Cost accounting is an exceptionally important element of a company's operations and product strategy. The estimated cost of a product greatly influences the price a company

---

[22]For an insightful discussion of the shortcomings of traditional cost accounting systems (and their impact on manufacturing), see Roger W. Schmenner, "Escaping the Black Holes of Cost Accounting," *Business Horizons,* January–February 1988, pp. 66–72.

charges for the product; estimated costs influence the decision to produce more or less of the product or whether to continue making the product at all. Estimated costs also influence investment decisions such as whether to build more manufacturing capacity for a product. Thus, accurate product cost accounting is vitally important.

However, today a growing number of accounting experts assert that the cost accounting systems used in many companies are outdated and obsolete. Consequently, these systems are distorting the true costs of products. The costs of some products are overstated; others are understated. The result, therefore, is that some winning products (those with true but undetected high-profit margins) are being dropped. Some losers (those with no real profit margin at all) are being kept. The irony of the situation is indeed cruel: some companies, convinced by their product cost estimates that they have a highly profitable product in hand, produce more and more while the product really is making no profit at all. The company ends up with many units manufactured and sold and little profits, and wonders why.

Many of these flawed cost accounting systems suffer from three shortcomings. The systems:

Misallocate overhead. Most systems allocate overhead across products based on direct labor—the number of direct labor-hours used to make the product. The more labor-hours consumed by the product, the greater the percentage of overhead allocated to the product. This policy is best when labor is the major cost of making a product. After all, products that consume the most direct costs should assume the most overhead. However, today this is no longer true. Some 25 years ago, direct labor accounted for 40 percent of production costs; today, it often accounts for less than 5 percent. So companies are allocating a major cost—overhead—based on a factor that is no longer representative of overall product costs.

The result: products made in high volumes appear more costly than they really are. Rockwell International made this discovery when it conducted a special study to determine why one of its top-selling axles was suddenly losing sales. The company found that it had been overcosting the high-volume axle by 20 percent and undercosting other lower-volume axles by 40 percent.

Neglect inventory carrying costs. Many systems don't consider the carrying costs of inventory that a product incurs, such as the carrying costs of parts and finished goods. As a result, many products that take up much inventory space are portrayed by the cost accounting system as less costly than they really are.

Neglect up-front and post-production costs. In costing products, many systems ignore the pre-production expenditures such as research and development and costs that follow the product's manufacture such as distributing and marketing. These costs can range from less than 10 to over 25 percent of a product's total costs.

Why have these systems not kept up with the times? Many observers believe that for most upper-level managers, cost accounting is dull. It lacks the excitement of developing a new product or marketing strategy. Thus, top management hasn't given the needed attention or funding to keep the system accurate and current. However, many companies are waking up to the costly flaws in their systems. More than 30 major manufacturing companies including General Electric, Eastman Kodak, and Rockwell International are participating in a joint project to update and retool their accounting systems.

Source: Adapted from Fred S. Worthy, "Accounting Bores You? Wake up," *Fortune,* October 12, 1987, p. 43ff.

FINANCIAL CONTROLS

Financial control methods aid managers in acquiring, allocating, and evaluating the use of financial resources, such as cash, accounts receivable, accounts payable, inventories, and long-term debt. The methods also enable managers to achieve acceptable liquidity, solvency, and profitability standards. Regardless of their size and type, organizations must be able to pay short-term obligations (liquidity) and long-term obligations (solvency). They also must pay dividends or distribute profits to the owners (profitability). In addition, the assets of an organization must be protected from theft, unlawful conversion, and misuse.

A complete treatment of financial control cannot be given here. A survey of some methods are presented below, however, to highlight the general principles of financial control.

Precontrol of Financial Resources

A primary means for precontrolling financial resources are the various plans prepared during the planning phase. These plans are supported by *budgets* allocating funds to each major expense category and organizational unit. A primary responsibility of accounting personnel is to develop the procedures and processes that enable management to keep track of how financial resources are allocated and who is accountable for expending and safeguarding them.

Concurrent Control of Financial Resources

Planning and budgeting are ineffective unless they are supported by policies and procedures defining how and by whom ongoing transactions are to be handled. Concurrent control of financial resources is implemented primarily through *internal control.*

Internal control is a function and responsibility of accounting. Through the efforts of the organization's accounting unit, policies and procedures are adopted which safeguard assets and verify the accuracy and reliability of accounting data. The characteristics of effective internal control include the following:

1. No one person should have complete control over all phases of an important transaction. For example, the same individual should not be responsible for preparing purchase orders and for making out the checks in payment of those purchases.

2. The flow of work from employee to employee should not be duplicative; the work of the second employee should provide a check on the work of the first. For example, the check drawn to pay the vendor of materials should be cosigned by a second employee who verifies the accuracy and legitimacy of the transaction.

3. Employees who handle assets should not also be responsible for the recordkeeping on those assets. This provision is implemented when employees who receive and store materials do not also verify the receipt of those materials.

4. Definitions of job responsibilities must be clearly established, so one can fix accountability for each aspect of a financial transaction. In other words, the organizing function of management must be the primary source for this important aspect of internal control.

Effective internal control procedures can be established for each financial resource. Cash, accounts receivable, interest inventories, investments, accounts payable, sales, payrolls, and purchases all must be safeguarded through procedures conforming to the four characteristics of effective internal control.

Postcontrol of Financial Resources

A principal source of information from which managers can evaluate historical results is the firm's accounting system. Periodically, the manager receives a set of financial statements which usually includes a balance sheet, an income statement, and a sources-and-uses-of-funds statement. These statements summarize and classify the effects of transactions in terms of assets, liabilities, equity, revenues, and expenses—the major components of the firm's financial structure.

A detailed analysis of the information contained in the financial statements enables management to determine the adequacy of the firm's earning power and its ability to meet current and long-term obligations. Financial ratios are an important tool for conducting a detailed analysis. A ratio is an index which relates two pieces of financial information to each other.[23] Analysts typically evaluate ratios in two ways. They conduct trend analyses by comparing the company's present and past ratios to identify changes in elements of the company's financial condition such as a declining profit margin. Analysts also compare a company's ratios to the averages of similar firms or to the averages of the industry in which the company competes. Financial ratios for numerous industries are published annually in several publications.[24]

Ratio analysis is a valuable tool for evaluating a company's financial condition.[25] However, it should be viewed as the first rather than final step in conducting a financial analysis. Ratios identify elements of a company's financial structure that need more indepth analysis, and they often raise many questions. However, ratios alone seldom provide complete answers.[26]

Ratios are typically calculated to evaluate three aspects of a company's financial condition: *profitability, liquidity,* and *solvency.*

Profitability.   The discussion of strategic planning in Chapter 6 described profitability measures. Whether the manager prefers the rate of return on sales, on owners' equity, or on total assets, or a combination of all three, it is important to establish a meaningful

---

[23]James C. Van Horne, *Fundamentals of Financial Management* (Englewood Cliffs, N.J.: Prentice-Hall, 1980), pp. 104–14.

[24]Industry financial ratios are published in a number of sources, notably *Dow Jones-Irwin Business and Investment Almanac* (published annually by Dow Jones-Irwin); *Key Business Ratios* (published annually by Dun & Bradstreet); and *Standard & Poor's Industry Survey* (published annually by Standard & Poors).

[25]For an overview of the use of financial ratios by business, see Paul Barnes, "The Analysis and Use of Financial Ratios: A Review Article," *Journal of Business Finance and Accounting,* Winter 1987, pp. 449–61.

[26]Garrison, *Managerial Accounting,* p. 800. For a study of the relationship between small business performance (among 400 retail pharmacies) and use of financial ratio analysis, see Joseph Thomas III and Robert V. Evanson, "An Empirical Investigation of Association between Financial Ratio Use and Small Business Success," *Journal of Business and Financial Accounting,* Winter 1987, pp. 555–71.

standard—one that is appropriate to the particular firm, given its industry and stage of growth. An inadequate rate of return can have negative effects on the firm's ability to attract funds for expansion, particularly if a downward trend over time is evident.

Liquidity.   The measures of liquidity reflect the firm's ability to meet current obligations as they become due. The widest-known and most often used measure of liquidity is the *ratio of current assets to current liabilities*. The ratio's standard of acceptability depends on the particular firm's operating characteristics.[27]

A more rigorous test of liquidity is the *quick ratio* or *acid test ratio*, which is the ratio of cash and near-cash items (current assets excluding inventories and prepaid expenses) to current liabilities.

The relationship between current assets and current liabilities is an important determinant of liquidity. Equally important is the *composition* of current assets. Two measures that indicate composition and rely on information found in both the balance sheet and the income statement are the *accounts receivable turnover* and the *inventory turnover*.

The accounts receivable turnover is the ratio of credit sales to average accounts receivable. The higher the turnover, the more rapid is the conversion of accounts receivable to cash. A low turnover would indicate a time lag in the collection of receivables, which in turn could strain the firm's ability to meet its own obligations. The appropriate corrective action might be a tightening of credit standards or a more vigorous effort to collect outstanding accounts.

The inventory turnover also facilitates the analysis of appropriate balances in current assets. It is calculated as the ratio of the cost of goods sold to the average inventory. A high ratio could indicate a dangerously low inventory balance in relation to sales, with the possibility of missed sales or production slowdowns. Conversely, a low ratio might indicate an overinvestment in inventory to the exclusion of other, more profitable, assets. Whatever the case, the appropriate ratio must be established by the manager, based on the firm's experience within its industry and market.

Solvency.   Another financial measure is *solvency,* the ability of the firm to meet its long-term obligations—its fixed commitments. The solvency measure relates the claims of creditors and owners on the assets of the firm. An appropriate balance must be maintained—a balance that protects the interests of the owners, yet does not ignore the advantages of long-term debt as a source of funds. A commonly used measure of solvency is the *ratio of profits before interest and taxes to interest expense.* This indicates the margin of safety, and ordinarily, a high ratio is preferred. However, a very high ratio combined with a low *debt-to-equity ratio* could indicate that management has not taken advantage of debt as a source of funds. The appropriate balance between debt and equity depends on a number of factors, and the issue is an important topic in financial management. As a general rule, however, the proportion of debt should vary directly with the stability of the firm's earnings.

---

[27]Insightful discussions on the shortcomings of the current ratio are provided by Mary M. K. Fleming, "The Current Ratio Reconsidered," *Business Horizons,* May–June 1986, pp. 74–77; and Joel M. Shulman and Ismael G. Dambolena, "Analyzing Corporate Solvency," *Journal of Cash Management,* September–October 1986, pp. 35–38.

Table 15–1 A summary of key financial ratios, how they are calculated, and what they show.

Ratio	How Calculated	What It Shows
Profitability ratios:		
1. Gross profit margin	$$\frac{\text{Sales} - \text{Cost of goods sold}}{\text{Sales}}$$	An indication of the total margin available to cover operating expenses and yield a profit.
2. Operating profit margin	$$\frac{\text{Profits before taxes and before interest}}{\text{Sales}}$$	An indication of the firm's profitability from current operations, without regard to the interest charges accruing from debt.
3. Net profit margin (or return on sales)	$$\frac{\text{Profits after taxes}}{\text{Sales}}$$	Shows aftertax profits per dollar of sales. Subpar profit margins indicate that the firm's sales prices are relatively low or that its costs are relatively high, or both.
4. Return on total assets	$$\frac{\text{Profits after taxes}}{\text{Total assets}}$$ or $$\frac{\text{Profits after taxes} + \text{Interest}}{\text{Total assets}}$$	A measure of the return on total investment in the enterprise. It is sometimes desirable to add interest to aftertax profits to form the numerator of the ratio, since total assets are financed by creditors as well as by stockholders. Thus, it is accurate to measure the productivity of assets by the returns provided to both classes of investors.
5. Return on stockholders' equity (or return on net worth)	$$\frac{\text{Profits after taxes}}{\text{Total stockholders' equity}}$$	A measure of the rate of return on stockholders' investment in the enterprise.
6. Return on common equity	$$\frac{\text{Profits after taxes} - \text{Preferred stock dividends}}{\text{Total stockholders' equity} - \text{Par value of preferred stock}}$$	A measure of the rate of return on the investment the owners of common stock have made in the enterprise.
7. Earnings per share	$$\frac{\text{Profits after taxes} - \text{Preferred stock dividends}}{\text{Number of shares of common stock outstanding}}$$	Shows the earnings available to the owners of common stock.
Liquidity ratios:		
1. Current ratio	$$\frac{\text{Current assets}}{\text{Current liabilities}}$$	Indicates the extent to which the claims of short-term creditors are covered by assets that are expected to be converted to cash in a period roughly corresponding to the maturity of the liabilities.
2. Quick ratio (or acid test ratio)	$$\frac{\text{Current assets} - \text{Inventory}}{\text{Current liabilities}}$$	A measure of the firm's ability to pay off short-term obligations without relying on the sale of its inventories.
3. Inventory to net working capital	$$\frac{\text{Inventory}}{\text{Current assets} - \text{Current liabilities}}$$	A measure of the extent to which the firm's working capital is tied up in inventory.

Table 15–1 *Concluded*

Ratio	How Calculated	What It Shows
Solvency ratios:		
1. Debt to asset ratio	$\dfrac{\text{Total debt}}{\text{Total assets}}$	Measures the extent to which borrowed funds have been used to finance the firm's operations.
2. Debt to equity ratio	$\dfrac{\text{Total debt}}{\text{Total stockholders' equity}}$	Gives another measure of the funds provided by creditors versus the funds provided by owners.
3. Long-term debt to equity ratio	$\dfrac{\text{Long-term debt}}{\text{Total stockholders' equity}}$	A widely used measure of the balance between debt and equity in the firm's overall capital structure.
4. Times-interest-earned (or coverage ratios)	$\dfrac{\text{Profit before interest and taxes}}{\text{Total interest charges}}$	Measures the extent to which earnings can decline without the firm becoming unable to meet its annual interest costs.
5. Fixed charge coverage	$\dfrac{\text{Profits before taxes and Interest + Lease obligations}}{\text{Total interest charges + Lease obligations}}$	A more inclusive indication of the firm's ability to meet all of its fixed-charge obligations.

Source: Arthur A. Thompson, Jr., and A. J. Strickland, *Strategy and Policy: Concepts and Cases* (Plano, Tex.: Business Publications, 1987), pp. 270–71.

The ratios discussed above are only some of the many methods used to evaluate the financial results of the firm.[28] Table 15–1 summarizes profitability, liquidity, and solvency ratios. Accounting as a tool of analysis in management has a long history predating scientific management. The point is here is that financial statement analysis as a part of the management process is clearly a postcontrol method.

MANAGEMENT SOLUTION

HARLEY-DAVIDSON'S ROAD TO RECOVERY

Once Harley-Davidson became fully aware of the severity of its problems, management moved quickly. A group of Harley executives pur-chased the company from AMF Inc. in 1981. The new owners then petitioned the Interna-

Continued

---

[28]Computer expert systems are being developed that conduct financial ratio analysis, and via a set of questions concerning a company's ratios compared to industry norms, provide judgments concerning the company's financial condition. For an example of how an expert system works for oil and gas companies, see James A. Sena and L. Murphy Smith, "A Sample Expert System for Financial Statement Analysis," *Journal of Accounting and EDP,* Summer 1987, pp. 15–22.

MANAGEMENT SOLUTION

Concluded

tional Trade Commission for protection from the Japanese in the form of increased import tariffs. In one of the strongest protectionist actions taken by the Reagan administration, the tariffs for imported motorcycles in the large-size segment of the U.S. market were increased in 1983 from 4.4 percent to 49.4 percent. This move bought Harley-Davidson some time; however, the tariffs were set to progressively decline and return to the 4.4 percent level by 1988.

Management then launched major efforts designed to improve inventory control, lower inventory costs, and boost product quality. A just-in-time inventory program was launched. Manufacturing employees were trained in the JIT concepts and designed a version of JIT that met the company's particular needs. Mindful of its parts inventory problems, the company focused on achieving total parts controls and on working with suppliers to achieve timely delivery of high-quality materials.

However, initially Harley erred in dealing with suppliers who were skeptical of the company's JIT commitment. Harley insisted on developing highly legalistic, 35-page suppliers contracts that focused mostly on the suppliers', not Harley's, obligations. Few suppliers signed. Realizing the shortcomings of its strategy, Harley then developed more informal, two-page contracts. They also sent teams of engineers and buyers to the suppliers' plants to help reduce the suppliers' own setup times, and to improve their parts designs.

Harley's JIT effort also focused on reducing setup times. The employees provided many of the ideas for changing procedures, fixtures, and equipment layout to speed the setup process. Eventually tools, dies, machines, and product parts were redesigned to facilitate faster setup. This effort paid off; setup times were reduced by an average of 75 percent across all machines.

Improved quality and quality control was another major objective. Toward this end, Harley's unionized work force agreed to be responsible for checking product quality while they work on the assembly line and to maintain their own machines (two Japanese techniques). Workers were trained in process quality control; Harley reduced its number of quality control inspectors from 100 to 10. Suppliers also agreed to establish the same process quality control techniques used by Harley-Davidson, and Harley provided the suppliers with the quality control training.

Within four years after the strategic turnaround was launched, Harley-Davidson Motor Co. achieved impressive results. Inventory was reduced by two thirds and the warehousing of raw materials, work-in-process, and finished goods inventory was eliminated. Defects per motorcycle were cut by 70 percent. Productivity improved 50 percent. Harley boosted its market share to over 20 percent.

In an unprecedented move, Harley petitioned the International Trade Commission in 1987 to end the import tariffs relief, and the Reagan administration obliged. Harley is no longer so protected, and competition from the Japanese is again at a fever pitch. Said Harley's CEO Vaughn Beals, "What we are talking about is war."

Source: Adapted from Mehran Sepehri, "Manufacturing Revitalization at Harley-Davidson Motor Co.," *Industrial Engineering*, August 1987, pp. 87–90, 92–93; Dexter Hutchins, "Having a Hard Time with Just-In-Time," *Fortune*, June 9, 1986, pp. 64–66; and Michael Kolbenschlag, "Harley-Davidson Takes Lessons from Arch-Rivals' Handbook," *International Management*, February 1985, pp. 46–48.

MANAGEMENT SUMMARY

☐ Effective control of production-operations and financial resources requires an appropriate mix of precontrol, concurrent control, and postcontrol methods and policies.

☐ Production-operations control requires methods, procedures, and policies for the input, transformation, and output elements of production.

☐ Precontrol of inputs attempts to ensure that there will be an appropriate quantity and quality of each resource. The economic order quantity (EOQ) formula is a widely used technique for determining how many and how often to purchase materials for production.

☐ Concurrent control in production-operations management is fundamentally a scheduling problem. Managers can use network and linear programming models to schedule the allocation of resources to different outputs.

☐ Just-in-time inventory management combines precontrol and concurrent control activities to minimize inventory and boost product quality, plant capacity, and productivity.

☐ Precontrol of financial resources is implemented through budgets, which specify standard levels for expense categories and organizational units.

☐ Concurrent control of financial resources depends on effective internal control procedures and policies.

☐ Financial statement and ratio analyses are important means for achieving postcontrol of financial resources. Managers calculate ratios to evaluate a company's profitability, liquidity, and solvency.

REVIEW AND DISCUSSION QUESTIONS

1. Describe the financial and production-operations control system you would set up if you were the manager of a fast-food establishment. Be as specific as possible.

2. Discuss the differences between precontrol of capital equipment and precontrol of materials. Your answer should take into account the differences in setting standards, obtaining information, and taking corrective action.

3. Describe how you would determine whether a firm has an adequate internal control system for sales, cash, and accounts receivable.

4. The EOQ model is a useful technique for controlling the quantity of materials purchased. Explain how the model could be used to control the quantity of materials to be manufactured.

5. Given the limitations of the EOQ model, how should the model best be used in precontrolling an organization's materials?

6. Some observers assert that just-in-time inventory management simply won't work in some manufacturing organizations. Provide an example of an organization that would support their contention.

7. Are the principles of JIT applicable in service organizations? Explain.

8. Liquidity, solvency, and profitability each measure different aspects of an organization's financial condition. Explain how it would be possible for an organization to have an imbalance of these three measures.

9. Of the ratios discussed in the chapter, many financial analysts believe that the current ratio is the most difficult to interpret. Why?

10. Why is production scheduling fundamentally a problem of resource allocation?

CASES

15-1 THE NUMMI EXPERIMENT

In the early 1980s, General Motors, battered by Japanese imports, realized a need to learn new ways to boost productivity and product quality. Many GM executives believed that they could learn much from the Japanese approach to making cars; however, they wondered whether the techniques would work with a unionized work force, and American managers and suppliers. Toyota wondered the same thing. Under protectionist pressure to make cars in the United States, Toyota was actively considering building manufacturing facilities in America. However, it first wanted to learn whether its techniques would work in the United States before taking such a giant step.

In 1984, these two companies combined resources to create New United Motor Manufacturing Inc. (NUMMI), a joint venture established to build subcompact cars. The venture is a bold experiment—to determine whether Japanese management works in the U.S. auto industry. If the experiment succeeds, both parties will gain, and the result could be a revolution in the way auto plants are managed and cars are made in America.

At the beginning of the venture, the challenge of achieving success was considerable. NUMMI is located in Fremont, California (near San Francisco), in an old GM plant that had been shut down in 1982 due to poor productivity and labor problems. At the peak of the discontent, daily absenteeism averaged 25 percent of the work force, and over 1,000 employee grievances were on file.

When NUMMI reopened the plant, 85 percent of the 2,500 employees were rehired from the plant's previous work force. NUMMI was faced with managing a once-hostile work force to meet a substantial challenge: produce a subcompact Chevy Nova that matches Toyota's Corolla (an almost identical model) in production cost and quality. Meeting the challenge would require new inventory and quality control methods, a new teamwork approach to assembly, and highly motivated American workers supervised primarily by Japanese managers. At NUMMI, Toyota is responsible for the daily management of the company; Toyota managers fill 35 of the company's 63 management positions. Sixteen slots are held by GM managers and 12 managers were hired by NUMMI. Eight of the 10 top-level managers come from Toyota. Toyota also performs all product engineering while GM handles marketing and distribution.

In 1985, Toyota, General Motors, and the United Auto Workers negotiated a unique labor contract for NUMMI. In the contract, the UAW made some considerable concessions. It agreed to reduce the number of job classifications from more than 80 to just 1 classification for production employees and 3 for skilled tradesmen. The union also committed to improving product quality. The employees received competitive pay.

In exchange, management agreed to a virtual guarantee of no layoffs. Management also agreed to consult with the union before suspending or firing an employee. Employees were also provided a greater involvement in decision making. Management thus received the work force flexibility (via few job classifications) it needed to implement the Japanese techniques. Workers obtained the decision-making involvement and job security needed to ensure that, in helping to boost productivity, they would not work themselves out of a job.

Employees were organized into work teams comprised of six to eight members. Each team is led by a team leader who is selected by management for his performance, communication, and teaching abilities. Hourly paid, team leaders receive about 50 cents more per hour for their extra responsibilities. Three teams comprise a group who is led by a salaried supervisor.

Each team's members were intensively trained in how to perform all of the jobs in the group's work area and in the techniques of quality control. Over 200 Toyota employees in Japan traveled to Fremont to train the employees. All team and group leaders also spent three weeks in Toyota's Corolla plant in Takaoka, Japan, learning the concepts and techniques of Japanese production management.

This intensive training enabled a team's members to rotate jobs, which they do frequently. It also provided teams with the authority to determine their work place and solve production problems. Importantly, ten members also were given the power to stop the production line if they spot a problem. Much of the in-process quality checking is done automatically by sensors on production equipment that shut the machine down when a defect is detected (the Japanese call this line-stop concept *jidoka*). However, the workers also serve as the plant's quality inspectors. While the typical GM plant has more than 80 quality engineers, NUMMI has none.

Ropes are hung throughout the plant. When an employee sees a problem, he tugs the rope, and electronic music begins playing to alert other workers. A red light on an overhead board illuminates the number of the employee's work station. The team leader goes to the trouble spot and often assumes the employee's work while he solves the problem. This situation occurs about 400 times each shift. About 200 times, the workers solve the problem fast enough to keep the line going (the line stretches about 1.3 miles); the remaining 200 times, the line stops but usually for no more than five seconds.

Besides superior quality control, the plant also focuses on superior inventory management. NUMMI maintains a just-in-time styled approach to inventory control. However, providing supplies "just-in-time" is quite demanding because some 1,600 of the 2,250 different parts needed to make Novas are shipped to Fremont from Toyota's plants and suppliers about 10,000 miles away. Toyota makes about 300 of these components; the rest are provided by its 70 suppliers located in or near Toyota City.

Toyota goes to great lengths to ensure parts arrive when needed. NUMMI's production schedules are set 12 weeks in advance. In Japan, parts from Toyota's plants and suppliers arrive hourly at Toyota's Kamigo Vanning Center where they are packed for shipping overseas to NUMMI. The most important component provided by Toyota in Japan are the engines which are assembled at Toyota's Shimoyama engine plant about 20 minutes from the center. Truckers make 16 trips to the center each day to meet their 900 engine delivery quota. What is the total time required to assemble an engine, transport to the center, pack the engine, take it to the Port of Nagoya, and load it on a ship? About six hours.

However, NUMMI's inventory system falls somewhat short of being truly JIT. The reason: severe weather sometimes delays the ships' deliveries of parts from Nagoya to the Port of Oakland in California. NUMMI thus holds two days' supply of inventory at the port and one day's supply at the NUMMI plant, just in case. When parts arrive at the Oakland port, truckers on average take about 10 minutes to enter the loading area, obtain a container's worth of cargo and leave for the 31 mile trip to NUMMI. The company is working to reduce that average time to less than five minutes.

NUMMI's 75 American suppliers who deliver 650 types of parts are provided with a seven-week advance schedule which is confirmed or revised daily. Parts are delivered by truck usually requiring a three-day trip from vendor to NUMMI's door.

Once at the plant, all parts—Japanese and American—are inspected and shipped to work teams hourly.

Has the NUMMI experiment worked? So far, signs spell success. Worker morale is high; absenteeism has dropped to about 3 percent. Management works to keep it that way by minimizing worker-management status differences. There is one parking lot (no executive parking spaces), one cafeteria, and with the exception of the president, all open offices for executives.

Auto experts consider the Chevy Nova to be the highest quality car that GM makes. The plant has come very close (within .25 defects) to achieving its goal of 1.5 defects per car. The Nova has the best ratings in consumer satisfaction and repair rates. The quality also matches Toyota's comparable Corolla produced in Japan; however, the plant's productivity is about 10 to 12 percent less than the productivity of Toyota's Corolla plant. NUMMI makes about 62 cars an hour. Yet, considering the plant's older condition and the workers' lesser experience, Toyota executives estimate that the productivity rates are about the same. These accomplishments have come without large-scale automation.

However, questions remain concerning whether this impressive record can continue. A projected worldwide glut in auto supply could spell problems in terms of employee layoffs and morale. The joint venture is scheduled to end in 1994.

Questions

1. Of the different techniques used by the Japanese in quality and inventory control, which do you believe are most useful? Explain.

2. Can the techniques be transferred beyond auto manufacturers to American industry at large? Discuss.

3. What are the major obstacles in making this transfer? How could the barriers be alleviated?

Source: This case is adapted from Bryan H. Berry, "What Makes the NUMMI Plant Different?" *Iron Age,* September 5, 1986, pp. 27ff; E. J. Muller, "NUMMI: How Toyota-GM Makes Cars by Crossing the Pacific, Just in Time," *Distribution,* October 1986, pp. 53ff; Mehran Sepehri, "Car Manufacturing Joint Venture Tests Feasibility of Toyota Method in U.S.," *Industrial Engineering,* March 1986, pp. 34–41; and Lauri Giesen, "Production Philosophy Gives NUMMI Efficiency," *American Metal Market,* October 6, 1986, p. 30.

15–2 A STRATEGIC CONTROL DECISION TASK

The plant manager of a major electronics manufacturer called a meeting with his immediate subordinates to discuss a major strategic control decision. The issue to be resolved concerned whether to go into the full-scale production and marketing of a new product, a miniature thermostat. The miniature thermostat, MT, had been under development for the past three years, and the manager believed that it was time to make a decision. The meeting was to be attended by the marketing manager, the production superintendent, the purchasing manager, and the plant cost accountant. The plant manager instructed each official to bring appropriate information and to be prepared to make a final decision regarding the MT.

Prior to the meeting, the plant manager noted the following facts concerning the MT:

1. Developmental efforts had been undertaken three years ago in response to the introduction of a similar product by a major competitor.

2. Initial manufacturing studies had indicated that much of the technology and know-how to produce the MT already existed in the plant and its work force.

3. A prototype model had been approved by Underwriters' Laboratories.

4. A pilot production line had been designed and installed. Several thousand thermostats already had been produced and tested.

5. Market projections indicated that a trend toward miniaturization of such components as thermostats was likely to continue.

6. The competitor who had introduced the product was marketing it successfully at a price of $0.80 each.

7. The cost estimates derived by the cost accountant over the past two years consistently indicated that the firm could not meet the competitor's price and at the same time follow its standard markup of 14 percent of the selling price.

Because of his concern for the cost of the MT, the plant manager asked the cost accountant to brief the group at the outset of its meeting. The accountant's data are shown in the following table.

	Actual Costs	Standard Costs
Direct labor	$0.059	$0.052
Direct material	0.340	0.194
Manufactured overhead (438% of standard direct labor)	0.228	0.228
Total manufacturing cost	$0.627	$0.474
Spoilage (10%)	0.063	0.047
Selling and administrative costs (40% of direct labor and overhead)	0.115	0.112
Total cost per MT	$0.805	$0.633
Required price to achieve 14% markup on selling price	$0.936	$0.736

The accountant noted for the group that the firm would not be able to manufacture and sell the MT for less than $0.805 each, given the present actual costs. In fact, meeting its markup objective would require a selling price of approximately $0.94 each, but that would be impossible, since the competitor was selling the same product for $0.80. She explained that if the MT could be manufactured at standard costs, it could compete successfully with the competitor's thermostat. She said that the company should abandon the MT if it could not be made at standard costs.

The marketing manager stated that the MT was an important product and that it was critical for the firm to have an entry in the market. He said that in a few years the MT would be used by all of the company's major customers and that the competition had already moved into the area with a strong sales program. He added that he did not place too much reliance on the cost estimates, because the plant had had so little experience with full-scale production of the MT and that in any case, standard costs, though appropriate for cost containment were inappropriate for decisions of this type.

The manufacturing superintendent stated that he was working with engineers to develop a new method for welding contacts and that if it proved successful, the direct labor cost would be reduced significantly. This would have a cumulative effect on costs, since overhead, spoilage, and selling and administrative expenses were based on direct labor. He also believed that with a little more experience, the workers could reach standard times on the assembly operations. He said that much progress in this direction had been made in the past four weeks.

The purchasing manager stated that material costs were high because the plant had not procured materials in sufficient quantities. She said that with full-scale production, material costs should decrease to standard.

Questions

1. If you were the plant manager, what decision would you make regarding the MT?

2. If you decided to manufacture the MT, would your decision indicate that the standard of 14 percent markup was not valid?

3. Trace the relationships between precontrol, concurrent control, and postcontrol as revealed by the facts of the case.

SIXTEEN

Managing Human Resources

LEARNING OBJECTIVES

After completing Chapter 16, you should be able to:

Define: *performance evaluation* in terms of its purposes.

State: the conditions necessary for effective human resource performance standards.

Describe: how managers combine precontrol, concurrent control, and postcontrol methods to manage human resource performance.

Explain: the advantages and disadvantages of traditional performance evaluation methods.

Discuss: how results-oriented and behavior-oriented methods overcome limitations of trait-oriented methods.

EVALUATING PERFORMANCE EVALUATION AT CONTROL DATA CORPORATION

Control Data Corp., a multinational computer and financial services company, has invested significant resources in its performance evaluation system. The company's managers were convinced that they could design and implement a system that would overcome the usual problems associated with performance evaluation. They believed that an effective performance evaluation system could be a valuable part of the company's effort to upgrade and develop employees' job-related skills and abilities. And it could serve as the basis for salary and promotion decisions.

Acting on these beliefs, Control Data devised a system with the following features:

1. *Performance appraisal forms.* Managers evaluate employees on the basis of criteria included on written forms. The content of appraisal forms directs the managers' attention to particular aspects and outcomes of the employees' performance. What is included on appraisal forms can make or break a performance evaluation system; it must therefore be designed with care. To develop the performance criteria, Control Data set up workshops that brought together employees and industrial psychologists. In this manner, the views and insights of employees who performed the jobs were carefully considered.

2. *The evaluation process.* Performance evaluation involves managers and employees and takes place over time. The process varies from organization to organization, but at Control Data it consists of the following managerial responsibilities:

a. Managers meet yearly with each of their subordinates to discuss job responsibilities and objectives. The result of these meetings are mutual agreements between each manager and each employee.

b. Managers constantly monitor each employee's performance to detect any potential deviations from progress toward the agreed-upon goals. Managers provide coaching and other supportive efforts to bring about corrective action.

c. Managers periodically complete the appraisal forms for each of their assigned employees. The forms require managers to evaluate overall performance and to identify what skills and abilities need improvement.

d. Managers have discussions with each of their employees to explain their evaluations and suggest what personal skills and abilities the employee should attempt to improve.

e. Managers determine salary levels and increments for each employee based on the performance evaluation information. Exceptional performance merits exceptional salary increments.

f. Managers meet again with each employee to explain the salary decision, including the factors they took into account.

Continued

MANAGEMENT INCIDENT

Concluded

3. *Support elements.* Control Data's evaluation system includes guides and policies, available to all employees, to explain and reinforce its importance. In addition, the company has developed an extensive training program to develop the skills of managers to be effective performance evaluators. The company also makes available training for employees who desire to overcome skill and ability deficiencies.

Control Data has a significant investment in its performance evaluation system, so its managers need to know whether the investment is paying off. Is the system effective? To find answers to their questions, Control Data managers now recognize that they somehow must develop a control system for a control system!

(The Management Solution to this Management Incident can be found at the end of this chapter.)

A manager's greatest responsibility is to select, direct, develop, and evaluate subordinates—the people of the organization. People are the sources of all productive effort in organizations. Organizational performance depends on individual performance.

In this chapter we apply the elements of the controlling function to human resources. You should develop greater understanding of how managers define standards, acquire information, and take corrective action in the process of managing human resources. The discussion is presented in three major sections: precontrol, concurrent control, and postcontrol of human resources. Although the discussion is framed by these three types of control, keep in mind that human resource control systems must be integrated both within the parts of the system and as parts of an overall management system.[1] The overall system is referred to as the human resource management program.

HUMAN RESOURCE MANAGEMENT FUNCTION

The HRM program at General Mills serves the needs of that organization and facilitates the accomplishment of its objectives. But without modifications, its program would probably not be well suited for Burger King or Eli Lilly. Each company develops its own HRM program after considering such factors as size, type of skills needed, number of employees required, unionization, clients and customers, financial posture, and geographic location.

The successful HRM program also requires the cooperation of managers, because it is they who must interpret and implement policies and procedures. Line managers must translate into action what a HRM department provides. Without managerial support at the top, middle, and lower levels, HRM programs cannot succeed. Therefore, it is important that managers clearly understand how to mesh their responsibilities with those of the HRM department.

Human resource management can be defined as the process of accomplishing organizational objectives by acquiring, retaining, terminating, developing, and properly using the human resources in an organization. The notion of accomplishing objectives is a major part of any form of management. Unless objectives are regularly accomplished, the organization ceases to exist.

The *acquisition* of skilled, talented, and motivated employees is an important part of HRM. The acquisition phase involves recruiting, screening, selecting, and properly placing personnel.

Retaining competent individuals is important to any organization. If qualified individuals regularly leave a company, it becomes continually necessary to seek new personnel. This costs money and is time consuming.

The opposite of retention is, of course, *termination,* which is an unpleasant part of any manager's job. Employees occasionally must be terminated for breaking rules, failing to perform adequately, or job cutbacks. The procedures for such terminations usually are specified by a HRM staff expert or are covered in a labor-management contract.

---

[1]Raymond E. Miles and Charles C. Snow, "Designing Strategic Human Resource Systems," *Organizational Dynamics,* Summer 1984, pp. 36–52.

Figure 16–1 An example of a personnel/human resource management department.

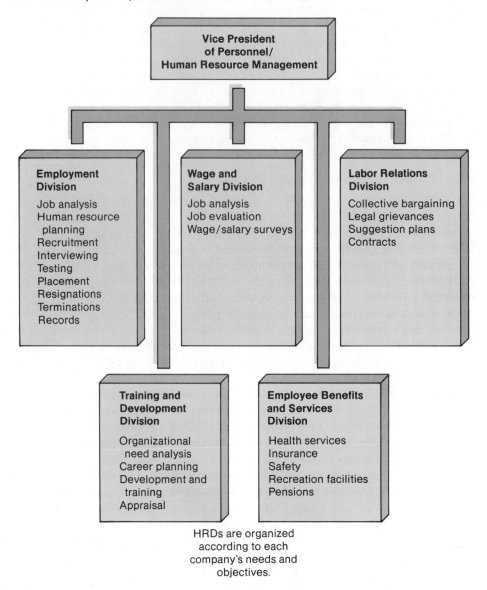

Vice President
of Personnel/
Human Resource Management

**Employment
Division**

Job analysis
Human resource
 planning
Recruitment
Interviewing
Testing
Placement
Resignations
Terminations
Records

**Wage and
Salary Division**

Job analysis
Job evaluation
Wage/salary surveys

**Labor Relations
Division**

Collective bargaining
Legal grievances
Suggestion plans
Contracts

**Training and
Development
Division**

Organizational
 need analysis
Career planning
Development and
 training
Appraisal

**Employee Benefits
and Services
Division**

Health services
Insurance
Safety
Recreation facilities
Pensions

HRDs are organized
according to each
company's needs and
objectives.

Developing personnel involves training, educating, appraising, and generally preparing personnel for present or future jobs. These activities are important for the economic and psychological growth of employees. Self-realization needs cannot be satisfied in an organization that does not have an efficient set of development activities.

The *proper use of people* involves understanding both individual and organizational needs so that the full potential of human resources can be employed. This part of human resource management suggests that it is important to match individuals over time to shifts in organizational and human needs.

HRM in larger organizations such as Alcoa, Bausch & Lomb, Polaroid, and Marriott is performed in a staff department like the one shown in Figure 16-1. Remember, however, that each company organizes its department according to its own set of needs and objectives. Each department activity utilizes some form of control. A few of the HRM activities and their control mechanisms will be discussed.

PRECONTROL OF HUMAN RESOURCES

Precontrol of human resources includes all those activities typically associated with *staffing* an organization.[2] The four principal staffing activities are *human resources planning, recruitment, selection,* and *orientation.*

HUMAN RESOURCE PLANNING

Human resource planning involves estimating the size and composition of the future work force. Through planning, managers can estimate what numbers and kinds of human assets will be needed. Human resource planning requires forecasting. Yet experience indicates that the longer the period predicted, the less accurate the prediction will be. Other complicating factors include changes in such areas as economic conditions, the labor supply, and competition.

Anticipating future business and environmental demands requires a planning system. The activities that a manager could follow in such a system include the following:

1. *Human resource inventory*—assessing the personnel skills, abilities, and potential present in the organization.
2. *Forecasting*—predicting future personnel requirements.
3. *Human resource plans*—developing a strategy for recruiting, selecting, placing, transferring, and promoting personnel.
4. *Development plans*—ensuring that properly trained managers are ready to take over vacant or new jobs.

To conduct these four activities, managers use formal and informal approaches to human resource planning. For example, some organizations rely on mathematical projections. They collect data on such factors as the available supply of human resources, labor-market composition, the demand for products, new research breakthroughs, and competitive wage and salary programs. From these data and previous records, managers then can use statistical procedures to make forecasts. Of course, unpredictable events can alter trends. But when such surprises are seldom, fairly reliable forecasts are possible.

---

[2]Judy D. Olian and Sara L. Rynes, "Organizational Staffing: Integrating Practice with Strategy," *Industrial Relations,* Spring 1984, pp. 170–83.

Estimating based on experience is a more informal forecasting procedure. Department managers and supervisors may be asked for opinions about future human resource needs. Some managers are confident in human resource planning; others are reluctant to offer an opinion or are not reliable forecasters.

The J. C. Penney Company, Inc., a large retail merchandiser, plans its human resource needs from information supplied by each retail store. Store managers from around the country provide information to a central data center that develops five-year projections for each position in the organization. The company's human resource needs are met primarily by promotion. Turnover is low. All J. C. Penney employees, meanwhile, are called *associates* to give them a sense of importance to the organization. Each employee is evaluated on her potential for being promoted, and these evaluations give the company a readily available, companywide inventory of human resources. A computer is used to match present and anticipated vacancies with available associates.

Recruiting Activities

If human resource needs cannot be met within the company, outside sources must be tapped. An attractive organization such as Alcoa keeps a file on applicants who sought employment with it over the past year. Even though these applicants were not hired, they frequently maintain an interest in working for a company with a good reputation and image. By carefully screening these files, some good applicants can be added to the pool of candidates.

Advertisements in newspapers, trade journals, and magazines notify potential applicants of openings. Responses to advertisements will come from both qualified and unqualified individuals. Occasionally, a company will list a post-office box number and not provide the company name. This form of advertisement is called a *blind ad*. Such advertisements eliminate the necessity of contacting every applicant. However, they do not permit a company to use its name or logo as a form of promotion. Some organizations are effectively using their own employees in newspaper and magazine ads. For example, a General Dynamics ad, while citing its employees as "19,000 reasons why business is good in San Diego," also calls attention to the employer's presence in the city. The ad also features employee security badges with photographs. Using employees in the ads personalized the company to recruits.[3]

The college campus is one of the most important sources for recruiting lower-level managers. Many colleges and universities have placement centers that work with organizational recruiters. The applicants read advertisements and information provided by the companies, and then they sign up for interviews. The most promising applicants are invited to visit the companies for more interviews.

To find experienced employees in the external market, organizations use private employment agencies, executive search firms, or state employment agencies. Some private employment agencies and executive search firms are called *no-fee agencies,* which means that the employer pays the fee instead of the applicant. An organization

---

[3]Bob Martin, "Recruitment AD Venture," *Personnel Journal,* August 1987, pp. 46–63.

is not obligated to hire any person referred by the agency, but the agency usually is informed when the right person is found.

There is an ethical theme in recruiting that must be considered. Some firms tend to hype a job or to mislead job applicants especially when there is a shortage of available talent. This type of behavior often backfires. The following Management Application suggests that there may be legal consequences associated with portraying jobs falsely.

MANAGEMENT APPLICATION

BEING ETHICAL ABOUT A JOB

To Lynda McDermott, the job offer sounded perfect. So she left her position at an accounting firm and became executive vice president of a consulting firm. The job was portrayed by her new boss as one that would allow her to play a major role in landing new business.

Eleven months later Lynda quit. Her boss, she says, had relegated her to administrative duties. "He's a wonderful salesperson," Lynda stated with some bitterness.

As Lynda sees it, she was a victim of a job bait-and-switch. Promised the world as an applicant, the new employee eventually realizes that the job is something quite different, leading to frustration, broken promises, and poor performance.

In a growing number of cases like Lynda's, disputes are ending up in court as parts of suits brought by previous employees. A troublesome case involved Ian Dowie, a former marketing vice president of Exxon. He won a $10.1 million fraud and breach-of-contract suit in federal court. Shortly after Mr. Dowie began work, the company reorganized its office-products unit and placed another manager above him. He was also passed over for other important jobs. Mr. Dowie's lawyer stated that, "He was promised certain responsibilities and they were reorganized out from under him."

Making promises that can't be delivered is referred to as the "courtship phenomenon." Recruiters paint the best picture they can about the job and their firm. These inflated claims can backfire and should not be made. What recruiters must do is to be perfectly honest, make no promises that can't be kept, and let the applicant talk to recent hirees. Any job has some shortcomings and these need to be communicated clearly before a person accepts or rejects a job offer.

Source: Adapted from Larry Reibstein, "Crushed Hopes: When a New Job Proves to Be Something Different," *The Wall Street Journal*, June 10, 1987, p. 25.

Individuals responsible for recruiting are faced with legal requirements. For example, a certain percentage of minority group members and women must now be recruited for positions that have seldom been filled by these people. These requirements are enforced by laws administered by the Equal Employment Opportunity Commission (EEOC). The federal government attempts to provide equal opportunities for employment without regard to race, religion, age, creed, sex, national origin, or disability through Title VII of the Civil Rights Act of 1964 and the Equal Employment Opportunity Act of 1972.[4] These laws have broad coverage and apply to any activity, business, or industry in which a labor dispute would hinder commerce. The laws also cover state and local governments, governmental agencies, and agencies of the District of Columbia.

Some of the specific provisions of the Equal Opportunity Act of 1972 are:

- It is unlawful for an employer to fail or refuse to hire or to discharge any individual, or otherwise to discriminate against any individual with respect to compensation, conditions, or privileges of employment because of race, color, religion, sex, age, or national origin. This applies to applicants for employment as well as current employees.

- Employers may not limit, segregate, or classify employees in any way that would deprive them of employment opportunities because of race, color, age, religion, sex, or national origin.

- The EEOC now has the power to file action in a federal district court if it is unable to eliminate alleged unlawful employment practices by the informal methods of conference, conciliation, and persuasion.

- Employment tests may be used if it can be proven that they are related to the job or promotion sought by the individual. Tests should be validated for each company.

- No discriminatory statements may be included in any advertisements for job opportunities.

The EEOC attempted at first to encourage employers to follow the guidelines of the law. Now the EEOC is more aggressive and asks employers to prepare *affirmative action programs;*[5] the employer must spell out how the company plans to increase the number of minority and female employees. If EEOC investigators do not like the distribution of employees, they can propose adjustments. The employer may then state why these adjustments can or cannot be made.

Even if the EEOC does not get involved with an employer, an individual who feels that discrimination is taking place may sue. The number of complaints of job discrimination has increased from 8,800 in 1966 to over 80,000 in 1987.[6] However, as of January 1988, the EEOC is bringing only approximately 400 suits per year against employers.

The hiring practices of airlines have been the subject of two important court decisions on recruitment. One held that female gender is not a bona fide occupational qualification for the job of cabin flight attendant. Another held that an airline's policy that stewardesses must be single is unlawful. No other female employees were subject to the policy, and there was no formal policy restricting employment to single male stewards. Another court ruled it illegal to fire a female employee because she is pregnant and

---

[4]Kenneth Sovereign, *Personnel Law* (Reston, Va.: Reston Publishing, 1984).

[5]Paul S. Greenlaw, "Affirmative Action or Reverse Discrimination," *Personnel Journal,* September 1985, pp. 84–86.

[6]Correspondence and discussions with EEOC (Washington, D.C., January 1988).

Table 16–1 Some legal guidelines for the selection step in staffing.

Selection Screening Steps	Legal Activities	Illegal Activities
Tests	Can be used if they have been validated	Cannot be used when there is no relationship between test results and performing the job
Interview information	To ask if a person is a U.S. citizen	To require citizenship or to ask proof of citizenship
	To ask about convictions for crime	To ask if person has ever been arrested
Age	To require proof of age after hiring	To require birth certificate
Racial identity	To keep records on racial and ethnic identity for purposes of reporting	To ask for race, creed, or national origin in application or interview

unmarried. A sex discrimination case against a New York law firm was settled, before a court ruling, when it agreed to recruit, hire, and promote women attorneys on the same basis as men.

The legal procedures regarding equal employment opportunities and recruitment are important to employers. Organizations have to adjust to and work with these laws. Although adjustments are sometimes difficult, they seem to be a better alternative than becoming involved in long and costly court battles. Providing equal opportunities to all qualified job applicants makes sense both legally and morally. The vast majority of managers in organizations believe that all citizens have a right to any job they can perform reasonably well after a sufficient amount of training.

Selection Activities

The *selection* of people depends largely on organizational needs and on compliance with legal requirements. Discriminatory practices in recruiting, testing, and offering a job are illegal, as defined in the Civil Rights Act of 1964 and the Equal Employment Opportunity Act of 1972. A few of the important legal guidelines affecting the staffing selection step are described in Table 16–1.

The actual selection process is a series of steps. It starts with initial screening and ends with the orientation of newly hired employees. Figure 16–2 presents each step in the process. Recognizing human resource needs through the planning phase of staffing is the point at which selection begins. Preliminary interviews are used to screen out unqualified applicants. This *screening* often is the first personal contact a person has with an organization. If the applicant passes the preliminary screening, she then usually completes an application.

Applications.   The *application form* is used to obtain information that will be helpful in reaching an employment decision. An application should include questions that can be used, if even in a general sense, to predict job success. The appropriate questions

Figure 16–2
Selection steps.

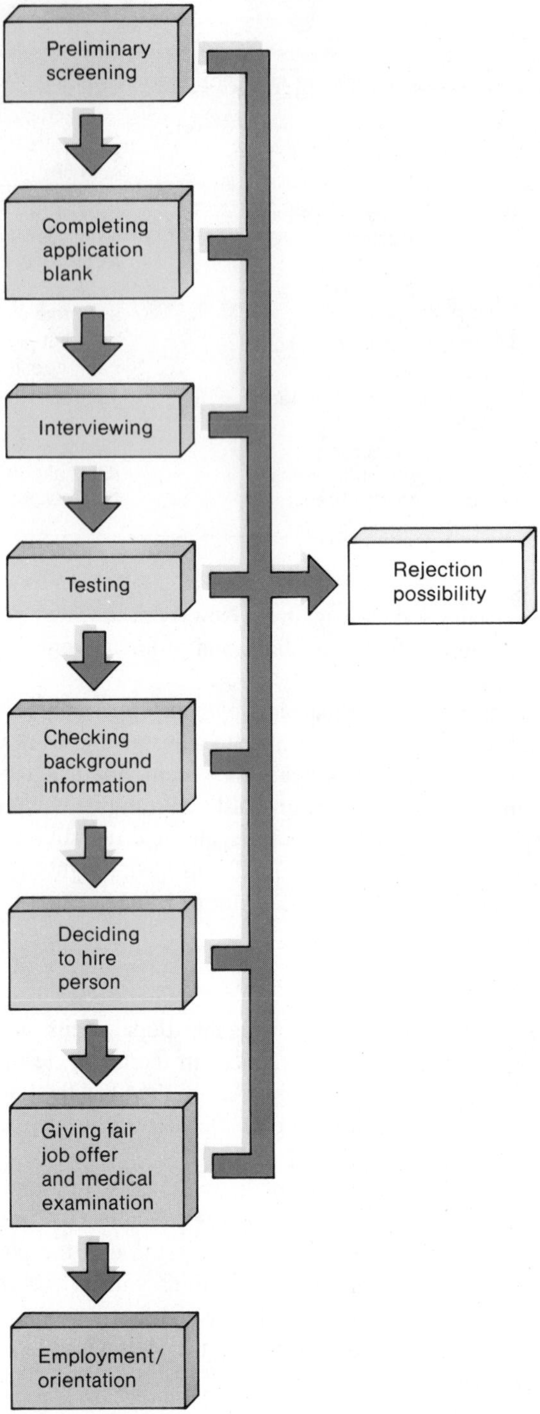

Preliminary screening

Completing application blank

Interviewing

Testing

Rejection possibility

Checking background information

Deciding to hire person

Giving fair job offer and medical examination

Employment/ orientation

can be developed only after a careful job analysis. An application form should be complete yet concise, so it does not burden the selection step with unnecessary information.

Two approaches are used widely to analyze application blank responses. In the *clinical method,* the interviewer carefully analyzes answers and attempts to gain a sense of a person's attitudes, personality, and career goals. Clinical analysis should not be attempted by untrained personnel. It also should not be considered a perfect analysis of an applicant's credentials.

The *weighted application method* is the second approach. For some jobs and organizations, certain items in a person's background—such as education and previous work experience—may be more important than others. Suppose that, through careful analysis, it is determined that the most successful sales personnel for an engineering firm are college educated, have at least eight years of field sales experience, are in excellent health, and have been raised in the sales territory. Managers could use this information as part of the selection process. Like the clinical method, the weighted application approach is not perfect. It can, however, increase the organization's ability to hire individuals who have the best chance to succeed.

Interviews.   Interviews are used throughout the selection process. Interviewers usually first acquaint themselves with the job analysis information. Second, they review the application blank information. Third, they typically ask questions designed to give better insight into the applicants, and they add this information to that on the application blank.

Three general types of interviews are used: structured, semistructured, and unstructured. In the *structured interview,* the interviewer asks specific questions of all interviewees. In the *semistructured interview,* only some questions are prepared in advance. This approach is less rigid than the structured interview and allows the interviewer more flexibility. The *unstructured interview,* meanwhile, allows the interviewer the freedom to discuss what even he thinks is important. Comparing answers across interviewees is rather difficult, however.

Some firms are now using computers to administer structural employment interviews. Although it does not replace the face-to-face interview, the computer can provide a base of information about each applicant before the interviewer meets the applicant. An applicant can typically complete a 100-question computer-aided interview in less than 20 minutes.[7]

Testing.   In recent years, *selection tests* have been a common method of screening applicants. Selection tests are costly, time consuming, and have legal implications.[8] But they do have several advantages:

---

[7]Douglas D. Rodgers, "Computer-Aided Interviewing Overcome First Impressions," *Personnel Journal,* April 1987, pp. 148–52.

[8]G. Stephen Taylor, "Personality Tests for Potential Employees: More Harm than Good," *Personnel Journal,* January 1988, pp. 60–64.

1. Improved accuracy in selecting employees. Individuals differ in skills, intelligence, motivation, interests, needs, and goals. If these differences can be measured, and if they are related to job success, then performance can be predicted to some extent by test scores.

2. Objective means for judging. Applicants answer the same questions, under test conditions, and their responses are scored. One applicant's score then can be compared to the scores of other applicants.

3. Information on the needs of present employees. Tests given to present employees provide training, development, or counseling information.

Despite these advantages, tests have been—and probably will remain—controversial. Key legal rulings and fair-employment codes have helped create strict procedures for developing tests. The following criticisms have been directed at testing programs:

1. Tests are not infallible. Tests reveal what persons *did* do in a testing situation, not what they could do on the job. Some of the best test performers may be the poorest job performers.

2. Tests are given too much weight. Tests cannot measure everything about a person. They can never substitute for good judgment.

3. Tests discriminate against minorities. Ethnic minorities, such as blacks and Mexican-Americans, may score lower on certain paper and pencil tests because of cultural bias. The Civil Rights Act of 1964 prohibits employment practices that artificially discriminate against individuals on the basis of test scores.

The U.S. Supreme Court made a landmark ruling related to tests in the *Griggs v. Duke Power Company* case in 1971.[9] Six years earlier, Duke Power had established a policy requiring job applicants to satisfactorily pass a number of tests and have a high school education to qualify for placement and promotion. A group of black employees challenged these requirements, arguing that they were denied promotions because of the testing policy. The Supreme Court ruled that neither the high school requirement nor the test scores showed a relationship to successful job performance.

Organizations using any test now must carefully examine how the scores are used. And test results must be validated. There must be statistical proof that test scores are related to job performance. Testing, however, still can be an important part of the recruiting process.[10] It also is a major tool for making decisions.

Toyota, as the following Management Application indicates, uses a vigorous testing program for applicants for jobs in their Georgetown, Kentucky, plant.

---

[9]Bently Baranabus, "What Did the Supreme Court Really Say?" *Personnel Administrator,* July–August 1971, pp. 22–25.

[10]Cristina G. Banks and Loriann Roberson, "Performance Appraisers as Test Developers," *Academy of Management Review,* January 1985, pp. 128–42.

MANAGEMENT APPLICATION

TAKING SOME SELECTION LESSONS FROM THE JAPANESE

Applying for a job at the Toyota Motor Corporation plant in Georgetown, Kentucky, involves a tough selection process. Mike Warren spent 25 hours being screened. He underwent paper and pencil tests, workplace simulations, and a probing interview. He scored high and was hired as a manager in quality control.

A battery of tests is required for anyone who would handle a fender or is a manager in the office. Is it because the Japanese are scared of the American worker? Is it the concern about labor unions? Or is it that the Japanese make a big commitment to their employees so when they hire them they want to make sure they'll work out for life? Perhaps it is for all of these reasons.

Toyota says it is testing and screening so thoroughly because it wants to find workers who still conform to the Japanese emphasis on teamwork, corporate loyalty, and versatility along the production line.

Although the testing is difficult, some 90,000 applications poured in for the approximately 3,000 jobs. In job-hungry Kentucky, people are willing to undergo tests to land a job. The Toyota selection methods are now being adopted by American automakers. General Motors, for example, joined Toyota in carefully assessing job applicants in Fremont, California, as the two companies reopened a plant through a joint venture.

Although General Motors appears to approve of the Toyota selection process, Honda does not like testing. Honda has hired hundreds of workers for its Marysville, Ohio, plant. They, however, do not use tests. Honda does, however, put every job applicant through three comprehensive interviews.

Source: Adapted from Richard Koenig, "Toyota Takes Pains, and Time, Filling Jobs at Its Kentucky Plant," *The Wall Street Journal,* December 1, 1987, pp. 1 and 29.

The hiring decision.   Once the preliminary screening steps are completed—evaluating the application blank, interviewing, and testing—and the organization considers making an offer, a *background check* usually is made. The background check consists of verifying various facts and collecting additional data from references and previous employers. The organization also attempts to gather facts about the applicant's previous record of job performance. If reference checks yield favorable information, the line manager and an employment division representative usually meet to decide the type of compensation and benefit offer that will be made.

Orientation Activities

Most large companies have a formal *orientation* for new employees. New employees usually know something about their organization, but they often do not have specific information. Orientations customarily provide information about working hours, pay, parking, rules, and available facilities. The orientation information should be furnished by line managers. The personnel department typically coordinates the orientation, but the manager of the new employee is the key person in the process.

If new employees are properly oriented, several objectives can be accomplished. First, start-up costs can be minimized. A new employee can make costly mistakes unless tasks, expectations, procedures, and other matters are properly explained. Anxieties can be reduced and realistic job expectations can be created by a good orientation.[11]

CONCURRENT CONTROL OF HUMAN RESOURCES

Concurrent control of human resources consists primarily of actions by supervisors who *direct* the work of their subordinates. As noted in Chapter 14, *direction* refers to the acts of managers when they undertake (1) to instruct subordinates in the proper methods and procedures and (2) to oversee their work to ensure it is done properly.

FEEDBACK CONTROL OF HUMAN RESOURCES

Many actions and activities are involved in the feedback control of human resources. Together they comprise the managerial practice known as *performance evaluation*. Performance evaluation is the focus of the remainder of this chapter.

Purposes of Performance Evaluation

Performance evaluation processes and procedures accomplish two broad, and several specific, purposes. The two broad purposes are termed (1) *judgmental* and (2) *developmental*.[12]

Judgmental purposes.   When performance evaluation results are the bases for salary, promotion, and transfer decisions, judgmental purposes are being served. The immediate objective is to improve performance by rewarding high performers. Managers who use performance evaluation for judgmental purposes must evaluate performance accurately and precisely and distribute rewards on the basis of performance. Failure to do so undermines the judgmental purposes and causes employees to be cynical about the process.

Managers become judges when judgmental purposes are sought. Subordinates being evaluated, meanwhile, recognize that their financial and career interests are at stake. So they tend to play passive, reaction roles and are frequently defensive. The atmosphere in which performance evaluations are undertaken is often colored by suspicion and distrust. Managers and subordinates alike are uncomfortable about the process, particularly when the information about performance is potentially inaccurate and when the performance standards are invalid.

---

[11]John P. Wanous, *Organizational Entry: Recruitment, Selection, and Socialization of Newcomers* (Reading, Mass.: Addison-Wesley Publishing, 1980).

[12]Evelyn Eichel and Henry E. Bender, *Performance Appraisal: A Study of Current Techniques* (New York: American Management Association, 1984).

Developmental purposes.   The second broad purpose of performance evaluation is to improve performance through self-learning and personal growth. The *developmental purpose* is accomplished when employees are made aware of their strengths and weaknesses and of ways to improve their skills and abilities.

The focus of attention is less on the appraisal of past performance and more on the improvement of future performance. The managers' roles in the process are to counsel, guide, and generally be helpful as subordinates seek, through active involvement, a better understanding of their potential for improved performance. Managers should avoid judgmental terms such as *good-bad, positive-negative,* and *right-wrong*. Instead, they should help employees identify areas in need of improvement.

The two general purposes of performance evaluation are not mutually exclusive. Managers must, however, identify the purposes of performance evaluation and provide for those purposes by adopting appropriate procedures.

Performance Standards

The performance evaluation program at any level within the organizational hierarchy must, at some point, focus on *performance standards*. In performance evaluation, the standard is the basis for appraising the effectiveness of an individual employee.

Requirements of a performance standard.   At least four requirements must be met before a measure can qualify as a performance standard. First, the measure must be *relevant* to the individual and the organization. Determining what is relevant is itself controversial. Some person or group must make a judgment about what constitutes relevance.

Second, the standard must be *stable,* or reliable. This involves agreement of different evaluations at different points in time. If the results from two different evaluations diverge greatly, the standard is probably unreliable.

Third, a performance standard must *discriminate* between good, average, and poor performers.

Finally, the standard must be *practical*. It must mean something to the rater and the ratee.

Single or multiple standards.   Ample evidence supports arguments for either single or multiple standards. In some situations, especially at the policymaking level, a single standard is needed to reach a managerial decision. In cases involving promotion, salary and wage decisions, transfer and counseling, multiple standards can be useful in illustrating why a particular decision is made or why a specific development program is recommended. It is extremely difficult to make a promotion decision on the basis of a single criterion.[13]

Managers ordinarily evaluate performance in several key areas of work. Figure 16–3 summarizes a survey that sought to determine the extent to which factors such

---

[13]See Frank J. Landy and James L. Farr, "Performance Rating," *Psychological Bulletin,* February 1980, pp. 72–107.

Figure 16–3 The most frequently used performance standards.

	White Collar Workers	Blue Collar Workers
Quality	93%	91%
Quantity	90	91
Job knowledge	85	85
Attendance	79	86
Initiative	87	83
Cooperation	87	83
Dependability	86	86
Need for supervision	67	77

Source: Bureau of National Affairs, "Employee Performance: Evaluation and Control," *Personnel Policies Forum*, February 1975.

as quantity and quality of work were used in performance evaluation. The results clearly indicate the importance of *quality* and *quantity* of work for white-collar and blue-collar workers alike. Ninety percent or more of the survey respondents indicated that they used these two factors when evaluating performance. Notice also the extensive reliance on personality traits and characteristics (initiative, cooperation, dependability, and need for supervision).

Administering Performance Evaluation

Although developing a systematic program for performance evaluation is extremely important, other managerial practices regarding performance evaluation are just as significant. Managers must decide (1) who will do the rating, (2) who will be rated, (3) when the rating should take place, and (4) how to perform in the evaluation interview.

Who should rate?   Five possible parties can serve as raters: (1) the supervisor or supervisors of the ratee, (2) organizational peers, (3) the ratee, (4) subordinates of the ratee, and (5) individuals outside the work environment. In most situations, the rater is the immediate supervisor of the person rated. Because of frequent contact, she is assumed to be most familiar with the employee's performance. In addition, many organizations regard performance evaluation as an integral part of the immediate supervisor's job. The supervisor's evaluations often are reviewed by higher management, thereby maintaining managerial control over the evaluation program.

A form of peer evaluation is used at Romac Industries, Inc., in Seattle. This company permits all employees at six months on the job to vote on the raises of other employees. When an individual requests a raise, his picture is put on the bulletin board along with information about the raise. The employees then vote whether to grant the raise. Management reserves the right to veto the results, but the essence of the policy is to allow peers to evaluate peers.

Interest in using self-evaluations has grown. The major claims in support of this approach are that self-evaluation improves the employee's understanding of job performance, increases the personal commitment of employees because of their participation in the process, and reduces the hostility between superiors and subordinates over ratings. Some employers fear, however, that self-ratings will be unusually high.

In organizations that enjoy a high level of trust, subordinates sometimes can rate their managers. Organizations with a history of antipathy between managers and nonmanagers, however, should not expect to obtain valid information by such means.

Support has emerged for increased use of multiple evaluators. The major advantage of using a combination of superior, peer, and self-ratings is that a great deal of information is gained about the employee.[14] In making decisions about promotion, training and development, and career planning, a manager needs as much information as possible to suggest the best courses for the employee.

When to rate.   There is no specific schedule for rating employees. In general, however, one formal evaluation a year is provided for older or tenured employees. Recently hired employees usually are evaluated more frequently than others. The time to rate will depend on the situation and on the intent of the evaluation. If performance evaluations are too far apart or occur too frequently, the ratee may not be able to use the feedback to make improvements.

An evaluation program conducted solely to rate employees soon will lose any potential value or motivational impact unless it is integrated with the main emphases of the organization. The judgmental and developmental purposes best show through when both the ratee and the rater understand each other's roles in the process. The rater must clarify, coach, counsel, and provide feedback. On the other hand, the ratee must understand rater expectations, her own strengths and weaknesses, and the goals to be accomplished. These various roles can become clear if the performance evaluation program is considered a continual process that focuses both on task accomplishments and on personal development.

The evaluation interview.   Regardless how individual job performance information is collected, the rater must provide formal feedback to the ratee. Without formal feedback, the ratee will have difficulty making the modifications necessary to improve performance, difficulty matching his individual job performance expectations with those of the rater, and difficulty assessing the progress being made toward accomplishment of career goals.[15]

The feedback interview should be part of any performance evaluation program from the beginning.[16] The interview should focus on the job performance of the ratee. Generally, raters feel uncomfortable about discussing the problems of those they rate.

---

[14]Eichel and Bender, *Performance Appraisal,* report considerable use of multiple raters in their survey of current practices.

[15]David M. Herold, Robert C. Liden, and Marija L. Leatherwood, "Using Multiple Attributes to Assess Source of Performance Feedback," *Academy of Management Journal,* December 1987, pp. 826–835.

[16]J. L. Pearce and L.W. Porter, "Employee Response to Performance Appraisal Feedback," *Journal of Applied Psychology,* April 1986, pp. 211–18.

Table 16–2 Guidelines for preparing and conducting an appraisal interview.

Preparing for the interview:
1. Hold a group discussion with employees to be evaluated and describe the broad standards for their appraisals.
2. Discuss your employees with your own manager and several of your peers.
3. Clarify any differences in language between the formal written appraisal and the interview.
4. If you are angry with an employee, talk about it before the interview, not during the interview.
5. Be aware of your own biases in judging people.
6. Review the employee's compensation plan and be knowledgeable of his salary history.
7. If you already have given the employee a number of negative appraisals, be prepared to take action.

Conducting the interview:
1. Focus on positive work performance.
2. Remember that strengths and weaknesses usually spring from the same general characteristics.
3. Admit that your judgment of performance contains some subjectivity.
4. Make it clear that responsibility for development lies with the employee, not with you (the rater).
5. Be specific when citing examples.

On the other hand, ratees often become defensive when raters point out weaknesses or failures. As criticism increases, the defensiveness of subordinates increases. Furthermore, praise in the feedback sessions is often ineffective, since most raters first praise, then criticize, and finally praise to end the session. Ratees become conditioned to this sequence.[17]

Too often, performance evaluation interviews focus on the past year or on plans for the short run. Rarely do a manager and subordinate discuss careers.[18] But managers should understand the requirements for the various career tracks within the organization. The manager should be able to help create challenging but not unattainable job tasks for subordinates. This will help prepare subordinates for future jobs requiring more skills and abilities. Managers should discuss the lifelong sequence of job experiences of subordinates as part of the performance evaluation feedback interview. Only when career goals are considered can the evaluation process become a developmental experience as well as a judgmental analysis of job performance.

Although the particular needs of each organization, manager, and individual must be considered, some general guidelines can be suggested. In Table 16–2, suggestions for preparing and conducting the appraisal interview are stated.

---

[17]Douglas Cederblom, "The Performance Appraisal Interview: A Review, Implications, and Suggestions," *Academy of Management Review,* April 1982, pp. 219–27.

[18]G. W. Dalton, P. H. Thompson, and R. L. Price, "A New Look at Performance by Professionals," *Organizational Dynamics,* Summer 1977, pp. 19–42.

Traditional Performance Evaluation Methods

Managers usually attempt to select a performance evaluation procedure that will minimize conflict, provide ratees with relevant feedback, and contribute to the achievement of organizational objectives. Basically, managers must try to develop and implement a performance evaluation program that also can benefit other managers, the work group, and the organization.

As with most managerial procedures, there are no universally accepted methods of performance evaluation to fit every purpose, person, or organization. What is effective in IBM will not necessarily work in General Mills. In fact, what is effective within one department or one group in a particular organization will not necessarily be right for another unit or group within the same company.

Graphic rating scales. The oldest and most widely used performance evaluation procedure, the graphic scaling technique, has many forms. Generally, however, the rater is supplied with a printed form, one for each subordinate to be rated. The form lists a number of job performance qualities and characteristics to be considered. The rating scales are distinguished by (1) how exactly the categories are defined; (2) the degree to which the person interpreting the ratings (e.g., the superior) can tell what response was intended by the rater; and (3) how carefully the performance dimension is defined for the rater.

Each organization devises rating scales and formats that suit its needs. Figures 16–4 and 16–5 are examples of types of rating forms used in many organizations. The one shown in Figure 16–4 is a more general form than that in 16–5, which is used by a state university to evaluate technical and staff personnel. Each form attempts to clarify the meanings of each of the rating factors. Users of the form in Figure 16–5 know that the rating scale is 1 (unacceptable) to 4 (superior) for each of the three factors. Note also that Figure 16–4 contains many of the factors listed in Figure 16–3, which typically are used in business organizations. The rating form in Figure 16–5 makes explicit the weights of each factor. When the form has been completed, the employee receives an overall score indicative of performance during the period covered by the evaluation.

Ranking methods. Some managers use a rank order procedure to evaluate all subordinates. The subordinates are ranked according to their relative value to the company or unit on one or more performance dimensions. The procedure followed usually involves identifying the best performer and the worst performer. These are placed in the first and last positions on the ranking list. The next best and next poorest performers then are filled in. This continues until all subordinates are on the list. The rater is forced to discriminate by the rank-ordering performance evaluation method.

Some problems are associated with the ranking method. One is that ratees in the central portion of the list likely will not be much different from one another on the performance rankings. Another problem involves the size of the group of subordinates being evaluated. Large groups are more difficult to rank than small groups.

Weighted checklists. A *weighted checklist* consists of a number of statements describing various types and levels of behavior for a particular job or group of jobs.

Figure 16–4   Typical graphic rating scale.

Name _____		Dept. _____			Date _____	
	Outstanding	Good	Satisfactory	Fair	Unsatisfactory	
Quantity of work Volume of acceptable work under normal conditions Comments:	☐	☐	☐	☐	☐	
Quality of work Thoroughness, neatness, and accuracy of work Comments:	☐	☐	☐	☐	☐	
Knowledge of job Clear understanding of the facts or factors pertinent to the job Comments:	☐	☐	☐	☐	☐	
Personal qualities Personality, appearance, sociability, leadership, integrity Comments:	☐	☐	☐	☐	☐	
Cooperation Ability and willingness to work with associates, supervisors, and subordinates toward common goals Comments:	☐	☐	☐	☐	☐	
Dependability Conscientious, thorough, accurate, reliable with respect to attendance, lunch periods, reliefs, etc. Comments:	☐	☐	☐	☐	☐	
Initiative Earnest in seeking increased responsibilities; self-starting, unafraid to proceed alone Comments:	☐	☐	☐	☐	☐	

Each statement has a weight or value attached to it. The rater evaluates each subordinate by checking the statements that best describe the behavior of the individual. The check marks and the corresponding weights then are summated. Figure 16–5 illustrates a form of the weighted checklist.

The weighted checklist makes the rater think in terms of specific job behavior. However, this procedure is difficult and very costly to develop. Separate checklists usually are established for each job or group of jobs.

Descriptive essays.   The essay method of performance evaluation requires that the rater describe each ratee's strong and weak points. Some organizations require every rater to discuss specific points, while others allow the rater to discuss whatever she believes is appropriate. One problem with the unstructured essay evaluation is that it provides little opportunity to compare ratees on specific performance dimensions. Another limitation involves the variations in the writing skills of raters. Some simply are not very good at writing descriptive analyses of subordinates' strengths and weaknesses.

Figure 16–5
Personnel
evaluation.

Name _____   Social Security No. _____

Job title _____

Bureau/center _____

	Rating × Weight = Score	
1. Demonstrated personal characteristics Consideration should be given to job knowledge, judgment, communication skills, attitude, ability to deal with people (superiors, subordinates, clients, and other university personnel), initiative, and so on.	____ 20% ____	
2. Performance of assigned duties Consideration should be given to the degree of program goal accomplishment, quality service provided, quantity of program activities (work load and clients generated), degree of supervision and/or guidance required, quality of reports, contribution to public relations, improvements generated in program to which assigned, clients/students' reactions, and so on.	____ 60% ____	
3. Contribution outside area of assigned duties Consideration should be given to suggestions for furthering the Office for Research, contribution to new program development, public relations activities, contribution to improving relations with the college and university, and state agencies.	____ 20% ____	

Total score   ____

Comments: _____

_____

_____

_____   _____
        Date   Signature

Rating errors.   The numerous traditional performance evaluation methods each have problems and potential *rating errors*. The major problems and errors can be *technical* in the form of poor reliability, poor validity, little practicality, or rater misuse. In some situations, raters are either extremely harsh or easy in their evaluations. These are called *strictness* or *leniency* rater errors. The harsh rater tends to give lower-than-average ratings to subordinates. The lenient rater tends to give ratings higher than average. These kinds of rating errors typically result because the rater applies his own personal standards to the particular performance evaluation system being used. For example, the words *outstanding* or *average* may mean different things to various raters.

Rating errors can be minimized if:

1. Each dimension addresses a single job activity rather than a group of activities.
2. The rater can observe the behavior of the ratee on a regular basis.
3. Terms such as *average* are not used on rating scales, since different raters react differently to such words.
4. The rater does not have to evaluate large groups of subordinates. Fatigue and difficulty in discriminating among ratees become major problems when large groups of subordinates are evaluated.

5. Raters are trained to avoid leniency, strictness, and other rating errors.

6. The dimensions being evaluated are meaningful, clearly stated, and important.

Another possibility is to use forms of performance evaluation that attempt to minimize rating errors.[19] Two of the more recently developed approaches are *behaviorally anchored rating scales (BARS)* and *management by objectives (MBO)*.

Nontraditional Performance Evaluation Methods

In an effort to improve traditional performance evaluations, some organizations have used various behaviorally based and goal-setting programs. The behaviorally based programs attempt to examine what the employee does in performing the job. The objective, or goal-setting, programs typically examine the results of accomplishments of the employee.

Behaviorally anchored rating scales.   Behaviorally anchored rating scales (BARS) are constructed through the use of "critical incidents."[20] *Critical incidents are examples of specific job behaviors that determine various levels of performance*. Once the important areas of performance are identified and defined by employees who know the job, critical incident statements are used to discriminate among levels of performance. The form for a BARS usually covers 6 to 10 specifically defined performance dimensions, each with various descriptive behaviors. Each dimension is based on observable behaviors and is meaningful to the employees being evaluated.

An example of BARS for a competence performance dimension for engineers is presented in Figure 16–6. The dimension is defined for the rater; the behaviors define the particular response categories for the rater; and the response made by the rater is precise and easy to interpret. The feedback provided by the BARS is clear and meaningful. For example, if the ratee is given a 1.5 on this dimension, she is provided with the specific behavior that the rater evaluated.

A number of advantages are associated with the use of BARS. Since job-knowledgeable employees participate in the actual development steps, the final evaluation form should be acceptable as a measure of actual performance.

The use of BARS also provides valuable insight into developing training programs. The skills to be developed are specified in terms of actual behavioral incidents rather than abstract or general skills. Trainees in a BARS-based program could learn expected behaviors and how job performance is evaluated.

A behaviorally anchored evaluation system may minimize rating errors. However, some critics of BARS have presented results indicating that the approach is not always

---

[19]Stuart Murray, "A Comparison of Results-Oriented and Trait-Based Performance Appraisals," *Personnel Administrator*, June 1983, pp. 100–5.

[20]P. C. Smith and L. M. Kendall, "Retranslation of Expectations: An Approach to the Construction of Unambiguous Anchors for Rating Scales," *Journal of Applied Psychology*, April 1963, pp. 149–55.

Figure 16–6
A BARS
performance
dimension.

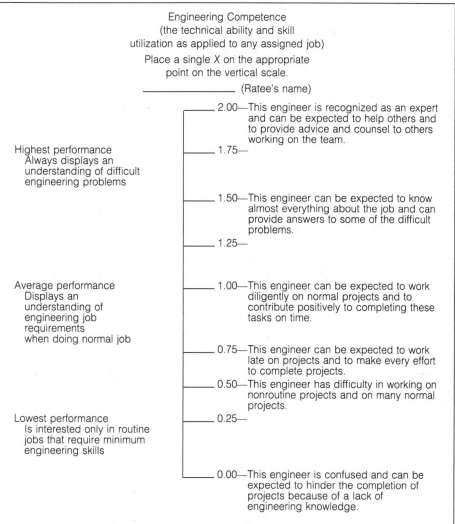

Engineering Competence
(the technical ability and skill
utilization as applied to any assigned job)

Place a single X on the appropriate
point on the vertical scale.

_____ (Ratee's name)

2.00—This engineer is recognized as an expert
and can be expected to help others and
to provide advice and counsel to others
working on the team.

1.75—

Highest performance
Always displays an
understanding of difficult
engineering problems

1.50—This engineer can be expected to know
almost everything about the job and can
provide answers to some of the difficult
problems.

1.25—

Average performance
Displays an
understanding of
engineering job
requirements
when doing normal job

1.00—This engineer can be expected to work
diligently on normal projects and to
contribute positively to completing these
tasks on time.

0.75—This engineer can be expected to work
late on projects and to make every effort
to complete projects.

0.50—This engineer has difficulty in working on
nonroutine projects and on many normal
projects.

0.25—

Lowest performance
Is interested only in routine
jobs that require minimum
engineering skills

0.00—This engineer is confused and can be
expected to hinder the completion of
projects because of a lack of
engineering knowledge.

the most relevant, stable, and practical. These critics also suggest that more research comparing BARS with the traditional evaluation methods is needed.[21]

Despite the time, the cost, and the procedural problems of developing and implementing BARS, this system seems to have some advantages. Specifically, a BARS

---

[21]D. P. Schwab, H. G. Henneman III, and T. A. DeCotiis, "Behaviorally Anchored Rating Scales: A Review of the Literature," *Personnel Psychology,* Winter 1975, pp. 549–62.

program could minimize subordinates' defensive attitudes toward evaluation. By being involved in the development of BARS, subordinates can make their inputs known. These inputs can be incorporated into the final BARS. The BARS development steps could include both superiors and subordinates. In a sense, then, all parties involved can contribute to the creation of the evaluation criteria (dimensions) and the behavioral incidents that are used to define each level of performance.

Another advantage of using BARS is that the evaluation program concentrates on job-specific and job-relevant behaviors. Many performance evaluation programs are abstract and meaningless to either the ratees or the raters. Thus, when giving feedback to ratees, the raters must convert the ratings to examples of actual job behavior. There are, in many cases, variances in the raters' ability to make these conversions from the rating scale to meaningful job behaviors. The BARS already contain behaviors that the superior can use in developing the evaluation counseling interview.

Management by Objectives

In the traditional and BARS evaluation programs, the rater is making judgments about the performance of *activities*. Many managers believe that a *results-based* program is more informative. One popular results-based program is called *management by objectives* (MBO). This program typically involves the establishment of objectives by the supervisor alone or jointly by the supervisor and the subordinate.

A high-powered, computer-generated MBO system is being used at Cypress Semiconductor Corporation in San Jose, California, which is described in the following Management Application.

MANAGEMENT APPLICATION

A FAST TRACKING MBO SYSTEM IN ACTION

In a conference room in the San Jose, California, headquarters of Cypress Semiconductor Corporation, the company's seven vice presidents sit in tense silence. Every week, at exactly noon, T. J. Rodgers, president and CEO, assembles the vice presidents for a status report on the grade of each department in the company. These sessions mean that there is no escaping the late report on the marketing project, the increased absenteeism in the clerical department, or the overrun production budget. The harsh light of a computer-generated projector beams down detailed charts on the status of each executive's weekly goal and performance.

At Cypress they refer to the program of weekly reviews as "TURBO MBO"—a computer-driven information review that tracks the goals of every company employee. Stanley Meresman, Cypress's vice president of finance and administration, for example, is responsible for five to seven of his goals every week, plus another 100 goals on behalf of the 20 people reporting to him.

T. J. Rodgers has the pulse of the entire firm at his fingertips. With the touch of a few keys on his personal computer, Rodgers can call up any one of about 4,500 weekly goals for his 670 employees. He believes that this is the only way to stay on top of the company's day-to-day operations.

The results at Cypress have been impressive. Last year, while most of the semiconductor industry was taking losses, Cypress earned $13.4 million on revenues of $50.9 million. Rodgers believes that his "TURBO MBO" system has enabled the firm to introduce one-third more changes than otherwise would be possible.

The Cypress system does have its detractors. Keeping track of every minute and every output is offensive to some employees. One former employee stated, "I am a self-motivated, professional engineer. I was offended that others were keeping track of exactly what I was doing all the time." Despite some detractors, T. J. Rodgers continues to use his high-powered, computer-driven "TURBO MBO" system. He feels that by keeping such a close tab on goals, there will be a minimum number of surprises. He needs to be informed to compete and respond in the dynamic semiconductor industry.

Source: Adapted from Steve Kaufman, "Going for the Goals," *Success*, January/February 1988, pp. 38–41.

MBO is far more than just an evaluation approach. It usually is a part of an overall motivational program, planning technique, or organizational change and development program. Here, we will only introduce the idea of MBO as an alternative to traditional performance evaluation methods.

An MBO performance evaluation program focuses on the employee's achievements. The key features of a typical MBO program include the following:

1. The superior and the subordinate meet to discuss and set objectives for the subordinate for a specified period of time (e.g., six months or one year).

2. Both the superior and the subordinate attempt to establish objectives that are realistic, challenging, clear, and comprehensive. The objectives should be related to the needs of both the organization and the subordinate.

3. The standards for measuring and evaluating the objectives are agreed upon.

4. The superior and the subordinate establish some intermediate review dates when the objectives will be re-examined.

5. The superior plays more of a coaching, counseling, and supportive role and less of a judgmental role.

6. The entire process focuses on results and on the counseling of the subordinate, and not on activities, mistakes, and organizational requirements.

MBO-type programs have been used in organizations throughout the world.[22] Approximately 40 percent (200) of *Fortune's* 500 largest industrial firms report using MBO-type programs. As with the performance evaluation programs already discussed,

---

[22]Dale D. McConkey, *How to Manage by Results* (New York: AMACOM, 1983).

Table 16–3 Managerial points of interest when selecting a performance evaluation program

	Programs					
Points of interest	Graphic Rating Scales	Ranking	Checklists	Essay	Bars	MBO
Acceptability to subordinates	Fair	Fair/poor	Fair	Poor	Good	Generally good
Acceptabilty to management	Fair	Fair/poor	Fair	Poor	Good	Generally good
Useful in reward allocations	Poor	Poor	Fair	Fair	Good	Good
Useful in counseling and developing subordinates	Poor	Poor	Poor	Fair	Good	Good
Meaningful dimensions	Rarely	Rarely	Sometimes	Rarely	Often	Often
Ease of developing actual program	Yes	Yes	Yes	No	No	No
Development costs	Low	Low	Low	Moderately high	High	High

there are both advantages and potential disadvantages associated with the use of MBO. The fact that MBO stresses results is a benefit that can also be a problem. Focusing only on results may take attention away from the process of accomplishing the objectives. A subordinate receiving feedback about what has been achieved still may not be certain about how to make performance corrections. A manager may tell a subordinate that the quality control goal was missed by 3.5 percent, but this type of feedback is incomplete. The subordinate who has failed to meet the quality control goal needs guidance and advice on how to accomplish it in the future.[23]

Other problems linked to MBO programs include improper implementation, lack of top-management involvement, too much emphasis on paperwork, failing to use an MBO system that best fits the needs of the organization and the employees, and inadequate training preparation for employees who are asked to establish goals.[24]

A final limitation of MBO is that comparisons of subordinates are difficult. In traditional performance evaluation programs, all subordinates are rated on common dimensions. Since, in MBO, each individual usually has a different set of objectives, it is difficult to make comparisons across a group of subordinates. The superior must make reward decisions not only on the basis of objectives achieved but also on the

---

[23]James S. Russell and Dorothy L. Goode, "An Analysis of Manager's Reactions to Their Own Performance Appraisal Feedback," *Journal of Applied Psychology*, February 1988, pp. 63–67.

[24]J. M. Ivancevich, "Different Goal-Setting Treatments and Their Effects on Performance and Job Satisfaction," *Academy of Management Journal*, September 1977, pp. 406–19; and J. M. Ivancevich, J. H. Donnelly, Jr., and J. L. Gibson, "Evaluating MBO: The Challenges Ahead," *Management by Objectives*, Winter 1976, pp. 15–24.

basis of his *conception* of the kinds of objectives that were accomplished. The rewarding feeling of having achieved objectives generally will wear thin among subordinates if the accomplishment is not accompanied by meaningful rewards.

A Review of Potential Performance Evaluation Programs

Table 16–3 summarizes the main points of the various approaches discussed. A performance evaluation system may be more useful in some organizations than in others because of the types of individuals doing the rating or because of the criteria being used. All of the programs discussed in this chapter have costs and benefits. Performance evaluation is an integral part of managing within organizations. So recognizing the strengths, weaknesses, and best uses for a particular program is an important job for managers.

MANAGEMENT SOLUTION

CONTROL DATA'S FOURTH PERFORMANCE EVALUATION FEATURE

To decide whether Control Data's performance evaluation system came up to expectations, the company's managers devised a monitoring and tracking process. This fourth feature of the system enables managers to assess effectiveness in terms of the degree to which both managers and employees are satisfied. The process includes three monitoring techniques:

1. *User-reactions questionnaire.* Periodically, a random sample of managers and employees completes a short questionnaire. The respondents indicate how satisfied they are with various aspects of the process. The questionnaire is particularly useful for detecting dissatisfactions with the ability of the system to determine employee strengths and weaknesses that can be exploited or improved in training. The questionnaire also provides information to gauge the relevance of performance criteria for measuring job performance. The information obtained is valuable feedback which enables managers to fine-tune the performance evaluation system.

2. *Policy tracking systems.* The company routinely tracks the relationship between performance evaluation outcomes and the personnel actions that result from it. Salary and promotion actions depend on performance, and managers must demonstrate that their actions reflect their performance judgments. The company also tracks the relationship between training and performance improvements. It is concerned with how well an employee's deficiency is improved through the training experience.

3. *Diagnostic feedback system.* The company developed a management information system that provides managers with norms to evaluate their own evaluation decisions. The norms enable managers to judge how well they differentiate among different levels of performance and avoid some of the many rating errors common when judging the performances of large numbers of individuals. The information system enables managers to compare their evaluation and salary decisions to those of other managers.

Continued

MANAGEMENT SOLUTION

Concluded

Control Data's response to the challenge to develop procedures for evaluating its performance evaluation system reflects understanding that this fourth feature is a natural extension of the other three. An effective performance evaluation system consists of an integrated set of parts, each making a different, yet compatible, contribution to the effectiveness of the overall system.

Source: Adapted from Luis R. Gomez-Mejia, Ronald C. Page, and Walter W. Tornow, "Improving the Effectiveness of Performance Appraisal," *Personnel Administrator,* January 1985, pp. 74–85.

MANAGEMENT SUMMARY

☐ Evaluating the performance of human resources is a key managerial responsibility. Effective performance evaluation can help accomplish such goals as increased motivation and improved knowledge.

☐ To be effective as a management control activity, performance evaluation must be based on specific standards. These performance standards must be relevant, stable, practical, and capable of distinguishing different levels of performance.

☐ To administer a performance evaluation program, managers must make several key decisions, including who should do the rating, when to rate, and how the evaluation interview will be performed.

☐ Traditional performance evaluation methods use some form of rating scale that requires managers to rate their subordinates on a number of dimensions.

☐ In reaction to some of the problems inherent in traditional performance evaluation methods, two recently developed methods, behaviorally anchored rating scales and management by objectives, have been widely adopted.

☐ Behaviorally anchored rating scales use critical incidents or specific job behaviors that determine different levels of performance.

☐ Management by objectives requires that managers and their subordinates mutually set objectives and standards for specified time periods.

REVIEW AND DISCUSSION QUESTIONS

1. Explain why both developmental and judgmental purposes are difficult to achieve in performance evaluation.

2. In your view, if a manager must choose between using performance evaluation for either developmental or judgmental purposes, which should be chosen? Explain.

3. Explain why rating errors occur and why they cause problems in performance evaluation.

4. What would be some reasons why a firm such as General Dynamics in San Diego would use present employees in their recruitment ads?

5. What role does the government play in human resource management activities and programs? Should its role be larger or smaller? Discuss.

6. Describe and distinguish between the various traditional performance evaluation methods.

7. Explain the differences between behaviorally anchored rating scales and traditional rating scales.

8. Explain the importance of each key decision that managers must make when administering a performance evaluation program.

9. What type of questions could be more easily asked by using a computer system than by using a traditional one-on-one interviewing format?

10. Explain the basic features of a management by objectives performance evaluation program.

CASES

16–1   EVALUATING MANAGERIAL PERFORMANCE

Steven Patrick was anxiously waiting for the Monday morning staff meeting to begin. He had only recently been promoted to corporate director of personnel, and today he would present a new idea to the rest of the corporate staff. This would be the first time that he had done so. In the six months since Steven had taken the new job and had begun attending the weekly staff meetings, he had remained silent except when responding to a direct question from one of the other corporate-level managers.

The staff meeting convened, and its chairperson, the executive vice president, called upon Steven to present his idea.

"As you know," said Steven, "the personnel division has the responsibility for developing procedures to evaluate the performance of line managers throughout the company. We view this responsibility in terms of the larger issue of developing the skills and abilities of line managers. Historically, this company has relied on evaluation by superiors, but I would like to suggest that the real source of information about how managers perform is their subordinates. As a company, we have not attempted to obtain information from the people who report to managers. Many companies, including some of our competitors, attempt to obtain information from subordinates.

"I am proposing that we consider a procedure for obtaining information that will enable us to know the strengths and weaknesses of each manager as viewed by those who report to him. The procedure is relatively simple. Each manager will meet with his people. A trainer from the personnel division will also be present at this initial meeting. The manager must assure his people that the purpose of the meeting is to obtain their cooperation in a process which will help him become a better manager. Any subordinate must feel free to refuse to take part in the process.

"Once the manager has met with his people and has explained what is going on, one of my trainers will meet with each subordinate who has agreed to participate and will have the subordinate complete a questionnaire. (A sample questionnaire is shown in Exhibit 16–1.) The specific questions to be included in the questionnaire will relate to the manager's performance of assigned activities, including his manner of dealing with people. Each subordinate will rate the manager on each activity on a numerical scale and will explain the basis for the rating to the trainer. To protect the subordinates from any real or imagined threat for participating, the responses will remain anonymous when they are reported to the manager. Only the trainer will know the source of any comments.

"After the trainers have obtained information from the subordinates, they will meet with each manager. The managers will be given all of the information obtained, and they will discuss it with the trainer. The purpose of this session and of others to follow is to prepare a plan that will enable each manager to take corrective action. The corrective action can range from a simple change in the manager's behavior if he has unknowingly been relating to people in objectionable ways, to a training program designed to develop the manager's skills and knowledge.

"Let me conclude by saying that we in personnel believe that this procedure will provide valuable information to our managers. It will also be possible to take the corrective action necessary to improve the performance of line managers. The only unresolved issue is that of standards. We will obtain numerical ratings for each manager, but we will have nothing to compare them to except those of other managers. If this group accepts the feasibility of this plan, our next step is to develop standards for managerial performance. I believe that to be the responsibility of top management, as represented by this group."

Questions

1. If you were a line manager, how would you react to Steven's plan? Would you consider it threatening? Why?

2. Do you see any problems in a procedure that attempts to obtain data for performance evaluation *and* personal development?

3. If you were Steven, how would you go about obtaining the performance standards? What type of control does Steven's plan represent?

Source: This case is adapted from Gerald W. Bush and John W. Stinson, "A Different Use of Performance Appraisal: Evaluating the Boss," *Management Review*, November 1980, pp. 14–17.

Exhibit 16–1

The Appraisal Rating Form

SECTION I, II

From your perspective and working relationship with Gerry Bush over the time span you have worked with him, you are asked to rate his performance in all of the following JOB COMPONENTS and INTERPERSONAL RELATIONSHIP areas. Please use the five point scale provided by placing an X in the appropriate box.

SECTION I—PRINCIPAL JOB COMPONENTS

   I. HUMAN RESOURCES FUNCTIONAL LEADER

      1. Appropriate involvement in each H.R. functional area:

	Low				High
	1	2	3	4	5
Labor relations	[ ]	[ ]	[ ]	[ ]	[ ]
Salary administration	[ ]	[ ]	[ ]	[ ]	[ ]
Benefits	[ ]	[ ]	[ ]	[ ]	[ ]
EEO	[ ]	[ ]	[ ]	[ ]	[ ]
Personnel planning	[ ]	[ ]	[ ]	[ ]	[ ]
International personnel	[ ]	[ ]	[ ]	[ ]	[ ]
Career development	[ ]	[ ]	[ ]	[ ]	[ ]
Annuitants	[ ]	[ ]	[ ]	[ ]	[ ]
Placements	[ ]	[ ]	[ ]	[ ]	[ ]

(continued)

Exhibit 16–1 (*concluded*)

	Low				High
	1	2	3	4	5

SECTION I—PRINCIPAL JOB COMPONENTS

2. Directing and coordinating Strategy Center/Corporate Human Resources projects where there is a need for a common view point. [ ] [ ] [ ] [ ] [ ]

3. Resolving unproductive conflict between Strategy Centers and Corporate Human Resources departments. [ ] [ ] [ ] [ ] [ ]

4. Understanding of corporate executive viewpoints regarding future Human Resources Policy development and providing direction to Human Resources groups accordingly. [ ] [ ] [ ] [ ] [ ]

5. Promoting the Human Resources function with Corporate and Strategy Center Executives and building support for proposed Human Resources Policy and strategy recommendations. [ ] [ ] [ ] [ ] [ ]

II. CORPORATE HUMAN RESOURCES MANAGER

1. Focuses attention of subordinates on important work priorities. [ ] [ ] [ ] [ ] [ ]

2. Encourages/leads inter-Human Resources discussion, collaboration between Corporate Human Resources groups on work projects or in resolving day-to-day issues. [ ] [ ] [ ] [ ] [ ]

3. Follows up on work projects. [ ] [ ] [ ] [ ] [ ]

4. Rejects inadequate work. [ ] [ ] [ ] [ ] [ ]

5. Rewards good work. [ ] [ ] [ ] [ ] [ ]

6. Handles unproductive conflict between Corporate Human Resources groups. [ ] [ ] [ ] [ ] [ ]

7. Ensures that subordinates are kept informed on important developments affecting their functions. [ ] [ ] [ ] [ ] [ ]

III. H.R. CONSULTANT/ADVISER-CORPORATE EXECUTIVE

1. Keeps corporate executive informed on internal and external H.R. issues of major significance to the corporation. [ ] [ ] [ ] [ ] [ ]

2. Directs H.R. personnel's attention to important issue raised by the executive and requiring immediate action. [ ] [ ] [ ] [ ] [ ]

IV. H.R. CONSULTANT/ADVISER—STRATEGY CENTER EXECUTIVE

1. Understands major H.R. issues or concerns of the Strategy Center Executives. [ ] [ ] [ ] [ ] [ ]

2. Provides advice or marshalls internal or external consulting resources to address major Strategy Center H.R. issues. [ ] [ ] [ ] [ ] [ ]

V. COMPANY REPRESENTATIVE

1. Handles interactions with government regulatory agencies effectively on behalf of the corporation. [ ] [ ] [ ] [ ] [ ]

2. Represents the corporation effectively internally with employee groups. [ ] [ ] [ ] [ ] [ ]

3. Represents the corporation effectively externally with business or educational institutions. [ ] [ ] [ ] [ ] [ ]

SECTION II—INTERPERSONAL RELATIONSHIPS

I. The effectiveness of leadership style exhibited in such business situations as Human Resources Council meetings. [ ] [ ] [ ] [ ] [ ]

II. The extent to which appropriate functional or business information is communicated, measured in terms of:

Quantity [ ] [ ] [ ] [ ] [ ]

Quality [ ] [ ] [ ] [ ] [ ]

III. The level of trust existing in your relationship with him. [ ] [ ] [ ] [ ] [ ]

IV. The level of openness existing in your relationship with him. [ ] [ ] [ ] [ ] [ ]

V. The "ease" of interaction existing in your relationship with him.   [ ] [ ] [ ] [ ] [ ] [ ] [ ] [ ]

VI. The level of support he gives you on assignments/projects.   [ ] [ ] [ ] [ ] [ ] [ ] [ ] [ ]

VII. The level of supervision and encouragement he gives you on assignments/projects.   [ ] [ ] [ ] [ ] [ ] [ ] [ ] [ ]

SECTION III—PERFORMANCE IMPROVEMENT INFORMATION
Considering the rating analysis you completed in Sections I and II and thinking more specifically about the job performance, complete the following subsections:

A. Identify minimally three work activities or practices which the senior vice president could do *more of* to improve job performance.

B. Identify minimally three work activities or practices which the senior vice president should do *less of* that would improve job performance.

C. Identify minimally three work activities or practices which the senior vice president is currently handling *just about right.*

16–2 GOAL SETTING AT TENNECO

Tenneco is a large, diversified company operating in eight major industries. Among the Tenneco companies are J. I. Case, manufacturer and marketer of farm and construction equipment; Newport News Shipbuilding and Dry Dock Company; Walker Manufacturing Company and Monroe Auto Equipment Company, manufacturers of automotive equipment; Packaging Corporation of America, a supplier of paperboard, folding cartons, and corregated containers; Tenneco Oil, producer, refiner, and marketer of petroleum and related products; Tennessee Gas Transmission Company, marketer of a wide range of industrial chemical products; and Tenneco West, which produces and markets agricultural products. Tenneco employs about 85,000 people, of which 15,000 are managers and professionals.

A task force with representatives from each divisional company of Tenneco recommended to the president that a performance planning and evaluation (PP&E) and goal-setting program be implemented. The president, in support of the PP&E program, stated:

> If we fail to offer maximum opportunity to any one person in our organization, we are failing in one of our basic management responsibilities. . . . Accordingly, I expect this philosophy and method of management to receive enthusiastic support at all levels within Tenneco.

Simply stated, Tenneco's top management wanted the PP&E program to create an atmosphere that encouraged self-motivation and personal satisfaction.

The PP&E program involved the diagnosis of each job by incumbents, who were then expected to broadly define the key responsibilities of their jobs. Next, specific objectives and priorities of these objectives were spelled out. Emphasis was placed on work performance and personal-development objectives. Many goal-setting programs place primary emphasis only on the work objectives, disregarding development objectives. This is not the case in the PP&E program. A balance between work performance and personal-development objectives is reached through dialogue, transaction, and agreement between the supervisor and each subordinate. The supervisor and each subordinate are expected to work out the balance in a formal meeting.

After one year, the results of the subordinate's actual performance and development progress are measured against stated objectives and priorities. The performance evaluation session focuses on results, with special attention paid to specific plans and accomplishments in personal development. This special concern about personal development highlights the most unique feature of the Tenneco PP&E program, which has some other important features:

1. Active top-management support displayed by participation of senior executives in all phases of PP&E.
2. The use of external evaluations to monitor the impact, if any, of PP&E on attitudes and performance of participants.
3. The use of data collected by external evaluators to make modifications. Presently, each company is able to develop its own feedback plan. Feedback in the PP&E programs means the use of the evaluator's information, collected and related to the divisional company management, to make modifications.

The Tenneco PP&E system contains areas in which subjective measures and judgments are used. However, the care exercised in planning, implementing, supporting, and evaluating the PP&E program appears to have had some impact on the attitudes of Tenneco managers about goal setting. Tenneco managers seem stimulated and interested in performance and personal-development goal setting. The secret may be that goal setting is used not only to assess performance contributions but also to develop managers for more responsible duties in the future.

Questions

1. What advantages were there in using a task force with representatives from each divisional company to develop performance planning and evaluation (PP&E) at Tenneco?
2. Does Tenneco's president seem concerned about the development of people? How did you reach this conclusion?
3. What would be the value of Tenneco's top management supporting the PP&E program?

Source: This case is based on the experiences and research of John M. Ivancevich, J. Timothy McMahon, J. William Striedl, and Andrew D. Szilagyi, Jr.

EXERCISE

16-1 A CONTROL PROCEDURE: YOUR PERSONAL PERFORMANCE APPRAISAL

Purpose: The purpose of this exercise is to apply performance appraisal guidelines to your own activities and objectives.

Setting Up the Exercise:

1. Write a paragraph (150 words or less) describing a successful you. What would make you successful? Select school, your job, your family, or personal life as a reference point. In your paragraph, list the outcomes (results) that would mean you were successful (e.g., *school*—grade point average, 3.3, graduated with honors, receiving highest grade on final; *job*—promoted to next level in two years, receiving recognition, receiving large merit increase).

2. For the reference point (choose one), select five areas of major concern and the measure of success you would use. Determine whether the measures of success are subjective or objective. Do they have a time frame?

Major Area of Concern	How Is Success Measured?	Subjective/ Objective	Time Frame Yes/No
1. _____ _____	_____ _____	_____	_____
2. _____ _____	_____ _____	_____	_____
3. _____ _____	_____ _____	_____	_____
4. _____ _____	_____ _____	_____	_____
5. _____ _____	_____ _____	_____	_____

3. Develop the major areas of concern into specific personal objectives—one for each major area of concern. The objectives should be one *single* sentence, clearly stated, with a time period specified. Rank the objectives from the most important to the least important.

Ranked Objectives

1. _____
2. _____
3. _____
4. _____
5. _____

4. The instructor will form groups of three students to share their success stories, measures of success, and objective statements. Are there differences in what are considered success measures, objectives, and priorities?

A Learning Note: Even self-performance appraisal is a control procedure. It serves to direct individual behavior toward objectives that are meaningful, clear, comprehensive, and challenging. Explicit objectives that are well stated must be carefully worked on. Skill in developing objectives can be improved with practice. Good objectives can be helpful in planning, organizing, and controlling behavior and attitudes.

SEVENTEEN

Organizational Change and Development

LEARNING OBJECTIVES

After completing Chapter 17, you should be able to:

Define: the term *organizational development,* from a manager's perspective.

State: the primary differences between the structural, behavioral, and technological change approaches.

Describe: the limiting conditions which can affect the outcomes of organizational change implementation.

Explain: why some employees resist change in organizations.

Discuss: the timing and scope dimensions of implementation.

TIMES OF CHANGE AT BANK OF AMERICA

When Bank of America was established in California in the early 1900s, the bank quickly acquired the reputation as an innovator in the banking industry. Its founder, A. P. Giannini was the first to advertise, a practice then considered unethical for banks. He introduced the concept of branch banking and pioneered the practice of moving bank executives' offices from private back rooms to up front where the customers come in for service. Giannini set his desk near the front door.

Giannini took another gamble—he financed Walt Disney's "crazy" idea of producing the first full-length feature cartoon, *Snow White and the Seven Dwarfs*. As a result of a close working relationship with Walt Disney, today Bank of America is the one bank allowed to provide banking services at Disneyland.

By the 1940s, over one third of all banking Californians were Bank of America customers. However, in the decades following Giannini's death in 1949, Bank of America's culture and operations changed. Innovation was less welcomed; a bureaucratic structure was ill-equipped to deal with intensifying competition brought about by deregulation in the 1970s.

By the early 1980s, management knew the company was in trouble. A series of interviews with employees determined that the company's culture communicated a clear message to employees: don't take risks, focus on short-term profits, don't worry about personal performance, and "be nice"—don't openly and frankly evaluate strategies, plans or products. In essence, play it safe. Management decided that the time was ripe for a change.

(The Management Solution to this Management Incident can be found at the end of this chapter.)

This chapter explores the processes of organizational change. As even the casual reader of management literature soon realizes, the term *organizational development* (OD) has a variety of meanings. In its most restrictive sense, organizational development refers specifically to a form of sensitivity training. In a larger and more encompassing sense, it refers to any systematically planned, programmatic effort to improve the effectiveness of an organization through the application of behavioral science concepts, theories, and approaches. The development effort may focus on the way in which the organization is structured, the behavior of employees, or the technology used to get the work done.[1]

The growing realization that organizations can become more effective through managerial applications of behavioral science knowledge has spawned a wealth of literature.[2] This chapter presents some of the established ideas from this literature, in the context of practical management. To provide a theme, the material is presented in terms of a model describing the important factors of the development process. For simplicity, the phrase, *the management of change,* is used to include the concept of organizational development in its broadest sense.

A MODEL FOR MANAGING CHANGE

The management of change is a systematic process that can be broken down into subprocesses, or steps. Figure 17–1 summarizes this process. It consists of eight steps linked in a logical sequence. A manager should consider each of these steps, either explicitly or implicitly, when undertaking a change program. The prospects for success are enhanced if each successive step is taken explicitly and formally.

In describing alternative change techniques and strategies, we do not propose that some alternatives are superior to others. No one change technique or change strategy can be thought of as superior without knowledge of the specific situation.

The knowledgeable manager recognizes the possible alternatives and is not committed to one particular approach to the exclusion of all others. At the same time, the effective manager avoids the pitfalls of stagnation. Thus, the management of change implies that the manager should adopt a flexible, forward-looking stance. Such a stance is essential in the change process outlined in Figure 17–1. Each step of the process is discussed in this chapter.

FORCES FOR CHANGE

There are two types of forces for change: external forces and internal forces. The *external* forces are change in the marketplace, the technology, and the environment; these usually are beyond the control of the manager. *Internal* forces operate within the firm and to some extent can be controlled by managers.

---

[1]See Wendel L. French, Cecil H. Bell, and Robert A. Zawacki, eds., *Organization Development* (Plano, Tex.: Business Publications, 1983).

[2]Wendy Pritchard, "What's New in Organization Development," *Personnel Management,* July 1984, pp. 30–33; and Stephen R. Michael, "Organizational Change Techniques: Their Present, Their Future," *Organization Dynamics,* Summer 1982, pp. 67–80.

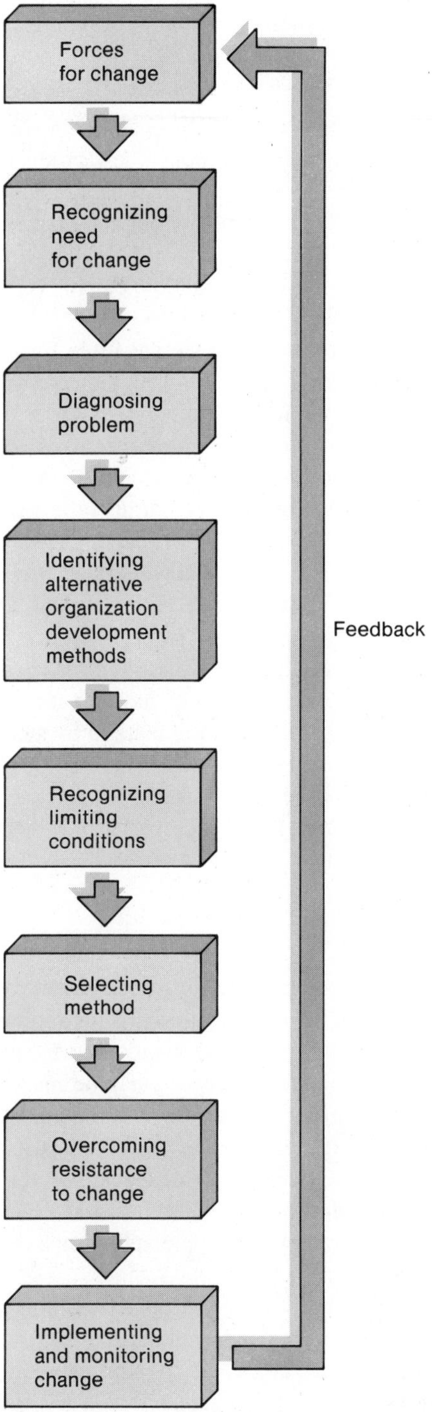

Figure 17–1
The management of change.

Forces for change

Recognizing need for change

Diagnosing problem

Identifying alternative organization development methods

Recognizing limiting conditions

Selecting method

Overcoming resistance to change

Implementing and monitoring change

Feedback

External Forces

Managers of business firms must respond to changes in the *marketplace,* the first external force for change. Competitors introduce new products, increase advertising, reduce prices, or improve customer service. In each case, a response is required, unless a manager is content to permit the erosion of profit and market share. Customer tastes and incomes also change. The firm's products may no longer have customer appeal. Or, customers may become able to purchase more expensive, higher-quality forms of the same products.

Changes in *technology* are the second external force for change. The knowledge explosion since World War II has brought new technology to nearly every management activity. Modern computers have made possible high-speed data processing and the solution of complex production problems. New machines and new processes have revolutionized manufacturing and distribution. Computer technology and automation have affected not only production techniques but also the social conditions of work. New occupations have burst forth, and old occupations have faded away. Sooner or later, delaying adoption of new technology that would reduce costs and improve quality will be reflected in the financial statement. Technological advance is a permanent fixture in contemporary society.

Environmental changes are the third external force for change. Managers must be tuned in to societal movements over which they have no control but which control the fates of their firms. The 1960s and 1970s were marked by a distinct increase in social activity. Sophisticated mass communications and international markets created enormous potential, but they also posed a great threat to managers unable to understand their significance. These pressures for change reflect the increasing complexity and interdependence of modern living.

Internal Forces

The forces for change within the organization can be traced to *processes* and *people*. Processes that facilitate change include decision making, communications, and interpersonal relations. Breakdowns or problems in any of these processes also can bring forces for change. Decisions may not be made, may be made too late, or may be of poor quality. Communications may be short circuited, redundant, or simply inadequate. Tasks may or may not be completed or even started because the person responsible did not receive the instructions. Because of inadequate or absent communications, a customer's order is not filled, a grievance is not processed, an invoice is not filed, or a supplier is not paid. Conflicts between people and groups reflect breakdowns in the interaction among individuals.

Low levels of morale and high levels of absenteeism and turnover are symptoms of people problems. A wildcat strike or a walkout may be the most tangible sign of a problem. Such tactics usually are employed because they arouse the management to action. Most organizations inevitably maintain a certain level of employee discontent; yet it is dangerous to ignore employee complaints and suggestions. But the process of change includes the *recognition* step and this is the point at which management must decide to act or not to act.

RECOGNIZING THE NEED FOR CHANGE

Managers learn of the magnitude of the forces for change through information. Financial statements, quality control data, and budget and standard cost information are important media through which both external and internal forces for change are communicated. These sources of facts and figures often are integrated elements of a refined management information and control system. Declining profit margins and market shares are tangible signs that the firm's competitive position is deteriorating and that change may be required.

Unfortunately, the need for change goes unrecognized in many organizations until some major catastrophe occurs. The employees strike or seek the recognition of a union before management finally concedes that action is needed. Talented managers leave the organization because they are not delegated authority and responsibility. A plant is forced to close because of high federal fines for polluting the environment. Managers must recognize the need for change by some means and must be able to diagnose the exact nature of the problem.

DIAGNOSING THE PROBLEM

Before appropriate action can be taken, managers must first diagnose the symptoms of the problem, then determine the problem itself. Unless the problem is readily apparent to all observers, experience and judgment are critical at this stage. However, managers often disagree as to the nature of the problem. There is no magic formula for *diagnosis*. The objectives of this step can be described by three questions:

1. What is the problem itself, as distinct from its symptoms?
2. What must be done to resolve the problem?
3. What outcomes (objectives) are expected from the action, and how will their attainment be measured?

The answers to these questions can come from management information and decision support systems in some organizations. However, managers may find it necessary to generate specific information through special committees or task forces. Meetings between managers and employees provide a variety of points of view and can be evaluated by a smaller group. Technical operational problems may be easily diagnosed, but subtler problems usually entail extensive analysis. One approach to diagnosing such problems is the *attitude survey*.

An attitude survey is a questionnaire designed to tap employee opinion about a wide variety of issues and aspects of the workplace. The questionnaire permits the respondents to evaluate and rate: (1) management, (2) pay and pay-related items, (3) characteristics of the organization's culture, (4) working conditions, and (5) other job-related items. The data is collected from employees, analyzed in detail, and fed back to various organization members. The survey's objective is to pinpoint the problem or problems as perceived by members of the organization. Subsequent feedback discussions of the survey results, at all levels of the organization, can give insight into

---

Table 17–1   Goal factors.*

Having gone through several work-planning and goal-setting (WP&G) sessions with your supervisor, you have established a set of goals for your job, which are in your WP&G contract. Listed below is a set of statements which may or may not describe your feelings about the entire WP&G process. Please read each statement carefully and then circle the one number from the seven alternatives which *best* describes your degree of agreement or disagreement with the statement. Please remember that there are no right or best answers. We would like your first impression to the question. Please answer each question.

	Strongly Disagree			Neutral			Strongly Agree
1. I receive a considerable amount of feedback concerning my overall performance on goals.	1	2	3	4	5	6	7
2. I am allowed a significant degree of influence in determining the results of my work.	1	2	3	4	5	6	7
3. The results expected for my work are extremely clear and help me know exactly what my job is.	1	2	3	4	5	6	7
4. The feedback I receive concerning my performance is well organized and helpful.	1	2	3	4	5	6	7
5. It takes a high degree of skill on my part to attain the results expected for my work.	1	2	3	4	5	6	7
6. I am not very committed to the WP&G goal-setting process.	1	2	3	4	5	6	7
7. It takes a lot of effort on my part to attain the results expected for my work.	1	2	3	4	5	6	7

*The complete questionnaire contains 34 questions.

the nature of the problem.[3] A sample of a questionnaire survey on the characteristics of a recently implemented goal-setting program is shown in Table 17–1.

Because of the increasing frequency of mergers, participative management, and other factors, an increasing number of companies are regularly conducting attitude surveys. IBM surveys its work force of more than 3,000 members every two years; Sears Roebuck, General Motors, Ford Motor, and Citicorp regularly obtain input from their employees.[4] Hartmarx Corporation surveys its 25,000-member work force every three years. The company analyzes results via computer and then personnel staff members meet with employees in small groups to obtain further employee input concerning their responses.[5]

---

[3]James F. Gavin and Paul A. Krois, "Content and Process of Survey Feedback Sessions and Their Relation to Survey Responses," *Group and Organizational Studies*, June 1983, pp. 221–47. Also see Ned Rosen, "Employee Attitude Surveys: What Managers Should Know," *Training and Development Journal*, November 1987, pp. 50–52.

[4]Thomas M. Ronen, "Do They Like Us? Attitude Surveys Arouse New Interest," *Industry Week*, October 14, 1985, p. 28.

[5]Larry Reibstein, "A Finger on the Pulse: Companies Expand Use of Employee Surveys," *The Wall Street Journal*, October 27, 1986, p. 23.

Attitude surveys are an effective way to obtain employee opinion on issues of interest; however the method is costly, averaging from $50,000 to $125,000 per survey project if handled by external consultants and from $25,000 to $70,000 if done internally.[6] Companies who conduct surveys also should be prepared to act on the survey's findings because surveying the work force generally raises employee expectations that management will respond to their complaints and concerns.

To ensure the survey's effectiveness, a number of companies obtain widespread employee participation in the survey's development. At GTE Corporation, for example, employees from all levels of the organization serve on the survey's steering committee. GTE also believes that a potential obstacle to survey effectiveness is a manager's impression that the survey is a witch hunt to identify poor performers. To eliminate this potential barrier, GTE assures each manager that responses from her subordinates won't be shared with upper-level management without her permission.[7]

Finally, the diagnostic step must specify *objectives* for change. Given the diagnosis of the problem, managers must establish objectives to guide the change and evaluate its outcome. The objectives can be shaped in terms of financial and production data, such as profits, market shares, sales volume, productivity, and scrappage. They also can be stated as (1) attitude and morale objectives that are derived from attitude survey information or (2) personal development objectives meaningful to the members of an organization. For example, objectives can focus on the personal growth or re-education of one employee or a group of employees. Whatever the objectives, they must contribute to profitability, competitiveness, flexibility, and efficiency.

IDENTIFYING ALTERNATIVE CHANGE TECHNIQUES

The particular change technique chosen depends on the nature of the problem. Management must determine which alternative is most likely to produce the desired outcomes.[8] In this section of the chapter, a number of change techniques are described. They are classified according to the major focus of the technique; namely, to change structure, people, or technology.

Structural Change

Logically, organizing follows planning, since the structure is a means for achieving the objectives established through planning. *Structural change,* in the context of organizational change, refers to managerial attempts to improve performance by altering the formal structure of task and authority relationships. But because structure creates human and social relationships that members of the organization may value highly, efforts to disrupt these relationships may be resisted.

---

[6]Ibid.; and Dale Feuer, "Employee Attitude Surveys: How to Hand off the Results," *Training,* September 1987, pp. 51–54, 58.

[7]Feuer, "Employee Attitude Surveys," pp. 53, 58.

[8]John M. Nicholas, "The Comparative Impact of Organization Development Interventions on Hard Criteria Measures," *Academy of Management Review,* October 1982, pp. 531–42.

Structural changes alter some aspects of the formal task and authority system. The design of an organization involves the specification of jobs, the grouping of jobs into departments, the determination of the size of the groups reporting to a single manager, and the distribution of authority—including the provision of staff assistance. Changes in the nature of jobs, bases for departmentation, and line-staff relationships are, therefore, structural changes.

Changes in the nature of jobs.   Changes in the nature of jobs originate with new methods and new machines. Work simplification and job enrichment are two examples of methods changes. Work simplification increases specialization, whereas job enrichment decreases it.

A job can be changed by altering (1) the job description, (2) the role expectations of a position, (3) the relationships among positions, and (4) work flow patterns. For example, a change in a job description means that the duties to be performed and the manager's expectations about the duties are changed. A purchasing agent had his job description changed in an area involving his latitude for making purchasing decisions. After the change, he was able to make any purchasing decision without checking immediately with his manager. This change was structural. His increased authority also meant that he would have to work on Saturday evenings. This was a role expectation for purchasing agents who had full purchasing decision authority.

Changes in the bases for departmentation.   Chapter 7 examined the process of combining jobs into groups. Opinion is growing among managers and researchers that grouping jobs on the basis of function, territory, product, and customer does not occur in an orderly fashion. The classification system of various departmental arrangements is not a very accurate description of the organization of the 1980s. What is found at Tenneco Inc., Shell Oil Company, the Buick Division of General Motors, Zenith Radio Corp., and other organizations is a hodgepodge of various types of departmentation.

Departmentation in the 1980s seems to be based largely on a contingency perspective. The situation, people, resources, and external organizational forces appear to dictate largely what basis of departmentation will be used. The multiproducts and multi-industry organization require a significant amount of managerial coordination. Thus, experiments with different forms of departmentation and various managerial hierarchies are being conducted.

Changes in line-staff relationships.   These changes normally include two techniques. The first and most common approach is to create staff assistance as a temporary or permanent solution. One response of manufacturing firms to the problem of market expansion is to create separate staff and service units. These units provide the technical expertise to deal with the production, financial, and marketing problems posed by expansion.

An illustrative case is a company that had grown quite rapidly after its entry into the fast-foods industry. Its basic sources of field control were area directors who supervised the operations of the sales outlets of a particular region. During the growth period, the area directors had considerable autonomy in making the advertising decisions for their regions. Within general guidelines, they could select their own advertising media and formats and set their own advertising budgets. But as their markets became saturated and competitors appeared, corporate officials decided to centralize the advertising function in a staff unit located at corporate headquarters. Consequently, the area directors' authority was limited, and a significant aspect of their jobs was eliminated.

A final illustration of changes in line-staff relationships is based on the experience of a large insurance company. It hired a management consulting firm to analyze the problems of a deteriorating market position. The consulting firm recommended that the company undertake a program of decentralization by changing a staff position to a line position. This recommendation was based on the consultants' belief that in order to increase premium income, the company must have its best personnel and resources available at the branch office level. Accordingly, the consultants recommended that assistant managers become first-level supervisors reporting to branch managers. The reorganization required significant changes in the jobs of assistant managers and managers throughout the organization.

These examples indicate the range of alternatives that managers must consider. Certainly, there are many more possibilities. Elements of structural change often include plans, procedures, the span of control, and levels of organization. The point that should be taken, however, is not that any list of structural change approaches is incomplete, but that all structural parts are interrelated. Job changes do not take place in a vacuum; on the contrary, the change affects all surrounding jobs. The management of structural change must be guided by the point of view that all things are connected.

Behavioral Change

Behavioral change techniques are efforts to redirect and increase employee motivation, skills, and knowledge bases. The major objective of such techniques is to coordinate performance of assigned tasks. The early efforts to change employee behavior date back to scientific management work-improvement and employee-training methods. These attempts primarily were directed at improving the skills and knowledge bases of employees. The employee counseling programs that grew out of the Hawthorne studies were (and remain) primarily directed at increasing employee motivation.

Training and development programs for managers typically have emphasized supervisory relationships. These programs attempt to provide supervisors with basic technical and leadership skills. Since supervisors are concerned primarily with overseeing the work of others, these traditional programs emphasize techniques for dealing with people problems: how to handle the malcontent, the loafer, the troublemaker, the complainer. The programs also include conceptual material dealing with communications, leadership styles, and organizational relationships. The training methods involve role-playing, discussion groups, lectures, and organized courses offered by universities, consultants, and training corporations.

As the following Management Application notes, the president of Honeywell, Inc., attributes much of the success of organizational change at Honeywell Information Systems to a unique management training program.

MANAGEMENT APPLICATION

LEARNING THE BASICS AT HONEYWELL INFORMATION SYSTEMS

In the early 1980s, Honeywell Information Systems, a division of Honeywell Inc., was in a slump. After 11 years of toe-to-toe competition with IBM, the division's revenue growth was declining while costs were increasing. Morale was low. Results from an attitude survey indicated that employees believed that the division was characterized by little strategic planning or teamwork, and a short-term focus on performance.

To stabilize the company's financial condition, management cut costs, implemented layoffs, and closed some operations and consolidated others. However, these actions were at best only a short-term solution. Honeywell needed a new long-term vision. Management's answer: instead of simply making and selling computer hardware and software, Honeywell should develop computer systems that provide solutions to customer's operations and control problems (a systems solution strategy). Management also realized that the division's highly authoritative culture needed to be changed to a participative, team-oriented one.

Implementing this strategy and cultural change required many divisionwide changes. Honeywell's president, James J. Renier believes that perhaps the most important action taken in the division's organizational change effort involved "sending (managers) back to school to learn the basics."

School convened at Gainey Farm, a conference center in southern Minnesota. There, the division's Executive Leadership program was launched in November 1983 with a week-long session attended by the division's 25 top managers.

School began on Sunday evening when each manager was asked to tell two true stories about the company: one that symbolized a value worth keeping and another that illustrated an attitude that should be eliminated from the company's culture. On Monday, the managers discussed the division's culture and politics and the problems facing management from a leadership perspective. The program's coordinators provided the managers with survey feedback from their subordinates concerning their management style.

Working in teams, the 25 managers spent Tuesday discussing the division's current approaches to performing major management tasks. Each team determined the changes that were needed to develop a positive culture and then illustrated the changes in skits presented before the other teams. Next, the managers completed a rigorous obstacle course on the center's grounds. The teamwork exercise ended with the most demanding task: hurdling a 12-foot wall, an activity designed to boost cooperation and trust.

On Thursday, the participants again closely examined the division's current culture and identified the values that needed to be established. They then projected the values into the future by writing articles about the division to be published in *Business Week* or *Fortune* in the next three years. The managers then drew up a list of objectives that when realized would make the fictitious stories a reality. On Friday, the workshop ended with an overall discussion of the workshop and challenges to come.

Honeywell Information Systems has repeated the Gainey Farm process in workshops conducted for the division's upper and middle management. By the mid-1980s, the division's sales were breaking old records and profits had substantially increased.

Source: Adapted from James J. Renier, "Turnaround of Information Systems at Honeywell," *Academy of Management Executive*, February 1987, pp. 47–50.

Training continues to be an important technique for introducing behavioral changes. In some applications, training has taken on a form quite different from that which developed under classical management theory. The vast majority of organizational development change techniques have been directed at changing the behavior of individuals and groups through problem solving, decision making, and communication. Team building, sensitivity training, and transactional analysis—the most commonly used change approaches—will be discussed in more detail.

Team building.   The purpose of team building is to enable work groups to do their work more effectively—to improve their performance.[9] The work groups may be established, or relatively new, command and task groups. The specific aims of the intervention include setting goals and priorities, analyzing the group's work methods, examining the group's communication and decision-making processes, and examining the interpersonal relationships within the group.[10] As each of these aims is undertaken, the group is placed in the position of having to recognize explicitly the contributions, positive and negative, of each group member.[11]

The process by which these aims are achieved begins with *diagnostic* meetings. Often lasting an entire day, the meetings enable each group member to share with other members his perceptions of problems. If the group is large enough, subgroups engage in discussion and report their ideas to the total group. These sessions are designed for expression of the views of all members and to make these views public. That is, diagnosis, in this context, emphasizes the value of "open confrontation" of issues and problems that were previously discussed in secrecy.

Identifying problems and concurring on their priority are two important, initial steps. However, a *plan of action* must be agreed on. The plan should call on each group member, individually or as part of a subgroup, to act specifically to alleviate one or more of the problems. If, for example, an executive committee agrees that one of the problems is lack of understanding of and commitment to a set of goals, a subgroup can be appointed to recommend goals to the total group at a subsequent meeting. Other group members can work on different problems. For example, if problems are found in the relationships among the members, a subgroup can initiate a process for examining the roles of each member.

Team-building interventions do not always require a complex process of diagnostic and action meetings. For example, the chief executive of a large manufacturing firm recognized that conflict within her executive group was breeding defensiveness among the functional departments. She also recognized that her practice of dealing on a one-to-one basis with executive group members, each of whom headed a functional department, contributed to the defensiveness and conflict. Rather than viewing themselves

---

[9]Richard W. Woodman and John J. Sherwood, "Effects of Team Development Intervention: A Field Experiment," *Journal of Applied Behavioral Science,* April–June 1980, pp. 211–17; and R. Wayne Boss, "Organizational Development in the Health-Care Field: A Confrontational Team-Building Design," *Journal of Health and Human Resources Administration,* Summer 1983, pp. 72–91.

[10]An excellent framework for developing a team-building program is provided by Cynthia Reedy Johnson in "An Outline for Team Building," *Training,* January 1986, pp. 48ff.

[11]Richard L. Hughes, William E. Rosenbach, and William H. Glover, "Team Development in an Intact, Ongoing Work Group," *Group and Organizational Studies,* June 1983, pp. 161–81.

as team members with a stake in the organization, the department heads viewed one another as competitors. The chief executive's practice confirmed their belief that they managed relatively independent units.

To counteract the situation, the chief executive adopted the simple expedient of requiring the group to meet twice weekly. One meeting focused on operating problems, the other on personnel problems. The ground rule for these meetings was that the group must reach a consensus on each decision. After one year of such meetings, company-oriented decisions were being made, and the climate of interunit competition had been replaced by one of cooperation.

Team building also is effective when new groups are being formed. There are often problems when new organizational units, project teams, or task forces are created. Typically, such groups have certain characteristics that must be altered if the groups are to perform effectively. For example, the following combination of characteristics will lead to real problems:

1.   Confusion exists as to roles and relationships.
2.   Members have a fairly clear understanding of short-term goals.
3.   Group members have technical competence that puts them on the team.
4.   Members often pay more attention to the tasks of the team than to the relationships among the team members.

The result is that the new group will focus initially on task problems but ignore the relationship issues. By the time the relationship problems begin to surface, the group is unable to deal with them, and performance begins to deteriorate.

To combat these tendencies, a new group should schedule team-building meetings during the first weeks of its life. The meetings should take place away from the work site; one- or two-day sessions often are sufficient. The format of such meetings varies, but essentially their purpose is to provide time for the group to work through its timetable and the roles of members in reaching the group's objectives.[12] An important outcome of such meetings is to establish an understanding of each member's contribution to the team and of the reward for that contribution. Although the reports of team building indicate mixed results, the evidence suggests that group processes improve through team-building efforts.[13] This record of success accounts for the increasing use of team building as an organizational development method.[14]

Sensitivity training.   This technique attempts to make the participants more aware of themselves and of their impact on others. "Sensitivity" in this context means sensitivity to self and to relationships with others. An assumption of sensitivity training is that poor task performance is caused by the emotional problems of the people who

---

[12]For other strategies for team-building effectiveness, see Paul S. George, "Team Building without Tears," *Personnel Journal,* November 1987, pp. 122ff.

[13]Kenneth P. de Meuse and S. Jay Liebowitz, "An Empirical Analysis of Team-Building Research," *Group and Organizational Studies,* September 1981, pp. 357–78.

[14]W. J. Heisler, "Patterns of OD in Practice," in *Organization Development,* ed. Daniel Robey and Steven Altman (New York: Macmillan, 1982), pp. 23–29.

must collectively achieve a goal. Thus, if these problems can be treated, a major impediment to task performance is eliminated. Sensitivity training stresses the *process* rather than the *content* of training and *emotional* rather than *conceptual* training. It is clear that this form of training is quite different from the traditional forms, which stress the acquisition of a predetermined body of concepts with immediate application to the workplace.[15]

The process of sensitivity training includes a group of managers (the training group, or T-group) who, in most cases, meet away from their place of work. Under the direction of a trainer, the group usually engages in a dialogue with no agenda and no focus. The objective is to provide an environment that produces its own learning experiences. The unstructured dialogue encourages one to learn about the self in dealing with others. One's motives and feelings are revealed through behavior toward others in the group and through the behavior of others.

Research on the effectiveness of sensitivity training as a change technique so far suggests mixed results. A detailed review of 100 research studies found that sensitivity training was most effective at the personal level.[16] The studies reviewed compared the influence of 20 or more hours of training on the participants' attitudes or behaviors. The review concluded that sensitivity training:

1. Stimulated short-term improvement in communication skills.
2. Encouraged trainees to believe that they controlled their behavior more than others did.
3. Was likely to increase the participative orientation of trainees in leadership positions.
4. Improved the perceptions of others toward the trainee.

Managers should examine this technique critically to determine what kinds of behavioral changes are desirable and what kinds are possible. Certain conditions could limit the range of possible changes. In this light, managers must determine whether the changes induced by sensitivity training are instrumental for organizational purposes and whether the prospective participant could tolerate any anxiety generated by the training.

Transactional analysis.   Transactional analysis (TA) is another approach to behavioral change. It was first developed by Eric Berne for use in group therapy. TA is a method for analyzing and understanding human behavior. The foci are the personality, the manner in which people interact (transactional analysis), the ways people structure their time, and the roles people learn to play in life (life scripts).

Transactional analysis training is used by organizations to improve understanding and interaction. Typically, a training program examines the features of transactional

---

[15]Elliot Aronson, "Communication in Sensitivity Training Groups," in French, Bell, and Zawacki, *Organization Development*, pp. 249–53.

[16]Peter B. Smith, "Controlled Studies in the Outcomes of Sensitivity Training," *Psychological Bulletin*, July 1975, pp. 597–622; and Carl A. Bramlette and Jeffrey H. Tucker, "Encounter Groups: Positive Change or Deterioration? More Data on a Partial Replication," *Human Relations*, April 1981, pp. 303–14.

analysis. Trainers attempt to change the participants' inappropriate interaction patterns to help improve personal development and organizational performance. A first step in TA training is to develop the participant's understanding of his ego state.

Berne theorizes that the personality consists of three ego states. He defines ego as "a consistent pattern of feeling and experience directly related to a corresponding consistent pattern of behavior."[17] Managers cannot direct ego states, but they can observe behavior and make inferences.

One ego state is called the Parent. This ego state arises from the manner in which our parents reared us. The Parent in us provides advice, guidelines, regulations, and discipline for others. The Adult ego state is our dispassionate and objective side. It uses facts, information, and analysis to reach a decision. The Child ego state reflects the natural impulses, attitudes, and activities that are learned from childhood experiences. This ego state can range from listening and responding to whining and hostility.

These three ego states (Parent, Adult, Child) exist in everyone, according to Berne. Ideally, if our Adult state is in control, we are aware of our Child and Parent states. However, Berne emphasizes that all three ego states are necessary.

The Adult develops later in life than the Parent and the Child. The usual response to some stimulus is a Child or Parent reaction. Therefore, Berne recommends that the best way to become Adult (objective and analytic) is to become aware of Parent and Child signals. Parent signals include sighing and patting someone on the head or back; using such words as *pal, lazy, stupid,* and *nonsense;* or exclaiming, "Not again!" A few typical Child signals are tears, pouting, temper tantrums and statements like "I wish," "I want," and "I don't care." The more a person is aware of such Parent- and Child-type signals, the stronger the Adult becomes, which is more applicable to work and co-worker relationships in organizations.

Transactional analysis only recently has been applied in organizations as a behavioral change approach.[18] Most of the research results are anecdotal or self-reported responses after one- to three-day TA training sessions. Therefore, it is not possible to strongly encourage or discourage its use in organizations. At present, there are significant amounts of both criticism and support for TA training.

Technological Change

Technological change includes any application of new ways of transforming resources into products or services. In the usual sense of the word, technology means new machines—lathes, presses, computers, and the like. But the concept can be expanded to include all new techniques, whether or not they include new machines. From this perspective, the work improvement methods of scientific management can be considered technological breakthroughs. However, in this section, only those changes that can be linked to the introduction of a machine or a worker-machine process are discussed.

---

[17]Eric Berne, *Transactional Analysis in Psychotherapy,* (New York: Grove Press, 1961); and Eric Berne, *What Do You Say After You Say Hello?* (New York: Grove Press, 1972).

[18]Heinz Weihrich and Andre-Sean Signy, "Toward System-4 through Transactional Analysis," *Journal of Systems Management,* July 1980, pp. 30–36.

Technological change involving computers and robotics is being implemented by a growing number of manufacturing and service organizations. In service firms, computers now either perform or assist employees in performing a wide variety of tasks such as processing customer banking transactions, life insurance policies, and hospital admissions. Robots are also performing service jobs. One major fast-food chain, for example, is installing robots in its outlets that will assemble hamburgers. Another chain is considering installing a completely automated hamburger preparation center.[19] At the NBC television network, robots—not people—now operate the cameras that telecast "Nightly News," the network's evening news program.[20]

Manufacturing processes are also being computerized. In many plants, computers now control large parts of the manufacturing process such as materials handling, quality testing, and assembly. Some companies have created *flexible manufacturing systems*. These systems produce a part or product entirely by automation. From initial design to delivery, the unit is untouched by human hands.[21]

These technological changes have occurred largely because of the potential of high technology to lower production costs, to boost productivity, and to improve quality.[22] However, although computer and robotics technologies have affected over half of America's jobs, the rate of hi-tech implementation in U.S. organizations has fallen far short of projections. The reason: many high-tech changes haven't delivered expected results.[23]

Many observers believe that the disappointing performance of such technological change is due to management's neglect of the structural and behavioral changes that must accompany technological change. Specifically, employees' jobs have not been redesigned in a way that both makes the best use of new technology and addresses the employees' social and psychological needs. A mismatch exists between technology and how workers perform their jobs, and how managers supervise the workers. Consequently, technology's potential isn't realized.[24]

This neglect is costly because computerizing the workplace requires major structural and behavioral changes for success to occur.[25] Changes are necessary in a number of areas including:

Job design.
When a manufacturing process is highly automated, computers control many manufacturing functions. The overall process becomes much more integrated

---

[19]Rick Van Warner, "Robotics: An Alternate Labor Source," *Nation's Restaurant News,* August 17, 1987, p. 18.

[20]"Robotic Cameras: Cutting out the Middle Man," *Broadcasting,* December 7, 1987, p. 96.

[21]See Mark A. Vonderembse and Gregory S. Wobser, "Steps for Implementing a Flexible Manufacturing System," *Industrial Engineering,* April 1987, pp. 38ff.

[22]Otis Port, "High Tech to the Rescue," *Business Week,* June 16, 1986, pp. 100–3.

[23]John Hoerr and Michael A. Pollock, "Management Discovers the Human Side of Automation," *Business Week,* September 29, 1986, pp. 70ff; Gordon Bock, "Limping Along in Robot Land: A Once Helpful U.S. Industry Goes Awry," *Time,* July 13, 1987, pp. 46–47; and Ruth Simon, "The Morning After," *Forbes,* October 19, 1987, pp. 164ff.

[24]Ron Zemke, "Sociotechnical Systems," *Training,* February 1987, pp. 47ff.

[25]Ibid., Hoerr and Pollock, ibid., pp. 71; and Richard E. Walton and Gerald I. Susman, "People Policies for the New Machines," *Harvard Business Review,* March–April 1987, pp. 98–106.

such that jobs can't be defined individually and isolated. The new technology creates work modules (clusters of tasks) that are often more effectively performed by teams of employees.

For example, in one axle plant that implemented a highly automated manufacturing technology, management established "shift operation groups"—teams each comprised of 20 employees (12 system attendants, four electricians, and four machine repairmen). Each team was responsible for from four-to-five machine functions, working to ensure that their part of the manufacturing process operated smoothly.[26] Shenandoah Life Insurance Company used a team-based strategy to reap the benefits of computerization. Their approach is described in the following Management Application.

MANAGEMENT APPLICATION

OVERCOMING THE PITFALLS OF IMPLEMENTING NEW TECHNOLOGY

In the early 1980s, Shenandoah Life Insurance Company, like many other firms, looked to new technology for boosting productivity. The company implemented a $2 million computer system to speed the firm's policy and claims-handling processes. However, once the system was in place, management discovered that the computer had little real impact on productivity. For example, the task of converting one policy required the efforts of 32 employees across three departments and some 27 days to complete.

Shenandoah had a problem: It had implemented high-tech but ignored the firm's highly bureaucratic, assembly line style system of work. Employees were still "passing papers from person to person" but this time electronically, said one observer. The technological and social systems of work didn't mesh.

The company subsequently made some major changes. Employees drawn from several departments were organized into semi-autonomous work teams. For example, one team of six clerical employees was formed for processing all life and health insurance policies in Virginia (Shenandoah Life Insurance is based in Roanoke).

The team has much autonomy in fulfilling this responsibility. Working as a team, the members assign tasks within the group, train one another, and make the final hiring decision concerning new members. There is no formal team supervisor; instead, the group can consult with advisers (such as the personnel director, the manager of methods and procedures) concerning particular problems.

Management also placed team members on a pay-for-learning compensation system. A member's pay is based on the number of tasks which he can competently perform. Members are encouraged to learn all the tasks and earn the top compensation rate. The team determines whether a member has learned a task well enough to receive a higher rate of pay. To facilitate team learning, the members designed their work environment so that they would face each other, conference table style, while working.

Once the company implemented a team approach to work design, the computer system took off. With teams devising ways to use the computer effectively in the context

---

[26]Walton and Susman, ibid., p. 100.

of a flexible work environment, the time required to process a policy was reduced from 27 to 2 days. The company is also processing 50 percent more applications with 10 percent fewer employees. Service-related customer complaints have been virtually eliminated.

Source: Adapted from John Hoerr and Michael A. Pollock, "Management Discovers the Human Side of Automation," *Business Week*, September 29, 1986, pp. 70–74; and John Myers, "Beyond Productivity," *Best's Review*, November 1984, pp. 130ff.

Employee training.   Workers must be highly skilled to handle the substantial team responsibility for a major part of the manufacturing process. Team members must understand the technology to oversee machine functions and be skilled in diagnostic problem solving and communicating to quickly correct the glitches that sometimes occur. Thus, technological change essentially alters the amount and type of training that employees receive.

Compensation.   Like Shenandoah Life Insurance Co., many companies with a highly automated manufacturing process and employee teams have implemented a pay-for-knowledge compensation system. Individualized pay approaches, such as a piece rate system, don't work because the contributions of individual employees are difficult to measure. The pay-for-knowledge approach boosts team flexibility.

Management style.   Because of the nature of their responsibilities, teams working with highly automated processes often have much more authority in performing their tasks than do individuals in more traditional, assembly line-designed jobs. This increase in employee autonomy changes the nature of the manager's job. The emphasis shifts from supervision and control to coaching and consultation.[27] Technological change also requires that managers broaden their knowledge to include a thorough understanding of the new technology.[28]

Technological innovations can change other aspects of the workplace. The changes can alter working conditions, the social relations among workers, career patterns, and promotion procedures, to name a few. The degree and extent of any changes in behavior and structure depend on the magnitude of the technological change. Essentially, the decision to adopt a technological change must involve consideration of the numerous behavioral and structural impacts that often occur. Those impacts must, in turn, be reconciled with the conditions that limit the scope and magnitude of the proposed change.

The three major alternative approaches to change—structural, behavioral, and technological—attempt to improve performance by improving communication, decision making, attitudes, and skills. These approaches are based on the assumption that changes in structure, behavior, and technology can result in improvements for the

---

[27]Zemke, "Sociotechnical Systems," pp. 49.

[28]Walton and Susman, "People Policies for the New Machines," p. 102.

Figure 17–2 Three change approaches.

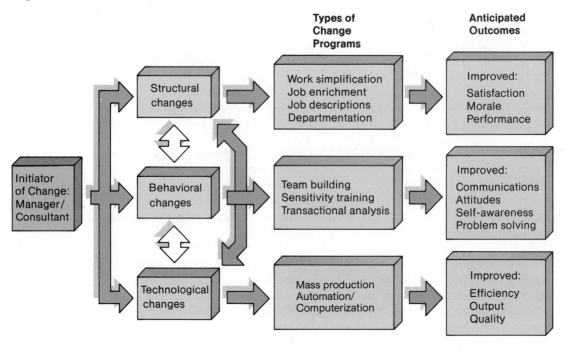

organization, individuals, and groups. The three approaches are presented in Figure 17–2 as a system. That is, changes in one area are related to changes in other areas. The anticipated outcomes of this system of interrelated changes include the factors shown in Figure 17–2. Accomplishing all of the anticipated outcomes would be worthwhile for any manager. However, any successes may be limited because of implementation problems, resistance to change, and various other conditions.

Two Trends in Organizational Change

Forces primarily in the external environment during the 1980s have encouraged two types of change in U.S. organizations: *downsizing* and *participative management*. Each type of change usually brings about changes in the structural, behavioral, and technological aspects of the organization.

Downsizing.   Declining revenues and increasing costs, mergers, and rising international competition have intensified the need for organizations to be more efficient and productive. Many companies have responded to this need by *downsizing*. This major action involves reducing the size of the work force, and often closing some operations and consolidating others.[29] CBS, Cessna Aircraft Corp., and Union Carbide are just a few of the major companies that have implemented this change strategy. From 1985 through 1988, AT&T eliminated about one fifth of its positions (75,000 jobs) in its work force reduction effort; DuPont has cut over 11,000 positions from its payroll.[30]

The core task of the downsizing effort is determining what operations should be closed and which positions should be eliminated in the organization. Many companies identify units to be closed based on an analysis of each unit's financial performance and the company's projected future demand for its services. Market analysis of a product or service's future demand is conducted when a unit's operations are tied to marketed output. Concerning positions, the content of jobs are analyzed to identify those that can be eliminated or consolidated with other positions.[31]

Once the downsizing decisions have been made, the most traumatic aspect of downsizing occurs—the actual shutdown of operations and employee layoffs. Some companies have attempted to help affected employees through this transition by providing advance notice, severance pay, extended health care benefits, and outplacement services. In a study of downsizing organizations, the Conference Board found that over half of the companies provided employees with at least three months advance notice; about 80 percent of the companies extended health benefits one year or more beyond the severance date.[32]

However, despite organizational efforts, the period is exceptionally traumatic for employees who leave and for those who remain. Many management experts believe that downsizing is the primary contributor to a decline in employee loyalty in organizations.[33] Thus, once the actual downsizing decisions have been made, the organization is faced with rebuilding the company. Structural changes in job content, work flow, and organizational design must be implemented. Management also must focus on rebuilding commitment among retained employees, many of whom question the company's commitment to them.

This task can be particularly challenging. Companies have responded in a number of ways. For example, when Eaton Corporation eliminated one third of its work force and operations in the mid-1980s, management took a number of actions to maintain a productive relationship with retained employees. The company stressed open, two-way communication throughout the downsizing period and thereafter, informing employees of the company's actions and reasons for them. Performance-based compensation and promotion from within the company have also been emphasized.[34]

---

[29]Walter A. Kleinschrod, "Sizing up Downsizing," *Administrative Management,* May 1987, p. 56.

[30]John J. Keller, "AT&T: The Making of a Comeback," *Business Week,* January 18, 1988, pp. 56ff; and Ron Zemke, "Delayed Effects of Downsizing," *Training,* November 1986, pp. 57ff.

[31]See Kevin W. Tourangeau, "Downsizing: A Structured Approach for Lasting Gains," *National Productivity Review,* Summer 1987, pp. 257–65.

[32]Perry Pascarella, "When Change Means Saying: 'You're Fired'," *Industry Week,* July 7, 1986, pp. 47ff.

[33]See Stanley J. Modic, "Is Anyone Loyal Anymore?" *Industry Week,* September 7, 1987, pp. 75ff.

[34]"Eaton's Answer to the Death of Loyalty," *Industry Week,* September 7, 1987, pp. 76–77.

In sum, downsizing is an often essential organizational change for companies striving to remain competitive in demanding external environments. However, the change is necessarily a painful one in many respects. Effective downsizing requires careful analysis of the companies operations and a well-planned implementation that minimizes unnecessary human costs.

Participative management. An increasingly competitive external environment demands that organizations produce better products and services and be more efficient in doing so. To meet this requirement, a rising number of companies are turning to employees, seeking their ideas and inputs and giving workers more autonomy in doing their jobs.

In many cases, employees are making decisions in their work that previously were the domain of management. We have seen examples of this type of employee participation and autonomy in our previous discussions of just-in-time inventory management, total quality control, and other organizational activities.

In these and many other instances, participative management has been implemented by redesigning jobs from an individual to team-based orientation. This structural change gives the responsibility for a major segment of work to a team of employees who often have the authority to schedule their own work, establish and monitor team performance measures, select and train their members, and solve production problems.

Participative management has been credited with improving production and service quality and efficiency in a number of companies. However, this type of change often encounters several obstacles. A frequent problem is opposition to the change from managers who fear a loss of authority and power. Accustomed to a more authoritative style of management, some supervisors have difficulty in being more participative in their relationships with subordinates and adopting a coaching rather than telling management style. Some employees also have difficulty in assuming the greater responsibility that participation requires. However, when these and other challenges are overcome, participative management has produced some impressive results.[35]

RECOGNIZING LIMITING CONDITIONS

The selection of a change technique is based on diagnosis of the problem, but is also tempered by the conditions at the time. Three such conditions are the *leadership climate, the formal organization,* and *the organizational culture.*

Leadership climate refers to the nature of the work environment that results from the leadership style and the administrative practices of managers. Any change program not supported by management has only a slim chance of success. Management must be at least neutral toward the change. By not supporting the change, or by being unenthusiastic about it, a manager can undermine the efforts to change because she is in an authority position. The style of leadership itself may be the subject of change; for example, sensitivity training is a direct attempt to move managers toward a certain

---

[35]See Tom Peters, *Thriving on Chaos* (New York: Alfred A. Knopf, 1987), pp. 281–377; and Bill Sapori, "The Revolt against Working Smarter," *Fortune,* July 21, 1986, pp. 58–62.

style—open, supportive, and group centered. But the participants in sensitivity training may be unable to adopt such styles if these are incompatible with the styles of their own superiors.

The *formal organization* must be compatible with proposed change. This includes the effects on the organizational environment resulting from the philosophy and policies of top management, as well as legal precedent, organizational design, and the system of control. Of course, each of these sources of impact may be the focus of the change effort. The important point is that a change in one must be compatible with all of the others. For example, a change to technology that eliminates jobs contradicts a policy of guaranteed employment.

The *organizational culture* refers to the impact of group norms and values and informal activities on the organizational environment. The impact of traditional behavior, sanctioned by group norms but not formally acknowledged, was first documented in the Hawthorne studies. A proposed change in work methods or the installation of an automated device can run counter to the expectations and attitudes of work groups. If such is the case, the manager implementing the change must anticipate resistance.

When managers evaluate the strength of limiting conditions, they are simultaneously considering the problem of objective setting. Many managers have been disappointed by change efforts that fell short of their expectations. Particularly frustrated are those managers who cannot understand why the simple issue of a directive does not produce the intended response. Thoughtful managers will recognize that even as they attempt to make changes, other conditions enforce stability. The realities of limiting conditions are such that managers often must be content with modest change or even no change at all.

If a manager implements change without considering the constraints imposed by prevailing conditions within the present organization, the original problem may only get worse. Such change may actually result in further problems. Taken together, these constraints constitute the climate for change—positive or negative.

RESISTANCE TO CHANGE

Most organizational change efforts eventually run into some form of employee resistance. Change triggers rational and irrational emotional reactions because of the uncertainty involved. Instead of assuming that employees will resist change or react in a particular manner, it is better to consider the general reasons why people resist change.

Why People Resist Change

Explanations of why people resist change take into account the following four reasons.[36]

---

[36]Four reasons are discussed in John P. Kotter and Leonard A. Schlesinger, "Choosing Strategies for Change," *Harvard Business Review,* March–April 1979, pp. 10–14. The discussion of resistance to change is based on this article.

Parochial self-interest.   Some people resist organizational change out of fear of losing something they value. Individuals fear the loss of power, resources, freedom to make decisions, friendships, and prestige. In cases of fearing loss, individuals think of themselves and what they may have to give up. The fearful individual only has his parochial self-interest in mind when resisting change. The organization and the interests of co-workers are not given much priority.

Misunderstanding and lack of trust.   When individuals do not fully understand why the change is occurring, and what its implications are, they will resist it. Misunderstanding the intent and consequences of organizational change is more likely to occur when trust is lacking between the person initiating the change and the affected individual. In organizations characterized by high levels of mistrust, misunderstandings likely will be associated with any organizational change.

Different assessments.   Since individuals view change differently—its intent, potential consequences, and personal impact—there are often different assessments of the situation. Those initiating changes see more positive results because of the change, while those being affected and not initiating the changes see more costs involved with the change. Take, for example, the introduction of robots. Management might view the change to robots as a benefit, but subordinates likely would consider the robot introduction to be a signal that they will lose their jobs.

The initiators of change often make two overly broad assumptions: (1) they have all the relevant data and information available to diagnose the situation; and (2) those to be affected by the change also have the same facts. Whatever the circumstances, the initiators and the affected employees often have different data and information. This leads to resistance to change. However, in some cases, the resistance is healthy for the firm, especially in the situation where the affected employees possess more valid data and information.

Low tolerance for change.   People resist change because they fear they will not be able to develop the new skills necessary to perform well. Individuals may understand clearly that change is necessary, but they are emotionally unable to make the transition. For example, this type of resistance is found in offices that introduce computerized word processing systems. Some secretaries, and even their bosses, resist changes that are clearly necessary to improve office productivity.

A low tolerance for change also is found in individuals who resist change to save face. Making the necessary adjustments and changes would be, they assume, an open admission that some of their previous behavior, decisions, and attitudes were wrong.

Minimizing Resistance to Change

Resisting change is a human response, and management must take steps to minimize it. Reducing resistance can cut down on the time needed for a change to be accepted or tolerated. Also, the performance of employees can rebound more quickly if resistance is minimized.

A number of methods have been useful in decreasing resistance to change. They are examined below.

Education and communication.   One of the most common ways to reduce resistance is to communicate and educate before the change occurs. This helps people prepare for the change. Paving the way, showing the logic, and keeping everyone informed helps cut down resistance.

Participation and involvement.   Bringing together those to be affected to help design and implement the change likely will increase their commitment. If individuals feel their ideas and attitudes are being included in the change effort, they tend to become less resistant and more receptive.

Facilitation and support.   Being supportive is an important management characteristic when change is implemented. It is essential for managers to be supportive (e.g., showing concern for subordinates, being a good listener, going to bat for subordinates on an important issue), and helping facilitate the change when fear and anxiety are at the heart of resistance.

Negotiation and agreement.   Resistance can be reduced through negotiation. Discussion and analysis can help managers identify points of negotiation and agreement. Negotiated agreement involves giving something to another party to reduce resistance. For example, convincing a person to move to a less desirable work location may require paying a bonus or increasing monthly salary. Once this negotiation agreement is reached, others may expect the manager to grant similar concessions in the future.

Manipulation and co-optation.   *Manipulation* involves the use of devious tactics to convince others that a change is in their best interests. Holding back information, playing one person against another, and providing slanted information are examples of manipulation. *Co-opting* an individual involves giving him a major role in the design or implementation of the change. The ethical problems associated with manipulation and co-optation are obvious and should preclude the widespread use of these techniques.

Explicit and implicit coercion.   In using explicit and/or implicit coercion, the manager engages in threatening behavior. She threatens the employees with job loss, reduced promotion opportunities, poor job assignments, and loss of privileges. The coercion is intended to reduce a person's resistance to the management-initiated change. Coercive behavior can be risky because it can generate bad feelings and hostility.[37]

IMPLEMENTING AND MONITORING THE CHANGE PROCESS

The implementation of proposed change has two dimensions: *timing* and *scope. Timing* is knowing when to make the change. Introducing a new electronic cash register system

---

[37]For a discussion of the positive role that change resistance plays in the organizational change effort, see Perry Pascarella, "Resistance to Change: It Can Be a Plus," *Industry Week,* July 27, 1987, pp. 45ff.

in a retail store would not be a good idea during the Christmas season. *Scope* is knowing how much of a change to make. The matter of timing is strategic; it depends on a number of factors, particularly the organization's operating cycle and the groundwork that has preceded the change. A change of considerable magnitude should not compete with ordinary operations. It might be easier to implement during a slack period. On the other hand, if the change is critical to the survival of the organization, then immediate implementation is in order.

The scope of the change depends on the change strategy. The change may be implemented throughout the organization and become established quickly. Or it may be phased into the organization level by level, department by department. The strategy of successful change utilizes a phased approach that limits the scope but provides feedback for each subsequent implementation.

The provision of feedback information is termed the *monitoring* phase. Figure 17–1 shows that information is fed back into the forces-of-change phase because the change itself establishes a new situation that might create problems.

The stimulus for change is a deterioration of performance objectives and standards that can be traced to structural, behavioral, or technological causes. The standards may be any number of indicators, including profit, sales volume, productivity, absenteeism, turnover, scrappage, and costs. The major source of feedback on those variables is the firm's management information system. But if the change includes the objective of improving employee attitudes and morale, the usual sources of information are limited, if not invalid.

To avoid the danger of overreliance on productivity data, the manager can generate ad hoc information to measure employee attitudes and morale. A benchmark for evaluation would be available if an attitude survey had been used in the diagnosis phase. The definition of acceptable improvement is difficult when attitudinal data are evaluated, since the matter involves "how much more" productive they should be. Nevertheless, if a complete analysis of results is to be undertaken, attitudinal measurements must be combined with productivity measurements.[38]

MANAGEMENT SOLUTION

BANK OF AMERICA LAUNCHES ORGANIZATIONAL CHANGE STRATEGY

Bank of America's first step toward organizational change was to conduct a "root value study"—to identify and examine the values of its founder, A. P. Giannini, values that had somehow been forgotten since his passing.

Continued

---

[38]William M. Vicars and Darrell D. Hartke, "Evaluating OD Evaluations: A Status Report," *Group and Organizational Studies*, June 1984, pp. 177–88.

MANAGEMENT SOLUTION

Concluded

Top management then decided to adopt these values via a set of new organizational goals. Essentially the objectives called for Bank of America to "put the customer first" in the company's decision making; respect employees and recognize and reward their good performance; emphasize the use of technology in operations and customer service; and communicate the company's strategy to employees and build a sense of teamwork within the organization.

Bank of America's top executives then set about communicating these goals and ideas for change throughout the company. Sam Armacost, Bank of America's CEO at the time, presented the objectives to the company's top 100 managers at the company's Management Forum meeting. The 100 managers then held sessions with employees within their units, discussing the new objectives and ways to achieve the goals.

Major changes occurred in several areas including compensation, performance evaluation, staffing, career progression, and training. Every manager completed a week's training in management and leadership fundamentals that reinforced the company's new values and goals. At the top of the organization, CEO Armacost cre-ated an Eagle pin which is a replica of part of Bank of America's logo. He or a member of the top-management team personally presented the pin to employees whose high performance symbolized the company's values. The company also more tightly linked compensation bonuses to achieving demanding objectives.

Some time after Bank of America launched its change effort, management surveyed employees on several questions and compared the post-change responses with pre-change answers. Changes seemed to have occurred in some areas. For example, since the change effort, significantly more employees believe that their managers work with them to set performance goals. Significantly more employees also believe that they are given an opportunity to express themselves when their superiors meet with them to review their performance evaluation results.

The organizational change effort is continuing at the company.

Source: Adapted from Robert N. Beck, "Visions, Values, and Strategies: Changing Attitudes and Culture," *Academy of Management Executive*, February 1987, pp. 33–41.

MANAGEMENT SUMMARY

☐ Organizational change is often inevitable. It also is necessary to improve the overall performance of the organization. Research has shown that planned change is more likely to bring about performance improvement than unplanned change.

☐ Employees resist the introduction of changes in structure, behavior, and technology. People resist change for economic reasons and for psychological reasons such as insecurity. Managers must be alert to any

□ indication of resistance and they should also prepare subordinates for change.

□ Before selecting change techniques, a manager must first recognize the need for change and conduct a thorough diagnosis so that problems can be uncovered.

□ In recent years, many companies have introduced computers and robotics (technological change) into their production and service operations. However, often results have been unimpressive due to the neglect of needed structural and behavioral changes to maximize the effectiveness of high technology.

□ The selection of a change technique should also consider limiting conditions in the organization such as the leadership climate, the formal organization, and the organizational culture.

□ Successful organizational change requires that the scope (amount) of change is accurate and that the change is implemented at the right time.

□ To monitor change, managers must collect data about whether objectives are being accomplished. Judging a major change a success even after one year's time is often premature.

REVIEW AND DISCUSSION QUESTIONS

1. Some experts believe resistance to change is a natural human tendency based primarily on the fear of the unknown. Why do people resist structural, behavioral, and technological changes?

2. In your opinion, which force in the external environment exerts the most powerful influence on organizational change? Explain.

3. Some organizational change experts assert that top-level executives are often the last to recognize the need for change. Why is this sometimes the case? Discuss.

4. How does a manager become attuned to the internal and external sources of change in an organization?

5. The following comment was overheard: "Structural, behavioral, and technological changes are all geared toward one major outcome, improved productivity. Thus, the best way to improve production output is to use the optimal mix of change strategies,

and this means everything available." Why is this statement incorrect?

6. Timing is the selection of the appropriate moment to initiate a change. Why is timing so important in implementing change?

7. Does implementing computerized technology in a plant's manufacturing operations exert more impact on structural or behavioral change? Explain.

8. The initiator of change may be a manager or an outside consultant. Does it make a difference if the initiator is not an employee of the organization?

9. Why is the use of sensitivity training as a behavioral change technique often criticized for creating stress and anxiety?

10. Attitude surveys are one approach to diagnosing organizational problems. What other tools or approaches could management use to perform the diagnostic task?

CASES

17–1 THE TRAINING DEBATE

An interesting debate is emerging in a number of companies concerning management training. The issue is: Does management have the right to put employees through training that is physically or psychologically uncomfortable, training that in some cases seeks to alter their fundamental beliefs?

The source of this debate is a growing number of highly unconventional management training programs offered by outside training organizations. Though still a minority in a large training industry, these unusual programs are gaining in popularity. For example:

At a ranch near Sante Fe, New Mexico, managers from Hewlett-Packard, GM, Dow Chemical, and many other organizations attend the Pecos Learning Center, run by the Wilson Learning Corp. There, the managers go through a series of exhilarating physical tasks such as launching themselves off a cliff, climbing up telephone poles, and traveling on the "zip line," a cord stretched in midair from one to the other side of the Pecos Valley. The managers travel the line by hanging onto a pulley. The exercises are safe; a safety harness protects each participant.

The camp's activities are designed to bond executives together. Camp officials say that overcoming physical fear is exhilarating and relaxes managers to talk about their work and lives. Many participants are pleased with their camp experience. However, some participants have questioned the training. Although the exercises are voluntary, they say they felt pressured to do things they found frightening. They also believed the personal discussions were intrusive.

Another form of training is provided by the MSIA (pronounced messiah) that is run by the Mystical Traveler Consciousness organization. It offers three courses entitled Insight I, II, and III. Courses I and II are "intensive-growth experiences"; course III teaches the mystical principles of the organization's leader.

The Church of Scientology has established two subsidiaries that provide training and consulting services for companies. The content of one of its programs was recently the core of a dispute involving Loretta Garrett, a former head of the sales department of Megaplex, a phone-answering service in Atlanta. At the urging of her boss, Ms. Garrett attended a Church of Scientology course. According to Ms. Garrett, the course focused in part on the principles of Scientology. She was urged to "admit guilt because sales were poor" and to get "past the analytical brain to clear the inner brain, where the poor sales were caused."

Ms. Garrett declined her boss's request that she have her personality "audited" at the local Scientology mission. Ms. Garrett quit; her boss told her she was fired. Ms. Garrett has since filed a complaint with the Equal Employment Opportunity Commission.

Perhaps the most publicized incident of employee rebellion against unconventional training occurred at Pacific Bell, a subsidiary of Pacific Telesis. Top management hired associates of Charles Krone, a prominent corporate trainer, to help develop a new culture for the company. Krone's associates worked two years at Pacific Bell to implement principles designed to condition people to "rethink the way they think," to find new ways to solve problems. Resentment among the work force grew.

At the request of the California Public Utilities Commission, another consulting group surveyed the work force. Results indicated that employees were angry over the principles, and the implied threat that those who didn't adopt the principles would not advance in the company. Employees also were angry over the practice of "facilitators" attending meetings as "thought police" to ensure that the employees were following the Krone principles. The California commission also discovered that the Krone program cost $40 million. The program was suspended; Pacific Bell's president retired early.

Many observers assert that when management embarks on training that involves psychological stress, it may well be liable for any ill effects on its participants. Asserts Richard Ofshe, a psychologist at the University of California at Berkeley, corporations are building "an enormous potential liability" with training that involves participant stress. In recent years, the number of individuals requiring psychiatric treatment due to management training programs is on the rise, according to the American Foundation in Boston and the Cult Awareness Network in Chicago.

Questions

1. As a manager who supports unconventional training, what would be your arguments for establishing such training for your managers?

2. As a manager who opposes unconventional training, provide a response to the arguments you've developed for question 1. Which position would you personally take?

3. A number of management trainers assert that any effective training program involves some stress. Do you agree? Explain.

Source: Adapted from Jeremy Main, "Trying to Bend Managers' Minds," *Fortune*, November 23, 1987, pp. 95ff.

17–2 RESISTING BETTER WORKING CONDITIONS

Sixteen employees of an engineering drafting company worked in the Southgate office of the firm. The office was a single room 36 feet by 46 feet. The drafting technicians, as they were called, liked their cozy office because they worked close to other technicians and away from the engineers, who were housed two miles away at an office in Northline shopping mall.

The company completed construction of a new office complex that housed all of its drafting technicians, engineers, and clerical personnel. Finally, after three years of being separated, all 96 of the organization's employees were able to work together under one roof. The new office complex was modern and had new furniture, full carpeting, a cafeteria, and a relaxation reading room. An architectural design firm set up the work area and decorated the offices. The drafting technicians and the engineers worked next to each other and, in fact, had small private offices for four- to six-person teams. The president of the firm, Jon Thorton, was very pleased with the appearance of the new offices and thanked the architectural designers for doing such an outstanding job.

Six months passed after the new offices were opened, and Thorton was puzzled about the poor performance of all the drafting technicians and many of the engineers. Absenteeism and turnover had increased, and the quality of completed work generally was poor.

Thorton met with Ralph Stello, the engineering supervisor, and Sherry Caldwell, the director of technical services, to analyze what had gone wrong. Sherry believed that the routine and the work pattern had been broken by the new office arrangement and that the technicians were resisting the change. Ralph agreed with her analysis. It also was Ralph's opinion that the engineers and technicians should be assembled to discuss the problems.

Questions

1. Why is the organization faced with the problems presented in this case?
2. Is Sherry Caldwell accurate in her assessment of what went wrong with the change?
3. What recommendation should be followed at this time to improve the situation?

EXERCISES

17–1 PAPER PLANE CORPORATION

Purpose: To work on a task and use the functions of planning, organizing, leading, and controlling.

Setting Up the Exercise: Unlimited groups of six participants each are used in this exercise. These groups may be directed simultaneously in the same room. Approximately a full class period is needed to complete the exercise. Each person should have assembly instructions and a summary sheet, which are shown below, and ample stacks of paper (8½ by 11 inches). The physical setting should be a room large enough so that the individual groups of six can work without interference from the other groups. A working space should be provided for each group.

- The participants are doing an exercise in production methodology.
- Each group must work independently of the other groups.
- Each group will choose a manager and an inspector, and the remaining participants will be employees.
- The objective is to make paper airplanes in the most profitable manner possible.
- The facilitator will give the signal to start. This is a 10-minute, timed event utilizing competition among the groups.
- After the first round, each six-member group should report their production and profits to the entire group. They also should note the effect, if any, of the manager in terms of the performance of the group.
- This same procedure is followed for as many rounds as there is time.

Data Sheet

Your group is the complete work force for Paper Plane Corporation. Established in 1943, Paper Plane has led the market in paper plane production. Presently under new management, the company is contracting to make aircraft for the U.S. Air Force. You must establish an efficient production plant to produce these aircraft. You must make your contract with the Air Force under the following conditions:

1. The Air Force will pay $20,000 per airplane.
2. The aircraft must pass a strict inspection made by the facilitator.
3. A penalty of $25,000 per airplane will be subtracted for failure to meet the production requirements.
4. Labor and other overhead will be computed at $300,000.
5. Cost of materials will be $3,000 per bid plane. If you bid for 10 but only make 8, you must pay the cost of materials for those you failed to make or which did not pass inspection.

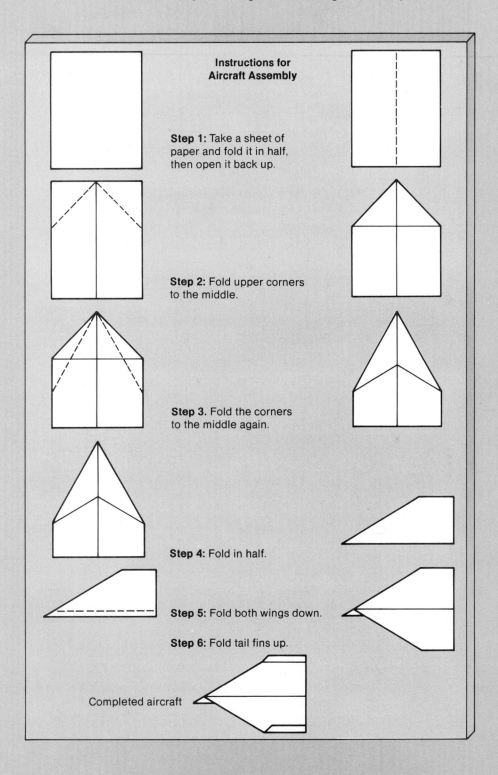

Instructions for Aircraft Assembly

Step 1: Take a sheet of paper and fold it in half, then open it back up.

Step 2: Fold upper corners to the middle.

Step 3. Fold the corners to the middle again.

Step 4: Fold in half.

Step 5: Fold both wings down.

Step 6: Fold tail fins up.

Completed aircraft

Summary Sheet

Round 1:

Bid:_____Aircraft @ $20,000 per aircraft = _____

Results:_____ Aircraft @ $20,000 per aircraft = _____

Less: $300,000 overhead_____ × $3,000 cost of raw materials

_____ × $25,000 penalty

Profit:_____

Round 2:

Bid:_____Aircraft @ $20,000 per aircraft = _____

Results:_____Aircraft @ $20,000 per aircraft = _____

Less: $300,000 overhead_____ × $3,000 cost of raw materials

_____ × $25,000 penalty

Profit:_____

Round 3:

Bid:_____Aircraft @ $20,000 per aircraft = _____

Results:_____Aircraft @ $20,000 per aircraft = _____

Less: $300,000 overhead_____ × $3,000 cost of raw materials

_____ × $25,000 penalty

Profit:_____

17–2 CONTROLLING THE APPEARANCE OF EMPLOYEES

Purpose: This exercise should increase the students' understanding of organizational control and how it can control behavior.

Setting Up the Exercise:

1. The class will be divided into groups of about six students each. Each group will be assigned to one of the following organization types:

    a. Computer sales organization.

    b. Fire department.

    c. Restaurant.

    d. Insurance organization.

    e. Charity (e.g., American Heart Association).

    f. Bank.

    g. Lawn and gardening retail store.

    h. Stereo equipment store.

    i. Real estate firm.

    j. Medical outpatient clinic.

2. Each group should develop a set of organizational policies that focus on the appearance of employees. Appearance refers to the overall appropriateness of the dress and hairstyle of employees.

3. A spokesperson will be appointed by each group to make a report of the appearance policies to the entire class. The spokesperson should present the group's recommendations, the factors used as guidelines in reaching the group decision, and how the group felt about organizations being involved in the formulation of appearance policies.

A Learning Note: This exercise should illustrate that appearance is a nonquantifiable characteristic. That is, the policy will be difficult to reach agreement on and to communicate effectively to others.

17–3 THE NEED FOR CHANGE

Purpose: To develop an understanding of how various change techniques can be used to solve a staffing problem and to illustrate how resistance to change can affect the outcome of an organizational change.

Setting Up the Exercise:

1. Establish groups of five or fewer students. Each group is to prepare a short consultant's report concerning the Southeast Par Telephone staffing situation. Specifically, the president wants the consultants to determine the organization's problem and to develop a solution that results in the fewest complaints.

The exercise is more informative if one group of students from the class serves as evaluators of the presentations. This group would be the panel reviewing the analysis of the other groups.

2. The Southeast Par Telephone situation is as follows:

Over the past three years, Southeast Par Telephone Co. has had a terrible record of recruiting young, qualified management trainees for positions in the accounting, operations, traffic, and maintenance departments. The company has a reputation of paying well and treating employees well, but it also is considered to be an organization with limited advancement opportunity.

The company is searching for young men and women between 21 and 35 years old, with college degrees (preferably some graduate education), who are willing to work different shifts during the two-year training cycle.

The unemployment rate in the city is 5.1 percent, which is below the national average, and the company is located eight miles west of the city. Management is puzzled about the company's inability to bring in qualified people for well-paying trainee positions.

3. Each group should develop a consultant's report which emphasizes the problem, the diagnosis that should be used, the most feasible change strategy, and the anticipated resistance consequences of the change strategy.

4. Each group should select a spokesperson to make a short presentation of the group's report to the entire class.

5. The evaluating group then should select the best consultants' report and discuss with the entire class why it was selected.

A Learning Note: This exercise will illustrate how different diagnoses result in the adoption of different change techniques.

COMPREHENSIVE CASE

17–1 SUPRA OIL COMPANY

John Nichols, a university research worker, had a talk with Mr. Bennett[1] about the headquarters sales organization of the Supra Oil Company, one of the largest integrated oil companies in the country. Excerpts from the conversation follow:

Nichols: You mentioned that you're planning to make some organizational changes here at headquarters. I wonder if you could tell me something about that.

Bennett: Well, sure I will, I don't want to take too much credit for this thing, but it sort of got started because in the last couple of years I've been doing some beefing around here about the fact that I was being kept terribly busy with a lot of the operating details of the sales organization. You can see what I mean by looking at the organization chart we have been working under. [Mr. Bennett produced a chart from his desk drawer and indicated all the people who currently were reporting to him.] [See Exhibit 17–1 for a copy of this chart.]

You can see that with all these people looking to me for leadership, I am not in a position to give them the right kind of guidance that I think they should have on their jobs. I just couldn't take the time. It didn't work too badly some time ago, but since I've been made a member of the board of directors, those activities have taken more of my time. What with being on additional committees and things of that kind, I just couldn't give 17 headquarter division managers the amount of help and attention that they really need. I think one of the things that they miss is that they're not in close enough touch with me or anybody else higher up the line, so that we can be in a good position to appraise their work. We hear about it from some of the field people when they are doing a lousy job, but we don't hear much about it if they're doing a good job. Occasionally, a field man will report that he is getting a lot of help from some staff outfit here, but that's rather rare. So we don't have a very good basis for appraising the good things that they do. So we started talking about what might be done to straighten this out.

Our plans are taking pretty definite shape now. Let me show you what we have in mind. [Mr. Bennett sketched on a pad of paper a diagram to indicate the planned organizational changes.] [See Exhibit 17–2.] You see, we will have two regional managers instead of three. We'll be making one of the present regional managers the manager of the headquarters sales divisions. Those are the divisions that specialize in promoting and selling our different specialty products. Then we'll set up a new job for Wingate, who has been acting as an administrative assistant here at headquarters. He'll take charge of a good number

---

Exhibit 17–1 Partial organization chart of the sales department.

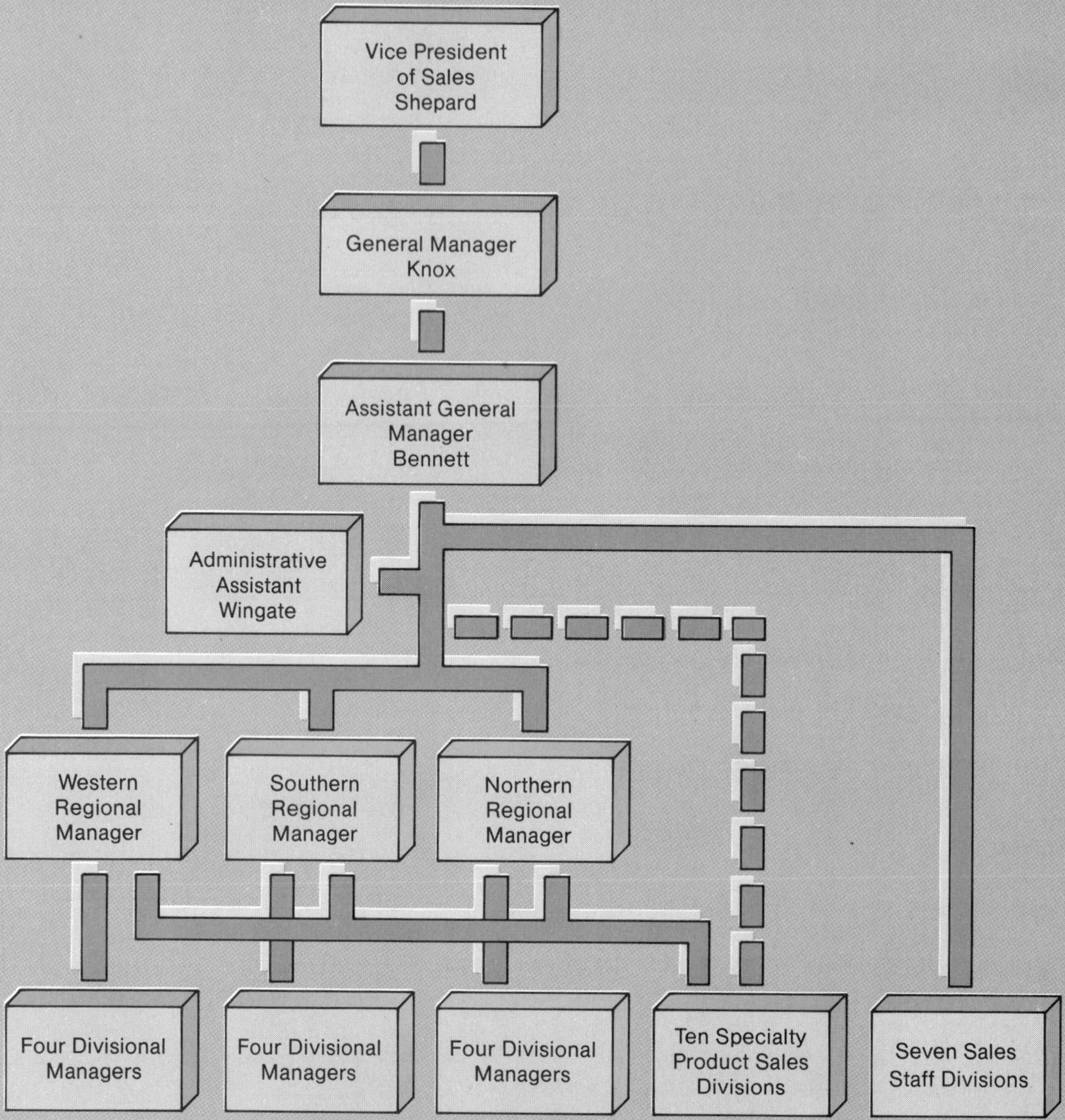

of headquarters sales staff divisions that were reporting directly to me. Those are staff divisions like price analysis and advertising. We will also give each of the two remaining regional managers an assistant manager. Those will be new positions, too.

Nichols: How did you get these plans started?

Exhibit 17–2 Proposed organization chart of the sales department.

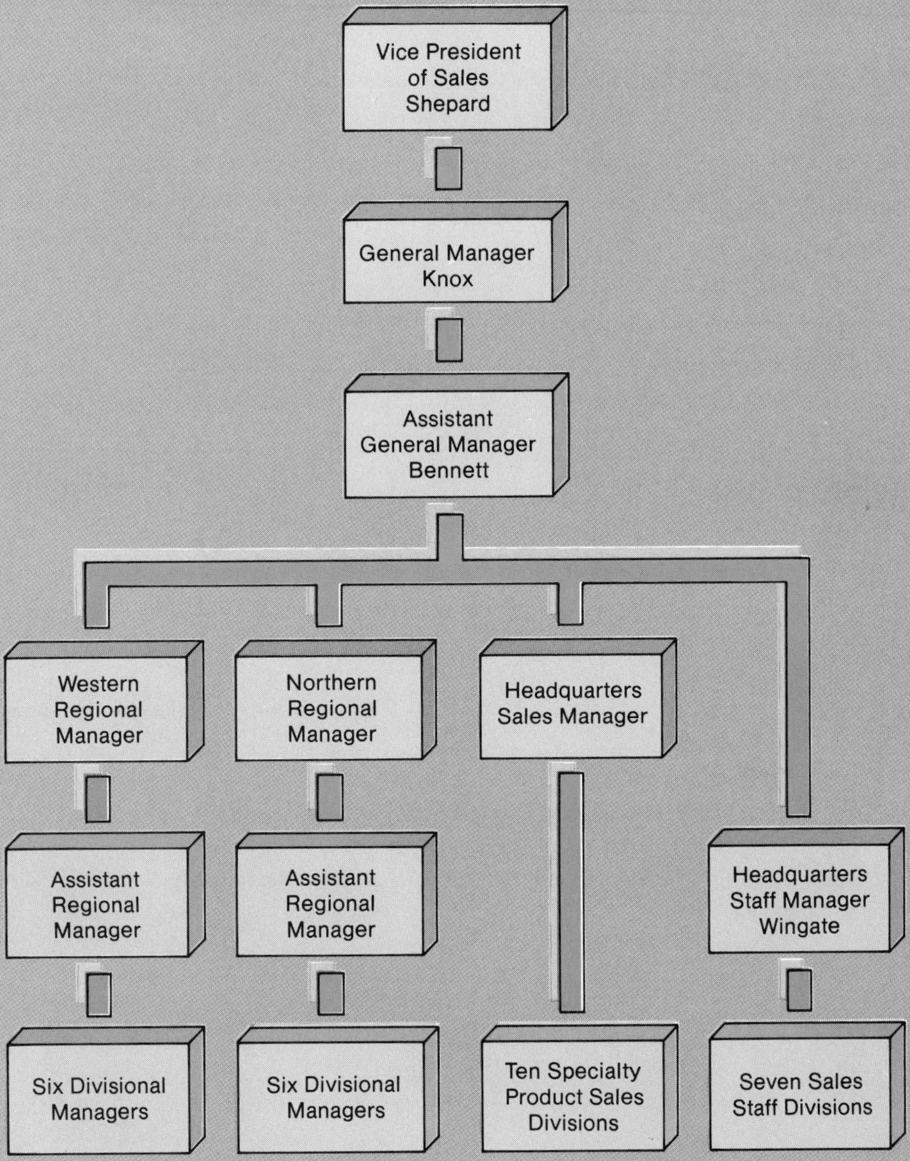

Bennett: I raised it with Shepard [vice president of sales] quite a while back.

Nichols: Would you say that was maybe six months ago?

Bennett: I think it probably was six months ago. Shepard's first reaction was unfavorable. You see, I expected him to feel that way because he was the one who had the most to do with setting up our current organizational plan. But I approached him on it two or three times and complained a little bit and kept raising the question, and finally he said, "Well, I'm going to be leaving here pretty soon. You people have got to live with the organization. If you think it would work better some other way, I certainly won't object to your changing it." Well, that sort of thing gave me the green light, so then I went ahead and raised the question with Mr. Weld [president]. That is, Mr. Knox [general sales manager] and I did. The first time we went to him, we talked about it in general terms. He said he thought it sounded like a pretty good idea and asked that we come back with two or three alternative ways of doing the thing in very specific terms. We talked to him once since then and, as a matter of fact, I'm going to see him this afternoon to see if he'll give us a final OK to go ahead with these plans.

Nichols: If you get his approval, what would you predict—that it might be another month before the change actually takes place?

Bennett: Well, I would say so. I think if we've got this thing going in a month that we will be doing pretty well. I'm going to want to talk to my regional managers and then the headquarters divisional managers about this, but they should buy it all right. I think it will be a fairly simple job to sell it to them. You see, they will in effect be getting more chance to have access to their boss. I think it will work out much better, and they will see the point to it.

Nichols: You say that you are making one less region and making the third regional manager the head of—I guess you are calling him the headquarters sales manager. Are all three of those jobs going to continue to be on an equal level?

Bennett: Yes, they will, but actually this job of headquarters sales manager will be sort of a training position for somebody to step into my job here as assistant general sales manager. That's what we have in mind. I think it will be a good assignment for training for my job. Then, too, we're going to be able to open up a couple of new positions here: the assistant regional managers. I think that is going to be very useful from a management development standpoint. You see, one of our problems is that a number of the top executives here are all about the same age. You see, Knox and myself and the three regional managers are all about the same age, and then the heads of a lot of our headquarters divisions here are men of about our age who—well, they won't retire immediately, but they don't have a terribly long time to go. So we can't look to too many of those people to be our successors here at headquarters. We want to bring in some people from the field who will step in here as assistant regional managers in training for the job of regional managers.

Nichols: I take it, then, that you will be picking the people for those jobs from your field division men on the basis of talent and ability rather than on the basis of seniority.

Bennett: Yes, that's right, we're going to pay very little attention to seniority in picking them. As a matter of fact, the two people we have in mind are two of our newest division managers, but they are both very able people. We think this will give us a chance to give them a good training for future development here.

This change that we are proposing, however, will not drastically change anybody's status here at headquarters, and I don't think it is going to cause as much trouble to put it in. You see, nobody will be jumped over the head of anybody else ahead of them in the management line. We think it's going to help a lot to have an assistant regional manager in here, because it means that both he and the regional manager will be able to spend more time out with the field organization. One will be able to cover matters here at headquarters while the other is gone.

Nichols: Does that mean that your field people will be getting more top-level supervision as a result of this change?

Bennett: Well, in a sense that's true, of course, but it won't be taking any authority or responsibility from the field people. We just feel that they will be in closer personal contact with the people here at headquarters. We think it is very necessary that we do more of that. You see, if our regional managers and assistant managers can get out in the field and meet with the people, they will have a better basis for appraising different people who come along, and they can make sure we get the best people in the jobs that open up. Sometimes it's pretty hard to tell here at headquarters just who some of the best people are out in the field. You see, some division may have a job open up, and they will have a candidate for that job whom they will recommend highly for the promotion. That may be all well and good, but we want to know whether or not there may be a better man in some other division whom we aren't hearing about who might be shifted over for that promotion. You can't blame the division people for that sort of thing, because they will have their favorite candidate and will, of course, be recommending him. We've made a few mistakes along the way because of this sort of thing, and if we have more personal contact, we will be able to do a better job of it.

Nichols: Will this mean that you will be able to spend more time in the field?

Bennett: Yes, I do hope that it will mean that. I think I ought to get out in the field more to keep in touch with what's going on in the market. It's really pretty hard to keep in touch with things while you are spending your time here at headquarters. You know, I want to get out and talk to people and see what they are talking about and see what kind of problems they are up against.

Nichols: I've heard several comments on this business of getting a feel for the market by getting out in the field. I take it that this is quite a different process from keeping in touch with the market on what you might call a statistical basis?

Bennett: Well, yes, it is. You see, I can look at the reports here in the office, and I may see that some district or some division is not doing too well at all on the basis of the figures in comparison with the competition. But I don't know just what the story is behind those figures. On a personal basis, I could probably begin to get some answers to it. It could be any one of a number of things. I might go out there and find that it's a temporary situation because the competition is, in effect, going out and buying the business away from us, or I might find out that our people are not being very smart or aggressive about promoting our products, or I might find out that they do not know some of the facilities we have available that would help them compete for the business. You see, one way we can compete for the business is the fact that this company has available some pretty good capital resources; and if we don't have good outlets in a given district, we're often in a position to offer to put up some capital to get some better outlets. That way we can do a better job of competing for the business, and sometimes the local people don't know that these possibilities exist, or perhaps they're a little reticent about putting up proposals. Or even if they do put up proposals, if we haven't been out in the field to see for ourselves what's going on, we probably don't do as good a job of appraising the proposals they do put up.

Nichols: In other words, the figures tell you that maybe something ought to be checked into, but you've got to go out and talk to people to find out what is really going on?

Bennett: Yes, that's right. You have to take a personal look. You can find out a lot faster than you can by correspondence just what is going on and what can be done about it.

Nichols: Won't this reorganization mean that some of the people both here and in the field will have new bosses now?

Bennett: Yes, that's right, but it's not too drastic a change. You see, we used to have only two regional managers some time ago. I guess we shifted off that system some four or five years ago. When I was out in the field as manager of a division, I was reporting in to the northern regional manager, who was Mr. Shepard at that time. Then I was brought in here as his assistant for the whole region. It was about that time that we set up this business of having three regions and I was named one of the regional managers, and at that time, Mr. Shepard became general manager.

Nichols: Well, it sounds as if that previous move might have been motivated somewhat by a desire to develop people and perhaps give you a chance to take over a regional managership before you might otherwise have had a chance to.

Bennett: Yes, I think that's right. At that time, that move was the way we could open things up for further management development, and now we are sort of doing it the other way around. Everybody knows that the arrangement we are now proposing may well be changed again in a few more years.

We like to change the organization around a little bit like this from time to time, just to let people know that we are not going to be static about things. Of course, we want to do it in a way so that some of our senior people do not get bypassed or jumped over by some of the younger ones, because that not only bothers the individual but it also hurts morale further down in the organization. You see, when some of the people further down see some of that sort of thing happening, they are apt to conclude that it might happen to them someday, and it's pretty discouraging to them. The way we are doing it now, we can bring up some younger people without jumping over anybody's head who is senior.

I think an organizational change of this kind is also useful in that it indicates to some of our younger people that they need not feel discouraged if they are in a position where someone is above them in line who shows no signs of being promoted on up. This situation might make a person feel that he is being blocked from future promotion by his boss. But he is encouraged when he sees an occasional organizational shift of this kind, because it makes him realize that things can happen in the future that might shift the organization around to a point where he can be sprung loose for a move on up, even though his boss may not be promotable.

Nichols: Then I take it that one of the predominant thoughts in this whole reorganization was one of management development?

Bennett: Oh, that's certainly true. That was one of the prime reasons we're proposing this, because we think it will help us develop our managers, and this gives us a way of doing it without upsetting the organization too much.

That afternoon Mr. Bennett kept the appointment with Mr. Weld that was mentioned in the conversation above. Upon entering Mr. Weld's office, Mr. Bennett handed Mr. Weld a copy of the revised sales organization chart.

Bennett: Here's a final version of our reorganizational plans. Do you think it is all right to go ahead on this?

Questions

1. Will the changes at Supra Oil be viewed as change just for the sake of change? As Bennett stated, "We like to change the organization around a little bit like this from time to time . . . "
2. How will the proposed changes affect the control systems at Supra Oil?
3. Suppose the change takes place at Supra. Would Bennett's performance as assistant general manager be easier to evaluate under the new system?

Source: *Supra Oil Co.* (9-557-005) Copyright © 1957 by the President and Fellows of Harvard College. Reprinted by permission of the Harvard Business School. This case was prepared by Paul R. Lawrence under the supervision of Milton P. Brown.

PART VI

The Management Process

1. Planning function
2. Organizing function
3. Leading function
4. Controlling function

Managing the Multinational Company

1. Environmental differences
2. Managing the MNC

Social Responsibility and Management Ethics

1. The meanings of social responsibility
2. Management ethics

Developing Management Careers

1. Career development
2. Human resource development

Management and Entrepreneurship

1. The entrepreneur
2. Entrepreneurship and the functions of management
3. Special challenges of entrepreneurship

MANAGING FOR PERFORMANCE: TRENDS AND PERSPECTIVES

INTRODUCTION TO PART VI

Part VI, Managing for Performance: Trends and Perspectives, contains four chapters.

The inclusion of material contained in the four chapters is based on the following rationale:

The last section of a management textbook should integrate the main ideas that have been developed in the preceding chapters. Ideally, this should be in the context of the important issues managers confront. This ideal is achieved by presenting the contributions and relevance of the management functions to the issues of managing multinational companies, social responsibility and management ethics, developing management careers, and creating and managing a new business enterprise.

The *multinational company* is an increasingly important form of organization. Managers who must plan, organize, lead, and control organizations that cross national boundaries face diverse cultures, governmental practices, and employee attitudes. Although the managerial functions and principles are applicable regardless of setting, the form they take must be compatible with the setting. The importance of multinational corporations will be an important management issue during the 1980s.

Every day newspapers report incidents involving organizations that some people would call socially irresponsible and unethical. Future managers must have some bases for understanding *social responsibility and management ethics*. Managers must understand their responsibilities for instilling acceptable ethical standards in their organizations and have guidelines for socially and ethically responsible behavior.

A properly designed organization must be maintained and adapted. One important means through which management ensures that the right people are performing the appropriate jobs is through the *development of management careers*. The human resources of organizations are crucial to performance, and it is becoming more and more apparent that organizations have an important stake in developing their employees to their fullest potential. The practices currently in use in career planning and development are the subjects of the chapter on management careers.

Finally, management and entrepreneurship are discussed in a new chapter for this edition of the book. It is entrepreneurial behavior and practices that have helped many firms to survive and to become intense competitors. The kinds of behaviors and practices that have been successful are presented.

The figure on the facing page summarizes the concept of this, the last part of the text.

EIGHTEEN

Managing the Multinational Company

LEARNING OBJECTIVES

After completing Chapter 18, you should be able to:

Define: what is meant by a *multinational company* (MNC).

State: the three primary decisions involved in becoming an MNC.

Describe: the different strategies for entering an international market.

Explain: the impact of culture, economics, and politics on managerial performance in an MNC.

Discuss: the performance of the management functions in an international environment.

MCDONNELL DOUGLAS' BID FOR CHINA'S BUSINESS

For decades, China lay beyond the grasp of international business. Staunchly Communist and led by a government that viewed free enterprise with contempt, China remained a lesser developed country in need of technological, economic, educational, and other development.

However, in recent years, China has experienced economic reforms that have resulted in a growing acceptance of free enterprise, imports, and direct investment by foreign countries. With one billion consumers (a quarter of the world's population) and a wide variety of needs that characterize a developing country, China is an enticing and possible market for many international businesses. However, it remains highly bureaucratic with many difficult challenges awaiting businesses who try to pry open the door to China trade.

In the late 1970s, McDonnell Douglas, a major aircraft manufacturer, sought to be one of the first companies to do business with China. The company wanted to obtain the largest order for commercial airplanes ever placed by the Chinese government. They assigned the formidable task to one individual, Gareth C. C. Chang, an energetic, determined 37-year-old Chinese-born and American-educated vice president at the company. Chang set out to secure the contract.

(The Management Solution to this Management Incident can be found at the end of this chapter.)

So far in this text, we have talked about the principles and functions of management primarily in the context of a domestic environment. We have implicitly assumed that in a given organization, management occurs within the boundaries of one country. In this chapter, we extend the parameters of management into the international environment and discuss how the managerial principles and functions apply when an organization decides to expand its operations and product or service into an international market.

This discussion is highly relevant because increasingly, organizations are becoming international in their operations and perspective.[1] The total amount of international trade has increased sevenfold since 1970.[2] Today, more than one fourth of all the goods produced worldwide cross national borders. Businesses in the United States are also venturing overseas in growing numbers. Those who aren't directly marketing their output internationally are nevertheless involved in international business in the sense that they are competing with foreign companies. Scan the aisles of your local consumer electronics, computer, or even clothing stores and the message is clear: international competitors are a major presence in many American markets. Whether a U.S. company operates at home or abroad, managing a business successfully requires understanding competitors with different outlooks, backgrounds, and strategies.

Why have a growing number of American businesses become so involved in international business? The reason is simple; many international markets provide substantial opportunities and returns for those businesses with the ability and determination to succeed in an often unfamiliar environment. Specifically, many companies venture abroad because of declining markets at home and brighter opportunities overseas. For some companies, the U.S. market for their product may be maturing or even in decline while the market in an overseas country is just taking off. Some businesses venture abroad to use excess manufacturing capacity. Some companies such as Caterpillar Tractor, establish manufacturing facilities worldwide partly to achieve substantial economies of scale which provides them with a significant cost advantage over competitors.[3] Other companies go international to alleviate the risk of operating in only one geographical market.[4]

Whatever the specific motive, businesses internationalize to reap potential rewards that are not so readily available at home. However, venturing into an international market is an exceptionally challenging strategy. Such is the case because once a company decides to do business abroad, it confronts an entirely new set of circumstances. In many countries, a business will find that consumer preferences are different. Marketing (i.e., pricing, promotional strategies, advertising, and distribution systems) is unfamiliar as are financial markets and accounting systems. The motivations and

---

[1]Michael I. Kirkland, Jr., "Entering a New Age of Boundless Competition," *Fortune*, March 14, 1988, pp. 40ff.

[2]John A. Young, "Global Competition: The New Reality," *California Management Review*, Spring 1985, pp. 11–25.

[3]James F. Bolt, "Global Competitors: Some Criteria for Success," *Business Horizons*, January–February 1988, pp. 34–41.

[4]John D. Daniels and Lee H. Radebaugh, *International Business: Environments and Operations*, 4th ed. (Reading, Mass.: Addison Wesley Publishing, 1986), pp. 544–55.

perspectives of host country employees may substantially differ along with personnel policies that are typical for doing business. The country's political environment and the relationship between business and government may distinctly differ from the political climate and relationship in the United States. A wide gap may exist between the culture at home and the culture in the international market. In sum, doing business abroad often requires setting aside many of the time-tested assumptions of doing business and building a new set of assumptions for an unfamiliar and often unsettling environment.[5]

This chapter will approach the topic of international management by focusing on three topics: (1) the aspects of an organization's decision to enter an international market, (2) the primary elements of the international environment and their impact on business, and (3) the application of the key managerial functions in an international context.

THE MULTINATIONAL COMPANY

A firm doing business in two or more countries is referred to as a *multinational company* (*MNC*). Typically, such firms have sales offices and, in many cases, manufacturing facilities in numerous countries. They view their scope of operation as global in nature. American firms such as Pfizer Inc., Hoover Co., Mobil Oil Corp., and the Otis Group, Inc., currently sell the majority of their output outside the United States. American firms such as Xerox Corp., Coca-Cola, Dow Chemical Co., IBM, and Chrysler Corp., currently earn more than half of their profits outside the United States.

One way to appreciate the truly multinational nature of many business firms is to examine foreign companies that have entered the United States, and American firms that are owned by foreign multinationals. Figure 18–1 presents some familiar names in each of these categories.

As competition intensifies, American firms must become more adept in international business. The necessity of avoiding costly mistakes and pressure from experienced competitors requires managers who can direct effective performance in an MNC.

THE MNC DECISION

The decision to become an MNC is truly a major one. Although the choice incorporates consideration of many factors, the move to becoming an MNC essentially encompasses three primary decisions.

The International Market to Be Served

Selecting the country (or countries) as the site for international expansion involves considering many aspects of the country's environment. Many international businesses emphasize the market size in the prospective host country (both current and potential

---

[5]For a discussion of the risks involved in multinational business, see Richard Capstick, "The Perils of Manufacturing Abroad," *International Management*, March 1978, pp. 43–46.

Figure 18–1   Some well-known multinational companies.

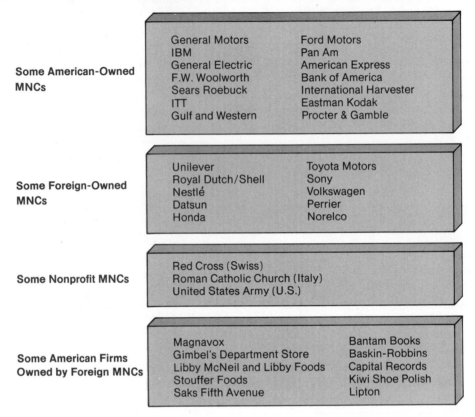

Some American-Owned MNCs	General Motors IBM General Electric F.W. Woolworth Sears Roebuck ITT Gulf and Western	Ford Motors Pan Am American Express Bank of America International Harvester Eastman Kodak Procter & Gamble
Some Foreign-Owned MNCs	Unilever Royal Dutch/Shell Nestlé Datsun Honda	Toyota Motors Sony Volkswagen Perrier Norelco
Some Nonprofit MNCs	Red Cross (Swiss) Roman Catholic Church (Italy) United States Army (U.S.)	
Some American Firms Owned by Foreign MNCs	Magnavox Gimbel's Department Store Libby McNeil and Libby Foods Stouffer Foods Saks Fifth Avenue	Bantam Books Baskin-Robbins Capital Records Kiwi Shoe Polish Lipton

size), the country's consumer wealth (per capita income), and the ease of doing business in the market. In assessing this latter criterion, organizations consider such factors as geographical location, language commonality, governmental relations with business, and the availability of employees with the skills which the business will require.[6] Overall, evaluating the prospective host country's cultural, economic, and political environments are important steps in the host country selection. These factors will be discussed in more detail later in the chapter.

The Products or Services to Be Marketed

What products or services should an organization establish in an international market? In answering this question, many firms opt for the *shot-in-the-dark* method.

---

[6]Daniels and Radebaugh, *International Business*, pp. 544–48.

They simply select one or more of their products (or services) that have done well in their domestic market and introduce it into the chosen international market. Kellogg's Corn Flakes, Coca-Cola, and McDonald's hamburgers were introduced in this manner.[7]

A growing number of companies are utilizing more analytical and deliberate approaches to product or service selection. Some firms utilize a *phased internationalization* approach. They travel to the selected host country and conduct product-market research to determine consumer needs in the overall product area in which the company does business. Then the company returns home with the research and designs a product that fits the consumers' needs. The new product (often some variation of the company's product line) is then introduced into the host country. Ferrero's Tic Tac breath mints and IDV's Bailey's Irish Cream liqueur are products which were specifically developed and marketed based on research of multiple international markets.[8]

Regardless of the approach taken by an organization, a successful international product or service requires that primary attention be given to the needs, preferences, and idiosyncrasies of the consumers in the selected host country. Many hugely successful American products have failed abysmally in international markets because U.S. companies simply ignored international consumer differences.

Other products which initially failed later found success once the manufacturer made some seemingly slight though important changes. Consider S. C. Johnson & Son's Lemon Pledge furniture polish. After the product sold poorly in Japan among older consumers, the company conducted marketing research and found that the polish smelled like a latrine disinfectant used throughout Japan during World War II. Johnson & Son reduced the lemon scent in the polish and sales boomed.

Mattel's Barbie doll was another faltering product in Japan until marketing research determined that few Japanese identified with the Americanized doll. For the Japanese, Barbie was too tall, too long-legged and her blue eyes were the wrong color. Mattel produced a Japanized Barbie—shorter with brown eyes and a more Asian figure. Thereafter, two million Barbies were sold in two years.

Even name changes can produce positive results. Pillsbury changed its "Jolly Green Giant" name in Saudi Arabia once it found that the name translated to "intimidating green ogre"; in China, Coca-Cola instituted a name change after it found that in Chinese, "Coca-Cola" means "bite the wax tadpole."[9]

Adapting products to meet international consumer tastes is one characteristic of businesses that have achieved substantial success in international markets. Their approach to business abroad is discussed in the following Management Application.

---

[7]Martin Van Mesdag, "Winging It in Foreign Markets," *Harvard Business Review,* January–February 1987, pp. 71, 73.

[8]Ibid.

[9]John Thackray, "Much Ado about Marketing," *Across the Board,* April 1985, pp. 38–46; Vernon R. Alden, "Who Says You Can't Crack Japanese Markets?" *Harvard Business Review,* January–February 1987, pp. 53–56; and John S. Hill and Richard R. Hill, "Adapting Products to LDC Tastes," *Harvard Business Review,* March–April 1984, pp. 92–101.

MANAGEMENT APPLICATION

˙THE INTERNATIONAL WINNERS

A growing number of U.S. companies are succeeding in international markets, earning profits overseas that substantially contribute to the company's overall financial performance. One analysis by *Fortune* magazine has found that these "international winners" utilize a surprisingly similar formula in establishing business overseas. In *Fortune*'s view, this formula involves several rules:

Be patient.   Regardless of the mode of market entry, profits are usually long in coming in different countries because of differences in culture, employment practices, and consumers—in short, usually very unfamiliar ways of doing business. In Japan, a U.S. operation requires 10 years or more before becoming profitable. Many international winners initially lost money but continued on because of the often substantial profits to be made.

Don't rush into an overseas market.   Most winners were painstakingly careful before establishing a business overseas. Many managers first visited the host country several times, talked with potential suppliers, and analyzed market demand and cultural differences. In short, they studied every aspect of business before taking the plunge.

Hire host country citizens to manage the business.   This practice provides a company with managers who thoroughly understand the market and prevailing business practices. It also eases government concern about foreign intrusion into the country's business community. Many companies emphasize hiring talent overseas. IBM, for example, has vigorously recruited at Japanese universities for years. Engineering students rate IBM among the three best employers in Japan. IBM also focuses on hiring women for management positions in Japan where few women are permitted to become managers. There, women rate IBM as the best place to work.

Thoroughly educate these managers about the company's culture.   Many successful companies have established training centers for their expatriate managers. Hewlett-Packard brings its recruits to corporate headquarters in Silicon Valley for education in the company's management principles.

Alter your products and marketing to fit the market.   Many U.S. companies have experienced the failure of marketing an American product in a country where customs find the product utterly foreign and unacceptable. International winners accommodate the international consumer's needs. Hewlett-Packard, for example, manufactures computer keyboards that accommodate European traditions. Kellogg found that Japanese consumers had problems speaking the Japanese translation of the famous "snap, krackle, and pop" slogan for Rice Krispies. In Japan, Rice Krispies now go "patchy, pitchy, putchy."

Boeing scored a major success with its marketing of the Boeing 737 plane in undeveloped countries. Boeing analyzed the runways in these countries and found they were too short and soft to accommodate the 737 and most other U.S. commercial jets. They also studied the flying techniques of Third World pilots (e.g., Boeing found they tend to land hard, bounce the plane, and land off the runway). Boeing responded by redesigning the wings to allow shorter landings, more powerful engines for faster take-offs, and low-pressure tires so the plane wouldn't bounce on hard landings. The Boeing 737 is now the world's best-selling commercial jet in aviation history.

Source: Adapted from Andrew Kupfer, "How to Be a Global Manager," *Fortune*, March 14, 1988, pp. 52ff; and Kenneth Labich, "America's International Winners," *Fortune*, April 14, 1986, pp. 34ff.

The Mode of Entry into the International Market

Once the market and product/service for international expansion have been selected, an organization must decide specifically how it will enter its selected market. There are three basic strategies for market entry which are illustrated in Figure 18–2. Each strategy results in greater commitment to the international venture.

Export.   Exporting involves selling a product in the international market without establishing manufacturing facilities there. Exporting encompasses promotion to stimulate demand for the product, collecting revenues, making credit arrangements from sales, and shipping the product to the market.

Most companies secure an *agent* to handle some or all of these tasks. However, once they become accustomed to the exporting business, a number of companies assume most or all of these tasks, often establishing a staff in the host country. Exporting is a very popular approach for entering international markets. Table 18–1 shows the top 10 exporters in the United States and illustrates the profitability which this approach can provide.

Exporting is the least complicated and least risky strategy for entering a foreign market. The strategy involves little or no change in the organization's basic mission, objectives, and strategies since all production continues at home. If problems arise in the host country, an exporting organization can easily exit the market. However, exports are subject to tariffs and other import costs imposed by the host country which can lessen exporting profits and competitive advantage. Moreover, when an agent is used to handle the exporting tasks, the organization has little control over the overall exporting situation; that is, such factors as product price, advertising, and distribution.[10]

Foreign activities.   As the importance of exports increases, the firm may decide that it now can justify its own foreign subsidiary. This decision usually involves establishing production and/or marketing facilities in the host country. This strategy differs from *direct investment* because it entails some type of association with a local firm or individual. This type of association usually takes the form of *licensing* or a *joint venture*.

When a firm negotiates a licensing agreement, it is granting the right to produce the firm's product to an outside company in the host country. A firm may also grant an outside company the right to use the firm's intangible assets such as patents or

---

[10]James M. Livingstone, *The International Enterprise* (New York: John Wiley & Sons, 1975).

Figure 18–2 Evolving into a multinational corporation.

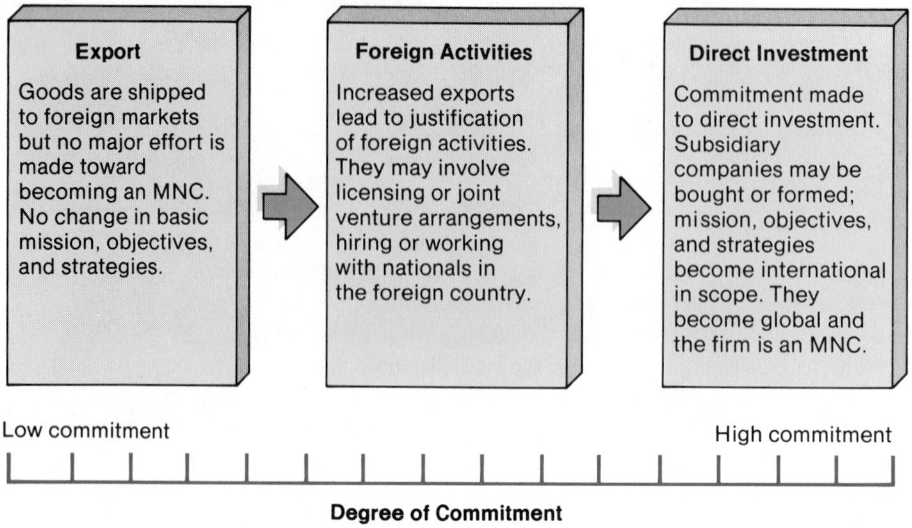

Export	Foreign Activities	Direct Investment
Goods are shipped to foreign markets but no major effort is made toward becoming an MNC. No change in basic mission, objectives, and strategies.	Increased exports lead to justification of foreign activities. They may involve licensing or joint venture arrangements, hiring or working with nationals in the foreign country.	Commitment made to direct investment. Subsidiary companies may be bought or formed; mission, objectives, and strategies become international in scope. They become global and the firm is an MNC.

Low commitment   High commitment

Degree of Commitment

technology. In the 1950s, many U.S. firms transferred technology to Japanese companies via licensing agreements. The licensing firm usually receives a flat payment plus royalties from the sale of the goods that are produced using the licensed technology.

Licensing can be an effective way to obtain profits from product sales without establishing and managing facilities in the host country. However, in licensing, a firm loses some control over the asset that is licensed. The company also runs the risk of the outside licensee eventually becoming a competitor.

In the joint venture arrangement, a business joins with local investors to create and operate a business in the host country. Each investor is a partner and shares the ownership of the new venture. Joint ventures are a quite popular strategy for launching a business abroad; over 40 percent of America's largest industrial corporations maintain international joint ventures.[11] They are especially popular with U.S. investors in countries such as China and Japan where the business and cultural environment is quite unique to the United States.[12] In recent years, the joint venture has become the cornerstone of McDonald's global expansion which is discussed in the following Management Application.

---

[11]A. K. Janger, *Organization of International Joint Ventures* (New York: The Conference Board, 1980).

[12]For an excellent study and discussion of the motives and use of joint ventures in China, see John D. Daniels, Jeffrey Krug, and Douglas Nigh, "U.S. Joint Ventures in China: Motivation and Management of Political Risk," *California Management Review,* Summer 1985, pp. 46–58.

Table 18-1 America's top 10 exporters.

Company	Products	Export Sales*	Percent of Total Sales
General Motors	Motor vehicles and parts, locomotives	$8,366,100	8.14%
Boeing	Aircraft	$7,330,000	44.86
Ford Motor	Motor vehicles and parts	$7,244,000	11.55
General Electric	Aircraft engines, medical systems	$4,348,000	12.35
IBM	Computers and related products	$3,058,000	5.97
DuPont	Specialty chemicals and energy products	$2,960,000	10.90
Chrysler	Motor vehicles and parts	$2,810,800	12.48
McDonnell Douglas	Aerospace and information systems	$2,804,800	22.15
United Technologies	Jet engines, helicopters, cooling equipment	$2,126,043	13.57
Eastman Kodak	Photographic equipment and supplies	$2,044,000	17.70

*In thousands of dollars.

Source: "The Bright Future of Service Exports," *Fortune*, July 20, 1987, p. 73. Copyright 1987 by Time, Inc. Reprinted by permission of the publisher. All rights reserved.

MANAGEMENT APPLICATION

MCDONALD'S GOES "BIGGU MAKKU"

For years, McDonald's was content with continually growing profits selling the "Big Mac" and its other products only within the United States. However, in recent years, the maturing fast-food market has sent America's top burger maker overseas. Today, more than 2,000 McDonald's outlets operate outside the United States. The company is now opening new international outlets at a rate of over 200 a year. McDonald's is particularly popular in Europe and Japan (where customers stop at "Makudonarudo" for a "biggu makku").

However, success overseas can be quite challenging. It requires that McDonald's establish outlets that embrace the high-energy culture of the company and maintain the rigorous production standards that are the core of the company's famous efficiency and product consistency. That can be difficult to do in highly different cultures.

McDonald's strategy is to establish joint ventures with partners who are carefully selected on the basis of hard work, dedication, and an entrepreneurial, upbeat approach to the business, and to insist that the partners maintain production standards. However, the partners are provided the freedom to be creative in marketing, new products, and aspects of the outlet's decor. Such autonomy enables the partner to develop an outlet to appeal to local tastes and culture.

For example as noted in Chapter 2, McDonald's outlets in Brazil sells Big Macs; they also market a soft drink that contains guarana, an Amazonian berry. Walk into a McDonald's in Annonay, France, and you'll see beer on the menu next to milk shakes. Music from Mozart and Brahms plays over the restaurant's speaker system.

McDonald's is satisfied with its strategy; however, the company faces major challenges in duplicating its highly effective supply system overseas. Its specifications for beef, condiments, and other supplies are very precise, which is essential to maintain product consistency. Few overseas suppliers are willing to purchase equipment to meet McDonald's specifications. As a result, McDonald's has at times invested in its own production facilities. After a futile search for a suitable hamburger bun in Great Britain, McDonald's created a joint venture there to build a large bakery to make the buns. In Thailand, McDonald's works with farmers to teach them how to grow Idaho russet potatoes. McDonald's grows its own potatoes in 18 countries.

The overseas challenge is demanding, and profit margins are slimmer because of the higher real estate costs and frequent need to import supplies. It also takes at least five years before any overseas outlet turns a profit. However, selling the "Biggu Makku" abroad is fast becoming an even greater ingredient in McDonald's future success.

Source: Adapted from Kathleen Deveny, "McWorld?" *Business Week,* October 13, 1986, pp. 78ff.

The popularity of joint ventures is largely due to the substantial advantages which the strategy can provide. A joint venture is a lower-cost and lesser-risk approach to establishing production and marketing operations abroad compared to foreign direct investment. Substantial gains can be reaped when partners with complementary abilities pool their skills and resources in making and selling a product. For example, several U.S. companies such as Kentucky Fried Chicken have achieved success in the challenging Japanese markets via joint ventures. These companies provide financing and technology while the Japanese partner provides the personnel and knowledge of the Japanese markets and business practices.[13]

However, the failure rates of joint ventures are disturbingly high. Approximately 40 percent of these international arrangements fail; most ventures last only from three to four years.[14] At the core of the arrangement's problems are the difficulties of joint ownership and management. Usually two partners from different countries and cultures must work together in setting venture objectives, strategy, and in operating the new business. Emerging differences in management and cultural styles can create major conflicts between the parties as can differing objectives for the venture. Several U.S.-

---

[13]Several excellent articles are available on the advantages, problems, and shortcomings posed by joint ventures. Among the more noteworthy are: Carmela E. Schillaci, "Designing Successful Joint Ventures," *The Journal of Business Strategy,* Fall 1987, pp. 59–63; Marjorie A. Lyles, "Common Mistakes of Joint Venture Experienced Firms," *Columbia Journal of World Business,* Summer 1987, pp. 79–84; F. Kingston Berlew, "The Joint Venture—A Way into Foreign Markets," *Harvard Business Review,* July–August 1984, pp. 48ff; and Oded Shenkar and Yoram Zeira, "Human Resources Management in International Joint Ventures," *Academy of Management Review,* July 1987, pp. 546–57.

[14]Kathryn R. Harrigan, "Joint Ventures that Endure," *Industry Week,* April 20, 1987, p. 14. Also see L. G. Franko, *Joint Venture Survival in Multinational Corporations* (New York: Praeger Publishers, 1971).

Table 18–2 Direct investment in other countries (In millions of dollars).

	1960	1970	1980	1986
United States	$2,940	$7,589	$19,220	$28,050
Japan	79	355	2,385	14,480
West Germany	139	876	4,180	8,999
Britain	700	1,308	11,360	16,691
Canada	52	302	2,694	3,254
France	347	374	3,138	5,230
Italy	−17	111	754	2,661

Source: "Entering a New Age of Boundless Competition," *Fortune,* March 14, 1988, p. 46. Copyright 1988 by Time, Inc. Used with permission of the publisher. All rights reserved.

Japanese joint ventures have run asunder because of conflicting objectives. America's business culture tends to emphasize profitability as a key objective; in Japan, the overriding business objective is growth in market share. Thus, conflict emerges when a U.S. partner wants to take its share of venture profits back to corporate headquarters in the United States, while the Japanese partner wants to reinvest profits for growth.[15]

Given the inherent difficulties with joint ventures, success requires a careful analysis and selection of the joint venture partner. Selection should be based on such factors as compatibility of venture objectives, similar value systems, and mutual respect. Agreements should be reached concerning mechanisms for resolving disagreement and the specific roles of each partner in managing the business.[16]

Direct investment.   The strongest commitment to becoming a global enterprise is made when management decides to begin producing the firm's products abroad with no association with a host country investor. This entry strategy is booming in international business; Table 18–2 depicts its rate of growth among seven countries over 36 years. The United States currently accounts for about 40 percent of all direct investment worldwide.

Businesses that build and/or buy manufacturing facilities abroad do so for a number of reasons. In some cases, direct investment reduces manufacturing expenses due to lower labor and other costs. This benefit triggered the booming growth of the maquiladoras industry along the Mexican border which is profiled in Case 18–1 at the end of this chapter. Direct investment also enables a business to avoid the tariff and other government-imposed costs associated with exporting. The strategy is an effective means for building major national markets and for maintaining total control over international operations. Also, larger benefits can be gained by establishing a local presence via direct investment. By paying taxes in the host country and providing local employment, a foreign business can build confidence among consumers and

---

[15]Schillaci, "Designing Successful Joint Ventures," p. 61; Lyles, "Common Mistakes of Joint Venture Experiment Firms." p. 80; and Berlew, "The Joint Venture," p. 48.

[16]John S. McClenahen, "Alliances for Competitive Advantage," *Industry Week,* August 24, 1987, pp. 33–36; and J. Peter Killing, "How to Make a Joint Venture Work," *Harvard Business Review,* May–June 1982. pp. 120–27.

receive more equitable treatment from the host government.[17] However, direct investment entails a full commitment to an international venture. When problems arise in the host country (e.g., market decline, economic depression, government instability), leaving the country is often quite difficult and costly.

In summary, the exporting, foreign activities and direct investment strategies for market entry offer different strengths and shortcomings. As one moves along the continuum from exporting to direct investment (depicted in Figure 18–2), commitment to the venture and control over international operations increases. Risk due to this greater commitment also tends to increase.

THE INTERNATIONAL ENVIRONMENT

The decision to become an MNC and thereafter effectively managing in an international setting requires careful assessment of the international environment. Due appreciation must be given to the differences that exist there relative to an organization's domestic environment.

Environmental factors, which bear great impact on managerial performance in a domestic setting, are magnified many times in the international market. In assessing the international environment, many factors should be evaluated. However, the host country's *culture, economics,* and *politics* should be given special attention. Although other environmental differences may exist, these three have the greatest impact on managerial performance in MNCs. How effectively managers respond to these differences often determines the success or failure of the MNC itself.

Culture

Culture is a very complex environmental influence, encompassing knowledge, beliefs, values, law, morals, customs, and other habits and capabilities an individual acquires as a member of society. These elements of culture can all vary a great deal across societies. If an MNC is global in nature, management must adapt its managerial practices to the specific and unique aspects of culture in each host country. An MNC's management must be culturally sensitive in its business practices and learn to bridge the cultural gap that exists between its ways of management and business and those of the host country. In making these adjustments, an MNC's management must be aware that cultures are *learned,* cultures *vary,* and cultures *influence behavior*.

Cultures are learned. Cultures include all types of learning and behavior, the customs that people have developed for living together, their values, and their beliefs of right and wrong. A culture is the sum of what humans learn in common with other members of the society to which they belong.

Cultures vary. Different societies have different cultures. Different objectives are prized, and behavior that is valued in one society may be much less important in

---

[17]Robert Grosse and Duane Kujawa, *International Business: Theory and Managerial Applications* (Homewood, Ill.: Richard D. Irwin, 1988), pp. 91–93.

another. This cultural diversity affects individual perception, and therefore, individual behavior.

Two examples illustrate the substantial differences in Eastern and Western cultures. In Asian countries, for instance, a major cultural rule of behavior in society is to maintain and "save face," essentially to preserve an individual's self-respect, pride, and dignity. This principle governs the ways that Asians communicate and interact with other people. For example, if an American business owner asks a Taiwanese for the location of a particular restaurant and the Taiwanese does not know, he will lie rather than admit his ignorance. Conceding ignorance causes embarrassment and loss of face. While American culture prizes individuality and frankness, the Asian culture emphasizes conforming to society. Individualism is shunned because by disagreeing with others' behavior, individualism insults others and causes their loss of face. Frank criticism is avoided because criticizing others causes a loss of face. Asians avoid demonstrations of anger because it is viewed as a humiliating loss of dignity.[18]

In Japan and other Asian countries, the culture emphasizes the social relationship as the foundation of business. Consequently, when an American business executive negotiates a joint venture with a prospective Japanese partner, they will discover that the Japanese will spend much time asking questions about the American's family and other subjects that seemingly have nothing to do with the joint venture. The American executive seeks to obtain a legal contract which American culture views as the foundation of the business relationship. However, the Japanese attempt to establish some foundation of a mutual relationship of personal trust and understanding which they view as the core of the business relationship. The time-consuming questions are an attempt to do so.

While the U.S. business executive seeks the certainty and protection of a legal contract, the Japanese view contracts as a hindrance. As the factors affecting the venture change over time, the Japanese reason, so will the relationship. A legalistic, unchanging contract is an unnecessary obstacle to the venture's natural development. Thus, while American business executives emphasize detail in the contract, the Japanese work to keep the document as general as possible. American business executives often have difficulty understanding these major cultural differences which have undone many joint venture relationships.

Cultures influence behavior.   Diversity in human behavior can be found in almost every human activity. Religious ceremonies, beliefs, values, work habits, food habits, and social activities vary endlessly with culture environment. The differences in behavior between peoples of different countries arise from differences in culture rather than differences in people.

Culture can affect behavior in many ways. For example, although human needs may be inherently similar, the cultural environment determines the relative importance of needs and the means through which they are satisfied.[19] Recall for a moment the

---

[18]John A. Reeder, "When West Meets East: Cultural Aspects of Doing Business in Asia," *Business Horizons,* January–February 1987, pp. 69–74.

[19]George W. England, *The Manager and His Values* (Cambridge, Mass.: Ballinger/Lippincott, 1975); and John Fayerweather, *International Business Strategy and Administration* (Cambridge, Mass.: Ballinger/Lippincott, 1978), pp. 449–57.

Table 18–3 Attitudes toward competition in three different cultures.

Nature and Effect of Competition	Typical American Viewpoints	Typical European Viewpoints	Typical Japanese Viewpoints
Nature of competition	Competition is a strong moral force: it contributes to character building.	Competition is neither good nor bad.	There is conflict inherent in nature. To overcome conflicts, man must compete, but man's final goal is harmony with nature and his fellowman.
Business competition compared	Business competition is like a big sport game.	Business competition affects the livelihood of people and quickly develops into warfare.	The company is like a family. Competition has no place in a family. Aggressive action against competitors in the marketplace is in order for the survival and growth of the company.
Motivation	One cannot rely on an employee's motivation unless extra monetary inducements for hard work are offered in addition to a base salary or wage.	A key employee is motivated by the fact that he has been hired by the company.	Same as the European viewpoint.
Reward system	Money talks. A person is evaluated on the basis of his image (contribution) to the company. High tipping in best hotels, restaurants, and so on, is expected.	An adequate salary, fringe benefits, opportunities for promotion, but no extra incentives— except in sales. Very little tipping (service charge is included in added-value tax).	Same as the European viewpoint.
Excessive competiton	Competition must be tough for the sake of the general welfare of society. No upper limit on the intensity and amount of competition is desirable.	Too much competition is destructive and is in conflict with brotherly love and Christian ethic.	Excessive competition is destructive and can create hatred. Only restrained competition leads to harmony and benefits society.

Table 18–3 (*concluded*)

Nature and Effect of Competition	Typical American Viewpoints	Typical European Viewpoints	Typical Japanese Viewpoints
Hiring policy	Aggressive individuals who enjoy competition are ideal employees. Individuals who avoid competition are unfit for life and company work.	Diversity of opinion. How competitiveness or aggressive behavior of an individual is viewed varies with national ideology and the type of work. In England, it is not a recommendation to describe a job applicant as being aggressive.	Individuals are hired usually not for specific jobs but on the basis of their personality traits and their ability to become an honorable company member. Team play and group consensus are stressed.

Source: Hugh E. Kramer, "Concepts of Competition in America, Europe, and Japan," *Business and Society,* Fall 1977, pp. 22–23.

different needs in Maslow's hierarchy of needs discussed in Chapter 12. One study of 116,000 employees in one U.S. MNC with locations across 50 countries found that employees differed in need importance in different countries. Employees in the Netherlands and Scandinavian countries, for example, valued social needs more highly than self-actualization needs (which contradicts Maslow's theory).[20] An individual's need for achievement has also been found to differ among cultures.

Culture also influences attitudes of individuals concerning the importance of work, authority, material possessions, competition, time, profit, risk taking, and decision making. Many employees in Israel, Austria, New Zealand, and Scandinavian countries, for example, prefer consultative over unilateral decision making. In some cultures, time is measured in days and years rather than hours which can substantially affect work scheduling and control. In some countries especially Muslim societies, the culture does not emphasize self-determination which is a strong cultural norm in the United States. People believe that fate rather than self-initiative determines the future. This belief has a major impact on business planning, objectives, and work.[21]

In some areas of the world, hard work is viewed as good, while in other areas, it is viewed as something to be avoided. Authority is perceived as a right in some nations but must be earned by demonstrated ability in others such as the United States. Table 18–3 presents attitudes in three different cultures (American, European, and Japanese)

---

[20]Geert Hofstede, "National Cultures in Four Dimensions," *International Studies of Management and Organization,* Spring–Summer 1983, p. 68 as cited in Daniels and Radebaugh, *International Business,* p. 99.

[21]Endel-Jakob Kolde, *Environment of International Business* (Boston: Kent Publishing Co., 1982), pp. 29–32; Daniels and Radebaugh, *International Business,* pp. 93–102; and Stephan H. Robock, Kenneth Simmonds, and Jack Zwick, *International Business and Multinational Enterprises* (Homewood, Ill.: Richard D. Irwin, 1977), pp. 309–40.

toward competition and illustrates how these attitudes influence managerial behavior, motivational approaches, reward systems, staffing practices, and leadership styles.[22]

Economics

The *economic influences* of a host country substantially affect MNC performance. Its income levels, economic growth, inflation rates, and the country's balance of payments can significantly affect an MNC's sales, earnings, and business practices. The MNC must constantly be aware of each host country's economic stability. The rate of inflation and currency stability must be closely monitored.

In terms of economic and overall development, countries are classified either as a *developed country* or a *less developed country (LDC)*. Compared to a developed country, a LDC has a lower level of economic development. It usually has a low gross national product, little industry, and underdeveloped educational, distribution, and communication systems. Comprising 80 percent of the world's population, LDCs have an unequal distribution of income that keeps many of these people in deep poverty.

Although LDCs comprise most of the world's population, only about 25 percent of the world's international business activity occurs in these countries.[23] However, the amount of international activity is increasing. In particular, a growing number of American companies are establishing direct investments in LDCs to obtain the advantages of much lower labor costs. This trend and the debate which it has triggered is discussed in the following Management Application.

MANAGEMENT APPLICATION

THE HOLLOW CORPORATION

An increasing number of companies are looking overseas for the manufacturing component of the products they sell. They obtain parts or whole products from makers in low labor cost countries to capitalize on the costs which lower the product's cost of goods sold. Many of these companies become "hollow"; they maintain marketing, financial, and other activities in the United States, but with reduced or nonexistent manufacturing activities.

Some examples: Virtually all of General Electric's consumer electronics products are made in Asia. Once the largest customer of American-made steel, Caterpillar Tractor now looks overseas for much of its steel. At Nike, manufacturing activities are limited; it employs only 100 manufacturing people among its 3,500-member work force. Liz Claiborne has 250 among its 3,000 employees.

This "outsourcing" strategy is profitable for the company; however, it is damaging to the United States, some observers believe. They assert that outsourcing robs the

---

[22]Also see David Granick, *Managerial Comparisons in Four Developed Countries: France, Britain, United States and Russia* (Cambridge, Mass.: MIT Press, 1972).

[23]Grosse and Kujawa, *International Business*, pp. 606–7.

United States of the strong industrial base it needs to prosper. For example, manufacturing activities provide business for many service companies (e.g., insurance, transportation, and even communications businesses). Transfer manufacturing abroad and with it goes demand for many service activities.

This type of de-industrialization, they assert, will weaken America's productivity and standard of living. According to productivity statistics, most gains in productivity and thus in standard of living come from the manufacturing, not service, sector. If America outsources its manufacturing, it will also lose the ability to innovate. If companies don't manufacture, they will lose the technological know-how and understanding of how new technology can be innovated. The best ideas come from manufacturing experience, not the laboratory.

Other observers disagree with this position, stating that while U.S. manufacturers are outsourcing, foreign countries are building manufacturing facilities in the United States. Further, the number of small manufacturing businesses is booming in this country.

Regardless of the impact of outsourcing on the U.S. economy and industry, the trend is likely to continue unabated. It is difficult for large U.S. corporations to resist outsourcing to such countries as China where workers are producing exceptionally high-quality products. Their wage is $1 a day.

Source: Adapted from "The Hollow Corporation," a special report in *Business Week*, March 3, 1986, pp. 57ff; and Susan Lee and Christie Brown, "The Protean Corporation," *Forbes*, August 24, 1987, pp. 76–79.

Economic relations between MNCs and LDCs often have been the subject of controversy. Many LDCs have strong feelings of nationalism. During the last 30 years, in their drives for political independence and freedom from foreign domination, many developing nations have felt the need to consolidate control of their economies by altering the past pattern of relationships with foreign firms. In some LDCs, extensive government regulations have been adopted with the ultimate purpose of limiting the growth of MNCs. More recently, however, there has been a movement away from this trend. The reasons for the shift are *changing attitudes* and *rising direct investment*.[24]

Changing attitudes.   Although charges of exploitation by MNCs still are made quite frequently, attitudes of both host governments and MNCs have changed. This has led to greater mutual understanding and accommodation in relations. Although host country fear of foreign domination still exists, it has eased substantially. Apparently, foreign governments realize that the relationship with MNCs need not be a no-win situation, but rather one of mutual gain.

Rising direct investment.   Improved relations have given rise to a doubling of direct investment compared to the early 1960s. Apparently, many MNCs believe the possible returns are worth the risk. Also, these direct investments do not reflect the flow of

---

[24]This section is based on *Transnational Corporations and Developing Countries: New Policies for a Changing World Economy* (New York: Committee for Economic Development, 1981), pp. 1–3.

other resources, such as managerial skills, technology, and marketing skills, which may overshadow the monetary contribution.

Despite greater mutual trust and a greater volume of investment, it would be wrong to assume that MNCs and developing countries have achieved total agreement on the questions of exploitation of resources and threats to sovereignty. These issues have divided them for years and, even today, opinions still diverge widely within each group.

At the heart of the controversy is a basic difference in perceptions and objectives. The MNCs, though they now are more willing to recognize their social responsibilities, still tend to concentrate on short-run performance criteria. Efficient and profitable operation is regarded as benefiting workers, customers, and suppliers directly, while the rest of the host country benefits indirectly through taxes.

Critics in the host country, on the other hand, point to undesirable political, social, and economic consequences. They charge that MNCs create many problems in developing countries struggling to achieve political and economic autonomy. In fact, similar arguments are made in discussions of the social responsibilities of business firms in the United States.

In response to these concerns, a number of large MNCs have launched efforts to aid in the development of the LDCs where they conduct international business. Ford Motor Company's South American subsidiary, for example, has constructed 128 schools in Mexico over the last 20-plus years. These schools educate about 170,000 children each year. Champion International Corp., subsidizes 13,000 meals each day for its Brazilian employees. Warner-Lambert's Tropicare Inc., provides training in primary health care in the four West African countries where it operates (Cameroon, Ivory Coast, Senegal, and Zaire). These efforts are not totally selfless; the MNCs realize that helping to solve the host country's developmental problems serves both the LDC's and the MNC's interests.[25]

Politics

The *political influences* in a host-country environment can substantially affect all of the managerial functions of an MNC and can frequently determine the ultimate success of an MNC's international operations. Our discussion of the political environment will focus on two topics: the characteristics of the host country government that most affect an MNC and the concept of *political risk* including how MNCs forecast and cope with political uncertainty in their international settings.

Concerning the host government, three factors most significantly influence an MNC's operations and performance.

Governmental attitudes toward imports and direct investment. Host country governments express their attitudes concerning international imports and investments with actions that can greatly help or hinder an MNC. Governments who encourage

[25]Ann McKinstry Micou, "The Invisible Hand at Work in Developing Countries," *Across the Board,* March 1985, pp. 8–15.

investment often provide incentives to persuade foreign companies to establish manufacturing facilities there. Such incentives are often provided by LDCs who want access to the technology, capital, jobs, and educational and managerial skills that an MNC can provide. Singapore, for example, offers low-interest government loans, tax holidays, and accelerated depreciation to foreign investors from certain industries. India provides capital grants to companies that will build manufacturing facilities in certain depressed areas of the country. Malaysia waives taxes for as long as 10 years for companies who also locate in certain areas.[26]

Although LDC governments are often eager to attract certain foreign investors, they will also set requirements that seek to obtain as much value from the MNC while not compromising the country's sovereignty. These requirements take on a variety of forms. Many LDCs, for example, require a "fadeout" where the majority ownership of the MNC's facility in the host country is transferred to a host country investor within a certain number of years. Other LDCs such as India set a strict limit on foreign ownership of an MNC facility. India limits foreign ownership of a local facility to 40 percent and must approve the operation's production capacity and entry into new markets. IBM left India after the government refused to agree to IBM's worldwide policy of total ownership of its subsidiaries. Coca-Cola Co. left India because it refused to comply with the government's requirement that the company disclose its Coke formula to its Indian partners.[27]

LDCs may also require that an MNC hire a specified number of local citizens for employee and management positions to boost the area's employment. Other LDCs require that the MNC sell its technology to local businesses. Many host countries restrict the amount of funds that an MNC can transfer out of the country. To obtain access to markets in developed countries, some LDCs such as Colombia require that for every good imported by a resident MNC, the MNC must export a Colombian good of equal or higher value.[28]

Both LDC and DC governments often seek to restrict the import of certain goods that compete with host country businesses. In these cases, barriers are established to discourage imports. A government may impose a tariff on certain imported goods which is a tax calculated as a percentage of the product's value. These tariffs raise the import's sales price which provides domestic competitors with a competitive advantage. In Japan, for example, imported cookies, crackers, and baked goods are taxed in the amount of 20 percent of their value. A tariff of 25 percent of value is applied to imported ham and bacon.[29]

To further aid domestic competitors, a government may provide them subsidies such as low-cost loans and tax breaks or a quota may be set on a product which limits

---

[26]Robert Weigand, "International Investments: Weighing the Incentives," *Harvard Business Review,* July–August 1983, pp. 146–52.

[27]Dennis J. Encarnation and Sushil Vachani, "Foreign Ownership: When Hosts Change the Rules," *Harvard Business Review,* September–October 1985, pp. 152–60.

[28]Grosse and Kujawa, *International Business,* pp. 219–27.

[29]David Gerstenhaber, "Japan's Markets Are Ripe for U.S. Exports," *The Wall Street Journal,* September 14, 1987, p. 21.

the number of goods that can be imported. Another barrier is to require inspection standards that are cost prohibitive for potential imports.

Efficiency of government.

Many American business executives become disillusioned with the inefficient bureaucracies they must deal with in many countries. Often, little assistance is provided by foreign governments to American businesspeople. Customs-handling procedures are inefficient and burdensome, and market information is nonexistent. Systems of law in each country also can be quite different. For example, the United States has developed its legal system by means of English *common law*. The courts are guided by principles derived from previous cases. In much of Europe and Asia, however, the legal system is one of *civil law*. In such systems, judges are less important, and the bureaucrat (civil servant) is extremely important. Unfortunately, American managers have found that many of the inefficiencies and obstacles in local governments tend to disappear when a suitable payment is made to some civil servant. In many nations, such bribes are considered a part of doing business. For example, during the late 1970s, the Northrop Corp. was accused of spending a substantial part of $30 million over approximately five years for bribes and kickbacks. One factor that emerged during congressional hearings was that such payments were considered in the Middle East to be traditional peculiarities of business practice.[30]

Out of the above and some 400 other cases came the Foreign Corrupt Practices Act, which was passed into law in 1977. For the first time in U.S. history, it became a crime for corporations to bribe an official of a foreign government in order to obtain, or retain, business in another country. More specifically, the law requires publicly held companies to institute internal accounting controls to ensure that all transactions are made in accordance with management's specific authorization and are fairly recorded.

Meanwhile, in West Germany, France, and Great Britain, payments of bribes abroad in business dealings remain not only legal but tax deductible. This practice obviously places the United States at a disadvantage in certain areas.

Government stability.

The stability of the host country government is perhaps the characteristic that bears the greatest impact on an MNC. Such is the case because highly unstable governments that are subject to volatile change can upend an MNC's operations. The most extreme impact of government instability can occur when an unstable government changes hands. In such cases, the MNC may face *expropriation* where the new leaders in power seize the MNC's facility without compensation. *Nationalization* may occur where the government forces the MNC to sell its facility to local buyers. Since World War II, most takeovers of MNC facilities have occurred in LDCs, particularly in Latin America. Since the early 1970s, manufacturing facilities have been the most susceptible to government takeover.[31] Beyond these more dramatic

---

[30]For an excellent account, see "Northrop Corporation: Development of a Policy on International Sales Commissions," in *Marketing and Society,* ed. R. D. Adler, L. M. Robinson, and J. E. Carlson (Englewood Cliffs, N.J.: Prentice-Hall, 1981), pp. 329–51.

[31]Daniels and Radebaugh, *International Business,* p. 552.

events, government instability can render substantial changes in MNC taxation, product pricing, employment of managers from the MNC's corporate headquarters, and other important aspects of doing business.

Government instability and the uncertainty of other elements of the political environment introduce a degree of *political risk* into an MNC's operations in a respective host country. Political risk refers to unanticipated changes in the host country's political environment that affect MNC operations. *Macro risk* involves political changes that affect all multinational corporations operating in a host country; *micro risk* are changes that affect certain industries or firms. Saudi Arabia's nationalization of all foreign operations in the country's oil industry in 1974 is one example of micro political change.[32]

Terrorism is an increasingly important element of political risk abroad. Terrorism can be defined as "the use or threat of use, of anxiety-inducing . . . violence for political purposes . . ."[33] International terrorism has assumed many forms such as attacks on military bases, airplane hijackings, the bombing of foreign embassies, and the kidnapping of political officials and business executives.

Although acts of terrorism are usually highly publicized, the actual number of terrorist incidents worldwide is not substantial. In 1986, for example, 3,000 terrorist acts occurred worldwide including 763 against businesses (mostly in Latin America). Sixty-seven incidents were targeted at U.S. businesses abroad.[34] Figure 18–3 provides a summary of terrorist incidents across continents for the first three quarters of 1985.

However, although the number is less than one might expect, terrorist incidents have been increasing from 12 to 15 percent each year during the last decade, and the number is continuing to climb. The nature of the terrorist acts have also become much more deadly.[35] These developments concern MNCs especially given that many companies are ill-equipped to handle a terrorist incident when one occurs. Moreover, when terrorism strikes an MNC, neither the host country government nor the U.S. government is likely to intervene and provide assistance. The MNC's management is on its own.

In deciding whether to establish operations in a country, few MNCs neglect the presence of political risk. Rather, most conduct *political risk analysis* which involves identifying and assessing the sources of risk and the probabilities that adverse political change will occur in the prospective host country. Several methods of analysis are available. Some MNCs visit the prospective host country and meet with government officials, business executives and other nationals to obtain their own first-hand assessment of the political environment.

Some MNCs employ panels of individuals who are experts on the country. They rate the country on a given number of political risk factors (such as the history of

[32]Robock, Simmonds, and Zwick, *International Business and Multinational Enterprises,* pp. 292–94.

[33]Edward F. Micklous, "Tracking the Growth and Prevalence of International Terrorism," in *Managing Terrorism: Strategies for the Corporate Executive,* ed. Patrick J. Montana and George S. Roukis (Westport, Conn.: Quorum Books, 1983), p. 3.

[34]Lennie Copeland, "Terrorism: The Mouse that Roared," *Personnel Administrator,* September 1987, p. 71.

[35]Ibid., pp. 70, 71.

Figure 18–3 Terrorism against business.

	Latin America	Europe	Asia	Mideast	Africa	North America
Bombings	443	101	76	29	20	2
Kidnappings	12	2	2	1	1	0
Attacks on installations	56	6	8	3	5	0
Assassinations	7	10	1	0	0	0
Highjackings	0	2	1	3	0	0
TOTAL	518	121	88	36	26	2

Source: "Business Copes with Terrorism," *Fortune*, January 6, 1986, p. 48. Copyright 1986 by Time, Inc. Used with permission of the publisher. All rights reserved.

government stability, the role of the military in the host government, and the government's attitude toward foreign investors). Some businesses also produce and publish risk ratings on nations. Business International (BI), for example, rates 70 countries on 55 political risk factors. The ratings are provided by BI's specialists who live in the countries they assess. The ratings are published for BI's subscribers.[36]

Rather than hire external experts or rely solely on published risk ratings, a growing number of companies are designing political risk analysis programs that meet the MNC's specific needs. Dow Chemical, for example, maintains its economic, social and political risk program (ESP). Six to eight line managers trained in political and economic analysis, along with executives from the respective country, provide specific risk analyses on a country. Xerox maintains its Issues Monitoring System which regularly identifies the 10 most important political issues for each host country where Xerox operates. Xerox's managers in the respective country assess the issues, evaluate their potential impact on Xerox, and then offer strategies for dealing with the issues. Using these strategies, "external relations" objectives are then set for each local manager. Part of the manager's yearly bonus is based on the accomplishment of the objectives.[37]

Regardless of the method of analysis used, the findings are incorporated into the MNC's decision making about operating in the host country. Beyond this analysis, MNCs also take actions to hedge against political risk. Some MNCs restrict operations to joint ventures where a local partner shares the risk. They may develop the operation by local borrowing which builds alliances with local banks. MNCs may spread the risk by locating plants in several countries, reducing their dependence on one host country. Many MNCs also obtain insurance policies (available from Lloyd's of London

---

[36]William D. Guth, *Handbook of Business Strategy* (Boston: Warren, Gorham, and Lamont, 1983), p. 136.

[37]Thomas W. Shreeve, "Be Prepared for Political Changes Abroad," *Harvard Business Review,* July–August 1984, pp. 111–18.

and other companies) which provide coverage against expropriation, damages due to war, terrorism, and other politically related losses.

Companies are also developing strategies for coping with the threat of terrorism. Some MNCs (e.g., IBM and Exxon) are maintaining low profiles in high-risk countries. The U.S. flag is not flown at these facilities. Businesses such as Goodyear Tire and Rubber Co., are reducing the size of corporate signs displayed at their company sites.[38] More companies are boosting security measures at their MNC facilities and hiring counterterrorism consulting firms to train employees in how to deal with a terrorist attack if it occurs.

In many MNCs, top-level management is establishing crisis management teams (much like those discussed in Chapter 2) to deal with terrorist incidents. Company plans consider the patterns of terrorism which are surprisingly consistent in different areas of the world. For example, airplane hijackings are the most popular terrorist technique in the Middle East; in Western Europe, U.S. banks and computer companies are popular targets and the bomb is a favorite terrorist weapon. Kidnappings are popular in Latin America where terrorists kidnap for money to finance political activities. In the Mideast, terrorists, usually well funded by local governments, kidnap foreigners to obtain release of political prisoners.[39]

High-level executives who are potential kidnapping targets are receiving special training in a growing number of large, visible U.S. MNCs. Companies are also sending drivers who chauffeur their executives to counterterrorism schools. There, they learn such techniques as escape tactics and battering through blockades (many terrorist experts believe that executives are most vulnerable to attack when driving to and from work).[40]

THE MANAGEMENT FUNCTIONS IN INTERNATIONAL MANAGEMENT

The management functions of planning, organizing, leading, and controlling must be applied efficiently (as adapted to the particular situation) in all managerial situations, but particularly international management. How each function can be applied in differing foreign environments is discussed below.

The Planning Function

The objectives of a multinational company cannot be the same as those of a domestic corporation. There are too many possibilities of conflict between corporate objectives and the economic and political objectives of the countries in which the firm operates. In many nations, the role played by government in planning helps heighten the possibility of conflicts with an MNC. For example, Japan's Ministry of International Trade

---

[38]Brian O'Reilly, "Business Copes with Terrorism," *Fortune*, January 6, 1986, p. 48.

[39]Ibid., pp. 48, 50.

[40]"Multinational Firms Act to Protect Overseas Workers from Terrorism," *The Wall Street Journal*, April 29, 1986, p. 33.

Table 18–4 The planning environment in domestic versus global settings.

Domestic Setting	Global Setting
Similar culture	Diverse cultures
Limited language differences	Multilingual
One economic system	Multiple economic systems
One political system	Numerous political systems
One basic legal system	Diverse legal approaches
One monetary system	Multiple monetary systems
Similar markets	Diverse markets

and Industry plans the nation's economy to the point of specifying five-year percentage growth rates in exports of specific products.

In certain situations, a country may have objectives—such as a favorable balance of payments or an improved standard of living for its citizens—that do not coincide with the corporate objectives of the MNC. A common source of conflict is that in order to achieve a profitable objective, some of the foreign subsidiary's earnings must be returned to the MNC's headquarters. This outward flow of earnings could have negative impact on the host country's balance of payments. For this and similar reasons, some nations place restrictions on multinational companies, as we have previously discussed.

Civil servants hold influential positions in foreign bureaucracies. Thus, they often dominate the planning functions of many countries. Managers of multinational companies must become acquainted with the attitudes and practices of these individuals, for an important reason. The civil servants often establish the conditions under which the managers must do their planning.

Table 18–4 presents some of the differences that can complicate the planning environment for a multinational manager. The greater the number of differing factors, the more complex the planning environment.

The Organizing Function

After a company decides to go multinational and its planning function is well along, it must devise an organizational structure. The structure must provide a network of jobs and authority for achieving the organizational objectives. As with planning, organizational structures in the international arena often must adjust to local conditions. Organizational effectiveness depends greatly on flows of information. And these flows become more difficult to maintain as geographically dispersed decision centers are established. Consequently, an MNC must build effective worldwide communication to transmit information throughout the organization.

Multinational companies usually employ the basic organizational structures discussed in this textbook. Let us briefly examine each one.

Product design.   An MNC following the *product-design structure* assigns to a single unit the operational responsibilities for a product or product line. Product-design struc-

Figure 18–4 Product organization design.

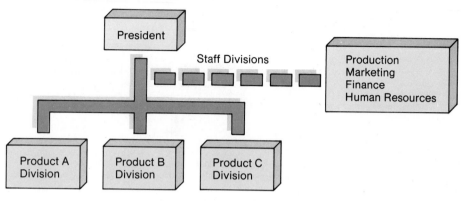

ture is widely used in multinational companies that have diverse product lines being marketed in geographically dispersed areas. Such multinationals as Sperry Rand Corp. and Clark Equipment Company use this design, illustrated in Figure 18–4.

Geographic design.   To use this design, a multinational company groups all functional and operational responsibilities into specific geographical areas. The geographic design is used widely and by such organizations as International Telephone and Telegraph Corp. and Charles Pfizer Corporation, which do not have highly diversified product lines. The area managers are given decentralized decision-making authority, and they coordinate practically all of the operations within their geographic areas. The geographic design is illustrated in Figure 18–5.

Functional design.   When an MNC uses *functional design,* managers at the corporate headquarters, who report to the chief executive, are given global responsibilities for such functions as production, marketing, and financing. Each manager has the authority to plan and control worldwide operations within the function she manages. The functional design is useful for an MNC with a very limited product line, because duplication of effort can be avoided. Extractive industries such as oil and gas often use this design, illustrated in Figure 18–6.

No organizational structure is suitable in all cases, for multinationals or for companies that operate only at home. You saw in Chapter 7 that organizational design is affected by numerous factors. A multinational company in a high-technology industry, for example, probably would not organize around geographic regions. More likely, it would use a functional design. A company with relatively inexperienced managers, meanwhile, probably would not use a product design.

Another factor that influences the organizing function of a multinational company is the degree to which management is home-country oriented, host-country oriented, or world oriented. How management views itself and the organization will affect how it organizes the firm in foreign countries. Table 18–5 shows how management's

Figure 18–5 Geographic organization design.

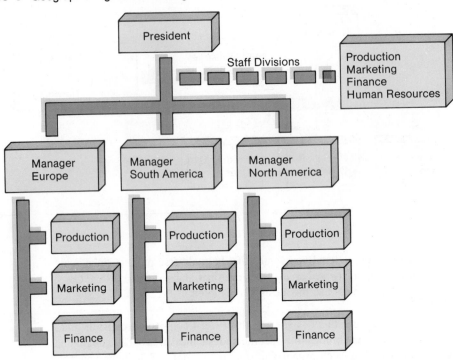

particular orientation can influence the organizational design. The figure also demonstrates the impact that the company's orientation can have on decision making, control, performance evaluation, communication, and staffing.

The Leading Function

Leadership approaches vary in effectiveness from nation to nation because styles of leadership and motivation incentives are influenced by a variety of factors. So effective management of an MNC requires managers to understand the needs and expectations of the people in the nations where the firm operates. Earlier, we noted that attitudes toward work, competition in the workplace, and authority vary greatly among cultures. Thus, leadership styles that might be effective in America, Canada, Great Britain, and parts of Western Europe probably would not work as well in Mexico, Africa, Turkey, Taiwan, or South America. In other words, cultures not only differ greatly, but so may the dominant needs of the people in different countries.

Because substantial differences can exist between the leadership styles and ways of doing business in many countries, a primary issue in managing the MNC's facility in a host country is whether local or expatriate managers should staff the facility. An *expatriate* is an MNC employee transferred to the facility from the MNC's home base

Figure 18–6 Functional organization design.

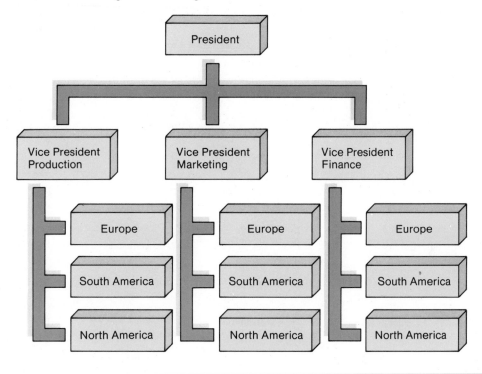

or from a facility in some other country. Well over 250,000 U.S. citizens work as expatriates in MNC facilities abroad.

The staffing decision requires evaluating many factors which both favor and disfavor the use of expatriates abroad. A number of these factors are shown in Table 18–6. Importantly, the use of expatriates ensures that the MNC facility has the necessary managerial skills to oversee the operation. This advantage is noteworthy especially in LDCs where there exists a shortage of managerial skills. However, the use of expatriates is much more costly than hiring local managers; many MNCs estimate that expatriates are three times more expensive than are locals. The high costs are due to the double taxing of an expatriate's compensation, and extra costs such as educational and family-related expenses.[41]

Although many MNCs staff a substantial number of management positions with expatriates, the failure rate of U.S. expatriate managers overseas is significant. Experts estimate that on average, 30 percent of all expatriate assignments end in failure often with the manager returning home sooner than planned.[42] Several reasons account for

---

[41]Grosse and Kujawa, *International Business,* pp. 480–81.

[42]See Rosalie L. Tung, "Expatriate Assignments: Enhancing Success and Minimizing Failure," *Academy of Management Executive,* May 1987, pp. 117–26.

Table 18–5 Management orientation and impact on the organizational design.

Organizational Design	Home-Country Oriented	Host-Country Oriented	World Oriented
Complexity of organization	Complex in home country, simple in subsidiaries	Varied and independent	Increasingly complex and interdependent
Authority; decision making	High in headquarters	Relatively low in headquarters	Aim for collaborative approach between headquarters and subsidiaries
Evaluation and control	Home standards applied for persons and performance	Determined locally	Find standards which are universal and local
Rewards and punishments; incentives	High in headquarters, low in subsidiaries	Wide variations; can be high or low rewards for subsidiary performance	International and local executives rewarded for reaching local and worldwide objectives
Communication; information flow	High volume to subsidiaries; orders, commands, advice	Little to and from headquarters, little between subsidiaries	Both ways, and between subsidiaries; heads of subsidiaries part of management team
Staffing, recruiting, development	Recruit and develop people of home country for key positions everywhere in the world	Develop people of local nationality for key positions in their own country	Develop best people everywhere in the world for key positions everywhere in the world

Source: Adapted from Howard V. Perlmutter, "The Tortuous Evolution of the Multinational Corporation," *Columbia Journal of World Business,* January–February 1969, p. 12.

such disappointing performance. Often the expatriate has a problem adjusting to the cultural and business environment in the host country. Family-related problems are also a frequent factor. Some expatriate managers also lack the special characteristics and abilities that an overseas assignment requires such as communication skills, flexibility, adaptability to change, emotional maturity, and the ability to work with people with different backgrounds, perspectives, and culture. These human relational skills are not emphasized by many MNCs in the selection of individuals for expatriate assignments overseas.[43]

---

[43]Ibid. Also see John S. McClenahen, "Why U.S. Managers Fail Overseas," *Industry Week,* November 16, 1987, pp. 71ff.

Table 18–6 Factors affecting the employment of expatriates or local nationals in a host country facility.

Factors Favoring Expatriates

Expatriates possess technical and managerial skills.

Using expatriates enhances communications between the parent and the subsidiary.

The presence of expatriates promotes the foreign or MNC image.

Parent/subsidiary relations are facilitated by the presence of expatriates familiar with the corporate culture.

The assignment of expatriates is part of their professional development program, and it improves senior management's decision making.

Factors Favoring Local Nationals

The total compensation paid to local nationals is usually considerably less than that paid to expatriates.

No host country cultural adaptation is necessary when local nationals are used.

Using local nationals is consistent with a promote-from-within policy.

No work permits are needed with local nationals.

Using local nationals promotes a local image.

Using expatriates with special employment contracts rather than local nationals may run afoul of local equal employment opportunity regulations.

Source: Robert Grosse and Duane Kujawa, *International Business: Theory and Managerial Applications* (Homewood, Ill.: Richard D. Irwin, 1988), p. 480. Reprinted with permission of the publisher.

The Controlling Function

Evaluating and controlling performance is essential to the success of MNCs. Obviously, the more global the operation, the more difficult the controlling function becomes. The control concepts discussed in earlier chapters are also applicable to MNCs; however, the control function is not used in some countries to the same degree it is used in the United States, because of cultural differences. Such concepts as performance appraisals and quality control may have little meaning in certain countries. But the implementation of control in the international environment requires the same three basic conditions employed domestically: *standards, information,* and *action.*

In establishing *standards* for MNCs, consideration must be given not only to overall corporate objectives but also to local conditions. This often involves bringing local managers into the planning process. As citizens of the country in which they work, these individuals can provide vital input. They can help establish standards of performance that contribute to organizational objectives without causing intercultural conflict.

Information reporting actual performance and permitting appraisal of that performance against standards is necessary. Problems can occur here which may not appear in domestic organizations. For example, should profitability be measured in local currency or the home currency? The value of different currencies may cause headquarters to arrive at different performance measures than those of local managers. Finally, the long distances involved can cause managers to fill information systems with a great deal of irrelevant information or too much information. Management information systems must be designed or altered to minimize the amount of information necessary for control.

Managerial *action* to correct deviations is the final step of the controlling function. The possibilities range from total centralization of decisions (all operating decisions are made at corporate headquarters) to a situation where international units are independent and autonomous. In the majority of cases, most action is taken by international managers with specific guidelines from corporate headquarters.[44] Effective managerial control of a global enterprise is extremely important—and extremely complex.

THE MNC AND THE CONTINGENCY APPROACH TO MANAGEMENT

The MNC is the type of organization that virtually demands a contingency approach to management. In fact, the MNC presents a special challenge to managers. Effective managerial performance in the international environment means managers must carefully consider the same factors outlined in the opening section of this book. What works in one part of the globe may be a failure or worse, a disaster, in another part.[45] The contingency approach to management, with its emphasis on adaptability, is the key to effective international management.

MANAGEMENT SOLUTION

CHINA SIGNS A $1 BILLION CONTRACT FOR COMMERCIAL AIRCRAFT

Chang worked six years with the Chinese government including its leader, Deng Xiaoping, to obtain the $1 billion contract, the largest sale ever granted to any U.S. company by the Chinese government. Chang's achievement did not come easily.

To obtain the sale, Chang's efforts included spending 10 months touring China's aviation facilities to provide the government with a candid evaluation of the country's aviation capabilities. Chang found that technologically the

country's planes were current circa 1960. This finding intensified the government's realization of the need to advance the state of its aviation capabilities which helped Chang in his efforts to obtain the contract.

However, like most developing nations, China wanted more than the most advanced aircraft. The government wanted McDonnell Douglas to provide the technological and managerial know-how to build the planes. In fact, China wanted
Continued

Continued

---

[44]See Guvene G. Alpander, "Multinational Corporations: Homebase-Affiliate Relations," *California Management Review*, Spring 1978, pp. 47–53, for some examples.

[45]See Cecil G. Howard, "The Returning Overseas Executive: Cultural Shock in Reverse," *Human Resource Management*, Summer 1974, pp. 22–26; and "Bayer's Formula for Product Innovation," *International Management*, February 1978, pp. 18–22.

MANAGEMENT SOLUTION

Concluded

to build some of the planes with McDonnell Douglas overseeing their efforts.

McDonnell Douglas agreed. Under the 12-year agreement, the company is providing 30 to 45 jet aircraft to China. Five planes have been built at McDonnell Douglas' facility in Long Beach, California. However, the remaining planes are being built by Shanghai Aviation, the Chinese government-owned aviation manufacturer, at the Chinese facility under a coproduction agreement. McDonnell Douglas has assigned 42 managers to Shanghai Aviation to train and work with the Chinese managers, employees, and technicians. Many of the Chinese managers have been trained at McDonnell Douglas' California facility. All of the planes will be inspected by the Federal Aviation Administration and must be passed by the FAA.

In addition, Chinese engineers are participating in McDonnell Douglas' development of a new generation MD aircraft, and the engineers may help to construct the new plane.

Since the agreement, Chang has become president of the McDonnell Douglas China subsidiary. Presently, his most challenging task has been to help turn Shanghai Aviation into a facility that can manufacture planes of the quality that will pass FAA standards. Cultural differences between American and Chinese managers have been faced. McDonnell Douglas has found Chinese workers to be hard working, eager, intelligent, but reluctant to make decisions. However, both American and Chinese employees are learning to work together, deal with conflict, and face decision-making tasks.

McDonnell Douglas is confident that the agreement will result in a productive, long-lasting relationship with the Chinese government. However, the company also realizes that any further sales will also require sharing McDonnell Douglas' technology and managerial expertise with its new customer.

Source: Adapted from Louis Kraar, "How One Man Landed China's $1 Billion Order," *Fortune*, August 18, 1986, pp. 46ff.

MANAGEMENT SUMMARY

- ☐ The global enterprise, or multinational company (MNC), presents a challenge to future managers—the challenge to perform the managerial functions effectively in an international environment.

- ☐ The decision to become an MNC involves determining the international market to be served, the products or services to be produced and marketed, and the strategy of entry into the selected market.

- ☐ The MNC decision requires evaluating the primary characteristics of an international setting—its cultural, economic, and political environments.

- ☐ Differences in culture can result in differing attitudes toward the importance of work, competition, authority, material possessions, risk taking, time, profits, and other factors.

- ☐ Economic differences in income levels, growth trends, inflation rates, balance of payments, and the stability of the currency and overall economy can significantly affect MNC performance.

☐ A government's attitude toward imports and direct investment, and government efficiency and stability are important characteristics of a country's political environment.

☐ The MNC requires a contingency approach to management. The contingency approach, with its emphasis on adaptability, can be the key to effective international management.

REVIEW AND DISCUSSION QUESTIONS

1. What major factors draw a company into international business? Discuss and provide examples where possible.

2. Do you believe you would be effective as an expatriate manager? If so, discuss why. If not, identify and discuss the reasons why.

3. The chapter discusses cultural, economic, and political aspects of the international environment that substantially affect the performance of an MNC. Are there other factors? Discuss.

4. How does the contingency approach to management (Chapter 1) relate to managing an MNC? Explain.

5. Based on your knowledge of international management, outline a training program that would effectively prepare U.S. managers in an MNC for an expatriate assignment in Japan.

6. Do the social responsibilities of managerial actions differ for MNCs in their domestic and international operations? Discuss.

7. Of the four managerial functions (planning, organizing, leading, controlling), which function do you believe is the most challenging to effectively perform as an MNC in different international environments? Explain.

8. Many risk experts assert that accurate political risk analysis is a very difficult task. Why?

9. If you have visited a country besides the United States, briefly consider the characteristics of the country's culture which you observed. How would these characteristics affect managing a U.S. facility in the country?

10. "How effective an individual is in international management will be determined by how well he or she can adjust to local conditions." Do you agree? Discuss.

CASES

18–1 THE MAQUILADORAS

Located in four Mexican towns along the 2,000-mile Mexico–U.S. border are what Texas Governor Bill Clements asserts is "the best-kept industrial secret in the United States." The secret is the maquiladoras, foreign (mostly U.S.) owned and managed factories that assemble parts transported across the border into products. Once assembled, the products are shipped back to the United States for sale.

In a few years, this maquila industry along Mexico's border has grown to over 1,000 maquiladoras in Tijuana, Nogales, Juarez, and Matomoros. (*Maquiladoras* is "handwork" in Spanish.) The plants employ over 300,000 Mexicans.

The reason for this booming industry: astoundingly low labor costs. Mexico is a lesser developed country, and its peso has been devalued several times. As a result, the country's minimum *daily* wage is less than $3, and a weekly paycheck is less than $15. These labor costs are less than half of the prevailing wages in Hong Kong, Singapore, South Korea, and other low-labor-cost countries where U.S. companies have constructed assembly plants. The U.S. manufacturers pay no tariffs on the parts shipped into Mexico as long as the assembled products are reimported to the United States. Duties on reimported parts are very low.

In short, the maquiladoras are enabling U.S. manufacturers to substantially reduce their production costs. As a result, literally hundreds of U.S. companies have set up assembly shops in Mexico. For example, General Motors has established 17 plants for its labor-intensive assembly work such as cutting and sewing car seats.

Asian and especially Japanese companies are also fast establishing maquiladoras in the border towns. Over 30 Japanese manufacturers already assemble there. Hitachi, for example, assembles about 100,000 color TV chassis in its Tijuana maquiladora each year. The chassis are then transported to Hitachi's plant in Anaheim, California, for final assembly. Matsushita has a plant in Tijuana where 1,600 Mexican workers assemble TV chassis. Sony, Sanyo, and 100 other Japanese manufacturers are expected to either build more or expand their maquiladoras in the next few years.

The maquiladoras movement has likewise provided benefits for the Mexican economy. They are transforming the four Mexican communities which were once tourist towns, into industrial centers. The maquiladoras also provide badly needed employment for Mexican workers. In Mexico, earning $15 a week provides a middle-class existence for many citizens who otherwise would remain unemployed. The output from the maquiladoras is second only to oil as Mexico's top foreign exchange earner.

However, the work is long and demanding for the $15 weekly paycheck. Employees work about 49 hours a week in a factory which is typically a one-story, windowless, concrete building. Inside, the surroundings are clean but spare, often comprised of long tables, chairs, and parts bins. There, employees across the plants assemble a wide array of products—computer keyboards, toys, carburetors, refrigerators, garage door openers, and even waterbeds. A few plants sort coupons; one plant even sorts walnuts. Over one third of the assembly work in the maquiladoras involves the production of clothing.

For management, operating the maquiladoras, while profitable, can also be challenging. Most of the American managers live in the United States just across the border. Each of the major Mexican maquiladoras communities is located less than an hour's driving time from a large U.S. community. Tijuana, for example, is about a half hour's drive from San Diego. Each day, the managers commute; the drive back often requires hours due to the customs inspection of cars traveling from Mexico into the United States. Electrical blackouts are also common, and telephoning a Mexican border town from the United States often requires 15 to 20 attempts.

Turnover at the maquiladoras is also a problem, often running from 70 to 100 percent each year. Younger, unskilled employees continually seek better working conditions and a shorter distance from their home (often in the mountains) to work. The companies won't increase the minimum wage to attract recruits; rather they will offer extras such as inexpensive food in the factory cafeteria, attendance bonuses, discounts on bus rides to work, and Michael Jackson records.

The maquiladoras industry will continue to grow at a projected rate of over 12 percent each year. However, concern is mounting among the AFL-CIO union organization and other U.S. groups that the establishment of maquiladoras by U.S. companies is contributing to unemployment in the United States. Said one union official, "The more maquiladoras the companies build, the more layoffs and the fewer jobs there are for Americans."

Questions

1. From an international management perspective, what other challenges are involved in managing a maquiladora?

2. In your opinion, is the union concern about maquiladoras merited? Explain.

3. Some observers respond to the union concern asserting that maquiladoras actually help employment in the United States. Do you agree? If so, how?

Source: Adapted from Brian O'Reilly, "Business Makes a Run for the Border," *Fortune,* August 18, 1986, pp. 70ff; Eugene Carlson, "Japanese Companies Increase Presence Near Mexico Border," *The Wall Street Journal,* December 22, 1987, p. 19; and Kathleen K. Wiegner, "How to Mix Sake and Tequila," *Forbes,* March 23, 1987, pp. 48ff.

18–2 GENERAL METROPOLITAN LTD. EXPANDS TO THE UNITED STATES

In 1948, Sir Maxwell Joseph purchased a hotel in London. From that beginning, he built General Metropolitan Ltd. into one of Great Britain's largest and most diversified companies. In the early 1980s, it achieved almost $7 billion in sales from a broad range of businesses: hotels, liquor, food, gaming, and leisure products. In fact, the company had become so successful that Sir Maxwell Joseph decided it was too big for Great Britain. In 1980, 88 percent of its profits came from its home base, and it had been blocked by law from making any new significant acquisitions. Besides, Great Britain's economy held little promise for additional growth.

As a result, Grand Met decided to enter the largest consumer market in the world: the United States. In the early 1980s, Grand Met acquired Liggett Group Inc., which was to become its vehicle for expansion into the United States. Liggett is a consumer-oriented firm, with Liggett & Myers Tobacco Co., Inc., Alpo dog food, sporting goods operations, and soft drink bottling and liquor distribution businesses.

Grand Met had a three-part plan for expansion in the United States. First, it hoped to broaden its U.S. sales of liquor, which included Grand Met's own brands such as J&B Rare Scotch. Second, Liggett was to be the base for adding companies in the food ingredients industry (it soon gained three U.S. ingredient producers). Third, it planned to buy upper-class hotels in major U.S. cities and convert them to the Grand Met format that had been successful in Great Britain and Europe.

Grand Met management believed that its expertise in consumer markets would be an asset in the United States. However, it planned to use U.S. management, a new tactic for Grand Met. During the 1970s, Grand Met had attempted direct expansions into Italy and France, but it was unable to compete with local industry. An executive stated, "We learned the sheer danger of assuming you can understand another country from here. We learned you have got to go in and make a partnership."

Questions

1. What is your opinion of Grand Met's entry strategy into foreign markets? What other approaches could it have used? Do they offer any advantages?

2. What is your opinion of Grand Met's policy of utilizing local managers? Can you foresee any problems?

3. What are some of the problems Grand Met faced before its Liggett acquisition and will face as a result of the acquisition? How are they similar to those faced by American MNCs?

Source: This case is adapted from "Grand Metropolitan: A British Giant Expands into U.S. Consumer Markets," *Business Week*, August 24, 1981, pp. 54, 59.

EXERCISE

18–1 LAUNCHING AN INTERNATIONAL BUSINESS

Purpose: This activity is designed to enhance your understanding of the key elements of the international environment and their impact on expanding a business internationally.

Setting Up the Exercise: The instructor will divide the class into groups comprised of four students each. Each group should complete the following project:

1. Assume that your group is the top-management team of a manufacturing company. Your team's first task is to select a product which your company manufactures. Once you've selected the product, assume that your company makes the product domestically and wants to expand production overseas. Specifically, your company seeks to produce and sell the product in a Latin American, European, or Asian country.

2. Select a country for your international expansion. Once you've identified the nation, conduct an assessment of the country as an international market for your product. Do so by:

   a. Conducting library research on the cultural, economic, and political aspects of the country's environment.

   b. In reviewing your research, answer the following questions:

      (1) What is the level of demand for your product in this potential market?

      (2) In what ways do the cultural, economic, and political aspects of the country's environment facilitate the success of your product in the market?

      (3) In what ways do these environmental aspects hinder the success of your product?

      (4) In your team's opinion, what are the primary challenges in establishing manufacturing facilities and launching your product in this market?

3. Prepare a five- to seven-page typed report which provides an overall profile of your selected market and presents your responses to these questions. Be prepared to discuss your overall findings in class discussion.

A Learning Note: This exercise effectively illustrates the importance of the international environment in launching manufacturing and marketing activities in an international market. Students should quickly realize the complexities involved in expanding business abroad which is one major reason why a number of overseas ventures fail.

NINETEEN

Social Responsibility and Management Ethics

LEARNING OBJECTIVES

After completing Chapter 19, you should be able to:

Define: *social responsibility* in terms that reflect your view of the role of corporations in society.

State: how a manager's ethics affect decisions regarding social responsibility.

Describe: the various internal and external beneficiaries of a company's socially responsible actions.

Explain: the primary characteristics of the metrocorporation, and the traditional and well-tempered corporations.

Discuss: the purpose and content of a *corporate code of ethics* and the problems inherent in making a code work in organizations.

A CASE OF CONSUMER DECEPTION AT BEECH-NUT

For years, Beach-Nut® Nutrition Corporation had maintained a nationwide reputation for producing high-quality baby food with all-natural ingredients. Its most successful product line was apple juice which was extensively marketed as containing pure "100% fruit juice."

However, in the early 1980s, Beech-Nut's director of research and development seriously questioned whether the company's best-selling product was indeed all natural. Jerome J. LiCari had tested the juice's ingredients extensively. Although no test then existed that would unquestionably determine whether the ingredients were pure apple juice, LiCari's tests built a substantial case that the ingredients purchased from Beech-Nut's supplier were likely phony.

LiCari was aware that the supplier had denied Beech-Nut officials permission to inspect the supplier's concentrate processing facility. He also knew that the supplier was providing the product's ingredients at costs that were 20 percent below the market.

In 1981, LiCari wrote a memo which summarized his tests and concluded that the "tremendous amount of circumstantial evidence" comprised a "grave case" against Beech-Nut's supplier. LiCari sent the memo to Beech-Nut's top management and waited for a response.

(The Management Solution to this Management Incident can be found at the end of this chapter.)

The terms *social responsibility, business ethics,* and *management ethics* appear frequently in popular and technical literature. Every day, newspapers report business activities considered by some people to be socially irresponsible and unethical. Yet others think such actions are quite proper, both from a social and ethical standpoint.

One purpose of this chapter is to provide bases for understanding the meanings and implications of social responsibility and ethics by reviewing (1) society's expectations for corporate and managerial behavior and (2) changing business ethics. Corporate and managerial decisions and actions occur within a dynamic and complex social context. Thus, when you understand the meanings of *social responsibility* and *business ethics,* you recognize that they change with time and circumstance.[1]

This chapter also provides guidelines to help managers determine what is socially and ethically responsible behavior. Managers must be aware of their own responsibilities for instilling acceptable ethical standards throughout their organizations. They also must create or continue organizational procedures and policies that encourage disclosure of unethical behavior. Laws should establish the minimum standards for what is responsible and ethical in business and managerial behavior. In other words, legality must be the recognized threshold of all managerial and organizational action.

THE MEANINGS OF SOCIAL RESPONSIBILITY

A recent review of literature identified at least nine meanings for social responsibility.[2] These nine meanings can be classified in three general categories: *social obligation, social reaction,* and *social responsiveness.*[3]

Social Responsibility as Social Obligation

This view holds that a corporation engages in socially responsible behavior when it pursues profit only within the constraints of law. Because society supports business by allowing it to exist, business is *obligated* to repay society by making profits. Thus legal behavior in pursuit of profit is socially responsible behavior, and *any behavior that is illegal or not in pursuit of profit is socially irresponsible.*

This view is particularly associated with economist Milton Friedman and others who believe that society creates firms to pursue one primary purpose—to produce goods and services efficiently and maximize profits.[4] As Friedman has stated, "There is one and only one social responsibility of business—to use its resources and engage in activities designed to increase its profits so long as it stays within the rules of the

---

[1] Ronald L. Crawford and Harold A. Gram, "Social Responsibility as Interorganizational Transaction," *Academy of Management Review,* October 1978, p. 880.

[2] Archie B. Carroll, "A Three-Dimensional Conceptual Model of Corporate Performance," *Academy of Management Review,* October 1979, pp. 497–505.

[3] Suggested by S. Prakash Sethi, "A Conceptual Framework for Environmental Analysis of Social Issues and Evaluation of Business Response Patterns," *Academy of Management Review,* January 1979, pp. 63–74.

[4] Milton Friedman, *Capitalism and Freedom* (Chicago: University of Chicago Press, 1962).

game, which is to say, engages in open and free competition without deception or fraud."[5]

The proponents of social responsibility as social obligation offer four primary arguments in support of their view. First, they assert, businesses are accountable to their shareholders, the owners of the corporation. Thus, management's sole responsibility is to serve the shareholder's interests by managing the company to produce profits from which the shareholders benefit.

Second, socially responsible activities such as social improvement programs should be determined by law, by public policy, and by the actions and contributions of private individuals. As representatives of the people, the government (via legislation and allocation of tax revenues) is best equipped to determine the nature of social improvements and to realize those improvements in society. Businesses contribute in this regard by paying taxes to the government which rightfully determines how they should be spent.

Third, if management allocates profits to social improvement activities, it is abusing its authority. As Friedman notes, these actions amount to taxation without representation. Management is taxing the shareholders by taking their profits and spending them on activities that have no immediate profitable return to the company. And management is doing so without input from shareholders. Because managers are not elected public officials, they are also taking actions that affect society without being accountable to society. Further, this type of nonprofit-seeking activity may be both unwise and unworkable because managers are not trained to make noneconomic decisions.

Fourth, these actions by management may work to the disadvantage of society. In this sense, the financial costs of social activities may over time cause the price of the company's goods and services to increase, and customers would pay the bill. Managers have acted in a manner contrary to the interests of the customers and ultimately the shareholders.

Although many people disagree with this meaning, *social responsibility* can refer to behavior directed exclusively (but legally) toward the pursuit of profit. A manager can, with some justification, state that he has discharged his *obligation* to society by creating goods and services in exchange for profit within the limits defined by law.

Social Responsibility as Social Reaction

A second meaning of social responsibility is behavior that is in reaction to "currently prevailing social norms, values, and performance expectations."[6] This pervasive view emphasizes that society is entitled to more than the mere provision of goods and services. At minimum, business must be accountable for the ecological, environmental, and social costs incurred by its actions. At maximum, business must react and contribute

---

[5]Milton Friedman, "The Social Responsibility of Business Is to Increase Its Profits," *New York Times Magazine,* September 1970, pp. 33, 122–26.

[6]Sethi, "A Conceptual Framework," p. 66.

to solving society's problems (even those that cannot be directly attributed to business). Thus, this viewpoint holds that corporate contribution to charity *is* socially responsible.

A somewhat restrictive interpretation of social responsibility as social reaction is that it involves only voluntary actions. This interpretation seeks to separate corporate actions that are *required* by economic or legal imperative from those that are initiated by voluntary, altruistic motives. This narrower view implies that a corporation pursuing only socially obligated behavior is not socially responsible because behavior is required, not voluntary.

Keith Davis, a leading spokesman for the view that social responsibility extends beyond the law has stated, "A firm is not being socially responsible if it merely complies with the minimum requirements of the law. . . . Social responsibility goes one step further. It [social responsibility] is a firm's acceptance of social obligation beyond the requirements of the law."[7] A firm that accepts social obligation only in reaction to pressure groups, consumer boycotts, or adverse publicity is not socially responsible, in this view.

Whether the firm's actions are voluntary or not, a broader interpretation of the social reaction view identifies actions that exceed legal requirements as socially responsible. Typically, these actions are reactions to expectations of specific groups: for example, unions, stockholders, social activists, and consumerists. Because these groups expect more than legal minimums, firms can simply decide not to react. Favorable reaction, however, is considered the socially responsible response.

The essence of this view of social responsibility is that firms are reactive. Demands are made of them by certain groups, and the firms are socially responsible when they react, voluntarily or involuntarily, to satisfy these demands.

Social Responsibility as Social Responsiveness

According to this view, socially responsible behaviors are anticipatory and preventive, rather than reactive and restorative.[8] The term *social responsiveness* has become widely used in recent years to refer to actions that exceed social obligation and social reaction.[9] The characteristics of socially responsive behavior include taking stands on public issues, accounting willingly for actions to any group, anticipating future needs of society and moving toward satisfying them, and communicating with the government about existing and anticipated socially desirable legislation.

A socially responsive corporation actively seeks solutions to social problems. Progressive managers, according to this view, apply corporate skills and resources to every problem—from run-down housing to youth employment, from local schools to small-business job creation. Such behavior reflects the "true" meaning of social re-

---

[7]Keith Davis, "The Case for and against Business Assumption of Social Responsibilities," *Academy of Management Journal,* June 1973, p. 313.

[8]Sethi, "A Conceptual Framework," p. 66.

[9]Peter Arlow and Martin J. Gannon, "Social Responsiveness, Corporate Structure, and Economic Performance," *Academy of Management Review,* April 1982, p. 235.

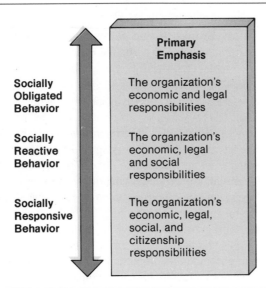

Figure 19–1
A continuum
of social
responsibility.

sponsibility for social-responsiveness advocates, and when corporate executives commit their organizations to such endeavors, they are likely to receive substantial public approval.

The social-responsiveness view is the broadest meaning of social responsibility. It places managers and their organizations in a position far removed from the traditional one of singular concern with economic means and ends. This view rests on two premises: (1) corporations *should* be involved in preventing, as well as solving, social problems; and (2) corporations "are perhaps the most effective problem-solving organizations in a capitalist society."[10]

A Continuum of Social Responsibility

The three general meanings of social responsibility can be depicted as a continuum, shown in Figure 19–1. At one extreme of the continuum is social obligation—business behavior that reflects only the firm's economic and legal responsibilities. Occupying the middle position is social reaction—behavior demanded by groups with a direct stake in the organization's actions. The furthest extreme, social responsiveness, is behavior that reflects anticipatory, proactive, and preventive expectations.

A corporation can choose to operate anywhere along the continuum. To be socially reactive, however, implies the firm's acceptance of social obligation. Similarly, to be socially responsive requires both social-obligation and social-reaction behavior.

---

[10]H. Gordon Fitch, "Achieving Corporate Social Responsibility," *Academy of Management Review,* January 1976, p. 45.

SPECIFIC SOCIALLY RESPONSIBLE ACTIVITIES

So far, the discussion has revolved around *abstract* concepts of social responsibility. However, an organization translates its particular concept of social responsibility into concrete expressions of social responsibility via specific, deliberate activities.

Socially responsible activities can be classified in different ways. One such classification provides eight categories of socially responsible actions. A business can take socially responsible actions in terms of its *product line* by manufacturing a safe, reliable, and high-quality product and in its *marketing practices* by, for example, being truthful and complete in its product advertising. Socially responsible activities in *employee education and training* can include effectively preparing employees to perform jobs well and retraining rather than laying off employees when new technology is implemented. Concerning *environmental control,* a business may be socially responsible by implementing production technology that reduces the amount of pollutants produced by manufacturing processes.

Actions in *employee relations, benefits, and satisfaction with work* can include providing benefits that accommodate important but unfulfilled employee needs such as providing an on-site day-care facility for parent employees. In the area of *employment and advancement of minorities or women*, businesses may choose to be socially responsible by focusing efforts on hiring and professionally developing minorities. Efforts to provide a clean, safe and comfortable working environment are socially responsible activities in the realm of *employee safety and health.*

Some businesses, especially large corporations, focus socially responsible efforts in the area of *corporate philanthropy,* by making donations to universities, arts and cultural foundations, the underprivileged, community development projects, and other groups and causes in society. Today, corporations and foundations provide about 11 percent ($10 billion) of all financial philanthropic contributions made in the United States. Corporate giving also occurs via donations of volunteered employee time, equipment, loaned facilities, and low-rate loans to nonprofit organizations.[11]

As these categories indicate, the objectives and types of socially responsible activities can vary widely. The following Management Application provides a brief look at 10 very different socially responsible efforts.

MANAGEMENT APPLICATION

10 ACTS OF SOCIAL RESPONSIBILITY

Organizations approach social responsibility with richly differing objectives, activities, and interests. To provide a look at how corporate involvement in social responsibility varies, here is a brief overview of efforts by 10 corporations.

---

[11]Stanley J. Modic, "Movers and Shakers," *Industry Week*, January 18, 1988, pp. 47ff.

Time Inc.   The publisher of *Time* magazine maintains a "Time to Read" literacy program in 18 sites across the United States. The program trains volunteer tutors (many are Time employees) to teach participants to improve reading skills. Learners receive a subscription to *Time* and to one other magazine published by Time Inc. The program is active at Camp Hill, Pennsylvania, where Time retirees and employees tutor inmates of the State Correctional Institution.

G. D. Searle.   The pharmaceutical manufacturer provides heart and high blood pressure medications free to needy patients who have no medical insurance and can't afford the drugs. G. D. Searle spends about $10 million on the program.

Digital Equipment.   In 1983, employees at Digital's Hudson, Massachusetts, semiconductor plant asked the computer manufacturer to look into the puzzling high number of miscarriages experienced by women working on the semiconductor assembly line. The company responded by funding a study conducted by the University of Massachusetts which identified a 39 percent miscarriage rate on the line compared to 18 percent for the plant overall and 10 to 20 percent among the public. While the study was conducted, Digital encouraged all pregnant women on the line to transfer to another job and provided transfers for all concerned women of childbearing age. Employees were fully informed of the study's results before publication; AT&T responded to the findings by banning pregnant employees from its chip assembly lines.

Levi Strauss.   Soon after the recent passage of immigration laws, Levi Strauss published "Ten Steps to Citizenship," a 36-page special edition of the company newspaper targeted at illegal aliens in the company's work force. The edition described the steps required to obtain U.S. citizenship. Levi Strauss has also provided loans to employees in the company's Texas and New Mexico facilities who are seeking amnesty under the law.

Ralston Purina.   The world's largest pet food manufacturer maintains a "Pets for People" program in more than 70 cities. The program works with local humane organizations to place pets with senior citizens. Every adopter of a pet receives a supply of Ralston Purina pet food; the company also pays $100 of the adopter's pet costs (e.g., expenses for shots, neutering).

AT&T.   The telecommunications company is the first major employer in the United States to offer an anti-apartheid matching savings plan for its employees. Employees who invest their savings in the plan may select a portfolio that excludes investments in any businesses that operate in South Africa. For every $1 an employee invests, AT&T matches with 67 cents.

Travelers.   The insurer has launched a part-time employment program for retirees from its own company and other organizations. Several hundred retirees work part-time at the Travelers' corporate headquarters in Hartford, Conn.

Scott Paper.   The paper products manufacturer maintains the seven-product line "Helping Hands," which is a charity effort. For every product sold, Scott donates five cents to one of six national charities.

McDonald's.   McDonald's is the first fast-food chain to provide its menu in Braille at all of its locations.

Dollar Dry Dock Savings Bank.   This New York bank issues a VISA credit card which pictures a drawing of a Vietnam war veteran. Every time a customer uses the credit card, the bank makes a donation to the Vietnam Veterans of America. The bank also donates $4 of the $20 annual card fee to the veterans association.

Source: Adapted from "Company Performance Roundup" reports prepared by Milton R. Moskowitz, *Business and Society Review*, 1987–1988 issues.

Another way to classify socially responsible actions is according to the *beneficiaries* of each action. In some instances, the organization's *customers* benefit; in other instances, the *employees* benefit. Beyond employees and customers are definable interest groups, such as racial and ethnic groups, women's groups, and governmental agencies. In a sense, these groups are organizations that transact business with the corporation. The focus of these transactions is not exchange of economic goods and services, but exchange of concessions based on relative power. In addition to customers, employees, and interest groups, there are abstract beneficiaries, such as future generations, society at large, and the common good. Activities such as giving grants to the arts are directed to these beneficiaries. For simplicity, two general classes of beneficiaries can be identified: *internal* and *external*.

INTERNAL BENEFICIARIES

Three groups of internal beneficiaries are apparent: *customers, employees,* and *stockholders* (owners). These groups have immediate and often conflicting stakes in the organization. Corporate activities in response to each group can be classified as obligatory, reactive, or responsive.

Responsibilities to Customers

Much of the discussion about the responsibility of business toward its customers is critical.[12] One target of criticism has been the business organization's responsibilities regarding products and marketing.

One social obligation of business relates to product characteristics: quality, safety, packaging, and performance. The relative importance of these characteristics varies among products over time. Even within one industry, the relative importance shifts. For example, Ralph Nader's book, *Unsafe at Any Speed* in 1965 raised the issue of automobile safety.

The safety issue reached its highest point in public awareness in the late 1970s when the Ford Motor Company paid approximately $500 million in liability damages because of accidental deaths and injuries to drivers and passengers of defective Ford

---

[12]The following discussion is based on Frederick D. Sturdivant, *Business and Society: A Managerial Approach,* 3d ed. (Homewood, Ill.: Richard D. Irwin, 1985).

Pinto automobiles. The public was incensed when a Ford internal memo containing a cost/benefit analysis of repairing versus not repairing the defective cars leaked out.[13] According to the memo, repairing the defective cars (at $11 per car) would cost Ford $137 million. If the defective cars were not recalled and repaired, the memo stated that 180 burn deaths would likely occur and would cost $200,000 each (this cost estimate is probably based on estimated insurance payments). The memo further stated that 180 burn injuries would likely occur and would cost $67,000 each. According to the memo, not repairing the cars would cost Ford about $49 million to compensate for death and injury. Ford Motor Co. did not recall the cars.[14]

Other companies, however, have been socially responsive concerning product safety. Levi Strauss, for example, spent considerable sums to reduce the formaldehyde content of its Sta-Prest slacks well below legally mandated levels. The company acted to eliminate any potential harm to consumers. John Deere has maintained a tradition of industry leadership in product safety. The company was the first tractor manufacturer to provide a rollover protective structure for its tractors which pioneered industry standards for user protection in farm and construction equipment.

Laws and regulations establish the bases for judging product safety, but market and competitive forces often set standards for product quality. A case in point is the American automobile industry. In the early 1980s, this industry faced declining demand for its products, due partly to a recession and high interest rates, but also to competition from Japanese auto manufacturers.

The success of Japanese automobiles rests largely on their superior quality. American consumers believe that Japanese cars are of better quality than American cars, and they express this judgment in their buying decisions. The response of American auto manufacturers has been to implement quality control programs and to publicize those programs in advertisements.

The issue of social responsibility toward customers is relatively fixed at one extreme (as in instances where specific legal directives define product safety) and quite fluid at the other (as in instances where there are general expectations regarding price/quality relationships). Many firms choose to meet their responsibilities to customers by responding promptly to complaints, by providing complete and accurate product information, and by implementing advertising programs that are completely truthful regarding product performance.

Responsibilities to Employees

Management's responsibilities to employees can be minimally discharged by meeting the legal requirements that relate to employee/employer relationships. Such laws address issues associated with, for example, the physical conditions of work (particularly the safety and health issues), wage and hour provisions, and union and unionization.

---

[13]Mark Dowie, "Two Million Firetraps on Wheels," *Business and Society Review,* Fall 1977, pp. 67–72.

[14]Ibid, p. 69.

The thrust of these laws is to encourage management to create safe and productive workplaces within which an employee's civil rights are not violated.

In addition to these responsibilities, the modern corporate practice of providing fringe benefits—retirement funds, health and hospitalization insurance, and accident insurance—has extended the range of socially obligated activity. In some instances, these practices are in response to concerted employee pressure, typically through union activity.

A company may assume other socially responsible activities such as providing comprehensive employee training, career development, counseling, and establishing employee assistance programs (EAPs) to help employees with drug and alcohol problems. Today, over 9,000 U.S. businesses including more than 30 percent of the Fortune 500 companies have established EAPs.[15] A growing number of businesses are also providing day-care assistance for employees; over 3,000 companies now offer day-care services and financial assistance or referral services for child care (a 50 percent increase in company participation since 1984).[16]

These socially responsible efforts are socially reactive in nature if they are responses to pressures from employees or external parties. The efforts are socially responsive if the organization proactively initiates these activities in the absence of any substantial pressure. However, it is important to note that like many socially responsible actions, activities taken in the interest of employees can also benefit the organization. For example, several companies that have proactively established day-care centers report substantial improvement in attendance and productivity rates among participating parent employees.[17]

Responsibilities to Stockholders

Management has a responsibility to disclose fully and accurately to stockholders its uses of corporate resources and the results of those uses. The law guarantees stockholders the right to financial information and establishes minimum levels of public disclosure. The fundamental right of a stockholder is not to be guaranteed a profit, but to be guaranteed information on which a prudent investment decision can be based. The ultimate action a stockholder can take is to sell the stock.

Many argue that a manager's preeminent responsibility is to the stockholder. In their opinion, any managerial action exceeding socially obligated behavior and benefiting any group other than stockholders is a violation of the stockholder's trust and, therefore, the corporation's social responsibility. We will confront this view later in discussing the origins of the various arguments surrounding corporate involvement in any cause outside of its economic or legal interest.

---

[15]"Battling the Enemy Within," *Time,* March 17, 1986, pp. 52ff.

[16]Veronica J. Schmidt and Norman A. Scott, "Work and Family Life: A Delicate Balance," *Personnel Administrator,* August 1987, pp. 40–46.

[17]Fern Schumer Chapman, "Executive Guilt: Who's Taking Care of the Children?" *Fortune,* February 16, 1987, pp. 30–37.

The internal beneficiaries of corporate actions are the focus of much of management's socially obligated behavior. In their relations with customers, employees, and stockholders, managers are most likely to be judged socially responsible. The relationships between the corporation and its internal beneficiaries are so circumscribed by law, regulation, and custom that the corporation is bound to act out of legal obligation. To do so is no special accomplishment for the corporation. To fail to act within the law, whether intentionally or not, can lead to legal action against the corporation and its management. Therefore, corporations have greater opportunities to be socially reactive and responsive in matters involving *external beneficiaries*.

EXTERNAL BENEFICIARIES

The external beneficiaries of corporate behavior are of two types, *specific* and *general*. Both types benefit from the organization's actions, even though they may have no direct or apparent stake in it.

Specific External Beneficiaries

Modern societies consist of a great diversity of special-interest groups working to further the well-being of their members. These groups often represent rather well-defined populations seeking to redress historical grievances: racial and ethnic minorities, women, the handicapped, and the aged. They pursue their interests by bringing political and popular opinion to bear on corporate actions. Some groups succeed in having laws implemented that motivate corporations to support their efforts. For example, equal employment opportunity and affirmative action legislation obligates corporations to recruit, hire, and develop women and members of minority groups. The fundamental contention of these groups is that they have been discriminated against in the past and that corporations have played major roles in that discrimination. Thus, corporations must take some responsibility to erase the vestiges of historical discrimination and to create a new environment of equal access to employment opportunities and economic advancement.

Corporate actions involving specific external beneficiaries can be obligatory, reactive, or responsive. The corporation can be judged irresponsible, both socially and legally, if it violates these laws. But beyond minimal compliance, a corporation has considerable latitude in its implementation of affirmative action programs. How rapidly it fills its managerial ranks with minorities and women is largely a matter of discretion, as long as good faith can be demonstrated. A corporation can be deemed socially reactive if it goes beyond the letter of the law in implementing affirmative action. Socially responsive behavior not only seeks solutions to the immediate problems, but attempts to go to the very heart of the causes. Such behavior could include making special efforts to do business with minority-owned businesses, creating programs to train the chronically unemployed, and initiating career development programs for women. When such efforts are not prompted by law or pressure, they are clearly socially responsive.

The most important characteristic of these actions—whether they are obligatory, reactive, or responsive—is that the economic, social, and political well being of a specific group—and, hence, of all society—is enhanced through the corporation's efforts.

General External Beneficiaries

Programs involving general external beneficiaries often are considered to be practicing social responsibility because they elicit corporate efforts to solve or prevent general social problems. Companies have launched efforts to solve or prevent environmental or ecological problems such as water, air, and noise pollution, and waste and radiation disposal. Actions by Johnson Wax Company in the mid-1970s provide an example of activity in this area. When the first scientific research was published concerning the destructive impact of fluorocarbons on the atmosphere's ozone layer, Johnson Wax immediately withdrew all of its fluorocarbon products worldwide, years before the FDA banned fluorocarbon use. Company officials report that they initially lost business and angered some manufacturers; however, the organization chose to act quickly because it believed the product withdrawal was in society's best interests.[18]

Other organizations have acted to upgrade education, the arts, and community health through gifts and donations of executive time. For example, New York Life is one of a growing number of companies that are donating funds for AIDS research and public education programs. New York Life donated over $1 million to fund an AIDS public information advertising campaign in New York and sponsored a fund-raising benefit which raised $2 million for AIDS research.[19]

Some organizations have launched efforts to improve the quality of governmental management through leaves of absence for executives to take government positions. Other organizations have contributed to philanthropic causes such as United Way to help upgrade the quality of community life. Companies have also made contributions to overall community development. One notable example is the "Minnesota 5 Percent Club," a group of 45 companies. Each member donates at least 5 percent of its taxable profits to the development of the twin cities, Minneapolis-St. Paul.[20]

Corporations have considerable freedom in this area of social responsibility. They can choose which specific problems to become involved with—or, they can choose not to become involved at all. But business leaders recognize the growing importance of issues such as the condition of the environment. For example: "In recent industrial history, few public policy issues have had the social, political, and economic impact that this one [health, safety, and the environment] is having on many companies."[21]

---

[18]Tad Tuleja, *Beyond the Bottom Line* (New York: Facts on File Publications, 1985), p. 78.

[19]Milton R. Moskowitz, "Company Performance Roundup," *Business and Society Review*, 1987, p. 69.

[20]James O'Toole, *Vanguard Management: Redesigning the Corporate Future* (Garden City, N.Y.: Doubleday & Co., 1985), p. 359.

[21]Francis W. Steckmest, *Corporate Performance: The Key to Public Trust* (New York: McGraw-Hill, 1982), p. 109.

This statement appears in a publication prepared for the Business Roundtable, a group of influential executives whose views are representative of business leaders in general.

But why do corporations engage in behavior that cannot be related, except remotely, to their primary economic and legal responsibilities? It is a matter of fact that they do, and they do so in an atmosphere of controversy.

THE CONTEMPORARY VIEW OF CORPORATE SOCIAL RESPONSIBILITY

Since the early 1970s, society has developed the attitude that corporations must react to problems created by their own actions. This attitude has supported the idea that corporations should be proactive, that they should respond to a wide range of social problems because they have the expertise and power to do so.

The current debate on the "social responsibility of business" is not concerned with obligatory behavior; business must be law-abiding. The debate seldom is couched in terms of reactive behavior, that business should be responsible for its actions. Rather, the concern is with socially responsive behavior, and the debate turns on two points: (1) one's view of the role of corporations in society, and (2) one's view of managerial ethics.

Two views of the role of corporations in society described here are irreconcilable. Both reflect extreme viewpoints.[22]

The *traditional corporation* is an instrument of a single group—the shareholders— and has one clear-cut purpose: to conduct business for profit. The prior claim of the stockholders on earnings after taxes is unquestioned, and management does not have to balance interests in distributing the earnings. This traditional view recognizes only legal social responsibilities and leaves public interests to the care of the state. This view of the corporation emphasizes social obligations.

The competing view is the *metrocorporation,* which assumes limitless corporate social responsibility. In this type of corporation, managers accept accountability to many segments of society. The metrocorporation is far removed from the strict, limited objective of the traditional corporation: profit for the stockholders. The metrocorporation emphasizes its rights and duties as a "citizen" in its relationships with the various groups in its environment. This view emphasizes reactive and responsive behavior, and it finds strong support among the most vocal contemporary proponents of social responsiveness.

The manager must reconcile the extremes represented by these two views. The following statement, however, urges equal respect for both views:

> The large business corporation is here to stay. It is an indispensable
> instrument for getting done some of the things that people want done. It
> is neither the exclusive instrument of one class of interests nor an

---

[22]This discussion is based on Richard Eells and Clarence Walton, *Conceptual Foundations of Business* (Homewood, Ill.: Richard D. Irwin, 1961), pp. 468–76.

> indiscriminant roster of "social" interests. Like other large organizations,
> the corporation has to be tempered to the times; and as a viable
> instrument it must adapt to the changing requirements of our free,
> complex, and interdependent society.[23]

A position somewhere between the extremes of the traditional corporation and the metrocorporation will take into account public expectations, yet will not infringe on management's responsibilities to the stockholder. This viewpoint upholds a concept called *the well-tempered corporation.*[24] Proponents of this view maintain that stockholders' claims are more likely to be met if a firm develops a position as a socially responsible organization. But the definition of a socially responsible firm changes as rapidly as the values of our society do. The following statement is a realistic response to the question, "What is a socially responsible firm?"

> The answer to this question will change and eventually must be answered
> by society itself. It may be best to define the socially responsible firm as
> one that anticipates what the public will expect from it and attempts to
> meet these demands before the public focuses its criticism upon it. In a
> nutshell, the socially responsible firm is one that is responsive to (even
> anticipates) the demands of society, not only economic ones, but social
> and environmental ones as well.[25]

As this statement indicates, the emerging view of the corporation in society emphasizes anticipation and responsiveness rather than obligation and reaction. Society expects corporations to take an active role in solving a range of problems seemingly unrelated to their primary missions.

The well-tempered corporation viewpoint reflects the pervasiveness of big business. The corporate form of ownership has provided the legal and organizational means to serve mass markets. Large organizations have the resources to acquire modern technology, to attract capital investment, and to take risks. But the very strength of corporations—their size—has become a source of corporate weakness: public demands. As business faces new crises and as expectations for corporate behavior are debated, the ethics of managers ultimately become the final standards for corporate social responsibility.

MANAGERIAL ETHICS

The word *ethics* commonly refers to principles of behavior that distinguish between what is good, bad, right, and wrong.[26] Ethics are used by managers as guidelines in making decisions that affect employees, the organization, consumers, and other parties. The importance of ethics increases in proportion to the *consequences* of the outcome

---

[23]Ibid., p. 474.

[24]Ibid.

[25]R. Joseph Monsen, *Business and the Changing Environment* (New York: McGraw-Hill, 1973), p. 121.

[26]Verne E. Henderson, "The Ethical Side of Enterprise," *Sloan Management Review,* Summer 1982, p. 38.

of a decision or behavior. As a manager's actions become more consequential for others, the more important are the ethics of that manager.

The role and state of ethics in American businesses have become a growing concern among managers and the public in the 1980s. Several factors have contributed to this concern. Scandals involving unethical activities by several major corporations (e.g., General Electric, E. F. Hutton, General Dynamics, and others) have been widely publicized.[27] One ethics expert has reported that over the past decade, two thirds of the Fortune 500 companies have been involved in illegal behavior.[28] Studies also indicate that many managers feel pressured by their employers to commit ethically questionable acts. In one survey study of 1,500 top-, middle-, and first-level managers, more than 40 percent of the respondents reported they had compromised their personal principles to meet an organizational demand.[29] These developments have led many individuals and managers to believe that ethics in business has declined over the last decade.[30]

Second, business ethics has become a topic of concern because businesses are realizing that ethical misconduct by management can be extremely costly for the company and society as a whole. E. F. Hutton and General Electric, for example, each paid several million dollars in criminal penalties and fines for their managers' misconduct. At the same time, the dynamics of ethics in management decision making is an often complex phenomenon.

Such is the case because determining what is and isn't ethical is often difficult to do. In some situations, the task is easy. We know, for example, that accepting bribes from a supplier is clearly unethical as is falsifying records or dishonest advertising in promoting a product. However, more often the ethics of a business situation are more complex. Every day, managers face ethical questions that have no easy answers. What for example, is a "fair" profit? What is a "just" price for a product? How "honest" should a company be with the press?

Because the ethics of a business situation are often complex, managers sometimes differ in their views of what actions are ethical. Currently, several ethical issues are being debated in the business environment. For example, managers are grappling with the ethics of employee surveillance (monitoring their computer work and telephones to measure employee productivity), and with the ethical questions of conducting polygraph tests of job applicants.[31] One upcoming ethical controversy in the U.S. business

---

[27]For example, see Larue T. Hosmer, *The Ethics of Management* (Homewood, Ill.: Richard D. Irwin, 1987), pp. 151–52; and Larue T. Hosmer, "The Institutionalization of Unethical Behavior," *Journal of Business Ethics*, 1987, pp. 439–47.

[28]This finding is the conclusion of Professor Amitai Etzioni which is reported by Saul Gellerman in "Why 'Good' Managers Make Bad Ethical Choices," *Harvard Business Review*, July–August 1986, p. 85.

[29]Barry Z. Posner and Warren H. Schmidt, "Ethics in American Companies: A Managerial Perspective," *Journal of Business Ethics*, 1987, pp. 383–91.

[30]See Roger Ricklefs, "Executives and General Public Say Ethical Behavior Is Declining in U.S.," *The Wall Street Journal*, November 1, 1983, pp. 23ff, and "Public Gives Executives Low Marks for Honesty and Ethical Standards," *The Wall Street Journal*, November 2, 1983, pp. 29ff; and Stanley J. Modic, "Are They Ethical?" *Industry Week*, February 1, 1988, p. 20.

[31]John Hoerr, "Privacy," *Business Week*, March 28, 1988, pp. 61ff.

community is the projected future use of genetic testing by employers. This issue is discussed in the following Management Application.

MANAGEMENT APPLICATION

THE ETHICS OF GENETIC SCREENING

Medical science has recently made much progress in estimating an individual's susceptibility to certain diseases by studying genetic makeup. Today, a person's predisposition to heart disease, certain cancers, Alzheimer's disease, sickle cell anemia, and many other illnesses can be determined by studying genetic makeup present in a tissue or blood sample.

This advancement is stirring an ethical debate in the business community concerning the use of genetic tests in the workplace. Testing proponents assert that employees should be tested in businesses where they are exposed to chemicals and other potential hazards in the workplace. The tests would enable a business to identify individuals who are highly susceptible to illnesses related to potentially hazardous exposures and to prohibit those workers from jobs involving such exposure. This move would reduce a high-risk employee's chances of illness and lower the company's health costs.

This concern about occupational illness is well founded. Each year, over 850,000 workdays are lost in the United States due to acute work-related illnesses experienced by more than 125,000 workers.

However, many observers oppose genetic screening. They argue that the tests are an invasion of privacy and would be used by businesses as a basis for denying employment and for dismissals. If the tests are allowed, opponents assert, all companies would use the tests, not just businesses where employees are exposed to potential hazards. Many companies would deny employment or would not promote those determined as high risks for illnesses such as Huntingdon's disease or Alzheimer's disease. These illnesses occur in later years and are not occupation related.

Opponents also assert that test results would be used by insurance companies to deny individuals coverage or to charge high premiums for coverage of certain illnesses which high-risk individuals have not contracted. Neither businesses nor insurance companies have a right to such genetic information, they argue.

Today, the use of genetic screening is so controversial that few companies will admit to conducting research into developing specific genetic tests for potential work-related illnesses. In 1980, DuPont was much criticized for testing black employees for sickle cell anemia, a test which the company now performs only upon the employee's request. No laws are presently on the books concerning an employer's right to conduct genetic screening, nor have tests been developed for widespread use. However, progress in test development is quickening. It is only a matter of time before the issue of genetic testing in the workplace becomes as timely and hotly debated as drug testing is today.

Source: Adapted from John Hoerr, "Privacy," *Business Week,* March 28, 1988, pp. 61–65, 66; and Allan L. Otten, "Price of Progress: Efforts to Predict Genetic Ills Pose Medical Dilemmas," *The Wall Street Journal,* September 14, 1987, p. 23.

Figure 19–2   An ethics test.

Many situations in day-to-day business are not simple right-or-wrong questions, but rather fall into a gray area. To demonstrate the perplexing array of moral dilemmas faced by 20th-century Americans, here is a "nonscientific" test for slippage. . . . Don't expect to score high. That is not the purpose. But give it a try, and see how you stack up.

Put your value system to the test in the following situations:

Scoring Code: Strongly Agree   = SA
                Agree   = A
                Disagree   = D
                Strongly Disagree   = SD

	SA	A	D	SD
1. Employees should not be expected to inform on their peers for wrongdoings.	—	—	—	—
2. There are times when a manager must overlook contract and safety violations in order to get on with the job.	—	—	—	—
3. It is not always possible to keep accurate expense account records; therefore, it is sometimes necessary to give approximate figures.	—	—	—	—
4. There are times when it is necessary to withhold embarrassing information from one's superior.	—	—	—	—
5. We should do what our managers suggest, though we may have doubts about its being the right thing to do.	—	—	—	—
6. It is sometimes necessary to conduct personal business on company time.	—	—	—	—
7. Sometimes it is good psychology to set goals somewhat above normal if it will help to obtain a greater effort from the sales force.	—	—	—	—
8. I would quote a "hopeful" shipping date in order to get the order.	—	—	—	—
9. It is proper to use the company WATS line for personal calls as long as it's not in company use.	—	—	—	—
10. Management must be goal oriented: therefore, the end usually justifies the means.	—	—	—	—
11. If it takes heavy entertainment and twisting a bit of company policy to win a large contract, I would authorize it.	—	—	—	—
12. Exceptions to company policy and procedures are a way of life.	—	—	—	—
13. Inventory controls should be designed to report "underages" rather than "overages" in goods received.	—	—	—	—
14. Occasional use of the company's copier for personal or community activities is acceptable.	—	—	—	—
15. Taking home company property (pencils, paper, tape, etc.) for personal use is an accepted fringe benefit.	—	—	—	—

Score Key: (0) for Strongly Disagree (1) for Disagree (2) for Agree (3) for Strongly Agree

If your score is:

     0 Prepare for canonization ceremony
 1– 5 Bishop material
 6–10 High ethical values
11–15 Good ethical values
16–25 Average ethical values
26–35 Need moral development
36–44 Slipping fast
    45 Leave valuables with warden

Source: Lowell G. Rein, "Is Your (Ethical) Slippage Showing?" *Personnel Journal*, September, 1980.

Figure 19–3
An ethical
framework.

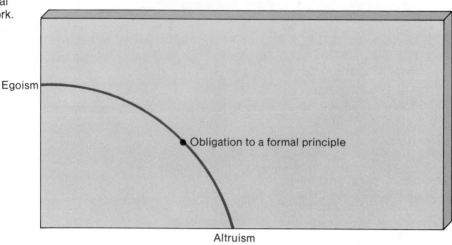

Source: Based on Grover Starling. *The Changing Environment of Business* (Boston: Kent Publishing, 1980), p. 255.

Because the ethics of managerial decision making are often complex and managers often disagree on what comprises an ethical decision, two subjects are particularly relevant: (1) the basis that the individual manager can use in determining which alternative to choose in a decision-making situation; and (2) what organizations can do to ensure that managers follow ethical standards in their decision making. These two topics are addressed in the following section.

ETHICAL STANDARDS

Managers must reconcile competing values in making decisions. They make decisions which have consequences for (1) themselves, (2) the organization that employs them, and (3) the society in which they and the organization exist. For example, managers can be called upon to make decisions that can be good for them, but bad for the organization and society. Figure 19–2 presents an ethics test. By completing it, you can experience first-hand the difficulty of defining ethical standards.

Philosophers, logicians, and theologians have studied ethical issues. Their ideas provide guidelines, but guidelines only, for making value-laden decisions. Figure 19–3 depicts a simplified model of ethical behavior with three different bases for determining ethical guidelines in decision making.[32]

Maximum personal benefits (egoism), depicted on the vertical axis, can be a manager's sole basis for decision making. A completely selfish manager would always

---

[32]This discussion is based on Grover Starling, *The Changing Environment of Business* (Boston: Kent Publishing, 1980). pp. 252–58.

select the alternative that is most personally beneficial. An extreme view of this ethical approach is that one should always seek that which is pleasurable, and conversely, one should avoid pain. A manager driven by egoism would evaluate decision alternatives in terms of personal benefit—salary, prestige, power, or whatever she considers valuable. If the action happens to also be beneficial to the organization and society, all is well and good. But these other benefits are incidental; personal welfare is the manager's top priority.

Some observers believe that investment bankers involved in illegal insider trading apply an egoist approach to their business behavior. Insider trading is discussed in the following Management Application.

MANAGEMENT APPLICATION

INSIDER TRADING

Traditionally, the U.S. stock market has been governed by a golden rule of sorts. All investors are equal players. No one benefits from advance information about which companies are about to acquire other businesses or which firms are about to sell. In the 1980s, however, a growing number of investment bankers—"insider traders"—have violated the law and have changed the investment climate on Wall Street.

The scenario of insider trading is simple. Suppose, for example, you are the top management of a corporation and have made the decision to acquire another company (the target). Your investment banker will arrange the financing of the deal and the formal transaction. By law, all communications between you and your banker are confidential. However, the banker secretly shares your intentions with an outside party who then quickly buys many shares of the target's stock. You then make your bid for the target company offering to buy its stock at an above-market price (i.e., to obtain the shares you need to gain control of the company). Unknown to you, the other party sells you his shares which were recently purchased at a much lower price. He makes a tidy bundle on the sale and splits the profit with your investment banker.

This is one of several scenarios that is often played in insider trading. All involve illegally sharing confidential information for profit. Since 1977, more than 150 insider trading suits have been brought by the Securities and Exchange Commission, a vast increase over the 47 suits filed from 1950 to 1977.

This increase indicates a major decline in business ethics among investment bankers and traders on Wall Street. Some observers assert that the decline is due to three factors. A first factor is the declining loyalty of investment bankers to the banks they work for. The average tenure of many bankers at one bank is from three to five years. Job hopping reduces the commitment to an employer and concern about the impact of questionable activity on the bank's reputation.

Second, the nature of the relationship between the investment bank and its clients has changed. In times past, most corporations had long-term relationships with one or perhaps two investment banks. In these cases, the CEO often dealt directly with the bank's chief. However, since the early 1980s, corporate clients have required that investment banks compete on price. The value and trust inherent in long-term relationships have diminished. Many companies maintain price-based relationships with multiple bankers which, many observers assert, facilitates a climate where the drive for profit overwhelms any concern about the other party's welfare.

A third factor is simply greed. The booming waves of acquisitions in the late 1970s and 1980s and the megadollars paid for businesses have tempted many players in the stock market to forgo ethics for major profits.

Regardless of the reasons, many observers assert that the wave of insider trading has created a climate where no one trusts anyone on Wall Street.

Source: Adapted from Bryan Burrough, "Fates Are Disparate for Those Charged with Insider Trading," *The Wall Street Journal,* November 18, 1987, pp. 1, 20; and Myron Magnet, "The Decline and Fall of Business Ethics," *Fortune,* December 8, 1986, pp. 65ff.

Maximum social benefits (altruism), depicted on the horizontal axis, also can be the sole consideration in decision making. An altruistic individual will select courses of action that provide maximum social benefit. A manager who follows this ethical guideline would measure right and wrong as the "greatest happiness to the greatest number." As a practical matter, decisions based only on altruistic concerns are particularly difficult to make. For example, altruism provides no means for judging the relative benefits to individuals, unless one is willing to assume that each has the same interest and benefit in a decision.

Obligation to a formal principle is shown between the extremes of egoism and altruism. Egoism holds that an act is good only if the individual benefits from it. Altruism holds that an act is good only if society benefits from it. The criteria for both ethical guidelines are the consequences. In contrast to them, the ethic of adhering to a formal principle is based on the idea that *the rightness or wrongness of an act depends on principle, not consequences.*

Those who adhere to principle in judging their actions could, for example, follow the Golden Rule: "Do unto others what you would have them do unto you." Or they might decide that each action should be judged by the principle: "Act as if the maxim of your action were to become a general law binding on everyone."

But the idea that actions can be judged by one principle is unacceptable to many individuals. Some prefer a *pluralistic* approach comprising several principles arranged in a hierarchy of importance. For example, one writer proposes that the following principles can guide managers in decision making: (1) place the interests of society before the interests of the organization, (2) place the interests of the organization before managers' private interests, (3) reveal the truth in all instances of organizational and personal involvement.[33] These three principles provide guidelines, but not answers. The manager must determine the relative benefits to society, company, and self. The determination of benefits and beneficiaries, however, is seldom simple accounting. But the advantage of a pluralistic approach to ethical decision making is that the decision maker, *with intentions to do right,* has the basis for evaluating decisions.

---

[33]Robert W. Austin, "Code of Conduct for Executives," *Harvard Business Review,* September–October 1981, pp. 53.

The Organization's Role in Ethical Behavior

The approaches to developing guidelines for ethical behavior have so far focused on the individual manager. Many observers assert that the organization should play a major role in ensuring that its managers act ethically in managing the firm. The organization's participation is understandable given that it is the organization which is ultimately responsible for the consequences of the decisions that its managers make.

Although a company is ultimately responsible, surprisingly few organizations have traditionally provided managers with specific guidelines concerning ethics in decision making. However, given the increasing concern about ethics in organizations, a growing number of companies are attempting to provide guidance for their managers.[34]

At the core of many corporate efforts is the development of a corporate *code of ethics* (often called a *code of conduct*). Typically established by top management, a code is usually comprised of a written statement of a company's values, beliefs and norms of ethical behavior.[35] Johnson & Johnson Co.'s "credo" is one example of a corporate code of ethics and is shown in Figure 19–4. Like many codes, J&J's credo specifies its values and beliefs concerning its relationships and responsibilities toward its different constituents (i.e., customers, employees, community, and shareholders). The credo also states Johnson & Johnson's objectives concerning each constituency and norms of behavior such as "supporting good works and charities" and "encouraging civic improvements." (James Burke, chairman of Johnson & Johnson, credits the credo with providing the source of direction for the company's successful handling of the Tylenol product-tampering crisis discussed in Chapter 11.)

Ideally, a code of ethics should provide employees with direction in dealing with ethical dilemmas, clarify the organization's position regarding areas of ethical uncertainty, and overall achieve and maintain ongoing conduct which the organization views as ethical and proper.[36] However, often codes do not achieve these purposes. For example, a recent study found that organizations with ethics codes were more often found in violation of federal regulations than were organizations with no established codes.[37]

Codes are often ineffective because, once they are established in written form, management does not follow through and proactively implement the code in the organization. The written code lies dormant and ultimately serves little more than a public relations purpose. However, organizations have achieved effective, "living" codes of ethics typically by following a multistep implementation strategy. They first translate values and beliefs into specific ethical standards of behavior. Some standards may exist in the code itself; however, often even more specific standards for particular

---

[34]John A. Byrne, "Businesses Are Signing up for Ethics 101," *Business Week*, February 15, 1988, pp. 56–57.

[35]Earl A. Molander, "A Paradigm for Design, Promulgation, and Enforcement of Ethical Codes," *Journal of Business Ethics*, 1987, pp. 619–31.

[36]Fred Luthans, Richard M. Hodgetts, and Kenneth R. Thompson, *Social Issues in Business* (New York: Macmillan, 1984), pp. 97–105.

[37]Rick Wartzman, "Nature or Nurture? Study Blames Ethical Lapses on Corporate Goals," *The Wall Street Journal*, October 9, 1987, p. 21.

Figure 19–4
Johnson &
Johnson's code
of ethics.

Our Credo

We believe our first responsibility is to the doctors, nurses and patients,
to mothers and all others who use our products and services.
In meeting their needs everything we do must be of high quality.
We must constantly strive to reduce our costs
in order to maintain reasonable prices.
Customers' orders must be serviced promptly and accurately.
Our suppliers and distributors must have an opportunity
to make a fair profit.

We are responsible to our employees,
the men and women who work with us throughout the world.
Everyone must be considered as an individual.
We must respect their dignity and recognize their merit.
They must have a sense of security in their jobs.
Compensation must be fair and adequate,
and working conditions clean, orderly and safe.
Employees must feel free to make suggestions and complaints.
There must be equal opportunity for employment, development
and advancement for those qualified.
We must provide competent management,
and their actions must be just and ethical.

We are responsible to the communities in which we live and work
and to the world community as well.
We must be good citizens — support good works and charities
and bear our fair share of taxes.
We must encourage civic improvements and better health and education.
We must maintain in good order
the property we are privileged to use,
protecting the environment and natural resources.

Our final responsibility is to our stockholders.
Business must make a sound profit.
We must experiment with new ideas.
Research must be carried on, innovative programs developed
and mistakes paid for.
New equipment must be purchased, new facilities provided
and new products launched.
Reserves must be created to provide for adverse times.
When we operate according to these principles,
the stockholders should realize a fair return.

Johnson & Johnson

Used with permission of Johnson & Johnson Co.

situations are developed. For example, a specific behavioral standard for Johnson and Johnson's credo objective of high product quality may be immediately reporting to management any evidence or concerns that a product is below the company's quality standards.[38]

These more specific standards may be incorporated as a supplemental part of the

---

[38]Luthans, Hodgetts, and Thompson, *Social Issues in Business*, p. 104.

ethics code. In this regard, Cummins Engine Company provides its employees with the *Cummins Practices,* a set of policies which details rules of conduct for a wide range of business situations including questionable payments, supplier selection, employee participation in political campaigns, and gifts. Each situation is fully discussed and includes the employee's relevant responsibilities and a list of individuals to contact if the employee needs further guidance.[39]

The code and standards are communicated to employees in written form and often in sessions with management. At John Deere, the company's code is present in the form of the "Green Bulletin," a green loose-leaf booklet kept on nearly every manager's desk.[40]

Besides translating the code into behavior standards, companies with effective ethics codes have determined the actions to be taken when code violations occur, have communicated the penalties to employees, and have implemented the penalties to ensure code compliance. Xerox Corp., for example, has dismissed employees for violations that are serious (taking bribes) and relatively insignificant (petty cheating on expense accounts). Chemical Bank has likewise fired employees for violating the code even when such violations were not unlawful. In both cases, actions were taken to communicate the company's commitment to the code and the importance of maintaining ethical behavior.[41]

Beyond these steps to ensure effective code implementation, other actions are often necessary to develop a companywide commitment to ethical behavior. Many ethics experts assert that top management must be committed to the effort; the CEO, as the most visible organization member, should embody the code's standards through behavior and personal example. Many organizations also periodically conduct ethics seminars to keep employees sensitive to the place of ethics in the company and to help them develop skills in handling ethical dilemmas. At Allied Corp., for example, managers who participate in the company's ethics seminars submit case studies of ethical problems which they've experienced on the job. The cases are then presented anonymously and discussed by participants.[42]

Many companies with effective ethics programs emphasize the importance of setting realistic performance objectives for subordinates.[43] Setting unreasonable goals is an effective way to promote unethical behavior to achieve those objectives (e.g., cutting corners, making ethical compromises) especially when the performance goals are tightly linked to rewards. Establishing the position of ethics advocate is another often-recommended action.[44] The ethics advocate is normally a top-level executive who, in

---

[39]Oliver F. Williams, "Business Ethics: A Trojan Horse?" *California Management Review,* Summer 1982, pp. 14–23.

[40]O'Toole, *Vanguard Management,* p. 52.

[41]Byrne, "Businesses Are Signing Up for Ethics 101," p. 57.

[42]David Freudberg, "Ministering to the Corporation," *Across The Board,* November 1984, pp. 14ff.

[43]Archie B. Carroll, *Business & Society: Managing Corporate Social Performance* (Boston: Little, Brown, 1981), pp. 78–79.

[44]Ibid., p. 85.

a sense, serves as the organization's full-time ethical conscience. The advocate evaluates the organization's actions from an ethical perspective and vigorously and openly questions the ethical implications of proposed plans of action.

ETHICS AND SOCIAL RESPONSIBILITY

The relationship between a manager's ethical standards and social responsiveness should be apparent. Ethics serve as bases for assessing the "rightness" of potential actions. In a sense, ethical standards are filters that screen actions according to relative rightness. The ideas that have been developed so far in these discussions of social responsibility, expectations for corporate behavior, and ethics are integrated in Figure 19–5.

In this summary, the corporation is seen as a *means* for achieving the *ends* of various claimants. Social responsibility involves deciding *what* means and *whose* ends are right and good. Ultimately, corporate managers must decide the relative rightness of each demand, and ethical standards are the bases for their decisions.

MANAGEMENT SOLUTION

BEECH-NUT PLEADS GUILTY TO FOOD AND DRUG LAW VIOLATIONS

Top management did not respond to LiCari's memo and according to LiCari, when he discussed the memo with John F. Lavery, the company's operations head, Lavery threatened to fire him. After next discussing the situation with the company president Neils L. Hoyvald, LiCari resigned.

However, Beech-Nut's problems had just begun. Soon thereafter, Beech-Nut was approached by a private investigator hired by a group of pure apple juice suppliers to investigate Beech-Nut's supplier (who also sold concentrate to other manufacturers). The investigator informed Beech-Nut that a new test had clearly established that the supplier's concentrate was fake; it was comprised of cheaper substitutes. The investigator asked Beech-Nut to join the manufacturers in a suit against the supplier.

Beech-Nut refused and continued to sell the now clearly phony product as pure apple juice. Beech-Nut had $3.5 million worth of apple juice

concentrate in inventory. According to a Beech-Nut executive, Beech-Nut's president ordered the inventory be sold "fast, fast, fast" at substantial price discounts. Much of the juice was sold outside the United States. Beech-Nut issued a national recall of its apple juice products and sued its supplier but continued to market mixed juices made from the phony concentrate.

In November 1986, a federal grand jury issued a 470-count indictment charging Beech-Nut and executives Lavery and Hoyvald with felony acts and intentional violation of the U.S. food and drug laws in selling phony apple juice. Beech-Nut has pled guilty to 215 felony counts and incurred $25 million in fines, declining sales, and legal fees. Beech-Nut's market share in apple juice has declined by about 20 percent. Its sales in 1987 approached a record low.

Why did Beech-Nut act so unethically? Observers suggest that Beech-Nut's top manage-
Continued

Figure 19–5 The corporation's social responsibility and managerial ethics.

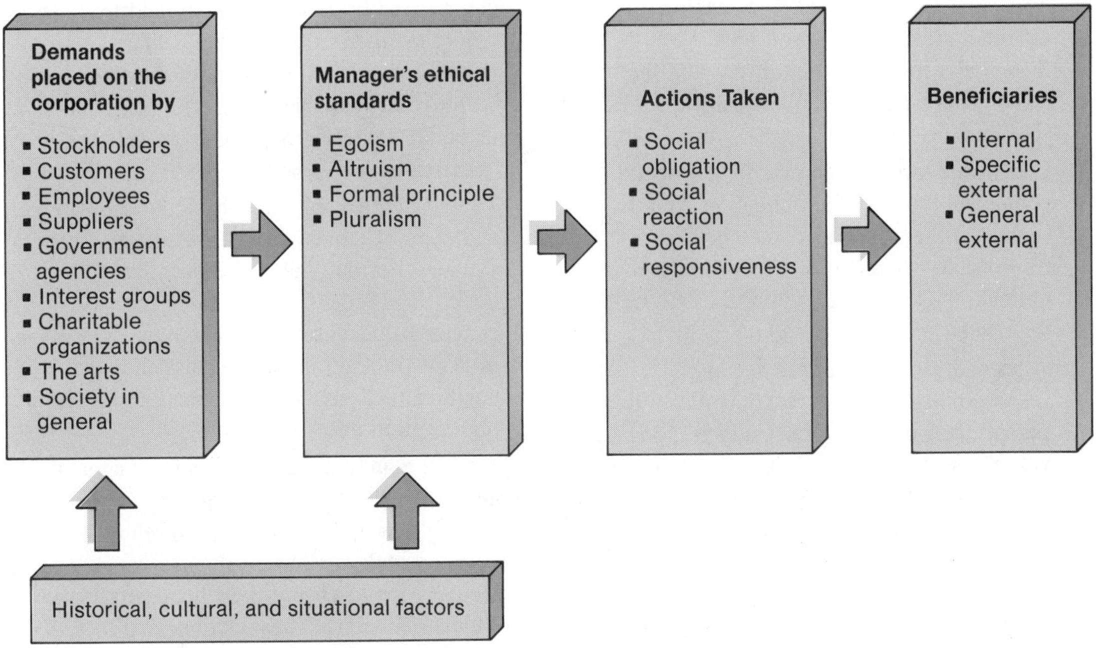

Demands placed on the corporation by
- Stockholders
- Customers
- Employees
- Suppliers
- Government agencies
- Interest groups
- Charitable organizations
- The arts
- Society in general

Manager's ethical standards
- Egoism
- Altruism
- Formal principle
- Pluralism

Actions Taken
- Social obligation
- Social reaction
- Social responsiveness

Beneficiaries
- Internal
- Specific external
- General external

Historical, cultural, and situational factors

MANAGEMENT SOLUTION

Concluded

ment was under substantial pressure to improve the company's dismal financial performance, and the much cheaper concentrate saved considerable sums. They also assert that Beech-Nut's executives rationalized their actions, arguing that other competitors were selling phony juice and that the adulterated apple juice, while not pure, was safe for its infant consumers. However, industry sources report that less than 5 percent of the apple juice on the market is phony. More-

over, while evidence does not clearly establish that the adulterated juice is hazardous, neither does it establish that the juice is safe for babies to consume because its long-term effects are as yet unknown.

Nestlé Corp., Beech-Nut's parent company, is financially supporting an aggressive courtroom defense of Lavery and Hoyvald.

Source: Adapted from Chris Welles, "What Led Beech-Nut down the Road to Disgrace," *Business Week*, February 22, 1988, pp. 124ff.

MANAGEMENT SUMMARY

☐ The term *social responsibility* has many different meanings. So you must keep the differences in mind when discussing the issue. The various meanings can be sorted into three categories.

☐ One of the three categories defines social responsibility as social obligation. In this sense, business is considered socially responsible when it meets its primary obligation—to pursue, within the law, a profit for owners.

☐ A second category defines social responsibility as social reaction. From this perspective, business is socially responsible when it reacts to prevailing social norms, values, and expectations. The business must sense, understand, and react to society's expectations.

☐ A third category defines social responsibility as social responsiveness. This category includes obligatory and reactive behavior, but goes on to state that corporations should be proactive and take action to prevent social problems.

☐ Socially responsible activities may be categorized by type of activity and by those who benefit from the activities. The beneficiaries may be internal (customers, employees, and shareholders) or external (specific interest groups or more general beneficiaries).

☐ There is increasing concern about the role and state of ethics in U.S. businesses because of the belief that business ethics have declined in recent years. Managers are concerned because of the complexity of ethics in decision making and because the costs of unethical actions can be substantial for the organization and society.

☐ Managers may use the concepts of egoism, altruism, pluralism, or obligation to a formal principle in their approaches to ethics in decision making. More organizations are also taking steps to ensure their managers make ethical decisions. These actions can include establishing and enforcing a corporate code of ethics, setting realistic performance goals for employees, providing ethics training for decision makers, and creating the position of an ethics advocate.

REVIEW AND DISCUSSION QUESTIONS

1. Explain why corporations have "social responsibilities." How does society express its expectations for corporate behavior?

2. Is it possible for a corporate executive to be both unethical personally and ethical professionally? Which are more demanding—the ethics of personal life or the ethics of professional life?

3. Identify organizations in recent events whose actions you believe to be notable expressions of social responsibility.

4. What are the basic arguments for and against each of the three meanings of social responsibility?

5. To which beneficiaries of corporate behavior is management primarily responsible? Explain your answer. Does your answer reflect *your* ethical standards?

6. Some management experts assert that ethics codes are of little value in organizations because a manager's ethics are mostly a product of his own individual values, not a written code developed by top management. Do you agree? In your opinion, are there

limits to a code's effectiveness in organizations? Explain.

7. Are society's expectations for corporate social responsibility likely to change in the 1990s? Discuss.

8. Opponents of the social obligation perspective of social responsibility assert that an organization's socially responsive activities can be directly profitable for the company and thus they don't compromise management's obligations to shareholders. Provide an example that supports this view.

9. Explain how a manager's ethics affect decisions regarding social responsibility.

10. Many observers who believe that business ethics have declined over the last decade also assert that ethics in society overall have declined at the same time. Do you agree? Explain.

CASES

19–1 BUILDING ETHICS AT GENERAL DYNAMICS

For years, General Dynamics Corporation enjoyed a productive relationship with the federal government as the nation's largest defense contractor. However, through much of the 1970s and early 1980s, General Dynamics came under heavy fire for allegedly overcharging the government. At one point, the Pentagon froze all payments to the company to retrieve almost $250 million paid in overcharge billings, according to a federal investigative agency. Criminal charges were filed against General Dynamics by the Justice Department.

Most observers assert that something was clearly wrong in the ways of doing business at General Dynamics. Company officials agreed. Top management set about building a strong sense of ethical conduct at the company via several steps:

A written code of conduct.   The core of the company's efforts is a 20-page publication that provides guidelines for ethical conduct in business situations and decision making. The "blue book" describes employee's responsibilities for maintaining the company's stipulated ethical standards and penalties for violating those standards. The book also specifies individuals with whom employees can discuss problems or questions concerning the application of the company's code. Importantly, the code contains a "squeal clause" which protects employees who identify individuals who are violating the ethical standards.

About 103,000 employees of General Dynamic received a copy of the blue book in sessions with their supervisors. In the sessions, the standards were discussed along with how to apply them in different on-the-job situations. Employees were also asked to sign an acknowledgement card stipulating that they understood the code of conduct and that the code is company policy. Most workers have signed the cards although signing is not required. However, reading the blue book and signing an acknowledgement card is a prerequisite of employment for job applicants.

Ethics training.   General Dynamics conducted ethics awareness seminars for all employees. The workshop's format included a film concerning the company's values, exercises about ways to resolve ethical dilemmas encountered on the job, and information and discussion about the company's overall ethics program. Seminars for upper-level managers included participation in case studies of ethics.

Ethics program directors.   About 40 employees serve as ethics program directors throughout the company. They answer employees' questions about the company's code and counsel employees on how to handle particular ethics dilemmas. Each director reports directly to the respective subsidiary president.

Program structure.   General Dynamic's overall ethics program is coordinated by a full-time corporate ethics director. He works with the company's ethics steering committee which is comprised of the major functional department directors of the company.

The committee provides overall direction for the program and policy development. The company's board of directors also maintains a committee on corporate social responsibility which reviews and approves ethics policy for General Dynamics. Members of this committee are all directors from outside the company.

Ethics hotline.   General Dynamics has established 30 hotlines throughout the company and a toll-free number for calling corporate headquarters. Ethics program directors operate the hotlines. In one year of the hotline's operation, over 3,600 calls were received. Over two thirds were requests for information or counsel in handling ethical dilemmas; the remaining contacts concerned reports of potential misconduct. In that year, General Dynamics imposed more than 100 sanctions for misconduct. The sanctions ranged from warning to dismissal and referral for criminal prosecution.

Has the ethics program worked? After conducting a companywide survey and an internal audit on the program, management thinks that the company has achieved a greater awareness of the importance and role of ethics in everyday work at General Dynamics.

Questions

1. Evaluate the ethics program at General Dynamics. What are the program's strong points? What changes could be made to make the program more effective?

2. Some observers assert that including a "squeal clause" in a company's code of ethics promotes employee spying on peers which is unethical. Do you agree? Discuss.

3. Although most employees signed the acknowledgement card, some did not. In your opinion, why would some people refuse to sign? Are these reasons legitimate?

Source: Adapted from William H. Wagel, "A New Focus on Business Ethics at General Dynamics," *Personnel*, August 1987, pp. 4–8.

19–2 A DREAM BECOMES A NIGHTMARE FOR ELI LILLY AND CO.

In 1982, Eli Lilly and Co. introduced a new drug, Oraflex. It was heralded as a miracle drug because one tablet per day eased the pain and inflammation of arthritis. Even more promising to the elderly was the chance—suggested in Lilly's publicity campaign—that the drug could arrest the disease. After only 320 days on the U.S. market, 500,000 people were taking the medication.

Tragically, soon the dream would become a nightmare. In Great Britain, where the drug had been on the market for two years, there were reports of side effects such as internal bleeding and kidney and liver problems. Officials in Britain stopped sales, citing reports of more than 3,500 adverse reactions and 61 deaths. Lilly pulled Oraflex off the U.S. market.

Then began what has become a familiar pattern—one that will change drastically if a proposed federal product liability law is enacted. (Under the proposed law, companies like Lilly would face punitive damages only once.) For now, however, lawyers for more than 280 people who say they or their relatives were injured have begun trying to determine if Lilly rushed the drug to market knowing there were questions about Oraflex's safety. If this is the case, Lilly will be liable for punitive damages in every case.

Most states do not limit the amount of punitive damages because they are designed to make examples of companies that are reckless and to deter others from disregarding safety. So it is the success or failure of the punitive claims in early trials, when a company faces multiple suits, that often sets the value of damages for the cases that follow.

Unfortunately for Lilly, lawyers found evidence that one of Lilly's executives in charge of research and regulatory matters knew of, but did not report to the U.S. Food and Drug Administration, 25 deaths associated with the drug. When the first Oraflex case came to trial in 1983, jurors awarded $6 million in punitive damages to the son of a woman who died after taking the drug.

The company appealed, saying the jury did not understand the scientific evidence. But that first verdict took much of the fight out of the company's defense. It soon settled at least seven cases, one for $500,000.

Questions

1. Should a company face punitive damages only once where negligence has been proved, even if there is a possibility that the total punitive damages may exceed the net worth of the company?

2. In the case where a product is defective but negligence is not present, should a manufacturer be liable for punitive damages?

3. What does this case illustrate about the problem of social responsibility and management ethics?

Source: "The Miracle Drug that Became a Nightmare for Eli Lilly," *Business Week*, April 30, 1984, p. 104.

EXERCISE

19–1 ETHICAL DILEMMAS

Purpose: This activity is designed to illustrate the complexity of ethical decision making and how people can differ in their views of what is and is not ethical behavior.

Setting Up the Exercise: Presented below are four situations often encountered in the workplace which pose ethical issues. Read each scenario and place yourself in the position of the respective decision maker. What would you do? Write your decision for each scenario on a sheet of paper.

The Roundabout Raise

When Joe asks for a raise, his boss praises his work but says the company's rigid budget won't allow any further merit raises for the time being. Instead, the boss suggests that the company "won't look too closely at your expense accounts for a while." Should Joe take this as authorization to pad his expense account on grounds that he is simply getting the same money he deserves through a different route, or not take this roundabout "raise"?

   Your decision:

The Faked Degree

Bill has done a sound job for more than a year. Bill's boss learns that he got the job by claiming to have a college degree, although he actually never graduated. Should his boss dismiss him for submitting a fraudulent resumé or overlook the false claim since Bill has otherwise proven to be a conscientious and honorable worker, and making an issue of the degree might ruin Bill's career?

   Your decision:

Sneaking Phone Calls

Helen discovers that a fellow employee regularly makes about $100 a month worth of personal long-distance telephone calls from an office telephone. Should Helen report the employee to the company or disregard the calls on the grounds that many people make personal calls at the office?

   Your decision:

Cover-Up Temptation

Bill discovers that the chemical plant he manages is creating slightly more water pollution in a nearby lake than is legally permitted. Revealing the problem will bring considerable unfavorable publicity to the plant, hurt the lakeside town's resort business and create a scare in the community. Solving the problem will cost the company well over $100,000. It is unlikely that outsiders will discover the problem. The violation poses no danger whatever to people. At most, it will endanger a small number of fish.

Should Bill reveal the problem despite the cost to his company, or consider the problem as little more than a technicality and disregard it?

Your decision: _____

Once everyone has completed the scenarios, your instructor will discuss the class responses to each situation. The instructor will also provide you with the general responses of about 1,500 adults and 400 middle-level managers. They completed the exercise as a part of *The Wall Street Journal/Gallup* poll on ethics in America.

Compare your responses to those of the general public and the executives. What factors account for any differences in how you responded compared to their decisions?

A Learning Note: This exercise aptly demonstrates the complexities of ethical considerations in decision making and the sources of the complexities: (1) the differing perspectives among individuals concerning what is ethical; (2) their differing interpretations and assessments of situations; and (3) differing goals, needs, and values.

Source: The scenarios are used by permission of *The Wall Street Journal,* Dow Jones and Company, Inc., November 5, 1983, pp. 29ff. All rights reserved.

TWENTY

Developing Management Careers

LEARNING OBJECTIVES

After completing Chapter 20, you should be able to:

Define: *career development* in terms of individual and organizational processes.

State: the specific problems that recent hirees and midcareer managers face.

Describe: the practices and policies managers can use to counteract career problems.

Explain: why managing dual-career employees is becoming a widespread managerial issue.

Discuss: the difficulties associated with devising career paths for a specific individual.

ORGANIZATIONAL INVOLVEMENT IN EMPLOYEE CAREER DEVELOPMENT

Assisting individuals with their career development plans and planning can be a powerful tool for integrating organizational and individual goals. But the managerial challenge is to design a program that will enable individuals to plan their careers with realistic information about career path opportunities that exist within a particular organization. At the most basic level, individuals must know and understand how their goals fit with those of their supervisors and work groups. In the absence of such information, individuals cannot find their places in the organization and, consequently, will never be able to make optimal contributions to it.

One R&D organization implemented a career development program in one of its divisions. The management of the division initially perceived the program to be an attempt to get nonsupervisory employees to take responsibility for their own career development. Eventually, however, the program provided not only opportunities for individual growth, but also as a way for supervisors to support employees' career goals and to disseminate organizational goals and objectives.

Another initial focus of the program was to improve peer relations among the nonsupervisory personnel. Managers and supervisors perceived poor peer relation to be a problem, but it was later discovered that the nonsupervisory personnel did not see the same problem. What they did see as a problem was the unfair way that supervisors assigned jobs and distributed rewards. Nonsupervisory employees perceived the problem to be poor employee-supervisor relations, not peer relations. The program then became a catalyst for managing employee-supervisor relations because effective career development cannot proceed in the context of arbitrary job and reward assignment environment.

These changes in management's expectations for what a career development program can accomplish were the result of how the program was designed. Rather than imposing the program, management designed the program only after involving managers, supervisors, and nonsupervisory personnel in a needs assessment phase. It was during this phase that it became obvious that an individual's career goals and strategies can be developed only with participation of the individual's supervisor who can represent the organization's goals and strategies. The information obtained in the design phase enabled management to think in terms of a program that could go beyond the usual expectations for a career development program. But what would be the features of the program?

(The Management Solution to this Management Incident can be found at the end of this chapter.)

An important management responsibility is to develop subordinates to their fullest potential. Organizational change and growth require managers to focus on developing people and placing them in key positions. Organizational growth through expansion, mergers, and acquisitions *creates* new management positions and *changes* the responsibilities of existing positions. Capable people must be available to fill the new and bigger jobs. Even organizations facing a stable or contracting future must recognize the link between performance and human resources development.

As organizations change, so do their employees. A recently hired manager has different needs and aspirations than does the midcareer or the preretirement manager. All of us move through a fairly uniform pattern of phases during our *careers*. The different phases produce different opportunities and stresses, all of which have implications for job performance. Effective managers understand these implications and try to help employees who wish to confront and deal with their careers and personal needs.

Managers should be concerned with their own career goals and with paths leading to those goals. Yet, managers often lack the ability and the information necessary to develop their career plans systematically and explicitly. But we see more and more evidence of a growing interest in helping individuals identify their goals and understand how to reach them.

This chapter reviews some of the career-developing issues. The framework guiding the presentation is shown in Figure 20–1. Note that two aspects of human resource and career development are (1) human resource planning and (2) formal training and development programs. Each of these topics was covered extensively earlier in the text. So discussion in this chapter will stress their interrelationships.

THE CONCEPT OF CAREER

The concept of career has many meanings. The popular meaning is probably reflected in the idea of career upward mobility—making more money; having more responsibility; acquiring more status, prestige, and power. The concept of career can apply to life pursuits other than business employment. For example, homemakers, mothers, and volunteer workers have careers. They, too, advance in the sense that their talents and abilities to take on larger responsibilities grow with time and experience. Clearly, the mother of married children plays a far different role than she did when her children were preschoolers.

Here, our discussion will center on the careers of those in occupations and professions. The definition of career that we use follows closely the one recently devised by Douglas T. Hall. Accordingly:

> The career is the individually perceived sequence of attitudes and
> behaviors associated with work-related experiences and activities over the
> span of the person's life.[1]

This definition emphasizes that the term *career* does not imply success or failure, except in the judgment of the individual. It also emphasizes that a career consists of

---

[1]Douglas T. Hall, ed., *Career Development in Organizations* (San Francisco: Jossey-Bass, 1986).

Figure 20–1   Career and human resource development.

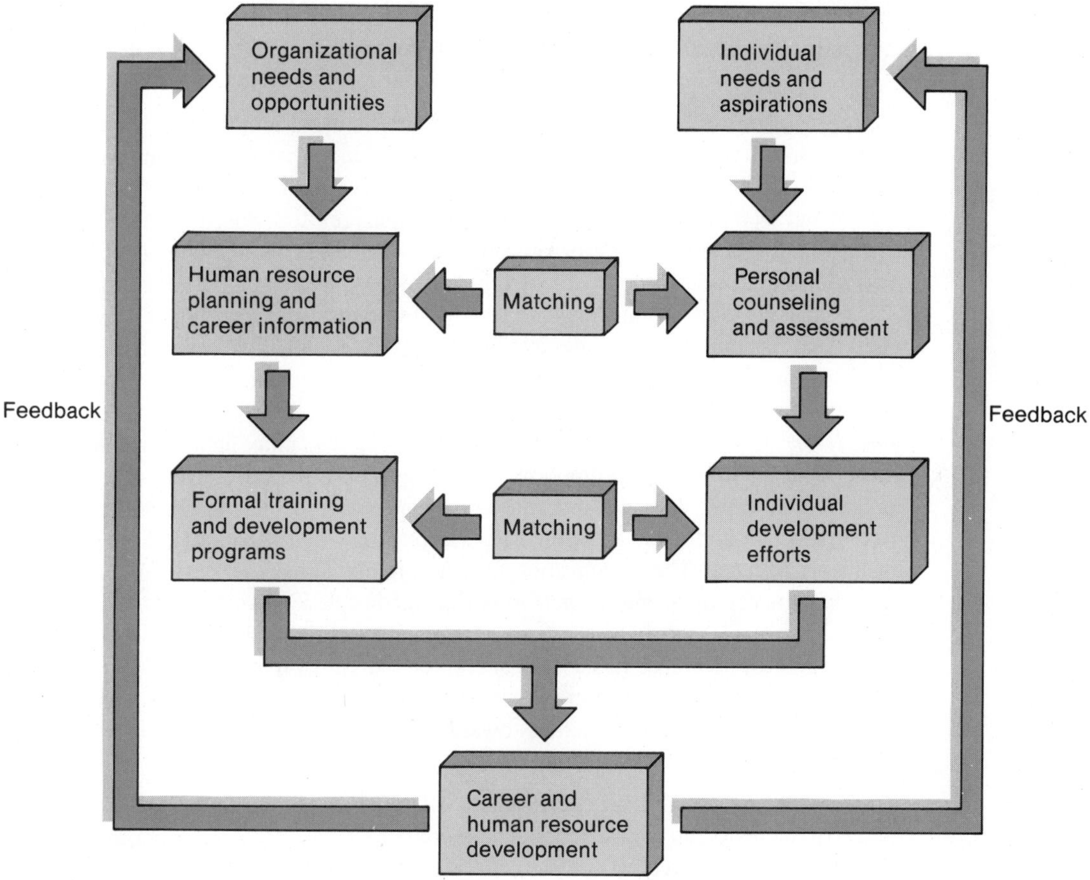

Source: Based on John C. Aplin and Darlene K. Gerster, "Career Development: An Integration of Individual and Organizational Needs," *Personnel*, March–April 1978, p. 25.

both attitudes and behaviors, and that it is an ongoing sequence of work-related activities. Yet, even though the concept of career is clearly work-related, it must be understood that a person's nonwork life and roles also play a significant part in it. For example, the attitudes of a 50-year-old midcareer manager about a job advancement involving greater responsibilities can be quite different from those of a manager nearing retirement. A bachelor's reaction to a promotion involving relocation is likely to be different from that of a father of school-age children.

Career Effectiveness

In organizational settings, career effectiveness is judged not only by the individual, but also by the organization itself. But what is meant by career effectiveness? Under what circumstances will individuals state that they have had "successful" or "satisfying" careers? And will the organization share the individuals' views about their careers? Although numerous criteria of career effectiveness could be listed, four important ones are performance, attitude, adaptability, and identity.

Career performance.   Salary and position are the usual indicators of career performance. Specifically, the more rapidly one's salary increases and one advances up the hierarchy, the higher the level of career performance. As one advances (is promoted), the greater is the responsibility in terms of employees supervised, budget allocated, and revenue generated. The organization is, of course, vitally interested in career performance since it bears a direct relation to goal attainment. That is, the rate of salary and position advancement reflects in most instances the extent to which the individual has contributed to the attainment of the organization's objectives.

Two points should be discussed now. First, to the extent that the organization's performance appraisal system does not fully recognize performance, individuals may not realize this indicator of career effectiveness. Thus, individuals may not receive those rewards, salary and promotion, associated with career effectiveness because the organization either does not or cannot provide them. Second, the organization may have expectations for the individual's performance which the individual is unwilling or unable to meet. The organization may accurately assess the individual's potential as being greater than present performance, yet because the individual has interests beyond his or her career (e.g., family, community, religious interests) performance does not match potential. In such instances, the individual may be satisfied with career performance, yet the organization is disappointed. This mismatch occurs as a consequence of the individual's attitudes toward the career.

Career attitudes.   This aspect of career effectiveness refers to the way individuals perceive and evaluate their careers. The more positive are these perceptions and evaluations, the more effective are the careers. Positive attitudes have important implications for the organization as well because individuals with positive attitudes are more likely to be committed to the organization and to be involved in their jobs. The manner in which individuals develop positive career attitudes is a complex psychological and sociological process; a full development of that process is beyond the scope of this discussion. However, it is evident that positive career attitudes are maintained to the extent that career demands and opportunities are consistent with individuals' interests, values, needs, and abilities.

Career adaptability.   Few professions are stagnant and unchanging. On the contrary, the condition of change and development more accurately describes contemporary professions. Changes occur in the profession itself requiring new knowledge and skills to practice it; for example, medicine and engineering have and will continue to advance in the utilization of new information and technology. Other professions likewise have changed markedly. Individuals unable to adapt to these changes and to adopt them in the practice of their careers run the risk of early obsolescence. It goes without saying that organizations benefit through the adaptiveness of its employees. An expression of the mutual benefits derived from career adaptability is the dollars expended by organizations for employee training and development. Thus, career adaptability implies the application of the latest knowledge, skill, and technology in the work of a career.

Career identity.   Two important components comprise career identity. First is the extent to which individuals have clear and consistent awareness of their interests, values, and expectations for the future. Second is the extent to which individuals view their lives as consistent through time, the extent to which they see themselves as extensions of their pasts. The idea expressed in this concept is, "What do I want to be and what do I have to do to become what I want to be?" This question expresses for the individual the meaning of Maslow's concept of self-actualization as the highest order source of motivation. Individuals who have satisfactory resolutions to this question are likely to have effective careers and to make effective contributions to the organizations which employ them.

Effective careers in management, then, are likely to occur for individuals with high levels of performance, positive attitudes, adaptiveness, and identity resolution. As a career, management is not peculiar. The same criteria for effective careers in any profession apply to management. Moreover, effective management careers are without doubt linked to organizational performance.

Career Stages

The idea that individuals go through distinct but interrelated *career stages* is widely recognized and accepted. The simplest version of the concept includes four stages: (1) the prework stage (attending school), (2) the initial work stage (moving from job to job), (3) the stable work stage (maintaining one job), and (4) the retirement stage (leaving active employment).[2]

Most working people prepare for their occupation by undergoing some form of organized education in high school, trade school, vocational school, or college. Then they take a first job, but the chances are that they will move to other jobs in the same organization or in other organizations. Eventually, they settle into a position in which they remain until retirement. The duration of each stage varies among individuals, but most working people go through all of these stages.

Studies of career stages have found that needs and expectations change through the stages.[3] Managers in American Telephone & Telegraph Company (AT&T) expressed considerable concern for security during the initial years on their jobs. This phase,

---

[2] Paul H. Thompson, Robin Zenger Baker, and Norman Smallwood, "Improving Professional Development by Applying the Four-Stage Career Model," *Organizational Dynamics*, Autumn 1986, pp. 49–62.

[3] Douglas T. Hall and Khalil Nougaim, "An Examination of Maslow's Need Hierarchy in an Organizational Setting," *Organizational Behavior and Human Performance* 3 (1968), pp. 12–35; and Raymond E. Hill and Edwin L. Miller, "Job Change and the Middle Seasons of a Man's Life," *Academy of Management Journal*, March 1981, pp. 114–27.

termed the *establishment* phase, ordinarily lasted through the first five years of employment. Following the establishment phase is the *advancement* phase, stretching approximately from age 30 to age 45. During this period, the AT&T managers expressed less concern for security and more concern for achievement, esteem, and autonomy. Promotions and advancement to jobs with responsibility and opportunity to exercise independent judgement are characteristics of this phase.

The *maintenance* phase follows the advancement phase. This period is marked by efforts to stabilize the gains of the past. Although no new gains are made, the maintenance phase can be a period of creativity, since the individual has satisfied many of his psychological and financial needs in earlier phases. Each individual and each career is different, but it is reasonable to assume that self-fulfillment is the most important need in the maintenance phase. But many people experience what is termed the *midcareer* crisis during the maintenance phase. Such people do not receive satisfaction from their work, and consequently, they may experience physiological and psychological problems.[4]

The maintenance phase is followed by the *retirement* phase. The individual has, in effect, completed one career, and she may move on to another one. During this phase, the individual may have opportunities to experience fulfillment through activities that were impossible to pursue while working. Painting, gardening, volunteer service, and quiet reflection are some of the many positive avenues retirees take. The relationship between career stages and needs is summarized in Figure 20–2.

The fact that individuals pass through different stages during their careers is clear. It is also understandable that individual needs and motives are different from one stage to the next. But managing the careers of others requires a more complete understanding of these stages.

Professionals are one group of individuals whose careers are of special significance to the performance of modern organizations. Knowledge workers—such professionals as accountants, scientists, and engineers—are the fastest-growing segment of the work force, recently pegged at 32 percent (blue-collar workers made up 33 percent).[5] These professionals spend their careers in large, complex organizations after obtaining advanced training and degrees. Organizations expect these knowledge workers to provide the innovativeness and creativity necessary for survival in dynamic and competitive environments. Obviously, the performance levels of professional employees should be of utmost concern for the organization's leaders.

The effective management of professionals begins by understanding the crucial characteristics of the four stages of professional careers. By the same token, professional employees can avoid a number of disappointments and anxieties if they also understand more about their career stages.

---

[4]John Veiga, "Plateaued versus Non-plateaued Managers: Career Patterns, Attitudes and Path Potential," *Academy of Management Journal,* September 1981, pp. 566–78; and John W. Slocum, Jr., William L. Cron, and Linda C. Yows, "Whose Career Is Likely to Plateau?" *Business Horizons,* March/April 1987, pp. 31–38.

[5]Gene W. Dalton, Paul H. Thompson, and Raymond L. Price, "The Four Stages of Professional Careers—a New Look at Performance by Professionals," *Organizational Dynamics,* Summer 1977, pp. 19–42.

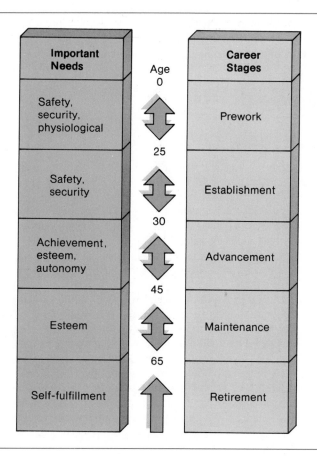

Figure 20–2
Career stages
and important
needs.

Important Needs

Age
0

Safety, security, physiological

25

Safety, security

30

Achievement, esteem, autonomy

45

Esteem

65

Self-fulfillment

Career Stages

Prework

Establishment

Advancement

Maintenance

Retirement

Stage I. Young professionals enter the organization with technical knowledge, but without an understanding of the organization's demands and expectations. Consequently, they must work fairly closely with more experienced persons.[6] The relationship that develops between the young professionals and their supervisors is an *apprenticeship*. The central activities in which apprentices are expected to show competence include *learning* and *following directions*. To move successfully through Stage I, professionals must be able to accept the *psychological state of dependence*. And some professionals cannot cope with being placed in a situation similar to that which they experienced while in school. They find that they are still being directed by an authority figure after anticipating that their first job would provide considerably more freedom.

[6]David M. Hunt and Carol Michael, "Mentorship: A Career Training and Development Tool," *Academy of Management Review,* July 1983, pp. 475–85; and Kathy E. Kram and Lynn A. Isabella, "Mentoring Alternatives: The Role of Peer Relationships in Career Development," *Academy of Management Journal,* March 1985, pp. 110–32.

Stage I job requirements prepare the individual for the more demanding and responsible work of the organization. The following Management Application describes some of the job activities of an aspiring professional in a stock trading firm.

MANAGEMENT APPLICATION

FIRST A CLERK, THEN A TRADER

Many jobs enable individuals to "learn by doing." This approach to job preparation works very well in environments which permit some degree of error and for individuals who can perform challenging unfamiliar tasks, accept criticism, correct mistakes, and work long hours. But in the high-stakes, high-risk environment of the stock trading firm, learning by doing could be disastrous. Successful job performance in a trading firm requires nearly instantaneous decisions in which there is little room for error. In fact, it would be foolish for a trading firm to issue a trader badge to a new job recruit no matter how bright, energetic, and enthusiastic. Instead of learning by doing, new employees "learn by observing."

To learn by observing requires employees to perform rather menial tasks. They spend the day adding, subtracting, transmitting phone messages, folding, sorting, tallying, and taking lunch orders. In short, they perform the duties typically assigned to a clerk. These experiences bear little resemblance to those ordinarily associated with professional training programs. Nevertheless, individuals enter the profession with the full knowledge that entry to the trading floor requires that they first demonstrate full knowledge of the technical and professional requirements of trading before they begin trading, not while they are trading. Although the experience of being a clerk may test the individual's humility, it is also the stepping stone to an important profession.

Source: Adapted from Anonymous, "I Diligently Remain a Clerk," *Business Today*, Winter 1987, p. 30.

Stage II. The professional employee next advances into Stage II, which calls for working independently. But passage to this stage depends on having demonstrated competence in some specific technical area. The technical expertise may be in a content area, such as taxation, product testing, or quality assurance, or it may be in a skill area, such as computer applications. The professional's primary activity in Stage II is to be an *independent contributor* of ideas in the chosen area. The professional is expected to need much less direction from others. The *psychological state of independence* may pose some problems because it contrasts with the state of dependence required in Stage I. Stage II is extremely important for the professional's future career growth. Those who fail at this stage do so either because they do not have the requisite technical skill to perform independently or because they do not have the necessary self-confidence.

Stage III. Professionals who enter Stage III are expected to become the mentors of those in Stage I. They also tend to broaden their interests and to deal more and more with people outside the organization. Thus, the central activities of professionals at this stage are *training* and *interactions* with others. Stage III professionals assume *responsibility for the work of others,* and this characteristic of the stage can cause considerable psychological stress. In previous stages, the professional was responsible for his or her own work. But now the work of others is of primary concern. Individuals who cannot cope with this new requirement may decide to shift back to Stage II. Individuals who are happy watching others move on to bigger and better jobs may be content to remain in Stage III until retirement.

Stage IV. Some professional employees remain in Stage III; for them Stage III is the career maintenance phase. Other professionals progress to yet another stage. This stage is not reached by all professionals because its fundamental characteristic is *shaping the direction of the organization itself.* You may think of such activity as the work of only one individual in an organization—the chief executive. In fact, it may be undertaken by many others. For example, key personnel in product development, process manufacturing, or technological research may be Stage IV types. As a consequence of their performance in Stage III of their careers, Stage IV professionals direct their attention to long-range strategic planning. In doing so, they play the roles of manager, entrepreneur, and idea generator. Their primary job relationships are to *identify* and *sponsor* the careers of their successors and to interact with key people outside the organization.

The most significant shift for a person in Stage IV is to accept the decisions of subordinates without second-guessing them. Stage IV professionals must learn to influence events and others through such indirect means as idea planting, personnel selection, and organizational design. These shifts can be difficult for an individual who has relied on direct supervision in the past.

The concept of career stages is fundamental to understanding and managing career development.[7] It is necessary to comprehend *life stages* as well. Individuals go through career stages as they go through life stages, but the interaction between career stages and life stages is not easy to understand.

Life Stages

Our understanding of the stages of life for children and youth is relatively well developed compared to our understanding of adult life stages. The field of psychology has provided much insight into the problems of childhood, but far less insight into the problems of adulthood. Adulthood is now thought to be defined by rather distinct phases. The demands, problems, and opportunities presented in these phases must be considered by managers concerned with developing the careers of their subordinates.

One view of the life stages emphasizes developmental aspects. That is, each life stage is marked by the need to work through a particular developmental task before

---

[7]Meryl Reis Louis, "Managing Career Transition: A Missing Link in Career Development," *Organizational Dynamics,* Spring, 1982, pp. 68–77.

the individual can move successfully into the next stage.[8] The stages and their developmental tasks are described below.

Adolescence.   For most people, this stage occurs from age 15 to age 25. Prior to this stage is *childhood*. Since our primary concern is the life stages as related to the career stages, childhood is relatively unimportant for our purposes. Achieving *ego identity* is essential for normal progression through adolescence. Adolescents are concerned with settling on a particular career or occupational choice. They can become confused by the apparent gaps between what they think they can do and what they think they must do to succeed in a career. The latter years of the adolescent stage usually coincide with initial employment, and if ego identity has not been achieved, one can expect difficulties during this first career opportunity.

Young adulthood.   The years between 25 and 35 ordinarily entail the development of *intimacy and involvement with others*. During this life stage, individuals learn to become involved not only with other persons but also with groups and organizations. How successfully individuals pass through this phase depends on how successful they were in establishing their ego identities as adolescents. In terms of career stages, young adulthood corresponds with the *establishment* of a career and the initial stages of *advancement*. There may be conflicts between life stage demands and career stage demands if, for example, the career stage requires behaviors inconsistent with establishing relationships with others.

Adulthood.   The 30 years between 35 and 65 are devoted to *generativity,* a term that implies concern for actions and achievements that will benefit *future generations.* Individuals in this life stage emphasize the productive and creative use of their talents and abilities. In the context of work experience, adulthood involves building organizations, devising new and lasting products, coaching younger people, and teaching others. This life stage coincides with the later years of the advancement career stage and the full duration of the maintenance stage. Successful development of the adulthood stage depends on having achieved ego identity and commitment to others, the developmental tasks of the preceding two stages.

Maturity.   The last life stage is maturity. People pass through this stage successfully if they achieve *ego integrity;* that is, if they do not despair of their lives and of the choices they have made. In a sense, this stage represents the culmination of a productive and creative life served in the interests of others to the satisfaction of self. This life stage coincides with the retirement career stage.

The relationships between life stages and career stages are shown in Figure 20–3. Successful careers evidently are a result, in part, of achieving certain career stages at certain ages. For example, a study of scientists in two research and development companies attempted to determine the relationship between performance and career

---

[8]Erik H. Erikson, *Childhood and Society* (New York: W. W. Norton, 1963).

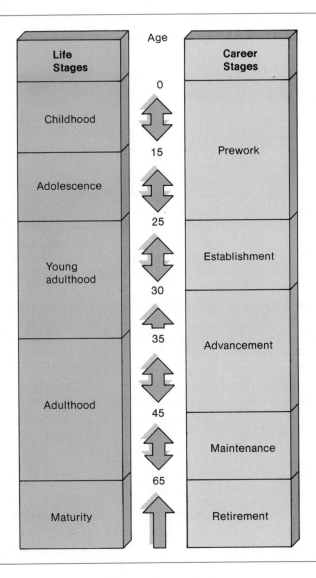

Figure 20–3
The relationships between career stages and life stages.

stage for those over 40. The results are shown in Table 20–1. In these two companies, it is apparent that individuals whose career stages were not in step with their life stages were relatively low performers.

Notice that all of the employees over 40 who are classified as at Stage I of their careers were considered to be below-average performers. For whatever reasons, these employees were unable to establish themselves as independent contributors of ideas and thus to move on to Stage II. Perhaps they had been unable to achieve ego identity during the early stages of their lives. Managers must recognize the interaction between career stages and life stages in designing effective career development programs.

Table 20–1 Relationship between age, career stage, and performance (40 years or older).

	Stage I	Stage II	Stage III	Stage IV
Above-average performance	0%	18%	79%	100%
Below-average performance	100	82	21	0

Two points in the careers of individuals are particularly crucial for career development. The *recent hiree* begins his career with a particular job and position. Experiences on this first job can have considerable positive and negative affects on future performance. The *midcareer* person is subject to pressures and possibilities different from those of the recent hiree, but she is also at a critical point. The following sections describe several career development problems of recent hirees and midcareer managers.

CAREER DEVELOPMENT FOR RECENT HIREES

Recently hired employees face many anxious moments. They have selected their positions based on what they expect the organization to demand of them and what they expect to receive for meeting those demands. Young managers, particularly those with college training, expect opportunities to utilize their training in ways leading to recognition and advancement. In too many instances, recently hired managers are soon disappointed with their initial career decisions. Although the specific causes of early-career disappointments vary from person to person, some general causes have been identified.[9]

Causes of Early-Career Difficulties

Studies of the early-career problems of young managers typically find that those who experience frustration are victims of "reality shock." These young managers see a discrepancy between what they thought the organization was and what it actually is. Several factors contribute to reality shock, and it is important for young managers and their managers to be aware of them.

The initial job challenge.   The first jobs of young managers often demand far less of them than they are able to deliver. Consequently, young managers believe that they are unable to demonstrate their full capabilities and that, in a sense, they are being stifled. This is especially true if the recruiter has been overly enthusiastic in selling the organization to the managers when they were recruited.

---

[9]Daniel C. Feldman and Jeanne M. Brett, "Coping with New Jobs: A Comparative Study of New Hires and Job Changers," *Academy of Management Journal*, June 1983, pp. 258–72.

Some young managers are able to *create* challenging jobs even when their assignments are fairly routine. They do this by thinking of ways to do their jobs differently and better. They may also be able to persuade their managers to give them more leeway and more to do. Unfortunately, many young managers are unable to create challenge. Their previous experiences in school were typically experiences in which challenge had been given to them by their teachers. The challenge had been created *for* them, not *by* them.

Initial job satisfaction.   Recently hired managers with college training often believe that they can perform at levels beyond those of their initial assignments. After all, they have been exposed to the latest managerial theories and techniques, and in their minds at least, they are ready to run the company. They are sure to be disappointed and dissatisfied, however, when they discover that others do not share their self-evaluations.

Initial job performance feedback.   Feedback on performance is an important managerial responsibility. Yet, many managers are inadequately trained to meet this responsibility. They simply do not know how to evaluate the performances of their subordinates. This deficiency is especially damaging to new managers. They have not been in the organization long enough to be socialized by their peers and other employees. They are not sure of what they are expected to believe, what values to hold, or what behaviors are required of them. They naturally look to their own managers to guide them through this early phase. But when their managers fail to evaluate their performance accurately, they do not know if they are meeting the organization's expectations.

Certainly, not all young managers experience problems associated with their initial assignments. But those who do and who leave the organization as a consequence of their frustrations represent a waste of talent and money. Thus, it is apparent that the cost of losing capable young managers outweighs the cost of efforts and programs designed to counteract initial job problems.

Table 20–2 presents some advice for young managers from a well-known management writer.

How to Counteract Early-Career Problems

Managers who wish to improve the retention and development of young management talent have several programs and practices from which to choose.

Realistic job previews.   One way to counteract the unrealistic expectations of new recruits is to provide realistic information during the *recruiting* process. Through *realistic job previews* (RJPs), recruits are given opportunities to learn not only the benefits they may expect from the job and the organization but also the drawbacks. Studies have shown that the recruitment rate is the same for those who receive RJPs as for those who do not. More important, those who do receive RJPs are more likely

---

Table 20–2   Some advice for beginning managers.

Remember that good performance that pleases your superiors is the basic foundation of success, but recognize that not all good performance is easily measured. Determine the real criteria by which you are evaluated and be rigorously honest in evaluating your own performance against these criteria.

Manage your career; be active in influencing decisions, because pure effort is not necessarily rewarded.

Strive for positions that have high visibility and exposure where you can be a hero observed by higher officials. Check to see that the organization has a formal system of keeping track of young people. Remember that high-risk line jobs tend to offer more visibility than staff positions like corporate planning or personnel, but also that visibility can sometimes be achieved by off-job community activities.

Develop relations with a mobile senior executive who can be your sponsor. Become a complementary crucial subordinate with different skills than your superior.

Learn your job as quickly as possible and train a replacement so you can be available to move and broaden your background in different functions.

Nominate yourself for other positions; modesty is not necessarily a virtue. However, change jobs for more power and influence, not primarily for status or pay. The latter could be a substitute for real opportunity to make things happen.

Before taking a position, rigorously assess your strengths and weaknesses, what you like and don't like. Don't accept a promotion if it draws on your weaknesses and entails mainly activities that you don't like.

Leave at your convenience, but on good terms without parting criticism of the organization. Do not stay under an immobile superior who is not promoted in three to five years.

Don't be trapped by formal, narrow job descriptions. Move outside them and probe the limits of your influence.

Accept that responsibility will always somewhat exceed authority and that organizational politics are inevitable. Establish alliances and fight necessary battles, minimizing upward ones to very important issues.

Get out of management if you can't stand being dependent on others and having them dependent on you.

Recognize that you will face ethical dilemmas no matter how moral you try to be. No evidence exists that unethical managers are more successful than ethical ones, but it may well be that those who move faster are less socially conscious. Therefore, from time to time you must examine your personal values and question how much you will sacrifice for the organization.

Don't automatically accept all tales of managerial perversity that you hear. Attributing others' success to unethical behavior is often an excuse for one's own personal inadequacies. Most of all, don't commit an act which you know to be wrong in the hope that your supervisor will see it as loyalty and reward you for it. Sometimes he will, but he may also sacrifice you when the organization is criticized.

Source: Ross A. Webber, "Career Problems of Young Managers," *California Management Review,* Summer 1976, p. 29. Reprinted with permission.

---

to remain on the job and to be satisfied with it than are those who do not.[10] A number of organizations practice "telling it like it is," including the Prudential Insurance Company of America, Texas Instruments Incorporated, and the U.S. Military Academy.

---

[10]John P. Wanous, *Organizational Entry* (Reading, Mass.: Addison-Wesley Publishing, 1980); Paula Popovich and John P. Wanous, "The Realistic Job Preview as a Persuasive Communication," *Academy of Management Review,* October 1982, pp. 570–78; and James A. Breaugh, "Realistic Job Previews: A Critical Appraisal and Future Research Directions," *Academy of Management Review,* October 1983, pp. 612–19.

In addition to the concern of specific firms for accurate depiction of job demands, industries have expressed similar concerns. Some of them have implemented industrywide programs to develop realistic job information. The following Management Application describes some of the things the retail industry is doing to combat the problems of unrealistic job expectations.

MANAGEMENT APPLICATION

REALISTIC EXPECTATIONS IN THE RETAIL INDUSTRY

Spokespersons for the retail industry have lamented the problems associated with high attrition rates among executive trainees hired right out of universities and colleges. Entry executive-level jobs in the industry require long hours, frantic pace, and physical work that discourage many trainees, causing them to quit the industry at the rate of 40 percent during their first five years. As the industry began to recognize the costs of this turnover, it realized that its recruiters should describe more accurately the nitty-gritty of retailing so as to prepare the trainees for the reality of their jobs.

Major retailers such as Allied Stores Corporation have implemented programs to present balanced information. They invite college professors to their stores to meet their former students and to hear how and what they are doing. They also go to campuses to hold information forums for students and faculty. The purpose of these sessions is to present both sides of the story, that retailing is hard work and that early years are filled with long hours of frustrating and not-so-glamorous work, but that long-run rewards do come. The effort is designed to provide newly recruited executive trainees with accurate expectations of their futures.

Source: Adapted from Marion L. Salzman, "In Search of Tomorrow's Excellent Managers," *Management Review*, April 1985, p. 43.

A challenging initial assignment. Managers of newly hired workers should be encouraged to assign them the most demanding available jobs. Successful implementation of this policy, however, requires managers to take some risks, since they are accountable for the performance of their subordinates. If the assignments surpass the abilities of the subordinates, both the managers and the subordinates share the cost of failure. Thus, most managers prefer to bring their subordinates along slowly by giving them progressively more difficult and challenging jobs, but only *after the subordinates have demonstrated their abilities*. Newly hired managers have *potential for performance*, but have not *demonstrated performance*. Thus, it is risky to assign an individual to a task for which there is any significant probability of failure. But studies have indicated that managers who experienced initial job challenge were more effective in their later years.

Demanding bosses. A practice that seems to have considerable promise for increasing the retention rate of young managers is to assign them initially to demanding supervisors. In this context, demanding should not be interpreted as autocratic. Rather, the type of boss most likely to get new hires off in the right direction is one who has high but achievable expectations for their performance. Such a boss instills in the young managers the understanding that high performance is expected and rewarded and, equally important, that the boss is always ready to assist them through coaching and counseling.

The programs and practices created to retain and develop young managers—particularly recent hires with college training—can be used separately or in combination. A manager would be well advised to establish policies that most likely would retain those recent hires with high potential. Such policies include realistic job previews coupled with challenging initial assignments supervised by supportive, performance-oriented managers. Although such practices are not perfect, they are helpful not only in retaining young managers but also in avoiding the problems that may arise during the middle phases of a manager's career.

CAREER DEVELOPMENT FOR MIDCAREER MANAGERS

Managers in the midstages of their careers ordinarily are key people in their organizations. They have established a place for themselves in society as well as at work. They occupy important positions in the community, often engage in civic affairs, and are looked on as model achievers in our achievement-oriented culture. Yet, every year popular and scholarly articles and books discuss the midcareer crisis and the middle-aged drop-out.[11] Executives disappear from their jobs and are later found driving taxis, teaching in ghettos, or at worst, wandering on skid row. Such lost talent is expensive to replace, and more and more organizations are initiating practices to deal with the problems of the midcareer manager.

The Midcareer Plateau

Managers face the *midcareer plateau* during the adult stage of life and the maintenance phase of careers. At this point, the likelihood of additional upward promotion may be quite low. Two reasons account for the plateau. First, there are simply fewer jobs at the top of the organization, and even though the manager has the ability to perform at that level, no opening exists. Second, openings may exist, but the manager may lack either the *ability* or the *desire* to fill them.[12]

Managers who find themselves stifled in their present jobs tend to cope with the problems in fairly consistent ways. They suffer from depression and poor health, and harbor fear of and express hostility toward their subordinates. Eventually, they may "retire" on the job or leave the organization permanently. Any one of these coping

---

[11]John Bardwick, *The Plateauing Trap: How to Avoid It in Your Career* (New York: AMACOM, 1986); and Janet P. Near, "Work and Nonwork Correlates of the Career Plateau," *Academy of Management Proceedings*, 1983, pp. 380–84.

[12]Thomas P. Ference, James A. F. Stoner, and E. Kirby Warren, "Managing the Career Plateau," *Academy of Management Review*, October 1977, p. 604.

mechanisms results in lowered job performance and, of course, lowered organizational performance.

The midcareer, middle-age crisis has been depicted in novels, movies, dramas, and psychological studies. Although each individual's story is different and unique, the scenario has many common features. Of course, not all managers respond to their situations in the same ways. Some, perhaps most, cope constructively. But to the extent that effective managers experience disruptive psychological, physical, and professional traumas, organizational performance will suffer. The cost of impaired managerial effectiveness indicates that organizations should implement programs to counteract midcareer plateau problems.[13]

How to Counteract Midcareer Problems

Counteracting the problems that managers face at midcareer involves providing *counseling* and *alternatives*.

Midcareer counseling.   Organizations such as IBM, Du Pont, Alcoa, and Western Electric Co., Inc. employ full-time staff psychiatrists to assist employees in dealing with career, health, and family problems.[14] In the context of such counseling, midcareer managers are provided with professional help for depression and stress. Since midcareer managers usually are well educated and articulate, they often only need someone to talk to, someone skilled in the art of listening. The process of verbalizing their problems to an objective listener is often enough to enable midcareer managers to recognize their problems and to cope with them constructively.

Midcareer alternatives.   Effective resolution of midcareer crises requires acceptable alternatives. The organization cannot be expected to go beyond counseling or personal and family problems. But when the crisis is precipitated primarily by career-related factors, the organization can be an important source of alternatives. In many instances, the organization simply needs to accept career moves that are usually viewed as unacceptable.

Three career moves with potential for counteracting the problems of midcareer managers are lateral transfers, downward transfers, and fall-back positions.[15]

Lateral transfers involve moves at the same organizational level from one department to another. A manager who has plateaued in production could be transferred to a similar level in sales, engineering, or some other area. The move would require the manager to take time to learn the technical demands of the new position, and during that time there might be reduced performance. But once qualified, the manager would bring the perspectives of both areas to bear on decisions.

---

[13]Norihiko Suzuki, "Mid-Career Crisis in Japanese Business Organizations," *Journal of Management Development* (1986), pp. 23–32.

[14]Manfred F. R. Kets de Vries, "The Midcareer Conundrum," *Organizational Dynamics*, Autumn 1978, p. 58.

[15]Douglas T. Hall and Francine S. Hall, "What's New in Career Management," *Organizational Dynamics*, Summer 1976, pp. 21–27.

Downward transfers are associated in our society with failure; an effective manager simply does not consider a move downward to be an acceptable alternative. Yet downward transfers are in many instances not only acceptable, but entirely respectable, alternatives, particularly when one or more of the following conditions exist:[16]

The manager values the quality of life afforded by a specific geographic area and may desire a downward transfer if it is required to stay in or move to that area.

The manager views the downward transfer as a way to establish a base for future promotions.[17]

The manager is faced with the alternatives of dismissal or a downward move.

The manager desires to pursue time-consuming, nonjob-related activities—such as religious, civic, or political activities—and for that reason may welcome the reduced responsibility (and demands) of a lower-level position.

The use of *fallback positions* is a relatively new way to reduce the risk of lateral and downward transfers. The practice involves identifying in advance a position to which the transferred manager can return if the new position does not work out. In this way the organization informs everyone affected that some risk is involved, but the organization is willing to accept some responsibility for it, and returning to the fallback job will not mean failure. Companies such as Heublein, Procter & Gamble, Continental Can Co., and Lehman Bros. Corp. have used fallback positions to reduce the risk of lateral and upward moves. The practice appears to hold considerable promise for protecting the careers of highly specialized technicians and professionals who make their first move into general management positions.

The suggestion that organizations initiate practices and programs to assist managers through midcareer crises does not excuse managers from taking responsibility for themselves. Individuals who deal honestly and constructively with their lives and careers will take steps early on to minimize the risk of becoming obsolete or redundant. At the outset of their management careers, they can begin to formulate their *career plans and paths*. Often they will be assisted in this process by their organizations.

CAREER PLANNING AND PATHING

Career planning involves matching an individual's career aspirations with the opportunities available in an organization. *Career pathing* is the sequencing of the specific jobs associated with those opportunities. The two processes are intertwined. Planning a career involves identifying the means for achieving desired ends, and, in the context of career plans, career paths are the means for achieving aspirations. Although career planning is still a relatively new practice, many organizations are turning to it as a way to *proact* rather than *react* to the problems associated with early and midcareer career crises.

---

[16]Douglas T. Hall and Lynn A. Isabella, "Downward Movement and Career Development," *Organizational Dynamics,* Summer 1985, pp. 5–23.

[17]Betsy D. Gelb and Michael R. Hyman, "Reducing Reluctance to Transfer," *Business Horizons,* March/April 1987, pp. 39–43.

Successful career planning and career pathing place equal responsibility on the individual and the organization. The individual must identify his or her aspirations and abilities and then recognize what training and development are required for following a particular career path. The organization must identify its needs and opportunities through human resource planning and provide career information and training to its employees.[18]

Such companies as Weyerhaeuser, Nabisco Brands, Inc., Gulf Oil Corp., Exxon Corporation, and Eaton Corporation use career development programs to identify the pool of talent available for promotion and transfer opportunities. Companies often restrict career counseling to managerial and professional staff, but IBM, GE, TRW Inc., and Gulf Oil provide career counseling for both blue-collar and managerial personnel.

Career Planning

Individual and organizational needs and opportunities can be matched in a variety of ways. Two widely used approaches are (1) informal counseling by the personnel staff and (2) career counseling by supervisors. These approaches are often quite informal. Somewhat more formal and less widely used practices involve workshops, seminars, and self-assessment centers.

Informal counseling.   The personnel staffs of organizations often include counseling services for employees who wish to assess their abilities and interests. The counseling process also can move into personal concerns, and this is proper since, as you have seen, life concerns are important factors in determining career aspirations. In this context, career counseling is viewed by the organization as a service to its employees, but not as a primary service.

Career counseling by supervisors usually is included in performance appraisals. The question of where the employee is going in the organization arises quite naturally in this setting. In fact, the inclusion of career information in performance appraisal predates the current interest in career planning. A characteristic of effective performance evaluation is to let the employee know not only how well he has done, but also what the future holds. Thus, supervisors must be able to counsel the employee in terms of organizational needs and opportunities not only within the specific department but throughout the organization. Since supervisors usually have limited information about the total organization, the company often must adopt more formal and systematic counseling approaches.

The extreme of informal counseling activities is self-counseling. Self-counseling often includes paper-and-pencil, self-assessment tests which enable individuals to better understand their strengths and weaknesses, likes and dislikes, and other personal characteristics. As noted in the following Management Application, such tests are available by mail.

---

[18]Cherlyn Skromme Granrose and James D. Portwood, "Matching Individual Career Paths and Organizational Career Management," *Academy of Management Journal,* December 1987, pp. 699–720.

MANAGEMENT APPLICATION

CAREER COUNSELING BY MAIL

Individuals seeking career counseling can obtain a self-assessment test that they can complete in the privacy of their homes. The test is available from National Computer Systems, Inc., P. O. Box 1416, Minnetonka, Minnesota 55440, at a cost of $34.95. The multiple-choice test measures different interests, work values, personal traits, and verbal and numerical abilities. It takes about three hours to complete and the responses must be returned to the vendor. Then the computer matches the individuals' answers to thousands of other people who report that they are happy and satisfied with their chosen profession. Within a few days a report is sent which interprets the responses and suggests 10 to 15 careers that match the individuals' responses.

Such tests can be instructive and can identify areas of interest that might have gone unrecognized. They are convenient and relatively inexpensive, but many experts would argue that they should not substitute for professional career counseling. Other experts point out that these kinds of self-analysis can be instructive and can suggest avenues of opportunity that could be explored without making a major commitment in time and money.

Source: Adapted from John A. Byrne, "This Test May Tell You to Switch Careers," *Business Week,* September 21, 1987, p. 125.

Formal counseling.   Workshops, assessment centers, and career development centers are being used increasingly in organizations. Typically, such formal practices are designed to serve specific employee groups. Management trainees and high-potential or fast-track management candidates have received most of the attention to date. However, women and minority employees are now receiving greater attention. Career development programs for women and minority employees are viewed as indications of an organization's commitment to affirmative action.[19]

One example of a formal organizational career planning system is Syntex Corporation's Career Development Center. The center is the result of the realization that the managers in Syntex were unable to counsel their subordinates, because they were too caught up in their own jobs. The center's staff first identifies the individual's strengths and weaknesses in eight skill areas Syntex believes to be related to effective management. These eight areas are (1) problem analysis; (2) communication; (3) goal setting; (4) decision making and conflict handling; (5) selecting, training, and motivating employees; (6) controlling employees; (7) interpersonal competence; and (8) the use of time. On the basis of scores in the eight areas, each manager sets career and personal goals. The center's staff assists the manager to set realistic goals that reflect her strengths and weaknesses in the eight areas.

---

[19]Edward G. Verlander, "Incorporating Career Counselling into Management Development," *Journal of Management Development* (1986), pp. 36–45; and B. Kaye, "Career Development Puts Training in Its Place," *Personnel Journal,* February 1983, pp. 132–37.

Organizations can use a variety of practices to facilitate their employees' career plans. One of the oldest and most widely used practices is some form of *tuition aid program*. Employees can take advantage of educational and training opportunities available at nearby schools, and the organization pays some or all of the tuition. J. I. Case, a Tenneco company with corporate offices in Racine, Wisconsin, is one of many organizations that provide in-house courses and seminars, as well as tuition reimbursement, for courses related to the individual's job.

Another practice is *job posting;* that is, the organization publicizes job openings as they occur. The employees thus are made aware of the opportunities. Effective job posting requires more than simply placing a notice on the company bulletin board. At a minimum, job posting should meet the following conditions:

1. It should include promotions and transfers as well as permanent vacancies.
2. The available jobs should be posted at least three to six weeks prior to external recruiting.
3. The eligibility rules should be explicit and straightforward.
4. The standards for selection and the bidding instructions should be stated clearly.
5. Vacationing employees should be given the opportunity to apply ahead of time.
6. Employees who apply but are rejected should be notified of the reason in writing, and a record of the reason should be placed in their personnel files.[20]

Career Pathing

Career planning results in placing an individual into the first job of a sequential series. From the perspective of the organization, career paths are important inputs for work force planning. An organization's future work force depends on the projected passage of individuals through the ranks. From the perspective of the individual, a career path is the sequence of jobs he undertakes to achieve personal and career goals. It is virtually impossible to integrate completely organizational and individual needs in the design of career paths. Yet systematic career planning can potentially close the gap between the needs of the individual and the needs of the organization.

Traditional career paths have emphasized upward mobility in a single occupation or functional area.[21] When recruiting personnel, the organization's representative will speak of engineers', accountants', or salespersons' career paths. In these contexts, the recruiter will describe the different jobs along the ladder pointing progressively upward in an organization. Each job, or rung, is reached when the individual has accumulated

[20]David R. Dahl and Patrick R. Pinto, "Job Posting: An Industry Survey," *Personnel Journal,* January 1977, pp. 40–42.

[21]Kevin J. Nilan, Sally Walls, Sandra Davis, and Mary E. Lund, "Creating a Hierarchical Career Progression Network," *Personnel Administration,* June 1987, pp. 168–83.

Figure 20–4 Career path, general management.

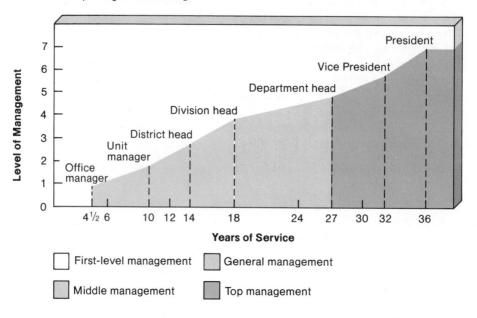

Source: Based on William F. Glueck, *Personnel: A Diagnostic Approach* (Plano, Tex.: Business Publications, 1978), pp. 272–73.

the necessary experience and ability and has demonstrated that he or she is ready for promotion.

Implicit in such career paths, however, is the attitude that one has failed if she does not move on up after a certain length of time. Such attitudes make it difficult to use lateral and downward transfers as alternatives for managers who no longer wish to pay the price for upward promotion.

An alternative to traditional career pathing is to base career paths on real-world experiences and individualized preferences. Paths of this kind have several characteristics:

1. They include lateral and downward possibilities as well as upward possibilities, and they are not tied to normal rates of progress.

2. They are tentative, and responsive to changes in organizational needs.

3. They are flexible enough to take into account the qualities of individuals.

4. Each job along the paths is specified in terms of *acquirable* skills, knowledge, and other specific attributes, not merely in terms of educational credentials, age, or work experience.[22]

---

[22]James W. Walker, "Let's Get Realistic about Career Paths," *Human Resource Management,* Fall 1976, pp. 2–7.

Realistic career paths, rather than traditional ones, are necessary for effective employee counseling. In the absence of such information, the employee can only guess at what is available.

An example of a career path for general management in a telephone company is depicted in Figure 20–4. According to the path, the average duration of a manager's assignment in first-level management is four years—two and one-half years as a staff assistant in the home office and one and one-half years as the manager of a district office in a small city. By the 14th year, the average manager should have reached the fourth level of management. The assignment at this level might be that of division manager of the commercial sales and operations division. Obviously, not all managers reach the fifth level, much less the seventh, that of the company president. As one nears the top of an organization, the number of openings declines and the proportion of candidates to positions increases.

SOME DIFFICULT CAREER AND HUMAN RESOURCE DEVELOPMENT ISSUES

Organizations that undertake career development programs are certain to encounter some difficult issues along the way.[23] The following problems are based on the actual experiences of some organizations.

Integrating Career Development and Human Resource Planning

The relationship between career development and human resource planning is obvious. Career development provides a *supply* of talents and abilities; human resource planning projects the *demand* for talents and abilities. It would seem logical that organizations undertaking one of these activities would undertake the other. Surely, it makes little sense to develop people and then have no place to put them, *or* to project needs for people but have no program to supply them. In fact, some organizations do have one program, but not both.

Even companies that make use of both career development programs and human resource planning have difficulty in integrating the efforts of the two. One reason is that each is done by different specialties. Career development often is done by psychologists, and human resource planning is the job of economists and systems analysts. Practitioners of these two disciplines have difficulty in communicating with each other. Their training and backgrounds create potential barriers to effective communication.[24]

A second reason for failure to integrate the efforts of career development and human resource planning is related to the *organizational structure*. Career planning usually is the function of *personnel departments*. Work force planning is the function of *planning staffs*. The two activities are carried out in two organizationally distinct units.

---

[23]This section is based on Hall and Hall, "What's New in Career Management," pp. 27–30.

[24]Mary Ann Von Glinow, Michael J. Driver, Kenneth Brousseau, and J. Bruce Prince, "The Design of a Career-Oriented Human Resources System," *Academy of Management Review*, January 1983, pp. 23–32.

The manager responsible for both units may be the chief executive officer or a group executive with many other responsibilities, as well.

Managing Dual Careers

As more and more women enter the working world and pursue careers, managers increasingly will confront the problems of *dual careers*. The problems arise because the careers of husbands and wives may lead them in different directions. An obvious problem can arise when the organization offers the husband or wife a transfer (involving a promotion), but it is rejected because the required relocation is incompatible with the spouse's career plans. One study reports that one in three executives cannot or will not relocate because this would interfere with the career of the spouse.[25] Thus, organizations *and* individuals lose flexibility as a consequence of dual careers.

At present, more than 46 million employed men and women are two-career couples, and both the number and the proportion of dual-career couples will most likely increase. The problems associated with this phenomenon are relatively new, but those who have studied these problems offer the following advice:

1. An organization should conduct an employee survey to gather statistics and information regarding the incidence of dual careers in its *present* and *projected* work force. The survey should determine *(a)* how many employees are at present part of a two-career situation; *(b)* how many people interviewed for positions are part of a dual-career situation; *(c)* where and at what level in the organization the dual-career employees are; *(d)* what conflicts these employees now have; and *(e)* whether dual-career employees perceive company policy and practices to be helpful to their careers and careers of their spouses.

2. Recruiters should present realistic previews of what the company offers dual-career couples. Orientation sessions conducted by personnel departments should include information to help such couples identify potential problems.

3. Career development and transfer policies must be revised. Since the usual policies are based on the traditional one-career family, they are inapplicable to dual-career situations. The key is to provide more flexibility.

4. The company should consider providing career couples with special assistance in career management. Couples usually are unprepared to cope with the problems posed by two careers. Young, recently hired couples are especially naive in this regard.

5. The organization can establish cooperative arrangements with other organizations. When one organization desires to relocate one dual-career partner, cooperative organizations can be sources of employment for the other partner.

6. The most important immediate step is to establish flexible working hours. Allowing couples the privilege of arranging their work schedules so that these will be compatible with family demands is an effective way to meet some of the problems of managing dual-career couples.[26]

---

[25]Francine S. Hall and Douglas T. Hall, "Dual Careers—How Do Couples and Companies Cope with the Problem?" *Organizational Dynamics*, Spring 1978, pp. 57–77.

[26]Ibid., pp. 72–76.

It would be a mistake to believe that dual-career problems exist only for managerial and professional personnel. More and more nonmanagerial personnel also are members of two-career families. Managers will confront problems in scheduling overtime for these people and in transferring them to different shifts. Like the needs of managerial and professional people, the needs of blue-collar workers must also be considered.

The issues of managing dual careers, both from the couple's and the organization's viewpoint, are only beginning to emerge. Managers of the 1980s will find these issues to be among their most significant career development challenges.

Dealing with Government Affirmative Action Programs

The initial thrust of affirmative action programs is to recruit and place women and minority employees into managerial and professional positions. Many organizations have been successful in that effort, but their success has created additional problems. For example, the career development needs of women and minority employees require nontraditional methods. A potential explosive additional problem is coping with the reactions of white male employees.

The key to meeting the career development needs of women and minority employees is to integrate recruitment, placement, and development efforts. For example, Virginia National Bankshares, the holding company of Virginia National Bank (VNB), has 155 offices throughout Virginia. Despite the fact that 72 percent of its employees are women, only 25 percent of them are in management positions. To correct the imbalance, VNB started a program designed to move more women into management. VNB appointed an advisory board consisting of eight women from various specialties within the bank. The advisory board interviewed all present female managers to determine what women considered to be their problems. The board then surveyed 109 nonmanagerial women to find out how many actually aspired to be managers.

The advisory board discovered that a large number of women were willing to undergo whatever training was necessary to move into management. The board also identified three crucial problem areas which had to be resolved before these women could realize their aspirations: (1) misconceptions about and outdated attitudes toward women, (2) lack of lending experience among women, and (3) lack of management skills among women. The bank's management accepted the advisory board's recommendation that a rotational program be implemented. Women would be placed in all major credit areas throughout the bank. They would be trained in three lending skills: accounting, economics/finance, and financial statement analysis. They would spend one month in each credit area: branch management, credit review, marketing, branch lending, commercial loans, mortgage loans, and national accounts. In addition to the rotational program, the bank began sponsoring seminars prepared by the National Association of Bank Women and conducting life planning seminars to help women function effectively in their careers and in other areas of their lives.

The VNB program is representative of career development designed to meet the specific needs of specific employees in a specific situation. Traditional programs are directed toward mainstream employees and are often too general in focus and content to meet the needs of women and minority employees. Although the VNB program's target group was women, its principles could be equally applicable to minority employees.

In the midst of affirmative action concerns, the employees most likely to feel threatened are white males of average competence. The threat is most keenly felt when the economy slows down and the few promotions available go to women and minority employees. White males are not much comforted to be told that such practices are temporary and are intended to correct past injustices. The white male of average competence is the one who often "loses" the promotion. Above-average white males usually will progress; below-average performers will always lag behind. So what can managers do to help the average performers?

No company practice can guarantee that average male employees will cooperate with affirmative action programs. But some practices offer promise. First, the company should provide open and complete information about promotions. Instead of being secretive about promotions (in the hope that if white males aren't told that they are being passed over, they won't notice it), the organization should provide information that permits white males to see precisely where they stand. If given such information, they will be less likely to overestimate their relative disadvantage and will be able to assess their position in the organization more accurately.

A second practice that seems promising is to make sure that white males receive as much career development assistance as other groups. White males may also need information about occupational opportunities *outside the company*. Since they perceive their upward mobility as being temporarily stifled by the company's affirmative action efforts, the average white males should be given the opportunity to seek career mobility elsewhere. But the management of any company that is sincerely pursuing affirmative action through career development must not expect all employees to go along with and support the effort. Vested interests are at stake when one group progresses at the expense of another.

MANAGEMENT SOLUTION

THE INDIVIDUAL DEVELOPMENT PLAN (IDP) WORKSHOP

The division's management decided on a workshop to include a series of related activities. Each of the activities was to accomplish certain objectives in the context of the entire program. The workshop's first activity was the division leader's presentation of the division's mission, goals, and overall strategy. The presentation outlined current and future major projects and anticipated job requirements as well as the division's philosophy of career development. Prior to attending the workshop, participants had received from their supervisors answers to some important questions, including: "What are the major goals for the work group and how can I support you to meet those goals? What do you see as the major results for my job in the next 12 months? How can you support me to achieve those results? What are my major competencies? What, in your view, is an outstanding employee?"

The workshop activity included group discussion of the division leader's presentation and the responses of supervisors to the key questions

Continued

MANAGEMENT SOLUTION

Concluded

not above. The participants completed a variety of self-assessment inventories to assist them to discern their values and appropriate strategies for achieving them. The participants took all this information as important imput in the development of their own individual development plans (IDP).

The IDP identifies what each individual can and should do to achieve career aspirations. It identifies development needs for performance improvement and job competency and specific actions to take to improve any deficiencies. It also identifies the assistance required of the supervisor and other division-controlled support such as job assignments, training, and information. The IDP also identifies all of the obstacles that must be overcome if the individual is to accomplish the plan. Completing the IDP

was the last activity of the workshop, and all the other activities led up to this important exercise. Following the workshop, individuals discussed their IDPs with their supervisors.

Through the participation of all key individuals throughout the organization, the career development workshop became more than a career planning exercise. Instead, it became an important strategy for integrating organizational and individual goals. In addition, it serves as an important activity for identifying and managing key work-related problems that can stifle not only the organization's purposes, but the individual's ambitions as well.

Source: Adapted from Donna R. Christensen, "Organizational Involvement: The Key to Employee Career Development," *Management Solutions*, May 1987, pp. 38–41.

MANAGEMENT SUMMARY

☐ Providing career development programs for employees is an important managerial responsibility. The effective performance of individual tasks depends, in part, on the balance between individual ability and task demands.

☐ Career development recognizes the changing needs of the organization and the individual. Organizations change in response to environmental pressures and opportunities. These changes alter organizations' needs for management talent. Individuals typically change as they grow and develop their talents and abilities.

☐ The unique career problems of recent hirees should be counteracted by the use of specifically designed practices and policies.

☐ Midcareer employees often face severe personal stress. Enlightened management practices will encourage such employees to face their situations and to exercise options offered by the organization.

☐ Effective career development programs provide opportunities for both the individual and the organization to achieve goals and objectives. It is impossible for the individual to develop a career in an organization without information on the organization's goals and objectives. Likewise the organization cannot plan its future human resource needs without information pertaining to existing employees' goals and objectives.

☐ Several issues loom as difficult career

development problems. The most important ones are managing dual careers, meeting development needs of women and minority groups, and integrating human resource planning and career development programs.

REVIEW AND DISCUSSION QUESTIONS

1. What is your career plan? How many of your friends seem to know what they want from their careers? Why do most young people seem to have trouble defining their career objectives?

2. Referring to question 1, what information would you like to have which would enable you to more adequately plan your career? What are the sources of this information? Why do you not now have this information?

3. What conflicts do you think you will have when you take your first job upon graduation? For which of these conflicts can you now plan and anticipate appropriate coping responses?

4. To what extent are you willing to relocate for the sake of your career? If you are relatively unwilling to relocate, what personal factors account for that reluctance and what are the implications for your career aspirations?

5. How can you learn the career paths in a

particular organization? Is this the kind of information you would want to get when you interview for a job? What questions would you ask to get this information?

6. Is it important to you that the organization in which you take your initial job have a career counseling program? Why?

7. Do you believe that you can cope with the problems of a dual-career situation? If so, what experiences in life have prepared you to cope with the problems? If not, why not?

8. How could a university business school prepare its students for the problems they will encounter as young hirees? Do college graduates generally have unrealistic expectations for their first jobs? Explain.

9. Explain why some white males of average competence consider affirmative action programs to be reverse discrimination. Do you share their view?

10. Explain why it makes economic sense for an organization to take an active part in the career planning process for its employees.

CASES

20–1 CAREER DEVELOPMENT PRACTICES AT AT&T, IBM, AND HEWLETT-PACKARD

The contemporary emphasis on career development includes the concept of career mobility. Where once it was thought that factors such as dedication, allegiance, and loyalty were important for career success, it is now thought that *concern for results* and *desire for responsibility* are key factors. The de-emphasis on company loyalty has accelerated during the 1970s to the point that companies are now becoming concerned with the consequences of the change.

Some of the consequences are directly measurable. For example, since 1960, the turnover among managers out of college less than five years has increased by 500 percent. The typical company can expect to lose 50 percent of its college recruits within five years of hiring them. These numbers translate into higher training costs, higher salaries, and lower productivity. The economic effects of these consequences are sufficiently large to stimulate countermeasures in some of America's best-known corporations.

AT&T attempts to match its needs for future executive leadership with the needs of individuals who seek that kind of leadership. AT&T's campus recruiters are directed to seek out those individuals who are predisposed to accept the company's operating style and fundamental beliefs. AT&T had compared its current group of recruits with those it had hired 20 years ago. Both groups expressed strong desire for achievement, but the current group scored only half as high in "deference to authority" and twice as high on "loyalty to peers." The results were interpreted to mean that the 1980s college recruit has little regard for where the achievement is realized, whether at AT&T or some other company. Thus, AT&T turned the attention of its campus recruiters toward those who are "our [AT&T's] kind of people."

IBM, long noted for its success in imbuing its executives with the corporate credo, has had no particular difficulty with managerial turnover. In fact, IBM's turnover has been cut in half since 1960. The philosophy at IBM is that company loyalty has to be earned. W. E. Burdick, vice president for personnel, states, "We'd be foolish to expect an MBA to walk in through the door and be loyal. Loyalty is something you've got to win." One feature of the IBM career development program is that each promotion up the executive ladder requires an additional training visit to the company's management-development center in Armonk, N.Y. The newly promoted manager is not only trained in the job requirements of the new position but also reindoctrinated in company philosophy: "Dignity and Respect for the Individual. Pursuit of Excellence. Dedication to Service." And, one might add, loyalty to IBM.

Hewlett-Packard Co.'s approach to acquiring company loyalty emphasizes sharing company successes with those who helped produce those successes. The company's headquarters are in the Silicon Valley area of California. It is here that microprocessor production has flourished and where the turnover of engineering personnel averages 60 percent. Yet, Hewlett-Packard's turnover is but 10 percent. The secrets, according to David Packard, chairman of the board, are profit participation and decentralized operating control. The company has 40 divisions, and each has its own research and development resources. According to Packard, creative people need the freedom to create technological breakthroughs that contribute to company profitability; those who develop the breakthrough share in that profitability.

These practices are successful means for instilling loyalty in career-oriented individuals. However, as one crusty CEO states, "When it comes to establishing loyalty, I have yet to find a substitute for fear." The fear referred to is the fear of unemployment brought about by a prolonged recession. As 1981 drew to a close, for instance, holiday and seasonal news was being pushed off the evening news by reports of mass layoffs of white-collar employees. It would be an interesting study to find out whether loyalty was a criterion for keeping one's job in those reported instances.

Questions

1. Compare the loyalty-building practices of the three companies. In what specific ways are they different; in what ways are they the same?

2. Is company loyalty necessary for achieving career effectiveness from the individual's perspective? From the organization's perspective?

3. What specific factors would cause you to be loyal to a particular organization?

Source: This case is adapted from Roy Rowan, "Rekindling Corporate Loyalty," *Fortune*, February 9, 1981, pp. 54–58.

20–2 CAREER DEVELOPMENT AT THE U.S. GENERAL ACCOUNTING OFFICE

The U.S. General Accounting Office (GAO) recently devised a career development program. Although the primary purpose of the program is to assist employees make appropriate career decisions, GAO's experience indicates that an organization must first develop the ability of managers to "do" career development. GAO's managers are no different from those in other organizations. They are caught up in the day-to-day routine and fail to budget time to consider the longer-run issues of their subordinates' futures. GAO believes that career development is an important managerial responsibility.

The first step in implementing the program was to assess the needs of managers. The following were identified:

1. Managers need to know more about the theory and practice of career development.

2. Managers need to know about opportunities throughout GAO, not just in that part where they presently work.

3. Managers need access to career development information that exists in both line and staff units.

4. Managers need to take a more active role in career counseling and to recognize nontraditional as well as traditional career paths.

5. Managers must be assured that top management is committed to organizationwide career development and that time devoted to it is considered worthwhile.

GAO met these needs in a variety of ways, but chief among them was a new workshop designed specifically for managers. The workshop is titled: Career Development Orientation for Managers.

The three parts of the workshop are: (1) philosophy, concepts, and overview; (2) Individual Career Planning Process; and (3) Organizational Career Development Process. Each of these parts draws upon materials widely available in the career development literature, but the specific circumstances and experiences of GAO are highlighted. For example, part 1 emphasizes the philosophy of career development at GAO, rather than dealing with issues at an abstract level.

Some of the questions raised in part 1 include:

1. What is career development?
2. Who should be responsible for it?
3. Should career development address individual or organizational needs?
4. Do career development programs raise false expectations?
5. What are the characteristics of individuals who can make effective use of career development programs?

Admittedly these questions are difficult to answer, but GAO believes that they must be addressed in order to proceed with the next two parts.

Part 2 instructs managers in the content of career counseling exercises which GAO's own counseling and career development staff provides. The exercises were done by managers so that they would know what their own subordinates would experience. The exercises consisted of four widely used career counseling steps: (1) understanding self, including one's values, needs, skills, and abilities; (2) understanding one's environment including job options, educational and training options, financial considerations, and projected skill needs; (3) taking action which consists of planning the future course of events related to development of self to take advantage of environmental opportunities; and (4) life management including the whole range of nonwork related events, activities, and experiences of individuals.

The activities of part 2 are person oriented. To do them effectively requires expertise and training in psychology. Thus, GAO does not hold managers responsible for leading their subordinates through the four steps. The manager's role is that of a referral agent seeing to it that individuals who desire the counseling experience are provided it.

The third part of the workshop, Organizational Career Development Process, emphasizes the stake of GAO in employee career development. This part mirrored part 2 in that it consists of four steps. The four steps are: (1) understanding organizational needs including identification of specific deficiencies within GAO to carry out an effective career development program, (2) understanding organizational environment including present and potential job opportunities and career paths within GAO, (3) organizational action planning requiring managers to identify the specific steps they will take to implement career development in their own units, and (4) problem recognition and referral requiring managers to be alert and sensitive to signs of employee mental and psychological well-being.

The completion of the workshop for managers signaled the beginning of the implementation of career development in GAO. The program is judged by management to be very timely. In view of limited growth in GAO with the consequent limited number of career advancement opportunities, the necessity of matching individual and career needs is even more important.

Questions

1. Evaluate the GAO career development program.
2. What would be your answers to the five questions raised by the participants in part 1 of their training program?
3. What should be the policy of organizations in mature and declining industries toward career development?

Source: Adapted from I. Marlene Thorn, Francis X. Fee, and Jane O'Hara Carter, "Career Development: A Collaborative Approach," *Management Review*, September 1982, pp. 27–28, 38–41.

EXERCISE

20–1 CAREER PLANNING

Purpose: The purpose of this exercise is to provide experience in thinking about what is important in one's life and career.

Setting Up the Exercise:

1. Each student will complete the following steps:
   a. Draw a horizontal line that depicts the past, present, and future of your career. On that line, mark an X where you are now.
   b. To the left of the X, on the part of the line that represents your past, identify events in your life that provided real and genuine feelings of fulfillment and satisfaction.
   c. Examine these historical events and determine the specific causes of your feelings. Does a pattern emerge? Write as much as you can about the events and your reactions to them.
   d. To the right of the X, on the part of the line that represents your future, identify career-related events that you expect to provide real and genuine feelings of fulfillment and satisfaction. You should be as explicit as possible when describing these events. If you are only able to write such statements as, "Get a job" or "Get a big raise," your career expectations are probably vaguely defined.
   e. After you have identified future career-related events, rank them from high to low according to how much fulfillment and satisfaction you expect from each.
   f. Now go back to step c and rank those historical events from high to low according to how much fulfillment and satisfaction each provided. Compare the two sets of ranked events. Are they consistent? Are you expecting the future to be the same or different from the past in terms of sources of feelings of fulfillment and satisfaction? If the future, expected sources are quite different from the past, actual sources, are you being totally realistic about the future and what you want from your career?
2. Each individual should answer the following questions and share answers with others:
   a. Which one of the six steps was most difficult to complete? Why?
   b. What are the principal categories of fulfillment and satisfaction? Can all these sources be realized in a career? Which ones are most likely to go unrealized in the career of your choice?

    c. Do you desire a career in management? Is your answer based on consideration of the potential sources of fulfillment and satisfaction that you value? Explain.

A Learning Note: This exercise will demonstrate the difficulties of identifying what we want from our careers. Most of us have vague and ill-formed notions of what careers are all about until we actually begin on a career path. Discussions with others about sources of career satisfaction can be very helpful.

TWENTY ONE

Management and Entrepreneurship

LEARNING OBJECTIVES

After completing Chapter 21, you should be able to:

Define: the risks of entrepreneurship.

State: the primary reasons why individuals become entrepreneurs.

Describe: the actions required for effective start-up planning.

Explain: the special challenges that many entrepreneurs face during their careers.

Discuss: the functions of organizing, leading, and controlling in the context of entrepreneurship.

TAKING THE PLUNGE, BEFORE 21

At 15, Barry Minkow was frustrated. He had great ambition, but little respect. As a teenager with a small build, he was often bullied by other students at his military school. His family sometimes didn't have much money. Once when the phone bill was unpaid and the family lost its phone service, Minkow was ashamed. "What do you say to your friends when they call you and find out that your service has been cut off?" he asked. "I mean, what do you do?"

For years, Barry's mother managed a carpet cleaning business. Barry spent much time there, learning the nuts and bolts of the business. He believed he could run the business as well as anyone, probably better.

However, creating a business is an exceptionally challenging undertaking. The odds of long-term success are slim, even for adults with years of business experience. The task is particularly demanding for a 15-year-old who must develop credibility among adults to attract customers and who must manage individuals who are many years his senior.

Barry weighed the pros and cons of launching a business, and at 15, took the plunge.

(The Management Solution to this Management Incident can be found at the end of this chapter.)

Peruse the latest issues of *The Wall Street Journal, Fortune, Business Week,* and other major business periodicals. Watch the evening's national news broadcast, and the impression is clear: big businesses provide the foundation of our economy. Exxon, Sears, IBM, Citicorp and other huge corporations generate the jobs, revenues, and financial strength that is central to our economic well-being.

However, this impression, while clearly conveyed, is misleading and incomplete. The missing key contributor is small business. The gas station, corner grocery store, clothing boutique, medical clinic, and any number of other small businesses you see in a given day produce on a national scale about half of the nation's gross national product. Every year, the country's some 14 million small businesses generate over 80 percent of the new jobs in the United States. Altogether, America's small business community is the world's fourth greatest economic power, behind the economies of the United States, Japan, and the Soviet Union.[1]

At the helm of many, if not most, of these companies is the *entrepreneur,* the individual who, propelled by an idea, personal goals and ambition, brings together the financial capital, people, equipment, and facilities to establish and manage a business enterprise. As the creators and navigators of small business, entrepreneurs direct a dominant force in the U.S. economy.

In starting and managing a business, the entrepreneur faces challenges that are unique to those of his big-business counterpart, the nonfounder CEO of a large, ongoing corporation. Unlike the corporate CEO, the entrepreneur, at least in the early stages of the business, is deeply and personally involved in every aspect of the enterprise. The entrepreneur applies the four management functions in creating, building, and shaping the business. As a result, the organization significantly reflects his needs, goals, and values.[2] The entrepreneur also copes with far greater personal and professional risk. In most cases, his personal financial resources will be lost if the business fails. Unlike large corporations, there is no supply of resources to cushion the effects of mistakes or unexpected developments. Most small businesses are initially run on a shoestring budget which heightens the importance and stresses of the entrepreneur's decision making. The entrepreneur is also strictly and singularly accountable for the business's success or failure. There is usually no board of directors to share the burden of responsibility.

This chapter presents a discussion of entrepreneurship, specifically focusing on the entrepreneur, the entrepreneurial tasks presented in the framework of the four management functions (planning, organizing, leading, and controlling), and special challenges facing the entrepreneur. We devote a chapter to this topic because of the

---

[1]George Melloan, "Small Firms Brace for Legislative Attack," *The Wall Street Journal,* May 5, 1987, p. 37; and "Millions of New Jobs to Be Created in '86, Survey Shows," *Mobile Register,* March 31, 1986, p. 3A.

[2]Several studies have examined the impact of an entrepreneur's personal characteristics on the firm (e.g., firm growth, structure, flexibility). For two insightful examples, see Norman R. Smith and John B. Miner, "Type of Entrepreneur, Type of Firm and Managerial Motivation: Applications for Organizational Life Cycle Theory," *Strategic Management Journal* 4 (1983), pp. 325–40; and Graeme Salaman, "An Historical Discontinuity: From Charisma to Routinization," *Human Relations* 30, no. 4 (1977), pp. 373–88.

entrepreneur's considerable economic and social importance in the United States and because of the growing prevalence of entrepreneurship. Every year, more than 1 million individuals assume the challenge and risks of creating a business in the United States. At some point in your career, you may well become one of them.

THE ENTREPRENEUR

Management scholars and observers have differed in their definition of an entrepreneur. Many view an entrepreneur as the creator, owner, and chief executive of a business enterprise. Some perspectives have emphasized financial risk as a key characteristic of the entrepreneur. A more recent perspective distinguishes between the small business owner and the entrepreneur. The small business owner establishes and manages a business to attain personal objectives. The business is an extension of the owner's needs, goals, and personality. The business's growth is not a primary objective. In contrast, the entrepreneur creates a business to build the enterprise for growth and profit. She uses a deliberate, planned approach that applies strategic management concepts and techniques. The entrepreneur is also highly innovative, creating new products and markets and applying creative strategies and ways of managing.[3]

Our perspective assumes the more general definition of the entrepreneur as the creator and manager of a business; however, this discussion will emphasize the innovative, growth-oriented entrepreneur. Bill Gates, profiled below, is the 33-year-old cofounder of Microsoft® and is an example of this type of entrepreneur.

ENTREPRENEUR PROFILE

BILL GATES: THE MOST POWERFUL MAN IN THE COMPUTER INDUSTRY

When IBM was fast developing its first personal computer in 1980, it asked 24-year-old Bill Gates, cofounder of a small software company, to quickly write a software program that would provide the PC with an operating system. Believing his small company wasn't up to the task, Mr. Gates declined and suggested a competitor. Within days, he reconsidered, found a Seattle programmer who had written a program called Q-DOS (the "Quick and Dirty Operating System"), and bought the program's exclusive rights for $50,000. Mr. Gates gave the software a new name, MS-DOS®, purchased a tie, flew to IBM's PC headquarters, and secured a contract.

That bit of luck and ingenuity put Mr. Gates and his company, Microsoft Corp., on the map. MS-DOS became the industry standard for personal computers; it is the operating system used by about 60 percent of all PCs sold in the United States and provides Microsoft with half of its yearly revenues. However, unlike many software firms, Microsoft's fortunes aren't solely reliant on one product.

---

[3]James W. Carland, Frank Hoy, William R. Boulton, and Jo Ann C. Carland, "Differentiating Entrepreneurs from Small Business Owners: A Conceptualization," *Academy of Management Review*, April 1984, pp. 354–59.

Rather, Microsoft provides most of the computer languages that professional programmers use on IBM and Apple computers. As a result, the company has set industry standards for many programming languages, for programs that manage PC peripheral devices and networks, and for the inner workings of all 10 million IBM PCs and countless compatibles. Such has made 33-year-old Mr. Gates the most powerful individual in the personal computer industry and his 45 percent share in the company worth about $1 billion.

Observers attribute Mr. Gates' success to his technical genius, limitless energy, obsessive perfectionism, shrewd negotiating abilities, and business acumen. Unlike many founders of computer firms, Mr. Gates possesses the rare combination of technical genius and professional management skills that enabled his company to make a smooth transition from a fledgling start-up to a professionally managed, fast-growing firm.

At Microsoft's headquarters in Redmond, Washington, Mr. Gates leaves management tasks to two skilled, professional managers while he focuses on technology, setting the company's strategic direction, and overseeing all major product development projects. Tall, bespectacled, and a Harvard University dropout, Mr. Gates is a demanding taskmaster and sets rigorous standards for his programmers. His typical workday runs from 9:30 A.M. to midnight. The company's attitude emphasizes challenge and informality, where many of the 1,500 employees wear jeans and gather frequently for picnics and parties. Although programmers could earn more elsewhere, turnover is less than 10 percent, well below the industry average.

Because Microsoft is so dominant in the PC industry, competitors—and sometimes computer company clients—complain about Mr. Gates' intimate knowledge of many companies' products and long-term strategy that is necessary in developing operations software for a major product. Some claim a conflict of interest exists. Others wonder whether Microsoft, involved in so many projects, has spread itself too thin. However, the company's success shows no signs of ebbing. Mr. Gates is fast pursuing his vision—to bring computing power "to the masses."

Source: Adapted from Brenton R. Schlender, "Microsoft's Gates Uses Products and Pressure to Gain Power in PCs," *The Wall Street Journal*, September 25, 1987, pp. 1, 5; and Richard Brandt, "The Billion-Dollar Whiz Kid," *Business Week*, April 13, 1987, pp. 68ff.

The Risks of Entrepreneurship

At least during the early stages of his enterprise, the entrepreneur works in the domain of a small business. Combining definitions provided by the Small Business Administration and the Committee for Economic Development, a small business is an organization that is privately owned (usually by top management), not dominant in its market, maintains local operations (though it may serve a much larger market), and employs less than 500 people.[4] Half of the small businesses in the United States have annual sales of less than $500,000 and employ 10 or fewer individuals.

---

[4]*Meeting the Special Problems of Small Businesses* (New York: Committee for Economic Development, 1974), p. 14; and *The State of Small Business: A Report to the President* (Washington, D.C.: U.S. Government Printing Office, March 1983), p. 28.

Table 21–1 Business failures in nine industries.

	Age of Company When It Failed		
	5 Years or Less	6 to 10 Years	More Than 10 Years
Agriculture, forestry and fishing	29.1%	23.0%	47.9%
Mining	49.1	28.7	22.2
Construction	43.6	30.0	26.4
Manufacturing	51.5	23.7	24.8
Transportation and public utilities	53.1	23.4	23.5
Wholesale trade	51.2	24.5	24.3
Retail trade	61.5	22.3	16.2
Finance, insurance and real estate	52.3	25.3	22.4
Services	60.6	22.0	17.4
Total	54.5%	24.1%	21.4%

Source: 1986 data from Dun & Bradstreet's "Business Failures Record." Table reprinted from "Down to Earth Advice for Angels," *Changing Times*, January 1988, p. 72. Reprinted with permission.

In launching her small business, the entrepreneur usually faces substantial *business risk*. Such is the case because, although well over 1 million new businesses are started each year (an estimated 1.3 billion in 1988), the failure rates of young companies are disturbingly high.[5] According to research by the Small Business Administration, from 25 to 33 percent of all independent small businesses fail during the first two years of operation.[6] Eight of every 10 businesses end within 10 years.[7] Table 21–1 shows the failure rates of businesses in nine industries during 1986.

Besides considerable business risk, entrepreneurs face significant *financial risk* as they typically invest most if not all of their financial resources in the business. They take a *career risk* when leaving a secure job for a venture with a highly uncertain future. They also incur *family and social risks* because the demands of starting and running a young business consume 60- to 80-hour workweeks that leave little time for attention to family and friends. The demands of entrepreneurship often strain marriages and friendships. They also assume a *psychological risk*—the risk of a deep sense of personal failure if the business does not beat the odds and succeed.[8] One highly successful entrepreneur succinctly summed up the considerable personal risks of entrepreneurship by describing the emotions of launching a business as "entrepreneurial terror."[9]

---

[5]David L. Birch, "The Truth about Start-ups," *Inc.*, January 1988, pp. 14–15.

[6]Jeremy Main, "Breaking Out of the Company," *Fortune*, May 25, 1987, p. 83.

[7]Richard Greene, "Do You Really Want to Be Your Own Boss?" *Forbes*, October 21, 1985, pp. 86, 87.

[8]Patrick R. Liles, *New Business Ventures and the Entrepreneur* (Homewood, Ill.: Richard D. Irwin, 1974), pp. 14–15.

[9]Wilson Harrell, "Entrepreneurial Terror," *Inc.*, February 1987, pp. 74–76.

The Motivations of Entrepreneurs

Given the sizable risks, time, and energy requirements of entrepreneurship, why do so many individuals take the entrepreneurial plunge every year? While the potential costs are high, the rewards can also be substantial. Entrepreneurs launch businesses because of one or more entrepreneurial motivations.

For independence. "Being my own boss" is a powerful motivator for many entrepreneurs who seek the freedom to act independently in their work. As heads of business, they enjoy the autonomy of making their own decisions, setting their own work hours, and determining what they will do and when they will do it.

For personal and professional growth. The challenges of building a business innately involve individual growth. To be successful, an entrepreneur must be able to cope with risk, uncertainty, and stress, handle many different interpersonal relationships, and manage a business with limited resources. Many individuals become entrepreneurs to experience this growth and the fulfillment gained from building a business into a purposeful, productive entity.

For a superior alternative to a dissatisfying job. Many entrepreneurs establish businesses as an alternative they perceive as superior to a highly dissatisfying job. A survey of the CEOs of the Inc. 500, the 500 fastest-growing U.S. private companies, found that frustration with working in large companies was the primary motivator for starting a business.[10] The CEOs were dissatisfied with the slow decision making, bureaucracy, and their limited autonomy as managers in larger corporations. Other entrepreneurs who were plateaued in their previous jobs, have launched businesses as a second career, contributing to a growing number of "late bloomer" entrepreneurs.[11] These entrepreneurs bring to their ventures years of business experience and professional contacts.

Many female entrepreneurs report poor advancement opportunities as their major reason for launching a business.[12] One third of the female members of the Inc. 500 cite their inability to move up as a major motivator for becoming an entrepreneur (twice the percentage of male members).[13] Other women have tired of the "corporate grind" that can be exceptionally difficult for women managers with children. They view running a business as ultimately providing the needed flexibility for having both a professional career and children. These trends have contributed to a boom in women entrepreneurship; today women own 28 percent of all U.S. businesses and account for

---

[10]Curtis Hartman, "Main Street, Inc.," *Inc.*, June 1986, p. 52.

[11]Main, "Breaking Out of the Company," p. 83. See also Faye Rice, "Lessons from Late Bloomers," *Fortune,* August 31, 1987, pp. 87–91; and Harry Bacas, "Leaving the Corporate Nest," *Nation's Business,* March 1987, pp. 14ff.

[12]See Susan Fraker, "Why Women Aren't Getting to the Top," *Fortune,* April 16, 1984, pp. 40–44; and Alex Taylor III, "Why Women Managers Are Bailing Out," *Fortune,* August 18, 1986, pp. 16–23.

[13]Hartman, "Main Street, Inc." p. 54.

one third of all start-ups each year.[14] One such entrepreneur is Liz Claiborne, considered by many to be America's most successful woman entrepreneur.[15] She is profiled in the following Entrepreneur Profile.

ENTREPRENEUR PROFILE

LIZ CLAIBORNE: THE "GREAT PATHFINDER"

When Liz Claiborne created her apparel manufacturing company in 1976, her goal was simple: create clothes for the professional woman and develop a small business under the Liz Claiborne label.

However, very quickly, her talents and penchant for quality produced something far more than originally planned. In 11 years, Liz Claiborne Inc., became a Fortune 500 company, producing annual revenues of over $800 million. The company currently ranks among America's 10 most admired corporations (number 5) according to Fortune's prestigious annual survey. At 58, Ms. Claiborne is widely considered to be America's most successful female entrepreneur, *the great pathfinder* as she is frequently called in the "rag" trade. The reason: as president and co-chairman (she shares the chairmanship with her husband, Arthur Ortenberg), Ms. Claiborne has shown just how profitable an apparel maker can be. Her company's 10.9 percent return on sales is by far the industry's best, four times the average of her top 10 competitors.

Ms. Claiborne's strategy for success is simple: (1) design colorful, fashionable clothes for the professional woman whose figure is full rather than model thin. (2) Ensure the clothes are of high quality, timely but not faddish. (3) Design for six seasons rather than four so customers can actually buy winter clothes in winter, summer clothes in summer. (4) Keep quality high but maintain low prices by contracting all manufacturing to clothes makers in low-labor-cost countries primarily in the Far East. (5) Exercise strict control over how the clothes are displayed and sold by retailers (because her clothes sell so well, Ms. Claiborne exercises far more control in this regard than do other top apparel designers).

Because her company has boomed in size, Ms. Claiborne no longer has time to design but rather supervises her team of 14 designers. Described as shy and intense, Ms. Claiborne's current project is the opening of her new chain of retail stores called First Issue, which will carry a line of casual clothes sold at prices lower than typical for Claiborne clothes. Unlike other designers who move into direct retailing, the clothes that will be designed by Liz Claiborne's designers won't carry her label to avoid cannibalizing sales from her lines in other department stores (and incurring the wrath of her retailers).

---

[14]"Starting Their Own," *Nation's Business*, May 1987, pp. 23–24. Also see "Women-Owned Companies," *Inc.*, January 1987, p. 11.

[15]Liz Claiborne is one of a number of entrepreneurs who launched a business with a spouse. For a look at profiles of successes, failures, and the special challenges experienced by married co-founders of businesses, see Marie Jeanne Juilland, "The Good, the Bad, the Ugly," *Venture*, January 1988, pp. 39ff; and Teresa Carson, "Honey What Do You Say We Start Our Own Company?" *Business Week*, September 15, 1986, pp. 115, 118.

She and Mr. Ortenberg are also working on the task of executive succession, grooming a team of managers who will run the company with the same team approach used so effectively by Ms. Claiborne and her husband. Though most of her moves have been exceptionally successful, Ms. Claiborne is reluctant to diversify further: "I worry about the label being everywhere."

Source: Adapted from Patricia Sellers, "The Rag Trade's Reluctant Revolutionary," *Fortune,* January 5, 1987, pp. 36–38; and "Store Wars," *Forbes,* January 11, 1988, p. 75.

For income.   Many entrepreneurs are enticed by the hefty profits that a highly successful business can provide, although the odds of such considerable success are slim. Others are motivated by making their own money in business. However, surprisingly, many entrepreneurs do not rate money as a primary motivator for starting a business. The surveyed Inc. 500 entrepreneurs, for example, ranked money fourth in importance (behind frustration, independence, and controlling one's life).

For security.   Given the substantial risks and uncertainty of entrepreneurship, personal security may seem an unlikely motivator. However, in a time of much corporate downsizing and layoffs, some entrepreneurs view running their own business as a more secure alternative, especially those in the middle and latter stages of their corporate careers.

Entrepreneurial Characteristics

A number of studies have been conducted to determine whether entrepreneurs distinctly differ in personality and other characteristics from managers and the public at large. Drawing generalizations from this body of research is difficult because studies differ in their definitions of entrepreneur.

However, assuming a general definition of entrepreneur, some research support exists for a number of characteristics.[16] Studies have found that entrepreneurs possess a significantly greater need for independence and autonomy, compared to managers. Other studies picture the entrepreneur as having a substantial need to achieve, and a tolerance of ambiguity—the ability to handle uncertain and ambiguous situations. Many entrepreneurs also have high energy and endurance, substantial self-esteem, and strong dominance; that is, a need to take charge, control, and direct others. Several studies also find that the entrepreneur has a lower need for social support compared to managers. She is not a team player or joiner. Figure 21–1 shows some distinct differences in the characteristics of surveyed Inc. 500 CEOs and the CEOs and senior executives of Fortune 500 companies.

---

[16]This discussion is drawn primarily from Donald L. Sexton and Nancy Bowman, "The Entrepreneur: A Capable Executive and More," *Journal of Business Venturing* 1, no. 1 (1985), pp. 129–40.

Figure 21–1 Differences in personal characteristics between entrepreneurs and Fortune 500 senior executives.

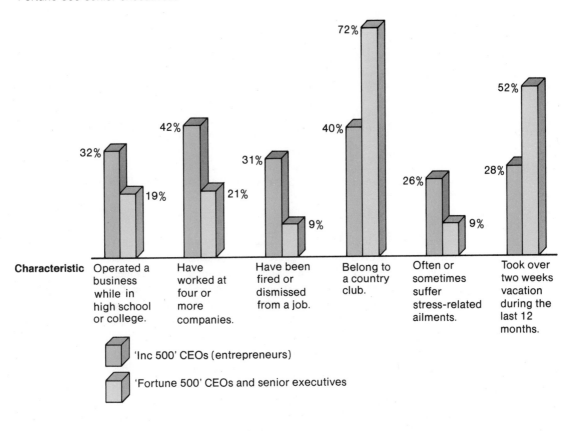

ENTREPRENEURSHIP AND THE FUNCTIONS OF MANAGEMENT

Creating and building a successful enterprise requires, above all, effectively performing the four management functions—planning, organizing, leading, and controlling. As research clearly indicates, poor management and management inexperience are the primary causes of new venture failure.[17] In 1986 alone, 9 of every 10 closings were attributed to inadequate management.[18] Thus, knowing the purpose and principles of

---

[17]For example, see *USA Today*, March 13, 1987, p. 13.

[18]Dun & Bradstreet, *Business Failures Record* (New York: Dun & Bradstreet Business Economics Department, 1986).

Table 21–2 Assess your entrepreneurial potential.

		Yes	No
1.	Are you a self-starter?	———	———
2.	Do you have a positive, friendly interest in others?	———	———
3.	Are you a leader (do you inspire confidence and loyalty)?	———	———
4.	Can you handle responsibility (do you enjoy taking charge)?	———	———
5.	Are you a good organizer?	———	———
6.	Are you prepared to put in long hours?	———	———
7.	Do you make up your mind quickly?	———	———
8.	Can people rely on you?	———	———
9.	Can you withstand setbacks without quitting?	———	———
10.	Can you adapt to changing situations?	———	———

Source: S. Norman Feingold and Leonard G. Perlman, "A Quiz for Would-Be Entrepreneurs," *Nation's Business*, March 1986, pp. 26–27.

each function and applying them well is critical to new venture success. By now, you are well versed in each function. Therefore, our discussion of the four functions focuses on how they apply to the special task of launching a small business.

However before we begin, it is important to briefly discuss the critical first step which precedes planning, the first entrepreneurial task. This first step is the *entrepreneur decision*, specifically deciding whether to establish a business or to become an entrepreneur.

Making the right decision requires a clear understanding of entrepreneurship and the requirements for success. Above all, the decision should be based on an accurate self-assessment of individual skills, abilities, and shortcomings. This is so because initially the entrepreneur *is* the business. He makes all the decisions, initiates critical business relationships, and performs the management functions. The entrepreneur's strengths and limitations will directly and profoundly affect the enterprise. Take a minute and answer the questions in Table 21–2 for a brief self-assessment of your entrepreneurial potential.

Many management observers agree that success requires certain entrepreneurial attributes. The entrepreneur must be motivated to make a profit because profitability (not self-fulfillment, independence, or other motivations) is essential for survival. The entrepreneur must be an effective planner, organizer, problem solver, and decision maker and be able to manage people well. Experience in the business is a virtual must as is a talent for getting along with people and the ability to handle stress. The entrepreneur must have nerve, be prepared to bounce back from inevitable setbacks, and be willing to devote long hours to the business.[19] Now, count the number of your affirmative answers to the self-assessment quiz. If you gave six or more unconditional yes responses, you have definite entrepreneurial potential.

---

[19]Harry Bacas and Nancy L. Croft, "Go Out on Your Own?" *Nation's Business*, March 1986, pp. 18–21.

Planning

Of the four management functions, planning probably contributes the most to new venture performance. Planning provides a well-thought-out blueprint of action for the critical first months of the new business. This activity is vital because when resources are so slim in the early days of the business, mistakes can be costly, even fatal to the business. Careful planning reduces the chances of major mistakes; it also forces the entrepreneur to examine the business's external environment, competition, potential customers, and the strengths and limitations of the new business.[20] However, despite the importance of planning, many entrepreneurs don't like to plan because they believe planning hinders their flexibility.[21]

The entrepreneur performs two types of planning. *Start-up planning* occurs before the enterprise opens for business. Thereafter, the entrepreneur performs *ongoing planning* which provides further strategic and operational direction for the established business. Chapters 3 and 6 address this latter type of planning which will not be discussed here.

Start-up planning essentially involves providing comprehensive, well-thought-out answers to the following five questions:

1.   What product or service will the business provide?
2.   What market will be served?
3.   How will the business be established?
4.   How will the business be operated?
5.   How will the business be financed?

What product or service will the business provide? and What market will be served?   These two questions are addressed jointly because answering one requires consideration of the other. Doing so also avoids a classic flaw of many new-product entrepreneurs: the assumption that a good product will automatically sell itself and that a ready-made market exists. The entrepreneurial graveyard is filled with unique, creative products that died for lack of customers.[22]

Many entrepreneurs address the product question by first conducting a widespread information search to identify opportunities. Numerous resources exist for this task: the business section of the newspaper, business magazines, and trade journals that focus on one industry are a few published sources of ideas. The Small Business Administration provides free, informative publications on many types of businesses.[23]

---

[20]See Erik Larson, "The Best-Laid Plans," *Inc.*, February 1987, pp. 60–64; and Bruce G. Posner, "Real Entrepreneurs Don't Plan," *Inc.*, November 1985, pp. 129–35.

[21]Richard L. Osborne, "Planning: The Entrepreneurial Ego at Work," *Business Horizons*, January–February 1987, pp. 20–24.

[22]Larson, "The Best-Laid Plans," p. 63.

[23]The SBA publishes a *Starting Out Series* on many types of businesses and a *Management Aids Series* of booklets on marketing and all major aspects of small business management. These booklets are available free at your regional field SBA office.

Table 21–3 Start-up statistics.

Ten Most Frequently Started Businesses	Survival Rank
1. Miscellaneous business services	132
2. Eating and drinking places	161
3. Miscellaneous shopping goods	159
4. Automotive repair shops	78
5. Residential construction	141
6. Machinery and equipment wholesalers	138
7. Real estate operators	38
8. Miscellaneous retail stores	100
9. Furniture and furnishings retailers	206
10. Computers and data processing services	163

Ten Businesses Most Likely to Survive	Start-up Rank
1. Veterinary services	125
2. Funeral services	158
3. Dentists' offices	108
4. Commercial savings banks	93
5. Hotels and motels	27
6. Campground and trailer parks	166
7. Physicians' offices	35
8. Barbershops	151
9. Bowling and billiards places	118
10. Cash grain crops	197

Source: Based on rankings of 236 types of businesses (approximately 1.4 million firms in the United States from 1978 to 1987). Reprinted from David L. Birch, "The Truth about Start-ups," *Inc.*, January 1988, p. 14. Reprinted with permission.

Discussions with bankers, business consultants, and large businesses, and trade shows can also provide direction.

Once a large list of prospective businesses is developed, the list is reduced by considering each business' feasibility and compatibility with the entrepreneur's goals and strengths. Concerning goals, for instance, does the entrepreneur want a business that is relatively easy to establish, one with few barriers to entry? Or is stability (long-term survival) or profit growth the primary objective? These considerations are critical because few businesses satisfy all three criteria. In one study of 1.4 million ventures (236 types of businesses), the researchers found that, as shown in Table 21–3, businesses with relatively easy start-up ranked low on long-term survival; those with high survival rates were the ones that were less frequently launched. High-growth ventures (such as basic steel and electronic component manufacturers) ranked low on both stability and ease of start-up.[24]

Concerning personal strengths, the entrepreneur compares each prospect's key ability requirements with her own strengths. For example, people skills are particularly essential in a clothing retail store while technical abilities are vital in a computer repair service.

---

[24]Birch, "The Truth about Start-ups," pp. 14–15.

Table 21–4 Successful new-product/service ideas.

Area	Idea
Health/fitness	An exercise studio for large women. Women at Large Systems Inc. (Yakima, Washington), found a successful market niche—overweight women who feel uncomfortable at regular aerobics classes. The company also offers fashion shows, makeup, and hair design. National franchise is coming soon.
	Low cholesterol eggs (190 to 200 mgs compared to 275 mgs for normal eggs) produced by altering the chicken's environment with special lighting, purified air and water, special feed and insulation from radiation. They cost 25 to 30 cents more per dozen. Environmental Systems Inc. (Lancaster, Pennsylvania)
Special occasions	An 8-foot personalized card (for birthdays, anniversaries, etc.) placed in the front yard at night, removed 24 hours later. The cost is $35. Yard Cards (Belleville, Illinois)
Evening wear	Evening gown rentals for big occasions. Gowns priced at $500 to $5,000 rent for $75 up plus a $200 minimum deposit (three-day rental). One Night Stand (New York City) carries 600 gowns, sizes 4–18.
Baby products	Toddler Casseroles—microwave dinners for children, ages 9 months to 3 years. Kid-sized servings in beef, turkey, and chicken with grains and vegetables. Cost: $2.50 each. Growing Gourmet Inc. (Walnut Creek, California)
Auto parts	An Alter-Break device to automatically adjust an auto carburetor. About the size of a cigarette package, it attaches to the carburetor. A microchip inside detects when to make the adjustment. Cost is about $50. Nutronics Corp. (Longmont, Colorado)
Paintings	Custom ceiling designs. StellarVision (Portland, Ore.) paints star constellations on bedroom ceilings with phosphorescent paint. Sleep under the stars for a cost of $49.95 per ceiling. Service in seven states.

Source: Adapted from "100 Ideas for New Business," *Venture,* December 1987, pp. 35ff.; "The Franchisor 50," *Venture,* February 1987, pp. 39ff; "Exercise Studios—and More for Larger Women," *Venture,* March 1988, pp. 40, 41; "Yard Cards Inc.: A Giant Surprise for All Occasions," *Venture,* April 1988, p. 11; "Dresses Perfect for a One Night Stand," *Venture,* May 1988, p. 14; "Dialing for Diapers," *Venture,* May 1988, p. 15.

Effectively answering these questions requires conducting an analysis of each business' market. This market evaluation involves assessing four factors: (1) the market's size—assessing past and projected sales trends, the life-cycle stage of the product/ service, and business survival rates; (2) the competition—determining the bases of competition (price, quality, image, customer service?), and the strengths and limitations of competitors; (3) customers—assessing average income; and (4) market share— determining the share of the market which a new business can reasonably obtain.[25] There are many free sources of information to assist this task. For example, the Chamber(s) of Commerce in the prospective market can provide published market data; other census and market information is available in the local library. For a fee,

[25]Leon C. Megginson, Charles R. Scott, Jr., Lyle R. Trueblood, and William L. Megginson, *Successful Small Business Management* (Plano; Tex., Business Publications, 1988), pp. 87–88.

market research firms can provide valuable information as can telephone, mail, and on-the-street surveys conducted in the market.

Most entrepreneurs launch a business that offers a product or service that is already available in the market. However, some businesses are based on a totally new product or service idea. These ideas sometimes produce the largest business successes; consider, for example, the weed-eater, personal computer, garage door opener, and microwave oven (some other successful new product/service ideas are summarized in Table 21–4). Market analysis is more challenging in this case. Because the product or service is new, there is no market data on demand or pricing. The entrepreneur must determine whether demand exists and if so, what customers would pay. Market surveys are essential to answer these questions.[26]

Regardless of whether the product or service is new or already exists, the entrepreneur should select a business that has a healthy market, is financially feasible, and matches his own objectives and abilities.

How will the business be established?   This question asks how the entrepreneur will enter the business. Three strategies are available: buyout, start-up, and franchise.[27]

The entrepreneur may *buy out* and acquire an existing company in the chosen business and market. This strategy affords a speedy entry into a business and market; the staff, facilities, supplier and distribution networks are immediately provided once the buyout contract is signed. A company with a solid track record and consumer image provides advantages that normally require years to develop. However, companies for sale can possess major and sometimes hidden problems. The entrepreneur must deal with what she has purchased; she can't develop all aspects of the business exactly as she prefers. An effective buyout requires careful selection of a company, a thorough evaluation of the company's strengths and weaknesses, and obtaining a fair price for the business.

In the *start-up,* the entrepreneur creates the business from scratch. He has the freedom to define and build the business largely according to his preferences. However, as previously discussed, the time, effort, requirements, and risks of start-ups are usually high.

In the *franchise,* the entrepreneur (franchisee) provides a product or service under a legal contract with the franchise owner (franchisor). The franchisor provides the distinctive elements of the business (the name, image, signs, facility design, patents), an operating system, and other services. To obtain a franchise, the entrepreneur pays an initial fee (typically ranging from $2,500 to $150,000) and thereafter a percentage royalty on sales (usually from 5 to 15 percent). The entrepreneur operates under the rights and restrictions of the contract.

Franchises are an increasingly popular form of new business. Over 500,000 franchise

---

[26]For an excellent, down-to-earth approach for assessing the feasibility of a new product/service idea, see Wilson Harrell, "But Will It Fly?" *Inc.*, January 1987, pp. 85ff.

[27]This discussion is based on Megginson et al., *Successful Small Business Management,* pp. 88–95, 130–44; and John G. Burch, *Entrepreneurship* (New York: John Wiley & Sons, 1986), pp. 101–26, 130–37.

Table 21–5 Top 10 franchises in the United States.

Franchise	Parent Company	Industry
1. Domino's Pizza	Domino's Pizza Inc.	Fast food
2. Chem-Dry	Harris Research Inc.	Maintenance/cleaning
3. McDonald's	McDonald's Corp.	Fast food
4. Subway Sandwiches & Salads	Doctor's Associates	Fast food
5. Jazzercise	Jazzercise, Inc.	Health/fitness
6. Packy the Shipper	PNS Inc.	Business services
7. Jani-King	Jani-King Int'l	Maintenance/cleaning
8. Novus Windshield Repair	Novus Franchising, Inc.	Auto maintenance
9. Burger King	Pillsbury Co.	Fast food
10. Coverall	Coverall North America	Maintenance/cleaning

Source: "The Franchise 100," *Venture*, November 1987, p. 42.

outlets currently operate in the United States.[28] Table 21–5 shows the top-10 franchises in the United States. Franchises are popular because they are less risky than start-ups or buyouts. During the first five years of operation, about 65 percent of all start-ups fail; only 5 percent of franchises close, according to the SBA.[29] This lower failure rate is primarily due to the support the franchisor provides the entrepreneur—usually management and employee training, operations and accounting systems, a recognized brand name, reputation, and financial, marketing, and management assistance. Tom Monaghan, the creator of America's top franchise, has built a franchise empire based on strong support for franchisees. His profile is given below.

ENTREPRENEUR PROFILE

TOM MONAGHAN: THE PRINCE OF PIZZA

Times were not always so enjoyable for Tom Monaghan, founder of Domino's Pizza. When he launched this business on a $900 investment in 1960 near Eastern Michigan University, college students would play pranks. Everyone in a dorm would order pizzas at the same time. Or often while Mr. Monaghan was making deliveries in a dorm, students would steal the pizzas still in his delivery truck. To stop the problem, the former Marine would hide in the truck and ambush the robbers with a mallet or a Coke bottle. "It made me so mad," he recalls, "people were threatening my livelihood, and it was a campus sport."

However, Mr. Monaghan's tenacity paid off. After years of steady expansion (and a comeback from near-bankruptcy in 1970), Domino's Pizza is today the world's largest home delivery pizza chain. The company maintains 4,300 outlets of which two thirds

---

[28]Dennis Holder, "Franchise Fever Catches On," *Working Woman*, July 1986, pp. 35–36.

[29]Ibid.

are franchises. Many observers credit the company's success to several factors, notably Mr. Monaghan's unrelenting energy and optimism and a keen understanding of what it takes to deliver a hot, good-tasting pizza and make a profit.

During his almost 30 years in business, Mr. Monaghan has maintained a simple business concept. Domino's Pizza sells only one basic pizza (three sizes with up to 11 toppings) and Pepsi. The company has no sit-down service and guarantees a 30-minute delivery or provides a discount on the pizza (drivers meet the guarantee on 90 percent of the orders).

The company works to keep its franchises efficiently run and the franchise owners, store managers, and employees well-trained. Only store managers may apply for a franchise, and if they qualify, they are rigorously trained in all aspects of franchise management at one of Domino's Pizza's regional training centers. Employees are trained on the job by store managers equipped with a variety of training aids provided by the corporate training staff, including videocassette training tapes that are upbeat and musical (MTV-styled). Performance standards are demanding (e.g., the order taker must answer a call within three rings and take the order within 45 seconds; the oven tender must cut and box one pizza by the count of 15).

Mr. Monaghan also rewards his managers well. Senior executives drive company-provided BMWs; top-performing store managers and franchise owners take weekend cruises on the company's million-dollar yacht, receive trips to Hawaii, or spend time at the company's plush corporate retreat. Any manager who exceeds the company's weekly sales record (currently about $62,000) receives a $12,000 Swiss gold wristwatch, the same style that the CEO wears. Mr. Monaghan once bet an overweight vice president that the man could not run a marathon by the end of the year. Mr. Monaghan lost the wager—and paid the runner $50,000.

At 51, Mr. Monaghan is a bit of a maverick. Once a child who spent many years in an orphanage or foster homes, he spends his money rather than accumulating it. In 1983, he bought the Detroit Tigers baseball team. He maintains an $18 million collection of classic cars, and once threw a $1 million, three-day Halloween party for friends and associates. He also generously donates to charity. One of his several projects is the development of a small community in the mountains of Honduras. Mr. Monaghan has funded a Catholic mission, medical clinic, and factory there—and opened a Domino's Pizza outlet.

As for Domino's Pizza, the company has opened a new $150 million headquarters facility which features museums, a farm, jogging trails, and a sports medicine center. The company will soon open the Leaning Tower of Pizza—a 35-story executive conference facility that leans 15 degrees to the east. Mr. Monaghan's business objective: to open 10,000 outlets by 1990.

Source: Adapted from Wendy Zellner, "Tom Monaghan: The Fun-Loving Prince of Pizza," *Business Week*, February 8, 1988, pp. 90, 93; and Susan Ager, "An Appetite for More than Pizza," *Nation's Business*, February 1986, pp. 81–83.

Although a franchise can provide substantial benefits, the strategy also possesses shortcomings. The entrepreneur greatly depends on the franchisor's ability, reputation, and support. Not all franchisors provide entrepreneurs with needed assistance. Poor relations between the entrepreneur and franchisor can quickly erode the entrepreneur's business. Also, the entrepreneur's creative freedom is usually inhibited by the franchise contract. The franchisor usually decides what to sell, the sales price, and many other aspects of the business.

Ensuring a successful franchise requires carefully evaluating the prospective franchisor (the franchisor's growth rates, performance, reputation, degree of support) and the franchise contract. Many entrepreneurs obtain franchisor evaluations from the company's other franchisees and examine the franchisor's depth of management (e.g., McDonald's maintains one manager for every 20 franchisees).[30] Many entrepreneurs also conduct their own market analysis in addition to reviewing the franchisor's assessment.

How will the business be operated? The entrepreneur answers this question by conducting planning in the business's various functions such as production, marketing, personnel, and research and development. Concerning production, for example, the entrepreneur determines who will supply materials and plans the layout of the production facilities. In marketing, the entrepreneur plans how the product will be distributed to retailers and promoted. Planning for operations also involves the other management functions (organizing, leading, and controlling).

How will the business be financed? Successfully funding a new business requires financial planning which is comprised of three steps: (1) estimating the business' projected income and expenses; (2) estimating the required initial investment; and (3) locating sources of funding.[31] In estimating the new venture's income and expenses, the entrepreneur uses the sales projection from his market analysis and approximates cost of production and other operating expenses drawing from past experience and industry research. These projections are typically done at least for the first year of business.

The start-up costs are also calculated. These expenses are one-time-only costs of establishing the business (e.g., installation of equipment, beginning inventory, licenses and permits). Estimates of start-up costs and ongoing income and expenses provide a projection of the amount of funding needed to launch the business and cover costs until the business is profitable.

Many entrepreneurs rely substantially on their own personal savings to launch their business. As shown in Figure 21–2, personal finances were used by almost three out of four founders of the Inc. 500 companies. A variety of other funding alternatives are often available. Commercial and investment banks, savings and loan associations, and the Small Business Administration are all frequently used sources of new venture funding. Venture capitalists, groups of investors who provide funding in exchange for a share of ownership in the company, are a possibility for ventures with substantial profit potential. And a number of communities provide loans to businesses they believe will boost the area's employment and contribute to the local economy.[32]

---

[30]Jeannie Ralston, "Promises, Promises," *Venture*, March 1988, pp. 55–57.

[31]Megginson et al., *Successful Small Business Management*, pp. 112–14.

[32]For an excellent overview of sources of new venture funding, see Marie-Jeanne Juilland, "Alternatives to a Rich Uncle," *Venture*, May 1988, pp. 62ff. Minneapolis is one community that provides substantial assistance for new businesses. A profile of the city's efforts is provided by Curtis Hartman, "Is It Easier than Ever to Start a Business?" *Inc.*, March 1987, pp. 69ff.

Figure 21–2 Sources of funding for new venture start-ups.

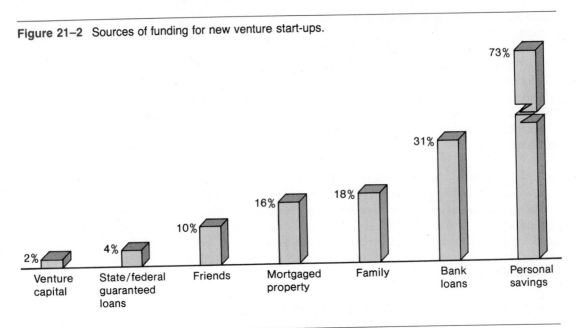

Source: Reported by the CEOs of the 1986 Inc. 500 firms. Some CEOs gave more than one response. Reprinted from Curtis Hartman, "Main Street, Inc.," *Inc.*, June 1986, p. 52. Reprinted with permission.

When approaching a prospective investor, the entrepreneur's chances of obtaining funding are enhanced by presenting a formal *business plan*. This document presents an overall analysis of the proposed business. It contains a description of the product/ service, a thorough analysis of the market, the entrepreneur's strategic objectives, the plans for each of the business's functional areas, a profile of the firm's management team, and importantly, the company's projected financial position and funding needs. Answers to the five questions of start-up planning provide the plan's content.

Many successful entrepreneurs consider the business plan to be the most important document an entrepreneur will ever write when launching a business.[33] It is the formal blueprint for the development of the new venture; prospective investors will scrutinize it closely before making a funding decision. Other important parties (e.g., suppliers and prospective major customers and managers) often will ask to see the plan before establishing a relationship with the new business.

Organizing

As we discussed in Chapters 7–9, the organizing function involves developing an organizational structure via job design, departmentation, determining span of control,

---

[33]For excellent, in-depth advice on how to prepare and present a business plan, see Burch, "The Truth about Startups," pp. 367–477.

and delegating authority. Ideally, these tasks provide a structure of relationships and authority that effectively coordinates the organization's efforts.

Although organizing activities are obviously important, they are often neglected by entrepreneurs in the early stages of the start-up. With limited resources and personnel, entrepreneurs focus on the immediate demands of generating sales and producing the product/service to meet the demand and to earn income. Organizational issues seem less important especially when the business is so small.

When entrepreneurs do explicitly address organizing tasks, the results are often more informal and flexible than in larger organizations. This informality is often intentional. For example, one study of successful growth-oriented entrepreneurs found that most of the founders intentionally avoided developing written job descriptions for their employees in the early stages of the firm's development. In more than two thirds of the cases, oral descriptions were maintained through the company's first major expansion.[34]

Written job descriptions were avoided because the entrepreneurs felt they would constrain the potential contributions and growth of employees while the firm was still small. None of the entrepreneurs wanted the employee's motivation and development to be hemmed in by the boundaries of a written description. The strategy also enabled the entrepreneurs to quickly change major job responsibilities when needed, which happens frequently when the organization is still taking shape.

Many of the entrepreneurs in the sample prepared an organization chart; however, the chart was viewed as a dynamic, continually changing picture of the company's structure. The chart also served an important purpose as a tool for continually assessing and re-evaluating the company. The study's researcher summed up the entrepreneurs' use of the organization chart stating that "It was more a means of thinking through key activities . . . a way to identify gaps and new needs—a tool for *thought*."[35]

As the firm grows in the number of employees, functions, and size of work groups and departments, job design, descriptions, and the overall structure of the business gradually becomes more formalized. However, initially the emphasis of organizing is on informality and flexibility to accommodate the dynamic change and adjustments that usually occur in the early stages of a new enterprise.

Leading

The entrepreneur's leadership task is identical to that of any CEO of a large corporation. She must encourage employees to work to achieve the business' goals by effectively communicating the tasks to be done, rewarding good performance, and creating an environment that supports the employees' efforts and individual needs.

However, some important differences exist between the small business entrepreneur and corporate CEO in performing the leadership function. First, in the newly launched business, the entrepreneur is solely responsible for effective leadership. There is no cadre of managers who share leadership responsibilities. Usually the entrepreneur is

---

[34]Thomas F. Jones, *Entrepreneurism* (New York: Donald I. Fine, 1987).

[35]Ibid., p. 168.

the organization's single boss. Leadership—effective or not—depends totally upon the entrepreneur.

Second, although leadership is a critical activity of the corporate CEO, quality of leadership is even more vital for the entrepreneur because there are no extra resources to compensate for the adverse effects of poor leadership (employee absenteeism, poor workmanship). Moreover, the entrepreneur's relationship with each employee bears a considerable impact on the firm. Consider that in a 10-employee company, each employee proportionately provides 10 percent of the firm's output. Therefore, the quality of the entrepreneur's personal or business relationship with an employee can have a major effect on the overall venture. Every individual's effort is critical to the firm.

In performing the leadership function, the entrepreneur usually must deal with one primary disadvantage. Given the firm's very limited financial resources, he usually cannot offer employees the salary and benefits that larger, more established firms can provide. Given the uncertainty of any new business, neither is long-term job security assured. These disadvantages may prevent the entrepreneur from obtaining the quality of employees he prefers.

However, the entrepreneur often possesses two important advantages. First, he is in a unique position to create an atmosphere in the company that promotes effective performance. Unlike the corporate CEO, the entrepreneur does not have to deal with prior company traditions and policies that may hamper motivation and performance. There are no established traditions, practices, or pre-existing norms of behavior. The venture is new and the entrepreneur is the firm's creator—and if he chooses—promoter and nurturer of employee excellence.

A second factor facilitates the entrepreneur's efforts in this regard. In the early days of a new, small business, the venture's employees often comprise a small group. Especially when the company's product is new and promising, a camaraderie and cohesiveness develop among members. Under a strong leader, the company's purpose is clearly communicated—make the product a success and put the venture on the map. In this type of highly challenging, stressful and familial environment, employees can become highly motivated, driven by the sense that "anything is possible." Such is particularly the case when part of the employee's income is tied to company profits. Perhaps this is one reason why 96 percent of the Inc. 500 companies include some sort of profit sharing as part of employee compensation.

The entrepreneur can create a climate of excellence and productivity in large part by setting a personal example in the ways he works and approaches the business, customers, and employees. Tom Watson of IBM, James Lincoln of Lincoln Electric, and Steven Jobs, cofounder of Apple Computer, are among those who utilized daily personal example as one way to motivate employees.

Although resources are limited, some entrepreneurs are creating innovative ways to facilitate effective leadership and motivation. Original Copy Centers Inc., a reproduction service in Cleveland, Ohio, assessed the needs of its 76 employees, who are mostly under 30 years of age and single. The company established a laundromat, exercise room, game room, and kitchen in its facility and provided employees with free coffee and private use of the company's personal computers. Although the company's compensation is no higher than the industry average, the work force is productive and the quality of work is exceptional. During the business's 12 years of operation, only three employees have quit.[36]

Smith & Hawken, an importer of garden tools, uses a technique called the "5-15 report" for maintaining open communication with employees (the "5-15" stands for 15 minutes to write and 5 minutes to read). Each week, every employee completes the three-part report by telling what he did during the week, describing his morale and that of his department, and providing one idea for bettering his job, department, or company. Management takes no longer than one week to respond to each idea. The technique is one way that Smith & Hawken keeps tabs on each employee's development, finds ways to improve the business, and provides needed support for the employees to do their jobs.[37]

Controlling

As we discussed in Chapter 14, the controlling function involves establishing standards, obtaining information that provides a comparison of actual with desired results, and taking actions to correct any adverse deviations from standards. In the small business, the controlling activities are particularly important, because in the initial stages of the venture, every aspect of the business is newly established. Given the newness of the business and its operations, mistakes are bound to be made. Because the business' resources are limited, it is essential that the entrepreneur detect and correct problems as quickly as possible. Effective controlling activities enable the entrepreneur to do so.

In the early stages of business, control systems are usually basic rather than sophisticated. However, most entrepreneurs develop financial, production, and inventory control systems that provide key indicators which they monitor weekly, even daily. These indicators include sales, production rates, inventory, accounts receivable, accounts payable, and importantly, cash flow and the cash flow outlook.[38] Ensuring that funds are on hand to pay immediate expenses is a particularly troublesome task, according to a survey of small business owners, as shown in Figure 21–3.[39]

A growing number of entrepreneurs are installing computerized control information systems to assist them in monitoring aspects of the company's performance and conducting financial and production analysis. Many software firms are developing programs specifically designed for a small business's control needs; this development along with the decreasing costs of computer hardware are making computerized control information systems a reality for small businesses.

Pacific Smelting, a manufacturer of zinc products based in Torrance, California, is one small business that has abandoned its manual recordkeeping for a computerized system. The manual system severely hindered the company's ability to determine

---

[36]Robert A. Mamis, "Details, Details," *Inc.*, March 1988, pp. 96–98.

[37]Paul Hawken, "The Employee as Customer," *Inc.*, November 1987, pp. 21–22.

[38]Dan Steinhoff and John F. Burgess, *Small Business Management Fundamentals* (New York: McGraw-Hill, 1986), p. 339.

[39]*The Wall Street Journal*, November 2, 1986, p. 35.

Figure 21–3 Entrepreneurial problems.

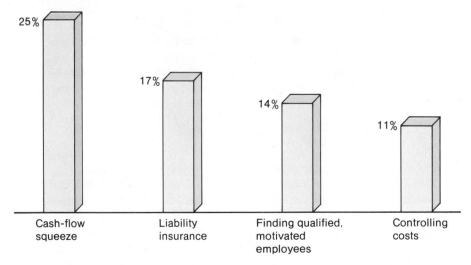

These percentages of surveyed small business owners said
the most important problems they face are:

25% — Cash-flow squeeze

17% — Liability insurance

14% — Finding qualified, motivated employees

11% — Controlling costs

Source: Reprinted from L. C. Megginson, C. R. Scott Jr., L. R. Trueblood, and W. L. Megginson, *Successful Small Business Management* (Plano, Tex.: Business Publications, 1988), p. 581. Used with permission.

which of its products were profitable, which customers were most important, and whether product pricing was accurate from a cost perspective. With its computer system, the company now can instantly obtain a broad range of control-related analysis including profit margins per sale and trend analysis of long-term changes in sales and profits across its product line. System analysis has led to the elimination of one product and revised product pricing to meet sales and profit objectives.[40]

Although control systems are used primarily to ensure that activities meet established standards, the systems serve another purpose for entrepreneurs who want their firms to grow. The systems facilitate growth by providing information that increases the entrepreneur's insights concerning the business's abilities and limitations. Said one entrepreneur: "By looking at information on sales growth, production efficiency, employee performance and staffing, and other factors, I gain a better idea of how my business can expand, and by how much. I have a much better understanding of what we can take on."

SPECIAL CHALLENGES OF ENTREPRENEURSHIP

At some point in their careers, entrepreneurs encounter major challenges that test their abilities and character. Three particular challenges merit special mention at this point.

---

[40]Mark Stevens, "Computerizing Your Business," *Working Woman*, September 1987, pp. 33f.

Growth of the Enterprise

A successful entrepreneur who creates a business for growth and profit inevitably discovers that the business she is running is dramatically different from the one she created. Because of growth, the company is no longer a shop with a handful of employees, a one-page customer list, and a single supplier and distributor. Rather, the company now employs several hundred workers in many departments. There are networks of suppliers and distributors and operations that run on a much larger scale.

Successfully managing a company with this type of growth requires a transition in management tasks and focus. Because of the company's greater size and complexity, coordination and control must be emphasized. Professional managers must be hired, and more sophisticated and formalized control systems and procedures must be developed and managed.[41]

The company's transition from a small shop to complex corporation also requires a major change in the entrepreneur's tasks and management style. To effectively lead the company, the entrepreneur can no longer make all decisions and maintain a hands-on involvement in all aspects of the business; the company is simply too big. Instead, she must delegate authority to subordinate managers and focus on coordinating their efforts. In this situation, many entrepreneurs find that their very skills which brought the company its early success are no longer effective. The company requires a new set of abilities from its CEO.

Do entrepreneurs effectively make this transition? Some, like Bill Gates of Microsoft, do. However, others have major difficulties in managing a much larger and more complex company.[42] Many have particular problems with delegating authority. As the creators of the business, they have a strong need to control its operations and find it extremely difficult to relinquish any decision making ("it's my baby," said one entrepreneur). Others find that they simply lack the professional management skills needed to run a complex business.

Some entrepreneurs, like Mitch Kapor, are uncomfortable with the environment of a big business. As founder of Lotus Development Corp., Kapor saw his computer software firm quickly grow from a small shop operation to a diversified, international corporation with more than 1,300 employees and $275 million in sales. Kapor found that "leading by coordinating" poorly matched his management skills, his desire to work with people in small groups, and his penchant for perfectionism.[43] Joseph Solomon, founder of Vidal Sassoon Hair Products, had similar problems when his company boomed in size. Solomon became frustrated because he missed the fast-moving, flexible, and more spirited, small group environment that his smaller company had provided.[44]

---

[41]See Neil C. Churchill and Virginia L. Lewis, "The Five Stages of Small Business Growth," *Harvard Business Review*, May–June 1983, pp. 30ff.

[42]For some interesting profiles, see Lucien Rhodes, "At the Crossroads," *Inc.*, February 1988, pp. 66ff; and Lucien Rhodes, "Kuolt's Complex," *Inc.*, April 1986, pp. 72ff.

[43]"Mitch Kapor," *Inc.*, January 1987, pp. 30ff; and Michael W. Miller, "Starting Over: High-Tech Entrepreneurs Who Have Left Their Old Firms Ponder Next Moves," *The Wall Street Journal*, September 8, 1987, p. 33.

[44]Jones, *Entrepreneurism*, pp. 248–50.

Entrepreneurs resolve this dilemma in several ways. Many learn to delegate, often by being careful in selecting those to whom they delegate, and by delegating gradually. Some, like Mitch Kapor, resign from their company or, like Joseph Solomon, sell their firm and start all over, launching a new venture. Other entrepreneurs avoid the dilemma entirely by deliberately restricting the size of their companies.[45]

Entrepreneurial Stress

All CEOs experience stress due to the burden of responsibility for managing a business. However, entrepreneurs, especially those who run small businesses, often experience particularly high levels of stress. The stress is partly caused by the risks the entrepreneur incurs in launching a business, and his sense of total accountability for its success or failure.

According to a study of 210 small business owners, other factors contribute to entrepreneurial stress.[46] Loneliness is a major source of stress (over half of the entrepreneurs reported they "frequently feel a sense of loneliness"). Loneliness arises because there is no one in the business or among friends or family with whom the entrepreneur can openly talk about the business and its problems and seek advice, especially in the early days of the company. No one is experiencing the same or even similar work activities or problems.[47]

Total immersion in the business, frustration with employee problems, and an overly high need for achievement can also contribute to entrepreneurial stress. Some entrepreneurs set unreasonable goals for themselves, push themselves too hard, and experience great frustration when they fall short of their expectations.[48]

There is no perfect cure for entrepreneurial stress. Indeed, many entrepreneurs believe that high stress is an inherent element of entrepreneurship, and many are capable of coping and even thriving on it. However, many entrepreneurs who view stress as a problem, have alleviated stress using a number of strategies such as making changes in their business routine (e.g., scheduling more time between meeting appointments and taking time off for exercise), setting time aside for social activities, and creating more opportunities for interacting with employees. Some entrepreneurs participate in local business organizations (such as the Rotary Club) that provide an opportunity to talk with other CEOs of noncompeting companies about their businesses.[49]

---

[45]For an interesting perspective from an entrepreneur who maintains a limited growth strategy, see Robert Mulder, "Sole Proprietor," *Inc.*, November 1986, pp. 96–98.

[46]See David E. Gumpert and David P. Boyd, "The Loneliness of the Small-Business Owner," *Harvard Business Review*, November–December 1984, pp. 18ff; and David P. Boyd and David E. Gumpert, "Coping with Entrepreneurial Stress," *Harvard Business Review*, March–April 1983, pp. 44ff.

[47]Ibid.

[48]Ibid.

[49]For insightful profiles of how four founders dealt with stress by changing their managerial lifestyles, see Joshua Hyatt, "All Stressed-up and Nowhere to Go," *Inc.*, January 1987, pp. 74ff; and John Grossman, "Burnout," *Inc.*, September 1987, pp. 89ff.

Selling the Company

Most of the U.S. businesses acquired today aren't large corporations; they are small, independent businesses, many of which were owned by entrepreneurs who were ready to sell their companies. Entrepreneurs decide to sell their businesses for several reasons. They may sell the company to retire and enjoy the financial returns the sale provides them or to use the profits to launch yet another company. An entrepreneur may sell the firm because, on the verge of retirement, she realizes that no qualified successor is available to assume leadership. This problem often arises among family-owned and managed entrepreneurships.[50] Or the entrepreneur may sell because the buyer can provide much-needed additional cash and other resources to fund the company's growth.[51]

Regardless of the motivation, the decision to sell the business introduces a complex acquisition process and concerns. Most entrepreneurs want their businesses to continue to thrive after the sale, and many are mindfully aware of the poor performance record of acquisitions. From half to two thirds of all acquisitions ultimately fail.[52]

Entrepreneurs approach selling their companies with many objectives; three are particularly important.

Locate the right buyer.   For entrepreneurs who are concerned about the company's future, this task involves finding a buyer with objectives for the entrepreneur's firm that are compatible with those of the entrepreneur. Compatibility is particularly important for entrepreneurs who want to continue to head the company after the sale.

Secure satisfactory terms of the sale.   These terms focus on price for the company, terms of payment, and special conditions concerning the company's employees and other aspects of the business. An entrepreneur's bargaining position is strengthened if his company possesses valuable resources such as an impressive record of financial performance, a strong reputation with customers, and difficult-to-replace assets (such as exceptionally talented management and strong, specialized R&D capabilities).

Obtain satisfactory autonomy.   Entrepreneurs who stay with the acquired firm usually seek to maintain as much autonomy as possible in managing the company after its sale.

For entrepreneurs who continue with the acquired company, managing the firm after the acquisition requires making some major adjustments. The entrepreneur must cope with lesser independence in running the business. Regardless of the amount of

---

[50]For a look at the special problems common in family entrepreneurships (and some solutions), see Patricia W. Hamilton, "The Special Problems of Family Businesses," *D&B Reports,* July–August 1986, pp. 18–21; Curtis Hartman, "Taking the 'Family' out of Family Business," *Inc.,* September 1986, pp. 70ff; and Sharon Nelton, "Strategies for Family Firms," *Nation's Business,* June 1986, pp. 20ff.

[51]See Beatrice H. Mitchell and Michael S. Sperry, "Selling out," and Sandra Salmans, "Cutting the Deal," *Venture,* January 1988, pp. 25–26, and 27ff.

[52]See S. E. Prokesch and W. J. Powell, Jr., "Do Mergers Really Work?" *Business Week,* June 3, 1985, pp. 88–94; and A. Bennett, "After the Merger, More CEOs Left in Uneasy Spot: Looking for Work," *The Wall Street Journal,* August 27, 1986, p. 15.

autonomy promised by the new owners, the entrepreneur must still report to a senior manager in the parent company, provide ongoing, detailed reports of the business, and account for its performance. This is often a difficult adjustment for entrepreneurs who previously only answered to themselves.[53] The entrepreneur's salary is also often reduced.[54] Many entrepreneurs have problems making these adjustments; consequently, many leave the acquired firm sooner than they expected.[55]

THE FUTURE OF ENTREPRENEURSHIP

The increasing trend of new business creation will likely continue in the 1990s as more people assume the risks for the potential personal and professional rewards of running a small business. Achieving success in this endeavor requires the ability to effectively implement the four functions of management especially during the early stages of the new venture when mistakes can be costly.

Perhaps above all, successful entrepreneurship requires a keen understanding of personal assets and limitations, and a strong commitment to the challenge. The adage "know thyself" aptly applies to anyone contemplating launching a business. If one day, you seriously consider this important step, thoroughly examine your motivations for starting a business, and the personal strengths and shortcomings you would bring to the enterprise. Self-understanding greatly improves the odds of building a productive company and reaping the substantial rewards of entrepreneurship.

MANAGEMENT SOLUTION

ZZZZ BEST COMPANY TOPS $4 MILLION IN SALES

Barry started his carpet cleaning business in his family's garage in Reseda, California, paying his father $150 monthly in rent. In five years, he built the business to an operation with 180 employees and branch operations in seven California towns. His parents now work for him. In 1987, sales exceeded $4 million.

His success can be attributed to several factors, notably hard work and ambition. A typical day begins at 4:30 A.M. at a local gymnasium, where he spends two hours body building (his build is no longer small). By 7 A.M., he is at work and logs in a 13-hour workday.

Barry's management style is aggressive (in his words, "my way or the highway"). All employees call him Mr. Minkow; indeed all of his managers are called *mister* which is a reflection
Continued

---

[53]R. H. Hayes and G. H. Hoag, "Post-Acquisition Retention of Top Management," *Mergers and Acquisitions,* Summer 1974, pp. 8–18.

[54]See Sanford L. Jacobs, "Unrealistic Expectations Pose Problems for Sellers of Firms," *The Wall Street Journal,* August 20, 1984, p. 17.

[55]Hayes and Hoag, "Post-Acquisition Retention of Top Management," p. 10.

MANAGEMENT SOLUTION

Concluded

of his military training, and in Barry's view a "great morale builder."

In his spare time, Barry teaches a course in entrepreneurship at a local college, telling young students that success is possible for entrepreneurs under the age of 21 who have the energy and drive. His statement is not an exaggeration. Some observers report a growing trend of entrepreneurship among high school and college students, evidenced in part by an increasing number of courses in entrepreneurship in high schools and colleges.

At 20, Barry's goal is to make ZZZZ Best the "General Motors of the carpet cleaning industry." He plans to take the company public and eventually establish franchises nationwide.

Note: Recent events have significantly changed this solution. Your instructor will provide specific details.

Source: Adapted from Nelson W. Aldrich, Jr., "Young Founders," *Inc.*, August 1986, pp. 63–65; and Cynthia Poulos and William Hoffer, "The Business Whiz Kids," *Nation's Business*, November 1986, pp. 20ff.

MANAGEMENT SUMMARY

☐ An entrepreneur is the creator and chief executive of a business enterprise. Entrepreneurs lead over 14 million U.S. businesses which provide more than half the nation's gross national product and over 80 percent of all new jobs.

☐ Despite the risks, many individuals launch new businesses each year for a number of reasons: to attain independence, personal and professional growth, income, and security or to achieve an alternative career which they view is superior to a dissatisfying job.

☐ Success in entrepreneurship requires careful start-up planning. This activity involves determining the product or service to be provided, the market to be served, and how the business will be established, financed, and operated.

☐ Although many entrepreneurs perform organizing activities in the early stages of their businesses, they often keep job descriptions and other organizational aspects of the firm flexible because of the dynamic change that the firm frequently experiences.

☐ Although often financially unable to provide compensation packages that strongly compete with larger, more established firms, the entrepreneur often has a special opportunity to develop an organizational culture that promotes employee productivity and excellence.

☐ Much of an entrepreneur's efforts in performing the controlling function centers on financial control, particularly ensuring that enough cash is on hand to cover immediate expenses.

☐ At some point in their careers, many entrepreneurs face the challenges of coping with entrepreneurial stress, making the transition from small business manager to large company CEO, and dealing with the tasks and concerns that surround selling the company.

REVIEW AND DISCUSSION QUESTIONS

1. Several studies have found that many entrepreneurs were the first-born child of their parents. Can you explain this relationship between birth order and entrepreneurship?

2. One management observer asserted: "Someone who opens a franchise really isn't an entrepreneur in the true sense. There's no creation of a business per se, no innovation." Do you agree? Explain.

3. In your opinion, which entrepreneurship task in the start-up phase of the business is the most difficult to complete successfully? Explain.

4. Hewlett-Packard, Land's End, David's Cookies, and Cuisinarts are all highly successful businesses that had no formal business plan when they were established. Does their success diminish the importance of a formal plan? Discuss.

5. In your view, what special problems face "late bloomer" entrepreneurs? What unique advantages do they bring to their businesses?

6. What are the drawbacks of maintaining orally communicated and flexible job descriptions in the early stages of a new business?

7. Suppose you are the head of a young, fast-growing computer software manufacturer. You are experiencing considerable stress from your job. What changes would you make to alleviate the problem?

8. What entrepreneurship tasks are unique to launching a new product or service as opposed to one that already exists in the market? Explain.

9. What special problems face the entrepreneur who needs highly skilled employees but lacks the financial resources to fund a strongly competitive compensation program? How can an entrepreneur deal with this problem?

10. Many acquisition observers assert that one reason so many acquisitions fail is that the acquired company is so much smaller than the buyer and the practices of the two firms so distinctly different. Explain.

CASES

21-1 HAIRDRESSING WITH A TWIST

Hair salons are not a glamorous business. Although the industry is growing (revenues have tripled in the last 10 years), it is dominated by small single shops that are poorly managed and marketed, with hairdressers that are inadequately trained and very underpaid. A few large chains exist but none have captured more than 2 percent of industry sales.

However, one company, Visible Changes Inc., is fast emerging as a comer in the industry with a sales performance that is unprecedented in the industry. While the average salon grossed $168,108 in revenues during 1986, the typical Visible Changes salon attained $885,387 in sales. Three of its 16 salons took in over $1.5 million. The company outshines the industry by every performance yardstick including average sales per customer which is about twice the industry average.

Visible Changes was founded in 1978 by John McCormack (chairman) and his wife, Maryanne. Mr. McCormack attributes his company's exceptional success partly to professional management. The salons are clean and classic looking; operations are streamlined and smoothly run. An advanced computerized information system keeps Mr. McCormack informed of the latest performance figures: yesterday's sales, for instance—per salon, per hairdresser, per product. Even a profile of yesterday's customers is available by age, gender, and birthday, and how all this compares with any previous days, weeks, or months.

However, that's not the real key to Mr. McCormack's success. The core is his hairdressers and a motivation/compensation program that directly links pay to performance. Every hairdresser earns everything he receives. All income—salary, commissions, even benefits—depends on performance. For example, each of the company's 300 hairdressers are paid based on commission, 25 percent on all walk-in customers (the basic haircut costs $19). However, Mr. McCormack believes that the key to an effective salon is excellent customer service by highly trained hairdressers. So he boosts the commission rates based on customer requests. If a hairdresser is requested by a customer, she earns a 35 percent commission on the fee. If requested more than 75 percent of the time, the hairdresser can charge a higher price, which by all indications, her customers are willing to pay. Thus, the hairdresser receives a higher income per customer.

Visible Changes hairdressers also sell hair products. They earn 15 percent commission on sales (the first $120 earned pays for health insurance). Each year, each hairdresser's performance is evaluated on a 10-point scale. Those who receive a top score receive a bonus that is 10 percent of their total pay for the year. Those who are among the company's 50 top product sellers or 50 most requested hairdressers receive a "superbonus." All employees receive profit sharing which amounts to 15 percent of everyone's gross pay for the year. The more business everyone brings in, the more everyone makes.

This system results in large incomes for hairdressers (and also the hair salon managers and receptionists whose pay is performance based). While the typical hairdresser in the industry earns $12,000 a year, a Visible Changes hairdresser earns about $33,000 a year. Some superstars like Tony Hatty who works at one of the company's salons in Houston, Texas (its home base), earn, with a 99 percent request rate, over $50,000 a year. Overall, the program is designed to attract and keep strong performers. Turnover is under 10 percent (the industry averages 30 percent).

Mr. McCormack, a former stockbroker and New York City police officer, believes the system emphasizes employee growth and development, and a focused attention to the customer. However, although the pay can be lucrative, performance standards are high. Employees must earn everything, even the right to attend the company's advanced training sessions (earned by achieving performance goals for two consecutive months). His current projects: Wisp International, which is marketing the company's computer system to other hair salons, and expansion. Mr. McCormack is giving his hairdressers the opportunity to open their own Visible Changes salons.

Questions

1. What entrepreneurial characteristics are needed to achieve the type of success which Visible Changes is experiencing?
2. Based on your own knowledge of hair salons (and Visible Changes), are hair salons a high-risk industry? Why or why not?
3. In your opinion, which management function (planning, organizing, leading, controlling) has played a primary role in Visible Changes' development?

Source: Adapted from Bruce G. Posner and Bo Burlingham, "The Hottest Entrepreneur in America," *Inc.*, January 1988, pp. 44ff.

21–2 WILL THIS BUSINESS SUCCEED?

Todd LeRoy and Michael Atkinson have launched a franchise business which they're certain will be a sure winner. The business, Associated Video Hut Inc., franchises video drive-through rental outlets.

Each "Video's 1st" outlet is a small Fotomat-type kiosk which a franchise owner buys and can place in a small shopping mall parking lot or in some other suburban, high-traffic area. There, customers can drive up to the kiosk window, review the list of titles shown on the promo board, pay the rental fee, and obtain a video cassette without leaving their car. The outlet specializes in hit movies, carrying only the current top titles (10 to 25 copies of each title) for a total inventory of 300 to 750 tapes. Because several copies of each title are available, customers are assured of obtaining the hit film they want.

Each film rents for $2.95 a day, more than the $2 a day rental which is the industry average. The two founders believe that customers will pay more for the time-saving

Exhibit 21–1 Competitive analysis.*

	Industry Average Performance for Video Retailer	Video's 1st Performance Assumptions
Store size	2,089 square feet*	48 square feet
Tapes stocked	3,478*	300
Individual titles stocked	2,417*	30
Tapes rented daily	185**	120
Percent of stock rented daily	5.3%**	40%
Rental price	$1.80**	$2.95
Wholesale tape cost (new releases)	$50**	$60
Resale price of used tapes	$16**	$20
Full-time employees	3*	1
Part-time employees	4*	4

*Video Software Dealers Association
**The Fairfield Group Inc.
Source: "Drive-In Movies," *Inc.*, February 1988, p. 43. Reprinted with permission.

convenience (just as people do at convenience food stores) and for the selection (hit films are difficult to rent at other video stores that carry only one or two copies). The kiosks are portable so if one location doesn't net much business, the franchise owner can easily move the shop to another site.

LeRoy and Atkinson believe their venture will succeed for the following reasons:

The market is there.   In 1987, consumers nationwide spent more than $4 billion in videocassette rentals, and in 1988 the rental revenues continued to climb for the several thousand video rental businesses in the industry. By 1995, an estimated 90 percent of all homes with TVs will also have a videocassette recorder. The founders believe that the rental industry should eventually top $15 billion in sales annually.

Low overhead.   LeRoy and Atkinson believe that most video rental stores incur unnecessary costs because they carry tapes that aren't rented. As shown in the competitive analysis in Exhibit 21–1, the average video rental store carries 3,478 tapes but only rents 12 percent of its inventory each day. The remaining tapes are unused, incurring high inventory costs as well as costs of the storage space (rent, utilities). The Video 1st concept eliminates this problem by keeping a limited inventory (350 to 700 cassettes) of high-volume tapes. Overhead is much lower. The two founders believe that their top competition is provided by the video superstores which carry virtually all titles and the "rack jobbers" which maintain limited inventory at gas stations, convenience stores, and other locations.

Franchise support.   The two entrepreneurs estimate that each kiosk will be highly profitable for a franchise owner (the pro forma statement is shown in Exhibit 21–2). These figures are estimates of an average month and annual totals for a kiosk's second year of operation. The founders estimate that a kiosk will break even if 150 tapes are

Exhibit 21-2 Video's 1st pro forma operating statement per kiosk.*

	Monthly Average ($)	Yearly Total ($)
Revenues:		
Tape rental fees (116 rentals per day @ $2.95)	$10,260	$123,117
Used tape sales (55 tapes per month @ $20)	1,100	13,200
Popcorn	150	1,800
Other	100	1,200
Total revenues	11,610	139,317
Cost of Sales:		
Prerecorded tapes (55 tapes per month @ $60)	3,300	39,600
Popcorn	93	1,116
Other	50	600
Total cost of sales	3,443	41,316
Gross profit	8,167	98,001
Operating expenses:		
Rent	500	6,000
Payroll (12 hours per day, seven days per week)	1,950	23,400
Payroll taxes	234	2,808
General (Insurance, supplies, utilities, miscellaneous)	505	6,055
Royalty payment (7% gross receipts)	813	9,752
Local advertising (2% gross receipts)	232	2,786
Corporate advertising (1% gross receipts)	116	1,393
Note payable, principal, and interest ($45,000 note @ 12%, five-year term)	1,000	12,000
Total operating expenses	5,350	64,194
Net income before taxes	2,817	33,807

*Depreciation and amortization not included.

Source: "Drive-In Movies," *Inc.*, February 1988, p. 43. Reprinted with permission.

rented each day (about 17 percent of its inventory). Given the pro forma projections, a franchise owner will earn $33,807, a pretax return on assets of at least 40 percent each year per kiosk if about 40 percent of a 300-tape inventory is rented every day. Franchise costs (which includes a kiosk, initial inventory, training, a grand opening, and sufficient working capital) will run about $88,000. The company will provide promotion materials (such as ads, four-color newletters for the franchisee's customers, and a list of movie titles for insertion into local newspapers). The founders will realize a profit of $23,500 per kiosk franchise excluding royalties.

Associated Video Hut has already opened two pilot stores and sold their first franchise to a group of investors in New York. They are negotiating with a Burger King multifranchise owner who wants to provide drive-through video rentals along with drive-through hamburgers. The founders' goal is to sell 5,000 kiosk franchises by the mid-1990s. To meet this objective, they are targeting individuals who want to set up at least three kiosks.

LeRoy and Atkinson recently presented their business plan to a group of new venture experts. "We keep asking people to shoot holes in the concept," asserted Atkinson, "and they can't do it." Some of the experts disagree.

Questions

1. Identify and assess the strengths and shortcomings of the concept behind Associated Video Hut.

2. Would you buy a "Video's 1st" franchise? Why or why not?

3. What suggestions can you provide to improve the business concept and operations?

Source: Adapted from Tom Richman, "Drive-In Movies," *Inc.*, February 1988, pp. 42ff.

(*Note:* Your instructor will provide a summary of the critiques of Associated Video Hut made by the expert panel.)

EXERCISE

21-1 PORTRAIT OF AN ENTREPRENEUR

Purpose: This activity is designed to enhance students' understanding of the entrepreneurial personality, and the motivations, challenges, and rewards of entrepreneurship.

Setting Up the Exercise: Your instructor will divide the class into groups of up to four members each. Each group's task is to identify a successful entrepreneur in your community and to interview the business leader. In your search for an entrepreneur, concentrate on identifying a successful small business which is directed by its founder. Perusal through the business section of recent issues of your community newspaper and a phone call to the local Chamber of Commerce should be helpful in locating an entrepreneur. (Don't underestimate your chances of obtaining an entrepreneur's cooperation. Experience with this exercise has shown that entrepreneurs typically enjoy talking about themselves and their businesses.) The interview should require from 30 minutes to one hour.

Here are some suggested questions to use:

1. What motivated you to start your own business?
2. How would you describe yourself to a stranger? (Are you self-confident, energetic, independent? Are you an optimist, a realist, a pessimist?)
3. In your opinion, what personality characteristics and abilities are essential for success as an entrepreneur?
4. How would you describe your leadership style?
5. Describe a typical workday.
6. What aspects of your work do you find the most satisfying? The most frustrating?
7. Which aspects of your work are the easiest for you? The most difficult?
8. Among your business' activities (operations, finance, marketing, personnel), which are you most involved in?
9. How much emphasis do you place on motivating employees?
10. What important lessons have you learned from your experience in creating and running your own business?
11. What advice would you offer to a young, prospective entrepreneur?

Once you've completed the interview, your group should develop an oral report which represents a profile of the entrepreneur which will be presented by your group's elected spokesperson. Each group will present its findings to the class. Your instructor will lead an open class discussion which draws together general common characteristics of entrepreneurs based on the interviews.

A Learning Note: This exercise should illustrate the common characteristics that entrepreneurs possess which include substantial energy, optimism, a practical, nuts-and-bolts approach to business, and ambition. Entrepreneurial differences should also emerge among the profiles especially between the entrepreneur driven by growth objectives, and those with other goals.

GLOSSARY OF TERMS

Activity The work necessary to complete a particular event in a PERT network. An activity consumes time, which is the paramount variable in a PERT system. In PERT networks, three time estimates are used for each activity: an optimistic time, a pessimistic time, and a most likely time.

Adapters Physical expressions used to adjust psychologically to the interpersonal climate of a particular situation. Frequently used to deal with stress (e.g., drumming fingers on a table). A form of body language.

Affect displays Usually subconscious expressions that directly communicate an individual's emotions (e.g., a "closed posture" which communicates defensiveness). A form of body language.

Affective attitude The part of attitude that involves a person's emotions or feelings.

Altruism An ethical standard which places highest value on behavior which is pleasurable and rewarding to society.

Appraisal costs Costs involved in directly evaluating product/service quality such as the costs of quality inspection and testing.

Attitude A person's tendency to feel and behave toward some object in some way.

Attribution An inference made by a person about his feelings or another person's feelings based on observed behavior.

Authority The legitimate right to use assigned resources to accomplish a delegated task or objective; the right to give orders and to exact obedience.

Behavior Any observable response given by a person.

Behavior modification An approach to motivation that uses operant conditioning. Operant behavior is learned on the basis of consequences. If a behavior causes a desired outcome (for managers), then it is reinforced (positively rewarded), and because of its consequences, it is likely to be repeated. Thus, behavior is conditioned by adjusting its consequences.

Behavioral approach to organizational design A design approach that emphasizes people and how the structure of an organization affects their behavior and performance. The advocates of a people orientation to design believe that the classical approach suppresses personal development because it is so rigid and restrictive.

Behaviorally anchored rating scales (BARS) A set of rating scales developed by raters and/or ratees that uses critical behavioral incidents as interval anchors on each scale. About 6 to 10 scales with behavioral incidents are used to derive the evaluation.

Biofeedback A technique, usually involving the use of some kind of instrumentation, in which the user attempts to learn to control various bodily functions such as heart rate and blood pressure.

Brand-switching model Provides the manager with some idea of the behavior of consumers in terms of their loyalty to brands and their switches from one brand to another.

Buffer A term used by the scholar James Thompson to describe the departments or units that are created to deal with environmental uncertainty and complexity.

Bureaucracy An organizational design that relies on specialization of labor, a specific authority hierarchy, a formal set of rules and procedures, and rigid promotion and selection criteria.

Business plan A written report that provides an overview and analysis of a proposed business. Includes a description of the prospective product or service, a thorough market analysis, the firm's strategic objectives, plans for each of the business' functional areas, a profile of the management team, and the venture's projected financial position and funding needs.

Buyout Entering a business by acquiring an existing company in the selected business and market.

Career An individually perceived sequence of attitudes and behaviors associated with work-related experiences and activities over the span of a person's life.

Career path The sequence of jobs associated with a particular initial job that leads to promotion and advancement.

Career planning The process of systematically matching an individual's career aspirations with opportunities for achieving them.

Career stages Distinct, but interrelated, steps or phases of a career, including the prework stage, the initial work stage, the stable work stage, and the retirement stage.

Carrying costs The costs incurred by carrying raw materials and finished goods in inventory. These include taxes and insurance on the goods in inventory, interest on the money invested in inventory and storage space, and the losses incurred because of inventory obsolescence.

Categorical imperative An ethical standard which judges behavior in terms of its consistency with the principle: "Act as if the maxim of your action were to become a general law binding on everyone."

Central tendency error The tendency to rate all ratees around an average score.

Changing external environment One in which there are rather frequent and expected changes in the actions of competitors, market demands, technology, etc.

Classical approach to organizational design Places reliance of such management principles as unity of command, a balance between authority and responsibility, division of labor, and delegation to establish relationships between managers and subordinates.

Closed system An approach that generally ignores environmental forces and conditions.

Code of ethics A written statement of an organization's values, beliefs, and norms of ethical behavior.

Coercive power The power of a leader that is derived from fear. The follower perceives the leader as a person who can punish deviant behavior and actions.

Cognitive attitude The part of attitude that involves a person's perceptions, beliefs, and ideas.

Cognitive dissonance A state in which there is a discrepancy between a person's attitude and behavior.

Command group The group shown on an organization chart that reports to a single manager.

Communication The transmission of information and understanding through the use of common symbols.

Competitive benchmarking Careful examination of a competitor's product to determine its costs and quality.

Computer skills Managerial skills comprised of a conceptual understanding of the computer and the ability to use the computer and software in performing aspects of the manager's job.

Conceptual management skill The ability to coordinate and integrate ideas, concepts, and practices. Such skill is most important to top-level managers.

Concurrent control The techniques and methods which focus on the actual, ongoing activity of the organization.

Conditions of certainty A situation in which a person facing a decision has enough information to know what the outcome of each alternative will be.

Conditions of risk A situation in which a person facing a decision can estimate the likelihood (probability) of a particular outcome.

Conditions of uncertainty A situation in which the decision maker has absolutely no idea of the probabilities associated with the various alternatives being considered. In such a situation, the intuition, judgment, and personality of the decision maker can play an important role.

Consideration Acts by a leader which imply supportive concern for the followers in a group.

Contingency management An approach that considers an organization's objectives, organizational and job design, human resources, environment, and managerial skills as interacting and affecting the type of management decisions made about planning, organizing, leading, and controlling.

Controlling function All managerial activity that is undertaken to assure that actual operations go according to plan.

Core job dimensions As proposed by Hackman and others, there are five core job dimensions which, if present, provide enrichment for jobs. The dimensions are variety, task identity, task significance, autonomy, and feedback.

Corporate philanthropy Financial donations by corporations to organizations for socially responsible purposes.

Cost-benefit analysis A technique for evaluating individual projects and deciding among alternatives. This technique is being adapted to the needs of public sector organizations to aid them in improving their performance.

Critical path The longest path in a PERT network, from the network beginning event to the network ending event.

Culture Culture is a very complex environmental influence which includes knowledge, beliefs, law, morals, art, customs, and any other habits and capabilities an individual acquires as a member of society. It is important to be aware that cultures are *learned*, cultures *vary*, and cultures *influence behavior*.

Decentralization The pushing downward of the appropriate amount of decision-making authority. All organizations practice a certain degree of decentralization.

Decision making The process of thought and deliberation which results in a decision. Decisions, the output of the decision-making process, are means through which a manager seeks to achieve some desired state.

Decoding The mental procedure which the receiver of a message uses to decipher the message.

Defensive behavior Behavior such as aggression, withdrawal, and repression which is resorted to by an individual when blocked in attempts to satisfy needs.

Delegation The process by which authority is distributed downward in an organization.

Departmentation The process of grouping jobs together on the basis of some common characteristic, such as product, client, location, or function.

Diagnosis The use of data collected by interviews, surveys, observations, or records to learn about people or organizations.

Differentiation The degree of differences in the knowledge and emotional orientations of managers in different departments of an organization.

Direct investment entry strategy The strongest commitment to becoming an MNC is when management decides to begin producing the firm's products abroad. This strategy enables the firm to maintain full control over production, marketing, and other key functions.

Direction A method of concurrent control which refers to the manager's act of interpreting orders to a subordinate.

Discounted rate of return The rate of return that equates future cash proceeds with the initial cost of an investment.

Distinctive competence A factor which gives the organization an advantage over similar organizations. Distinctive competences are what the organization does well.

Downsizing An organizational response to declining revenues and increasing costs that involves reducing the work force and often closing and/or consolidating operations.

Downward communication Communication that flows from individuals at higher levels of an organization structure to individuals at lower levels. The most common type of downward communication is job instructions that are transmitted from the superior to the subordinate.

Dual careers Situations in which both the husband and the wife are pursuing careers.

Egoism An ethical standard which places highest value on behavior which is pleasurable and rewarding to the individual.

Emblems Physical gestures that quickly convey an understood word or phrase (the OK sign with thumb and forefinger, for example). A form of body language.

Emergent leader A person from within the group who comes to lead or influence its members.

Encoding The converting of a communication into an understandable message by a communicator.

Entrepreneur An individual who establishes and manages a business.

EOQ model The economic order quantity model, which is used to resolve problems regarding the size of orders. A manager concerned with minimizing inventory costs could utilize the model to study the relationships between carrying costs, ordering costs, and usage.

Esteem needs The awareness of the importance of others and of the regard which is accorded by others.

Event An accomplishment at a particular point in time on a PERT network. An event consumes no time.

Expatriate An MNC employee transferred to a host country from the MNC's home base or from an MNC facility in another country.

Expectancy motivation model Views motivation as a process governing choices. In this model, a person who has a goal weighs the likelihood that various behaviors will achieve that goal and is likely to select the behavior that is expected to be most successful.

Expected time(t_e) A time estimate for each activity that is calculated by using the formula:

$$t_e = \frac{a + 4m + b}{6}$$

where a = optimistic time, m = most likely time, and b = pessimistic time.

Expected value The average return of a particular decision in the long run if the decision maker makes the same decision in the same situation over and over again. The expected value is found by taking the value of an outcome if it should occur and multiplying that value by the probability that the outcome will occur.

Expert power The power which individuals possess because followers perceive them to have special skills, special knowledge, or a special expertise.

Export entry strategy The simplest way for a firm to enter a foreign market is by exporting. This strategy involves little or no change in the basic mission, objectives, and strategies of the organization, since it continues to produce all of its products at home. The firm will usually secure an *agent* in the particular foreign market who facilitates the transactions with foreign buyers.

Expropriation Seizure of an MNC's property in a host country without compensation.

External change forces Forces for change outside the organization, such as the pricing strategies of competitors, the available supply of resources, and government regulations.

External communications Information that flows outward from the organization to the various components of its external operating environment. Whatever the type of organization, the content of this information flow is controlled by the organization (e.g., advertising in business organizations).

Failure costs The costs incurred by a defective product or service. Costs are internal (scrapped material and product reworking) and external (damaged reputation with consumers).

Final performance review The last step in the MBO process, a final meeting between the manager and the subordinate which focuses on performance over an entire period. The final performance review must accomplish two important purposes: (1) an evaluation of the objectives achieved and the relating of these accomplishments to rewards such as salary increments and promotion and (2) an evaluation of performance that is intended to aid the subordinate in self-development and to set the stage for the next period.

First-line management The lowest level of the hierarchy. A manager at this level coordinates the work of nonmanagers but reports to a manager.

Flexible manufacturing systems Production systems that manufacture a part or product entirely by automation.

Forecasting An important element of the planning function which must make these two basic determinations: (1) what level of activity can be expected during the planning period and (2) what level of resources will be available to support the projected activity. In a business organization, the critical forecast is the sales forecast.

Foreign subsidiary entry strategy As exports increase in importance to the firm, it may decide that it can justify its own foreign subsidiary. This decision usually involves joining with nationals in the foreign country to establish product and/or marketing facilities. It differs from direct investment in that some type of association is formed with a local firm or individual. This type of association usually takes the form of licensing or joint-venture arrangements. *Licensing* is granting the right to produce and/or market the firm's product in another country to an outside firm. *Joint-venture* arrangements involve foreign investors forming a group with local investors to begin a local business with each group sharing ownership.

Formal groups The established departments, units, and teams created by the managers in an organization.

Franchise A business wherein the entrepreneur (franchisee) provides a product or service under a legal contract with the franchise owner (franchisor). The franchisor provides the distinctive elements of the business (i.e., name, image, signs, facility design).

Friendship group An informal group that evolves because of some common characteristic, such as age, political sentiment, or background.

Generativity An individual's concern for actions and achievements that will benefit future generations.

Goal participation The amount of involvement a person has in setting task and personal development goals.

Grapevine An informal communication network in organizations that short-circuits the formal channels.

Grid training A leadership development method proposed by Blake and Mouton which emphasizes the necessary balance between production orientation and person orientation.

Group assets The advantages derived from the increase in knowledge that is brought to bear on a problem when a group examines it.

Group cohesiveness The attraction of individual members to a group in terms of the strength of the forces that impel them to remain active in the group and to resist leaving it.

Group development The phases or sequences through which a group passes, such as mutual acceptance, decision making, motivation, and control.

Group liabilities The negative features of groups, such as the group pressure that is expected to bring dissident members into line, the takeover of a dominant member, and the reduced creativity that results from the embarrassment of members about expressing themselves.

Group norm Agreement among a group's members about how they should behave.

Group politics The use of self-serving tactics to improve a group's position relative to that of other groups.

Groupthink A phenomenon that occurs when a group believes that it is invincible, turns off criticism, attempts to bring noncomplying members into line, and feels that everyone is in agreement.

Halo effects The forming of impressions (positive or negative) about a person based on an impression formed from performance in one area.

Halo error A positive or negative aura around a ratee that influences a rater's evaluation.

Hawthorne effect The tendency of people who are being observed or involved in a research effort to react differently than they would otherwise.

Hawthorne studies Management studies conducted at the Western Electric Hawthorne plant in a suburb of Chicago. The most famous studies that have ever been conducted in the field of management.

Horizontal communication Occurs when the communicator and the receiver are at the same level in the organization.

Human management skill The ability to work with, motivate, and counsel people who need help and guidance. Most important to middle-level managers.

Human resource planning Estimating the size and makeup of the future work force.

Illustrators Physical gestures that illustrate what is being said (extended hands to indicate the size of an object, for example). A form of body language.

Immediate performance measures Measures of results that are monitored over short periods of time, such as a day, a week, a month, or a year. These include measures of output, quality, time, cost, and profit. Immediate performance measures are not always easy to obtain.

Informal groups Natural groupings of people in response to some need.

Initiating structure Leadership acts which develop job tasks and responsibilities for followers.

Integration The degree to which members of various departments work together effectively.

Intelligence information Data on such elements of the organization's operating environment as clients, competitors, suppliers, creditors, and the government for use in short-run planning, and data on developments in the economic environment, such as consumer income trends and spending patterns, and in the social and cultural environment for use in long-run strategic planning.

Interest group An informal group formed to achieve some job-related, but personal, objective.

Intergroup conflict The disagreements, hostile emotions, and problems that exist among groups. These conflicts emerge because of limited resources, communication problems, differences in perceptions and attitudes, and a lack of clarity.

Intermediate performance reviews In the MBO process, periodic reviews of performance that monitor progress toward achieving the objectives that have been established and the action plans that have been developed. These reviews are an important element of control in management by objectives.

Internal change forces Forces for change that occur with the organization, such as communication problems, morale problems, and decision-making breakdowns.

Intertype competition Occurs between different types of institutions. Kellogg competes with Procter & Gamble for shelf space in supermarkets, and hospitals compete with private clinics for medical practitioners.

Intratype competition Occurs between institutions engaged in the same basic activity. Ford competes with General Motors for automobile customers. This is the form of competition that is described in economic studies.

Inventory models A type of production control model which answers two questions relating to inventory management: "How much?" and "When?" An inventory model tells the manager when goods should be reordered and what quantity should be purchased.

Investment decisions Commitments of present funds in exchange for potential future funds. Investment decisions are controlled through a capital budget.

Job analysis A process of determining what tasks make up the job and what skills, abilities, and responsibilities are required of an individual in order to successfully accomplish the job.

Job depth The relative freedom that a job holder has in the performance of assigned duties.

Job enrichment A strategy that seeks to improve performance and satisfaction by building more responsibility, more challenge, and a greater sense of achievement into jobs.

Job range The number of tasks assigned to a particular job.

Just-in-time inventory management An approach to inventory management designed to minimize inventory, boost plant productivity, and product quality.

Leader-member relations A factor in the Fiedler situational model of leadership which refers to the degree of confidence, trust, and respect that followers have in the leader.

Leadership In the context of management theory, the ability of a person to influence the activities of followers in an organizational setting. Management theory emphasizes that the leader must interact with his or her followers to be influential.

Legitimate power The power which rank gives a leader in the managerial hierarchy. For example, the department manager possesses more legitimate power than the supervisor because the department manager is ranked higher than the supervisor.

Less developed country (LDC) An LDC has a very low gross national product, very little industry or an unequal distribution of income with a very large number of poor.

Line functions Activities which contribute directly to the creation of the organization's output. In manufacturing, the line functions are production, marketing, and finance.

Listening skills The ability to focus on the communicator, block out distractions, and comprehend the communicator's message.

Macro-organizational design The design of an organization or a department.

Management The process by which people, technology, job tasks, and other resources are combined and coordinated so as to effectively achieve organizational goals.

Management development The process of educating and developing selected employees so that they have the knowledge, skills, attitudes, and understanding needed to manage in future positions.

Management functions The activities which a manager must perform as a result of position in the organization. The text identifies planning, organizing, leading, and controlling as the management functions.

Management information systems An organized, structured complex of individuals, machines, and procedures for providing management with pertinent information from both external and internal sources. Management information systems support the planning, control, and operations functions of an organization by providing uniform information that serves as the basis for decision making.

Management by objectives A planning and controlling method which comprises these major elements: (1) the superior and the subordinate meet to discuss goals and to jointly establish attainable goals for the subordinate; (2) the superior and the subordinate meet again afterward to evaluate the subordinate's performance in terms of the goals that have been set.

Managerial roles The organized sets of behavior that belong to the manager's job. The three main types of managerial roles discovered by such researchers as Mintzberg are interpersonal, informational, and decisional roles.

Matrix organizational design A design in which a project-type structure is superimposed on a functional structure.

Mechanistic system An organizational design in which there is differentiation of job tasks, rigid rules, and a reliance on top-management objectives.

Micro-organizational design The design of a job.

Midcareer plateau The point or stage, of a career at which the individual has no opportunity for further promotion or advancement.

Middle management The middle level of an administrative hierarchy. Managers at this level coordinate the work of managers and report to a manager.

Mission A long-term vision of what an organization is trying to become. The mission is the unique aim that differentiates an organization from similar organizations. The basic questions that must be answered in order to determine an organization's mission are: "What is our business? What should it be?"

Motion study The process of analyzing work in order to determine the most efficient motions for performing tasks. Motion study, a major contribution of scientific management, was developed principally through the efforts of Frederick Taylor and Frank and Lillian Gilbreth.

Motivation The inner strivings that initiate a person's actions.

Multinational company (MNC) An MNC is a business firm doing business in two or more countries.

Nationalization Occurs when a host country government forces an MNC to sell its facility to local buyers.

Need hierarchy A model that presents five levels of individual needs—physiological, safety, social, esteem, and self-actualization. According to Maslow, if a person's needs are unsatisfied, the most basic levels of needs will be more pressing than the other levels.

Negative reinforcement An increase in the frequency of a response which is brought about by removing a disliked event immediately after the response occurs.

Noise Interference with the flow of a message from a sender to a receiver.

Nonprogrammed decisions Decisions for novel and unstructured problems or for complex or extremely important problems. Nonprogrammed decisions deserve special attention of top management.

Nonverbal communication The transmission and receipt of messages by some medium other than verbal or written.

Open system An organization that interacts with its environment and uses the feedback received to make changes and modifications.

Operating management Manages the implementation of programs and projects in each area of performance, measures and evaluates results, and compares results with objectives.

Ordering cost An element in inventory control models that comprises clerical, administrative, and labor costs; a major cost component that is considered in inventory control decisions. Each time a firm orders items for inventory, some clerical and administrative work is usually required to place the order and some labor is required to put the items in inventory.

Organic system An organizational design with a behavioral orientation, participation from all employees, and communication flowing in all directions.

Organization strategies The general approaches that are utilized by the organization to achieve its organizational objectives. These approaches include market penetration, market development, product development, and diversification strategies.

Organization structure The formally defined framework of task and authority relationships. The organization structure is analogous to the biological concept of the skeleton.

Organizational change The intentional attempt by

management to improve the overall performance of individuals, groups, and the organization as a whole by altering the organization's structure, behavior, and technology.

Organizational communications Information that flows outward from the organization to the various components of its external operating environment. Whatever the type of organization, the content of this information flow is controlled by the organization (e.g., advertising in business organizations).

Organizational objectives The broad continuing aims which serve as guides for action and as the starting point for more specific and detailed operating objectives at lower levels in the organization. This book classifies organizational objectives into four categories: profitability, competitiveness, efficiency, and flexibility.

Organizational performance The extent to which an organization achieves the results that society expects of it. Organizational performance is affected in part by managerial performance.

Organizing function All managerial activity which results in the design of a formal structure of tasks and authority.

Payback period The length of time that it takes for an investment to pay for itself out of future funds.

Perception The process by which individuals organize and interpret their impressions of the environment around them.

Performance evaluation A postcontrol technique which focuses on the extent to which employees have achieved expected levels of work during a specified time period.

Personal-behavioral leadership theories A group of theories that are based primarily on the personal and behavioral characteristics of leaders. These theories focus on *what* leaders do and/or *how* leaders behave in carrying out the leadership function.

Personality The sum of an individual's traits or characteristics. These traits interact to create personality patterns.

Phased internationalization Designing a product or service for international expansion based on product-market research in the prospective host country and identified needs of host-country consumers.

Physiological (basic) needs Consist of needs of the human body, such as food, water, and sex.

Planning function All managerial activities which lead to the definition of objectives and to the determination of appropriate means to achieve those objectives.

Policies Guidelines for managerial action that must be adhered to at all times. Policymaking is an important management planning element for assuring that action is oriented toward objectives. The purpose of policies is to achieve consistency and direction and to protect the reputation of the organization.

Political risk Unanticipated changes in the host country's political environment that affect MNC operations. Can be *macro* (affecting all MNCs in a host country) or *micro* (affecting only certain industries or firms).

Political risk analysis Identifying and assessing the sources of political risk and the probabilities that adverse political change will occur in a particular location.

Position power A factor in the Fiedler situational model of leadership which refers to the power inherent in the leadership position.

Positive reinforcement An increase in the frequency of a response which results when the response is followed by a positive reinforcer.

Postcontrol The techniques and methods which analyze historical data to correct future events.

Power The ability to influence another person's behavior.

Precontrol The techniques that are used to maintain the quality and quantity of resources.

Prescriptive management Discovering and reporting how managers should perform their functions.

Prevention costs The costs of preventing product or service defects (for example, employee training.) The precontrol aspect of quality control.

Principle of management A generally accepted tenet which guides the thinking and on-the-job practices of managers.

Private sector organizations Profit-making organizations in the U.S. economy.

Profitability measures Profitability measures include the ratio of net profit to capital, to total assets, and to sales.

Programmed decisions Responses to repetitive and

routine problems, which are handled by a standard procedure that has been developed by management.

Project organizational design A design in which a project manager temporarily directs a group of employees who have been brought together from various functional units until a specific job is completed.

Projection The tendency of people to attribute to others traits which they feel are negative aspects of their own personality.

Proxemics An individual's use of space when communicating with others.

Public sector organizations Federal, state, and local governmental bodies.

Punishment The introduction of something disliked or the removal of something liked following a particular response in order to decrease the frequency of that response.

Quality audit A study of every factor that affects quality in an activity or process.

Ranking methods The ranking of ratees on the basis of relevant performance dimensions.

Rate of return The ratio of the annual returns to the initial cost of the investment.

Realistic job previews (RJP) The practice of providing realistic information to new employees. The recruiter tells it like it is to avoid creating expectations that cannot be realized.

Recency of events error The tendency to make biased ratings because of the excessive influence of recent events.

Recycling The process by which one MBO cycle gives way to another. The final performance evaluation session of one MBO leads directly into the establishment of objectives for the next cycle. Divisional or departmental objectives are established, individual objective-setting sessions are conducted, and the MBO process recycles.

Referent power The power of a leader that is based on the leader's attractiveness. The leader is admired because of certain personal qualities, and the follower identifies closely with those qualities.

Regulators Physical movements that regulate a conversation (for example, nodding the head to indicate understanding). A form of body language.

Reward power The power generated by the perception of followers that compliance with the wishes of leaders can lead to positive rewards (for example, promotion).

Rumor An unverified belief that circulates in an organization or in its external environment. Comprised of the *target* (the rumor's object), the *source* (the rumor's communicator), and the *allegation* (the rumor's point about the target).

Safety needs Refers to such needs as protection from harm, ill health, and economic disaster and to the need for job security.

Scalar chain The graded chain of authority through which all organizational communications flow.

School of management A body of knowledge, concepts, and procedures that is used by managers. The authors discuss three schools of management. The *classical* school focuses on the functions of managers and on how those functions can be applied efficiently. The *behavioral* school is particularly concerned about people and how they behave and respond in organizations. The *management science* school uses mathematical procedures and scientific methods to study organizations. Each of these schools has advocates who consider its view of managing to be the most accurate and successful. The authors' preference is to show how each of the schools makes a contribution to managing for performance.

Scientific management The practices introduced by Frederick W. Taylor to accomplish the management job. Taylor advocated the use of scientific procedures to find the one best way to do a job.

Self-actualization The need to fully realize one's potential.

Sensitivity training An organizational change approach that focuses on the emotions and processes of interacting with people.

Shot-in-the-dark method Method of choosing a product or service for international expansion by selecting a product that is successful in the home country market and introducing it abroad.

Situation analysis An attempt to understand the environment in which the organization's efforts will be expended; an important phase of the strategic planning process. Before a well-managed organization expends any effort, it conducts a situation analysis. This attempts to answer two questions for management: What should be done? What is it possible to do? The situation analysis is usually conducted in two phases: the internal analysis and the external analysis.

Situational theory of leadership An approach which advocates that leaders understand their own behavior, the behavior of their subordinates, and the situation before they utilize a particular leadership style. The application of this approach requires diagnostic skills in human behavior on the part of the leader.

Skill An ability or proficiency that a person possesses that permits him or her to perform a particular task.

Small business An organization that is privately owned, not dominant in its market, maintains local operations, and employs less than 500 people.

Social needs Needs for social interaction and companionship.

Sociogram A graphical presentation of pathways used for communication. A sociogram shows who is communicating with whom.

Span of control The number of subordinates who report to a superior. The span of control is a factor that affects the shape and height of an organization structure.

Stable external environment An environment in which there is little unpredictable change.

Staff functions Activities which contribute indirectly to the operation of the organization's output. Ordinarily, staff personnel advise line personnel.

Staffing A process that includes the forecasting of personnel needs and the recruitment, selection, placement, and training and development of employees.

Start-up planning Planning activities that occur before a firm opens for business. Involves determining the product or service the business will provide, the business' market, and how the business will be established, operated, and financed.

Stereotyping The attribution of a whole set of traits to persons on the basis of their membership in particular groups.

Strategic management Develops the mission, objectives, and strategies of the entire organization; the top-level decision makers in the organization.

Strategic planning The activities which lead to the definition of objectives for the entire organization and

to the determination of appropriate strategies for achieving those objectives.

Strictness or leniency rater errors Ratings that are lower or higher than the average ratings usually given because of the strictness or the leniency of the rater.

Structural change A planned change of the formally prescribed task and authority relationships in an organization's design.

Supportive relations The consideration and interest displayed by a manager toward subordinates.

System 4 Likert's people-oriented organization design, which emphasized open communication, supportiveness, inputs from employees to managers, and general supervision. The opposite extreme of System-4 is System-1 organization design.

Task group A formal group put together temporarily to complete a specific job or project.

Task structure Refers to the degree of routineness found in a job. A highly routine job is said to have high task structure.

Technical management skill The skill of working with the resources and knowledge in a specific area. Such skill is most important to first-level managers.

Technological change A planned change in the machinery, equipment, or techniques that are used to accomplish organizational goals.

Terrorism The use or threat of use of violence for political purposes.

Theory X-Theory Y McGregor's theory that behind every management decision is a set of assumptions that a manager makes about human behavior. The Theory X manager assumes that people are lazy, dislike work, want no responsibility, and prefer to be closely directed. The Theory Y manager assumes that people seek responsibility, like to work, and are committed to doing good work if rewards are received for achievement.

Time study The process of determining the appropriate elapsed time for the completion of a task or job. This process was developed as part of Frederick W. Taylor's effort to determine a fair day's work.

Top management The top level of an administrative hierarchy. Managers at this level coordinate the work of other managers but do not report to a manager.

Total quality control An approach to quality in organizations that seek to achieve continual quality improvement in all aspects of the organization and to involve employees substantially in the improvement effort.

Trait theory Attempts to specify which personal characteristics (physical, personality, mental) are associated with leadership effectiveness. Trait theory relies on research that relates various traits to effectiveness criteria.

Transactional analysis A behavioral change approach that is designed to give individuals insight into their impact on others and their interpersonal communication style.

Turbulent external environment An environment in which changes are unexpected and unpredictable.

Two-factor theory of motivation The theory, popularized by the work of Frederick Herzberg, that the absence of some job conditions dissatisfies employees but that the presence of those conditions does not build employee motivation and that the absence of other job conditions does not dissatisfy employees but that their presence builds employee motivation. The former conditions, called *maintenance* factors, include job security, work conditions, salary, and status. The latter conditions, called *motivators,* include achievement, recognition, advancement, and responsibility.

Unity of command A management principle which states that each subordinate should report to only one superior.

Unity of direction The process of grouping all related activities under one superior.

Upward communication Upward communication flows from individuals at lower levels of an organization structure to those at higher levels. Some of the most common upward communication flows are suggestion boxes, group meetings, and appeal or grievance procedures.

Value set A lasting set of convictions that are held by a person, an accompanying mode of conduct, and the importance of the convictions to the person.

Weighted checklist A rating system consisting of statements that describe various types and levels of behavior for a particular job. Each of the statements is weighted according to its importance.

Work overload There are two types of overload: *quantitative*—when a persor has too many different things to do or an insufficient amount of time to do the job; *qualitative*—when a person feels a lack of ability to do a part of the job.

NAME INDEX

SUBJECT INDEX

COMPANY INDEX